My World As A Jew

By the same author:

A Century of Judaism in New York
   (New York, Congregation B'nai Jeshurun, 1930)
Toward a Solution
   (New York, G. P. Putnam's Sons, 1940)
Shanah be-Yisrael, an account of Dr. Israel Goldstein's year of service as treasurer of the Jewish
   Agency
   (Jerusalem, World Confederation of General Zionists, 1950)
Brandeis University— Chapter of Its Founding
   (New York, Bloch Publishing Co., 1951)
American Jewry Comes of Age: Tercentenary Addresses
   (New York, Bloch Publishing Co., 1955)
Transition Years, New York–Jerusalem, 1960–1962
   (Jerusalem, Rubin Mass, 1962; published in Hebrew as *Shenot Ma'avar,* 1963)
Israel at Home and Abroad
   (Jerusalem, Rubin Mass, 1973)
Jewish Justice and Conciliation: History of the Jewish Conciliation Board of America, 1930–1968
   (New York, Ktav Publishing House, Inc., 1981)
Jewish Perspectives: Selected Addresses, Sermons and Articles, 1915–1983
   (in press)

Festschriften:

Two Generations in Perspective: Notable Events and Trends 1896–1956, essays dedicated to Dr. Israel
   Goldstein on the occasion of his sixtieth birthday
   (New York, Monde Publishers, Inc., 1957)
Studies in the History of Zionism (Pirké Meḥkar be-Toledot ha-Tziyyonut), essays presented to
   Dr. Israel Goldstein on the occasion of his eightieth birthday by the Hebrew University's Institute
   of Contemporary Jewry
   (Jerusalem, World Zionist Organization, 1976)

Dr. Israel Goldstein. Alfred Bernheim-Ricarda Schwerin photo, Jerusalem.

My World As A Jew

The Memoirs of Israel Goldstein

VOLUME 1

Herzl Press
New York • Cornwall Books • London

Cornwall Books
440 Forsgate Drive
Cranbury, NJ 08512

Cornwall Books
25 Sicilian Avenue
London WC1A 2QH, England

Cornwall Books
2133 Royal Windsor Drive
Unit 1
Mississauga, Ontario
Canada L5J 1K5

Library of Congress Cataloging in Publication Data

Goldstein, Israel, 1896–
  My world as a Jew.

  Includes index.
  1. Goldstein, Israel, 1896–   . 2. Rabbis—United
States—Biography.   3. Zionists—United States—
Biography.   I. Title
BM755.G63A37   1983   956.94'001'0924   [B]   82-42621
ISBN 0-8453-4765-9

Printed in the United States of America

Dedicated
To my beloved Bert
Who enriched my life by sharing it
And who imbued my days with
Her own keen perceptions and unswerving ideals

Remember the days of old,
Consider the years of many generations;
Ask thy father, and he will declare unto thee;
Thine elders, and they will tell thee
Deuteronomy 32: 7

Contents of Volume 1

Illustrations in this volume appear in three groups,
between pages 98–99, 162–163, and 258–259.

Foreword

On first giving serious thought to the writing of these memoirs, I was somewhat daunted by what would obviously be a task of considerable magnitude. The central problem, one which has accompanied me from the earliest planning stage down to the printed proofs, was how to compress the ramified activities, experiences, events, and encounters of more than six decades within the pages of this book. Fortunately, after a long process of condensation, that task has now been completed.

My generation was privileged to live through an era of more than ordinary consequence for mankind generally, two World Wars and a socio-economic revolution, and of fateful consequence for the Jewish people in particular, which, within the space of one decade, experienced the Holocaust of six million Jews and the birth of the Third Jewish Commonwealth. It is virtually impossible for any autobiographical work to do justice to the historical significance of that period. One can only be grateful for the *zekhut* of having lived and served throughout these years.

I make no apology for the fact that this is a first-person narrative, which, by its very nature, cannot claim to be detached and objective. My career has been one of public service and involvement, dominated by Jewish activities and responsibilities but also touching the broader human scene at many points. A substantial part of my life has been spent in travels far and wide, mostly connected with the discharge of public commitments, and the record is intended not only to shed light on remote areas and peoples but also to relate these, wherever possible, to distant fringes of the Jewish Diaspora where small *kehillot* are struggling to survive.

To some extent, these memoirs may help the reader to penetrate the psychology of the Jewish activist, or *Askan*, devoted to the welfare of his people, speaking out on its behalf and championing its cause. They may also contribute to a better understanding of the type of American rabbi who moved out of the sheltered environment of his synagogue in order to assume broader roles of Jewish leadership.

The main difficulty which I faced from the outset in writing these memoirs was the plenitude of material. For over sixty years, I have gathered a vast number and assortment of files and papers, have written and delivered literally thousands of reports, speeches, and sermons, have corresponded with hundreds of people in many countries, have kept regular and special diaries, have contributed to the proceedings of innumerable conferences, congresses, and ceremonial occasions, and have amassed a storehouse of documentation. All this material is now being transferred to the Central Zionist Archives in Jerusalem.

At various stages in the preparation of this book, I received help from the following individuals, to whom my grateful acknowledgement is due, since my extensive archives constituted important source material. I am indebted to Mrs. Ada Walk, who, having taken over from Mrs. Vera Prausnitz, and assisted by Mrs. Ursula Kroner, sorted out and classified my archives, working under the expert supervision of Dr. Michael Heymann, Director of the Central Zionist Archives in Jerusalem. Dr. Heymann's advice was helpful throughout. I am also under obligation to Mrs. Sylvia Landress, Director and Librarian of the Zionist Archives and Library in New York, and her capable assistants, for their frequent helpfulness.

A special word of appreciation is due to Dr. Menaḥem Kaufman, Administrator of the Institute of Contemporary Jewry at the Hebrew University of Jerusalem, for his aid in connection with the management of my archives.

To Dr. Michael J. Cohen, of Bar-Ilan University, I am obliged for having helped me by researching and condensing large quantities of material on the World Confederation of General (now "United") Zionists and on the Keren Hayesod—United Israel Appeal.

The chapter on General Zionism was read by Mr. Kalman Sultanik and that on the Keren Hayesod was read by Mr. S. J. Kreutner, both of whom offered valuable suggestions.

I am indebted to Mrs. Shulamit Nardi of Jerusalem for having read the first draft of the manuscript and for having offered many a helpful and perceptive observation.

A particular meed of acknowledgement is due to my good friend of blessed memory, the late Julian Meltzer of the Weizmann Institute in Reḥovot, who brought his considerable ability to bear on the task of threading together many disparate items from various sources and who edited a substantial portion of the text. His death, in the midst of these labors, was a loss both to Israel and to the journalistic profession.

To my faithful friend and distinguished colleague, Professor Moshe Davis, founder of the Institute of Contemporary Jewry at the Hebrew University of Jerusalem, I am grateful for the unstinted, valuable advice and constant encouragement which he has given me.

My special thanks and appreciation go out to Dr. Gabriel A. Sivan of Jerusalem, for helping me to complete these memoirs and for his definitive editing of the entire book. He rendered an additional service of importance in selecting and processing appropriate photographs to accompany the text. The arduous tasks which he undertook required patience and skill, which he invested generously. Dr. Sivan's broad Jewish and general scholarship, as well as his professional experience as an author and editor, including his contribution as one of the editors of the *Encyclopaedia Judaica*, have added an invaluable resource to the preparation of this book. I am particularly indebted to Dr. Sivan for his meticulous research and attention to detail, which have safeguarded the interests of historical and overall accuracy.

Dr. Mordecai S. Chertoff and Mr. Sam Bloch of the Herzl Press, New York, spared no effort to ensure that this two-volume work should reach a high standard of technical excellence.

Grateful acknowledgment is also due to Mrs. Pauline Cooper, my loyal and competent secretary in Jerusalem, who typed the bulk of the manuscript and who has borne cheerfully and efficiently with trying situations and idiosyncrasies. Mrs. Mimi Solomon, who for decades has served as my faithful and devoted secretary in New York, has continued to be of great assistance in this project, especially in gathering some of the material for the early portion of the book.

Finally, and above all, to Bert, my life companion, in whom "the heart of her husband doth safely trust," I offer these few words of loving appreciation. She has toiled at my side, in common fields of endeavor, several of which she graced in her own right, sharing my hopes and fulfillments but sometimes also my disappointments, and therefore has had a unique vantage point from which to offer helpful advice. Many of the discerning suggestions which she made have been embodied in the text.

There were others who assisted me in one way or another, directly or indirectly, by word of mouth or in writing. To all of these friends I am gratefully obliged.

The title which I have chosen for this autobiography, *My World As A Jew*, expresses what, I like to feel, has been the main content of my life and career.

These recollections may also be helpful, I trust, in providing our children and, especially, our grandchildren, Judith, Joyce, Margaret, Dan, Joshua, Michael and Kenneth Akiba, with some comprehensive idea of their family roots.

Jerusalem
December 1983
Kislev 5744

—ISRAEL GOLDSTEIN

1
The First Jewish Scenes: 1896–1914

The section of South Philadelphia in which I was born and grew up, during the two decades before America entered World War I, no longer exists as a recognizable Jewish entity. In my day, however, it was a pulsating, vital, and effervescent scene, typical of Jewish life in most metropolitan centers of the far-flung Dispersion. In point of fact, the neighborhood was not exclusively Jewish: its population included a large Polish Catholic admixture, and encounters between the two communities—sometimes friendly, but usually less so—were inevitable. Yet, from the standpoint of a cohesive Jewish existence, reminiscent of the Lithuanian and other North Russian *shtetlakh*, the hamlets, villages, and small towns of the "Old Country" in which our forebears had lived and from which they had come, it was in every respect a ghetto.

Our forerunners had brought with them a goodly spiritual heritage, substantially complementing the few wretched material possessions that were to start them off as residents of the New World. It was this spiritual baggage which sustained the newcomers during the early years of struggle in the *Goldene Medine*, the "golden land" to which they had come, full of hopes and dreams and no little trepidation. With typical Jewish persistence—for how else can our survival be explained?—they began to weave the picturesque threads of this heritage into the texture of an emergent American culture.

Foremost in that process of American Jewish acculturation was, of course, the synagogue—focus of vital Jewish life and activity. It was not only the *bet ha-knesset*, a place of assembly for the religious devotions and social intercourse of its congregants, but also a refuge where the newcomer could find comfort, fellowship, and support in the initial bleak period of settlement and readjustment. For the "old-timers" who had been in the *Goldene Medine* as long as three or four years (more than that almost made one a "founding father"), the *shul* was an extension of the home.

In any of the hundreds of synagogues scattered over the face of the North American continent, one could savor the nostalgia of age-old Jewish remembrance lodged deep in the national being, a sort of inherent awareness of the past, present, and future all rolled into one, which stems from the essence of the Jewish tradition. It

15

was a tradition and an awareness overshadowing all alien values and pressures of the new American cultural outlook.

The Jewish physical and spiritual experiences of the old homesteads in Eastern Europe, transplanted onto free American soil, were a psychological fact of life to the first generation of those who had fled from czarist oppression. From my childhood and early youth, I came into contact with the fringes of that experience and saw how it functioned in the consciousness of Jews living in my neighborhood.

There was an additional strand in the web of consciousness being woven in the mind of a young Jewish boy in the "Gentile" city of Philadelphia. That was the conspectus of the outside world, which, as the years advanced, gradually became more familiar to a lad accustomed only to the cultural ways and experiences of the ghetto. Thus, not until my later boyhood, when at public school, did I learn that I had been born during the second term of President Grover Cleveland, or that the twenty-fifth U.S. President, William McKinley, had been assassinated in September 1901, shortly after my fifth birthday.

Among the vivid memories of the American presidency that remain from my formative years in South Philadelphia, however, is the colorful figure of Teddy Roosevelt, who served in the White House from my fifth year until I became Bar Mitzvah. His flamboyant personality and his exploits were occasionally a topic of conversation among us junior fry, who heard stories of this no-nonsense President from our elders. Their interest in such matters is an example of the dual acculturation within the Jewish community, which at that time was growing as a result of mass immigration from Eastern Europe—alongside other new-settler communities such as the Polish, Italian, Greek, and Irish—and being forged in the crucible of late nineteenth- and early twentieth-century North American civilization.

All that background was a formative part of my early upbringing in the ghetto of South Philadelphia, just three long blocks from the Delaware River, which separated Pennsylvania's largest city from Camden, New Jersey.

The second strand in the web of my consciousness was the one that led to my Zionist activity. Four months and four days before I came into the world, a Jewish journalist and feuilletonist in Vienna, Dr. Theodor Herzl, whose interest in Jewish affairs had until then been minimal, wrote a pamphlet that literally rocked the Jewish world—or that segment of it which still felt the millennial yearning for a homeland. In this brief work, *The Jewish State*, published on February 14, 1896, Herzl issued a clarion call to the Jewish people to take their destiny into their own hands. Many cast him in a messianic role. During the eight short years when he flashed like a brilliant meteor across the firmament of Jewish and world history, Herzl established the political base of the State of Israel, which came into being fifty-two years later.

All that was only a distant vision for the infant son born on June 18, 1896, to David Goldstein and his wife, Fannie (née Silver), who had gravitated to Philadelphia in the previous five years from their separate hamlets in Lithuania.

Theodor Herzl has always remained prominent in my mind as one close in appearance to my father, Reb Yehudah Leib David Goldstein (né Wallach), although, of course, there the resemblance ended. Like Herzl, my father—as I remember him from childhood—was rather tall, with a handsome countenance, penetrating dark gray eyes and a rather abundant square beard, although he was balding. As the years went by, the beard became grayer and more neatly trimmed, but his handsome aspect and keen gaze never altered. My mother, Fannie, was shorter by several inches. She had a kindly face, with gray eyes, and it seemed to me that all the goodness in the world was wrapped up in her. With the passage of time, however, her appearance was marked by the outer symptoms of a heart condition which took its toll of her health and stamina. This ailment set in with the birth of my brother Isaac, who was my junior by four years, and it persisted throughout the rest of her life.

Father was twenty-five years old when he arrived at Ellis Island in 1893. Friends persuaded him to exchange his original surname, Wallach, for the better-known "Jewish" one of Goldstein. Untutored in the English language and American ways, he yielded to their advice in this, as in many other matters. So it was that, thanks to the pundits who had come to the United States before him, we youngsters became Goldsteins instead of Wallachs.

My father was born in 1868 in the hamlet of Stayachechik, in the "government" (province) of Vilna, Lithuania, where my grandfather eked out a living as a small-scale farmer. Wallach senior was an observant Jew, though not a learned one, but he was ambitious for his three sons and sent them to study at yeshivot in neighboring towns.

By the time my father was ten years of age, he was already a *yeshivah-bokhur*, a Talmudical student, in the larger township of Smorgon, some distance from his home. As was the custom for out-of-town pupils, he often slept on the yeshivah premises and the practice of *essen-teg* necessitated his eating daily meals at various homes in the Jewish community.

From Smorgon my father graduated, if that is the word, to a center of Jewish scholarship headed by one who became eminent in Jewish and Zionist history. This was the celebrated yeshivah of Lida, which in 1885 had come under the enlightened direction of Rabbi Yitzhak Ya'akov Reines. Some years later, in 1902, Rabbi Reines arranged the conference of Orthodox rabbis and laymen in Vilna at which the Religious Zionist movement, Mizrahi, was founded. It was at Lida that my father received *semikhah*, rabbinical ordination, and was also authorized to become a *shohet*, a ritual slaughterer of poultry. Both qualifications were to guide him in the choice of a vocation when he arrived on the shores of the New World—penniless but not friendless, to judge from the way his *landsleit* (countrymen) received him.

It was probably under the inspiration of the same *landsleit* that he settled in Philadelphia. There, in 1895, at the age of twenty-eight, when he had already been several years in the United States, he met a young woman nearly ten years younger than himself. Fannie Silver was born in Kobylnik, a village in the same "government" of Vilna where my father had his origins. With its fifty Jewish families, Kobylnik was a slightly larger *kehillah* than Father's hamlet, Stayachechik, which counted only twenty Jewish households. Kobylnik, incidentally, was known for its *blottes,* muddy paths and near-morasses, which persisted during the rainy season, when the river bordering the village overflowed. One of those dense forests common to northwestern Russia, and which are almost impenetrable to outsiders, lay in the vicinity of Kobylnik. Two generations later, that forest provided a hiding place for Jewish partisans during the Nazi occupation.

My mother's father, Shammai Silver, and her stepmother, together with their older daughter and son-in-law, were in charge of the dairy on the estate of the *poritz,* the Russian landlord. Mother's family consisted of three sisters and a brother, the siblings of the first wife, and two stepbrothers and a stepsister, born to her father's second wife. Shammai Silver was a devout, simple Jew, having no claims to scholarship but making up for this in piety. He spent most of his evenings, after the day's arduous toil in the dairy, reciting *Tehillim* (Psalms), the spiritual mainstay of many a humble Jew.

Like many others of his kind, on reaching the "golden land," my father began to earn his living as a peddler. We children listened with bated breath to the stories he and Mother told us of their years in Russia and of their early days in America. Father was fond of describing his first venture as a door-to-door salesman with basket slung over shoulder. That basket, crammed with a variety of goods, must have been a veritable department store for the connoisseur housewives upon whom he called. His limited knowledge of English was boosted by more experienced friends, "veteran" residents of two or more years' standing. They told him to answer any question by a potential customer with the stock phrase, "Look in the basket." His first sales contact was a kindly lady, who must have taken a liking to the handsome, bearded young man who had knocked at her door. She greeted him with a smile and asked, "Are you married and have you any children?" Father, well-rehearsed and eager to make his first stride along the intricate ways of American commerce, must have startled her when he replied: "Look in the basket!"

The peddler's trade was not for Father and he soon gave it up. Judging by the success that overtook other pioneers in that form of mercantile activity, he may well have forfeited the chance of becoming the owner of a large department store or even of a chain of stores. Nor was he inclined to follow the example of many other fellow immigrants in those early years by working in a tailoring sweatshop. He may thus also have lost the opportunity of becoming a captain of industry.

Instead of pursuing the mythical pot of gold at the rainbow's end, Father sought ways of making a living more suited to his training and more congenial to his temperament. So it was that he eventually became the *shammash* (sexton) in the Niezhiner Synagogue, a post he combined with *shehitah,* the ritual slaughtering of poultry in the yard of the synagogue. Those were his substantive functions, but my father was a man of parts in congregational life, so that many other tasks devolved upon him.

The Niezhiner *Shul* was the spiritual and physical center of Agudat Ahim Anshei Niezhin, the Fraternal Society of the Men of Niezhin. They followed the *Nusah ha-Ari,* a partly Sephardic prayer rite named for the illustrious kabbalist, Rabbi Yitzhak Luria, a mystic enveloped in legend who flourished in sixteenth-century Safed.

For my father, adopting this ritual must have necessitated a "conversion" from the Ashkenazi traditions in which he had been reared, but I rather suppose that purely economic factors were involved.

To the uninformed, the difference in ritual and practice may be slight and of no real consequence. Not so, however, to the cognoscenti. Such a change involved not only variations in the order of prayer, but also in the manner of "laying" *tefillin,* the phylacteries worn on the forehead and the left forearm during weekday morning prayers, as enjoined in Deuteronomy 6:8. The Hasidic way prescribed that the *tefillin* on the forearm be bound in a clockwise direction, whereas under Father's ancestral dispensation they were tied counterclockwise. Another innovation, as far as Father was concerned, was the more joyous approach to religious observances the Niezhiner congregants practiced, which attained heights of exhilaration on special occasions through the imbibing of spirituous refreshment.

The Niezhiner *Shul* was located in the heart of South Philadelphia's Jewish quarter, at Third and Fitzwater Streets, three blocks east of the Delaware River. A few blocks to the south, on the appropriately named South Street, was the neighborhood inhabited mostly by the Black community. Slightly to the north of South Street lay a large covered market occupying two whole blocks on Bainbridge Street. These details are sufficient indication that the whole district was an exotic one for a youngster to explore, in search of "broadening" experiences.

Our synagogue, on Third and Fitzwater, was a three-story building that had been converted from a former Polish church. The actual house of worship was one flight up, and above it were two floors with meeting rooms that were rented out to societies. This rental contributed to the meager budget of the congregation, supplementing the membership fees it was one of my father's duties to collect.

Taking care of these rooms formed another part of the sexton's duties. The quarters assigned to him (and later to his family) were in the basement. There my father brought young Fannie Silver, his twenty-year-old bride, when they were married in 1895. Her chores, in addition to raising a family, included helping Father to take care of the *shul* premises, while he ran the daily prayer services, provided *minyanim* (quorums) for *Yahrzeit* memorial observances on the appropriate anniversary, enforced payment of dues, attended to the arrangement of circumcisions, weddings, and funerals, and performed the hundred and one other services that devolved upon a *shammash.* I recall going with him on occasion to a funeral and then to the usual pot-cheese light refreshment after the interment, which served as a break from the wearying rides in horse-drawn carriages to the outer suburbs.

Father's full name, Yehudah Leib David, was given the Hebrew acronym *Yeled,* literally "youngster." He always signed his name in Hebrew as "Yeled Goldstein," betokening his youthful spirit.

It would be tempting to claim that I first saw the light of day, as the eldest child of Yehudah Leib David and Fannie Goldstein, within sound of the no-longer-sounding Liberty Bell, or near to where the founding fathers of American independence lived and labored some 120 years before my birth. But that would be topographically incorrect: the Niezhiner *Shul's* environment lay much farther south, bounded on the east by the Delaware River, several blocks away, and, on the south, by the "Dump," a huge junk and garbage pile that did little for the ecology of that section of Philadelphia.

Having entered this world in the basement of the Niezhiner *Shul,* I can literally claim to have been born into the synagogue—an institution that was to become the focus of my active professional life and the fulcrum of my spiritual and communal existence. In that cramped space, I acquired the rights and prerogatives accruing to the firstborn son according to Jewish custom and prescription.

Even as a very young child, I recall helping my parents to look after the premises. One satisfying recollection, which goes back more than three-quarters of a century, is of circulating among the male worshipers on Sabbaths and festivals, and offering them a *shmek tabak* (a whiff of tobacco) from the communal snuffbox, to add to their enjoyment of the prayer service. As a reward for the pinch of snuff, I would receive an affectionate pinch on the cheek.

When I was approaching the age of five and my brother, Isaac, was still a babe in arms, a remarkable new chapter opened in the lives of my mother and her two youngsters: her return and our first visit to Russia. Though now dimly and sketchily remembered, this was for me the second formative Jewish scene of my earliest years.

Life in the Shtetl

Although, of course, I was scarcely aware of that long voyage across the Atlantic and the North Sea and of the train journey from Hamburg to my young mother's birthplace in Lithuania, some residual memory of that second Jewish scene lingered in my consciousness. There remained with me a lively recollection of a number of circumstances which, though overlaid by the rush and tumble of events and encounters in the ensuing three-quarters of a century, still evoke a large measure of warm sentiment.

For one thing, I learned for the first time that I had grandparents and I actually met them. It is important for a child of five to know that his parents are themselves the offspring of *their* parents. This thought strengthens within the young child the sense of belonging and of tradition. Moreover, that awareness imparts greater validity to the Fifth Commandment, "Honor thy father and thy mother." The act of filial respect was fortified, I think, by the sudden realization that Mother and Father were at one time small children too. In the juvenile milieu I had come to regard as an almost exclusive preserve, my one-year-old brother, Isaac, was still a suspect intruder.

Our language at home in those days was Yiddish or *Mamme-loshen* (the "mother tongue")—that Middle High German dialect, commingled with many Hebrew and Slavic words, which became the lingua franca of millions of Ashkenazi Jews domiciled in various parts of the Diaspora. Up to the age of eight, or thereabouts, Yiddish was virtually my sole medium of communication. My parents were barely aware of English, knowing just enough to get by when they occasionally wandered into the Gentile environment of Philadelphia.

The journey to my mother's home in Lithuania must have taken several weeks, and my perceptions were probably sharpened by the change of atmosphere and clime. In later years, my mother would fondly recall the searching cross-examination to which I put her on meeting her father and stepmother, and all my aunts, uncles, and cousins. With such an abundance of relatives in the *shtetl*, Philadelphia soon faded into a wilderness bereft of close kith and kin, except for Father.

Another emotional acquisition was my first sight of the wide-open spaces of nature, an experience that impressed itself on my mind as I viewed the landscape and greenery that enveloped the village of Kobylnik. The frame houses and cobblestone streets of South Philadelphia had hardly prepared me for this.

The long voyage across the ocean to Russia was not just a family visit for Mother, although she had been away for nearly eight years. Such a vacation would have been a luxury far beyond my father's slender means. It was primarily intended as a health cure. Mother suffered from a rheumatic heart and had been advised to take the waters at Mount Clemens, a health resort in southeastern Michigan. By a fortunate coincidence, however, the mineral baths at Kemeri, a spa near Riga, the Latvian capital, had similar properties, together with an additional advantage Mount Clemens lacked: proximity to her kin, thus affording an opportunity to visit the old homestead. Since the cure, to be effective, had to be prolonged and—if taken in Michigan—would involve enormous expense, the opportunity of a reunion with her family, showing off the children and ensuring that they were taken care of while she was away at Kemeri, was more than my mother could resist. Apart from the family at Kobylnik, where my aunt and uncle assisted my grandparents in looking after the estate and the creamery belonging to the lord of the manor, her brother-in-law, Eli, was comfortably established as a lumber merchant in Svir, a larger town in the vicinity, where he had a substantial home.

There was an inauspicious beginning to our arrival in Kobylnik. Burdened with her luggage and two small children, one of them a babe in arms, my mother discovered to her horror when we disembarked that her trunk containing all the presents she was bringing to her family had disappeared. Imagine someone coming from the *Goldene Medine*, laden with her own and her children's belongings as well as gifts for her kin, losing all of this en route! Fortunately, everything was recovered.

Owing to her frail health, Mother had to remain at Kemeri, with intermittent visits to her kin, for nearly two and a half years. The separation from Father was an obvious hardship for her, but there were no hardships involved for a growing child. My time was fully occupied—exploring, learning, and absorbing, even at that tender age, the culture of the *shtetl*, that Jewish milieu from which my father and mother had brought their own spiritual baggage to America a decade earlier. I derived further enjoyment from learning to play the violin. It was a completely satisfying schedule for an eager child visiting an Old World that was so new to him.

A good portion of my time was spent with the family at Svir. My Uncle Eli, a learned man, enrolled me in the local *ḥeder*, although my *ḥeder* instruction had already begun in Kobylnik. Since my uncle had several daughters, and the house was equipped with a piano, it attracted young men of culture and proved to be a much more refined and erudite environment than my grandfather's homestead in Kobylnik. A cousin newly released from the Russian army, where he had received a musical training, taught me to play the violin. This apparently aroused hopes that I would develop into a musical prodigy, and I soon became the object of considerable adulation, apart from receiving special attention as a native-born American child.

Occasionally, my mother would take me to visit my paternal grandfather at Stayachechik, where he had a small farm. There, for the first time, I saw a field of grain and had the unique experience of mounting a horse, not without some trepidation. My paternal grandfather was, as I have indicated, no scholar but a simple, devout Jewish peasant, whose piety was as firm as the soil from which he gained a livelihood. My maternal grandfather, on the other hand, was the type of the *Tehillim* Jew.

Recalling his historic first conversation with Arthur James Balfour in 1906, when the British statesman was visiting Manchester, Chaim Weizmann mentions how, after exposing his views on Zionism, he was asked: "Are there many Jews who think like you?" To Balfour's question Weizmann replied: "I believe I speak the mind of millions of Jews whom you will never see and who cannot speak for themselves, but with whom I could pave the streets of the country I come from."

My grandparents were plain, God-fearing Jews, several million of whom then lived in Russia and elsewhere on the European continent. Few of them were men of the soil, but all—whether learned or not—were men of the spirit to whom Jerusalem may have been distant and unattainable, yet who pinned their faith on Zion's ultimate restoration. The soil of Russia, Poland, and other lands of the Diaspora was watered by their sweat and tears, but their prayers were vested in Zion, Jerusalem, and Eretz Yisrael. They were the real bedrock of Zionism: the faithful millions.

Between Svir and Kobylnik, I acquired my early Jewish education in the *ḥeder*. It was an all-day syllabus, beginning with the *siddur* (prayer book) and continuing with the *Ḥummash* (Pentateuch). Our knowledge of Hebrew was gained by way of translation into Yiddish, our daily vernacular. Tales of Jewish antiquity, to which we listened with rapt attention, were an introduction to the history of our people.

The *ḥeder* curriculum was not entirely limited to religious subjects. As Jewish children were not sent to Gentile schools, our teachers permitted us a smattering of Russian and elementary arithmetic. Most of the day, from morning until late afternoon, was spent in the *ḥeder*. During the winter months, when we stepped into the dark street, we carried lanterns to light our way home.

One more souvenir of that time deserves mention. My mother was extremely proud of her older son's accomplishment as a budding violinist. (I doubt if my performance was especially remarkable, but who can gainsay a mother's pride?) She would often put me on top of the highboy or chiffarobe that faced the window looking out on the street, and urge me: *"Shpil, Yisrolik, shpil!"*—"Play, little Israel, play!" I would then thrum part of a Jewish *lidel* or some chords of a secular melody, so that passersby below might hear and admire "the fiddler on the chiffarobe."

Although the Jews of Kobylnik, Stayachechik, and all the other Russo-Polish hamlets and villages in which they scraped a living remained within their own self-sufficient Yiddish-speaking little world, no one could fail to be aware of the Christian surroundings. Nor did the anti-Semitic animosity of our neighbors escape our notice. We small boys could not, of course, divine the reason for that hostility; all that we knew was that, as Jews, we were the target for popular resentment. By and large, the Christian community had little influence on our segregated Jewish existence. We heard the church bells, saw the ecclesiastical processions, and watched the bearded monks going by—sights and sounds to be endured in the knowledge that we were in *Golus,* an environment far more alien than anything I had experienced in America. I marveled at the tall black headgear of the Christian priests and their bejeweled vestments, as they walked along in their impressive parades. Nevertheless, we took care to keep out of their way, especially at Easter and Christmas.

In later years, I always had the feeling that my childhood experience in Russia was an important and formative one. It was my first exposure to the Old World and its values, and it helped me to gain a better understanding of them. It also added a dimension to my Jewish loyalties and sensibilities.

Returning from Russia nearly thirty months after we had arrived there, my mother had to steal with us across the border, for reasons I can no longer recall. Yet I still remember that ordeal—the atmosphere of stealth and fright, the band of shady characters on whom we had to rely so that we might be smuggled into Prussia one dark night.

Years later, when she was in a somber mood of reminiscence, my mother would sometimes dwell on the hazards of that homeward journey in 1903: a frail young woman encumbered with two small children and the accumulated possessions of her stay, obliged to make her way without a friendly hand as far as Hamburg, where we took ship for the United States.

Fortunately, we now traveled as second-class passengers, instead of in third class or steerage. It compensated for the discomforts we had endured on the way to Hamburg. Even then, amid the confusion and scramble of our transfer from train to ship, we almost lost my younger brother, Isaac, who was now well past his third year. Luckily, everything ended without mishap.

When I made return visits to Russia nearly thirty years later and, once again, in the summer of 1963, I tried to recapture some of that childhood experience of the *shtetl,* its family warmth and the vibrant *Yiddishkeit* that permeated every fiber of one's being—not merely the language but the very essence of a lifestyle that has remained part of my spiritual equipment. But alas! the *shtetl,* as tens of millions of Jews had known it in the course of generations, is now only a memory. The Nazi juggernaut crushed the *shtetlakh* and their people—my people—into oblivion. The Kobylniks, Svirs, and Stayachechiks may figure on the map, but they are no longer Jewish abodes. For those who once knew them, however, a savor of the vanished past—of *di alte Heym,* the Old Country—lingers on.

Philadelphia—Home of Liberty

Some time after my mother, brother, and I returned from Russia, an important innovation took place in our family life. The Niezhiner congregation was adjudged by its elders to have outgrown the original quarters at Third and Fitzwater Streets, and they decided to transfer to new and more commodious premises on Second Street, near Catherine Street, one block away from the former site. This new *shul* building had also served previously as a Polish church, and so there was a further *mitzvah* involved in converting the premises into a synagogue.

The more ample site had a garden in front and a large empty lot in the back. These were like green fields, compared to our previous cramped quarters.

Our location was an extension of the Polish neighborhood, into which Jewish families were gradually infiltrating. Wooden frame houses were the architectural standard, as the luxury of brick had yet to reach our district. One of the more affluent members of the congregation tried to get the best of both worlds by having the exterior of his wooden frame house overlaid with tin panels on which replica bricks were painted. It added an "upper-class" touch to this worthy's residence.

By contrast with the old building of the Niezhiner *Shul*, the new premises were spacious. The main structure contained vestry rooms on the ground floor, used by congregants for weekday services and as meeting places, while the synagogue proper was one flight up. The front garden afforded a touch of botanical splendor, thanks to an abundance of sunflowers in the appropriate season.

The vacant lot at the back enabled the boys to play, and had enough room at the side for an ample *sukkah* on the Tabernacles (Sukkot) festival. Our living quarters were in the three-story house adjoining the synagogue, and we occupied the top floor and attic. There was enough room to accommodate not only our own immediate family but also, at various stages, Aunt Cheskeh, Uncle Meyer, and Cousin Brayne when they also reached America. At the street level there was a store; the offices of the congregation's secretary, a Mr. Kratzok, were on the next floor; and higher up lived the sexton and his family. It was a hardship for my mother, whose constitution was never robust, to climb up all those flights of stairs, but she had no alternative.

To us lads the attic was a special boon, our stamping ground and private den. There we slept and did our school homework—by lamplight, of course, since the gaslight fixtures ended at the living quarters below. Thus, at the age of nine, I was elevated to the topmost heights of the Niezhiner *Shul* complex.

It was inevitable that the synagogue and its ambience, both religious and secular, should come to mean a great deal to me, to my brother Isaac and to my youngest brother, Morris, who managed to have been born in the old *shul* premises, shortly before the move to its new location.

Even if I knew little and cared less for the mundane problems that affected Agudat Aḥim Anshei Niezhin, the synagogue was our milieu and our world. Homiletic nourishment, the Yiddish *droshe*, was a treat reserved for rare occasions, but cantorial sustenance, *ḥazzanut*, was available frequently on Sabbaths, festivals and, above all, on the High Holy Days. My love of *ḥazzanut* dates back to those years of my boyhood.

Our beloved *shul*, in which religious devotion and piety were commingled with a genial community feeling, thus persisted as a kind of *shtetl* in an American setting. By the time I had come back from my sojourn in Lithuania, I was old enough to derive—consciously and subconsciously—meaningful values from that synagogue connection.

The move to larger premises made it possible to engage a permanent *ḥazzan*, and Cantor Ḥayyim Harris became part of our congregational life. Considerable as were his musical talents, they were excelled by his Jewish learning and Zionist devotion. Later on, when he gave up the cantor's profession, he became a pharmacist and one of the most dedicated Zionists in Philadelphia. On special occasions, Cantor Harris was accompanied by a choir, and I was mobilized to contribute my alto to the volume of choral decibels. Needless to say, it was an all-male choir.

From time to time, I attended other synagogues in order to hear famous cantors from New York officiating in Philadelphia. Our small *shul* was, of course, hardly important enough to be on their itinerary. To hear them, I would have to walk quite a distance to the *Russisher Shul* (B'nai Abraham) or to the Ḥasidic congregation, B'nai Reuven Anshei Sfard, but the effort was rewarding.

One *ḥazzan* whom I vividly remember was Cantor Isaac Schlossberg, known more popularly as *Sha'agat ha-Ari*—"The Lion's Roar." Others included Cantor Meisels of New York and *Der Blinder Khazzen*. Once I was privileged to hear Cantor "Nissi Belzer" (Nissan Spivak), who, under emotional tension, stuttered, but who skillfully managed to capitalize on his defect by integrating it into the staccato style of his rendition. Their melodies, their stirring supplications and vocal prowess, left an indelible impress on my young ear, mind, and heart.

As I grew older, there were also opportunities to hear good classical music in Philadelphia. After overcoming my initial fear of venturing forth from our own tightly knit section in South Philadelphia, I came to know and love the fascinating historic environments with their own unique flavor of the past. A twenty-minute walk on a Saturday afternoon would bring me to Independence Hall and the sight of its Liberty Bell, crack and all. Fifteen minutes beyond it was City Hall, the tallest building in Philadelphia, surmounted by the impressive statue of William Penn in his broad-brimmed Quaker hat.

On rare occasions, usually Sundays, there were visits to Fairmont Park and its famous zoo. Somewhat more distant was Willow Grove, where well-known bands played occasionally, including the one conducted by John Philip Sousa. Less frequently there were excursions to Chester, where there was good fishing in the Delaware River. Physical diversions, however, were necessarily indulged in without the knowledge—let alone the blessing—of my parents, hence they were relished all the more. Although I had little enough time to roam around much, as I grew older, there were intermittent opportunities for recreation.

One problem of which I was yet unaware was that of Black-White race relations. Philadelphia had a large Negro community, and it was taken for granted that our Black fellow citizens were mostly engaged in menial occupations. Our household could not afford hired help, except on rare occasions; at no time was the attitude of our parents disdainful. In the primary grades and in high school there were Negro pupils, yet I do not recall any racial strains. Black youngsters were among the best athletes in high school and we respected them for their prowess.

Nevertheless, there must have been a good deal of seething resentment among Negroes in the community, which had not yet come to the surface. The nearest thing to racial tension I sensed was when I chanced to be on South Street during the prizefight between Jim Jeffries, the White boxing champion, and Jack Johnson, his Black challenger. I remember how startled I was by the hostile racial character of the reactions when the Negro boxer scored his victory.

I was also becoming aware of developments in the political sphere. Philadelphia was under the firm control of Republican politicians. We saw little but heard much about our ward leaders, the Vare brothers. Mayor Rayburn headed the Republican municipal administration, Senator Penrose was the senior of the two politicians representing Pennsylvania. There had been much popular admiration for President Teddy Roosevelt, the Rough Rider, whose foreign policy was to "speak softly and carry a big stick." Enthusiasm subsided during the regime of his Conservative successor, William H. Taft, but Jewish esteem for Taft increased when, in 1911, with the overwhelming support of Congress, he abrogated America's commercial treaty with czarist Russia because of that country's refusal to honor passports held by Jewish citizens of the U.S.

Philadelphia Jewry had a rich history dating back to pre-Revolutionary times, when it constituted a sizable proportion of the 1,500 Jews then living in the nine colonies. There were a handful of Jewish families residing between the Schuylkill and Delaware rivers in the late 1730s, some years before the Spanish and Portuguese congregation, Mikveh Israel, was established.

A number of Jews born in the city or living there at the outbreak of the American War of Independence in 1776, as well as during the next few decades, achieved distinction among its roster of patriots. The most illustrious of these Jews were Lieutenant Colonels Solomon Bush and David Salisbury Franks, Major Benjamin Nones (who was, at various times, aide-de-camp to the Marquis de Lafayette and to George Washington), Haym Solomon, and the Reverend Gershom Mendes Seixas of Congregation Shearith Israel in New York, who was a voluntary exile in Philadelphia during the early 1780s. The exploits of such Jewish patriots brightened our history books and fired our boyish imagination.

A great deal could be said about the personalities who shaped the early history of Philadelphia Jewry. I have always attached particular significance to the splendid roles those early Jewish patriots played during and after the American Revolution. My birth and my formative years in what had been the focal center of American independence, as well as my awareness of the contributions made to that cause by the founding fathers of its Jewish community, have left their impress on my consciousness as an American Jew.

Schooldays and Classmates

Not yet eight years old when I returned from the rustic vistas of northern Russia to the urban purlieus of South Philadelphia, I must have been an odd child indeed— an American-born "greener" who had never attended school in the United States.

My fluent knowledge of Yiddish, moderate acquaintance with Hebrew, and inadequate Russian were poor recommendations when I was enrolled in the public school at Third and Catherine Streets. Without one word of English to sustain me, I had to endure the taunts and gibes of classmates who spoke English as readily as I spoke *Mamme-loshen*.

My school was within the perimeter of the Jewish "ghetto" and only two blocks away from the Niezhiner *Shul* where we lived. In that pervasive Jewish atmosphere of home and school, and of the *ḥeder* where I became an after-school-hours pupil, life was to some extent a modified version of my erstwhile *shtetl* experience.

The *ḥeder* was run by Samuel Markowitz and enjoyed a local reputation as a *ḥeder metukkan*, an improvement over the old-fashioned ones, since pupils were taught *dikduk*, Hebrew grammar. To my father, only the best was good enough for his firstborn, even if it did involve an outlay of fifty cents a week for five sessions of four hours each. It was sheer extravagance when he paid out another fifty cents weekly for violin lessons, to carry on the basic instruction I had acquired in Svir from my cousin, the flutist. Such expenditure carved a substantial slice out of my father's income, which at that time was seven dollars a week.

Father's reward for this musical extravagance came from a recital he arranged for me in the meeting room of our *shul*. At its conclusion, a medal was presented to the child prodigy. Only later did I discover that it was my fond parent who had ordered the medal in anticipation of his son's "virtuosity" and to encourage his musical progress.

The pressure of other educational commitments soon necessitated the relinquishing of my budding career as a violinist. More exacting disciplines demoted the violin to the lower regions of our dwelling, and there it remained as a souvenir of musical promise unfulfilled.

Our Jewish milieu was not without its hazards. A Polish Catholic parochial school was located nearby, and now and then some of us younger lads had to run the gauntlet. It was under the stress and fury of those occasions that I first became familiar with the principles of *haganah*, self-defense.

Conforming to Ḥasidic practice, our Sabbath afternoons were dedicated to *Oneg Shabbat*, enjoyment of the holy day, which included a learned discourse. Periodically, the Chief Rabbi of Philadelphia, Rabbi Bernard L. Levinthal, who was the outstanding Orthodox rabbi of his time in the United States, would come and deliver a *droshe* at the Niezhiner *Shul*, whose congregants would admire more than they could understand. His erudition and Torah wisdom passed over my head, but I listened intently all the same. I like to think that the subconscious effect he had on an impressionable youngster, even of my tender years, was one of the early influences of my childhood.

Apart from Chief Rabbi Levinthal, our visitors included an occasional *maggid*, more preacher than scholar, whose function placed him in a class of his own. The role of the *maggid* in East European *shtetl* life was a formidable one. Outstanding among the itinerant variety was Rabbi Ya'akov Krantz, the famous Dubner *Maggid*. They were the Jewish orators par excellence; and, from time to time, a dramatic touch or flourish helped to get some religious or ethical message across to their rapt listeners.

The difference between the rabbi preaching his sermon and the *maggid* relating his parable was that the former delivered a learned disquisition, whereas the latter spoke more to the heart. His homiletical style was fortified by *musar*, moralizing injunctions designed to induce a mood of repentance and of resolution to lead a better way of life. The *maggid* often had melody as well as morality. He delivered his message with a *niggun*, a song of the heart and to the heart.

Association with the synagogue also had its practical advantages for a lad whose upbringing was tinged with parsimony. Sukkot, Tabernacles, was a rewarding festival. My assignment was to bring the *lulav* and *etrog* (palm branch and citron) to the homes of well-to-do congregants on each workday morning of the festival week. For this service, grateful recipients awarded me tips ranging from a quarter to as much as a dollar. Quite apart from the financial return, visiting these homes and staying until the prayer and blessing were completed had the advantage of giving me some insight into the way other families lived.

At this age, I became increasingly aware of my father's many talents and occupations. He was much more than the sexton of our synagogue—he was its most learned layman and conducted a *shi'ur* (study session) in Talmud. Every few years there would be a *Siyyum ha-Shas* festivity marking the completed study of the entire Talmud. I recall attending at least two of these special occasions.

Father was also the congregation's most interesting personality. Men came to him for advice and women would ask him to *apshprekhen an ayn-horra*, to "ward off the evil eye," if a malady afflicted their children. When Jewish fraternal organizations became the vogue, he served as secretary of the B'rith Sholom Lodge centered in our community. In addition, he was also secretary of a local building and loan association.

In later years, I often reflected that a man of his personality and talents would have gone much farther in life had he not been tied down by family obligations that made it hazardous to sacrifice the present for the future.

Meanwhile, my own childhood was proceeding apace. My school day was a long one: 9:00 A.M. to 3:00 P.M. at public school and 4:00 P.M. to 7:00 P.M. at *ḥeder*, except on Fridays, Sabbaths, and festivals. Homework for school classes also took up no little of my time, so Shabbat provided a welcome break.

The Sabbath had, of course, a routine of its own. There were, first of all, the services on Friday night and Shabbat morning. In midafternoon came my father's *farherren*, or oral examination, to ascertain what Jewish knowledge I had imbibed during the previous week. In the late afternoon, between *Minḥah* and *Ma'ariv* services, came the *Se'udah Shelishit* ("Third Meal"), of which the basic gastronomical ingredient was herring; its main intellectual and spiritual ingredient, however, was Ḥasidut, the building of a mystical ladder from earth to heaven, which usually left me suspended midway. A boy of ten could hardly be expected to grasp such mysteries, but this lad was not too young to feel some kind of dreamy uplift and to be stirred by the spirited *Zemirot*, Sabbath table hymns, which preceded and followed the discourse.

I came to know our neighborhood well, or at least those sections of it bounded by the perimeter of two blocks north and south. My special interests were the grocery store and the pharmacy, to which I was most often sent on errands by my ailing mother. The woman who ran the grocery store, assisted by a feeble-minded daughter who had been abandoned by her husband, aroused my deep respect for the courageous way in which she faced her problems.

Tackling a crowded daily schedule, I was prevented from enjoying a game of baseball or any other activity on the sports field. Indeed, my father frowned upon all such exercises as *bittul zeman*, a waste of good studying time. Schoolmates of mine, who were not so parentally inhibited, played games in the empty lot near the *heder*, and I would often watch them with some feeling of envy.

To compensate for the lack of physical training, I stepped up my sedentary activities. Philadelphia was fortunate in having a Hebrew Education Society founded some sixty or more years earlier, in 1849, with the object of providing the poor Jewish immigrant with extension courses in the language, literature, general culture, and usages of the New World. Around the end of the first decade of this century, the society opened its premises on Catherine Street and there I spent many an hour during the week devouring books, mostly English but some in Yiddish, also taking some home by courtesy of the lending service.

My father looked somewhat askance at these bundles of "goyish" books I toted home, followed later by my brothers and, in due course, by my sister, Sarah. Isaac was now about five or six, while Morris was born a year after Mother had brought her two older boys back from Russia.

Nevertheless, our excursions into the bowers of English literature went unimpeded. My father eventually became keen on my hearing good English speakers and even urged me to attend the Sunday lectures of the Ethical Culture Society's branch in Philadelphia, evidently having no fear that I might be swayed by that society's un-Jewish doctrines. There also, I had my first experience of listening to elevating music.

In his eagerness to expose me to good cultural influences, Father even suggested that I go to hear the sermons preached by the two leading Reform rabbis in the city, Dr. Joseph Krauskopf and Dr. Henry Berkowitz. This demonstrated both tolerance and foresight on his part.

I think that by then my father had already weighed in his mind the possibility of my studying for the rabbinate. Untouched by the doctor-lawyer complex, he wanted me to hear worthwhile speakers and good music, and to become acquainted with an atmosphere of decorum, quite different from what prevailed in the Niezhiner *Shul*.

The Hebrew Education Society on Third and Catherine Streets brought us some notable personalities in the field of Yiddish culture. Among them was Dr. Nahman Syrkin, the eminent Labor Zionist. His daughter, Dr. Marie Syrkin, a gifted woman of letters, has been our Zionist colleague and friend these many decades. Among other appreciated guest lecturers was Jacob Gordin, the best-known Yiddish dramaturgist of his time, who adapted several of Shakespeare's plays for the Yiddish stage. One of these was his celebrated drama, *Der Yidisher King Lear*. Gordin also wrote a few plays of his own, of which I remember *Got, Mensh un Tayfel*. This lecture schedule at the Hebrew Education Society helped to broaden my Jewish cultural horizons.

My browsings in the pastures of religious learning under the tutelage of Samuel Markowitz lasted until I was ten, by which time I was conversant with the Torah, the commentary of Rashi (our outstanding Jewish Bible commentator), and the rudiments of Talmud. At that stage, Mr. Markowitz told my father, "This *ḥeder* can no longer teach anything to your son—take him to the Yeshivah Ketannah."

This institution, Philadelphia's junior Jewish Academy, had been founded by Chief Rabbi Bernard L. Levinthal and its official name was Yeshivat Mishkan Yisrael. At the time when I knew him, Rabbi Levinthal was in the prime of life, in his mid-forties, with a high forehead and a sparsely bearded face that radiated geniality and nobility. He headed the United Orthodox Hebrew Congregations of Philadelphia, and in 1902 had been among the founders of the Union of Orthodox Rabbis of the United States and Canada, later also of the American Mizraḥi Organization.

His elder son, Israel Herbert, who was about seven years older than I, studied for the rabbinate at the Jewish Theological Seminary in New York. Louis Edward, his younger son, was my senior by only a few years and I became a junior member of his Zionist circle. It included David Galter, who in the course of time served as editor of the Philadelphia weekly, *The Jewish Exponent*, and Louis Feinberg, who in later years became the beloved Conservative rabbi in Cincinnati, Ohio.

Lou Levinthal and I were eventually classmates at the University of Pennsylvania. He went on to study law, became an eminent jurist, and was judge of the Court of Common Pleas until his retirement in 1959. He preceded me as president of the Zionish Organization of America, served as Jewish adviser to General Lucius Clay in postwar Germany and was, for a number of years, chairman of the board of governors of the Hebrew University. Judge Levinthal eventually came to live in Jerusalem, where we saw a great deal of one another until his lamented death in 1976.

At the Yeshivah Ketannah, where I remained for the next two years, I went on with the study of Talmud. Holding my own against the older boys was no easy task. We all admired our Talmud teacher, Mr. Ganapolsky, the best in town.

On reaching the age of twelve, I entered Southern Manual Training High School, which had opened only one year before my enrollment, in the "deep south" of South Philadelphia, not far from the city "Dump." The inclusion of manual training in the curriculum was an innovation in the city. None of the pupils was less qualified or adapted for it than I. Fortunately, however, the listing of my name placed me alongside a Jewish lad named Greenspan, who was extremely adroit with his hands and excelled at manual crafts. We struck a bargain. He helped me in the workshop, I helped him with his Latin, and so we both managed to graduate together.

The fact is that I would have preferred to go to Central High School in North Philadelphia, which had a reputation for academic excellence and also awarded a B.A. degree to its graduates. A zoning law, however, obliged me, as a resident of South Philadelphia, to attend the new high school, for boys only, which was in its second year of operation. Since, in the eyes of my parents, time was of the essence, this school's three-year course had obvious advantages.

The student body at Southern Manual High comprised approximately the same number of Jews and non-Jews, the latter being mostly Italians and Irish, with a sprinkling of Negroes. I cannot recall a single anti-Semitic incident during my three years there, although one heard of such discrimination at other local schools. There were Jewish boys on the basketball and football teams. One of the basketball players, also a good student, was Robert M. Bernstein, who later became a very successful lawyer and one of the leading Zionists in Philadelphia.

Parallel with my studies at Southern Manual High, I was also enrolled at Gratz College, a training school for Jewish teachers. It was named for a noted local Jewish benefactor, Hyman Gratz, who had made a large bequest in 1856 "for the education of Jews residing in the City and County of Philadelphia." The college was opened only some forty years later, however, toward the end of 1897.

It may be said that I entered under "false pretenses" as the minimum age was fifteen and I was only twelve, but I was "12XL"—big and burly for my age, and far ahead of my years in schooling. This mixture of qualifications also enabled me to enter college at fifteen.

When I was admitted to Gratz College, its premises were uptown on Seventh Street, in the basement vestry of the building occupied by the historic Spanish and Portuguese congregation, Mikveh Israel. Its rabbi at that time was Leon H. Elmaleh. A year before my graduation, in 1909, Gratz College moved further uptown to new premises adjoining Mikveh Israel at Broad and York Streets, about four miles from my home. I now had to walk a great deal farther, since the carfare by trolley (then all of three cents) was beyond my means. As a result of walking to high school four miles each way, five days a week, and the same distance to Gratz College three times a week, my legs became the best developed part of my body and have stood me in good stead ever since.

Attendance at Gratz was a rare experience. The faculty members whom I recall were the Reverend Henry M. Speaker, who was principal; Arthur Dembitz, who taught a systematic course of Jewish history; Dr. Isaac Husik, who taught Hebrew and years later achieved eminence as a historian of Jewish philosophy; and Julius H. Greenstone, who lectured on Jewish religious ceremonies and taught pedagogy. They provided us students with a modern Jewish background in subjects that, upon graduation, we in turn were to teach. I use the term *modern* because grammar was taught there as a science. Our syllabus also included the principles of teaching, which was the raison d'être of the establishment. Those years at Gratz were an important preparation for my future career.

Another first for me was being taught by Dr. Husik to use the Sephardi pronunciation of Hebrew. That was partly because Gratz College had been founded by leaders of the Spanish and Portuguese mother congregation of Philadelphia Jewry. It was a helpful anticipation of Israeli Hebrew.

To study at Gratz was a new and important experience for a youngster reared in the Niezhiner *Shul*. It was a time that also brought new and lasting friendships. One of these was with Ida Bloom, who later married Rabbi Harry Davidowitz. They made their Aliyah to Palestine, where he divided his time between managing his father-in-law's plant for manufacturing artificial teeth and translating Shakespeare's plays into Hebrew, while Ida reviewed plays for *The Palestine Post*.

One of my extra-curricular preoccupations was Zionism, which had first impinged upon my juvenile consciousness some years earlier. When I was eight, shortly after we returned home from Russia, the sudden death of Theodor Herzl at the early age of forty-four struck the Jewish world like a thunderbolt. The founder of modern political Zionism was, as yet, a remote figure in my life, nor was I old enough to fathom the inner tensions of the Zionist movement, but I was distinctly impressed by the impact of Herzl's death on my father. To him, as to most Jews, it came as a devastating blow. The Jewish masses had been fired by the advent of this towering figure and by the new hope and vision of Jewish redemption he inspired. Herzl's sudden passing, under the stress of arduous tasks and controversies, gave rise to shock and grief throughout the Jewish world.

The Zionist presence in our home, as in most Jewish homes where we lived, was betokened by the blue and white *pushke* (collection box) of the Jewish National Fund, which had been established less than three years before Herzl's death. There it stood, beckoning for those coins which might eventually redeem a *dunam* of land or plant a forest on the soil of our ancient homeland.

When I was around twelve, Zionism became for me a personal experience and responsibility. Among my classmates at Yeshivat Mishkan Yisrael were several who gained distinction in various fields—Gershon Agronsky (later Agron), the journalist and founder of *The Palestine Post*, who was to become Mayor of Jerusalem; Koppel Pinson, the historian; Louis Fischer, an expert on Soviet affairs who was long sympathetic to Communism; and Samuel Noah Kramer, the world-renowned authority on ancient Sumerian culture. We were all near contemporaries and we moved within more or less the same adolescent orbit.

Gershon was one of my closest companions and our friendship, which later involved our wives, Ethel and Bert, remained lifelong. Gershon had come with his family from Russia. At seventeen, he was handsome, bright-faced, brash, quick-witted, and articulate. Louis Fischer, born in Philadelphia the same year as I, was for nearly three decades a leading apologist for the Soviet Union, and his books and lectures attracted wide attention.

Together with Gershon Agronsky, I became a Zionist politician at the age of twelve. We named our group the Hatikvah Club and at the beginning were under the tutelage of somewhat older young Zionists such as Louis Feinberg, David Galter, Louis Levinthal, and C. David Matt. Soon, however, we were on our own, facing the Zionist realities staunchly and combatively. Combatively, because our ventures sometimes led us into stormy conflicts. Gershon and I harangued young audiences at street corners. Some of us boys were also engaged in militant sorties against the Christian Mission to the Jews, which had its headquarters at Fifth and Catherine Streets, in the heart of South Philadelphia's Jewish quarter. This, we decided, was sheer chutzpah, and we reacted accordingly.

As a budding Zionist leader, I alternated with Gershon Agronsky in the presidency of the Hatikvah Club. Another political milestone achieved at this time was my being chosen by popular vote as "senator" to represent Section IV in Southern Manual Training High School's Class of 1911, the year in which I turned fifteen. This was as far as I ever got toward the U.S. Senate.

Stepping Stones

In the summer of 1911, at the age of fifteen, I finished both high school and Gratz College, and was admitted to the University of Pennsylvania.

Having been elected salutatorian of the Class of 1911 at Southern Manual High, I had to deliver the address at the commencement exercises. As a devotee of Shakespeare, whose literary treasures our English teacher, Professor Nieweg, had revealed to us, I took up his suggestion and chose as my theme the three hundredth anniversary of the Bard's death, although that occasion was still five years away.

An important new factor in my life at this time was the birth of my sister, Sarah, which enhanced my status as the oldest of four instead of three. The intrusion of a girl into the family did not bother me as much as it must have perplexed my younger brothers, Isaac and Morris, since I was busy and away from home most of the time. Often I regretted not having had the experience of growing up with a sister; what it meant to have an older brother in absentia, only little Sarah would know.

Our family circle now included three of my mother's brothers—Hirsch and Leibe Silver and their families, and Max Silver, who was still a bachelor. My cousin Morris, Hirsch's son, my senior by six months, was a staunch Zionist; my cousin Julius, Leibe and Esther's son, several years younger than I, already showed signs of great promise. His family eventually moved to Brooklyn. There were also female cousins, I should add, but with these relatives I had little converse in our male-dominated milieu.

Duly graduated from high school to college, I lacked one essential requirement—*kemaḥ*, adequate means, my father's being, of course, meager. He, after all, had to bring up the younger children. True, I was now competent to teach in a Jewish school, as a graduate of Gratz College, but this could only begin somewhat later. I needed employment, even if temporary, in order to earn a few dollars to see me through the summer. Luckily, I found a job as a stockboy in the stoves section of the Litt Brothers' department store. The pay was eight dollars weekly, with no work on Saturdays.

Fortune smiled more graciously upon me at the end of the summer, when a teaching post became available at the Sunday Hebrew school in Frankfort, a district in the northeastern part of the city. Following upon that, I took on a teaching assignment at the Hebrew Orphanage in suburban Olney—four afternoons weekly, four hours every afternoon, at the rate of fifteen dollars a week. This enabled me not only to pay my way through college but also to contribute to the family exchequer.

Evidently because of my size, I was assigned the top class at the orphanage and found that some of the pupils were not much younger than their teacher. If, despite our lecturers' urgings at Gratz College, I sometimes resorted to corporal punishment as a means of instilling discipline, this was only in self-defense.

Upon my admission to the university, therefore, in the fall of 1911, I was already pursuing a busy life of tuition—both at the receiving and at the giving ends. Regrettably, I was too young and too fully occupied to derive much advantage from the social life on the campus, where my fellow students were mostly three years my senior. Through force of circumstance, I devoted myself to my studies and to earning a livelihood. Nevertheless, I did find time for Friday afternoon concerts at the Academy of Music, where a seat in the top gallery, almost under the rafters, cost fifteen cents. It was worth that amount, no paltry sum in those days, to hear the Philadelphia Orchestra playing under the baton of famed maestros. Among the soloists, my preference was naturally for violinists rather than pianists, and Eugène Ysaye and Jan Kubelik impressed me most.

Another welcome relaxation was to attend a play at the famed Chestnut Street Theater. There was a stock company with Blanche Yurka as the leading lady. Occasional touring companies with star performers came to display their dramatic wares. A seat in the upper balcony cost the standard fifteen cents.

I was an especially ardent Yiddish theatergoer, partly because this secular diversion was "forbidden fruit." Only some years later did my father and mother themselves begin to frequent and enjoy the Yiddish Theater. For my earlier transgressions, and for my introduction to this new cultural medium, I have to thank my Uncle Max Silver. The first Yiddish play I saw was *Joseph and his Brothers*. Some of the actors who came to entertain audiences in Philadelphia were Jacob Adler, Madame Keni Lipzin, Boris Thomashefsky, David Kessler, Jacob Rosenthal, and, later on, Rudolph Schildkraut, whose background was the classical theater in Germany, as well as the comedians, Sam Kestin and Sigmund Mogulesco.

A serious turning point in the life of our family occurred when I was in my first year at the university. Father gave up his position in the Niezhiner Synagogue and took on a coal agency. Our family then moved to the Strawberry Mansion section of Philadelphia, a new middle-class Jewish neighborhood, where he bought a two-story brick home.

The new residence was a welcome improvement over our previous living quarters, but any enjoyment we felt was overshadowed by the illness that afflicted him for a long time. It was a persistent circulatory ailment, Reynaud's disease, which affected his left leg and may have resulted from excessive cigarette smoking. I became an amateur physician and consulted numerous medical books in the university library, searching for information about Father's ailment. He came under constant hospital treatment and underwent a series of amputations, starting with a toe and ending at the knee joint. The surgeon was John K. Mitchell, son of one of Philadelphia's most distinguished physicians and men of letters, Dr. S. Weir Mitchell.

After a year's ordeal in various hospitals, and having been fitted with a prosthetic limb, Father was allowed to go home and had to face a difficult period of adjustment. Much of his time was spent in the nearby B'nai Jeshurun Synagogue, where he conducted a class in Talmud. A few years later, Dr. Abraham A. Neuman was appointed rabbi of this congregation. He later became president of Dropsie College. Neuman, together with his successors, Rabbi Harry Davidowitz and Rabbi Max Drob, held my father in high regard.

I was a young man in a hurry, having decided to complete the four-year college course in liberal arts within three years. My self-imposed task was not made easier by my crowded Hebrew teaching schedule, which left little time for extra-curricular activities. I did join one group, however, a branch of the Menorah Association (then in its early phase on college campuses), which provided a forum for the discussion of Zionist and other Jewish issues.

The three years at college passed by quickly enough. I did rather well at the academic level and was elected to Phi Beta Kappa in my third and graduating year.

While still at Gratz College, I had come to the attention of Dr. Cyrus Adler, then president of its board of trustees. He continued to keep an eye on me at the University of Pennsylvania. The hours I spent in the library there also brought me into contact with Professor Morris Jastrow, the orientalist, who was also a leader in the Ethical Culture movement.

Around this time, my teaching post at the Hebrew Orphan Asylum out in Olney proved too arduous, because of the time consumed in traveling to and fro, so I relinquished it in favor of one at the Talmud Torah School in northeast Philadelphia, where Dr. Joseph Meadow was the principal.

As I approached graduation in the early months of 1914, shortly before my eighteenth birthday, I began pondering my future. I had no taste for business, law, or medicine. For a while, the idea of pursuing a career in social work appealed to me and I made extensive inquiries about the possibilities in that field. Then thoughts of the rabbinate began to occupy my mind more and more, as this was a calling that also provided opportunities for social and communal service. Five young Philadelphians, with whose families we had a close acquaintance, had graduated or were about to graduate that year from the Jewish Theological Seminary in New York, the rabbinical training school of Conservative Judaism. They were Israel Herbert Levinthal, son of Rabbi Bernard L. Levinthal; Milton Markowitz, son of my old *ḥeder* teacher; and C. David Matt, Morris Teller, and Oscar Levin. The Orthodox rabbinical school was the Rabbi Isaac Elchanan Theological Seminary (now Yeshiva University) in New York, while the Reform school was Hebrew Union College in Cincinnati.

For a number of reasons, my inclination was toward the Jewish Theological Seminary, where Professor Solomon Schechter, one of the great scholars of our age, was then president. He had joined the Seminary in 1902, at the invitation of several leading American Jews, including Judge Mayer Sulzberger of Philadelphia, and remained in office until his death in 1915.

Since my father had been closely connected with an Orthodox—indeed, a Hasidic—synagogue for so many years, he must have had reservations about his son making a career for himself in the non-Orthodox rabbinate. My own association with the Niezhiner *Shul* had endowed me with an Orthodox practice that was more habit than persuasion, but I had no deep theological commitments. Father was probably aware of this ambivalence on my part and, as he himself tended to become more liberal in his attitude as he grew older, he did not raise any objections when I opted for the Conservative seminary.

A decisive factor was the encouragement of Dr. Cyrus Adler, by now president of

Dropsie College, where, after graduating from the University of Pennsylvania in 1914, I took a summer course in Bible under Professor Max L. Margolis. Dr. Adler took a friendly interest in my career and advised me to go to New York. A year or two later, following the death of Professor Schechter, he became acting president of the Seminary, and I continued to enjoy his patronage.

Together with his cousin, Judge Mayer Sulzberger, and Judge Horace Stern, Dr. Adler was one of the top lay leaders of Philadelphia Jewry—the "uptown Jews" to whom we humbler residents of the southern purlieus looked up with great respect. I revered Judge Sulzberger from afar. With Judge Stern I had some communication when I taught at the Hebrew school in the Frankfort section of town, to which he would come in his capacity as president of the Hebrew Education Society, to address the closing exercises.

Toward the end of September 1914, therefore, I said goodbye to Philadelphia, not without some keenly felt nostalgia for my boyhood and youth there. Ten years had elapsed since my mother had brought her two small boys back from Russia, a decade that had been fruitful in many respects and during which I had forged a number of enduring ties and friendships.

Three other Philadelphians, older than myself, also enrolled at the Jewish Theological Seminary at that time. They were Bernard Heller, Nahum Krueger, and Reuben Rabinowitz, whose families were friendly with us. I was the youngest student in the Class of 1918.

Other boyhood friends I left behind. One was Gershon Agronsky, who was then beginning his career in journalism on the staff of the newly established *Yidishe Velt* in Philadelphia. Two years later, he set off for Montreal to enlist in the British-sponsored Jewish Legion, then trained in England and served in Palestine under General Allenby. Louis Fischer had also embarked on a writing career, which would eventually take him to Russia and win him fame as an authority on Soviet Communism. For a short while, he, too, served in the Jewish Legion. Eddie Davis, whose father was a regular visitor at our home, had begun studying law and dabbled in literature and drama.

I left Philadelphia for New York, deeply grateful that I had been born and raised in that City of Brotherly Love, which had played such an important part in America's growth and development. Its Jewish community, 175,000 out of a total population of a million and a half in 1914, was the third largest in the United States, exceeded only by the *kehillot* of New York City and Chicago. Both as a distinctive element in Philadelphia's history and as a mother community in American Jewry, its role was a notable one. I have always taken pride in being one of Philadelphia's native sons.

2

The Good Way: 1914–25

"Provide yourself with a teacher," Rabban Gamliel enjoins in the opening section of *Pirké Avot*, the Mishnaic "Chapters of the Fathers." That was precisely my aim when I entered the Jewish Theological Seminary as a youthful Bachelor of Arts, eager to drink deep at this fount of Jewish learning.

The Seminary occupied a three-story building at 523 West 123rd Street, just south of West Harlem. This structure barely accommodated the faculty and the seventy students who were enrolled in those days. Because the number of students was not large, most classes were attended by the entire student body.

There can be no doubt that we were well provided with a distinguished faculty that gave the JTS its reputation as one of the foremost institutions of Jewish learning in the world. It was headed by Dr. Solomon Schechter, who combined vast Hebrew erudition with a felicitous English style. The Seminary's fame rested upon Professor Schechter and four other scholars of renown, whom he had brought in: Professor Louis Ginzberg, in Talmud; Professor Israel Friedlaender, in Bible; Professor Alexander Marx, in history and Jewish bibliography; and Professor Israel Davidson, in medieval Hebrew literature. Like my fellow students, I was awed at the privilege of sitting at their feet.

Solomon Schechter had come to New York from the University of Cambridge, England, a dozen years before I enrolled, bringing with him most of his great library of discoveries from the Cairo Genizah, on which he was the world authority. A commanding, patriarchal figure, with a leonine head crowned by a mane of white hair, Professor Schechter had a broad, impressive beard, a regal countenance, and piercing blue eyes that gazed intently at one over the half-moon reading glasses. Except for those spectacles, he had the authentic appearance of a biblical prophet.

We listened reverently to his lectures on theology, although they were easier to read than to hear. Often I would sit passively, almost heedless of his flow of scholarship, basking in that inspiring presence. I could not help feeling that he barely knew or noticed me.

Professor Schechter had been Reader in Rabbinics at Cambridge. Leaving Germany for Britain in his midthirties, he acquired an impeccable, masterly English style rated second only to Israel Zangwill's in Anglo-Jewry, and he possessed a mordant wit that could demolish opponents with a phrase. His addresses at the annual Seminary graduation exercises at Aeolian Hall were eagerly anticipated, not only for their scholarly content but also for their incisive comments on timely and timeless Jewish problems. He brought to the American Jewish scene a breath of fresh air in Judaism and Zionism, as well as in Jewish scholarship, coupled with a gift for the striking utterance.

Because of his immense scholarship and worldwide reputation, Schechter seemed remote and inaccessible. It was rumored at the Seminary in my time that, without his wife, Mathilde, he would have been completely lost in the mundane aspects of life, such as food, dress, and the like.

Looking over his spectacles, he seemed to gaze far beyond the students in front of him. Schechter made an impressive figure in that portrait of him, swathed in his red Cambridge academic robe, which hung on one of the Seminary walls. We marveled at this Rumanian Jew who had shaken the world of Jewish scholarship by his discovery and interpretation of the Genizah fragments, which he rescued from the ancient Cairo Synagogue.

Solomon Schechter's arrival in the United States gave stimulus to the Conservative movement. In 1913, he founded the United Synagogue of America, as a federation of congregations with a common tie of loyalty to Conservative ("historical") Judaism, as distinct from Reform and Orthodoxy.

His advent also proved a boon to the fledgling Zionist movement in America. Schechter's chief contribution, however, was to Jewish learning and to the training of rabbis who would combine Jewish learning with modern culture and thus contribute to strengthening Judaism in America.

Professor Louis Ginzberg, who taught rabbinics, possessed a Talmudic erudition far beyond my ken. Below average in height, he had large piercing eyes, a piping voice marked by a slight German accent, and a friendly manner that balanced his innate remoteness. Louis Ginzberg's reputation as an *illui*, the leading Talmudist of his day, was enhanced by the fact of his descent from the prestigious Gaon of Vilna. We students regarded him as the most Orthodox star in the Seminary's constellation.

My own Talmudic equipment was deemed inadequate for Professor Ginzberg's class, so I was assigned to that of Professor Israel Davidson. He was at that time on his way to the topmost rung of scholarship in medieval Hebrew literature, although few of us then suspected that this was his forte, especially the Hebrew poetry of the Middle Ages. His monumental thesaurus of Hebrew poetry throughout the ages is still a classic. We appreciated Israel Davidson, however, for his delightful sense of humor.

Professor Israel Friedlaender's realm at the Seminary was biblical literature and exegesis. In the wider world of scholarship, however, he was also considered an authority on Arabic (including Judeo-Arabic) literature and on Semitics in general. An inspiring teacher, he lectured with style and erudition. Yet he was not only a scholar: he held and expounded views on current Jewish affairs and also played an active role in the communal life of New York Jewry. Professor Friedlaender meant even more to us as the Zionist par excellence among our teachers. It was from him that we learned about Aḥad Ha-Am (Asher Ginzberg), the great articulator of cultural and spiritual Zionism. His tragic end, in 1920, when he was murdered by bandits while on a mission for the Joint Distribution Committee in the Ukraine, deprived American and World Jewry of a Jewish luminary and dedicated servant of his people.

Another of our revered teachers was Rabbi Moses Hyamson, who joined the faculty in 1915, during my second year, as professor of Jewish legal codes. Though somewhat on the pedantic side, Hyamson was a gentle soul who, while lacking the power to inspire, commanded respect for his learning and piety. Professor Hyamson, formerly senior *dayyan* of the London Beth Din, had arrived from England in 1913, after an unsuccessful bid for the post of Chief Rabbi left vacant by the death of Dr. Hermann Adler. The successful candidate, Dr. Joseph H. Hertz, was the Seminary's first graduate. After having served as the leading rabbi in Johannesburg, South Africa, for about twelve years, Hertz accepted a call to Congregation Orach Chayim, a prominent Orthodox synagogue in New York, which he left upon his appointment to the Chief Rabbinate of the British Empire. Dr. Hyamson had then come to New York to fill the vacancy at Congregation Orach Chayim.

The most beloved of our teachers was the historian and bibliographer, Professor Alexander Marx, a large, hale, well-built man of jovial personality, whose hearty laugh could often be heard resounding through the halls of learning. A graduate of the Orthodox rabbinical seminary in Berlin (like Israel Friedlaender), and already a historian and bibliographer of repute, he had accepted Professor Schechter's invitation to teach Jewish history and to serve as librarian at the Seminary. Marx was an outstanding linguist, equally at home in classical and Semitic languages. A superb scholar, he lectured on history in a thorough and comprehensive manner, though not always as comprehensibly as we would have wished, because of his heavy German accent.

Professor Marx was a fine bookman, with an extraordinary knowledge of manuscripts. In the course of his half-century of service at the JTS (1903–53), he built up a massive library of some 165,000 books—there had been only 5,000 when he arrived—and the world's largest collection of Judaica manuscripts.

Most of my own intellectual stimulation, however, came from Rabbi Mordecai M. Kaplan, who was professor of homiletics. This subject naturally had the greatest attraction for most of the rabbinical students. Professor Kaplan had been on the faculty during the five years preceding my arrival at the JTS, and he was the youngest and most thought-provoking of our teachers. His course on Midrash was a fascinating excursus into that field. He taught us not only how to construct a sermon, but also to find new and deeper meaning in the text of the Torah. At about that time he was beginning to develop his philosophy of Judaism as an evolving religious civilization, a concept from which the Reconstructionist movement would eventually blossom. A lifelong Zionist, he spent a dozen of his later years in Jerusalem and maintained his literary output and his influence to the extraordinarily ripe old age of one hundred.*

Two other members of the faculty were Mr. A. Jaffe, who gave supplementary instruction in Talmud to those boys, like myself, who were in need of additional "toning up," and Mr. Walter Robinson, who was our instructor in elocution and public speaking.

All in all, therefore, we were exposed to as eminent a group of scholars as was feasible to gather under one roof, and we were not unmindful of that privilege.

Following the death of Professor Schechter in 1915, Dr. Cyrus Adler became acting president of the Seminary. He served as its president from 1924 until his death in 1940. His reputation as a scholar rested on his earlier years at the Smithsonian Institution in Washington, D.C., and as president of Dropsie College in Philadelphia.

Since Dr. Adler had been instrumental in bringing me to the JTS, I had a special reverence for him coupled with personal gratitude. His friendly guidance continued throughout my student career. Nevertheless, I could also judge him objectively (see chapter 15). As a human being, he seemed rather cold and aloof. As a Jew, he felt and exercised deep concern and a great sense of responsibility for the well-being of American Jewry and of the Jewish people everywhere. He had a prominent role in the affairs of the American Jewish community, but he was not a Zionist. Indeed, he frequently clashed with Zionist leaders, and I felt an emotional barrier between us on that score. I regarded him as a kind of Brahmin in Jewish life, a feeling enhanced by his aristocratic family connections in Philadelphia.

Within the walls of the Seminary on West 123rd Street, there was scarcely an echo of the world-shaking events precipitated by the outbreak of war in Europe. We students were old enough, of course, to sense the cataclysmic nature of the times, but it had little impact on our own lives until the United States declared war on the Central Powers, Germany and the Austro-Hungarian Empire.

There were eleven of us in the class of 1918. Solomon Goldman, a Brownsville boy, three years my senior, was impressively at home in modern Hebrew literature. He was also our most articulate Zionist. The best Talmudist among us was Solomon Metz.

Since the Jewish Theological Seminary was identified as a training school for Conservative rabbis, and since Dr. Schechter was the exponent par excellence of Conservative Judaism in America, it seemed rather paradoxical to me at the time that the leading trustees of the Seminary board should be such men as Louis Marshall, Jacob H. Schiff, and Felix M. Warburg, whose affiliation was with Reform Judaism. Their support was no doubt an expression of their enthusiasm for the Seminary as an institution of higher Jewish learning rather than as a school for the training of Conservative rabbis, yet the incongruity of this situation did not escape me.

*In March 1981, when these lines were written.

Subsistence was a problem that faced nearly all of my classmates. There were no tuition fees at JTS in those days, but there were also no dormitories. Some modest stipends were available, but, for the most part, we had to fend for ourselves and pay for our board and lodging—those of us, at least, who were from outside the New York area. Coming from lower-middle-class homes, we all looked for opportunities to earn a livelihood by giving private Hebrew lessons or teaching Hebrew school classes.

My own economic odyssey led me first to a Mr. Samuel Rottenberg in Brooklyn, a well-to-do manufacturer of knitted goods who was already making his mark as a patron of Jewish education in his community. I was engaged to tutor his three sons. Residence with the Rottenberg family was my first exposure to comfort, even luxury, but it was hard-earned luxury in that it meant having to cope with three husky, spirited youngsters who looked askance at Hebrew instruction as an unwelcome intrusion into their playtime. Besides, the oldest brother was too much for me to cope with physically. This lack of rapport between us was bad enough, but the long journeys between their home in Brooklyn and the Seminary on New York's West Side deprived me of two precious hours daily that might have been devoted to study. It was inevitable, therefore, that my hard-earned, unaccustomed luxury should have terminated after a short time.

Fortunately, an opening became available for a teacher at the weekday Hebrew school of a congregation in Washington Heights, a new upper-middle-class Jewish neighborhood, easily accessible by an extension of the subway. My robust physique again stood me in good stead: I was assigned to teach the top class, which consisted of twelve- and thirteen-year-old boys and girls. The principal, Rabbi Moses Rosenthal, a recent Seminary graduate, was also rabbi of the congregation.

What with teaching at this school and a few private lessons, my economic situation was better than that of most fellow students, but my work schedule was a demanding one.

A fellow Philadelphian, Milton Markowitz, son of my onetime *ḥeder* teacher, had just graduated from the Seminary and it was through him that I met his uncle, who lived a short distance away. There was room for a lodger at his home, a prospect that had obvious advantages—continued association with the Markowitz family, a short walk from the Seminary, and the fact that Morris Markowitz, Milton's uncle, had been praised as a Talmudic scholar by his brother, Samuel, in Philadelphia, who had taught me the rudiments of my Hebrew education. There were certain other advantages of which I became aware only after taking up residence in the household. One was the rare character of the *ba'alat ha-bayit*, Dora Markowitz, a true *eshet ḥayil*, or "woman of valor." Another, to which I accustomed myself gradually, though not reluctantly, was that the Markowitz household included five girls, Bessie, Rose, Bertha (Bert), Adele, and Grace. The third daughter, Bert, who was closest to my age, appealed to me in particular. She was bright, attractive, high-spirited, and endowed with a warm, outgoing personality. At the time, she was about to graduate from Hunter College.

The report I brought to my parents on my first visit home—that I was now esconced in the Markowitz residence—brought them a measure of reassurance.

My first year at the Jewish Theological Seminary was anything but a scholastic triumph. I must have regarded it as a welcome opportunity to relax after an intensive three years at college, together with my strenuous teaching schedule to earn a living. Father's protracted illness had also called for a special measure of solicitude on the part of the eldest son.

Consciously or not, I took that first year at the JTS somewhat lightheartedly. Encouraged by one of my Seminary classmates, I indulged in activities that scarcely taxed the intellect. They included running a small boat equipped with an outboard motor, enjoying an occasional vaudeville entertainment, and generally inclining more toward "L'Allegro" than toward "Il Penseroso."

In the midst of these diversions, Professor Mordecai Kaplan, then a vigorous man in his late thirties, invited me to go rowing with him one afternoon on Central Park Lake. Although no words of stern admonition accompanied this friendly gesture, our little excursion did provoke more reflection and stocktaking on my part.

I caught myself midway in that backsliding from academic application, in time to work seriously for the end-of-year exams. Not only did I pass them convincingly, I also managed to write a prizewinning essay for Professor Schechter on "The History of the Khazars." This belated spurt of academic ambition probably came as a surprise to more than one of my teachers.

Over the High Holy Days, it was customary for most JTS students to take on assignments in synagogues, helping to conduct the services and preaching sermons. The place assigned to me was a newly formed congregation in Camden, New Jersey, across the river from my native city. There I had my first practical experience in the pulpit.

It was with a chastened sense of purpose, determined to prove myself, that I entered upon my second year at the Seminary. In addition to my rabbinical studies, I started working for my M.A. degree at Columbia University. The interlude of revolt against the strict regime of my pre-Seminary days was over. This turnabout may well have been motivated not only by a wish to gain the respect of the faculty and of my classmates, but also—subconsciously perhaps—by an urge to impress the Markowitz household, especially the girl studying at Hunter College.

At the beginning of that second year, I found myself in the company of some new students of excellent caliber. Prominent among them was Louis Finkelstein, who had just been admitted to the JTS. This son of the outstanding Orthodox rabbi in Brownsville, New York, was already making his mark as a brilliant young Talmudic scholar.

A memorable circumstance marked that period in 1915, a few months after my nineteenth birthday. Our homiletics course provided that students, beginning with their second year, should preach Shabbat morning sermons before the Seminary congregation, which included members of the faculty and other worshipers living in the vicinity. These sermons had first to be delivered before the faculty and student body on the preceding Wednesday, when they would be criticized by the president, the professor of homiletics, the instructor in elocution, and the students. In the light of their comments, the novice preacher would make the necessary revisions and then deliver his sermon before congregants in the Seminary synagogue on the following Sabbath morning. All in all, it was something of an ordeal for any budding *darshan*.

That year, Professor Kaplan announced that the sermon themes should be of a biographical nature, dealing with the *Tanna'im*, the teachers of the early Talmudic period. The subject assigned to me was Rabban Gamliel of Yavneh. Each discourse was to include a survey of the *Tanna's* life, a selective study of his outstanding attributes, and an appropriate linkage of those attributes with the Jewish problems and issues of our time.

When my turn came to read the sermon before the jury, prior to its formal delivery at the larger Sabbath gathering, I was understandably nervous. Having presented my maiden effort, I waited anxiously to hear the reactions. Two or three of the students spoke first, offering some friendly criticism. Professor Kaplan spoke next, and his judgment was favorable. Then, with bated breath, we all awaited Professor Solomon Schechter's verdict. To my amazement and delight, it was enthusiastic. However surprised other people may have been, I was flabbergasted, and not a little mystified.

All this took place on November 17, 1915. I looked forward with expectation and new confidence to giving my sermon three days later, on the ensuing Sabbath. No one could then have foreseen the dire event that would befall us so swiftly, endowing that sermon with unexpected significance.

Early on Friday morning, November 19 (12 Kislev), Professor Solomon Schechter, our revered head, suffered a heart attack and passed away at the age of sixty-nine. His death shocked and appalled the whole of American Jewry. A "mighty cedar of Lebanon" had fallen.

At the funeral, held on the following Sunday, Rabbi Elias L. Solomon delivered the eulogy. Next day, the faculty met to consider what form of memorial observance to arrange at services on the ensuing Sabbath, before the Seminary congregation. On the initiative of Professor Mordecai Kaplan, and with the approval of the faculty, it was decided to invite me to deliver my sermon on Rabban Gamliel of Yavneh, as a memorial tribute to Professor Schechter of blessed memory. The sermon apparently had brought out points of resemblance between the lives of those two men—the severe standards they set for Jewish scholarship and leadership, their appreciation of the value of non-Jewish culture, and their passion for the unity of the Jewish people, transcending all personal considerations.

So, at last, it became clear to me—as to others—why Solomon Schechter had shown such enthusiasm for that sermon on Rabban Gamliel. Subconsciously, I had written it with Schechter in mind and he, subconsciously, must have reacted accordingly.

Speaking of Rabban Gamliel, I said:

His attitude toward the secular subjects of the day was remarkably liberal. His knowledge of mathematics and astronomy was so profound that it enabled him to compute the calendar, and his sympathy for Greek culture in general is attested by his son. . . .

In this attitude, Rabban Gamliel was not only in advance of his own times but far in advance of many in our own day who seem to think that secular knowledge, worldly culture, and good Jewishness cannot dwell harmoniously under one roof.

I went on to show how Rabban Gamliel, through his worldly wisdom and broad human sympathies, was able to gain recognition for his office and for his people among the ruling classes of Rome, and how we in our own day needed the same kind of recognition for our people and our religion.

I continued:

Jews need no longer keep their faith in the dark. It should be brought out into the broad daylight, to the full view of the Gentiles. They are interested to know about our religion, our history, our literature. . . . When telling them, we must speak in a way intelligible to them. We must ourselves have a good understanding of secular knowledge and culture; we must be educated in the history of the world, in the literature of the nations, in order to present our message to the world clearly and comprehensibly. . . .

Would that our spokesmen were men like Rabban Gamliel—not only devout Jews but also cultured, worldly Jews. There is a crying need for such leaders in our time. Moreover, present-day Jewish life in America is disorganized. We cannot hope to establish in this country the kind of unity which Rabban Gamliel of Yavneh established in his day. We cannot hope to have here such an institution as the Assembly of Yavneh, exercising not only religious but also civil authority. But we can dare to hope for leaders of Rabban Gamliel's caliber, and we need such leaders to give strength to Judaism in this country—leaders who are both Jewish and modern, who are ready to sacrifice their personal ambitions for the sake of their cause; leaders who can also be followers, who will not hesitate to retire from leadership when the circumstances require it, yet continue to take part in the councils of their people; leaders who will work not for their own honor, but for the honor of God and the welfare of Israel . . . as did Rabban Gamliel of Yavneh.

In delivering this Sabbath sermon after the memorial prayer, I added a brief personal eulogy of Solomon Schechter, after noting that mine had been the last student discourse that received his approval:

The uppermost ideal of Rabban Gamliel's life was the one which inspired our departed master, the ideal of a unified Israel. The hope of spiritual unity among our people was, for him, a major concern. To the promulgation of this hope, and to the nourishment of this ideal, he applied his brilliant mind and powerful pen. . . . Our departed master is a link in the golden chain of illustrious leaders of our people who lived for the glory of God and the unity of Israel.

The unusual combination of circumstances attending this, my homiletical debut, was recalled for years thereafter by those who had been present on that occasion.

Dilemmas and Decisions

It was during my second year at the Seminary that I began to be troubled about knotty points of Jewish theology and practice, and about my future course of preparation for the rabbinate. I started to feel uneasy over what was expected of a Conservative rabbi in regard to theology and ritual observance. Several other students in our class who were similarly troubled had, in fact, already defected from the Seminary and moved to Hebrew Union College in Cincinnati, the training school for Reform rabbis. One of them was my fellow Philadelphian, Bernard Heller; two others were Joseph L. Baron and William Schwartz.

I faced the same dilemma. A variety of doubts assailed me, yet Cincinnati held no allurement: Reform Judaism struck me as a synthesis of negatives, and I felt that I should be able to maintain my independence in the broad ranks of Conservative Judaism. It was my hope that, in a seminary with patrons such as Schiff, Marshall, Warburg, and the Lehmans, there might be no authoritarian domination.

What I disliked most of all about Hebrew Union College was the anti-Zionist atmosphere fostered by its president, Dr. Kaufmann Kohler. At the same time, however, I never quite overcame the feeling that I did not fit neatly into the pattern of Conservative Judaism. Thus, if I may run ahead of my story, there were many presidencies in American Jewish life that later offered themselves and that I accepted, yet I declined the presidency of the Rabbinical Assembly of America, the Conservative movement's rabbinate. I felt that I could not be considered, in thought and in practice, a normative representative of that trend in Judaism. All in all, however, I did feel more at home in the Conservative rabbinate than I would have felt in the Reform rabbinate of that period. I brought my congregation into the United Synagogue of America and I never severed my ties with the Rabbinical Assembly.

As students at the JTS, we frequently had confrontations with Reform Judaism. Often, on a Sabbath morning, some of us would stroll over to hear rabbis preach in those synagogues within walking distance. Although we had a high regard for the discourses of Rabbi Jacob Kohn of Temple Ansche Chesed, a Conservative congregation, we were deeply impressed by the preaching of Samuel Schulman, the Reform rabbi of Temple Beth-El. Our appreciation of Rabbi Schulman's sermons derived from their intellectual content, their learning, and their spirited delivery, but we often found ourselves in disagreement with his Reform doctrines and especially with his anti-Zionism.

My second year at the Seminary (1915) was marked by a good student record. I gained awards in homiletics and public speaking, as well as a prize for an essay on "The Aramaic Portion of the Liturgy," which I wrote for Professor Israel Davidson.

That was the year in which I took a momentous decision, although it was less spiritual than romantic in nature. Bertha Markowitz and I had been taking notice of each other for some time, and ere long we decided to announce our engagement. Bert, who graduated that year from Hunter College, had a background different from mine in many respects, but quite similar in others. Her parents, too, had emigrated from Lithuania at the end of the nineteenth century, but the towns from which they came—Keidan and Chekishok—were considerably larger than the *shtetlakh* where my parents had been born and raised.

Bert's father and mother had both come to the United States with their parents. Her maternal grandparents took up farming in upper New York State and were the only Jews cultivating the soil in their area. She spent a good part of her childhood with them and her love of the country never left her, even after she settled in an urban environment. Her early education in a one-room schoolhouse in Franklin Falls, near Saranac Lake, and later at a high school in Burlington, Vermont, where she was an outstanding pupil, was followed by a degree course at Hunter College in New York.

Unlike my own parents, Bert's father and mother spoke English among themselves at home and with their children. The Jewish training they gave her was considered unusual for a girl in those days. She had attended classes at the Uptown Talmud Torah in New York City and she later took some courses at the Teachers' Institute of the Jewish Theological Seminary. Upon graduating from Hunter College in 1915, Bert was qualified to teach in the public schools and was so employed during the period of our engagement.

It was a tense moment for both of us when we went to meet my parents in Philadelphia for the first time. They took to her at once, and so did my younger brothers, Isaac and Morris. My sister Sarah was still quite small at the time, but she had "a friend at court" in my fiancée, who prevailed upon my parents to be rather less strict in their upbringing of the only girl in the family.

As a second-year student at the JTS, now engaged to be married, I found it more difficult to work with my accustomed tempo and concentration, particularly since my earning capacity from Hebrew teaching had to be adjusted to new and demanding priorities. Our prospective marriage would require saving up considerable funds.

Toward the end of the year, I assumed a new responsibility as weekend student rabbi to the newly established congregation of B'nai Shalom at Rockville Center, Long Island. The Jewish migration out of crowded Brooklyn and into the "wide open spaces" of Long Island was then proceeding apace. New communities were being formed and beginning to develop; some became quite flourishing in the course of time. But this was still in the early stages of that city-to-suburbs exodus. The position I took involved conducting the religious services on Friday evenings, when I also delivered a sermonette, and teaching the children on Saturday mornings. It was by no means easy to muster a *minyan* for the prayer services, and we had to appeal to the communities in Lynbrook, Freeport, and other neighboring townships to rally round our synagogue, at Rockville Center, on Friday evenings.

The president of this fledgling congregation was Ben Markowitz, the younger brother in that household where I was the star boarder. It is not unlikely, therefore, that my success in obtaining the post of weekend rabbi resulted from more than the normal credentials.

All in all, it was a valuable experience for me, providing some initial contact with suburban Jewish families, albeit in weekly doses only, and enabling me to gain my first experience of the Jewish ministry.

My fiancée and her family were no less ambitious for my success than I was, so I had more than one reason for applying myself with redoubled zeal and energy to my study and teaching commitments.

An interesting Sunday school post that came my way, broadening my social horizon, was at Dr. Stephen S. Wise's Free Synagogue. The principal, Rabbi Louis I. Newman, a militant Zionist, later became the distinguished spiritual leader of Temple Rodeph Sholom in New York, after having ministered to San Francisco's leading Reform congregation. Once again, my physique helped to enhance my status and I was given the oldest class to teach. My pupils included two bright and charming girls—Justine Wise, the daughter of Dr. and Mrs. Stephen Wise, and Lucille Uhry, who later married Rabbi Newman.

As the months passed by, and my life was filled with new meaning and new challenges, I found ongoing satisfaction in study, teaching, and occasional diversion in music or the theater. On one occasion, I took my cousin, Bessie (Batya) Rothberg, to hear Sholem Aleichem himself read from his works.

At the end of my third year, I received the Steinbach Scholarship, the premier award at the Seminary, and became secretary of my class, taking an active part in student activities.

One impression of those wartime years that remained etched in my memory was of Eliezer Ben-Yehudah, the father of modern Hebrew, whom I often saw moving quietly among the bookshelves in the Seminary library. Short and slim, with a close-cropped head of graying hair and a neatly trimmed goatee beard, he wore pince-nez glasses. He had left Jerusalem at the outbreak of the war, when the Turkish governor of Palestine, Jamal Pasha, outlawed Zionism and expelled its advocates. Ben-Yehudah remained in the United States until 1919, when he returned to Eretz Yisrael. It was he, together with Menaḥem Ussishkin, that robust Zionist leader, who persuaded the first British High Commissioner, Sir Herbert Samuel, to recognize Hebrew as one of the three official languages of the new (mandated) Palestine, alongside English and Arabic.

Throughout this time, we students had paid scant heed to the hostilities in Europe, which were now in their third year. It was as if the war were raging on a different planet. Had it not been for the banner headlines in the daily press, we would scarcely have been aware of the peril to which Europe and European Jewry were exposed by the conflict. True, the American Jewish leadership was concerned and undertook relief operations in accessible areas, through the Jewish Joint Distribution Committee, but we knew little about this. It was a serious omission on the part of a training school for the rabbinate.

When the United States entered the war on the side of the Allied Powers in the spring of 1917, we felt, like all other Americans, that we had a stake in the defeat of Germany and the Central Powers. We were also anxious about the future of the Jews in Europe.

I recall vividly the tremendous excitement generated by the British Government's publication on November 2, 1917, of the Balfour Declaration, which favored "the establishment in Palestine of a national home for the Jewish people." It was as though trumpets had suddenly blared, heralding the Messiah. All of us at the Seminary were gripped by the significance of this event. For me, it awoke memories of the youthful enthusiasm expressed at the Hatikvah Zionist Society in South Philadelphia, almost a decade earlier. We seemed close to the *athalta di-ge'ulah*, the dawn of our long-awaited Redemption.

Curiously enough, however, although we students all considered ourselves to be Zionists, none of us felt the urge to enlist in the Jewish Legion of the British Army, as some of my contemporaries in Philadelphia had done. Solomon Goldman was most vocal in his Zionism, but my outward calm belied the agitation inside me. In retrospect, it seems almost incredible that our routine at the Seminary could have been unaffected, pursuing its normal placid course. That other cataclysmic event of November 1917, the Bolshevik Revolution, with all its implications for mankind and particularly for the largest Jewish community in the world at the time, caused no more than a ripple on the tranquil surface of our rabbinical training program.

There we were, living through the most dramatic epoch in centuries, yet giving scant thought to bright promises or to ominous portents. With one or two notable exceptions, our teachers—absorbed in the Jewish past, the sacred texts, and the tragedy-laden history of the People of the Book—seemed, as far as we could tell, oblivious of the unfolding tragedy of Europe's Jews and of the new glow of Zion's hope for the future.

In June 1917, I received the M.A. degree from Columbia University, where I had taken courses in history, philosophy, and comparative religion, including lectures by Professors Felix Adler, John Dewey, and A. V. Jackson. My thesis, supervised by Professor Jackson, was on "A Comparison between Buddhist Ethics and the Jewish Ethics of the Fathers." One of the faculty members who impressed me, although I did not study under him, was that eminent orientalist, Professor Richard James Gottheil. He had served as president of the American Zionist Federation from 1898 until 1904.

The fourth and graduating year of our class, starting early in the fall of 1917, found us casting around for permanent posts in the rabbinate. By then, I had given up my weekend position at Rockville Center and accepted one with a new congregation in Coney Island, a more densely populated Jewish area. There, too, religious services were held only on Friday evenings, but prospects for the immediate future seemed more promising here than at Rockville Center. The mixed choir and organ music were to my taste. Within a few months, however, I became disenchanted with this congregation, as I found no sign of any serious intention or desire to build up an active congregational unit with an educational program for the youth.

A vacancy occurred at Congregation Peniel in Washington Heights. I preached there on a number of Sabbaths and appeared to make a good impression, but my tender years were the main obstacle. The position was awarded to Rabbi Aaron Eiseman, who had ministered to Congregation Beth Israel, at Lexington Avenue and

72nd Street. This latter congregation, bereft of its rabbi and feeling the effects of Jewish migration westward from the Upper East Side, was now in quest of a student rabbi for the High Holy Days. It had a mixed choir, an organ, and family pews.

When the High Holy Day post was offered to me, I accepted. It was the most important congregational position for which I had been chosen until then. It had some fine old-established members, such as the Mark Abrahams and the Samuel Lustbader families, who later joined Congregation B'nai Jeshurun when it moved to the West Side. Eventually, Congregation Beth Israel sold its valuable property and dissolved.

It so happened that, in the fall of 1917, Bert and I attended the laying of the cornerstone for the new West Side edifice of Congregation B'nai Jeshurun. It had moved from its fourth site and was holding services on a temporary basis at Leslie Hall on Broadway, near 83rd Street. B'nai Jeshurun's new site at 88th Street, west of Broadway, was in the heart of a steadily expanding upper-middle-class Jewish neighborhood.

Both of us were interested to learn that this historic congregation was about to have a new lease of life on the West Side, now that it had sold its beautiful house of worship on Madison Avenue, near 65th Street, where its membership had been declining. Temporarily, Rabbi Bernard Kaplan acted as spiritual leader. The principal address at the cornerstone ceremony was given by the president of the Borough of Manhattan, Julius Miller.

On Shavu'ot, the Festival of Weeks (or Pentecost), I was invited to conduct the services and confirmation exercises at Temple Beth Elohim, located in a newly developing section of the Bronx. Established only recently, this congregation and its liberal features were to my liking.

Both the Shavu'ot services and the confirmation exercises I supervised there made a favorable impression. Judge Harry Stackell, president of the congregation, and the members of his board wanted me to stay on as their permanent rabbi, with effect from the ensuing Rosh Hashanah. I preferred, however, to wait and see what other opportunities might present themselves. It was nevertheless encouraging to have that offer of a permanent post.

Our graduation exercises at the Jewish Theological Seminary were scheduled for a month's time, in June 1918. I was the youngest of the eleven graduates, having celebrated my twenty-second birthday only a few days previously. The prizes I received that year included one in homiletics awarded by Professor Kaplan and another for the essay, "Modern Interpretations of the Book of Job in Comparison with the Medieval Jewish Commentators," which I had submitted to Professor Friedlaender. A culminating and unexpected honor was the faculty's decision that I be class valedictorian at the graduation exercises.

Aeolian Hall, the usual venue for these exercises, was crowded with parents, relatives, and friends of the new graduates, in addition, of course, to members of the faculty and the student body. In view of the circumstances, I felt more than a little nervous when taking my place on the podium. I had gone to considerable trouble in preparing successive drafts of my address, and my eagerness to deliver the final version was mixed with some degree of trepidation.

A few passages from that address may reflect not only my own emotions at the time, but also the Jewish and general atmosphere that prevailed as World War I was nearing its end.

I touched upon the current position of the American Jewish community, the challenges and opportunities that confronted it, the role of both synagogue and rabbi in molding the future of American Jewry, and the future potential of Eretz Yisrael after the Balfour Declaration, as well as its significance for American Jews and for Jewish life everywhere. My address also dwelt on the problems of postwar moral and spiritual reconstruction.

As I saw it, the dilemma in Jewish life was a confrontation between the defenders of the faith, who were stubbornly opposed to any change, and those who were bent on indiscriminately assimilating external culture, heedless of their first duty to assimilate their own. The first element seemed to make Judaism repellent to the younger generation, severing religion from life; the second ended up severing life from religion. Proceeding from that thought, I said:

> Here, then, is the problem which faces us as rabbis—to make the Jewish religion a part of life for the Jews, not only in the Synagogue but in all of their social relations, in every phase of their activity, be it physical, intellectual or recreational. This is the task which is incumbent upon the American rabbi.

Departing briefly from my main theme, I then referred to the issuance of the Balfour Declaration, embodying the hope for a restoration of Eretz Yisrael to the People of Israel, which had "quickened the Jewish pulse the world over." And I added:

> With a center for Judaism in the Jewish land, the constructive work of rabbis throughout the Diaspora will gain stimulus and animation. Thus, the upbuilding of Jewish life in this country will proceed all the more readily, it will take on warmth and color under the rays which will radiate from Zion.

The response to this valedictory, by the students, the faculty, and the audience, gave me considerable satisfaction and encouragement.

It so happened that one of those present in the audience was Sol M. Stroock, a leading member of the Seminary's board of trustees and honorary secretary of Congregation B'nai Jeshurun. The new premises of B'nai Jeshurun at 88th Street and West End Avenue, where my fiancée and I had attended the cornerstone laying the previous autumn, had been completed in May 1918, and the elders had been interviewing a number of candidates for its ministry, including men of standing in the rabbinate, both Reform and Conservative. Apparently, however, they had not found any one candidate upon whom they could agree.

At the suggestion of Mr. Stroock, the board of the congregation invited me to occupy their pulpit on the last Shabbat in June. Following that visit, I was invited to preach again on the next Sabbath. As a result of that second sermon, I was offered the position for a trial period of six months, at a salary beyond what was normal for a rabbinical novice. Such an offer from a prestigious congregation in New York was far beyond my expectations.

I might add, parenthetically, that because of the fortuitous link between my valedictory and this prestigious offer, it was felt by the student body that it created an unfair advantage for the valedictorian. Their point, in my judgment, was well taken. So mine was the valedictory to end valedictories.

Despite the attractions of B'nai Jeshurun, I had mixed feelings about the matter, being none too sure of my qualifications for the post in view of my comparative youth. Nor was I certain that I would prefer B'nai Jeshurun to Beth Elohim in the Bronx. The latter congregation seemed to offer more of a challenge to a young rabbi. It had a warmer, more responsive Jewish community, in its formative stage, with younger men in the leadership, and it was located in an area where it could draw upon many young families and a considerable youth constituency.

Wrestling with this new dilemma in my life, I sought the advice of Dr. Cyrus Adler at the Seminary.

"Look, Dr. Adler," I said, "there are young people in the Bronx, and it seems to be a wonderful opportunity from the spiritual angle. Congregation B'nai Jeshurun is an elderly one, and I feel sure they can have any rabbi they like in America."

Cyrus Adler saw things differently, however, believing that I should accept the call for the sake of the Seminary as well as for my own good. There was also another consideration. He wanted to make sure that Congregation B'nai Jeshurun would remain within the ranks of Conservative Judaism and would affiliate with the United Synagogue of America.

I took his advice. So it was that, at the age of twenty-two and on six months' probation, I became the rabbi of the oldest Conservative congregation in the United States. At the end of my trial period, I was elected by the board for a five-year term.

The new synagogue edifice on 88th Street had an imposing exterior and an exquisite interior design. The architects had endeavored to incorporate motifs found in ancient Semitic art. Its seating capacity was approximately 1,200, including the balcony. Conforming to the non-Orthodox pattern, there were family pews, a mixed choir, and an organ. Many upper-middle-class Jewish families were taking up residence in the neighborhood, and so B'nai Jeshurun held the promise of becoming a vital center of Jewish life and cultural activity.

The congregation had been established in 1825 as an offshoot of the Spanish and Portuguese Congregation Shearith Israel, as soon as there were enough Ashkenazi families to organize a congregation of their own. It was thus seven years short of its first century when I accepted the call. Many prominent figures in American Jewry had been in touch with the congregation at one time or another. Among them was the redoubtable Mordecai Manuel Noah, who contributed to its establishment and who, in 1828, delivered the main address on the first anniversary of the original (Elm Street) synagogue's consecration.

The roster of those who had served the congregation as rabbis in the course of its history included several outstanding men whose personalities had left their imprint on the American Jewish scene. Among them were Morris J. Raphall, who had come over from England in 1849 and who had achieved a nationwide reputation in the United States as a scholar and orator; Henry S. Jacobs, who became the first president of the New York Board of Jewish Ministers in 1881; and Stephen S. Wise, who served his novitiate at B'nai Jeshurun and who, years later, was to become the foremost spokesman of American Jewry. Among the more recent incumbents were Rabbis Joseph Mayer Asher, Judah Leon Magnes, and Joel Blau.

Bert and I had been engaged for three years by now and we had already made our plans to marry upon my graduation. Some time before the board of Congregation B'nai Jeshurun invited me to become their rabbi, we had decided to hold the wedding ceremony at Temple Ansche Chesed, which was close to the Markowitz home. Its scholarly rabbi, Dr. Jacob Kohn, had graduated from the Jewish Theological Seminary more than a decade before me.

Following my new appointment, the venue of our nuptials obviously had to be B'nai Jeshurun. Ours was the first wedding ceremony to take place in the new synagogue edifice. On July 21, 1918, Bert and I were united in wedlock by my favorite teacher at the Seminary, Professor Mordecai M. Kaplan, in the presence of a large congregation that included our parents, brothers, sisters, other relatives and friends, and a number of B'nai Jeshurun trustees and congregants.

Our honeymoon was spent visiting the Thousand Islands in northern New York State, the Great Lakes, the Adirondacks town of Keeseville just south of Plattsburg, New York, where Bert was born, and the city of Burlington, across the Vermont state line, where she had attended high school while living wtih her maternal grandparents.

The High Holy Days of 1918 ushered in the rabbinical career for which I had been consciously training during my four years at the Seminary, and subconsciously from the years of my synagogue-oriented childhood in South Philadelphia. The fact that my congregation, B'nai Jeshurun, had family pews, a mixed choir, and an organ did not appear to faze my Orthodox father, who accepted the situation with unexpected equanimity. Indeed, years later, when my youngest brother, Morris, chose to enter the Reform rabbinate by way of Hebrew Union College, Father seemed reconciled even to that deviation. I suspect that an even-handed scepticism lay behind his attitude toward both departures from Orthodoxy.

In a way, my father's reaction illustrated the basic problem of Conservative Judaism, at least in that period. Did the term *Conservative* mean "Conservative Reform," or was it intended to stress the importance of *conserving* Jewish values and traditions in a modern age that beckoned in the opposite direction?

The establishment of the United Synagogue by Professor Solomon Schechter in 1913 was meant to strengthen the forces of "historic" Judaism. At that time, few of its constituents favored an organ and family pews in which men and women sat together. When urging me to accept the post of rabbi at B'nai Jeshurun, Dr. Cyrus Adler had rightly apprehended that its lay leaders might not be averse to joining the

Reform movement, represented by the Union of American Hebrew Congregations, and that, by serving as their rabbi, I would keep them within the fold of Conservative Judaism, albeit as one of its more liberal constituents.

I considered myself honor-bound to bring the congregation into the ranks of the United Synagogue and succeeded in doing so in the first year of my ministry, with the help of Rabbi Samuel M. Cohen, the first executive director of the United Synagogue. This was B'nai Jeshurun's first affiliation with any organized group of synagogues since its withdrawal from the Union of American Hebrew Congregations thirty-two years earlier, in 1886.

The problems I faced at the commencement of my rabbinate were manifold, and they might have baffled someone older and more experienced than myself. I tackled them in earnest at the end of my probationary period, following my election as rabbi of the congregation for a five-year term, on January 1, 1919.

This may be as good a place as any for some personal observations about the career that I chose. There are some rabbis whose primary interest is Jewish scholarship and who utilize their leisure hours to deepen their Jewish knowledge. More than a few such men have adorned the American rabbinate. Some have left the ministry after years of devoted service to their congregations and have taken up posts in institutions of higher learning.

One notable example is Professor Louis Finkelstein, who came to the Seminary a year after me and who impressed us with his Talmudic knowledge and scholarly bent. Upon graduation, he ministered to a congregation for a number of years, but was obviously destined for an academic career. When Dr. Cyrus Adler became president of the Jewish Theological Seminary, he invited Dr. Finkelstein to join the faculty and also to assist him in the general administration of the Seminary. After the death of Cyrus Adler in 1940, Professor Finkelstein succeeded to the presidency and in 1951 he became chancellor of the JTS. He guided its fortunes with foresight, imagination, and distinction for over a quarter of a century.

Other rabbis choose to dedicate themselves largely to pastoral work and thus play a meaningful role in the lives of the congregational families. Others, again, excel as organizers and make a start by placing their own congregation and its affiliates—the sisterhoods, men's clubs, and young people's groups—on a sound organizational basis. Often they reach out into the wider community and become involved in the larger aspects of communal leadership. I have known instances (including my own, alas), which bear out the caution in Exodus Rabbah (*Va-Era* 6.2) that "one who occupies himself with communal matters forgets his learning." Perhaps that is the highest price of all that a rabbi must pay for his career of public service.

There are also rabbis who have developed a penchant for fostering good relations between Jews and Christians. In a sense, they become the Jewish apostles to the Gentiles. This, too, is a worthwhile contribution, since Jews are invariably a minority group in the Diaspora and need the goodwill of the majority.

A few rabbis have achieved prominence in national Jewish leadership and have even attained international renown. I refer to such eminent personalities as Stephen S. Wise and Abba Hillel Silver, who were conspicuous for their dedication to the cause of the Jewish people as a whole and who reached the front rank of World Zionism. Another eminent American rabbi, Judah Leon Magnes, left his pulpit to organize the New York Kehillah, later becoming chancellor (and then president) of the Hebrew University in Jerusalem. They, and several others like them, were able to impress themselves upon the American Jewish scene—and eventually upon the world Jewish scene—by virtue of their special qualities: dedication to service, an impressive personality, oratorical gifts, and organizational ability.

Jews outside the United States often wonder how it is that rabbis in the United States have come to play such an important part in areas of public life beyond the "four ells" of their calling. There are not many other Jewish communities in the world where a rabbi steps outside his normal sphere in order to engage in broad, extramural activities.

To my mind, this has been the case in America partly because talented Jewish laymen found their outlet in business and the professions, in politics and in municipal, state and national life. The entire field of Jewish communal service was long neglected by the ablest Jewish laity. Hence it was left to rabbis who had the inclination and the requisite ability, to assume responsible positions of leadership.

It is within that orbit of value judgment that I would place my own career from the time I enrolled at the Jewish Theological Seminary. Long before I was mature enough to formulate theological commitments, I was motivated by the desire to choose a career that would be a vehicle for public service. The atmosphere of my home life, the example of a few older boys from Philadelphia, and the influence of Dr. Cyrus Adler, however, combined to direct me toward the rabbinate. In my student years at the Seminary, I often considered the possibility of a career in Jewish scholarship, but the motivation of public service proved to be decisive.

The inception of my ministry coincided with the beginning of a period fraught with immense significance not only for the Jewish people, but for mankind at large. World War I was in its closing phase. It was already apparent that the Allied Powers would be victorious, but it had also become clear that the postwar world, shaken to its very foundations, would be faced by a fateful period of rebuilding. European Jewry stood in the greatest need of reconstruction. The Balfour Declaration, having aroused Jewish hopes for the rebuilding of Zion, was our one ray of consolation.

The installation of the recently appointed young rabbi of Congregation B'nai Jeshurun took place on December 13, 1918, with all due ceremonial, in the new West 88th Street edifice. Dr. Cyrus Adler, as head of the Jewish Theological Seminary, delivered the installation address. He dwelt on the challenges posed by the war and the approaching victory, as well as on those facing American Jewry and its rabbinate at such a time.

His personal references touched me deeply. "I knew [your rabbi] as a lad," he observed, "before he entered the Jewish Theological Seminary, and have watched his career ever since." Despite my hesitations and my preference for a smaller congregation, Dr. Adler had advised me to accept the call from B'nai Jeshurun, feeling sure I would prove equal to the task and that the lay leaders would extend their full cooperation. "Give this ungrudgingly and in full measure," he concluded.

In my inaugural address, I dealt first with the dilemma of the Jew in modern times. "In the nineteenth century," I said, "the problem was how to make the life of the Jew more modern, how to color it with the pigments of contemporary European culture and civilization. Today, in the twentieth century, the problem is not how to make the Jew's life more modern—it is modern enough—but how to make the life of the modern Jew more Jewish."

I went on to review the impact of the war on our situation in the United States:

The problem of religion in general, and the Jewish problem in particular, is still one of conserving our faith. If anything, it is now more important than ever. The hundred thousand Jewish boys who will return to their homes will look for spiritual guidance of a positive nature. They will not be satisfied with a devitalized Judaism. The religious reactions which they have experienced in the camps and trenches have been too strong to suffer dilution. If these boys are to be satisfied, it must be with a living faith, a faith having its roots in the life of a people, not in the pulpit of a temple; a faith which expresses itself in concrete symbols, not in abstract doctrines; a faith whose pulse-beat is neither too high, feverish and ecstatic, nor too low, dull and lethargic, but normal, alive and alert. . . .

It is not only the letter but the spirit which counts—the spirit of conserving Jewish values and serving the Jewish people. That criterion is broad enough and sound enough to embrace the bulk of our race. "All Israel are responsible for one another." Our common responsibility shall be the bond between us. To lead in such a common purpose is a sacred privilege.

Charting a Course

When I entered the rabbi's study at West 88th Street for the first time, there were two obvious tasks confronting me. One was to get acquainted with my new flock; the other was to study congregational and community problems in depth, and to establish harmonious relationships with people and organizations.

It did not take me long to discover that my path would be strewn with pitfalls. I was, for example, very conscious of my youth; in time, of course, congregants might come to like me, but would they pay heed to what I said? Another factor that disturbed me was the inherent conservatism of B'nai Jeshurun's membership at that time, which included a considerable number of successful businessmen and employers. Then, too, an *a priori* allergy to Zionism, typical of the dominant and older German Jewish element that had come over from the East Side, seemed likely to clash with my own firmly Zionist outlook. How much support I would receive from the newer membership, whose roots were mainly in Eastern Europe, could not easily be determined. Friction might also arise from my commitment to social service in its broadest sense, to a vital Jewish community, and to a decent society based on social justice.

The period immediately following my induction, therefore, found me preoccupied with parochial responsibilities, getting acquainted with the congregational families and with the larger community, and learning to work with the lay leadership of the congregation.

These lay leaders were the most immediate of my problems. Elderly and, by and large, of German Jewish extraction, they were (with a few honorable exceptions) not especially endowed with any culture—European, American, or Jewish. Their chief qualifications as policymakers were success in business and the professions and a willingness to devote time and service to the affairs of Congregation B'nai Jeshurun. Heading them was Sol M. Stroock, honorary secretary of the board of trustees and a man of distinguished pedigree, whose parents had also belonged to the congregation. Among other things, he was secretary of the board of trustees of the Jewish Theological Seminary. It was, of course, Mr. Stroock who had initially recommended my appointment as rabbi.

Other prominent members of the congregation were Louis S. Brush; Henry A. Dix, who would bequeath his substantial estate in Mt. Kisco, New York, to the Young Women's Hebrew Association; and Charles W. Endel, who had grown up in the congregation and now headed the Knights of Pythias in New York.

Some of the distinguished old families, such as the Lehmanns and the Elkuses, had left to join Temple Emanu-El. New families were also coming in, and many of these, Jews of Eastern European origin, were gradually changing the complexion of B'nai Jeshurun. In the meantime, however, I had to work with the old guard. For a novice such as I, this was no easy assignment.

During the months that followed my assumption of office, I was to realize that further pursuit of Jewish learning would not prove easy in the midst of a busy ministry, where the demands of organization and administration in synagogue affairs and any venture into the broader areas of communal service would leave little time to spare. I was never quite at peace with myself on that score. It was soon apparent, however, that my main talents and concerns lay in other directions—propounding the message of Judaism, making the congregation not just a unit for Jewish worship but also one for Jewish service, developing the religious classes into more than a Sunday school, integrating the life of the congregation within that of the larger community, Jewish and general, and winning the congregation over to the Zionist cause and for Zionist service. I also nurtured the hope that, beyond the confines of B'nai Jeshurun itself, I might become involved in the larger community, in Zionist and civic commitments, and in a broader effort to improve the quality of our social environment.

I had no doubt that a tough and, perhaps, long struggle lay ahead. Fortunately, no one queried my immediate targets. The experience I had already gained as a student rabbi now stood me in good stead.

The religious school had to be reorganized. The premises made available for this vital activity—a vestry room divided by movable partitions, and adjoining the janitor's quarters—contrasted shamefully with the magnificent house of worship. It gave evidence of the relative place assigned by the congregation's elders to the religious education of the children. The provision of adequate facilities and of American-trained Jewish educators had top priority at this stage. My choice for principal of the religious school was Goodman A. Rose, a student at the Jewish Theological Seminary. He was followed by Julius Silver, a graduate of the Teachers' Institute at JTS.

The religious services had also to be planned with a twofold aim in view: to satisfy the needs of the existing membership and to attract new families from the neighborhood. Congregation B'nai Jeshurun had developed the tradition of a beautiful musical service, led by a splendid cantor, organist, and choir. With the passing of its distinguished *ḥazzan*, Edward Kartschmaroff, a new cantor, Jacob Schwartz, had been chosen shortly before my arrival, and his glorious baritone voice added dignity to the service.

I took my responsibility as a preacher very seriously, knowing full well that in a metropolis such as New York the standing of the rabbi, both in his own congregation and in the wider community, rested primarily upon his preaching ability. On no occasion did I come to the pulpit unprepared. Gradually, B'nai Jeshurun's pulpit drew considerable attendances, both from the immediate neighborhood and from other sections of New York Jewry.

In order to provide for the religious needs of those who were unable to attend Sabbath morning services, I introduced special late Friday evening (after-dinner) services, at which there was a lecture-sermon dealing with Jewish ideology and with matters of current interest, whether Jewish or general. These lectures proved very popular. The innovation did not affect the central importance of the Sabbath morning services and their pulpit message.

The sisterhood of Congregation B'nai Jeshurun was its philanthropic arm. Behind it lay decades of social service activity in the community at large and of ongoing work for the congregation itself in the social sphere.

World War I was drawing to a close, but while it lasted my congregation, many of whose families had sons in the U.S. armed services, was active, like other congregations, in volunteer work for the war effort. This was undertaken primarily by our sisterhood, through its sewing circle and through a social committee that arranged dances in our vestry rooms for the men in uniform. B'nai Jeshurun families contributed to the Liberty Loan drives and Welfare Fund campaigns. At the same time, our sisterhood was constituted a Red Cross auxiliary branch for making bandages and hospital gauzes to be shipped overseas. At the religious services held on the High Holy Days, special accommodations were provided for Jewish servicemen.

The congregation operated as a West Side unit in the United War Campaign and in the Liberty Bond and Red Cross campaigns. In all of this activity, the rabbi was, of course, heavily involved.

After the armistice, a joint interfaith memorial service to honor the dead was held in the Catholic church located in our neighborhood. The address I delivered on behalf of the Jewish community was my first interfaith assignment as rabbi of B'nai Jeshurun.

Now that peace had been restored, I found it possible to concentrate much more on the internal needs of the congregation. It was soon apparent that the new families joining our congregation were inclined toward a more traditional form of service. Far from resisting this trend, I gladly responded to it. More Hebrew prayers were introduced and services were held each morning and evening.

I was also aware that the youth deserved special consideration in terms of the religious services. A junior congregation was therefore organized in 1922 and held its own services on Sabbaths and festivals; a year later, High Holy Day services for young people were introduced, and college students were invited to participate. From 1924, during the winter vacations, special Friday evening services for collegians were held. The tradition of a confirmation ceremony for girls on Shavu'ot was continued.

Thanksgiving Day services were held each year, in accordance with the congregation's long-standing practice, and other congregations in the vicinity were made welcome. Prominent laymen in the community, both Jewish and non-Jewish, were invited to deliver the addresses.

Similarly, on Friday evenings and Sabbath mornings, leading Conservative and Reform rabbis and Jewish laymen were invited to occupy the pulpit. Among them, in the early years, were Dr. A. A. Brill, Professor Israel Friedlaender, and Judge Julian W. Mack; Itamar Ben-Avi, son of Eliezer Ben-Yehudah and an eminent Palestinian journalist; and Dr. Chaim Weizmann, on one of his early visits to the U.S. The B'nai Jeshurun pulpit began to win a respected place and a wide following in the community.

The steadily expanding educational and social activities made it imperative to acquire new premises to house them. A reflection of the shortsightedness of the congregation's elders and, at the same time, an indication of their willingness to make amends is the fact that in 1920, just two years after their new synagogue had been dedicated, more adequate premises were acquired to house the religious school and youth activities. It was a three-story private dwelling on the corner of West End Avenue and 88th Street, adjoining the synagogue edifice.

The first director of this new Community Center was a JTS student, Louis M. Levitsky. He was succeeded, in turn, by Julius Silver, Morton Goldberg, and Albert Gordon. The Community Center became a hive of educational and social activities for the youth. From among the congregational families, Paul Tishman and Abe Wechsler volunteered to be club leaders.

I never relaxed my efforts to make Congregation B'nai Jeshurun more aware of its responsibilities in the field of Jewish education. At the end of 1922, for example, my annual report stressed that, "if parents would give the Hebrew training of their children the same attention they devote to those subjects which are only cultural luxuries, the next generation of American Jewry would have more to boast of." In the face of widespread indifference, my one hope was that some children might be galvanized to demand changes in their "de-Judaized" homes. Six years later, after a decade as rabbi, I called for the institution of a Sunday morning parents' discussion group, led by some qualified person, to reinforce Jewish religious awareness.

In the meantime, something remained to be done in order to enhance the beauty of the house of worship itself. The interior, of white plaster, and tastefully designed, needed to be ornamented with color and symbolism. I welcomed the opportunity to have a part in working out the decorative Jewish motifs.

By the early 1920s, I had reason to believe that the initial chapter of my ministry—dedicated to "lengthening the cords and strengthening the stakes" of the congregation in Jewish religious and cultural life—was an auspicious one. I felt that I could now afford to become involved also in the affairs of the larger community.

With the end of World War I in 1919, and the devastation it had wrought in Europe, the plight of European Jewry, especially in Russia and Poland, called for American Jewish aid on a massive scale. This was given primarily through the American Jewish Joint Distribution Committee.

Throughout the war years, while I was a student, the Zionist cause had no more powerful and eloquent advocate in America than Shmaryahu Levin, whose ship had returned hastily to New York with the outbreak of hostilities in August 1914. As a member of the Zionist Executive, he busied himself with propaganda work throughout the United States and established the Provisional Executive Committee for General Zionist Affairs, which Justice Louis Brandeis headed. This committee's major achievement was to save the Yishuv in Palestine by interceding with the U.S. State Department on Palestinian Jewry's behalf.

The Balfour Declaration of 1917 had, of course, given enormous impetus to the Zionist dream, which now seemed on the way to fulfillment. It was subsequently endorsed by President Woodrow Wilson and the U.S. Congress, thanks partly to the intercession of Justice Brandeis and Rabbi Stephen S. Wise, the leaders of American Zionism. It was clear that the Jews of America would have an important part to play in the future tasks of the World Zionist movement.

At the peace conference in Versailles, held at the end of the war, the representatives of American Jewry led the other Jewish delegations in their efforts to secure Jewish minority rights in the countries of Eastern Europe, and implementation of the Balfour Declaration with regard to Jewish rights in Palestine.

As a result of these vast new responsibilities, American Jewry felt a quickening of Jewish interest, activity, and commitment. It was inevitable that Jewish pride should have been stirred and Jewish self-consciousness reawakened. Such developments, together with improved economic conditions, were reflected in new standards of philanthropy for the needs at home and abroad, in the enlargement of Jewish educational facilities, in an expansion of the Zionist ranks, in the growing number of synagogues, and in the broadening of their function.

A new type of synagogue institution developed, known as the Synagogue Center. It was based on the premise that the synagogue should be the center of Jewish community life, not only a place of worship and religious education for the children but also one offering a wide program of general (educational, cultural, social, and even recreational) activities. Synagogue Centers began to arise in America, and this trend was naturally reflected in the development of my plans for Congregation B'nai Jeshurun.

The Keren Hayesod (Palestine Foundation Fund) campaign, proclaimed by Dr.

Chaim Weizmann in London at the first World Zionist Conference held after the war, in July 1920, conducted its inaugural fund-raising effort among the Jews of the United States in April 1921. A distinguished delegation arrived, headed by Dr. Weizmann, Menaḥem Ussishkin, and Professor Albert Einstein.

I threw myself and my congregation into the Keren Hayesod's fund-raising activity on New York's West Side, a new and flourishing Jewish neighborhood. This was the beginning of what was to become an ever-growing commitment on my part both to the Keren Hayesod and to the Keren Kayemet (Jewish National Fund). It also led to my involvement in the councils of the Zionist Organization of America, at first locally and then nationally.

Another eminent visitor whom I met in 1924 was the Palestinian educator, David Yellin. Then a man of sixty, he occupied a key position in the Yishuv as chairman of the Va'ad Leumi, the National Council of the Jews of Palestine. Yellin, who founded the Hebrew Teachers' Seminary that now stands in the Bet ha-Kerem suburb of Jerusalem, had come to deliver some lectures at the Jewish Institute of Religion in New York and at Columbia University.

The manifold schedule of extra-congregational activities, however, was not allowed to interfere with my first priority, the development of my congregation as a strong, vital unit of religious, cultural, Zionist, and philanthropic activity. Indeed, it was partly because of the rabbi's extramural activities that many new families became attracted to the congregation. Our congregational roster of members and seatholders doubled and trebled. Some purchased their pews outright; others rented seats from year to year.

The rabbinate, being virtually a full-time occupation, takes its toll of family life. Fortunately, in my case, Bert's unusual competence as a mother compensated for my unintentional neglect as a father. Our son, Avram Shalom, was born on July 3, 1919; our daughter, Vivian Rose, was born on May 14, 1922.

We sent our children to the progressive Walden School, and arranged for their Jewish education to be imparted under the wing of our congregational religious school and under private tutors. Each stage of their growth and development brought us joy and fulfillment.

Centenary of Congregation B'nai Jeshurun

The year 1925 was an important milestone in the history of the congregation, marking the hundredth anniversary of its founding. I saw in this historic landmark an opportunity not only to foster congregational pride and loyalty, but also to project the image of B'nai Jeshurun on a national and international scale.

The centennial was planned a full year in advance. A network of committees was organized, representing the men, women, and youth of the congregation. A centenary fund of $100,000 to promote Jewish education was projected. The entire year was to be punctuated by special events for all age groups. Sabbaths and festivals during the year were given a special jubilee character.

Among the guest speakers who addressed centennial functions were Dr. Cyrus

Adler, Mrs. Rebekah Kohut, and Rabbis Rudolph Grossman, Maurice H. Harris, Nathan Krass, and Stephen S. Wise. A public meeting of the Rabbinical Assembly of America, held in the synagogue to mark the congregation's centenary, was addressed by Dr. Cyrus Adler and Louis Marshall, and by Rabbis Adolph Coblenz of Baltimore, Louis Epstein of Boston, and Herman Lissauer of San Francisco.

At the Centennial Thanksgiving Service, which took place in the synagogue of the "mother" congregation, Shearith Israel, addresses were delivered by the rabbis of both congregations.

These hundredth anniversary festivities culminated in a banquet at the Hotel Astor, held on the night of Thanksgiving Day, November 28, 1925. It was a fitting climax to the year's celebration. Families whose antecedents in the congregation went back two, three, and four generations were there, as well as young people now about to assume congregational responsibility. Others present included leaders of sister congregations, the distinguished representatives of universities, theological seminaries, rabbinical bodies, and philanthropic institutions, eminent spokesmen of the Christian denominations and figures of renown in the nation's civil and political affairs. More than 600 guests were in attendance. The printed program carried a poem by the *rebbetzin* of the congregation, dedicated to its centennial.

Among the hundreds of congratulatory messages received were those from - Alfred E. Smith, Governor of New York; Dr. Joseph H. Hertz, Chief Rabbi of the British Empire; Dr. Nicholas Murray Butler, president of Columbia University; and the Reverend Dr. S. Parkes Cadman, president of the Federal Council of Churches in America. Felicitations were also extended by Congregation B'nai Jeshurun's seven older sisters in the United States.

In addition to the greetings of the rabbi and of Charles W. Endel, the president of the congregation, Mrs. Eva Levy, the president of the sisterhood, and Sol M. Stroock, who chaired the proceedings, addresses were delivered by William T. Manning, the Protestant bishop of New York; Monsignor Thomas A. Carroll, who represented Cardinal Patrick Hayes; Dr. Stephen S. Wise; Adolph S. Ochs, publisher of *The New York Times*; Dr. Cyrus Adler; R. S. Copeland, U. S. senator from New York; and Julius Miller, president of the Borough of Manhattan.

Messages poured in from the Yishuv in Palestine and from Jewish leaders all over the world, including the chief rabbis of Austria, Denmark, France, Italy, and Poland, and rabbinical leaders in Germany.

The congregation emerged from its centennial with its position strengthened and its prestige greatly enhanced. Emphasis throughout the celebration was given to Jewish unity across differences and to the American community in general.

The hundredth anniversary stimulated my own interest in the history of Congregation B'nai Jeshurun, as seen against the general background of American Jewish life. After several years of research and study, I wrote *A Century of Judaism in New York* and presented this doctoral thesis to Professor Alexander Marx of the Jewish Theological Seminary. On his recommendation, I was awarded the degree of Doctor of Hebrew Literature in 1927. My thesis was published in 1930, and it elicited favorable comment.

I concluded my book with the following observation:

What is the significance of a single Congregation's Centenary in the life of American Israel?

A century is a short span in the story of a people which counts its existence in terms of thousands of years. A single Congregation is but a speck upon the map of Universal Israel. When, however, a single Congregation has wrought a century of service to God—Israel—Humanity, it becomes a circumstance of no mean proportions. When, moreover, the scene of that circumstance is a nation and government so young that its own lifetime exceeds the Congregation's record by no more than half-a-hundred years, then the touch of romance is added to the achievement.

B'nai Jeshurun's century is like a mirror reflecting the broad background of Jewish life in New York and in America, out of which Israel has come to its present estate. Religious Freedom and Political Equality, Broadminded Neighborliness and Economic Opportunity, these ideals which have become American traditions are ingredients which have gone into the building of B'nai Jeshurun, even as they have entered into the building of American Israel altogether.

Acknowledging the Providence which has guided its career, grateful to America which has mothered its growth, and proudly cognizant of the Jewish loyalty and devotion which have through four generations sustained its high purpose, Congregation B'nai Jeshurun lifts its voice in Thanksgiving and Song.

The congregation's centenary provided fresh impetus for its growth and development. People applying to join had to be turned away for lack of accommodations.

Before long, the property adjoining the synagogue that had housed the religious school, as well as the sisterhood, men's club, and youth groups, proved inadequate. In 1926, the congregation sold this property and purchased a lot on 89th Street, directly contiguous to the rear of the synagogue. The cornerstone was laid, with appropriate exercises, on December 18, 1927. The building was dedicated on May 20, 1928, exactly ten years after the consecration of the new synagogue.

On the morning of that day, the children of the religious school marched from their temporary quarters at 78 Riverside Drive to the auditorium of the magnificent new Community Center, where the school's principal, Milton B. Perlman, conducted the exercises. The main dedication service was held in the auditorium that same evening, and Dr. Cyrus Adler delivered the principal address.

B'nai Jeshurun's new Community Center was acclaimed as one of the finest structures of its kind. The architects were those who had erected the synagogue edifice, and the style they chose was very similar. It was a six-story building, equipped with elevators, and it comprised an exquisite chapel, large social rooms, twelve spacious classrooms, a magnificent auditorium, social rooms for the sisterhood, men's club, and young people's groups, a roof garden ideal for the erection of a *sukkah*, and the superintendent's quarters. The basement contained sports facilities and had locker rooms and showers.

Altogether, therefore, this new building offered the congregation and the Jewish community a religious, educational, cultural, social, and recreational center of the highest standard in every respect. It accommodated two overflow religious services on the High Holy Days and overflow memorial services on the festivals, in addition to children's services on Sabbaths, festivals, and High Holy Days.

The broader significance of this institution was emphasized in my dedication address:

> The conception of the Synagogue's function has grown from a delimited notion of the Synagogue as a weekend prayer hall to the concept of the Synagogue as a full-time spiritual power house radiating energy into the life of the entire community—men, women and children.
>
> We have waited to see whether the Community Center idea can justify itself and whether our community has the strength, the enthusiasm, and the loyalty to support such an institution.
>
> We have erected this institution with a firm and generous hand, with faith in our people and with hope in our future.

Throughout the 1920s, I championed the cause of Jewish youth and urged that our young people be given a voice in the running of congregational affairs. In the face of a "hardening of the arteries" among Orthodox lay leaders and of a cold formalism in the Reform temple, how could young Jews be attracted to the synagogue and take their rightful place in synagogue life? The Young Israel movement, organized by young people for young people, was a timely response in the Orthodox camp. Such young "Jewish protestants" raised their voice, not because they cared so little about Judaism, but because they cared so much.

At this early stage in my rabbinical career, I served as president of the Young People's League of the United Synagogue from 1922 until 1925, and thereafter as honorary president for some years. This was the first national presidency to which I would be appointed. My involvement was not only a demonstration of my feeling that this national youth organization had a worthwhile part to play in the affairs of the United Synagogue. It also indicated that a rabbi should concern himself with the place of Jewish youth in the life and activity of his own congregation.

3

New Horizons, New Responsibilities: 1925–44

The planning, financing, and construction of B'nai Jeshurun's new Community Center and the writing of my book on the congregation's history especially preoccupied me during the latter part of the 1920s, but these tasks were accompanied by growing involvement in the broader aspects of community responsibility. Year by year, the more scholarly projects I may have hoped to undertake gave way to the calls of organizational, administrative, and fund-raising responsibilities in my congregation, and farther afield.

In 1925, I served as chairman of the West Side area of the United Palestine Appeal and of the Committee of Rabbis of Greater New York in the United Jewish Appeal campaign. I also traveled a good deal along the Eastern seaboard and in the Midwest, on behalf of the American Jewish Joint Distribution Committee, Keren Hayesod, Jewish Theological Seminary Endowment Fund, United Synagogue, and Young People's League of the United Synagogue.

That same year, after having served as secretary, treasurer, and vice-president of the New York Board of Jewish Ministers (later renamed the New York Board of Rabbis), which embraced Orthodox, Conservative, and Reform rabbis, I was elected to the presidency and served for two years (1925–27) in that capacity. Being president of this board was especially meaningful to me since the first incumbent, in 1886, had been one of my distinguished predecessors at Congregation B'nai Jeshurun, Rabbi Henry S. Jacobs.

It was my privilege, as president of the New York Board of Jewish Ministers, to give expression to our heartfelt and profound joy on the establishment of the new Hebrew University in 1925. The opening ceremony in Jerusalem took place on April 1, with Lord Balfour and Dr. Chaim Weizmann as the principal speakers. Dr. Weizmann's presence in New York a few weeks earlier enabled the board to tender a luncheon in his honor. He delivered an address on "The Hebrew University—Its Significance for the Spiritual Enrichment of Diaspora Judaism." A resolution was passed, declaring "this historic event to be a spiritual blessing for all mankind." The board designated March 28 as Hebrew University Sabbath, and on this occasion members delivered appropriate sermons to their congregations.

The ceremony on Mount Scopus was attended by leaders of the Zionist movement, spiritual and lay leaders of World Jewry, and representatives of British and other universities. Owing to my congregation's hundredth anniversary celebration, I was unable to attend these exercises. Rabbi Israel H. Levinthal conveyed the text of our resolution. It spoke of the dawn of a new era in the spiritual and cultural life of Israel and went on to envisage the unfolding by the Hebrew University of "the old yet ever new beauties of our Torah, so that, in the light of knowledge, we may once more proudly walk along our own broad, clear, distinctive Jewish way of life."

During my term of office, I conducted a series of symposia on "The Problems of the Jewish Ministry." This later appeared in book form, and it has been a valuable guide book to many young rabbis. Every topic was discussed, in turn, by an Orthodox, a Conservative, and a Reform rabbi, each of whom was especially qualified by his own experience to deal with the topic assigned to him. The concluding symposium in this series, on "The Responsibilities of the Rabbi's Wife," was conducted by three distinguished *rebbetzins*, Mrs. Rebekah Kohut, Mrs. Tamar de Sola Pool, and Mrs. Sarah Hyamson. In her summation, Mrs. Hyamson evoked no little amusement when she said that "the chief responsibility of the rabbi's wife is to take care of the rabbi."

Having brought my congregation into the United Synagogue of America, and through my presidency of the latter's Young People's League, I became more and more involved in its councils. I also visited a number of communities on behalf of the Seminary Endowment Fund, directed by Rabbi Max Arzt. It was a member of my congregation, Louis S. Brush, who in 1928 bequeathed a sum in excess of one and a half million dollars, which made possible the erection of the great buildings of the Jewish Theological Seminary of America.

During this period, it was also my task to head a successful fund-raising campaign for $50,000, to help maintain the Jewish Division of the New York Public Library. I undertook this effort at the invitation of Dr. Joshua Bloch, who had succeeded Abraham Freidus as head of the Jewish Division. The campaign treasurer was Dr. Carl Pforzheimer, a noted businessman and bibliophile, and our patrons and advisors included Dr. A. S. W. Rosenbach, the renowned book collector, of Philadelphia.

An important Jewish cultural event that claimed my attention was the visit of the Hebrew poet laureate, Chaim Naḥman Bialik, to the United States. His purpose was to win greater support for the Keren Hayesod, Jewish National Fund and Hebrew University campaigns. He addressed a gathering held in his honor on Saturday evening, March 6, 1926, at Temple Beth-El, an Orthodox congregation in Boro Park, Brooklyn. An illustrious figure, whom I revered and often heard in New York during the 1920s and 1930s, was the Reverend Zvi Hirsch Masliansky, an outstanding Zionist orator and *maggid,* who was idolized by the vast Yiddish-speaking public of his day.

There were doleful occasions, as well, in which I participated. Thus, in April 1926, it was my sad privilege to eulogize the foremost Yiddish actor, Jacob P. Adler:

The modern theater, as the medium for expressing an outlook on life, has often sounded not only the note of an individual, but the strain of a nation. The Yiddish theater had fulfilled this function to a special degree. Crude as the Yiddish drama had been, in the main, it nevertheless registered, with understanding, the pulse of the Yiddish masses—their romance, their national aspiration, their humor and their pathos. Jacob P. Adler's career spanned the history of the Yiddish theater; he was its prime personality. His own life was replete with dramatic situations. He was a Jew who carried within his heart Jewish passion and Jewish hope, Jewish pride, Jewish pathos and love of the Jewish people.

Other memorial addresses I had occasion to deliver in those years, at B'nai Jeshurun and elsewhere, were dedicated to Louis Marshall (September 1929), a great lawyer and a great Jewish leader; Cantor Josef Rosenblatt (June 1933), whose golden voice was matched by his golden heart; and Adolph S. Ochs (May 1935), who took an ailing newspaper in 1896 and made it into the greatest organ of public opinion, *The New York Times.**

In October 1927, I was elected president of Young Judea, the largest Zionist youth movement in America. Most of its membership of approximately 10,000 consisted of boys and girls in their late teens, while the officers were young people in their twenties. The executive director, Samuel J. Borowsky, was a gifted Hebraist and Jewish educator.

One of the activities in the Young Judea program took the form of an essay and public-speaking contest. The winner in 1927 was Esther Davis, a beautiful teenager, whose theme was "What Palestine Means to American Youth." The prize awarded to her was a transatlantic voyage by sea to Eretz Yisrael. On the boat she met Reuven Rubin, a young Palestinian painter, who was homeward bound after a successful exhibition in New York. That meeting led to their marriage in 1930. Rubin was destined to become an internationally renowned Israeli artist, and his gracious wife, Esther, played an important part in his life and success. I always felt proud to have had a fortuitous role in their romance.

As president of Young Judea, I paid my first visit to Palestine in the summer of 1928 and brought greetings to the Jewish Boy Scouts of Eretz Yisrael, as well as a gift of $5,000 for their new sports field and parade grounds. Bert accompanied me, since it was also our tenth wedding anniversary. The visit (which I describe elsewhere in these pages) left an indelible impression on both of us, intensifying our resolve to enlarge and deepen our service to the Zionist movement.

A year later, in 1929, having become active in the Zionist Organization of America, I headed the American Zionist delegation that had an urgent meeting in Washington with President Hoover and Secretary of State Stimson, following the anti-Jewish Arab riots in Palestine.

It came as a welcome assignment to be appointed first chairman of the Social Justice Committee of the Rabbinical Assembly of America, in 1931. The scope of my activities in this area was soon increased when I was appointed to a similar

*Tributes to Bialik, Ochs, Rosenblatt, and others appear in my book, *Toward a Solution* (1940). On "Yossele" Rosenblatt, see also chapter 17.

position in the Synagogue Council of America, comprising rabbinical and lay bodies of the Orthodox, Conservative, and Reform movements. Working alongside parallel groups in the Christian denominations, I became involved in current issues affecting industrial, interracial, and interfaith relations, the relationship of Church and State, and problems of world peace.

In 1928, I participated in the founding of the National Conference of Christians and Jews. Thereafter, I became actively involved in its programs, serving for a number of years on its executive and administrative bodies. Its original designation was the "National Conference of Jews and Christians," but the word order was eventually changed in deference to the numerical proportion of Christians to Jews.

Before lending myself to this movement, however, I had made certain that it had no missionary aims in view, especially since one of its main Christian advocates was suspect on that account. The Reverend John Herring, executive director of the NCCJ for the first eight months, and his successor, Everett R. Clinchy, won my confidence and the confidence of others that they had no ulterior motives.

Christian missionary activity had agitated the Jewish community shortly before the National Conference of Christians and Jews came into being. It fell to my lot to play some part in articulating Jewish reservations, when addressing the North American Home Missions in Atlantic City, New Jersey. I said that, in my view, Jews would respond to every sincere approach for Christian-Jewish goodwill, but that it must be a friendship between equals, each respecting the other's right to his own religious creed and practice, each following his own road to salvation.

The main address at the founding dinner of the National Conference of Christians and Jews in 1928 was given by an eminent American, Charles Evans Hughes, who a year or two later was appointed Chief Justice of the U.S. Supreme Court. It was my privilege to deliver the invocation. Over the years, I took an active part in the NCCJ and addressed many religious groups under its auspices. At times, I was critical of its tendency to shy away from Zionism and from the issues affecting Negroes. On the whole, however, the NCCJ performed a useful function and became a major factor in improving relations between Christians and Jews on the American scene. It introduced Brotherhood Week observances to mark Washington's birthday. It also dealt with objectionable material in textbooks used by children attending public schools.

At Congregation B'nai Jeshurun, the men's club, organized in 1928 for social, cultural, and philanthropic purposes, began sponsoring annual Interfaith Brotherhood Services, when awards were made to deserving persons in civic and religious life. As part of the nationwide celebration of George Washington's bicentennial, an observance was arranged by the New York Board of Jewish Ministers, on May 2, 1932, at the synagogue of Shearith Israel, mother congregation of American Jewry. Note was taken of the fact that, in 1789, the Reverend Gershom Mendes Seixas, minister of Shearith Israel, had been invited to take part in the inauguration of George Washington as first President of the United States. Participating in the 1932 bicentennial observance were that historic congregation's minister, the Reverend Dr. David de Sola Pool, and its minister emeritus, the Reverend Henry Pereira

Mendes. Representatives of leading Christian bodies attended the service at Congregation Shearith Israel, and a message was received from President Herbert Hoover.

One other aspect of interfaith activity engaged my attention from the late 1920s. It was stimulated by Kedar Nath Das Gupta, who had come from India to organize the World Fellowship of Faiths and the Union of East and West. On one occasion, in 1930, Das Gupta arranged a Rosh Hashanah observance in Grace Episcopal Church at 10th Street and Broadway, one of New York's aristocratic churches. Its minister was the Reverend Dr. S. Percy Grant, a highly regarded liberal clergyman. The celebration, at which I had been asked to respond on behalf of the Jewish community, was scheduled to take place on the evening immediately after the termination of the second day of Rosh Hashanah. It was to be attended by Hindus, Muslims, and Christians, as well as Jews, under the auspices of the World Fellowship of Faiths.

My wife and I traveled by subway from our home on the West Side and, as we emerged from the subway station into the street, we heard church bells playing the traditional synagogue melody of *En Kelohénu*. That unusual pre-welcome touched us as deeply as the splendid formal program awaiting us inside the church.

On another occasion, several years later, under the auspices of the Interfaith Fellowship, I was invited to address the Muslim Brotherhood at the feast marking the end of the month of Ramadan. Reciprocating the courtesy, I invited the leader of the Muslim Brotherhood, Dr. G. T. Kheirallah, a scholarly physician, to visit my congregation and take part in a Jewish-Muslim-Christian symposium marking the eight hundredth anniversary of the birth of Maimonides.

The lay leadership of B'nai Jeshurun was, on the whole, appreciative of my manifold outside activities, especially since new families were being attracted to the synagogue at the same time. The congregation's membership had increased considerably, its finances were in good order, and its reputation in the community was growing. Some grumbling could nevertheless be heard among the trustees, on two counts. First, my Zionist activities were not welcomed by the residue of German-Jewish families opposed to Zionism. Second, my liberal economic views and activities, on the side of labor, annoyed many of the leading members, who belonged to the employer class. This divergence of opinions sometimes provoked heated discussion.

To me, the issue at stake—freedom of the pulpit—was a fundamental one. Not being certain that I would have my way, I began to look around for alternative posts in New York and other cities. Opportunities were not lacking. Fortunately, however, B'nai Jeshurun's lay leadership became reconciled to my stand, partly for personal reasons and partly because of the American community's growing acceptance of the freedom of the pulpit, the rights of labor, and the validity of Zionism. Besides, growing concern with the strident Nazi menace in Europe, which conveyed its own sobering and frightening message, now outweighed other issues.

The pulpit of Congregation B'nai Jeshurun was winning the respect of the community and attracting people from many parts of New York City. In 1929, the late

Friday night service and lecture, inaugurated a decade previously, were discontinued in favor of Sunday morning lectures, preceded by a brief service. With this in mind, I prepared a special booklet entitled *Devotional Service for Secular Occasions*. These Sunday morning lecture-services were well attended. My frequent absences from the city, however, obliged me to discontinue them. In addition to the early Friday evening services, a late Friday evening (abbreviated) service and sermon, broadcast over one of the local radio stations, reached a wide audience.

Among my congregants at this time was the wife of Professor Richard Gottheil, who held the chair of Semitic languages at Columbia University and who had served as first president of the American Federation of Zionists. Both Mrs. Gottheil and her sister, Eva Leon, also a congregant, were ardent Zionists.

Unlike the Gottheils, whose family background was German in culture and Reform in religion, Eddie Cantor was of Orthodox Russian immigrant stock. His daughter, Marilyn, attended the religious school of Congregation B'nai Jeshurun. This famous American entertainer became deeply involved in the work of Youth Aliyah and undertook a mission to Great Britain on its behalf. Years later, during the 1940s, he also supported the efforts of the American Zionist Emergency Council.*

B'nai Jeshurun became known increasingly as *the* Zionist synagogue of New York. A succession of Zionist leaders, from Eretz Yisrael and other parts of the world, attended our Sabbath services. Dr. Chaim Weizmann was our guest of honor on the first day of Passover in 1928. Following the establishment of the State of Israel, many visiting Israeli statesmen attended our High Holy Day services. Levi Eshkol, then Israel's Minister of Finance, attended our Kol Nidré service in 1956. Other eminent Israelis who came to our services were Zalman Shazar, Moshe Sharett, and Golda Meir. On the High Holy Days, most of Israel's diplomatic representatives in New York usually worshiped with us.

Among other prominent Jewish leaders from abroad whom I welcomed to our synagogue over the years were Chief Rabbi Jacob Kaplan of France, in October 1956; Barnett Janner, M.P. (later, Lord Janner), who came in his dual capacity as president of the Board of Deputies of British Jews and as president of the Zionist Federation of Great Britain and Ireland, in January 1957, to address my congregation on the tercentenary of British Jewry; and Sir Isaac Wolfson, whom I often saw in New York.

Depression Years—The Fight for Social Justice

The severe economic depression that hit the United States in 1929 and had disastrous repercussions throughout the world was a grave test not only of the American economy, but also of its social and political institutions. The rosy period of the nation's expansion and of its social, cultural, and political advancement now came to a halt. The problem for most Americans was how to survive this crisis.

*For some impressions of Eddie Cantor, see chapter 17.

In that decade of 1930–40, the Jews of the United States had to grapple with the basic issues of economic retrenchment and of discharging at least some of the responsibilities they had assumed in better times.

For the Jewish people as a whole, this would be an era of foreboding and a prelude to disaster. World Jewry was destined to become the major victim of Hitlerism, which first engulfed Germany and Austria, then attacked the continent of Europe and thereby precipitated World War II. It was in this critical period that American Jewry was called upon to bear responsibilities more vast and clamorous than any it had been called upon to bear at previous times of crisis.

The role of a single congregation could only be miniscule, but the cumulative role of thousands of Jewish congregations in America was considerable. It was important to make them feel the responsibilities they were called upon to fulfill in the crises that affected both the American nation and the Jewish people. The American rabbinate during these years was a constructive factor, both in the congregational and in the communal areas.

Within my own congregation, B'nai Jeshurun, I had a manifold responsibility: to organize the men, women, and youth so that they would make their most effective contribution to the philanthropic and social needs of both the neighborhood and the city. They had also to play their part in the fund-raising campaigns for general unemployment relief, for the local Federation of Jewish Philanthropic Societies, and for the campaigns of the Jewish National Fund, the United Palestine Appeal, and the Joint Distribution Committee.

Although I had begun to play a larger role in Zionist affairs, moving into national and international Zionist responsibilities, I also felt bound, as an American, to shoulder urgent civic and national obligations.

Commencing in 1933, I served on the New York City Citizens' Committee on Unemployment Relief. That same year, I was appointed to the U.S. Department of Labor Committee on Immigration and Naturalization, the main purpose of which was to improve the facilities at Ellis Island. In 1935, I was appointed to the National Labor Relations Board and served as a public representative for the Second District of New York. Years later, in 1943, I served on a panel appointed by the U.S. Department of Labor, to fix minimum wages in the poultry industry, which was largely Jewish.

During the early 1930s, I joined the American National Civil Liberties Union, being drawn more and more to spheres of political action. It must be remembered that the impact of the Depression years, followed by President Franklin D. Roosevelt's New Deal, engendered a transformation of the American public psyche. There was a greater awareness of social and economic injustices that needed to be rectified.

Sporadic outbursts of anti-Semitism were a worrying feature of the 1920s and early 1930s. The American Jewish community had to face hostile agitation during the Red Scare that followed the Bolshevik Revolution in Russia, at the height of the Depression, and after the Nazi seizure of power in Germany.

An early manifestation of this anti-Jewish propaganda was the appearance, from

May to October 1920, of defamatory articles in *The Dearborn Independent*, a weekly financed by the automobile magnate, Henry Ford. These articles, which exploited the forged "Protocols of the Learned Elders of Zion," were later published as a collection entitled *The International Jew*. A lawsuit compelled Ford to terminate his anti-Semitic campaign in 1927 and to publish a retraction.

The Ku Klux Klan, a secret organization directed against Catholics, Jews, and Negroes, made a short-lived bid for power in some areas of the United States, but there were more enduring forms of discrimination in public life at this time. An unofficial *numerus clausus* operated against Jews in some universities and in commerce and the professions, while the Johnson Act of 1924 (controlling immigration on the basis of racial quotas) subsequently closed America's doors to many Jewish victims of the Nazi terror.

During the 1930s, Father Charles E. Coughlin of Detroit, the notorious "radio priest," poisoned the air with his anti-Jewish broadcast talks and the articles published in his weekly, *Social Justice*. Simultaneously, encouraged by the rise of Nazism, organizations such as the German-American Bund fostered race hatred with their uniformed parades and pamphleteering. Fortunately, however, such tactics were repudiated and condemned by most Americans of German descent. American Jewry successfully resisted and discredited these campaigns. They died down after the outbreak of World War II.

Like other rabbis in the United States, I dealt with these threats in my pulpit addresses. At the national level, I had occasion to combat anti-Semitism in my capacity as chairman of the Rabbinical Assembly's Social Justice Committee and, later, as chairman of the Social Justice Committee of the Synagogue Council of America.

One dominant issue of the mid-1930s was the right of labor to enter politics. There were labor leaders and intellectuals, Jewish and non-Jewish, who sponsored that cause. I had long shared their viewpoint and so became involved. We felt it to be timely and essential that labor should make its voice heard as a political force.

The American Labor Party in New York came into existence in 1936. Among its founders were three leading Jewish trade unionists, David Dubinsky, Jacob Potofsky, and Alex Rose. I was an active supporter until 1944, when it became evident that the ALP had fallen under Communist control. Breaking away in that year, we organized the American Liberal Party of New York. I was elected one of its honorary vice-chairmen and took part in all the ensuing political campaigns.

The officers and honorary officers of the Liberal Party included labor leaders such as David Dubinsky and Alex Rose and a group of intellectuals. Among these were former U.S. Assistant Secretary of State Adolf A. Berle; Professor William H. Kilpatrick, dean of American educators; Professor Reinhold Niebuhr, the eminent theologian and vice-president of Union Theological Seminary; Professor John Bennett, that seminary's dean; Dr. John L. Childs; and Dr. Sidney Hook, the noted philosopher.

The founders of the Liberal Party believed that New York's citizens needed a new instrument through which to make their views felt on political issues and social progress. Our platform called for government established on moral principles, with the public good as its central objective, and for the elimination of totalitarianism and reaction of every stripe.

To run ahead of my story, the Liberal Party played an important part in local and national affairs after World War II. Thus, on December 6, 1955, I spoke before the historic merger convention of the American Federation of Labor and the Congress of Industrial Organizations. While saluting the American labor movement as "the most reliable and the most effective force against Communism," I also cautioned against the resistance in some locals to the admission of members "without regard to race, creed, color or national origin." Nor could there be any justification, in my view, for only "one-way traffic between Religion and the unions." On the social plane, I declared:

> The trade union has most effectively resisted the dehumanization of the worker which has resulted from the industrialization of our society. It has restored the laborer to his true place—changing him from a mere cog in the industrial setup to an individual with the God-given power to control his own destiny.

The Liberal Party pioneered in progressive labor legislation and consumer protection. It was especially active in the fight for civil rights and liberties, striving to eliminate racial discrimination and segregation. Speaking from a Liberal Party platform on one occasion, I said that the Negro was "not the only victim of group discrimination, but the most conspicuous victim, the most numerous and the most abused. . . . The inequalities from which American Blacks suffer are a blemish upon the moral credentials of our nation, a hurtful relic of the slaveholder mentality, which Federal legislation is obligated to expunge."

On September 11, 1956, at a New York State convention of the party, I was accorded the privilege of nominating Adlai E. Stevenson as our candidate for the presidency of the United States. My association with the Liberal Party continued until we made Aliyah at the end of 1960.

As I have already indicated, my political activities did not go down well with some of my congregational elders. Occasionally, there were frank exchanges of opinion, when I took the opportunity of stating that I believed it to be my duty, as a spiritual leader, to champion the cause of the underprivileged in the social and industrial fields. The usual reaction to this was that "a rabbi should stick to religion and keep out of politics." I would then ask, "What is religion? Is it *apart from* life or is it *a part of* life?" Whereas, in the case of Zionism, I did succeed in winning over my congregation and its lay leadership, on political and social issues I succeeded only in winning the right to air my views from the pulpit and in the wider community.

The appointment by the Rabbinical Assembly of a special Committee on Social Justice, which I served as its first chairman, was an earnest of the Assembly's conviction that rabbis should educate their congregations in matters pertaining to the U.S. economy, decent labor and race relations, and international comity. On these and similar issues an authentic Jewish viewpoint could be expressed. In my chairman's report for 1932, I emphasized that "our label as a 'Conservative' group was never intended to designate conservatism in social and economic outlook." Our objectives included the promotion of a more friendly relationship between Jewish labor organizations and the synagogue, the establishment of appropriate agencies for resolving disputes of a nonreligious character between Jews, and the formulation of a policy on disarmament and world peace. Professor Mordecai M. Kaplan, then president of the Rabbinical Assembly, conducted a special seminar on economic issues.

My report for the following year concerned itself also with President Roosevelt's New Deal and with Jewish-Christian relations. Our committee insisted that "no arbitrary limit be placed on the rabbi's freedom of speech in his pulpit references to socio-economic evils" and pledged its support for a proposed five-day week and minimum-wage scales.

Dealing with religious matters, our committee urged the major churches to dissociate themselves from missionary activities aimed at Jews, called for an end to religious discrimination in employment, and advocated the abolition of sectarian (Christmas and Easter) festivities in public schools. Appreciation was expressed for the stand taken by American Christian groups against the persecution of the Jews in Nazi Germany.

One important outcome of this committee's work was the *Pronouncement on Social Justice,* which the Rabbinical Assembly adopted by a majority vote at its convention in July 1934, and which was then published as an official document.

Such involvements, which I was later able to broaden when I headed the Social Justice Committee of the Synagogue Council of America, brought me into contact and cooperation with the National Catholic Welfare Conference and the Federal Council of Protestant Churches. I had occasion to address many church, university, and other non-Jewish audiences and frequently discussed the relationship of Church and Synagogue and of these two with the State. The issues engaging our attention were related for the most part, however, to labor relations and to the Black community's underprivileged status in terms of housing, education, and employment. "Social discrimination, painful as it is, can be borne," I once told a Negro congregation in New York, " but political disfranchisement, economic oppression and educational discrimination are violations of fundamental human rights, which cannot be tolerated. America injures itself when it denies justice to one-tenth of its population."

It is my belief that American Jewry, individually as well as collectively, has sinned less against the Negro than have other sections of the U.S. population. On the whole, the Jewish posture has been a liberal one, not only because Jews themselves are often exposed to prejudice, but also because of the Jewish tradition rooted in the biblical precept: "Thou shalt not oppress a stranger: for ye must know the heart of a stranger, seeing ye were strangers in the land of Egypt" (Exodus 23:9.)

An opportunity to serve the cause of social justice on a local Jewish level, and in the Jewish tradition of bringing peace between man and fellow man, presented itself in 1929, when I became associated with the Jewish Court of Arbitration in New York. It was one of several such attempts to provide a free and appropriate framework for adjudicating and conciliating disputes arising between Jews. Such cases involved small-business disagreements, complaints of parents against children who refused to contribute to their support, marital problems, altercations in small Jewish congregations between religious functionaries and lay officers, as well as claims for sick benefits and for interment in Jewish cemeteries which arose in Jewish lodges and *landsmanshaften*. Actions in the municipal courts usually involved long delays and expensive litigation. Those who were not yet familiar with the American environment and the English language were at a special disadvantage. Moreover, there was often the motivation of avoiding the *ḥillul Hashem* involved in bringing unseemly Jewish quarrels to public attention.

The decisions of those tribunals were binding under the New York State Arbitration Law of 1920, which gave force to the decision of an arbitrator or arbitrators chosen by both parties to a dispute.

In 1930, I assumed office as president of the Jewish Court of Arbitration in New York. Its executive secretary was Louis Richman, a lawyer, and one of its principal sponsors was Judge Jacob Panken of the Family Court of the City of New York. Sessions took place for a number of years in the Municipal Courthouse on Madison Street, in the heart of the Lower East Side. Later, they were held at the Jewish Educational Alliance nearby, on East Broadway.

Soon after my election as president, we had the tribunal's name changed to "The Jewish Conciliation Court of America," in order to stress the less formal and more personal aspect of its program. In 1939, the word "Court" was replaced by "Board," thus emphasizing our role as voluntary conciliators.

The Board's clientele came from all parts of Greater New York. It largely comprised the first generation of Jewish immigrants and, in cases of support claims by parents against children, the first generation of American-born Jews. We had the full cooperation of the Yiddish press in publicizing our work and in broadening the range of our clientele. Since the parties to a dispute were not permitted to engage the services of a lawyer, litigants had direct contact with the adjudicators. There was a panel of three judges at every session. Each panel consisted of a rabbi (Orthodox, Conservative, or Reform), a lawyer or judge in one of the municipal courts, and a businessman. The constant amid the variables was the executive secretary, Louis Richman, who took time off from his own legal practice to serve without compensation.

Not a few of the cases brought before the Jewish Conciliation Board could not be settled merely by handing down a decision. Social-service assistance was needed. For a time, this aspect of our work was handled by members of the sisterhood of Congregation B'nai Jeshurun. In 1936, Ruth Richman, wife of the executive secretary, was engaged as social-service director. Some years later, Dr. Howard E. Berk, a trained psychiatrist, volunteered his expert services, attended every session, and took part in the proceedings as a consultant.

Since the "Jewish Court," as it was popularly known, needed judges of caliber, I succeeded in enlisting men and women of standing in the community. Among them was General David Sarnoff, president of the Radio Corporation of America, who readily availed himself of the opportunity to practice his fluent Yiddish.

It was a source of great encouragement that Justice William O. Douglas of the U.S. Supreme Court accepted our invitation to speak at the Board's thirty-fifth anniversary celebration, which also marked the twenty-fifth anniversary of my presidency. This function took place at the Jewish Educational Alliance, on January 17, 1954, with some of our clients as guests of honor. General Sarnoff, who chaired the proceedings, introduced himself in Yiddish as "a Jew from Minsk." Justice Douglas expressed appreciation for our work, in an address on "The Problems of the Little People." A few sentences may be worth quoting:

> The thing that has interested me particularly about the Board is that it has been more interested in justice than in law. Throughout the centuries, law has been trying to catch up with justice. . . . The work of the Conciliation Board, seeking to find what is the truth, trying to apply justice, is a great experiment in a busy community where there are many problems, local and international. It is important to take time out to make adjustments in the little problems of people. That, in the end, marks the difference between a society which administers to the needs of people and a society where sores and troubles fester, where the needs and aspirations of the ordinary man are neglected.

On June 20 of that year, our anniversary celebrations received special coverage by the National Broadcasting Company in an *Eternal Light* radio program entitled "Court without a Gavel," which dramatized our conciliation procedures. The title given to this broadcast aptly described the informal but effective nature of the Board's services to the Jewish public. This radio feature was repeated by the NBC in October 1965, to mark our forty-fifth anniversary.

Throughout the nearly four decades of my association with the Jewish Conciliation Board of America, I was fortunate to enjoy the enthusiastic support of rabbinical colleagues in New York, Orthodox, Conservative, and Reform, and of many prominent laymen. Rabbi Dr. Leo Jung of the Jewish Center (Orthodox) and Rabbi Dr. Julius Mark of Temple Emanu-El (Reform) served as vice-presidents. Jacob R. Schiff, followed by Israel, Nathan, and William Sachs, all prominent in the city's business life, held the post of treasurer. Louis Richman, who first brought me into the Board, continued as executive secretary until his death in 1956, when he was succeeded by his widow, Ruth Richman. Our patrons and supporters came from all segments of the Jewish community. We were also fortunate to have a distinguished non-Jewish patron in John S. Burke, president of the B. Altman Company and head of the Friedsam Foundation. After his passing, John S. Burke, Jr., continued his father's interest and support.

It was a welcome and meaningful experience for me to be involved in this unique area of Jewish social service.* Ministering to an upper-middle-class congregation, I particularly felt the need for contact with *Amkha*, the humbler Jewish masses. Especially because I was becoming more and more concerned with the larger problems of *Klal Yisrael*, the Jewish people in general, I felt it my duty to involve myself also in the problems of *Reb Yisroel*, the ordinary individual Jew.

An exotic cause that claimed my allegiance in the early 1930s was that of the Falashas, known as the "Black Jews of Ethiopia." Though shrouded in legend, the history of these Falasha tribesmen, then scattered around Lake Tana in northwestern Ethiopia, had long been familiar to travelers and explorers. One who made a study of them was the French Jewish orientalist, Professor Joseph Halévy, who spent some time among the Falashas in 1868 and collected a wealth of information. The Alliance Israélite Universelle sponsored his mission. Halévy passed on his commitment to Jacques Faitlovitch, a pupil of his at the Sorbonne. The latter dedicated his life to this remote outpost of Jewry.

Faitlovitch first went to Ethiopia as a young man, in 1904. He spent eighteen months among the Falashas (a name interpreted to mean "strangers"), investigating their religious traditions and practices. The Ethiopians generally trace their ancestry to King Solomon and the Queen of Sheba, but the Falashas claim descent from Jews who arrived by way of Egypt in Temple times. Professor Faitlovitch became convinced that they were descended from one of the "Lost Ten Tribes" of Israel. He found that the Falashas were exposed to the blandishments of Christian missionaries and he resolved to teach them the essentials of traditional Judaism and to reunite them with the Jewish people. They themselves were proud of their ancient Jewish heritage and wished to remain faithful to it. There were perhaps 70,000 Falashas at the time, living in conditions of squalor and destitution. They knew no Hebrew and spoke Amharic, the Ethiopian vernacular, but the language used in their prayers was Ghe'ez, the sacred tongue of Ethiopia. Centuries of isolation, marked by hostile religious pressure, had made them cling to a way of life prescribed in the Bible. They were oblivious of the Talmud and postbiblical (rabbinic) tradition.

On the initiative of Professor Faitlovitch, Pro-Falasha Committees were organized in various European Jewish communities before 1914. Then, during World War I, he came to the United States and established an American Pro-Falasha Committee. Some years later, while on another visit to the United States, he sought help for the establishment of a boarding school in Addis Ababa, the Ethiopian capital, where promising young Falashas would receive a Jewish education. A suitable plot of land for this school had been donated by Haile Selassie, the Negus or Emperor of Ethiopia, who had assumed the title of "Lion of Judah" upon his ascent to the throne.

*My recent book, *Jewish Justice and Conciliation* (New York, 1981), deals at length with the Jewish Conciliation Board and its case histories. It also contains a historical review of Jewish juridical autonomy. The subject was treated earlier and more briefly by me in an essay, "Modern Courts of Arbitration and the Jewish Historical Background," included in *Toward a Solution* (New York, 1940), pp. 303–21. See also chapter 16.

It was at this point, in 1930, that I entered the picture, when I went to hear a lecture given by Professor Faitlovitch in New York. His vivid and moving account of the Falashas excited my interest and converted me into an ardent advocate of their cause. At his urging, I accepted the chairmanship of the American Pro-Falasha Committee. We undertook the project of building and maintaining the school in Addis Ababa where Falasha boys would be taught Hebrew, Bible, and Jewish history, as well as certain handicrafts. I recall going to Tiffany's on Fifth Avenue and purchasing a miniature sculptured lion, which we inscribed as follows:

To the "Lion of Judah,"
in appreciation of his helpfulness to the Falashas.
From the American Pro-Falasha Committee.

This gift was taken to Ethiopia by Professor Faitlovitch, who, together with his former pupil, the new principal of the school, Taamrat Emanuel, attended Haile Selassie's coronation in November 1930.

Soon after the coronation ceremony, Taamrat Emanuel accompanied Professor Faitlovitch to New York, thus becoming the first of his people to arrive in the United States. I had suggested the advisability of bringing him, in order to increase the effectiveness of my fund-raising campaign. Taamrat Emanuel himself represented the best argument in favor of the work to which Dr. Faitlovitch had dedicated himself. Thanks to his mentor, he had acquired some degree of European culture and a modicum of Hebrew learning, which he in turn endeavored to instill in pupils attending the school in Addis Ababa. He thus exemplified what could be achieved for the Falashas under proper guidance and training.

A women's division of the Pro-Falasha Committee was established, comprising representatives of the Orthodox, Conservative, and Reform wings of American Jewry. Mrs. David E. Goldfarb was chairlady and Mrs. Samuel Spiegel and Mrs. Herbert S. Goldstein served as her deputies. Dr. Cyrus Adler, one of the first to encourage Faitlovitch, and Professor Mordecai M. Kaplan were among those who took a keen interest in our work. The Italian occupation of Ethiopia (1936–41) and World War II were a temporary handicap to these endeavors.

At a later stage, Professor Norman Bentwich rallied support in Great Britain and visited Ethiopia, where he spent some time among the Falashas. He was a tower of strength to Professor Faitlovitch.

When the war ended, Professor Faitlovitch settled in Tel Aviv and strove to gain wider support for this cause until his death in 1955. Fourteen years later, I was able to see the effects of worldwide Jewish apathy toward the Falashas and their perilous situation, when I visited Ethiopia in 1969 (see chapter 12).

A Zionist Mission

Since my early youth, Zionism had been integral to my spiritual, intellectual, and emotional being. Yet despite all the passion and purpose, I was not destined to tread the soil of Eretz Yisrael until my wife and I went there in the summer of 1928 (as previously mentioned), on the occasion of our tenth wedding anniversary.

It was hardly an auspicious time for a visit to Palestine. The adverse economic conditions, stemming from the crisis that had begun in 1923, accentuated the magnitude of the task that lay ahead in building the Jewish National Home. Unemployment was rife within the Yishuv. Veteran inhabitants as well as newcomers were feeling the pinch. Large numbers of workers had to subsist on the meager pay they received from government relief projects initiated during the tenure of the second High Commissioner, Lord Plumer. Financially, the Zionist Executive was in the doldrums. Zionist fund raising throughout the world was at a low ebb and, in spite of their valiant efforts to secure money and manpower, Dr. Chaim Weizmann and his associates were making little headway with the Jewish communities of the world, especially in America. The Yishuv was shouldering a heavy burden, both physically and psychologically. This could be attributed, in large measure, to the economic recession that hit Poland during the 1920s. Discriminatory Polish economic measures had driven many middle-class Jews from the country; with the gates of America barred to them, they gladly turned to Palestine, thus constituting the Fourth Aliyah. Such an influx caught the Zionist bodies by surprise, for at that point they had neither the means nor the capacity to deal with this situation. Clearly, all the high hopes and soaring ambitions of the previous decade were being put to a severe test.

Nevertheless, for my wife and me, it was a thrilling experience to view the Land of Israel, still barren in many parts, and especially the Jezreel Valley. As seen from the foothills below Nazareth, the Emek's new Jewish settlements were barely visible, yet we could already glimpse the flourishing potential behind the apparent desolation. Both Bert and I sensed that, before very long, these uninviting landscapes would be populated and filled with vegetation. We were awed and enraptured by the holy places in the walled Old City of Jerusalem; delighted to wander through the few paved streets of Tel Aviv, "the world's first all-Jewish city," streets clustered around Rothschild Boulevard; heartened to see the flourishing agricultural colonies of Judea; and overjoyed when we were reunited with old friends from Philadelphia who had made Aliyah, such as Ethel and Gershon Agronsky and Harry and Ida Davidowitz, and when we met leaders of the Yishuv.

More than anything else, that first trip through Palestine made us aware of the vast and complex problems the Zionist movement had to tackle, and of how much needed to be done—and could be done—to help turn the desert into a blossoming garden. I realized that no amount of speechifying on American platforms would adequately convey all of this, but I also had a much better idea of the mission I might be able to undertake if called upon to do so at some future date.

The weeks we spent touring Eretz Yisrael in 1928 reactivated and galvanized my Zionist commitment. In practical terms, this had begun when I worked for the Keren Hayesod campaign in 1921, soon after coming to Congregation B'nai Jeshurun. It had brought me into contact with local and world Zionist leaders, and I had served as president of Young Judea. Now that I was seeing it all with my own eyes, and not through the eyes of others, I felt that some greater task was required of me. It was not until four years later, in 1932, however, during my second trip to Eretz Israel, that my ruminations about playing a more effective role in *binyan ha-Aretz*, the redemption and upbuilding of the Land, were crystallized as a plan of constructive action.

More economic, social, and political changes had meanwhile taken place in America, Europe, and Palestine. The depression into which the United States had been plunged since 1928 had cut the ground beneath our feet. Many of my friends and congregants had been hard hit. A still graver menace, of worldwide significance, was Adolf Hitler's bid for power in Germany. A handful of farsighted statesmen, Winston Churchill chief among them, had begun to issue dire warnings. The Jewish communities of Europe were the most immediately and seriously endangered. The world in general, however, chose to live in a fool's paradise of indifference and complacency, ignoring the signs of coming disaster.

In the midst of all these pressures, my wife and I had decided that the Bar Mitzvah of our firstborn, Avram, should take place in Jerusalem. The family pilgrimage included, of course, his ten-year-old sister, Vivian. These days, such Bar Mitzvah excursions across the Atlantic are fairly commonplace; at that time, however, they were rare.

Our second pilgrimage to Eretz Yisrael began with a visit to the holiest of Jewish sites, *Ha-Kotel ha-Ma'aravi*, the surviving fragment of the Western Wall of the Temple. We went there late on Friday afternoon, accompanied by that grand lady and Zionist exemplar, Henrietta Szold. She was then in her early seventies, yet sprightly and energetic, fully occupied with the concerns of our people, pursuing a crowded daily schedule in Palestine that would have taxed the strength of a person half her age. Within a year, as the founder of Hadassah, she would become responsible for organizing Youth Aliyah and thus embark upon an undertaking that, under her loving care, would rescue tens of thousands of children from lands of peril and bring them to safety in the Land of Israel. She was a Jewish matriarch, adored by her people long after her death thirteen years later, at the age of eighty-five.

I made some notes of this visit to the Western Wall at the time and described the impression it made upon us:

> In some ways it is an inspiring spectacle; in other ways it is a grief and a humiliation. The plaintive notes of prayer rend the air with seeming futility. All around is filth. Arabs look on with disdain. They consider it to be their property, and that Jews pray there only on sufferance. British police officials patrol the area to make sure that there is no conflict. And yet, the Jew whose prayers cling to that Wall is the Jew whose persistent clinging to his people has held the thread of Jewish destiny intact, so that it was possible for the vision of a New Palestine to be conceived and translated.

Avram's Bar Mitzvah initiation in Jerusalem the next morning took place at the new Yeshurun Synagogue, whose name bore a resemblance to that of my synagogue in New York. Our son did his part very well, and impressed the congregants with his "Sephardic" pronunciation.

The reception at the hotel after the ceremony was attended by more than a hundred of our Palestinian friends, including Henrietta Szold, Rabbi Meir Berlin (later, Bar-Ilan), Justice Gad Frumkin, Dr. I. B. Berkson, head of the Va'ad Leumi Education Department, Hebrew University professors and labor leaders—altogether a cross-section of the many-sided Eretz Yisrael community. We were delighted that our son's Bar Mitzvah should have been marked by this assemblage betokening Jewish unity across differences.

In the afternoon, I took Avram and Vivian for a walk around Jerusalem, recapturing the thrill Bert and I had experienced on seeing these historic places four years earlier. We traced the ancient, lichen-covered walls of the Old City; we followed the Valley of Hinnom, source of the term *Gehenna;* we strolled past the age-old water pools that supplied the Jerusalem of David and Solomon; we entered David's Citadel and saw the spot where his son, Adonijah, proclaimed himself king while his father lay dying; and we returned toward evening, just as the full moon was creeping out from behind the hills of Moab. A fellow New Yorker remarked that it was "a promenade along the Broadway of Jewish history."

The feeling that dominated all others was that I was here not as a rabbi but as a Jew who, with his family, formed an integral part of the Jewish people. Both when I sat in the synagogue and when I strolled with my children around Jerusalem, I felt more keenly than ever before the power and depth of the Jewish tradition. It is axiomatic, if trite, to say that never is a Jew more at home than in Eretz Yisrael.

Leaving Haifa by boat, en route to Soviet Russia in that summer of 1932, I made a brief stop in Istanbul before proceeding across the Black Sea to Odessa and thence to Kiev, Minsk, and Moscow. My wife, son, and daughter had remained in Jerusalem, staying with Ethel and Gershon Agronsky and their family most of the time.

While waiting in Istanbul for the boat to Odessa, I made an effort to visit Leon Trotsky, once the most powerful Soviet leader after Lenin. Having quarreled with Stalin, and following his expulsion from the USSR in 1929, Trotsky had been granted asylum by the Turkish authorities on Prinkipo Island in the Sea of Marmora, near Istanbul. From there he had been conducting a one-man campaign against Stalin's tyrannical regime. Alluding to his main recreation in this isolated spot, Trotsky is said to have remarked, "If Lenin were still alive, he would be fishing here, next to me."

Although I posed no threat to Trotsky's security, my attempt to see him proved unsuccessful. I managed to reach the island of Prinkipo and the dilapidated villa in which he lived, but that was as far as I got.

In due course, the ship arrived and we sailed for Odessa. This was my first visit to Russia since the sojourn there with my mother and infant brother thirty years earlier. Contrary to the advice of some friends, I had stated candidly in my application for a visa that I was a clergyman. The necessary document was forthcoming, but my visit was subject to the official Intourist arrangements. Nevertheless, I was able to tour those synagogues in Odessa and Moscow which had not been converted to other purposes and to attend Sabbath services alongside the dejected local worshipers. Such visits had a counterpoint in the officially sponsored tours of antireligious museums and in visits to Kolkhoz collectives, workers' clubs, and the like.

It was a hard year for the USSR. Food shortages had given rise to widespread malnutrition. The extent of inefficiency and sheer neglect was astounding. New hotels and apartment buildings rapidly deteriorated, factories installed by German engineers were ruined after a year or two, but the enthusiasm of Soviet youth ran high, and it was contagious. As I recorded at the time, however, children had once been afraid of their parents; now parents were afraid of their children.

Jews and other believers were allowed to practice their religion, but every educational force and social sanction was employed to discredit religion. Zionist activity was a political offense. The Yevsektsiya, the Jewish section of the Communist Party, had displayed its zeal in this process of repression. Yiddish culture was encouraged, however, as part of a general policy of dealing with minority populations. Anti-Semitism, though officially outlawed, remained widespread. In areas such as the Crimea, where Jews constituted a substantial portion of the population, instruction in the schools was in Yiddish. To counteract Zionism, and as a protective measure against Japanese expansionism, the Government had announced the establishment of the "Jewish Autonomous Region" of Birobidzhan, on Russia's far eastern border with Manchuria.

Economically, Jews had suffered more than any other segment of the population because of their predominant status as middlemen. The American Jewish Joint Distribution Committee had received permission to help Russian Jews adopt an agricultural way of life in Crimea and the Ukraine. In the cities, where ninety percent of the Jews were to be found, many tried to eke out a livelihood by means of a private trade, which was permitted under certain limitations, but they were déclassé folk condemned to a miserable existence.

While in Moscow, I had the pleasure of visiting one of my old boyhood friends, Louis Fischer, with whom I had grown up in Philadelphia. He was now achieving an international reputation as an expert and commentator on Soviet Russia. From Moscow, the next stage of my journey took me to Warsaw. Here, the Jewish picture was markedly different. A score of Yiddish and Hebrew papers, dailies and weeklies, appeared in Warsaw, a bastion of religious Orthodoxy and Jewish nationalism. The ultra-Orthodox Agudas Yisroel was the strongest element there, closely followed by the various Zionist groups. At the same time, however, endemic Polish anti-Semitism was rampant and the authorities did nothing to suppress it. The realities of Jewish existence in Poland gave much ground for concern. Politically, this very large and important Jewish community was treated as an undesirable, alien intruder; economically, squeezed by government financial policies, it faced a grim, even hopeless future. The only solution, I felt at the time, was wholesale Aliyah to Eretz Yisrael.

At the end of August, I left Warsaw to attend an anti-war congress in Amsterdam, as a delegate of the World Fellowship of Faiths in the United States. This congress had been convened by Romain Rolland, the eminent French novelist and Nobel

Prize laureate, who had left-wing and pacifist leanings. In his novels, especially the ten-volume *Jean Christophe*, Rolland had portrayed Jewish idealists in a manner worthy of his own humanitarianism. My feeling about him was particularly apprecia-tive, since the journey to Holland had led me across Germany, where the growth of militant anti-Semitism was only too apparent. Hitler's National Socialist Party and its Nazi storm troopers already dominated the scene.

After a day or two in Amsterdam, I realized that the Communist delegates from a number of countries—Germany in particular—were virtually in control of the anti-war congress. This circumstance did not disturb me unduly at the time, since I felt, like many others (including Joseph Brodsky and Sherwood Anderson) among the American delegates present, that it was worth our while to cooperate with all who sought world peace. In reality, however, it was a congress against *imperialist* war. When we returned to the United States, the activists launched the American League against War and Fascism. I joined its executive committee, but later on, when the name of this body was changed to the "League for Peace and Democracy," and when I became convinced that it was really a Communist front organization, I bowed out. Like many other trusting liberals who threw themselves into the anti-war movement, I was taken in at first, but dissociated myself as soon as it became clear that we were being "used."

The most tangible and immediate outcome of my visit to Eretz Yisrael was my deeper involvement in the Jewish National Fund of America. During our visit to Palestine, Bert and I had studied the JNF land-redemption *(ge'ulat ha-Aretz)* pro-gram at closer hand. This made us realize more than ever before the practical, as well as the idealistic, value of its work.

We had managed to pack a good deal of travel into our schedule and, under the guidance of JNF officials and the inspiration of its stalwart president, Menaḥem Ussishkin, "The Zionist Rock of Gibraltar" as he was popularly known in the movement, we had absorbed a plethora of ideas, information, and impressions. For both Bert and me this was our real introduction to the practical aspects of Zionism, the building of the homeland in Eretz Yisrael.

Without my having realized it at the time, our second visit to Eretz Yisrael had prepared me for a new and important Zionist undertaking. Had anyone asked me beforehand, I would have insisted that there was no time to spare in my schedule for any additional responsibility.

Now conscious of the important role of the Jewish National Fund, I accepted the call extended to me at the end of 1933 to assume the presidency of the JNF in the United States, and to help strengthen it. Upon checking the figures, I found that the JNF's annual income from the American Jewish community amounted to less than $150,000. It derived mostly from coins placed in the familiar blue and white boxes, from flag day and flower day collections, and from planting trees in the soil of Eretz Yisrael.

The vision of Professor Hermann Schapira, outlined by him at the First Zionist Congress in 1897, was subsequently realized by the Fifth Congress in 1901 as the Keren Kayemet Le-Yisrael, the Jewish National Fund. It was an instrument for redeeming the ancestral land and for reclaiming it from rocks, sand, and swamps, by purchase and by intensive cultivation. In this way, the soil of Eretz Yisrael would be made available for agriculture by Jewish hands, the barren hills would be planted with forests, and the entire land would be developed anew as the inalienable property of the Jewish people. What better way, indeed, to fulfill practical Zionism? Yet, in 1933, this fundamental Zionist enterprise was receiving miniscule support from the richest Jewish community in the world! Something was very much amiss, I thought, and it would be my task to bring about a desperately needed change.

I had gone on record already as saying that "the Jewish National Fund is loved, but not adequately supported, by the Zionists of America." My decade as president of the American JNF was dedicated to testing its potential in the United States. By the time I retired from office in 1943, our yearly revenue had reached a peak of nine million dollars—two-thirds of the Keren Kayemet's annual world income.

The process of "agonizing reappraisal" began in the wake of Menaḥem Ussishkin's mission to the United States in December 1930, when he came to raise funds for extensive land development, especially in the Ḥefer Plain. He arrived with high expectations of American Jewry's capacity (indisputable) and willingness (untested) to underwrite a strategic land-redemption program. What he found, however, were antiquated fund-raising and publicity methods and an administrative staff that failed to measure up to expectations.

A special JNF conference held in Washington, D.C., in February 1931 had adopted a plan for more intensive land-purchase schemes by American Jewish communities, but nothing came of that resolve. At the end of his stay, Ussishkin left New York feeling bitterly disappointed with the American Jews from whom he had anticipated so much. He had already fared much better in Canada, where the far smaller community of 170,000 Jews managed to raise one million dollars for the redemption of Wadi Hawarith in the Sharon, now the fertile and populous Emek Ḥefer.

Two years after Ussishkin's departure, when I became president of the American JNF, it was immediately clear that personnel and methods had to be overhauled. My first step was to retire the old executive director and to appoint in his place a bright young man, Mendel N. Fisher, who had shown drive and promise as the Keren Hayesod's director in the southwestern United States. He proved to be dynamic and resourceful. The JNF's board of directors in the United States—mainly comprising representatives of the Zionist parties as well as a few chosen *ad hominem*, by the president, supported my plan of action. Together we began to plan our new strategy and organization.

Among those whom I brought into the board was Jacob Sincoff, a new member of my congregation, who later became its president. He did splendidly as associate treasurer, accompanied me in other Zionist commitments, and later assumed leading positions in the Zionist Organization of America, the United Palestine Appeal, United Jewish Appeal, and Israel Bonds. Another "find" was Maurice Levin, owner of Hearn's Department Store in New York, who made the first substantial gift to the

JNF, a donation of $65,000, and set a new standard of individual giving. Maurice Levin was more than a big contributor; he was a Jew of great heart and great vision. Years later, he and his stepbrother, Jacob M. Kaplan, also contributed generously to the establishment of the Hebrew University Dental School in Jerusalem.

On the organizational side, we developed regional bodies throughout the United States and initiated a series of regional conferences. We also devised attractive slogans to popularize tree planting on a wider scale—groves and forests—and, later, *Naḥalah* projects of land for agricultural settlement. A long-term "investment" scheme I promoted from the mid-1930s was JNF educational work, including publications and specific projects, in Jewish day schools and congregational Hebrew schools.

One of the initial difficulties I encountered was the opposition expressed by some of the American Zionist leaders to the "aggressive" new policies adopted by the JNF. They had come to regard the Keren Hayesod as the only important fundraising vehicle for the Zionist movement. That attitude had to be modified. I had numerous meetings with Judge Morris Rothenberg, Louis Lipsky and others, in order to hammer out a viable arrangement. I insisted that the United Palestine Appeal, which had been set up in 1925, should grant the JNF parity of status and income with the Keren Hayesod. It was agreed that these two Zionist funds should henceforth be equal partners in the United Palestine Appeal. We received the warm commendation of Ussishkin and his principal aides, chief among them Dr. Abraham Granovsky (Granott) and later Yosef Weitz. They felt satisfied that, at long last, the American affiliate was giving a good account of itself.

One of the great American friends of the Keren Kayemet was Justice Louis D. Brandeis, the Grand Old Man of American Zionism, who followed our work with interest and approval. More than once we sought and obtained his sound advice in developing our programs. I recall him vividly, a tall, lean, impressive figure of aristocratic mien. He was slow and thoughtful of speech, yet behind his gentle, soft-spoken manner lay an assurance and conviction as hard as steel.

I met Justice Brandeis for the first time in 1936, as president of the American JNF. His home in Washington, D.C., was modest, almost austere. Our conversation roamed over a wide area. I remember his mentioning the importance of Akaba (Eilat) for the Jewish National Home: David Ben-Gurion had enlightened him on that significant point. Brandeis showed himself to be a warm supporter of the Keren Kayemet land-redemption program, recognizing its basic importance for the future of the Yishuv.

At about this period, in the mid-1930s, I began to cultivate Senator Alben W. Barkley of Kentucky, a future Vice-President of the United States. It had become customary in the Zionist Organization, and especially in its fund-raising bodies, to have prominent U.S. senators and representatives address important gatherings. Senator Barkley was a leading American political figure and an effective platform personality. In the course of time, he developed a genuine understanding and appreciation of the Jewish National Fund and grew into one of its most eloquent advocates.

Among the more significant new techniques we fostered were the *Naḥalah* projects, involving the purchase of large tracts of land that were named for individual or for group donors. These commitments were for $25,000 or more. Many such *Naḥla'ot,* populated with flourishing settlements, now adorn the map of Israel. It was a new and exciting event for us when a *Naḥalah* of 1,000 *dunams* in honor of its president, Alfred M. Cohen, was endowed by the B'nai B'rith, a non-Zionist body that had become the leading Jewish fraternal organization in America and throughout the world. This broke new ground in more than one sense. The sum involved was $100,000, a record for those days, and endowments by other Jewish fraternal organizations soon followed.

Another important *Naḥalah* project was undertaken by the Labor Zionists in honor of Léon Blum, the distinguished Premier of France and one of the world's preeminent Socialist leaders. Our hope that this scheme would have the collateral effect of drawing in non-Zionist labor elements was indeed realized, and it achieved gratifying results. The Labor Zionists then undertook a similar project in honor of William Green, president of the American Federation of Labor. This, too, proved successful and attracted many Christian as well as Jewish labor supporters.

Thus, the JNF served to make new friends for the Jewish National Home while providing new and substantial resources for the land-redemption program.

Two years after I had assumed the presidency, the Keren Kayemet's office in Jerusalem announced its major scheme for the draining and reclamation of the marsh area around Lake Ḥuleh. We inaugurated a Ḥuleh "gift bonds" campaign that raised substantial sums in the United States. Eventually we were able to obtain a five-million-dollar loan repayable in ten years.

Ever since then, I have considered that my work for the Jewish National Fund was the greatest single Zionist service I was privileged to render in the United States, because it broke new ground. It also marked my entry into the wider national realm of Zionist affairs. In 1935, a year before my election as a vice-president of the Zionist Organization of America, I began a four-year term as chairman of the United Palestine Appeal and was appointed a ZOA delegate to the Nineteenth World Zionist Congress at Lucerne, Switzerland. This was my first exposure to the workings of a Zionist Congress. Subsequently, it was my good fortune to be a delegate to every Zionist Congress up to the time of my retirement from office in the Zionist movement, in 1971.

Our son, Avram, had just graduated from the Walden School in May 1935, at the age of fifteen. We felt that he was too young to go to college and decided to let him spend a year in Eretz Yisrael. Our daughter, Vivian, who was just thirteen at the time, insisted upon going as well. We therefore embarked on a family trip through England and then onward to Lucerne for the Zionist Congress. Toward the end of the Congress sessions, we put both children on the train to Marseilles, where they boarded the ship for Palestine.

I brought to the Congress a substantial check for the JNF, which I presented to Ussishkin. It helped considerably to change his impression of American Jewry.

At the 1938 convention of the Zionist Organization of America in Detroit, I was a candidate for the presidency of the ZOA. The opposing candidate, Rabbi Solomon Goldman of Chicago, had been a classmate of mine at the Jewish Theological Seminary. My supporters were led by Rabbi Abba Hillel Silver of Cleveland. Rabbi Goldman had the backing of Dr. Stephen S. Wise, Judge Harry Fisher of Chicago, Louis Lipsky, and the "inside" apparatus of the ZOA. I lost the election by a narrow margin and continued to serve in the office of vice-president and as president of the Jewish National Fund of America.

Prelude to Catastrophe

Throughout the 1930s, events in Europe had been overshadowed by the menace of Nazi Germany. Hitler's meteoric rise to power, the formation of the Rome-Berlin Axis, the civil war in Spain, the rape of Czechoslovakia, and, finally, the infamous Munich Agreement, which, according to Neville Chamberlain, would bring "peace in our time"—all these were components of the tragic overture.

On the American scene, indignation and protest greeted the onward march of Nazism, with its threat to democracy and world peace in general and to the Jewish people in particular. Liberal public opinion in the United States was articulated and led by President Franklin D. Roosevelt. American Jews had their own special grounds for alarm. Jewish public opinion was mobilized chiefly under the banner of the American Jewish Congress, headed by Dr. Stephen Wise. An anti-Nazi boycott of German goods was organized, in which liberal forces, both Jewish and non-Jewish, worked together. Those were days marked by protest rallies and by grave fears that the cataclysm of world war lay immediately ahead.

The pact signed at Munich on September 29, 1938, entailing the dismemberment of Czechoslovakia, heralded the approaching catastrophe. Throughout the free world, protest meetings were held and sympathy was expressed for the victims of appeasement and aggression. At one such meeting, held in Carnegie Hall, New York, when the principal addresses were delivered by the brother of President Eduard Beneš of Czechoslovakia and by Dr. Stephen Wise, it was my privilege also to take part.

Referring to the Nazi Golem threatening Europe and the free world, I warned that the Munich pact was not "peace with honor," as Chamberlain and Daladier had termed it. What honor could be salvaged from the capitulation of Great Britain and France belonged only to the Czechoslovak people. I continued:

> We believe that dictatorships, like the Golem, bear the seeds of their own destruction. And when that day of democracy's vindication will come, it will see the wrong of October 1, 1938, righted. . . . Perhaps a Jewish spokesman has a special right to utter a word of consolation and hope, seeing that the Jew is the victim of the same forces of reaction. We are brothers in sorrow. We can testify that a people lives as long as its memories and hopes are alive.

Almost on the eve of World War II came the opening of the Jewish Palestine Pavilion at the New York World's Fair held at Flushing Meadows, Long Island. The fair, held during Mayor Fiorello LaGuardia's administration, was under the general charge of former Police Commissioner Grover Whelan. A suave, handsome man, he had all the attributes of a diplomat and needed them to overcome the innumerable difficulties that arose before the fair could be inaugurated in 1938.

There were several outstanding national pavilions at the fair, and our Zionist exhibit was planned to display the whole range of Jewish achievements in the National Home. The construction of the Palestine Pavilion was made possible by the combined efforts of thirty American Jewish organizations, both Zionist and non-Zionist, which worked together in order to raise the necessary funds and administer the project. George Backer, a public-spirited citizen and Jew, was president of the board, I served as chairman, and the resourceful and tempestuous Meyer Weisgal was its executive director. He made a hurried trip to Palestine and came back with the architect Aryeh Elḥanani, who designed a splendid building for the pavilion, surmounted by a Menorah. Inside, there were ten exhibition halls depicting the progress made by the Yishuv during the past two decades in terms of agricultural settlement, urban development and cultural achievements.

For the cornerstone-laying ceremony, a rock was brought from the northernmost and most recent point of Jewish settlement in Eretz Yisrael, Kibbutz Ḥanita. The choice of such a rock, which had lain on the site of an ancient synagogue, was symbolic and imaginative. "This stone," I remarked at the ceremony, "has been for centuries a witness of Jewish desolation. Now it is a witness of Israel's renascence."

The Palestine Pavilion's opening day, May 28, 1939, was one of the major events of the fair. More than 100,000 people crowded the field, providing the largest attendance for any function in the World's Fair program. Special messages were received from President Franklin D. Roosevelt, Dr. Chaim Weizmann, and Dr. Isaac Halevi Herzog, the Ashkenazi Chief Rabbi of Palestine. "The Jews have never forgotten the land of their origin," Weizmann wrote. "They have displayed in this respect a steadfastness which has not its like in the history of mankind." The denial of Jewish rights in Eretz Yisrael was "of a piece with the general denial of human rights, which challenges international law and morality." Thus, he concluded, if the Palestine Pavilion should succeed in its aim, it would render a service "not only to the harassed Jewish people, but to the cause of world justice; for the Jewish problem is, in a sense, the touchstone of civilization."

So vast was the throng that it overflowed onto the platform intended for the VIPs. These included Professor Albert Einstein, Thomas Mann, the great German writer and Nobel laureate, Mayor LaGuardia, Grover Whelan, and other state and civic dignitaries, as well as the heads of those Jewish organizations that had brought the project into being. As the ceremonies were about to begin, and before escorting the VIPs to their seats on the platform, I went out to make sure that all was in readiness. To my consternation, I found that the places reserved for our eminent guests were *bezetzt*—fully occupied. My expostulations fell on deaf ears. The first determined squatter whom I approached told me that he was also a Very Important Person. "How come?" I asked, and he then explained with much self-importance that he headed a Zionist district in the Bronx. Similar responses were forthcoming from other interlopers. Finally, with a few well-chosen words, I managed to persuade them to vacate the platform, thus avoiding a most embarrassing situation.

New York's Mayor, Fiorello LaGuardia, stood within earshot of these irate dialogues, waiting impatiently to be seated. When I came back to escort the guests of honor, including him, to their places, the "Little Flower" (Fiorello) whispered huskily in my ear: "Dr. Goldstein, how do you Zionists expect to manage a state of your own if you cannot even manage a platform?" The official program, however, proceeded smoothly.

In the course of my address, I said:

> Facing the Temple of Religions, the Jewish Palestine Pavilion is significant to both Christian and Jew, whose respective faiths were cradled in the Holy Land. Situated on American soil, this building witnesses not only Jewish hope and achievement in Eretz Yisrael, but also the deep interest of the American people and Government in our hope and its fulfillment.

During the year or more in which the pavilion was open, it was visited by two and a half million men, women, and children of every race and creed. Among the Jewish leaders who came from overseas to see the exhibits were Dr. Weizmann, David Ben-Gurion, Vladimir Jabotinsky, and Eliezer Kaplan.

The pavilion amply fulfilled its purpose—to demonstrate to the world the achievements of the Zionist enterprise in Eretz Yisrael and its meaning for World Jewry. Thanks to its architectural design and craftsmanship, to the paintings and sculptures on display within, and to the impressive exhibits of Jewish industry, agriculture, cooperative endeavors, and cultural achievements, the Palestine Pavilion was a first-rate demonstration of what the Yishuv and the Zionist movement had already produced. It also conveyed a timely message—that the world of tomorrow, abounding in mechanical invention, would desperately need the spiritual nourishment and inspiration a Jewish Palestine could provide.

The twentieth anniversary of my rabbinate was marked by a special program of events at Congregation B'nai Jeshurun over the weekend of January 21–22, 1939. This culminated in a testimonial dinner, at which the speakers included Herman Levy, president of the Congregation; Prof. Louis Finkelstein, provost of the Jewish Theological Seminary, who delivered a gratifyingly warm address; Rabbi Isaac Landman, chief editor of the *Universal Jewish Encyclopedia*, who occupied a leading Reform pulpit in New York; Dr. Stephen S. Wise, then president of the American Jewish Congress; and my brother, Morris, who came from San Francisco. Messages of greeting were received from Governor Herbert Lehman, Mayor Robert F. Wagner, Rabbi Dr. David de Sola Pool, then chairman of the Synagogue Council of America, and President Thomas Gates of the University of Pennsylvania, my alma mater.

This was the first of several celebrations held by Congregation B'nai Jeshurun to mark various milestones in my rabbinate. I paid tribute, in my response, to the congregation's membership, saying that "even when they would not follow me, they tried to understand me, and when they could not understand, they respected my views."

At the end of 1940, my first volume of sermons and addresses, *Toward a Solution*, was published in New York by G. P. Putnam's Sons. Dedicated to my wife and children, it dealt with a variety of issues—from the Zionist movement to Jewish-Christian relations. "If the contents of the volume seem to be weighted on the side of Palestine and Zionism," I wrote in a foreword, "it is because of the deeply felt conviction that therein lies the center of gravity of the solution to the Jewish problem, a conviction which derives renewed cogency from the events and currents of our time."

The year 1939 had, in fact, begun on a gloomy note for the Jewish people and for Zionism. As a result of the *Kristallnacht* outrages by the Nazis on November 9–10, 1938, hundreds of synagogues were laid waste, thousands of Jews were deported to concentration camps, and incalculable damage was done to Jewish property. In the previous July, President Roosevelt had summoned an international conference at Evian-les-Bains, a small French town on the shores of Lake Geneva. Its purpose was to find a solution to the refugee problem. An intergovernmental committee was established with the object of providing further places of sanctuary for the victims of Hitlerism. In practice, however, only the Dominican Republic showed willingness to accept Jewish refugees. The resettlement plans, announced with so much fanfare at the Evian Conference, led only to disillusionment. It was a grim foretaste of the fate awaiting millions of Jews in Nazi-occupied Europe during World War II.

On the Zionist plane, we were being confronted with mounting evidence of the British Government's negative attitude toward the building of the Jewish National Home in Palestine. Successive commissions of inquiry and White Paper reports had advocated whittling down the pro-Jewish terms of the Mandate in response to Arab pressure and the machinations of anti-Zionist officialdom. In the wake of the Arab riots of August 1929, the Shaw Commission's findings and the Hope-Simpson Report of October 1930 led to the Passfield White Paper, severely limiting Aliyah and Jewish land purchases in Palestine. It all but repudiated the promises made by the Balfour Declaration. Dr. Chaim Weizmann gave dramatic expression to the outrage felt by World Jewry by resigning from his presidency of the Zionist Organization. Not until the Colonial Secretary, Malcolm MacDonald, had the White Paper drastically amended did Weizmann agree to withdraw his resignation.

Another Royal Commission, headed by Lord Peel, began its investigations in August 1936 and Weizmann appeared before it on three separate occasions. The Arab Higher Committee, however, boycotted the proceedings. In its report, the Peel Commission urged that Jewish land purchases in Eretz Yisrael be restricted and that Jewish immigration be curtailed for the ensuing five years. Nevertheless, the Zionist enterprise undoubtedly impressed the members of the Commission, who made the revolutionary proposal that Palestine be divided into self-governing Jewish and Arab territories. Sir Arthur Wauchope, the British High Commissioner, who was well disposed toward Zionism, endorsed the Peel Commission's report. The Arab Higher Committee, led by Haj Amin al-Husseini, the Mufti of Jerusalem, rejected it outright. A majority within the World Zionist Organization believed that the partition plan was at least worth exploring.

In the fall of 1938, this partition scheme was again put forward by the Woodhead Commission, but its findings were considered impracticable by the British Government.

In my presidential address before the Jewish National Fund of America's annual conference in New York, on November 29, I mentioned the fact that the Woodhead Report had appeared on the first day of my recent visit to London. "Dr. Weizmann had apprehended its contents," I said, "but not its cold, cynical tone. The partition scheme was abandoned, not because the Jews objected that they received too little, but because of the objections of those evil forces which stood behind the Arabs, the masters of Munich and the dictators in Rome and Berlin who were loath to see the prestige which might accrue to the Jewish people as a result of a Jewish State." Only Menahem Ussishkin, the head of the Keren Kayemet, had seemed untroubled as to the future.

A culminating stage in Whitehall's attempt to thwart the terms of the Balfour Declaration and the League of Nations mandate was reached in the first half of 1939, when the British Government called a round-table conference on Palestine, at St. James's Palace, London, where it hoped to resolve the problem of conflicting interests. Arab representatives categorically refused to take their seats next to Jews, and the two delegations had to be met with separately. A marked pro-Arab bias was evident throughout this abortive round-table conference. It resulted in the notorious MacDonald White Paper of May 17, 1939, which declared that it was "not part of the policy of His Majesty's Government that Palestine should become a Jewish State," but that a binational Palestinian state should be created, "in which the essential interests of both parties would be safeguarded." Jewish immigration was restricted to a maximum of 75,000 during the next five years, after which no more Jews were to be admitted to Eretz Yisrael without prior Arab agreement. Jewish land purchases and settlement projects were similarly curtailed.

A grave setback to all our hopes, this "great betrayal" was the more damnable in view of the obvious Nazi menace and the desperate efforts of German, Austrian, and other Jews in Central Europe to find refuge in Eretz Yisrael. The 1939 White Paper, which remained in force until the end of the British administration in Palestine nine years later, was a severe blow to the Jewish National Fund. Nevertheless, the JNF lost no opportunity to redeem every available *dunam* of land throughout the ensuing period. In the United States, we continually hammered home the challenge, stressing the paramount need to acquire whatever land could be purchased.

At the same time, our political response to the White Paper was firm and uncompromising. Thus, in the United States, a delegation of Zionist leaders, headed by Dr. Stephen Wise and by Rabbi Solomon Goldman, president of the Zionist Organization of America, registered its protest with the British ambassador in Washington. As vice-president of the ZOA and president of the Jewish National Fund of America, I was a member of that delegation.

I continued in the presidency of the American JNF, although my personal inclination was to retire after having set it on a new course. Nearly five years in office had convinced me that the leadership could be handed over to some other qualified person. Ussishkin, however, bade me stay on. Writing to me on June 10, 1938, he had stated:

> In several letters you have hinted, to my dismay, that the present might be the last year of your service to the Jewish National Fund of America as President. You know that I am not given to flattery, and you will believe that I fully mean it when I say that no other President in the history of the JNF in America has so strongly and effectively defended the interests of the Fund nor assured its expansion with such devotion, vision and practicality. . . . I can at present see no one in America to follow in your footsteps.

Such an appeal, from such a Zionist leader, was irresistible, and I remained president for another five years.

An atmosphere of grim foreboding surrounded us when my wife and I set sail for Europe in the summer of 1939. As one of the delegates of the ZOA, I was scheduled to attend the 21st World Zionist Congress in Geneva. Our trip began with a visit to the British Isles, during which we spent a week with the Reverend John Ross and his family in Belfast, Northern Ireland. The Reverend Ross, spiritual leader of the Belfast Jewish community, was the father of Hyman J. Ross, a prominent member of my congregation in New York and a devoted friend.

By the time we left Britain for Geneva, Europe was already on the threshold of World War II. Now, at last, our own lives were overshadowed by the menace of Nazism, even at the Zionist Congress. We were aware that delegates from Germany were terrorized into silence, fearing that Nazi spies might be keeping a close watch on what was said at the various sessions.

Joshua Heschel Farbstein, the veteran Polish Zionist leader, who had emigrated to Palestine in 1931, was chairman of the Finance and Budget Committee. He had attended the First Zionist Congress in Basle, was a founder and leader of the Mizrahi movement, and had served as president of the Zionist Organization and the Keren Kayesod in Poland, as president of the Warsaw Jewish community and as a member of the Polish parliament, the Sejm. Owing to his advanced age, Heschel Farbstein was unable to chair meetings of the Budget Committee, where Vera Weizmann also played a role, and so, as vice-chairman, I deputized for him, conducting the sessions in Yiddish.

One issue that aroused heated debate was that of "unofficial" rescue operations by Mosad Aliyah Bet agents in Central and Eastern Europe. These activities, resulting in increased "illegal" immigration to Eretz Yisrael, were disfavored by some Zionist leaders, including even Rabbi Abba Hillel Silver, who felt that efforts should be concentrated on changing the policy of the British Mandatory regime.

Fear and tension dominated the proceedings. No one present at that Geneva Congress is likely to forget the poignant and agonized closing session at which Chaim Weizmann, in a trembling and tear-laden voice, spelled out the doom confronting the trapped Jewish communities of Europe as he bade farewell to the delegates, especially those returning to Hitler's Third Reich. "I have no prayer but this," he said, "that we will all meet again alive."

Everyone was in a rush to leave. Bags were already packed, reservations on trains and ships had been made, but not all the ships were sailing on schedule and last-minute changes had to be made. Some of the delegates had gone even before the closing session ended. After leaving for home, most of the Polish and German representatives were never to be seen or heard from again.

By the time we reached Cherbourg to board our ship for America, war had broken out and we were fortunate to get back safely to New York.

So began the long nightmare of the supreme Jewish tragedy.

War Relief Campaigns

The new conflict that engulfed Europe in 1939 did not at first impinge unduly on the consciousness of the American people. True, there was now a much broader realization than in 1914 of the dangers implicit in a struggle that could hardly remain localized for very long, but there were many, such as Charles E. Lindbergh, who cautioned against involving the United States in a situation that was "none of our business." A substantial segment of American public opinion, which found organized expression in the "America First" movement, embraced the doctrine of isolationism so as to remain a safe distance from European entanglements. Those who favored the isolationist line poured scorn on President Franklin D. Roosevelt's thesis that Nazism was a threat to the entire free world and must be countered by some system of collective security among the democratic nations. Fortunately, other counsels prevailed and Roosevelt found general support for his policy.

Feelings were especially outraged by the cynical pact between Ribbentrop and Molotov, as a result of which the Nazi invasion of Poland from the West was followed by a Soviet attack from the East, leading to the new partition of Poland at the end of September 1939. Little more than two months later came the Soviet onslaught on Finland. A Finnish Relief Fund campaign was organized in the United States, and I chaired a sympathy meeting at Congregation B'nai Jeshurun on December 18, when contributions were made to the fund. On that occasion, a message was received from Herbert Hoover, former President of the United States, whom I had cabled a few days earlier, recalling my visit to him at the White House in 1929 and the splendid message of sympathy he had then conveyed, through me, to the Jewish victims of Arab terrorism in Palestine. I said, in the course of my remarks at this meeting, that, "as an American, I hail Finland for its courage as a small democratic nation which dares, in the midst of an intimidated Europe, to defend its liberties against overwhelming odds. Finland is the farthermost outpost of democracy today."

Despite international indignation, relief campaigns, and the Soviet Union's expulsion from the League of Nations, Finland was compelled to give way to Russian demands and sign a humiliating "peace treaty" in 1940. Speaking before the annual convention of the Mizraḥi Organization of America in Baltimore, on May 20 of that year, I drew attention to a grim contrast between the plight of the Finns and that of the Jews:

When the little Finnish nation of three and a half millions was invaded and attacked by a vastly greater power, the world's indignation was aroused, its sympathy flowed out and its generous help went forth to the victim. When, however, three and a half million Jews in Poland were consigned to massacre and spoliation, the world's conscience was not outraged, its sensibilities were not shocked and its practical sympathies were not aroused. The Jews of conquered Poland are deprived even of the privilege of a heroic death. Had three and a half million Jews lived on their national soil in Eretz Yisrael, there might be a different story to tell today. . . .

Not long after the outbreak of World War II, the Interfaith Committee for Aid to the Democracies was established in the United States, with the object of supporting President Roosevelt's policy of collective security. Its primary founders were the Reverend Dr. Henry A. Atkinson, an eminent Protestant clergyman, and Rabbi Stephen S. Wise. The Interfaith Committee's platform included the influencing of public opinion in favor of the Anglo-French alliance, thereby counteracting the considerable weight of isolationism and the impact of pro-German propaganda which Nazi sympathizers disseminated in the two years preceding the entry of the United States into the war.

Dr. Wise called a conference under the auspices of the American Jewish Congress, of which he was president, when over a thousand delegates came from most states in the Union. His motion that the American Jewish Congress should affiliate with the Interfaith Committee and establish a Jewish section of the British War Relief Society was adopted by acclamation. He and other Congress leaders then proposed that I be elected chairman of the Jewish Section. That new responsibility, together with other wartime commitments, ushered in a spate of activities that took me to many parts of the U.S.A.

The British War Relief Society in the United States had come into being in 1939 and was headed by Winthrop Aldrich, board chairman of the Chase National Bank, who later became U.S. ambassador to Great Britain. The executive director was Frederick W. Gehle, a vice-president of the bank. Under their leadership and with the help of a staff, effective service was rendered in having urgent necessities shipped to Britain for victims of the Nazi aerial blitzkrieg.

As I saw it, our unit's participation gave us an unusual opportunity to emphasize our dedication to the war effort as a Jewish community. There was an additional Zionist motivation. We felt that it would be helpful for Great Britain, the Mandatory power in Palestine, to be made aware of the part American Jews, and particularly American Zionists, were playing in the American effort for British War Relief.

To launch the Jewish Section, I called a conference of a score of national Jewish organizations, among them B'nai B'rith and the American Jewish Congress, at which our program was formulated. Our special tasks were the provision of mobile canteens to help feed civilians in British towns and cities devastated by the Luftwaffe, and the establishment of nursing homes for children evacuated to country areas from the blitzed cities. These canteens and nursing homes were to be made available to all, irrespective of race or creed. One important point we agreed upon related to *Kashrut* facilities for Jews.

The response from the American Jewish community was good. Many non-Jewish friends, sympathizers, and sponsors also contributed. I did a great deal of journeying to and fro and was able to note the favorable public reaction to our campaign.

The first of the children's homes we named for Sarah Delano Roosevelt, the President's mother, who had died shortly before. The President invited me to the White House and expressed his appreciation of this tribute to his late mother. The memorial album betokening our gift, which I presented to him then, is now in the Roosevelt Library at Hyde Park, New York.

Other homes were named for Lord Balfour, Justice Louis D. Brandeis, General Sir Archibald Wavell, Dr. Chaim Weizmann, and Rabbi Stephen Wise. The appropriate presentation was made to the president of the World Zionist Organization during one of his wartime visits to the United States, when he and Mrs. Weizmann attended a luncheon the British War Relief Society gave in his honor, attended also by the British ambassador to the United States, Lord Halifax. Subsequently, the society also honored me by setting up a home in my name at Porlock, in southwestern England, which accommodated children evacuated from Plymouth. Two more of these homes were established in honor of American war heroes, Colin Kelly and Meyer Levin.

Altogether, we were able to supply scores of mobile canteens and to establish eight children's nursing homes. It was an impressive undertaking by the American Jewish community.

By the spring of 1941, Axis forces were in control of Europe, from the borders of Spain and Turkey to the Soviet frontier. With a German army under General Erwin Rommel advancing toward the Egyptian border and Rashid Ali's pro-Nazi coup in Iraq, the European conflict assumed even more frightening dimensions. Having turned the United States into the "arsenal of democracy," President Roosevelt signed the Lend-Lease Act of March 1941, whereby massive supplies of war materials were delivered to Great Britain, which then "stood alone" against Hitler's "Fortress Europe." On August 14, this alliance was cemented by the Atlantic Charter, in which Roosevelt and Great Britain's Prime Minister Winston Churchill pledged themselves to "the final destruction of Nazi tyranny."

At that stage of the war, such a pledge was a valuable morale-booster, but its fulfillment seemed a distant prospect as the Nazi war machine ground on relentlessly. The situation in the Middle East was particularly ominous, with British troops on the retreat and tied down by the threat of a widespread Arab revolt. Disregarding Whitehall, British military intelligence entered into a secret alliance with the Yishuv and began training Palestinian Jews for guerilla warfare in the event of a Nazi invasion. Efforts for the creation of a Jewish Brigade, which had Churchill's backing, were nevertheless thwarted until the last phase of World War II, as a result of anti-Zionist pressures. Indeed, despite its disproportionately large contribution to the war effort, the Yishuv was destined to remain "the Forgotten Ally."

American isolationism, which had been losing ground since the Battle of Britain, melted away in 1941. With characteristic treachery and cynicism, Hitler turned his all-conquering armies against the Soviet Union at the end of June and fortified the Axis by an alliance with Japan, which launched a devastating attack on the U.S. fleet at Pearl Harbor in December, thereby bringing America into the war.

In October 1941, the Russian War Relief Committee was established and it received immediate Jewish support. We organized two separate bodies, the Jewish Council for Russian War Relief (founded early in 1942) and the American Committee of Jewish Writers, Artists and Scientists, which contributed to relief work among the distressed Russian civilian population. Those heading the Jewish Council included Professor Albert Einstein and Dr. Stephen Wise (honorary chairmen), Louis Levine (chairman), and Baron Edouard de Rothschild (honorary vice-chairman). The Interfaith Committee for Russian War Relief was also set up, with most Christian denominations participating except for the Roman Catholics, although Al Smith, a former Democratic presidential candidate and a Catholic, lent his personal support. As president of the Synagogue Council of America, I served as a vice-chairman of the Interfaith Committee, and held similar office in the Jewish Council for Russian War Relief and in the Jewish Writers', Artists' and Scientists' Committee.

Replying to criticism from some Jewish labor and Zionist quarters, I argued that the possibility of enhancing the credentials of Yiddish-speaking Communists in the United States was of minor importance compared with the very real possibility of securing an affirmative position on the Zionist program from groups working for Soviet-American friendship. There were other important considerations. Having been cut off from Russian Jewry for a quarter of a century, we now had the opportunity to resume contact with our brethren in the USSR and must make every effort to do so. There was, furthermore, the question of Soviet Russia's attitude toward Zionist aims in Palestine, and its potential importance after the defeat of the Nazis.

In Moscow, the Jewish Writers', Artists' and Scientists' Committee had its prototype in the Jewish Anti-Fascist Committee, which received considerable encouragement from Stalin and the Soviet hierarchy. Our own Jewish Council was instrumental in dispatching drugs, medical supplies, clothing, and food to the USSR, and we were permitted to direct our aid to any region of our choice.

On May 24, 1942, by courtesy of the National Broadcasting Company, special messages were relayed in Yiddish from the New York conference of the Jewish Council for Russian War Relief to a plenary session of the Jewish Anti-Fascist Committee in Moscow. I was invited to broadcast a message, together with Dr. Nahum Goldmann, Abraham Goldberg, and Stanley Isaacs, a former president of the Borough of Manhattan. In the course of my talk, I referred to the contribution made by the Yishuv in Eretz Yisrael to the Allied war effort, in terms of military personnel, industrial output, and agricultural productivity. American Jewry, I said, was pleased that contact with the Jews of the USSR, broken for over twenty years, had now been reestablished. I then continued:

> We look forward to our common victory and to the peace which will follow, when the right of the Jews to a National Home in Palestine will be recognized. We look forward to the day when the inscription on Hitler's tombstone will read: "My very last territorial demand." We shall not rest, we shall continue to do everything humanly possible to bring closer the day of a free Jewry and a free world.

In my capacity as chairman of the Jewish Section of British War Relief, I also participated in a dinner held in honor of Professor Einstein on October 25, 1942. On this occasion, I said:

> Russia is the keystone in the struggle of the United Nations against the most powerful foe that has ever attacked civilization. We American Jews extend our greetings to our fellow Jews in Russia, looking forward to the day of victory, when the pattern of the new world will be arranged. We trust that, with the help of the United States, Great Britain and Soviet Russia, the aspiration of the Jewish people for a Jewish Commonwealth in Palestine will be fulfilled and that, at the same time, Jews—wherever they dwell—will have full, unrestricted rights as human beings.

A high point in our activity was the visit one year later of two prominent Soviet Jews, Professor Solomon Mikhoels, the distinguished Yiddish actor, and Lieutenant Colonel Itzik Fefer, the eminent Yiddish poet. Mikhoels was chairman of the Jewish Anti-Fascist Committee, and both men came to the United States on a goodwill mission, as guests of the Jewish Council for Russian War Relief and the Jewish Writers', Artists' and Scientists' Committee. An enthusiastic crowd of 50,000 people welcomed them at the Polo Grounds, New York, on July 8, 1943. At a farewell dinner arranged in their honor on September 19, I took occasion to say:

> You have won thousands of new friends for the Soviet Union and substantial aid for its war relief activities. We are left wondering, however, about Soviet Russia's attitude toward Jewish religious life, Zionism and Zionists, and about the Hebrew language, as to whether they are still proscribed or discouraged. These uncertainties are the missing elements in the great common denominator which makes us brothers.
>
> If, in the great Soviet Union, in the great new world which will rise out of the ashes of this War, there can develop among Soviet Jewry an appreciation of the factors which we consider bone of the bone and flesh of the flesh of the Jewish future, we shall be brothers for all time.

At the end of World War II, in 1945, I again broadcast a message to Russian Jewry, stressing the fact that Soviet losses, in terms of human life and property, exceeded those of all the other Allies combined. "Only one other people has suffered greater decimation and devastation," I said, "namely, the Jewish people, with its six million slain." After paying tribute to the valiant Red Army, I expressed gratitude for having had the privilege to serve in the cause of Russian War Relief, and added a prayer "that, in the era of peace now beginning, there may develop a sense of fellowship between the USSR and the U.S.A. which will be a bulwark of world peace."

On December 20, 1945, I had an interview with Archbishop Alexei of Yaroslavl and Rostov, a visiting representative of the Russian Orthodox Church, at the Russian Cathedral in New York. Later, I took part in a reception tendered in his honor by the Interfaith Committee of the American Society for Russian War Relief. Archbishop Alexei emphasized that Nazi atrocities in Russia had been directed against the churches as well, but made a point of referring to Jewish suffering and to the valor displayed by Jews serving in the Red Army. I said that Jewish suffering at the hands of the Nazi regime had begun six years before the outbreak of war, and declared that the Jewish people felt grateful to the Soviet Union because of the refuge many Jews had found there. I also told the Archbishop about our part in the Russian War Relief campaign.

When he inquired about the attitude of American Jews toward the USSR, I said that it was a friendly one on the whole, but that there was resentment over Soviet antagonism toward the Zionist movement. That, he said, was a political question on which he was unable to express any opinion. Clearly, he was not free to state his own mind. I nevertheless suggested that it would be helpful, in improving American-Soviet relations, if a delegation of U.S. clergymen would visit Russia and, on its return, report that there was in fact freedom of religion in the USSR. He could give me only an evasive reply.

To those who had fondly believed in East-West rapprochement, and whose goodwill had been exploited by various Communist "front organizations," the descent of Stalin's Iron Curtain and the ensuing Cold War were disillusioning in the extreme. Any lingering notions of a change in Soviet totalitarianism were finally shattered, a few years after the war, when first Mikhoels and later Fefer headed the roster of prominent Russian Jews who were murdered during the anti-Semitic campaign that masqueraded as an "anti-cosmopolitan" purge. Only after the death of Stalin were our wartime guests "rehabilitated."

Mobilizing American Jewry

Immediately following the Japanese attack on Pearl Harbor and the entry of the United States into the struggle against the Axis Powers, I had thrown myself completely into the American war effort. Like every other rabbi, priest, and minister in the United States, I organized my own congregation first. It quickly became a beehive of activity. The ladies of our sisterhood worked valiantly, making up kits for servicemen, providing them with cigarettes, arranging dances for soldiers on leave and other benefit functions, and being generally helpful. The purchase of U.S. War Bonds was stimulated, and funds were raised for the Red Cross and United Service

Organizations. Three hundred and fifty of the boys and girls who had grown up in the B'nai Jeshurun community served in the U.S. armed forces. Seventeen of them, alas, never returned.

I also became actively engaged on another front of wartime service. As the Jewish co-chairman of the Commission on Religious Organizations attached to the National Conference of Christians and Jews, I took part with its president, Dr. Everett R. Clinchy, and with Dr. Robert W. Searle, Fathers Walsh and Ahearn, and other clergy in the interfaith teams that visited army camps, naval bases, and other military installations throughout the country. Together, we brought the message of American unity and interfaith comity, and we explained the moral and spiritual significance of the war against Nazism and Fascism. It was an opportunity to address tens of thousands of young Americans, many of whom had never seen or heard a rabbi before and some of whom may have had distorted ideas about Jews and Judaism.

Notwithstanding the pressures that wartime conditions laid upon the American Jewish community, its devotion to the Zionist cause did not flag during those eventful years. On the contrary, the times made our Zionist struggle an unprecedented challenge and opportunity.

On his return from the Geneva Zionist Congress in September 1939, Rabbi Solomon Goldman, president of the Zionist Organization of America, had enlisted the help of his colleagues in forming the nucleus of an emergency committee on which all the American Zionist bodies were represented. I became active in this committee. Despite irregular communication with Europe, the American Zionist Emergency Council (as it later became known) was able to maintain contact with Chaim Weizmann and his circle in London and also with the leaders of the Yishuv in Palestine.

The emergency situation we faced, as the Nazi terror engulfed a prostrate Europe, was aggravated by the British decision to enforce the White Paper regulations of May 1939 with rigor and heartlessness. Throughout the war years, a Royal Navy blockade prevented Jewish refugees from landing on the shores of Eretz Yisrael. Having escaped the clutches of their Hitlerite pursuers, these Jews found themselves again outlawed as "illegal immigrants." Tragic cases in point were those of three refugee vessels, the *Patria*, the *Salvador*, and the *Struma*.

In November 1940, nearly 2,000 "illegals" were packed into the S.S. *Patria* by the Mandatory government for deportation to the island of Mauritius in the Indian Ocean. An explosive charge planted by the Haganah, and meant only to disable the ship so as to prevent the deportation order, ripped through its hull and sank the vessel in Haifa harbor, resulting in the loss of some 250 lives. Early in the following year, the S.S. *Salvador* foundered off the Turkish coast after having been sent back to its port of departure in Bulgaria. Four-fifths of the 350 Jewish refugees on board were drowned.

Most horrifying of all was the fate of the S.S. *Struma*, an overcrowded and leaking boat that put into Istanbul in mid-December 1941. The 769 Rumanian Jews aboard underwent incredible privations for two months as the Turkish authorities refused to

1. Early years: With parents, David and Fannie Goldstein, in Philadelphia, ca. 1899.

2. On graduation from the University of Pennsylvania, 1914.

3. Bertha Markowitz (Bert Goldstein), on graduation from Hunter College, New York, 1915.

4. As the youthful rabbi of Congregation B'nai Jeshurun, New York, 1918.

5. At Congregation B'nai Jeshurun's centennial charity bazaar, Hotel McAlpin, New York, December 17, 1924. Rabbi Goldstein receives a "golden book" from Mrs. Jacob Schwartz containing names of workers for and patrons of the bazaar. Also shown are Cantor Jacob Schwartz and Charles W. Endel, president of the Congregation *(5th and 6th from left)*; John F. Hylan, Mayor of New York *(standing behind Rabbi Goldstein)*; and Mrs. Eva Levy, president of the Sisterhood *(between Rabbi Goldstein and Mrs. Schwartz)*.

6. Taamrat Emanuel, the gifted Falasha leader, on his visit to New York in 1931, during the author's chairmanship of the American Pro-Falasha Committee.

7. With Max Zaritsky *(seated right)*, president of the Hatters' Union of the American Federation of Labor, at a Jewish National Fund testimonial dinner honoring William Green *(seated left)*, president of the AFL, June 1940. Cosmo-Sileo photo, New York.

8. At world conference of the Jewish National Fund-Keren Kayemet Le-Yisrael, held in Lucerne, August–September 1935, during the 19th World Zionist Congress. Pictured *(left to right, with backs to wall)*: Eliahu Epstein, Menaḥem Ussishkin, the author, Dr. Abraham Granovsky, and Louis Rimsky. Keren Hayesod photo, United Israel Appeal Photo Archives, Jerusalem.

9. Jewish Palestine Pavilion at the New York World's Fair, 1939. Committee in session *(left to right, standing):* Joseph Schlossberg, Louis Lipsky, Jacob Fishman, Jacob Sincoff, Pierre van Paassen, Samuel Blitz, Mendel Fisher, Eddy Norman, and Meyer Weisgal; *(seated):* Dr. Chaim Weizmann, Grover Whelan, Dr. Stephen Wise, Judith Epstein, and the author. Keren Hayesod photo, United Israel Appeal Photo Archives, Jerusalem.

10. General view of the Jewish Palestine Pavilion, with U.S. and Zionist flags.

11. Opening ceremony, with the author delivering an address and *(seated, far left)* Louis Lipsky and Rabbi Bernard L. Levinthal of Philadelphia.

12. At opening ceremony *(seated, left to right):* Grover Whelan, Professor Albert Einstein, the author, and George Backer.

13. American Zionist leaders, protesting the 1939 White Paper restrictions on Jewish immigration into Palestine, outside the British Embassy in Washington, D.C., November 1940. Pictured *(left to right)*: Solomon Matz, Nellie Ziv, Rabbi Leon Gellman, Rabbi Isadore Breslau, Rabbi Solomon Goldman, Ḥayim Greenberg, Dr. Stephen Wise, Louis Segal, Herman Hollander, and the author.

14. Jewish Section of the Interfaith Committee for Aid to the Democracies (British War Relief). New York dinner in support of the Chaim Weizmann Children's Nursing Home in England, 1940. Pictured *(left to right in center)*: Sir Angus McIntosh, Vera Weizmann, Dr. Stephen Wise, Dr. Chaim Weizmann, and the author. Herbert S. Sonnenfeld photo, New York.

15. Jewish Section (British War Relief). The author's visit to the Israel Goldstein Children's Nursing Home in Porlock, during his wartime trip to Great Britain, March 1944. R. Kingsley Tayler photo, Minehead, England.

16. Wedding of daughter, Vivian Goldstein, and Paul Olum at Congregation B'nai Jeshurun, June 1942. The marriage canopy.

17. **Wedding of Vivian and Paul Olum.** Family group comprising *(left to right)* Mr. and Mrs. Jacob Olum, the bridegroom and bride, and Dr. and Mrs. Israel Goldstein.

18. **Biltmore Hotel Conference, New York, May 1942.** On dais *(left to right):* unidentified, the author, Judge Louis E. Levinthal, David Wertheim, Louis Lipsky, Meyer Weisgal, Dr. Stephen Wise, Dr. Chaim Weizmann *(speaking)*, David Ben-Gurion, Dr. Nahum Goldmann, Tamar de Sola Pool, Dr. Abba Hillel Silver, Benjamin Browdy, and Rabbi Leon Gellman (obscured). Isaac Naiditsch is seated 4th from the left in the front row. Zionist Archives and Library, New York.

allow them to disembark while the British grimly denied them even the hope of internment on Mauritius for the duration of the war. All efforts by World Jewry to save these unfortunates proved unavailing. On February 24, 1942, having been forced out of Istanbul, the *Struma* went down five miles off the Turkish coast leaving only one survivor.

Such incidents increased anti-British feeling in the Yishuv and shed light on subsequent operations by the two dissident Jewish underground movements, the Irgun Tzeva'i Leumi (Etzel) and the Lohamé Herut Yisrael (Lehi, or the "Stern Gang").

During the first few years of the war, I continued to serve as president of the Jewish National Fund of America, having also served as co-chairman and then chairman of the United Palestine Appeal. I became co-chairman of the United Jewish Appeal in 1939, when the UJA was reconstituted to include the American Jewish Joint Distribution Committee, the United Palestine Appeal, and the National Refugee Service. Despite the obstacles we faced and the restrictions under which we labored, important opportunities still existed in Eretz Yisrael. Thus, in the first week of January 1940, at a United Palestine Appeal–National Conference for Palestine gathering in Washington, D.C., I said in the course of my chairman's address:

> We should be guilty of a sin against our people if, because of *kotzer ru'ah*, not shortage of means and resources but shortage of spirit, vision and will, we should fail to make ours today every *dunam* which can be bought, every industrial position which can be won and every immigration influx which can be achieved.

Menahem Ussishkin's reproaches on this score were unceasing. Even after the publication of the 1939 White Paper, there had been more land available in Palestine than the JNF could find the money to purchase. Ussishkin, the unswerving, single-minded champion of *binyan ha-Aretz*, continued to issue exhortations until the day of his death, October 2, 1941. Paying tribute to his memory, at the fortieth anniversary conference of the JNF in New York on November 30, I recalled his admonition: "If the soil of Palestine will be ours, a dozen Passfields will not prevail against us; if not, a dozen Balfours will not help us." "Zionism's Man of Iron" had become a legend even in his lifetime and, I declared, "the entire development of the Jewish National Home, from 1919 to 1939, would be inconceivable without the foundations which Ussishkin and the Keren Kayemet laid."

It was a melancholy thought that American Jewry's now greatly increased contribution to the JNF, still less per capita than that of the much smaller Jewish communities in Great Britain or South Africa, might come too late.

One of the most successful Jewish National Fund projects undertaken during my administration was the President Franklin D. Roosevelt Golden Book inscriptions campaign, which raised over $100,000. On November 10, 1940, at a JNF conference in St. Louis, I had much pleasure in making a Golden Book presentation to FDR, which was accepted on his behalf by our good friend, Senator Alben W. Barkley, majority leader of the U.S. Senate. In the course of my presidential address at this conference, I reviewed the progress made in the six years of my administration, during which new fund-raising records had been achieved for the JNF, and I expressed our grave concern for the fate of our brethren in Nazi-occupied Europe. I also made glowing reference to the wartime role of the Yishuv in Eretz Yisrael, where 135,000 Jews had registered for military service, and dwelt on the need for more land purchases to facilitate agricultural and urban settlement, as well as the production of urgently required food supplies.

Among the distinguished overseas visitors in whose honor the American JNF arranged special functions during my presidency were Dr. Chaim Weizmann and the Ashkenazi Chief Rabbi of Palestine, Dr. Isaac Halevi Herzog. Weizmann utilized his periodical visits to promote our fund-raising campaigns in the United States. One such occasion that stands out in my memory was the dinner we held for the world Zionist leader at the Waldorf-Astoria Hotel in New York on June 10, 1942. The speakers were Sir Ronald Campbell, the British ambassador to the United States, Jan Masaryk, Foreign Minister of Czechoslovakia's Government in Exile, Judge Louis Levinthal, president of the ZOA, Dr. Abba Hillel Silver, and Dorothy Thompson, a noted Christian Zionist. As president of the JNF, I chaired the dinner and presented a Golden Book certificate to Dr. Weizmann.

Perhaps the most momentous JNF conference that took place during my administration was the one held in Detroit at the end of 1942, after Rommel's vaunted Afrika Korps had been crushed by the British Eighth Army under General Bernard Montgomery at El Alamein. In my presidential address before this conference, on December 26, I said:

> The 600,000 men, women and children of the Yishuv who, thank God, are not enslaved, can be counted on to defend their soil and their homes, like their counterparts at Stalingrad. But Eretz Yisrael has been saved. Our Zionist Executive is not a government-in-exile. The gallant sons of the Yishuv have helped to drive Rommel into headlong flight. Let it never be forgotten that the Jews of Palestine, in contrast to their neighbors, did not wait for the Axis forces to be routed before revealing their enthusiasm for the United Nations.

It followed, therefore, that Jewish rights in Eretz Yisrael should win unambiguous international recognition, alongside those of every freedom-loving people:

> Nations great and small are preparing the briefs of their peace plans. If the credits for a people's reconstruction are in proportion to the extent of its casualties and martyrdom, the world's obligations to the Jewish people are without parallel. And if a people's contribution to the winning of the war is a criterion, the Jewish people in every land has made as great a contribution, proportionately, as any in the roster of the United Nations. As indisputable as are our credits, so just are our demands—as individuals to whom equal political, economic and religious rights are due, and as a people, entitled like every people to a homeland where it can have the unrestricted right of entry and independence. Translated into political terms, that means a Jewish Commonwealth in Palestine. This bill of rights for

the Jewish people must be internationally guaranteed, and this guarantee, too, must be internationally implemented. These are fundamental Jewish demands.

Finally, in this Detroit address, I referred to the specific concerns of the Keren Kayemet within the larger context of Zionist work in Palestine, and in relation to our struggle against an iniquitous "reinterpretation" of the League of Nations Mandate:

> Land is our most effective political wedge at this time, in our unremitting fight against the White Paper policy. In prewar days there used to be another weapon, "Aliyah Bet," with which we resisted the restrictions on immigration. Now, because of war conditions, immigration is almost at a standstill; land purchase, however, is not. Two out of every three *dunams* purchased by the Jewish National Fund are in effect a nullification of the intent of the White Paper. The political importance of this program cannot be underestimated. Every Jew who redeems a *dunam* of land in Eretz Yisrael strengthens the economic bulwark, the political wedge and the national stake for Israel's future in Palestine. These considerations are commended to the attention of those Zionists who are prone to couple maximal demands upon the world with minimal demands upon themselves. We must be sure that our claims receive credence by virtue of our sacrifices. Let us not lose a single day in preparing for our *ge'ulah—Panu derekh*, prepare the way, remove the obstacles from the road of our people!

Thereafter, I continued for one more year to head the Jewish National Fund of America, until my election as president of the Zionist Organization of America in 1943. After retiring from my ten-year presidency of the JNF, I maintained my ties with it as honorary president of the Jewish National Fund in the United States.

If I were asked to single out the most important achievement in America on behalf of Zionism during the dramatic period between 1940 and 1945, I would unhesitatingly point to the Biltmore Program and the struggle for its implementation. That this ringing declaration of postwar Zionist policy should have come forth from a gathering convened on American soil had a deep significance of its own. Jewish communities in embattled Europe were unable to raise their voices; some of them were already being destroyed by the Nazis. Nor was British Jewry in a position to take a strong stand, with its National Government desperately engaged in fighting a relentless enemy. The Yishuv in Palestine also lacked political force. It thus fell to the Zionist leadership in America to take a bold initiative.

All of us were greatly impressed by David Ben-Gurion's dramatic pronouncement, "We shall fight with the British against Hitler as if there were no White Paper, and we shall fight the White Paper as if there were no war." It took immense courage to stand up and utter a challenge of such vast implications. The letter and spirit of the Biltmore Program echoed his enunciation.

This program took its name from the Biltmore Hotel in midtown Manhattan, which was the venue of the Extraordinary Zionist Conference called on May 9–11, 1942, by the American Zionist Emergency Council headed by Dr. Stephen S. Wise.

It was attended by Dr. Weizmann, president of the World Zionist Organization, David Ben-Gurion, chairman of the Jewish Agency Executive, and by a galaxy of American and Canadian Zionist leaders, including Dr. Nahum Goldmann, Louis Lipsky, Dr. Abba Hillel Silver, Rabbi Leon Gellman (Mizrahi), Tamar de Sola Pool (Hadassah), and Hayim Greenberg of the Labor Zionists. My old friend, Judge Louis E. Levinthal, president of the ZOA, opened the conference and helped to temper its stormier debates. I took part and spoke as president of the Jewish National Fund of America. Six hundred delegates participated.

The purpose of the Biltmore Hotel conference was to reaffirm Zionist aims, formulate the Zionist program, and determine the course of action the Zionist movement should pursue after the war. The principal debate revolved around Ben-Gurion's insistence that the aim of Zionism should be immediate Jewish self-rule in Palestine. Until then, Zionism's declared objective had never gone beyond the "Jewish National Home." Weizmann, though equally committed to the idea of a Jewish State, was less uncompromising in his stand and favored a policy of gradualism. He took issue with Ben-Gurion's maximalist approach. Delegates lined up on either side.

Ben-Gurion's program, which many, including Weizmann, thought premature or ill-advised, gave rise to heated exchanges. It called for unrestricted Jewish immigration, the establishment of a Jewish commonwealth in Eretz Yisrael, and recognition of the Jewish Agency as the sole authority in charge of the country's development. The defeat of Hitlerism, he declared, would not free the Jewish people from its misery; that was a dangerous illusion. The time had come for Jews to secure control of their own affairs and destiny. "A Jewish Palestine will arise," he affirmed. "It will be the pride of every Jew in the Diaspora and it will command the respect of every people on earth."

Abba Hillel Silver, who was soon to emerge as one of Ben-Gurion's principal allies, said that American Jews, comprising the largest free Jewish community in the world, had a vast and unique responsibility. "We must educate the masses of our people as to what Palestine means for the Jewish future, and work among American non-Jews as well. Jewish groups must act in unison. We must have an international source of authority during this emergency."

Speaking in my capacity as president of the Jewish National Fund of America, I emphasized my oft-repeated theme: the need to secure the funds for acquiring every available *dunam* of land in Palestine, since land ownership could be a key factor in determining the boundaries of the new Jewish State. Up to one million *dunams* of land could still be bought—more than the JNF had been able to acquire in all the forty years of its existence. "These lands in our possession," I declared, "would be a major credential for demanding a postwar immigration of large numbers of Jews into Palestine."

In spite of the differences of tone and approach, the Biltmore Conference as a whole adumbrated Jewish statehood in Eretz Yisrael. It was, in fact, Ben-Gurion's program that, in broad outline, the delegates adopted when they insisted on the establishment of Palestine "as a Jewish Commonwealth integrated in the structure of the new democratic world." The Biltmore Program, which was endorsed by the leading Zionist bodies in North America, Great Britain, and Palestine itself, reflected the determination of Jews everywhere to achieve national and territorial sovereignty in the revived ancient homeland. It also marked a shift in the Zionist center of gravity from London to New York and Washington. The ghastly fate of millions of Jews in Nazi-occupied Europe would, before long, underscore the meaning and resolve of that Zionist milestone.

In September 1942, I was elected for a two-year term to the presidency of the Synagogue Council of America, the overall religious body in the United States representing both the rabbinical and the lay congregational organizations of the Orthodox, Conservative, and Reform wings of American Jewry. It did not include the ultra-Orthodox elements. My executive assistant was Rabbi Ahron Opher.

Our work brought us into contact and cooperation with the corresponding Protestant and Catholic bodies, the Federal Council of Churches of Christ in America and the National Catholic Welfare Conference. We worked jointly in relation to the war effort and stressed the moral and spiritual postulates of American life, the quality of home and family, and the importance of religious worship and education. We also formulated a Declaration on World Peace. This affirmed that the moral law must govern the world order; that the rights of the individual must be assured; that the rights of oppressed, weak, or colonial peoples must be protected; that the rights of minority groups must be safeguarded; that international institutions to maintain peace with justice must be organized; that international economic cooperation must be developed; and that a just social order in each country must be achieved.

Coming in the midst of World War II, my term of office represented a special challenge and opportunity. Within the Jewish fold, the Synagogue Council sponsored the broadcasting of religious radio programs, the arrangement of conferences of Jewish religious leaders on the wartime tasks of the synagogue, and effective representation of the synagogue as such in the overall councils of the American Jewish community.

By virtue of its manifold activities, the Synagogue Council of America was able to open doors that would have remained closed to Jewish bodies of a nonreligious character.

In my capacity as president of the Synagogue Council, I was invited to deliver a prayer before the U.S. House of Representatives in Washington, on April 21, 1942. This was the first of seven similar occasions, extending to the 1970s, when it was my privilege to open with prayer a session of the U.S. Senate or House of Representatives.

On the home front, throughout the war years, while the Jewish chaplain played his part alongside our troops on the field of battle, other forms of service were open to civilians. As previously indicated, Jewish congregations organized U.S. Defense Bond purchases, promoted enlistment for Civil Defense, and provided hospitality and comforts for soldiers far from home. Rabbis accepted the challenge and opportunity, through their pulpit and personal contacts, to fortify civilian morale and to encourage generous responses to fund-raising appeals for the war effort and for

Allied war relief projects. The Synagogue Council of America, transcending the differences between its constituents, symbolized the impulse to work for common Jewish and civic objectives.

During my term of office as president of the Synagogue Council, I had occasion to write to Donald M. Nelson, chairman of the War Production Board, in connection with the approaching Jewish High Holy Days. Our request was that Jewish employees be enabled to take time off for their religious observances, such time to be made up thereafter so that their contribution to the nation's defense would in no wise be diminished. We received an affirmative response.

In September 1942, Dr. Joseph H. Hertz, the British Chief Rabbi, had sent an eve of Rosh Hashanah radio message to American Jewry and I had returned the compliment from New York through the facilities of the National Broadcasting Company. On October 3, 1943, I transmitted a similar radio message from the Jews of the United States to our brethren in Great Britain. I took the opportunity to thank British Jewry for the hospitality extended to our sons "over there," affirmed our common struggle against the "gangster nations" and our appreciation of the heroic British stand, and expressed the hope "that together we may find ways to rescue Jews from the hands of the Nazis." I also mentioned the resolution adopted by the American Jewish Conference (see below) demanding the establishment of a Jewish commonwealth in Palestine, as the logical sequel to the Balfour Declaration, and praying for victory, peace, and healing.

The facilities of the Office of War Information were placed at my disposal for another Rosh Hashanah message, which reached Europe, North Africa, and Eretz Yisrael.

A memorandum was submitted by the Synagogue Council to a conference of the United Nations Relief and Rehabilitation Administration (UNRRA) in Atlantic City on November 10, 1943. It called for special provisions to be made for the religious needs of the Jewish population in liberated countries after the war. Similar documents had already been submitted by Protestant and Catholic organizations on behalf of their adherents. We particularly stressed the need for surviving Jews and Jewish communities in Europe to be supplied with *kasher* food, to have their synagogues and religious schools reconstituted, and to be afforded the reestablishment of rabbinical and educational functions. Wherever spiritual leaders were not available, the Synagogue Council of America and other Jewish religious bodies would cooperate in providing suitable rabbis and ministers. The proposals contained in our memorandum were drawn up in consultation with the Religious Emergency Council of the British Chief Rabbinate and with the American Jewish Joint Distribution Committee.

On retiring from the presidency of the Synagogue Council in September 1944, I submitted a detailed report covering what had been, for the Jewish people, "the most catastrophic years in our tragedy-laden history." It mentioned, *inter alia,* our support for the war effort, the representations made on behalf of religiously observant workers in essential industries, our High Holy Day and festival radio transmissions to U.S. servicemen abroad and to Jews in occupied countries, the memorandum we had submitted to UNRRA, and the cooperation received from the Federal Council of Churches in urging that the Administration intercede on behalf of Jewish victims of Nazi terror. We had two specific achievements to our credit, of special importance to American Jews. One had been the stoppage of a bill in the New York State Legislature that would have opened schools on Saturdays for a program of work on farms during the summer, to help the war effort. On the positive side, we had drawn up special prayer services during the war, including a service for the (first) anniversary of the Warsaw Ghetto Uprising in April, as well as a service for D-Day in June. These were widely distributed.

All in all, the Synagogue Council of America made a worthy contribution to the part played by the American Jewish community during the war years.

The Holocaust: American Jewry's Response

Until Reinhard Heydrich and his Gestapo and SS associates met in the Berlin suburb of Wannsee on January 20, 1942, no overall plan had been formulated by the Nazis for the systematic destruction of European Jewry. Since the outbreak of World War II, special *Einsatzgruppen*—mobile units whose task it was to conduct mass executions—had been active as the armies of the Third Reich rolled onward through Eastern Europe. A major effort to convey information about these massacres had been made by the World Jewish Congress, which had listening posts in Geneva, Stockholm, and Lisbon. The WJC constantly endeavored to enlist the aid of Allied governments, as well as Jews, in its many rescue operations.

The Wannsee conference empowered "specialists" such as Adolf Eichmann to implement Hitler's cherished *Endlösung der Judenfrage*, his "Final Solution of the Jewish Problem," as the total annihilation of Europe's Jews was designated in Nazi jargon. Months would pass, however, before we received word of this new policy and before we could devise any strategy for effective action. It was only after the war that comprehensive accounts of the Holocaust, describing the behavior of the Allied "bystanders" as well as of the Nazis and their Jewish victims, appeared in print.*

Early in 1942, Thomas Mann, the eminent German writer, transmitted reports of the mass murders in his BBC talks from London, but the information was "unconfirmed," patchy, and so horrifying that many people dismissed it as exaggerated. Non-Jews especially tended to regard such reports as anti-German "atrocity propaganda." We knew that the Nazis had been killing Jews in large numbers ever since 1933, but it was hard to believe that a systematic program of genocide was being conducted against the Jews of Europe. Mounting evidence of the Holocaust soon dispelled our remaining illusions. On June 19, 1942, at a special press conference in London, the World Jewish Congress (British Section) publicized

*For part of the following account, I am indebted to Professor Melvin I. Urofsky, author of *American Zionism from Herzl to the Holocaust* (Garden City, N.Y., 1975), and to two works of relevance, *Unity in Dispersion. A History of the World Jewish Congress*, edited by Dr. A. L. Kubowitzki (Kubovy) (New York, 1948), pp. 155–96, and Arthur D. Morse, *While Six Million Died. A Chronicle of American Apathy* (New York, 1967).

certain grim facts that had come to its attention. Indignation ran high in Parliament, the churches, and the press.

Across the Atlantic, however, press reaction was initially skeptical and restrained. Major newspapers, such as *The New York Times*, chose to play down the story of Nazi mass murders. The American Jewish leadership thereupon undertook the launching of an unprecedented information campaign in the United States and the free world. On July 21, a mass demonstration was held at Madison Square Garden in New York, under the auspices of the American Jewish Congress, B'nai B'rith, and the Jewish Labor Committee. Dr. Stephen Wise presided. Messages were received from President Franklin D. Roosevelt, who promised that "a day of reckoning will surely come," and from Great Britain's Prime Minister, Winston Churchill, who stressed the contribution of the Yishuv in Palestine to the Allied war effort. The speakers at this rally included Governor Herbert H. Lehman of New York, Senator Henry Cabot Lodge, Mayor Fiorello LaGuardia, William Green, president of the American Federation of Labor, and Bishop Francis J. McConnell, head of the Methodist Church in New York.

The fast of Tish'ah be-Av, the Ninth of Av, commemorating the destruction of the First and Second Temples in Jerusalem, began on the following night. It was an appropriate occasion on which to link ancient and modern catastrophes—the destruction of the First Temple and Jewish Commonwealth in 586 B.C.E. and the second destruction in 70 C.E. with the current *Ḥurban* of our people in Nazi-infested Europe. As president of the Synagogue Council of America, I called upon our 1,300 rabbis to acquaint their congregants and their non-Jewish neighbors with the facts now in our possession, and to take the initiative in organizing protest meetings and appeals to the U.S. Administration to use its influence in halting the slaughter. Readings were prescribed for synagogue services on Tish'ah be-Av. The Orthodox rabbinate in the United States and Canada additionally urged those Jews who did not ordinarily fast on that day to do so. We received special messages from Chief Rabbi Isaac Halevi Herzog of Palestine, from Chief Rabbi Joseph H. Hertz of Great Britain, and also from leaders of the Protestant and Catholic churches in the United States. Responding to a proposal made by the Synagogue Council of America, Chief Rabbi Hertz called upon the whole of British Jewry to observe Tish'ah be-Av as a day of mourning for the Jewish victims of Hitlerism. The *Congressional Record* of July 20 included seven columns of background information on Nazi crimes against the Jewish people, based on material supplied by the Synagogue Council. A special prayer was also delivered before the House of Representatives on July 23, the day of the Jewish fast, by the Reverend Dr. James Shera Montgomery, the Congress chaplain.

Within the next few weeks, more precise details of the Holocaust began to filter through to us from across the Atlantic. On August 1, 1942, the World Jewish Congress representative in Geneva, Dr. Gerhart Riegner, learned from a confidential German source that Hitler had ordered the annihilation of all Jews in Europe, the means of destruction being Zyklon B gas. After checking this report with his other sources of information, Dr. Riegner was able to verify the basic facts regarding Hitler's "Final Solution." He then sent urgent cables to the U.S. Government and to the World Jewish Congress in London and New York. Although the U.S. State Department had already received similar reports from the Polish Government in Exile in London and from resistance groups, it dismissed the information as "fantastic" and suppressed Riegner's disclosure. For reasons of its own, the State Department also intercepted his cable to Stephen Wise. By this time, at least two million Jews had already perished and the gas chambers and crematoria now increased the efficiency of Nazi mass murder, which had hitherto relied on crippling slave labor, starvation, and machine guns.

On August 17, Riegner's cable reached Sydney Silverman, a Labor Member of Parliament who was chairman of the British Section of the World Jewish Congress. After an inexplicable lapse of some ten days, he transmitted its contents ("with all necessary reservation as exactitude cannot be confirmed") to Dr. Wise in New York, thus circumventing the State Department. Confronted by Wise, Sumner Welles, the U.S. Undersecretary of State, asked him not to publicize the ghastly details until they could be "verified." This meant that almost three months would elapse before the salient facts could be made known to the American public. At the same time, on October 7, President Roosevelt announced his Administration's readiness to help establish an international commission for the investigation of Nazi war crimes.

Generally speaking, the Allied governments were by no means eager to facilitate rescue attempts by the World Jewish Congress or other independent Jewish bodies, or even to emphasize the fact that Nazi atrocities were primarily directed against the Jewish people. Until the final stage of World War II, indeed, obstacles were placed in our way by unsympathetic officials. Henry Morgenthau, Jr., then U.S. Secretary of the Treasury, later accused certain State Department bureaucrats of suppressing the flow of information about the Holocaust so as to prevent an outraged American public from forcing their hand. The man responsible for much of this deliberate obstruction, it appears, was Assistant Secretary of State Breckenridge Long, whom Morgenthau charged with blatant anti-Semitism.

By November 1942, however, an overwhelming mass of affidavits and eyewitness testimony, compiled by Dr. Riegner and Richard Lichtheim (the Jewish Agency representative in Geneva), had reached Sumner Welles. He called Dr. Wise to Washington on November 24 and told him that the facts ascertained were even more appalling than Riegner's August report had led them to suppose, and that Hitler had given orders for the destruction of European Jewry to be completed by the end of the year. Accordingly, Sumner Welles now authorized Stephen Wise to release the full story to the American press.

Meanwhile, Dr. Wise had summoned a number of American Jewish leaders, including myself, to acquaint us with the latest information. Some Jewish groups were nervous about concerted public action and only informal discussions were held at first. Dr. Wise also met with U.S. Secretary of the Treasury Henry Morgenthau, Jr., and Supreme Court Justice Felix Frankfurter, in the hope that they might induce the President to take prompt and effective measures. On December 8, Stephen Wise headed a delegation that was received by President Roosevelt at the

White House. He was handed a memorandum entitled *Blue Print for Extermination*, and expressed shock at its contents, although the information had already come to his notice. Roosevelt promised that the U.S. Government and the United Nations would take all steps necessary to halt the Nazi program of genocide.

Extraordinarily enough, as Morgenthau was to relate,* the President had just come up with a fantastic scheme for the removal of Arabs from Palestine to some other part of the Middle East, and for their replacement by Jewish refugees. He anticipated the possibility of Jews becoming the majority and of Palestine gaining its independence under Christian and Jewish auspices. It was one of many unrealistic dreams.

Earlier in the year, President Roosevelt had indicated that the United States would join its Allies in setting up a War Crimes Commission, but the U.S. Administration deferred clarifying its position from June until October 1942. As a result of British pressure, both governmental and public, Roosevelt finally announced his decision on October 7, leaving the impression that America had taken the initiative in this matter. British public opinion strongly favored a comprehensive rescue operation and, by December 7, the London *Times* was asking what steps would be taken to prevent Hitler's "Final Solution," since no statement of any kind had yet been made to warn the Nazi leadership of Allied retribution. Ten days later, the Allied governments at last issued their joint declaration on the wholesale destruction of European Jewry. There was an emotional scene in Great Britain's House of Commons, where, in reply to a question by Sydney Silverman, M.P., Foreign Secretary Anthony Eden confirmed the worst reports of the Holocaust.

A dramatic eyewitness account of the mass slaughter had been brought from Eastern Europe by Jan Karski, a non-Jewish liaison officer of the Polish underground in Warsaw. Before escaping to London, he had smuggled himself into and out of the Warsaw Ghetto and the Belzec death camp in Poland. This testimony was presented to Roosevelt, Anthony Eden, and Jewish leaders in Great Britain and the United States, but the heroism displayed by Karski (now a professor at Georgetown University's School of Foreign Service in Washington, D.C.) has only been acknowledged in recent years. Apart from horrifying statistics, he brought a desperate appeal from the doomed Jews of Warsaw: if the Allies did not threaten the German people with mass reprisals and if they did not agree to ransom Jews from the Nazis, Jews in the free world should stage a hunger strike to arouse universal concern.

In the United States, a six-week period of mourning and intercession was proclaimed for the Jewish and non-Jewish victims of Hitlerite terror, persecution, and murder. As president of the Synagogue Council of America, I called upon rabbis to set aside Kislev 23, 5703 (corresponding to December 2, 1942), as a special day of mourning and prayer, to coincide with the date proclaimed for Jews throughout the world by the Chief Rabbinate in Eretz Yisrael. Demonstrations took place on all five continents. In New York City, half a million Jews stopped work for ten minutes,

---

*See John Morton Blum, *Roosevelt and Morgenthau. A Revision and Condensation from the Morgenthau Diaries* (Boston, 1970), pp. 518 ff.

radio silence was observed, and memorial services were held in synagogues. During the months that followed, scores of protest rallies took place throughout the United States and other countries of the free world.

Addressing the Detroit convention of the Jewish National Fund held on December 26, 1942, I said:

> This conference is the first national assembly of Jews to meet following the publication of the gruesome facts. Civilized nations have expressed their sense of shock, but one thing they have failed to do—speak to our afflicted, tempest-tossed people in the words proclaimed by the Statue of Liberty in New York harbor: "Send these, the homeless, tempest-tost to me." Would that the England of Cromwell, Milton and Balfour might speak in this hour of Jewish martyrdom and say, "Come home to your mother Zion!"
>
> For all our rivers of tears and oceans of blood, for all our gutted synagogues and desecrated scrolls, for all our slaughtered kinfolk and the agony of these black years, we can be consoled only if, in the land of our sunrise, our *Mizrah*, the sun of freedom will rise for us "with healing in its wings" and shine forth upon the world, bearing the message, *"Am Yisrael Hai!"*—"Israel Lives!"

While mobilizing American Jewry, we also made efforts to rouse public opinion in the wider, non-Jewish community and to enlist the cooperation of Christian organizations, clergy, and laity. Thus, on December 11, a Statement on Anti-Semitism was adopted by the Federal Council of Churches, condemning "the incredible cruelties toward the Jews in Nazi-occupied countries which have stirred the Christian people of America to the deepest sympathy and indignation." This statement urged member churches to intensify efforts for harmonious relations between Christians and Jews and called for the securing of "full justice for the Jews and a safe and respected place for them in Western civilization," with consideration to be given after the war to immigration opportunities to the United States and other lands. There was, however, no mention of Palestine in this otherwise welcome pronouncement. No less timely and encouraging was the full-page advertisement denouncing Nazi atrocities, placed in New York newspapers on December 28, 1942, by American citizens of German descent.

Some ten days later, on January 6, 1943, I led a Synagogue Council delegation that met with the leadership of the Federal Council of Churches and discussed the possibility of practical steps to rescue Jews trapped in occupied Europe. Our proposals dealt with efforts to halt the Nazi program of genocide; the rescue of Jewish children and other survivors through the intercession of neutral countries and the International Red Cross, as well as through the provision of entry visas to Palestine and the United States; opportunities for the permanent resettlement of refugees in various countries, notably Palestine (where the British White Paper restrictions would have to be overcome); and the education of Christian public opinion to an appreciation of the fearful Jewish tragedy and of the measures necessary for its alleviation. We reiterated our belief that the Federal Council of Churches could bring significant influence to bear in all these matters of desperate urgency, thereby indicating to the U.S. Administration that a substantial section of the American public fully supported the Jewish demand for swift action.

As president of the World Jewish Congress, Dr. Stephen Wise had established the Joint Emergency Committee on European Jewish Affairs for the purpose of undertaking rescue operations. It comprised spokesmen of the leading national Jewish organizations, among whom I represented the Synagogue Council of America. We were spurred on by the knowledge that time was slipping through our fingers and that we must respond immediately to the awesome challenge. The Synagogue Council set up its own Committee for Emergency Intercession, which organized and channeled Jewish protests against the apathetic reaction of the Allied Powers to the Holocaust in Europe.

We continued to maintain our pressure on the U.S. Administration throughout the war. On March 1, 1943, the American Jewish Congress staged a huge demonstration at Madison Square Garden: 22,000 people were packed into the hall and 15,000 more stood outside. With "Stop Hitler Now!" as its slogan, this rally was held jointly with the American Federation of Labor, the Congress of Industrial Organizations, and the Church Peace Union. Addresses were delivered by Dr. Chaim Weizmann, Rabbi Stephen Wise, Governor Thomas E. Dewey of New York, Mayor Fiorello LaGuardia, Senator Robert F. Wagner, William Green, and other leaders. Cables of support were received from the Archbishop of Canterbury and from Cardinal Hinsley in Great Britain. A twelve-point program of action, prepared with the help of World Jewish Congress experts, was adopted unanimously. It included the following urgent recommendations:

1. Approaches to the leaders of Nazi Germany by neutral governments, calling for the release of Jews and for their emigration to such places of refuge as might be provided.
2. The establishment of a number of such havens by the Allies.
3. Liberalization of U.S. immigration laws.
4. Sanctuary for Jewish refugees in Great Britain and its Dominions, and in the Latin American republics.
5. Opening the doors of Palestine to Jewish immigration.
6. The supply of identification papers to stateless refugees.
7. Backing for this program of rescue through UN financial guarantees.
8. A request to be sent to Washington, urging that all necessary steps be taken to provide food and other aid for the relief of those incarcerated in Nazi ghettos, and to secure the release and rescue of Jews from Nazi-occupied territories.

On the following day, Undersecretary of State Sumner Welles disclosed that a note had been sent to the British Government on February 25, proposing that the United States cooperate in organizing an intergovernmental committee for the study of methods to save "political refugees" in Europe. This was hardly the response for which we had been hoping. In mid-April, therefore, another mass rally took place at the Chicago stadium. Our demands were reiterated by speakers who included Judge

Joseph M. Proskauer, Senator Harry S. Truman, Dr. Stephen Wise, and Henry Monsky.

A leaflet incorporating our twelve-point rescue program was distributed nation-wide by the Synagogue Council, together with the suggested outline of a letter to be written to the recipient's senator and congressman as well as to the President, urging them to act upon these vital resolutions. At the same time, a motion, proposed by Majority leader Alben W. Barkley and adopted by the U.S. Senate, condemned the Nazi atrocities and demanded the trial and punishment of those responsible.

Soon after the March demonstration in New York came the announcement of an Anglo-American Conference on Refugees in Bermuda. This remote British island in the Atlantic had presumably been chosen with care, as a place where discussions might take place behind closed doors and without the irritating presence of Jewish delegations and lobbyists. Like President Roosevelt's international meeting at Evian in 1938, the Bermuda Conference of April 19–30, 1943, which (by a grim irony) coincided with the outbreak of the Warsaw Ghetto Uprising, proved a fiasco and "a facade for inaction." The man appointed by the State Department as secretary to the U.S. delegation was Robert B. Reams, an anti-Semitic "expert" on Jewish problems who had been doing his best to sabotage and obstruct American efforts to save Jewish lives. It was our feeling that the purpose of the Bermuda Conference was not so much to rescue Jews facing death in Europe as to rescue the State Department and the British Foreign Office from possible embarrassment and public censure.

By mid-1943, however, the "conspiracy of silence" had been broken to some extent. In September of that year, the U.S. Office of War Information decided to allocate time, in its overseas broadcasts, to information about the Holocaust and to warnings that the Nazi war criminals would be brought to justice. At long last, it seemed, the policy of inertia was being abandoned.

Three of Henry Morgenthau's non-Jewish aides, Randolph S. Paul, Josiah E. DuBois, Jr., and John W. Pehle, Jr., had succeeded in uncovering irrefutable evidence of State Department machinations against our rescue campaign. They urged that the "Jewish issue" be taken out of the hands of Breckenridge Long and his subordinates, and that a special government commission be empowered to implement effective rescue measures. In December 1943, Assistant U.S. Solicitor General Oscar S. Cox, one of the architects of Lend-Lease, aided by Professor Milton Handler of Columbia University's law school, began to utilize public pressure and concern for the establishment of such a commission. On January 22, 1944, the War Refugee Board was established "to rescue victims of enemy oppression who are in imminent danger of death, and otherwise afford such victims all possible relief and assistance consistent with the successful prosecution of the War." John Pehle, Jr., Assistant Secretary of the U.S. Treasury, became the director of the Board. It signaled a welcome departure from the previous attitude of indifference to the fate of European Jewry. Pehle and his colleagues ended the practice of suppressing unwelcome and unpleasant information about the *Sho'ah* (Holocaust).

Positive aid programs, inspired by some of the World Jewish Congress recommendations, were undertaken and forceful diplomatic action was initiated.

The War Refugee Board was mainly financed by the American Jewish Joint Distribution Committee, whose European staff, headed from 1942 by Dr. Joseph J. Schwartz, displayed exceptional courage and initiative in conducting rescue and relief work during World War II. Many of these heroic JDC officials, while striving to obstruct the Nazi murder apparatus, were themselves swept away in the avalanche. The JDC operated under severe limitations, yet managed to scrape together nearly $80 million for various rescue schemes—smuggling funds to the Warsaw Ghetto, negotiating the ransom of two trainloads of Hungarian Jews, and endeavoring to prevent further deportations. Such measures had the ultimate effect of saving perhaps as many as 100,000 Jewish lives, even if it was a case of "too little and too late."

Throughout this time, Henry Morgenthau, Jr., was the one member of President Roosevelt's cabinet who consistently pressed for a more vigilant and effective rescue program. He and Pehle managed to induce Roosevelt to issue a declaration on March 24, 1944, stating categorically that those implicated in the Holocaust would pay for their crimes. Unfortunately, this declaration came too late to prevent most of the slaughter. Efforts to enlist the support of Pope Pius XII proved unavailing. Here and there, individual Catholic prelates, notably Monsignor Angelo Roncalli, the apostolic delegate to Turkey (who was to become Pope John XXIII), interceded vigorously to halt the Nazi "resettlement" deportations from various countries. In the International Red Cross, despite the general policy of procrastination and reluctance to "endanger its status," a few determined administrators worked resourcefully to save Jews from the gas chambers. In Nazi-occupied Hungary, great heroism was displayed by a young Swedish diplomat, Raoul Wallenberg, who went to extraordinary lengths to pluck Jews from the trains and death marches bound for Auschwitz.

At a mass meeting held in Carnegie Hall on the first anniversary of the Warsaw Ghetto Uprising, April 19, 1944, I spoke of the now greater awareness in America of the Holocaust's dimensions. After the solemn kindling of a *Yahrzeit* candle in memory of Polish Jewry's martyrs who had died *al kiddush Hashem*, in sanctification of God's Name, I took occasion to say:

> The Battle of the Warsaw Ghetto will be remembered as one of the greatest demonstrations of spiritual courage in the annals of a people whose very survival is a phenomenon of the undefeated spirit. The men, women and youth who for forty days and nights resisted Nazi tanks, guns and incendiaries are to be remembered as the Maccabees and the Bar Kokhbas of our tragic time . . . They died defiant, resisting and heroic, exacting a heavy toll of the bestial foe. They died not only for the honor of Israel but for the honor of civilization.

Yet was hopeless resistance all that the surviving remnant of European Jewry could look forward to? Was everything humanly possible being done, I asked, to rescue as many as could be rescued? "We do not merely beg for crumbs of mercy.

We ask, as an ally not to be forgotten or ignored, that Jews who everywhere are on the side of the United Nations—without equivocation and without Quislings—and who have suffered incomparably heavier and more tragic casualties than any other ally, be not permitted to perish. We ask that Hitler, losing the war against the United Nations, be not permitted in the meantime to win his war against the Jewish people. There is not an hour to lose."

This *"J'Accuse!"* should also stir Jews to self-searching and to more determined effort. The last message from the lonely heroes in their Warsaw Ghetto bunker had contained a stinging reproach:

The blood shed by three million Polish Jews will pursue not only the Hitlerite beasts, but all those who, in their indifference and obstinacy, had only words to offer instead of deeds, to save a people doomed to extermination by Hitler's murderers. None of us, the last Mohicans of an extinguished people, will forget or forgive this.

President Roosevelt's declaration on Nazi criminality was disseminated by the British, but not by the Soviets. The latter, obstinately pursuing their own ideological aims, argued that "all Russians, not only the Jews, faced extermination." Yet when Eichmann's "trucks for Jews" proposal was under review in June 1944, Andrei Vishinsky, Deputy Foreign Minister of the USSR, dispatched a secret note to U.S. Ambassador Averell Harriman, insisting that all negotiations be halted. This put an end to the desperate mission of Joel Brand and sealed the fate of Hungarian Jewry. There is also reason to suspect that Soviet objections may, in part, have been responsible for the Allied refusal to destroy Auschwitz and Birkenau in a precision-bombing attack. Despite talk of the "great technical difficulties involved," operations of this kind had been conducted successfully in Western Europe. In one instance, Allied bombers had attacked a German prison in France and wiped out the guards while the detainees escaped unharmed. Where doomed Jews were concerned, however, a sudden paralysis of the will affected the decision makers.

From its head office in Geneva, and with the cooperation of its London and New York bureaus, the World Jewish Congress continued to explore ways of saving Jews in Nazi-occupied Europe. Dr. Aryeh L. Kubowitzki, secretary-general of the WJC, had been a vigorous advocate of such rescue efforts from the beginning of the war. Time and again, however, the WJC was frustrated by a reluctance on the part of the Allies to divert attention, even momentarily, from "pursuit of the war effort." Thus, early in 1943, Dr. Gerhart Riegner learned that about 70,000 Rumanian Jews deported to Transnistria could be ransomed from Ion Antonescu's pro-Nazi regime if an advance on the $35 million demanded would be placed in escrow with the Berne legation of the United States. President Roosevelt, Henry Morgenthau, and Cordell Hull gave their approval, but the rescue plan was sabotaged by State Department bureaucrats, aided and abetted by British Foreign Office personnel. More than once, such obstructionism nullified proposals of ours that received the green light from Washington.

The British displayed a split personality in face of the Holocaust. On the one hand, men such as Anthony Eden seemed genuinely horror-stricken by the mass destruction of Jewish lives; on the other hand, they would not countenance any organized rescue campaign that might prejudice "higher national interests." Ransom money "would fall into enemy hands," Jews released by their captors in the Balkans could not be transported to Palestine because "there simply were not enough ships to handle them" or because "Hitler would be sure to sneak his agents into the group." With callous consistency, Eden denied the requisite documents to French and Rumanian Jewish refugees. As Arthur D. Morse has concluded, "The possibility of mass rescue threatened England's Palestine policies; the vision of Jews streaming to Palestine seemed to upset Whitehall more than the vision of Jews walking to their death in the gas chambers."*

Today, some forty years after those dire events, there is a move to reexamine Jewish responses to the Holocaust, particularly as far as the American Jewish community is concerned. With the wisdom of hindsight, of course, it is easy to point an accusing finger at guilty parties in the United States and British wartime administrations, but the question still remains: Did Jewish and Zionist leaders in the free world do enough to make a burning issue of the rescue of Hitler's principal victims? I have an uneasy feeling that many occupying Jewish leadership positions at the time were misled by hollow assurances "from on high" and were lulled into complacency by eminent Jewish colleagues who innocently, but mistakenly, believed that they had found sympathetic ears in Roosevelt's administration.

Everyone—including the writer—who held a position of Jewish leadership, major or minor, during that tragic period of our history should feel, in retrospect, a sense of his own inadequacy and of contrition in the light of what transpired.

Thus, in the end, six million Jews perished while the United States dithered and temporized, while the British doggedly sealed off ports of embarkation, and while we Jews in the free world naïvely heeded assurances that "everything possible would be done" to save lives. Our protests and proposals were listened to politely, but were ignored. That the Jewish leadership of the United States failed to do more, when more might have been done to rescue the survivors in 1942 and 1943, is our self-indictment.

Zionist Activities during World War II

When Judge Louis Levinthal's tenure as president of the Zionist Organization of America drew to a close at the end of 1943, I was unanimously elected to succeed him. While resigning as head of the Jewish National Fund, I retained my presidency of the Synagogue Council until the end of my term in the following year. Thus it was that two top posts in the American Jewish community devolved upon me during the latter part of World War II, presenting exceptional challenges and opportunities for public service in a critical and dramatic period of American Jewish history.

*While Six Million Died, p. 335.

Over the years, Congregation B'nai Jeshurun had grown to accept—and even to welcome—my leadership positions. It was a source of deep satisfaction when, upon my election as president of the Zionist Organization of America, every congregational family enrolled in the ZOA and the blue and white Zionist flag was placed on B'nai Jeshurun's pulpit alongside the American Stars and Stripes.

Shortly before I became president of the ZOA, Dr. Abba Hillel Silver was elected co-chairman with Dr. Stephen Wise of the American Zionist Emergency Council, and chairman of its Executive Committee. The AZEC had been reorganized on an interparty basis to serve as a more effective instrument for the achievement of Zionist aims. The new allocation of responsibilities was designed to place the political direction of the American Zionist movement in the hands of Dr. Silver, who (from 1938 until 1943) had served as chairman of the United Palestine Appeal. Wise eventually resigned and Silver then continued alone as chairman of the AZEC. It was a conflict both of personalities and of policies, in which Abba Hillel Silver's activism gained ascendancy.*

Louis P. Rocker, a prominent New York stockbroker, was chairman of the ZOA Finance Committee during the early part of my administration. He had been a successor of mine as president of Young Judea and an active participant in the work of the Jewish National Fund, Keren Hayesod, and United Palestine Appeal. Years later, with his wife, Norma, who directed the Women's Division of Israel Bonds in New York, Rocker made Aliyah to Israel. Simon Shetzer was the ZOA's executive director when I became president. He died in office and was succeeded by Saul Spiro, who in turn was succeeded by Sidney Marks.

There were four promising young Zionists who came under my wing at this time and who went on to achieve positions of leadership in the American Zionist movement. The oldest, Isaac Imber, who had served as president of Masada, the ZOA youth organization, later became the U.S. representative of Rassco, the Jewish Agency Housing Corporation. Rabbis Seymour Cohen, Hertzel Fishman, and Joseph Sternstein began their Zionist careers during my presidency of the ZOA. Seymour Cohen was destined to become president of the Synagogue Council of America and of the Rabbinical Assembly. Joseph Sternstein served three decades later as president of the ZOA and then of the Federation of American Zionists. Hertzel Fishman made Aliyah to Israel, where he wrote several thought-provoking books, served in the Israel Ministry of Education, and was eventually chosen to represent the Conservative movement on the World Zionist Executive.

The membership of the Zionist Organization of America in 1943 was 68,000. My two principal objectives were to broaden and deepen the Zionist program, and to swell the ranks of the ZOA so that the organized Zionist movement in the United States could raise a more powerful voice in propagating the Biltmore Platform.

This second objective gained urgency as a result of the virulent anti-Zionist campaign then being waged by the self-styled American Council for Judaism. This noisy group, which threatened to exert an influence out of all proportion to its size,

---

*See chapter 4 and the character sketches in chapter 17.

had been set up earlier in the year by Lessing Rosenwald. He served as first president of the council and appointed Elmer Berger, a Reform rabbi, as its executive director. We had reason to fear the potential danger which the American Council for Judaism represented within the ranks of the Reform movement. In that same year, for example, Temple Beth Israel of Houston, Texas, passed a resolution excluding from its membership anyone who professed even the mildest interest in Zionism. When this obnoxious regulation came to light, I poured scorn on a Jewish congregation that rejected the sanctities of Judaism. "By these rules," I declared, "Moses, Isaiah and Hillel would be barred from full membership." Incredibly enough, the Houston Reform temple maintained its unyielding anti-Zionist stand until 1967.

One of the first steps I took, therefore, as president of the ZOA was to appoint Arthur Lelyveld, a gifted young Reform rabbi, as director of a special Committee on Unity for Palestine to combat the anti-Zionist militants. It was his first important Zionist assignment, and he discharged his responsibilities admirably. With the help of dedicated workers in critical areas of the United States, and through visits by outstanding Zionist speakers, the propaganda of our opponents was effectively counteracted.

The ZOA's ongoing program was conducted through various departments, each having its own chairman and, in most cases, its own full-time professional director. Political activities were coordinated with those of the American Zionist Emergency Council, then headed by Rabbis Stephen Wise and Abba Hillel Silver. The Palestine Economic Bureau, for investments in Eretz Yisrael, began to develop under David Tannenbaum; publicity and public relations were directed by Ernest E. Barbarash; and the ZOA Education Committee was chaired by Rabbi Simon Greenberg. The Hebrew Arts Committee, under the chairmanship of Rabbi Moshe Davis, fostered Jewishly motivated theatrical and dance groups among younger American Zionists.

We undertook an expanded publications schedule, which included a series of authoritative biographies of Zionist leaders, some little known to Jews in the United States. Among these were studies of David Wolffsohn by Rabbi Emil Cohn, and of Baron Edmond de Rothschild by Isaac Naiditsch. On one occasion, too, an award was given to Rabbi Harry Davidowitz, an American who had settled in Eretz Yisrael, honoring his Hebrew translation of Shakespeare's works. A major step was the appointment of Ludwig Lewisohn, the distinguished author and publicist, as editorial writer and literary editor of *The New Palestine*, which now appears as *The American Zionist*. Carl Alpert was managing director of this monthly until his wartime induction into the U.S. armed forces.

Other departments of the ZOA were responsible for membership and field service, Aliyah, a speakers' panel, and the Expansion Fund, which I launched to finance the entire program. This fund raised over $300,000 in two years. The American Zionist Youth Commission, conducted jointly with Hadassah, worked with and through Young Judea, Masada, Avukah, and Junior Hadassah. Finally, the ZOA Radio Project sponsored the production of a nationwide series of quarter-hour broadcasts entitled *Palestine Speaks!* Many stars of stage and screen took part in these transmissions. The Zionist aim of a Jewish commonwealth in Palestine thus made its impact on American public opinion through nationwide radio programs.

As a demonstration of practical support for the Allied war effort, the Zionist Organization of America conducted a mass campaign, in June 1944, to sell $25 million in U.S. War Bonds. This campaign, led by Edmund I. Kaufmann and Ernest E. Barbarash, surpassed all expectations and resulted in the sale of bonds worth more than $65 million throughout the United States. At a ceremony held on July 31, 1944, William C. Fitzgibbon, special assistant to the Secretary of the Treasury, presented the Treasury Department's highest citation to the ZOA. In accepting the citation on the ZOA's behalf, I noted that this was the largest sum ever raised by any single Jewish organization in the United States and that close to 500,000 Jewish boys were fighting in the American armed forces. "The least that we, their kin back home, can do is to provide the tools for victory," I said. "No people has made a heavier contribution to the victory of the United Nations, in proportion to its membership, and no people has suffered so heavy a toll." Having stressed the role of the Yishuv in all aspects of the war effort, I went on to emphasize the justice of the Zionist cause. "The establishment of Palestine as a Jewish commonwealth is postwar aim No. 1 of the Jewish people. No matter how great the military victory of the United Nations may be, the war will not have been won on the moral side unless this measure of justice will have been achieved."

When I relinquished the presidency in 1945, membership of the ZOA had more than doubled to reach 138,000, the largest increase in the organization's history.

By the middle of 1943, World War II had reached its decisive phase. Nazi Germany and Japan had scored awesome initial victories: the armies of the Third Reich had penetrated deep into Soviet Russia, Great Britain had been ravaged by the air attacks of Goering's Luftwaffe and its forces were engaged in desperate battles in the Middle East, while the seemingly irresistible Japanese were firmly entrenched from the borders of India to the Marshall Islands, across the Pacific, and southward to New Guinea. Yet this was also the year that marked the turning point of the war, as the Allied forces began to stem the Axis advance and to make important gains on land, at sea, and in the air. With the prospects of an Allied victory growing brighter, there was a revival of our hope that out of the titanic world struggle Zionism might at last achieve the fulfillment of its aim, a Jewish State in Eretz Yisrael.

The first step by the American Zionist movement was to work toward the establishment of a united Jewish front behind the Biltmore Program. Our efforts bore fruit when the American Jewish Conference assembled in New York, where its first sessions took place from August 29 until September 2, 1943. Representatives of 65 national Jewish organizations were present, as well as delegates from the 78 larger Jewish communities of the United States. Altogether, 501 delegates attended the sessions. It was in every sense a popular assembly, more than two million American Jews having taken part in the election of delegates to the Conference.

As national president of B'nai B'rith, Henry Monsky, a brilliant lawyer from

Omaha, Nebraska, played the leading role in organizing the American Jewish Conference. B'nai B'rith was a non-Zionist body, but Monsky himself made no secret of his own Zionist convictions. Meyer Weisgal was the energetic organizing secretary and Isaiah L. (Si) Kenen of Cleveland, Ohio, a gifted journalist and staunch Zionist, served effectively as the Conference's executive director.

Three major issues figured on the Conference agenda: the European Holocaust and problems concerning the rights and status of Jews in the postwar world; the implementation of the rights of the Jewish people with respect to Palestine; and the appointment of a delegation to carry out the Conference program in cooperation with the duly accredited representatives of other Jewish communities throughout the world.

As president of the Zionist Organization of America, I was elected co-chairman of the Interim Committee of the Conference, together with Henry Monsky and Louis Lipsky. We considered our primary task to be the creation of a representative American Jewish body that would define its position on the postwar aims of the Jewish people, both in Eretz Yisrael and in a reconstructed Europe. Although the full scope of the Holocaust was as yet unknown to us, we realized that the Jewish communities of Nazi-occupied Europe had already been overwhelmed by an unprecedented catastrophe, of which American Jewry was not fully aware and to which it was insufficiently responsive.

In the course of an address delivered before one of the opening sessions of the American Jewish Conference, on August 29, 1943, I pointed an accusing finger at our own great constituency of five million Jews:

> The American Jewish community, as a whole, has not been convulsed by the unprecedented tragedy which has fallen upon the Jews of Europe. One pogrom in Kishinev in 1903 shook American Jewry more profoundly than the mass murder of a million Jews in 1943.

I proceeded to berate those spokesmen for Western democracy who continued to pretend that the fate of the Jews was in no way different from that of any other small nation under the Nazi heel, and that their salvation must depend on the Allied war effort. Who else had been singled out for total destruction? Why did so many of our "friends" in high places turn a blind eye to the truth? "It is a stark fact," I declared, "that unless special and drastic measures of rescue are undertaken immediately, the victory of the United Nations will come too late to do the Jews in Nazi lands any good. They will all be dead." After outlining a five-point rescue program, I said that it would not be unreasonable to tell the U.S. Government: "If millions of American citizens were trapped in the Nazi charnel-houses, you would find a way to rescue large numbers, and without delay!"

This was the black cloud that hung over my period of leadership in the ZOA, the Synagogue Council, and the American Jewish Conference in the closing years of the war.

Among the national Jewish organizations represented at the opening sessions of the Conference had been the American Jewish Committee, headed by its newly elected president, Judge Joseph M. Proskauer. Though vehemently anti-Zionist, Proskauer had joined with Judges Irving Lehman and Samuel Rosenman in a declaration criticizing the severe limitations placed upon Jewish immigration into Palestine. When, however, the Conference went on record as supporting the establishment of a Jewish commonwealth in Eretz Yisrael, in a resolution adopted after Rabbi Abba Hillel Silver's masterly address, Judge Proskauer and his associates of the American Jewish Committee demonstrated their opposition by walking out of the hall. Seven weeks later, they withdrew their participation in the Conference.

The resolution on Palestine, which received overwhelming support, called for the fulfillment of the Balfour Declaration and the League of Nations Mandate, the immediate withdrawal of the 1939 White Paper, and the opening of the gates of Palestine to unrestricted Jewish immigration. It also demanded that the Jewish Agency for Palestine be recognized under the Mandate as the authorized representative of the Jewish people, and that it be vested with the authority to direct and regulate immigration into Palestine, to develop to the maximum the agricultural and industrial potential and the natural resources of the country, and to utilize its uncultivated and unoccupied lands for Jewish colonization and for the benefit of the country as a whole. "The measures here urged," this resolution affirmed, "constitute the essential prerequisites for the attainment of a Jewish majority and for the re-creation of the Jewish Commonwealth."

The Conference's approval for the resolution, by a substantial majority vote, confirmed the claim made consistently by the Zionist movement in the United States that it had the support of a great majority of American Jews. It was hoped that this fact would be taken into account not only in the United States, but also in Great Britain and wherever statesmen were considering the problems faced by Jewry in the postwar world. On the eve of the U.S. presidential elections in 1944, this policy statement was to gain the endorsement of both the Democratic and the Republican parties.

By the time the second session of the American Jewish Conference opened at the end of 1944, the full enormity of the *Sho'ah* had become public knowledge. We were pursued by the nightmare that, even then, many thousands of Jews were being slaughtered daily as Hitler's program of genocide ground on relentlessly, while leaders of the free world made no serious effort to halt it.

This new Conference session began at the Hotel William Penn in Pittsburgh on the afternoon of Sunday, December 3, 1944, just fifteen months after the first had been concluded in New York. Five hundred delegates attended. During the time that had elapsed between the first and second sessions, preliminary steps had been taken to put the Conference resolutions into effect. These included the formal submission of its entire program to U.S. Secretary of State Cordell Hull by a delegation that went to Washington the previous September, together with a statement calling for an international bill of rights and a memorandum on the punishment of war criminals. The documents were lodged with the State Department in August 1944, immediately prior to the Four-Power conferences at Dumbarton Oaks that led to the establishment of the United Nations Organization. On July 31, a mass meeting, organized by the American Jewish Conference in Madison Square Park, had overflowed into the streets of New York with tens of thousands of Jewish citizens in a rousing demonstration. This was a further opportunity to voice our demand that the United States and its Allies act swiftly to rescue those Jews who could still be saved from the Holocaust.

Together with Henry Monsky and Louis Lipsky, I had a share in all of these activities. The three of us shouldered what Lipsky called, in his opening address at the second Conference session, "the organized responsibility of the American Jewish community within specified areas of the postwar Jewish problems." Four more years were to elapse before the Conference, having seen the achievement of its principal aims, disbanded at the end of 1948. I shall return to these developments later.

Meanwhile, early in 1944, I had paid a visit of several weeks' duration to Great Britain, where I met with leading members of the government and with the heads of the Jewish community and the Christian churches (see chapter 4). Several months thereafter, in mid-October, the annual convention of the Zionist Organization of America provided an opportunity to report on the progress achieved by the ZOA and to discuss Jewish concerns about the present and the immediate future. In the course of my presidential address before this convention in Atlantic City, on October 14, I said:

> We mourn the nameless martyrs of Hitlerism. We salute the Jewish participants in the War, 1,500,000 in the armed forces of the United States, Great Britain and Soviet Russia. Palestinian Jewry's 40,000 volunteers—twenty-five percent of its adult male population—have enlisted in the fighting forces of Great Britain, and unnumbered thousands of Jews are among the guerilla fighters and underground movements of Europe.

Quoting a letter I had received from Rabbi Judah Nadich, Chief of Jewish Chaplains in the European Theater of War, I spoke of the Jewish Maquisards in France who had succeeded in hiding many Jewish children and in smuggling hundreds of them across the Spanish border, thus enabling them to reach Eretz Yisrael. I also referred to the Jewish Brigade, which the British had at last set up after years of stubborn refusal. All of this now entitled the Jewish people to a place at the peace conference, and in all bodies such as UNRRA where the problems discussed involved Jewish interests.

The victory of the Allies would find most of the Jews in Europe destroyed. "A surviving remnant of approximately one and a half million Jews will be found scattered over the continent," I cautioned, "many of them emerging from caves and forests. They will require food, shelter and healing." Supplementing whatever program of relief and rehabilitation the UN might provide, American Jewish philanthropy would flow toward them in unprecedented measure. More than philanthropy, however, would be needed: Jewish communal life would have to be restored. I proposed that a Zionist delegation from the United States visit the Jews of liberated Europe as soon as practicable.

Foreseeably, many Jews would refuse or find it impossible to return to their former homes. More than one potential haven had already given advance notice that Jewish mass immigration would not be tolerated. Hence, I said, one must reach an inescapable conclusion:

> There will be one country only to which the Jewish masses have a claim as Jews—Palestine. What a stain it is upon Britain's honor that many thousands who could have been rescued from Hitler-occupied countries were left to perish because the White Paper stood between them and Palestine! How long will that White Paper be allowed to stand in the way of evacuating Jewish refugees from Europe to Palestine? How long will the Intergovernmental Committee charged with finding a solution for the homeless continue to regard itself as an arm of the British Colonial Office?
>
> One of the first postwar responsibilities of the UN should be the facilitation of Jewish mass immigration into Palestine. There must be no more *Struma* incidents and no more deportations. Unless Palestine is set aside for all Jews who may want to go there, Hitler will have been presented with his only triumph.

It was a programatic speech, dealing with all the practical aspects of Jewish revival after the war. I also advocated the building of a richer, more contentful Jewish life in the United States as part of our Zionist task, to compensate in some measure for the *Hurban* in Europe. Repeatedly, however, "a Jewish commonwealth in Palestine" was my major theme and I called upon the U.S. Administration to throw its weight into the scales on our side. In conclusion, I emphasized the fact that a Jewish National Home was indispensable for the spiritual and cultural survival of the Jewish people, and that the war must not end without a moral as well as a military triumph over Nazism.

This address had wide reverberations. Soon afterwards, I received a gratifying letter from James Grover McDonald, onetime League of Nations High Commissioner for Refugees from Germany and a bitter critic of State Department policy, telling me how much he agreed with my presentation. A year later, he would be a member of the Anglo-American Committee of Inquiry whose findings on the Palestine question would dismay the British Labor Government, and he was destined to become the first U.S. ambassador to Israel.

On October 15, 1944, the day after my address, we received the following message from President Roosevelt to the ZOA convention:

> Please express my satisfaction that, in accord with traditional American policy and in keeping with the spirit of the Four Freedoms, the Democratic Party at its July convention this year included the following plank in its platform:
>
> "We favor the opening of Palestine to unrestricted Jewish immigration and colonization and such a policy as to result in the establishment there of a free and democratic Jewish Commonwealth."
>
> Efforts will be made to find appropriate ways and means of effectuating this

policy as soon as practicable. I know how long and ardently the Jewish people have worked and prayed for the establishment of Palestine as a free and democratic Jewish Commonwealth. I am convinced that the American people give their support to this aim; and, if re-elected, I shall help to bring about its realization.

Our dealings with Roosevelt throughout the Nazi period and the war made some of us wary of his promises. With elections close at hand, he was anxious to secure the American Jewish vote.

Meanwhile, the American Zionist Emergency Council, headed by Rabbis Abba Hillel Silver and Stephen S. Wise, was developing into a powerful political arm of the Zionist movement. The principal constituents of the AZEC were the Zionist Organization of America, the Hadassah Women's Zionist Organization, the Labor Zionists, and the American Mizrahi Organization. I had been a member of the original committee of eight that constituted the first nucleus of the AZEC. Others prominent in its leadership were Louis Lipsky, Herman Shulman, Rose Halprin of Hadassah, Rabbi Wolf Gold of Mizrahi, and Hayim Greenberg of the Labor Zionists.

Considerable effort was devoted to winning over Christian public opinion. The American Palestine Committee (APC), founded in 1932, was revived ten years later under the chairmanship of Senators Robert F. Wagner of New York and Charles McNary of Oregon. While Emanuel Neumann, who had originally taken the initiative in establishing it, was in Palestine, the APC remained dormant; but it underwent a revival after his return to the U.S. in 1941. It quickly gained the support of former U.S. Secretary of State Sumner Welles and was strengthened by hundreds of national figures, including senators and congressmen, university presidents, state governors and city mayors, editors and labor leaders. Helen Gehagan Douglas became the APC's national secretary.

I. L. Kenen of the AZEC played an important part in organizing the merger of the American Palestine Committee with the Christian Council on Palestine (CCP), founded in 1942, with the Reverend Dr. Carl H. Voss of Pittsburgh as its executive director. This second body mainly comprised Protestant ministers and functioned under the chairmanship of the Reverend Dr. Henry Atkinson, general secretary of the interfaith Church Peace Union. Among its most active supporters were two outstanding theologians, Professors Reinhold Niebuhr and Paul Tillich; Methodist Bishop Francis J. McConnell; Professor William F. Albright, the eminent archaeologist; and Daniel A. Poling, editor of the *Christian Herald*. Another prominent figure in the ranks of the CCP was Pierre van Paassen, the Unitarian writer and journalist.*

When the APC and the CCP merged in 1946, some 2,000 clergymen and religious educators in the United States affiliated with the new American Christian Palestine Committee. Its first chairman was the Reverend Dr. Henry Atkinson, the co-directors being Professor Howard M. LeSourd and the Reverend Dr. Carl Voss.

---

*On Pierre van Paassen, see chapter 17.

LeSourd, a distinguished Methodist, received several years' leave of absence from his post as dean of Boston University's Graduate School of Education to serve in the American Christian Palestine Committee, to which he brought immense drive and many famous names. Soon after the establishment of the committee, a telegram was sent to President Roosevelt and to Secretary of State Cordell Hull, requesting that the British Government be urged to abrogate the White Paper policy so that at least the remnant of European Jewry might be rescued and allowed to enter the Jewish National Home. The telegram further urged that all possible pressure be exerted on the regime of Admiral Horthy to stop the persecution and deportation of Hungarian Jews, and that the U.S. Administration open the gates of America to substantial Jewish immigration.

By 1946, when Dr. Carl Voss became chairman of its executive council, the American Christian Palestine Committee had a registered membership of 15,000 and had developed into an effective instrument for enlisting American Christian opinion in favor of the Zionist cause. In 1947, the Reverend Karl Baehr was appointed extension secretary and three years later he succeeded Howard LeSourd as the committee's director. Dr. Carl Voss raised his voice constantly on behalf of Zionism during the postwar years, and he remained a faithful, effective friend of the Jewish State.

The ultimate objective of the American Zionist Emergency Council was to win the support of the American people and Government for the Zionist program. It was no easy task at a time when enormous pressures were being exerted against us, especially by elements within the U.S. State Department itself, where (because of the oil lobby) we had many more opponents than supporters.

Significant progress appeared to have been made at the beginning of 1944, when the Palestine issue came before both Houses of Congress. On February 1, Senators Robert F. Wagner (Democrat) and Robert A. Taft (Republican) introduced into the U.S. Senate a resolution urging the American Government to use its good offices and take appropriate measures "to the end that the doors of Palestine shall be opened for the free entry of Jews into that country and that there should be full opportunities for colonization, so that the Jewish people may ultimately reconstruct Palestine as a free, democratic Jewish Commonwealth."

About a week later, the House of Representatives began its hearings on a Palestine resolution to similar effect. The chairman of the House Committee on Foreign Affairs was Representative Sol Bloom (Democrat) from New York, who favored the passage of this resolution. Together with Abba Hillel Silver, I was one of the American Zionist spokesmen who took part in these hearings. Dr. Silver delivered a characteristically forceful statement of our position.

Appearing before the Foreign Affairs Committee as president of the ZOA, I traced the history of Zionism in America, the role of the Keren Hayesod, Jewish National Fund, and Hadassah, and the effects of the White Paper policy in Palestine. On the record of the Yishuv during World War II, I observed that it had "made a greater contribution to the victory of the United Nations in the Near and Middle East than all the Arab states put together." American Jewry's attitude on the

Palestine question, I said, had been registered by the American Jewish Conference, the only all-embracing, democratically constituted body in American Jewish life. As co-chairman of the Interim Committee, I submitted to the attention of the House the resolution passed by the American Jewish Conference, urging that it now receive the approval of Congress. Such a step, I declared, "would lift the hopes of the surviving remnant of European Jewry; it would be in the best American tradition, combining Biblical Prophecy with humanitarian statesmanship."

The proposed resolution was finally adopted by the House of Representatives, marking an important step forward in our effort to gain the Administration's support for the Zionist political program. The U.S. State and War Departments nevertheless succeeded in having the resolution shelved. It was reintroduced in November 1944, when 400 out of the 535 members of Congress went on record as approving the Zionist call for immediate U.S. action in favor of a Jewish State in Palestine. President Roosevelt and the State Department then indicated their lack of enthusiasm for the resolution, and it was tabled.

Another important opportunity had presented itself in the summer of 1944, during the conventions of the two major American political parties. Stephen Wise cultivated his friends in the Democratic Party, buttonholing many of the delegates, and I assisted him in the lobbying. A pro-Zionist plank was inserted in the Democratic election platform. As a result of similar efforts by Abba Hillel Silver, supported by Emanuel Neumann, the Republican convention followed suit. Our joint efforts thus bore fruit, as the two major parties committed themselves to the principle of a Jewish commonwealth in Eretz Yisrael.

On the eve of President Roosevelt's departure for the "Big Three" Conference at Yalta with Churchill and Stalin, early in February 1945, he was inundated with telegrams and letters urging him to bring up the Palestine issue at that meeting and to secure a favorable decision by the two other leaders. Our hopes were dashed by the outcome of the talks at Yalta, and our feeling of disappointment was intensified by what occurred immediately after the conference. With much pomp and ceremony, the feudal ruler of Saudi Arabia was received by President Roosevelt on board an American warship, where matters of mutual interest were discussed. Clearly, Roosevelt was anxious to placate the oil-rich Arab monarch, especially with regard to Zionist aspirations in Palestine. Subsequently, in his report to Congress on March 1, 1945, the President declared that he had "learned more about the whole problem, the Moslem problem, the Jewish problem, by talking with Ibn Saud for five minutes" than he could have learned "in the exchange of two or three dozen letters."

Despite attempts to reassure the Zionist leadership, this statement gave rise to a furore and lost Roosevelt much of his credibility with the American Jewish public. On April 12, Roosevelt died suddenly and it remained for his successor, Vice-President Harry S. Truman, to assume the direction of affairs and to prove himself.

The most arduous part of our struggle still lay ahead.

4

A Noise of War: 1944–45

Setting out for England in February 1944, on a manifold official mission, I was not unaware of the difficult prospect of being there during a grim and exhausting struggle. It would certainly not be a junket. Winter, in any case, has never been a propitious season for visiting Great Britain. What with wartime conditions adding their own hardships and discomforts to a wretched climate, the outlook was far from beckoning.

It turned out to be both a sobering and an exhilarating experience. As an eyewitness, I felt compassion for those countless people who had lost close relatives on the battlefields and for the victims of the ferocious Nazi air raids on the home front. Yet the quality of endurance manifest on every hand aroused my deep admiration. How could any visitor to Great Britain in those days not have appreciated the indomitable spirit of the tough "island race," to use Churchill's phrase, which was fighting a war forced upon it by a totalitarian madman bent on world conquest?

Overseas air transportation in wartime was, of course, at a minimum. It required no little "pull" to get a civilian passage across the Atlantic on the army-operated Pan-American Clipper seaplane service, but my connection with the British War Relief Society helped to obtain the required priority.

Strapping myself in and looking around after boarding the commodious plane at LaGuardia Airport that gray morning of February 15, I caught sight of what must have been some very influential persons among the forty passengers. There was little time to observe them more closely, however, before we took off. The attention of all of us was focused on the receding airport buildings and the New York and New Jersey coastlines as our aircraft veered south across the ocean in the direction of the West Indies. We were to take the southern route to Europe.

My overseas journey had several objectives in view. First and foremost, as president of the Zionist Organization of America, I was anxious to consult with our colleagues of the Jewish Agency Executive about postwar Zionist prospects, as well as to sound out members of the British War Cabinet on their concept of the future of Palestine and the Jewish National Home. The proclamation issued by the Biltmore Hotel conference almost two years earlier had been displeasing to the British Government, needless to say, and we learned that no little resentment had been caused among some cabinet members, who felt that their country was being unnecessarily harassed by complicated political problems that properly belonged to postwar councils.

Two imperative factors pointed up the urgency of consultations incumbent upon the Zionist leadership. First was the fact that the five-year period predicated in the British White Paper of May 1939 for the grant of 75,000 immigration certificates (including 25,000 for refugees) would end on March 31, 1944, after which time Jewish immigration would be contingent on Arab consent. Moreover, reports of the Holocaust were then reaching us from Nazi-held Europe, although the full ghastly extent of that catastrophe had still to be revealed.

In addition to conferring with Dr. Weizmann and his colleagues, and with as many members of the Government as I would be able to reach, a further purpose was to inspect the children's homes set up by the Jewish Section of the British War Relief Society. Moreover, as president of the Synagogue Council of America and chairman of the Commission on Religious Organizations of the National Conference of Christians and Jews, I wanted to make contact with the heads of religious communities in the United Kingdom and with the NCCJ's counterpart, the British Council of Christians and Jews. All in all, it was an ambitious itinerary to complete during the few weeks which I intended spending in the British Isles.

The trip from New York to our first stopover at Hamilton, Bermuda, was uneventful enough. It had been scheduled as an overnight stay, but after landing at the USAAF base, built on a site leased from Great Britain, it emerged that we would have to make a longer sojourn of eighteen hours. I was given the opportunity of meeting the resident Jewish community on the island—just three families! They were all Zionists.

Some thirty hours later, after two intermediate halts in the Azores and Lisbon, our big bird came down in the midafternoon of February 18 at Poole, a seaside town near Bournemouth, on the south coast of England, a little more than two hours by rail from London. I was especially intrigued by the demeanor of the trio of customs and immigration inspectors who combed our baggage and examined our papers. When the last of them saw a reference to the Zionist Organization of America in my papers, he disclosed that Dr. Weizmann had come through this point of entry a few months previously.

"He was a great help to us in the last war, sir," he informed me, alluding to Weizmann's work on acetone as an ingredient for triggering cordite, which had won him renown almost three decades earlier. "I wonder if he's working on something that'll be of use in *this* war?"

I knew, of course, that Dr. Weizmann had submitted proposals to the British Government and President Roosevelt concerning the possible manufacture of synthetic fuel and rubber, but I felt neither disposed nor qualified to enter a "scientific" discussion, so merely hazarded the vague opinion that "he must be working on something."

After completing the formalities at Poole, I telephoned the Zionist offices in London to announce my arrival. Upon reaching Victoria Station that night, I was met by a Reverend Baum and his wife and by Major Isaac Levy, a Jewish chaplain to the British armed forces. How this trio could have detected anyone in the almost total blackout was beyond my understanding. Getting across London to Grosvenor House, my hotel on Park Lane, was like steering one's way through the nethermost regions of mythology; but the cabby, who was obviously used to this kind of Stygian navigation, duly and cheerfully deposited us on the broad doorstep of the blacked-out hotel.

My escorts assured me that Hitler's blitzkrieg had more or less been halted by the vigilant RAF air-defense system, and there had been a lull for the past year. Once inside the hotel, I found that while accommodation had been reserved for me, my choice of room could be made on arrival. In typically American tourist fashion, I asked for a room on the top floor.

This request was granted with surprising alacrity, although I had been given the impression that the hotel was crowded. When I entered the room, I saw that the curtains were tightly drawn and ascribed this to the statutory blackout. It quickly transpired that I had spoken too soon, and too guilelessly, at the reception desk below. Within a matter of minutes, the air-raid siren began to wail. The "Jerries," as London cockney slang dubbed them, had resumed their depredations. I was struck by the whimsical thought that they must have been tipped off about my arrival by the Mufti of Jerusalem, Haj Amin al-Husseini, who was then Hitler's guest in Berlin.

I could not resist the temptation to draw aside a small corner of one curtain to see what was happening. A searchlight played upon one tiny point in the evening sky— an enemy bomber plane—and I heard the anti-aircraft battery in Hyde Park, across the road from the hotel, spewing forth its deadly fire at the target. The noise of the artillery was deafening, a bass counterpoint to the clanging of fire engines in the street.

I doubt if I held the curtain fringe open for more than a minute. Had anyone seen me, I might have been pelted with expletives as a Yankee fool. Then the alarm rang through the hotel corridors. I went into the hallway and saw people running down the stairs. Joining them, I soon found myself in the air-raid shelters in the basement. Outside, firemen were going back and forth between the hotel and the street, extinguishing a couple of blazes nearby with quiet, well-practiced efficiency. On my way down from the top floor, I realized at last why it was largely unoccupied.

Such was my introduction to wartime London.

The Zionist Issue in Great Britain

Lavy Bakstansky, the general secretary of the Zionist Federation and director of the Joint Palestine Appeal, came round to the hotel later to greet me. I had brought a letter from the British ambassador in Washington, D.C., Lord Halifax, which "Bakky" thought could be useful, especially with the Foreign Secretary, Anthony Eden. As it later transpired, he was right in that assumption. "Bakky" also told me that I could be of service to the JPA in addressing meetings.

When I finally ventured into the street and saw the drawn faces and red-rimmed eyes of people who had obviously been on civil-defense duty, the wrecked buildings, and the still-smoldering embers, I realized what Londoners had been going through during the previous four years. Reflecting that the British were a tough and hardy folk to have endured this kind of battering, I wondered if their leaders would be as unyielding when it came to negotiating a territorial settlement for the battered Jewish people.

The headquarters of the Jewish Agency and World Zionist Organization at 77 Great Russell Street, in the heart of Bloomsbury, close to the British Museum and many buildings of the University of London, had miraculously escaped damage during the long series of air raids. Some of the nearby structures had been less fortunate and there were huge gaps where residences, hotels, and offices had once stood.

A familiar landmark, 77 Great Russell Street was then, and for some years after, the 10 Downing Street of the Zionist movement. This old-fashioned edifice, possibly the former townhouse of some peer or country gentleman, seemed in urgent need of renovation, but had been expanded to incorporate the next-door house (No. 75) so as to make more office space available. In New York, no Jewish organization of standing would have been content with such premises, but here in London even Government departments were housed unpretentiously.

Dr. Weizmann's large room was on the second floor at No. 77. Upon entering his office, a few days after my arrival in London, I found him sipping a cup of tea and gazing meditatively at the fireplace. The room was already a hive of activity long before eleven o'clock, when the Executive was scheduled to meet. Weizmann was listening to Moshe Shertok (later, Sharett), head of the Jewish Agency's Political Department in Jerusalem, who had come from Palestine with two other Executive members for a series of meetings. His colleagues were Rabbi Yehudah-Leib Hacohen Fishman (later, Maimon), the Mizrahi leader, and Dr. Emil Schmorak, a refugee Polish Zionist.

When fully assembled, the Executive, in addition to the Jerusalem trio, comprised Professor Selig Brodetsky, who had come down from Leeds, where he taught at the university; Berl Locker, the Po'alei Zion leader; Dr. Nahum Goldmann; Lavy Bakstansky and Ivor (Joseph Isaac) Linton, the chief secretaries; and Weizmann's two advisers, Mrs. Blanche Dugdale, Lord Balfour's niece, and Professor Lewis Namier of Manchester University. I was there by invitation, not being a member of the Executive.

It was a businesslike conference, sparing of rhetoric and precise in substance, and it went off like clockwork, with no untoward diversions. The main decision was to prepare a memorandum for the British Government, setting forth the Jewish Agency's position on immediate and long-range problems. It appeared that, owing to the slow progress of the Allied military campaign in Italy and, especially, because Arab threats and protests were gathering volume and momentum, Zionist prospects seemed to be in for a long, hard struggle.

When given the floor, I suggested that our Emergency Committee in New York be asked to help in preparing the memorandum, as we had staff experts and a great deal of material that might be useful. I reported that the feeling of the Zionist leadership in America was that the time had come to press the Zionist case. The American presidential elections were approaching and the Jewish vote might determine the balance in many communities. I added that I had come armed with many letters of recommendation and that, since my arrival a few days earlier, I had arranged to meet with various religious leaders—the Chief Rabbi, Dr. Joseph H. Hertz, the Archbishop of Canterbury, Dr. Geoffrey Fisher, and heads of the Council of Christians and Jews. I had already seen a senior official of the Ministry of Information, a Mr. Williams, who headed its Religious Affairs Department, and had discussed Palestine with him.

It was a delight to watch Weizmann's agile conduct of the meeting. He looked much better than when I had last seen him in New York some eighteen months earlier. I made a diary note at the time, which may be worth quoting:

> Here, in the midst of his colleagues, presiding at a meeting of the World Zionist Executive, Weizmann is in his element and at his best. Without the slightest appearance of intrusion, he peppers the discussions with keen wit, guides them with subtle skill and holds them in check with practical sagacity. With a delicately turned phrase he devastates a ponderous argument. His gift for understatement has a deadly effect. With a simple homely idiom he routs an opponent. He quotes his reply to a British statesman who had offered his assurance that the Jewish claims to Palestine would be dealt with after the War.
>
> "After the War," said Dr. Weizmann to him, "there will be a long queue of applicants, and we do not know what priority the Jewish people will get."

A week after my arrival, I saw Dr. Joseph H. Hertz, Chief Rabbi of the United Hebrew Congregations of the British Empire. This was my first meeting with the Jewish Theological Seminary's senior rabbinical graduate, who had formerly occupied distinguished Orthodox pulpits in Johannesburg, South Africa, and in New York.

I found him to be remarkably vigorous for a man of seventy. Although he did not believe in "religious flirtations," he was interested in our (American) National Conference of Christians and Jews. Asked about the Archbishop of Canterbury's position on Zionism, Hertz said that Dr. Geoffrey Fisher "had not declared himself." Hertz took his line from Weizmann and preferred not to interfere in such matters. Not being bound by local protocol, I felt it would do no harm if I broached these matters with the Archbishop when we met.

The following day, I attended Sabbath services at the Great Synagogue in Duke's Place. This historic house of worship had been devastated by Hitler's blitz and services were therefore held in temporary premises on the site. A plaque had been erected to commemorate the original structure, dating from 1692, and the consecration of a temporary building on November 7, 1943. This made a deep impression on me, since the portion for that week was *Terumah*, which deals with the construction of the Tabernacle. After the conclusion of the Torah reading, the rabbi, in his Prayer for the Royal Family, added a sentence (in Hebrew) from the liturgy of the

High Holy Days: "May it be God's will that their houses shall not become their graves."

Immediately after that weekend, I embarked on a long series of meetings with British political figures and also addressed a number of public and private gatherings.

One of my first engagements was an interview with a Mr. Hochler, the administrative head of UNRRA, who referred to the difficulty in securing entry into Palestine for Jewish refugees. He had no knowledge of U.S. Government pressure on the British to modify their current unrelenting policy, but assured me that UNRRA would finance the maintenance of refugees wherever they could be saved. I raised two specifically Jewish concerns, the first regarding diet and the second dealing with religious worship. *Kasher* food could be ordered in Great Britain or the United States, I pointed out, while it should be possible to construct mobile synagogues for the use of Jewish DPs. Mr. Hochler promised to investigate these matters.

The same evening, I attended a mass meeting called by the National Committee for Rescue from Nazi Terror, which took place at Central Hall, Westminster. A sprinkling of non-Jews was in the audience. The Archbishop of York expressed his feelings in no uncertain terms. "Never in history," he said, "have such diabolical crimes been committed and on so unprecedented a scale." Allied bombing of German cities, with all the casualties and destruction involved, was justified because it would hasten the liberation of millions of enslaved people. "We must let the Germans know what crimes are being committed in their name," he went on. "I am not able to draw a distinction between Nazis and the German people. These crimes are not committed by a few but by thousands, and they are known by many more [Germans]." It was not good enough to plead that resistance was impossible under the Gestapo: among the occupied nations there were many who were not deterred on that account. The Archbishop was convinced that British soldiers would never have committed such crimes and he pledged his support, as a Christian, for "this crusade to rescue these people as soon as possible."

The Chief Rabbi, Dr. Hertz, pointed out that the average Britisher, lacking visual evidence of the atrocities, simply could not believe that such things were possible. The press must therefore do much more to publicize the facts.

Hannan Swaffer, the eminent writer, brought in the issue of Palestine. British Government censors had been at pains to conceal Palestinian and Jewish contributions to the war effort, he affirmed. All press references to the twelve Jewish batallions that had fought their way from El Alamein to Italy had been deleted, for fear of offending the Arabs. "We have had to buy every Arab in this war," he charged. "Not one came to our side, whereas the Jews are naturally our allies. How long are we to be afraid of offending the Arabs?" It was an apposite question, all the more so when posed by a non-Jew.

The statements made at that meeting were very much in my mind when I saw Sir Herbert Emerson of the Intergovernmental Committee on the following day. He proved to be remarkably naïve, believing that fifty percent of the Jewish refugees would wish to return to their homelands. Palestine, he claimed, was no solution to the problem "because of the worldwide Muslim attitude." I then asked him, "What have *they* done for England in this war? Why are their leaders in prison?—Because they sided with the enemy!" He could offer no reply.

One week later, I left London for a short fund-raising tour of the provincial centers. Accompanying me on the train to the north of England was Bernard Cherrick of the JNF head office. A very fine type of Jew, he had served in the rabbinate for a time, but was skeptical about the Anglo-Jewish "ministry" and its communal status. After making his Aliyah three years later, Cherrick devoted his energies to the Hebrew University of Jerusalem, of which he is today vice-president.

My first port of call was Liverpool, which had (and still has) an excellent Zionist and fund-raising record. The devastation there was even worse than in London, especially in the city center and near the docks that provided Great Britain's main lifeline to America and the Atlantic convoys. When I arrived, the city was in chaos and supplies of gas and electricity had been disrupted. My youngest brother, Morris, had served as rabbi to the small Liberal (Reform) congregation in Liverpool at one time. While there, I took the opportunity of visiting the splendid Anglican cathedral, which had escaped the bombing. In spite of the blackout, about 400 people came to the JPA meeting I addressed in the evening—an excellent response under the circumstances. Several U.S. Jewish servicemen stationed in the area also attended this midweek function at the Greenbank Drive Synagogue, where Bernard Cherrick, who had grown up on Merseyside, was the other speaker.

From Liverpool I went on to Manchester, which had a much larger Jewish population, second only to London's. I met the Lord Mayor, a Labor man, who told me that he attended more Jewish than non-Jewish functions. About 300 people came to the JPA luncheon at which I spoke. Before leaving, I had an interview with a Mr. Crozier of *The Manchester Guardian* and we discussed Palestine, UNRRA, the American scene, and the effects of war on religion.

My third provincial meeting was further south, in Birmingham.

One of the main motivations that prompted me to seek the views of some of Great Britain's war leaders on their Government's policy toward our Zionist aims was the recognition, then already becoming widespread, that the United States was destined to play a crucial part in determining the outcome of the war—a conflict that had turned out to be much more difficult (and precarious) for the Allies than had seemed at the outset. American Zionists were considered in British official circles to be of some importance in the formulation of U.S. attitudes toward Great Britain. I intended, in my interviews, to refer to the conjuncture of affairs and to acquaint British VIPs with the views of a major segment of American Jewry.

The recent publication of British state papers by various independent historians has shed light on Whitehall callousness toward the fate of European Jewry in the final stages of World War II. At that time, of course, Jewish and Zionist leaders had only vague presentiments of what British policymakers were about.

Unlike most of his colleagues, Prime Minister Winston Churchill was well disposed toward Zionism and was concerned to save the remnant of Hitler's Jewish victims. At every turn, however, his directives appear to have been blocked by the machinations of senior officials and underlings. During my stay in Great Britain, Churchill was away at Marrakesh, in Morocco, recuperating from an illness, but I met every other available Government minister.

In my talk with Foreign Secretary Anthony Eden on March 13, I stated that not only American Jewry but American public opinion in general would react favorably to an annulment of the inhibiting clauses of the 1939 White Paper and to the reconstitution of Palestine as a Jewish commonwealth after the war.

Anthony Eden (later, Lord Avon) was a suave, handsome man of aristocratic lineage and the traditional public school and "Oxbridge" background, well versed in the arts of diplomacy and possessed of a smooth manner. Our interview had been arranged by the American ambassador, John G. Winant, who accompanied me and remained throughout the conversation, which lasted nearly an hour. I began by mentioning the activities of the Jewish Section of the British War Relief Society, and Eden expressed gratitude for our work.

Turning to political matters, I told the Foreign Secretary that the Zionists in America, which meant practically the whole of the Jewish community, had assumed the arduous duty of building up an amicable relationship between the U.S. and Great Britain. I dwelt on the pro-Zionist sympathy among American Christians in every walk of life and the friendly trend in the U.S. Congress. He listened politely to my inquiries as to what chance there was of the Jewish people securing a state in Palestine after the end of the war, but he remained noncommittal. When I asked bluntly what his attitude was, Eden parried the question by saying that Dr. Weizmann knew where he stood.

"I have spoken often to Dr. Weizmann," I said, "but I *don't* think he knows where you stand."

There was a short pause, but Eden did not reply. Instead, when I remarked that we were certain of Mr. Churchill's attitude, he answered, "You know that the Prime Minister is your friend. Weizmann comes to see him, and he talks to us and turns us inside out."

Incidentally, that value judgment was corroborated by one of Churchill's close friends and collaborators, Sir Robert (later, Lord) Boothby, who recorded the Prime Minister's response on one occasion during World War II, when he heard that Dr. Weizmann wanted to see him. "I cannot always see Weizmann when he needs me," Churchill stated. "He is my conscience and the last time I saw him, I spent three sleepless nights."

My talk with Anthony Eden ranged over many subjects. I described the situation in Poland and Rumania, and the grievous position of the Jewish communities there, at which he was visibly shocked. I touched upon the Lowdermilk Plan.* At one point he asked whether Palestine was large enough, and he spoke about the Arabs, to which I retorted that they had received nineteen-twentieths of what they had

---

*A scheme devised by Walter Clay Lowdermilk, an American soil-conservation expert, for irrigation of the Negev through a Jordan Valley Authority.

asked for. "Yes, but what will happen to the 300,000 [sic] Arabs in Palestine?" he insisted. Their position, I said, was better than ever. When Eden pointed out that 30,000 immigration certificates remained unused and were still available, I asked whether he would allow 100,000 Jews to perish if they could still be rescued from Europe after the available certificates had been used up. He replied that "a way would be found."

Eden then went on to speak about an Arab federation and, turning to Ambassador Winant, he said that they had tried to find a formula that would satisfy both sides, but that it had not come off. In the ensuing exchange, he asked Mr. Winant whether America would like to take over the Mandate, but the ambassador merely smiled and made no reply.

On the way out, Eden asked me how Russia stood. I was startled that he should have addressed that question to me, and I said so, but ventured a guess that the USSR would go along with any solution adopted by Great Britain and the United States. Before we parted, he put his arm around me and said that "everything would be fine." He was the epitome of politeness, if not of sincerity. Afterwards, John Winant, who had remained behind for a few moments, told me that Eden was consistent in avoiding commitments he felt Great Britain could not honor, and that he had said as much to him.

Clement Attlee, the Deputy Prime Minister, whom I met on the following day, was a different proposition altogether. Though a Labor leader and longtime Socialist, he was more the Fabian Society intellectual than the "horny-handed son of toil." Reticent to the point of coldness, he nevertheless proved to be more sympathetic and genial than I had expected.

When talking to Attlee and the other British statesmen, I had no hesitation in using the *shem ha-meforash* of the "Jewish State," and in asking for their views about its realization. They were cognizant of the fact that American Jews were playing an important part in the American war effort and were destined to play a significant role in postwar discussions.

Speaking of the White Paper, Attlee said that it could not be changed unless there was a new election, as some members of the Cabinet and of Parliament had voted for it. When I asked him whether I could say that he understood the Jewish problem and was trying to find a solution consonant with our thinking, he answered in the affirmative. Nevertheless, I left with the feeling that he would prove a hard nut to crack when official parleys began in earnest.

My schedule for March 14 included meetings with two other Laborites, Ernest Bevin and Herbert Morrison. Bevin, the trade-union leader, then Minister of Labor and National Service, was already a leading figure in the War Cabinet. A beefy-looking man of squat build and broad shoulders on which his head sat squarely, "Ernie" Bevin wore a habitually grim expression, the dourness of which was heightened by pursed lips. I found him somewhat perplexing and hard to figure out. He spoke quite openly from the first, and wanted to know why the Jews were always pressing for a solution of their own problems to the exclusion of general ones.

"I was in Whitechapel when the Passfield White Paper came out," Bevin said. "If those people could have laid hands on [Lord] Passfield, they'd have torn him limb from limb. You'd have thought there were no other problems in the world."

This observation came to my mind a year or two later, when he delivered himself of his notorious remark that the Jews "always push to the head of the queue."

Bevin minced no words, asking why the Jews insisted on Palestine. Was it big enough, and why should consideration not be given to other places? He described himself as an internationalist and said that Palestine would have to fit into the international picture. He also raised the question of dual loyalty, and I told him that Justice Brandeis had been both a great American and a great Zionist, and that Dr. Weizmann had perhaps done more for Great Britain than many eminent Englishmen. He concurred with these personal evaluations. At the same time, however, he was sorry that the Balfour Declaration had not been "settled" in World War I and would like to "settle" the question now. "I'll be damned if I'll allow British blood to be shed for either Jew or Arab," Bevin said heatedly. When I pressed him for his attitude toward a Jewish State, he replied forthrightly that he could not promise anything he was unable to carry out.

"Nevertheless, if I'm in office when the time comes," he said, "I'll see to it that justice is done to the Jewish people." Then, after a brief pause, he added, "*and* to the Arabs." This was not the time to issue declarations that might cause trouble, he concluded, while admitting that Zionism was "a good thing" because it gave the Jews status.

Thus, some of Ernest Bevin's later complexes were already apparent. His lack of sympathy for, or even understanding of, what Palestine meant to the Jewish people was obvious. He had no real appreciation of Zionist hopes and aspirations.

Herbert Morrison, the Home Secretary, was friendly and outgoing. He spoke of his visit to Palestine before the war and said that he had been impressed by the "new type of Jew" he found there. A number of Government ministers had been opposed to the 1939 White Paper, he went on, but it would be wrong to say that the policy was defunct. When I asked what would happen after the 30,000 certificates were used up, he said that a way would be found for a provisional solution.

One week earlier, I had had a brief interview with Sir Stafford Cripps, the Minister of Aircraft Production. He impressed me as a man of austere convictions, which accorded with his appearance. Though not antagonistic, he took an ambivalent stance, evidently influenced by the difficulties of the Arab problem. One could not impose a decision on a population that opposed them, he said. Moreover, he opined, the Christian community of Palestine had to be considered, as well as the Arabs and the Jews. Cripps himself was thinking in terms of a trilateral solution. A pious Christian Socialist, he was especially concerned with the moral aspect of postwar developments and pinned his hopes on some organization for world peace.

By far the most amicable among the bevy of statesmen whom I met was Leopold Amery, the veteran Conservative Party leader, who had long been one of Weizmann's intimate friends in the orbit of British public life. I found him to be cordial in disposition and ready to be helpful. Amery viewed Zionism from the standpoint of British interests. He indicated that there were some things he would like to say, but that his lips were sealed. The War Cabinet was constantly reviewing these questions, he said, but a statement at that particular time would make for controversy. They had been receiving cables of protest from India.

I later presented a summary of my impressions to the Zionist Executive in London. At the last Executive meeting I attended, on March 16, 1944, Weizmann stated that things were going fairly well at the upper level, but that there was a great deal of undermining by the lower echelons. He was afraid that conditions might be created which would render nugatory any decision reached at the top. There were people who were ready to sabotage official policy, as they had done over the past twenty-five years, but it was impossible to convey this to the Prime Minister. If the American Zionists could get President Roosevelt to communicate his views in his own way to Mr. Churchill, Weizmann said, it would be very useful.

I recall two public occasions during my sojourn in England when Dr. Weizmann was the guest of honor. One evening I was invited to a meeting of the Parliamentary Pro-Palestine Committee, which supported the Zionist cause, and heard Weizmann deliver an address. Those present literally hung on his every word, and I could not help feeling there was something peculiarly British—the dignity, soft-spoken manner and restraint, the charm and power of persuasion—in this Jew from Motele and Pinsk.

Another afternoon, toward the end of my visit, I was at the official inauguration of the Joint Palestine Appeal at the Grosvenor House Hotel. Simon (later, Lord) Marks presided, a short, dark-haired man with piercing eyes, who, with his brother-in-law, Israel Sieff (also later elevated to the peerage), had been brought into the Zionist movement in 1913. These two men were fervently devoted to Eretz Yisrael. Marks had been secretary to the Zionist delegation at the Versailles Peace Conference in 1919. He and Sieff built up the Marks and Spencer chain stores into a great retail merchandising empire. Simon Marks had the brusque manner of the prosperous businessman and he conducted the proceedings with great effectiveness.

There was a large and representative turnout at the informal luncheon, which raised the sum of £200,000. Chief Rabbi Hertz was the first speaker; his address was brief, pungent, and telling. I spoke after him and was followed by others. The climax came when Weizmann rose to address the gathering. It was a moving moment, as I recorded in my diary:

> As he rises to speak, there is tense expectancy. Most unoratorical of speakers, handicapped by a weak voice, he holds his audience by the simplicity and incisiveness of his speech. He holds his audience as much by what he is as by what he says. He seems more resolute and more demanding than the Weizmann of former years. The affliction of his people is on his face, as in his heart.

Further Wartime Encounters

Zionist affairs were not my only preoccupation during those weeks. One day I went to see General Dwight D. Eisenhower, whose appointment as Supreme Allied

Commander for the invasion of Europe had been announced that month. He was engrossed in plans and preparations for the eventual landing when I was received at his headquarters "somewhere in England." The U. S. ambassador, John G. Winant, was instrumental in arranging the interview.

I found General Eisenhower ensconced in modest quarters. He had been sipping a cup of tea when I was shown into his office, and I remarked how quickly he seemed to have assimilated British ways. He said that he worked hard into the late hours and found a cup of tea refreshing at this time of the day. "Ike" certainly gave the impression of being at the height of his powers.

Telling him about my work with British War Relief and the National Conference of Christians and Jews, I said that the latter had asked me to ascertain from him whether he was in favor of extending to this theater of war some of the activities in which the Conference was engaged in the United States. I went on to explain the spiritual issues of the struggle, as I saw them.

Eisenhower was restless and got up, pacing to and fro as he answered. "It happens that the closer men get to the battlefront, the less they know what they are fighting for," he said. "The moral factor is important. Cromwell's men went into battle singing hymns. It's not my business to make speeches. The general who talks too much loses his case. But my message is this: 'The spirit of unity among our troops, the spirit of unity at home, the spirit of unity between the home front and the battlefront—that's what we want.' So go ahead and talk to General Lee about how to work it out. It has my approval."

I commented: "This is one war about which the clergy can get enthusiastic."

Our conversation left me with the feeling that Eisenhower had intelligence, spirit, and physical power. I took up with General Lee and his staff the proposal Eisenhower had approved—interfaith teams of clergymen organizing programs for the armed forces—and it was put into effect later that year in the European Theater of Operations.

This wartime meeting led to further contacts years later, when Eisenhower became President of the United States.

Another leader, of a markedly different kind, whom I went to see in London was the Roman Catholic Archbishop of Westminster, Cardinal Griffin. The U.S. Chief of Army Chaplains was with him when I called. I talked about the (American) National Conference of Christians and Jews and its Committee on Religious Organizations, and touched upon the possibility of a British equivalent, suggesting that it would be worthwhile sending chaplaincy trios around the camps in Britain.

When I turned to the refugee problem and hinted that Palestine could provide the major solution to its Jewish aspect, the Catholic leader quickly shied away and said, "I must not interfere in political matters. If I do, I may lose my position." Answering my question as to interfaith relations in the United Kingdom, he said, "We're all at peace here."

Cardinal Griffin struck me as a person who felt rather insecure, but that might have been because he had assumed office only a short while previously and was therefore unwilling to undertake any risky commitments. The Catholics in Great

Britain did not appear to have the same degree of influence which they enjoyed in the United States.

On a parting note, when he wanted to know the nature of my status as president of the Synagogue Council of America, I replied, much to his amusement, that I was "a sort of Jewish archbishop with a tenure limited to two years."

An English divine of variant (Protestant) faith and disposition upon whom I called was the Dean of St. Paul's, Dr. W. R. Matthews. I had written him from the States, expressing sympathy when the Cathedral was bombed during the blitz. One afternoon, after an earlier meeting of the Zionist Executive, I took a taxi and went to "the City" to inspect the damage. It was considerable. Blocks around St. Paul's had been completely razed, leaving frightful gaps.

Dr. Matthews, who served with the Liberal (Reform) Jewish community's Rabbi Israel Mattuck as co-chairman of the British Council of Christians and Jews, said that he favored Zionism and thought the Jewish National Home would do for Jews throughout the world what a British embassy did for Britons abroad—give them status. Having invited me to address the executive of the CCJ while I was staying in London, he asked if there was anything he could do for me.

"With the coffers of the Chase National Bank, the physical protection of the U.S. Army and your spiritual protection," I responded, "I'm all set."

Dr. Geoffrey Fisher, the Anglican Archbishop of Canterbury, whom I met at the House of Lords, proved to be a man of liberal views and of great worldly as well as spiritual wisdom. He believed that the British Government could do much more for Jewish refugees and expressed opposition to the Palestine White Paper. While reluctant to take a public stand on the Mandate's transformation into a Jewish commonwealth after the war, he personally favored such a development and promised to use his influence, wherever possible, to promote this solution. "Anti-Semitism," he declared, "is primitive barbarism."

On February 21, a week after my arrival in Great Britain, the Reverend W. W. Simpson, secretary of the British Council of Christians and Jews, arranged a press conference to coincide with the observance of Brotherhood Week in the United States, where it had originated. Portions of our addresses at this press conference were cabled to the National Conference of Christians and Jews in the U.S. We urged the establishment of an International Conference of Christians and Jews to counteract nefarious elements sowing mistrust and discord. Such an organization could also sponsor interfaith pronouncements on peace aims, expressing the common views of the great religious traditions. Victory, we believed, must bring not only self-preservation but improved standards of living for the masses, thus justifying the wartime hardships and sacrifices.

The Reverend Simpson and I were privileged to have a share in organizing the International Conference of Christians and Jews, which came into being at Oxford in 1946.

Early in March, through the courtesy of the British Ministry of Health, I undertook a two-day journey to the children's nursing home bearing my name at Porlock, near

Bristol, in southwest England. My escort, a Mr. Carr, and I went in an ambulance driven by a New Zealand girl. En route to Somerset, we halted for refreshment at a Red Cross canteen in Devizes, a town in Wiltshire, where a Jewish girl from the Bronx, a Miss Druskin, was in charge. Over tea, she told us that 800 men from the nearby armored division camp made daily use of the canteen.

As we resumed our journey to Minehead, the nearest large town to Porlock, I reflected that obtaining the gasoline needed for the round trip was itself a considerable achievement in those days of strict rationing. Indeed, as souvenirs of the austerity conditions over there, I later brought home to New York ration books with coupons for food and clothing that were issued to residents and visitors—a grim reminder of what Britons had to endure. When I first went to register with the police, who issued these booklets to visitors from overseas, there was an amusing interlude with the constable who took the application form I had filled out. A stickler for proper form, he did not like my description of myself as a "clergyman." He crossed out the term and wrote instead, "Clerk in Holy Orders."

Porlock turned out to be a quiet, pretty village, nestling in the beautiful countryside inland from the Bristol Channel, and facing the rugged coast of Wales to the north. We stayed overnight at the Anchor Hotel, right on the Channel. It was ideal country for anyone wishing to find a retreat from the hurly-burly of war. The nursing home, which the Jewish Section of the British War Relief Society had established in my honor, was located in pleasant surroundings.

Over a hundred tots, ages four to six, were accommodated there, mostly fair-haired kiddies evacuated from Plymouth, which had been the *Mayflower*'s port of departure for the New World in 1620. There was not one Jewish child among these youngsters—a circumstance that made the Jewish commitment all the more appreciated.

The children had been well rehearsed for my visit. As soon as I entered the building, they greeted me with a spirited chorus of "Yankee Doodle." I was enchanted by this visit to a tranquil corner of the embattled British Isles.

Some of the titled patrons of the British War Relief Society with whom I came in contact knew Weizmann personally, but they seemed much more familiar with his scientific achievements and prestige as a Zionist leader than with the Jewish national cause itself. His was a unique position in Anglo-Jewry, a fact of which the average Britisher was fully aware.

Having met a number of Jewish boys serving in the U.S. armed forces in various parts of Great Britain, I made a point of conveying messages from them to their families in or near New York on my return. Among these American servicemen was Dr. Martin Cherkasky, a young army doctor, whose sister, Fannie, was the wife of my younger brother, Isaac. He happened to be stationed in London and I was delighted to locate him there and to bring him regards from home. Years later, in the United States, Dr. Cherkasky rose to eminence in his profession as director of the Montefiore Hospital in New York and as one of America's foremost hospital administrators.

One particular incident connected with my wartime visit to Great Britain had repercussions worth relating here. The BBC invited me to record a talk about the Purim festival for transmission to Nazi-occupied Europe and, in the hope that it would reach Jewish ears, I recounted the story of Esther and Mordecai to my invisible radio audience. I emphasized the way in which Providence had thwarted the vengeful Haman's plan to exterminate the Jews, and Queen Esther's role in saving her people from total destruction, and concluded my talk with a prayer for speedy deliverance and with the Hebrew phrase, *Am Yisrael Ḥai!*—"Israel shall live!"

Twenty years later, in the last week of January 1964, when I was in Brussels to open the campaign of the Keren Hayesod—United Israel Appeal, of which I was world chairman, there awaited me at my hotel a letter, which tells its own story.

Brussels, 27.1.64.

Dear Dr. Goldstein,

I do not think that we have ever met face to face, although I have heard many of your addresses in various countries. But there is one speech forever engraved in my memory, the one you delivered for the BBC in February 1944, which inspired me many years later to write an article printed in *Elseviers Weekly*, the most important weekly paper in Holland.

Thinking that this article may interest you, I have just translated it into English on the spur of the moment, so please forgive any grammatical errors.

I look forward to seeing and hearing you again tomorrow evening—under happier circumstances, thank God.

Yours faithfully,
R. Chanania

Twice Purim

Brussels
February 1944

It happened in the gloomy days of the German occupation, in that nerve-consuming war which seemed to have no end. . . .

I am alone in my dreary hiding place one chilly, gray February morning. It is cold, since the precious coal for my little stove has to be saved for the long hours of the winter evening.

Ten o'clock—time to listen in to the banned radio broadcast from London. Maybe there will be some news, anything that will give hope and strength to go on living in these times of misery and fear. Over the air, from across the Channel, comes the voice of the announcer in London: "In a few moments, the Reverend Dr. Israel Goldstein will speak to you about the Feast of Esther." It comes as a shock—Purim, today must be Purim! In my day-to-day existence I have forgotten that there are still festivals to be celebrated, traditions to be remembered.

Childhood memories rise before me. As in a dream, I see our whole family seated around the table, listening to my father as he reads the *Megillah*, the Scroll of Esther. I hear once more the Hebrew text relating in sing-song fashion how Ahasuerus, the king of Persia, during a sleepless night, had the royal chronicles read to him and discovered to his surprise that among his subjects there was a certain man who had rendered a great service to the king without asking for a reward. Ahasuerus then summoned this man, Mordecai the Jew, and became acquainted with his beautiful ward, Esther, who was chosen to be the king's wife. Esther succeeded in outwitting Haman, the Prime Minister, who sought to annihilate the Jewish people, and so it was that she rescued her kinfolk from certain death. . . . I awake from my reverie just as Dr. Goldstein is ending his talk with the words, *"Am Yisrael Ḥai!*—Israel shall live!"

Israel shall live? All I know is the Nazi manhunt—dragging Jews from their hiding places, rounding them up in the street; all I know today is the *Sammellager* [concentration camp]—Westerbork, Malines, Drancy—and the *Vernichtungslager* [death camp]—Bergen-Belsen, Auschwitz, Majdanek. Hitler-Haman, reigning over the major part of Europe, carries on with his process of extermination. Yet there *is* still a Free World, there *are* still Jews who celebrate Purim. Can there be grounds for hope? That would require a miracle, and miracles are so rare in our time; it is so difficult to preserve one's faith. . . .

Seven years have gone by and, in the home of Dr. Michael Amir, first Ambassador of the young State of Israel to the Benelux countries, Purim is being celebrated. Festive tables, beautifully decorated with the first spring flowers, are illuminated by candles burning in tall, antique candelabra. Wine sparkles in raised glasses as cheerful, laughing people exchange toasts with *"Le-Ḥayyim!"*

And suddenly, in my mind's eye, I am back in my dreary little hiding place, shivering with cold, as I press my ear to the radio and listen to that hope-inspiring voice from London. . . . The Miracle *did* take place.

R. Chanania

[Published in *Elseviers Weekly,* Amsterdam, March 21, 1959]

Needless to say, I was deeply moved by the knowledge that, in some small way, my words had been a source of comfort and encouragement to one of my people who survived the Nazi Holocaust. As recently as March 3, 1980, I deemed it appropriate to tell this story, in the course of an address delivered in my capacity of honorary chairman, at the sixtieth jubilee celebration of the Keren Hayesod in Antwerp.

Another incident during that crowded six-week stay had a somewhat ironical climax. One morning, I had a call from Rabbi Harold Reinhart, minister of the West London Synagogue of British Jews. His congregation, the first in England to espouse Reform, was located on Upper Berkeley Street, near Marble Arch in the West End, and one of its earlier distinguished incumbents had been the Reverend Morris Joseph. Though dubbed "Reform," it was actually Conservative Reform in comparison with the Liberal or Progressive synagogue. The senior rabbi of the latter was Rabbi Israel Mattuck, with whom the Reverend Maurice Perlzweig, first chairman of the World Jewish Congress (British Section), had been associated until he left for New York in 1942.

Reinhart, an American by birth, had served as a Reform rabbi in the United States and was a notorious anti-Zionist. His telephone call to so notorious a Zionist as myself came as a surprise, especially when he invited me to occupy his pulpit on the following Sabbath.

"You know, of course, that I intend to preach a Zionist sermon?" I cautioned.

"I don't care what you preach about," he replied in a solemn voice, "as long as your sermon doesn't exceed twenty minutes."

I accepted his invitation. The temptation of preaching from an anti-Zionist pulpit was one that could not be resisted. Since I had derived little comfort from meeting with Clement Attlee, Ernest Bevin, and several other members of the War Cabinet, my address was less than complimentary to His Majesty's Government.

Judging from the response at the end of the service, Rabbi Reinhart's flock appeared to have enjoyed the Zionist sermon. One leading congregant, I think he was a vice-president, indicated his pleasure by a poke in my ribs, adding in a far from sotto voce tone, "*Yasher ko'ah*—well done! You gave it to them good and proper!"

Apart from the Zionist Executive sessions I attended during my time in London, I also met with a number of leading Jewish personalities on other occasions. Such figures included Simon Marks, Barnett Janner, Isaac and Edith Wolfson, and Eva, Marchioness of Reading, the daughter of Sir Alfred Mond (first Lord Melchett), a great Jew and Zionist supporter. Though raised as a Christian, she had reverted to Judaism in the late 1930s and became an ardent Zionist. Lady Reading served later as chairman of the British Section of the World Jewish Congress.

I found opportunities for talks with Dr. Weizmann outside 77 Great Russell Street as well. He and his wife had their temporary London home at the Dorchester Hotel, only a couple of blocks from where I was staying on Park Lane. I strolled over for a cup of tea one afternoon and found him in a pensive, almost lugubrious mood. He was deeply distressed by some untoward developments—Ben-Gurion had resigned from the Zionist Executive and a rift within the movement threatened to shatter a desperately needed unity and harmony. Weizmann felt like giving up the helm altogether and devoting his time to scientific research, but we all persuaded him not to do so, pointing out that his withdrawal at such a time would be catastrophic for World Jewry. He said he felt that he was a "prisoner of war" who had to suffer for the sake of his people.

"It may be unduly bold of me, a younger man, to say it," I told Weizmann, "but you have no right as a Zionist to resign. It would be a major calamity for Zionism, especially at this juncture. You feel pessimistic, but let Churchill say the word you want to hear and everything will be different, and other things will seem of secondary importance. Ben-Gurion's resignation would be a blow, but if he resigns it will not be a world-shaking event. *Your* resignation will give aid and comfort to our enemies. You have no right to do it. We've been through terrible years," I added, "and you are entitled to the *nakhes* [personal satisfaction] of leading us to better times."

As he drew on the long cigarette holder in that well-appointed hotel sitting room, Weizmann seemed a melancholy figure. Still tormented by the personal misfortune Vera and he had sustained two years earlier, when their younger son, Michael, an

RAF flight lieutenant, died in aerial combat over the English Channel, he was also obsessed by the *Sho'ah* in Europe. Yet, as I noted at the time, even his sadness was serene and restrained.

Weizmann agreed to my proposal that representative American Zionists be coopted to the London and Jerusalem sections of the Executive, since it was likely that Washington would become a significant factor in future political decisions. Now that American Zionists were numerically the foremost group, he foresaw that they would take control at the first postwar Zionist Congress.

Our talk ranged over the general prospects of the world Jewish situation, postwar conditions for British Jewry and the whole gamut of the Jewish problem. He seemed most interested in gaining some insight into the American personalities with whom he was in diplomatic touch and was sure that the views of important Americans would influence the general picture. I left with the impression that Weizmann was oversanguine in his assessment of how far leading figures in the British Government could be counted upon to adopt a favorable Zionist policy after the war.

It transpired, of course, after the tumult and the shouting had died down, that his optimism had not been warranted nor his confidence in certain people justified. One of Weizmann's first greetings to me when I arrived in London had reflected his sense of apprehension at the stiffening American Zionist attitude toward President Roosevelt and his equivocal policies on the Jewish National Home issue. Weizmann was most perturbed by what he considered to be unnecessary "needling" of the United States Administration by the leaders of the American Zionist movement then functioning through the Emergency Council.

This process of needling, the refusal to be brushed aside with affable and often hollow assurances by our supposed friends in official Washington, represented quite a revolution in American Zionism. The masses felt that Dr. Abba Hillel Silver's advent to leadership, and the line he advocated and pursued, added a positive element that increased the chances of our achieving some fair measure of our aspirations. We realized that time was running out and that we had to obtain firm pledges during the war period, failing which they might never be forthcoming again.

Weizmann's temperament was uncongenial to needling tactics. As an illustration of his attitude, I remember that in our first talk after my arrival in England he made use of the (Yiddish) expression "We must be careful not to call out the bear from his lair!" To me, this remark spoke volumes.

Needling, the organization of mass pressure, characterized developments in American Zionism at the time. Jewish communities in major cities of the United States were being mobilized to influence their representatives in Congress. It was a battle for public opinion, in the hope of attaining success where diplomatic overtures to indifferent statesmen might not succeed. To many of us, this was legitimate use of the democratic process. I am convinced that the more forthright policy paid off. Yet to Weizmann, apparently, it was something new, undignified, and possibly even fraught with danger.

Abba Hillel Silver personified the growing militant tendency in American Zionism, which was to find strong expression at the 22nd World Zionist Congress in

Basle, almost three years later, in December 1946. Weizmann had rightly foreseen that American Zionists would assume a dominant role in the deliberations of the first postwar Congress. Their emergence as exponents of a more militant policy, to which he was opposed, led to his own removal from the presidency of the World Zionist Organization.

The seeds of that activism were born of the Jewish revulsion against the world's callous apathy toward Nazi genocide, and these seeds began to germinate in the program of the American Zionist Emergency Council under Dr. Silver's leadership. As previously indicated, a rift developed between Silver and Wise over the credibility of the promises made by President Roosevelt. Silver accused Wise of being "taken in" by Roosevelt, and Wise, who found it difficult to adjust himself to the new militancy, yielded the leadership to Dr. Silver.

Once Harry Truman entered the White House, a significant change occurred. If, at first, Truman expressed resentment against the Zionist leaders for pushing him too much, he later came to understand Jewish issues, to adopt a positive policy, and to stick to his guns.

I have already mentioned the mass meeting held at Carnegie Hall in 1938 to protest the Munich Agreement, which resulted in the first dismemberment of Czechoslovakia. In May 1943, while President Eduard Beneš was staying at the Waldorf-Astoria Hotel in New York, I wrote him a letter in which I referred to my "Word of Comfort to Czechoslovakians," one of the speeches made at Carnegie Hall, and sent him a copy of that address. "Now you are here," I said, "the resurgence of your country and your people seems assured."

Toward the end of my sojourn in England, I had a stimulating interview with President Beneš, then an exile in London. He foresaw the likelihood of vested interests manipulating popular anti-Semitism in countries such as Poland and Rumania, but discounted this possibility as far as the Czechs were concerned, although wartime Nazi policies might encourage racial animosities among the Slovaks. The emergence of a Jewish commonwealth in Palestine would, he believed, lend moral strength to the Jewish position in other countries. Those Jews who feared "dual loyalty" accusations were themselves guilty of a narrow and backward approach to the issue of Jewish national rights, he affirmed.

Beneš was convinced that there would be a favorable outcome to the Zionist struggle for Jewish self-determination and that a decision in principle would be taken by the Western Powers before the war ended. It was his considered opinion that the USSR would not oppose Zionist aspirations in Palestine. Speaking personally, the Czech statesman reaffirmed his friendship for the Jewish people, a friendship he had expressed publicly on many occasions.

My wartime stay in England lasted longer than I had planned, although the six weeks passed quickly enough in a crowded schedule of activities. I had booked accommodations for a much shorter period, but the letter given me by Lord Halifax worked like a charm, securing an extended use of my hotel room.

At a press conference held at 77 Great Russell Street on March 16, 1944, I took the opportunity of thanking all who had made my stay in Great Britain "enlightening and perhaps not unhelpful." I also referred to matters concerning British War Relief, interfaith relations, and Zionism. Noting the opposition of President Roosevelt and the U.S. Administration to the 1939 White Paper, I expressed my firm view that "the doors of Palestine should be open to as many Jews as knock for admission and can be absorbed in the country," as guaranteed by the Balfour Declaration and League of Nations Mandate. "Under Jewish enterprise," I stated, "Palestine can accommodate eventually a population of two million Jews without displacing a single Arab now living there." Resettlement of Jewish refugees in Palestine should form part of an eventual UN Refugee Resettlement Program. I also mentioned my meetings with U.S. Ambassador Winant, Czechoslovakia's President Beneš, Anthony Eden, Clement Attlee, Ernest Bevin, Leopold Amery, Herbert Morrison, Sir Stafford Cripps, and Sir Herbert Emerson. Finally, I expressed my profound faith in an Allied victory and in Anglo-American understanding and cooperation.

Eventually, in the latter half of March, I made my departure. On the way to Prestwick airport, in the west of Scotland, I met Rabbi Kopul Rosen in Glasgow. An impressive personality, he was for a time president of the British Mizraḥi and later the founder and principal of Carmel College, a Jewish "public school" run on Eton-and-Harrow lines near Oxford. I also visited Isaac Wolfson's mother, Mrs. Necha Wolfson, who lived in a beautiful home in Ayrshire, near the sea. A remarkable Jewish matriarch, she had raised eleven children—eight daughters and three sons. She possessed all the endearing traits of an *eshet ḥayil*, and her philanthropy and good works were boundless.

Our flight home was not without dramatic suspense. As the Air Transport Command plane was leaving Newfoundland, we noticed sparks on the starboard (right-hand) side of our aircraft. Fifteen minutes later, the pilot decided to return, but after twice circling over the airfield he went on again, as conditions were apparently unsuitable for landing.

Someone near the window, looking out, saw that the underside of the aircraft was red-hot. My fellow passengers, all pilots and aircrews returning to the United States in order to ferry American planes to England, broke out in song. As the only civilian aboard, I was surprised at my own calmness. I calculated that, if the aircraft were to blow up, the end would come almost instantaneously. "My competent wife will be able to manage," I thought to myself, "Avram and Vivian are no longer children. They can fend for themselves. And to end one's life on a mission for one's people is not a bad way to go."

Thus musing, I was alerted to the fact that the pilot had managed to extinguish the fire, and had announced that he would try to land in St. John's, Newfoundland. Fog was closing in, however, and it was hilly terrain, so we made for Boston, which also proved to be fogbound. Finally, our plane flew on to Washington, D.C., and landed safely there.

Ha-Gomel, the traditional thanksgiving benediction, was in my heart as we taxied along the runway toward the terminal.

The first body to which I reported on my mission to Great Britain was the American Zionist Emergency Council. This report may have played some part in helping Wise, Silver, Lipsky, and the other leaders of the AZEC to formulate policies, methods, and approaches. I also brought a message from Dr. Weizmann to the Jews of the United States, urging them to lend the weight of their support to the campaign for a Jewish commonwealth in Eretz Yisrael. At a Madison Square Garden rally in New York, I spoke about my recent visit to Great Britain and also presented a report to the Synagogue Council of America, dwelling on my contacts with religious personalities in England.

Alluding soon afterwards (in the March 31, 1944, issue of *The New Palestine*) to my high-level meetings in London, I stressed the clear feeling in British official circles that "a definitive solution of the Palestine problem should wait until the end of the European war." This view could not be accepted passively by the Zionist movement. "The postwar period will have its special problems and difficulties," I affirmed, "especially in the Near and Middle East. . . . One is not impressed by the argument that other problems, too, will await their solution until after the war. Exactly the contrary is the case. We see permanent commitments in the process of being made every day. Why must the agony of the Jewish people be prolonged? England, no doubt, can afford to wait. The Jews, alas, cannot."

A Peaceful Interlude

To come back to my family and to my congregation was always, for me, a welcome respite. By this time, our two children were already married and had embarked on fruitful careers in their respective fields.

Avram, our firstborn, had entered Harvard in 1936 and had graduated *magna cum laude* in 1940. Having been awarded his doctorate at the Harvard Medical School in 1943, he served in the U.S. Army Medical Corps during World War II. His first appointment, in 1946, was as an instructor in the Harvard Medical School, where he taught pharmacology.

Avram's first marriage, on September 5, 1940, was to Naomi Friedman of Brooklyn, who had graduated from Brooklyn College and Columbia and who later obtained her Ph.D. at Boston University. Our daughter-in-law's promising career ended tragically, however, with her death in an automobile accident on July 2, 1946. Two years later, her book, *The Roots of Prejudice against the Negro in the United States*, was published by Boston University Press.

On August 29, 1947, Avram married Dora Benedict of Cohasset, Massachusetts, a graduate of the Harvard Medical School, who was awarded her doctorate there in 1949. Avram had served as one of her instructors. Their children are Margaret, Daniel, Joshua and Michael.

Our daughter, Vivian, had graduated from Swarthmore College and Upstate Medical School in Syracuse, N.Y. She was subsequently awarded her doctorate in psychology, at Radcliffe College, in 1948. On June 8, 1942, Vivian married Paul

Olum, a former classmate of our son, Avram, at Harvard. Their children are Judith, Joyce and Kenneth Akiba.

Paul had graduated from Harvard *summa cum laude*, at the head of his class, in 1943. After further study at Princeton, he was awarded his doctorate in mathematics and physics, at Harvard, in 1947. During the war, he was recruited to work under Dr. Robert Oppenheimer on the Manhattan (Atomic Bomb) project at Los Alamos, New Mexico. After the war, Paul became professor of mathematics at Cornell University and head of his department there.

To run ahead of my story, I might add that in 1955 Avram moved to Stanford University, California, where he was appointed professor of pharmacology and chairman of the department. His wife, Dora, also became a professor of pharmacology in Stanford University's School of Medicine, and both of them have lectured on their respective fields of drug addiction and alcoholism in various parts of the world.

While Paul was teaching at Cornell, Vivian became adjunct associate professor of psychology there and conducted a private psychotherapy clinic for children. At the University of Texas in Austin, she later obtained another post as adjunct associate professor. Subsequently, Paul and Vivian moved to the University of Oregon, at Eugene, where he went on to become provost and she became associate professor of psychology.

Toward the end of May 1944, Congregation B'nai Jeshurun marked my twenty-fifth anniversary as rabbi. Guest speakers at the celebration were Professor Louis Finkelstein, president of the Jewish Theological Seminary, and Dr. Everett R. Clinchy, president of the National Conference of Christians and Jews. Messages of greeting were received from President Franklin D. Roosevelt, Great Britain's Chief Rabbi, Dr. J. H. Hertz, Dr. Chaim Weizmann, and Rabbi Stephen Wise.

In the early summer of that year, I paid a week-long visit to Mexico, on behalf of the ZOA and the Jewish National Fund of America. My crowded schedule, from June 27 to July 4, included meetings with a number of prominent Mexican statesmen—the Foreign Minister, the Minister of the Interior, and the Minister of Postwar Affairs. This last ministry deserved emulation by some of the larger democracies. I sought and received, to a degree, Mexican support for the Zionist program.

The Minister of the Interior was Miguel Alemán, who later became President of Mexico. He offered some interesting observations when dwelling on the role the Jewish community was playing in the economic development of the republic, stating that he favored larger Jewish immigration into Mexico, which needed manpower as badly as the United States had needed it in the previous century. He added that he wanted to keep out Nazis and Fascists.

I also called on the Archbishop of Mexico, Cardinal Luis Martinez, and told him about the work of the National Conference of Christians and Jews in the United States. I left with him a draft of the joint statement on postwar plans we were then engaged in composing.

Later that week, while lunching with Elias Sourasky, reputedly the wealthiest

Jew in Mexico, I was amused to learn how he had bought out a German bank in Mexico so as to replace its swastika emblem by a Magen David.

An interesting experience was my visit to the Mexican Indian synagogue on the outskirts of the capital. Theodore Reznikoff, chairman of the JNF in Mexico, was my guide. The leader of these mestizo *Israelitas*, a lawyer named Baltazar Ramirez, told us that the Indian "Jews" observed the Sabbath, circumcision, and *Kashrut*. They supposedly numbered about 3,000 in all, did not mingle with the immigrant Jewish population in Mexico, and claimed Spanish Marrano ancestry. Only about sixty-five *Israelitas* attended the Sabbath service to which I was escorted—fifteen men, twenty women, and thirty boys and girls. They used an Orthodox prayer book with a Spanish translation, but their services had organ accompaniment and a mixed choir. Rabbi Morris Clark, whom we met there, headed a Reform congregation in Pine Bluff, Arkansas, which was helping this community. He told me of the work he was doing among Mexican Indian "Jews" in the interior. It transpired that this sect was not recognized as Jewish by the Orthodox rabbinate. Señor Ramirez had "converted" his followers from an earlier Protestant allegiance.

It was an odd mixture of observances that Sabbath morning. The service began with *Mah Tovu*, "How goodly are thy tents, O Jacob." Selections from the *Sidrah*, the weekly Torah portion, were read, together with translations into Spanish, but the prescribed *Haftarah* reading from the Prophets was omitted. I noticed a Jewish National Fund blue and white box in the synagogue and saw their leader consulting a JNF calendar.

Invited to address them, I complimented the Indian congregation on its decorum and its interesting service. As the Portion of the Week was *Ḥukkat*, I mentioned that we were bound together as fellow Jews by many laws and statutes that had kept our people together as a distinct religious group. I urged them to teach their children more Hebrew and to join the Zionist Organization and acquire "Shekalim" in connection with the forthcoming World Zionist Congress.

The service, which lasted about an hour and a half, concluded with the priestly benediction, recited by their leader, Señor Ramirez, who flung a *tallit* over his head, like a *Kohen* blessing the congregation. This was followed by a hymn in Spanish, which he had composed, and the singing of *Hatikvah*.

That Sabbath morning in Mexico City provided an intriguing footnote to the romance of our faith in remote corners of the Dispersion.

The UN Conference at San Francisco

Toward the end of 1944, it was becoming increasingly evident that the war had entered its penultimate phase. Spirits rose high as people throughout the free world anticipated a speedy conclusion to the protracted conflict in Europe, where Allied armies were steadily overcoming the Nazi war machine.

Yet amid this general optimism, the Jewish people alone found little comfort. We knew only too well that millions of our brethren had been—and were still being—

annihilated by Hitler's fiendish cohorts. Here and there, it was possible to rescue surviving Jews by negotiating with some of the Führer's lieutenants and Axis partners, who sought to build up credit and cash against the day of reckoning, which could not be too far away. Allied warnings, in broadcasts to Europe, may have saved many lives.

Although the final convulsive struggle dragged on, it was obviously only a matter of weeks or a few months before the Third Reich would be overthrown. The death of Franklin D. Roosevelt in April 1945 came as a stunning blow. Preparations were underway to convene the founding conference of the United Nations, which Roosevelt, the leader of the victorious Allies, had been scheduled to address. The UN Charter, to replace that of the defunct League of Nations, was formulated on the basis of proposals agreed upon by representatives of the United States, the United Kingdom, the USSR, and China at Dumbarton Oaks, outside Washington, D.C., during the late summer and early fall of 1944. President Roosevelt had been associated with every stage of the preliminary discussions and the drafting of texts. His passing closed a dramatic chapter in the history of the American presidency.

The United Nations Conference, which opened in San Francisco on April 25, 1945, anticipated the end of the war. Its purpose was to formulate and adopt the basic charter of a world organization for "the maintenance of international peace and security" and for "the promotion of the economic and social advancement of all peoples." The "Big Three" talks at Yalta in February had stipulated that any country that declared war on Nazi Germany before March 1 would be entitled to representation at San Francisco. The conference remained in session for over a month. By June, the UN Charter had been promulgated.

Some forty nongovernmental organizations were also allowed to send "consultants" with the delegations. Half of this number came from the United States. Among the advisory bodies were the American Jewish Conference, the World Jewish Congress, and the Board of Deputies of British Jews, which combined forces in a joint committee; the Jewish Agency for Palestine; and the American Jewish Committee. As the interim chairmen of the American Jewish Conference, Henry Monsky, Louis Lipsky, and I went to San Francisco, where we joined the other Jewish participants. Those representing the Jewish Agency included Rabbi Stephen Wise, Dr. Nahum Goldmann, Arthur Lourie, and Eliahu Epstein (later, Elath); heading the American Jewish Committee nominees was Judge Joseph M. Proskauer.

The Jewish people, possessing no recognized territory of its own, had no national status at the conference. Thus, although we represented the great majority (eighty percent) of the Jews of the world, the most that we could do was to hover about, talking to statesmen in the lobbies or seeing them elsewhere by appointment.

On the Friday evening prior to the opening of the UN Conference, Rabbi Wise and I addressed a Jewish community service at Temple Sherith Israel, the oldest Jewish congregation in San Francisco, where my brother, Morris, served as rabbi.

Though interested in the general purposes of the new United Nations Organization, our Jewish delegation focused its particular concern on two proposed charters: one for an international bill of rights and the other for a system of international trusteeship. The American Jewish Committee was mainly concerned with the first proposal, while the Jewish Agency concentrated on the second. We of the American Jewish Conference and the Joint Committee supported both, but the trusteeship question especially preoccupied us.

With regard to the first issue, we wished to see in the UN Charter a clause explicitly safeguarding the rights of minority groups. Both our delegation and that of the American Jewish Committee worked strenuously to have such a clause adopted. Eventually, the "Big Four" (the U.S., Great Britain, China, and the USSR) agreed to a compromise formula which stated that the purposes of the UN should include "the promotion and encouragement of respect for human rights and for fundamental freedoms for all, without distinction as to race, language, religion or sex." The words *safeguarding* or *protection* had been replaced by *promotion and encourage-ment*—thereby weakening the clause—but the recast version might have been far worse, so we went along with it.

In concentrating on the trusteeship charter, we wished to make certain that Jewish rights in Palestine, as embodied in the Balfour Declaration and the British Mandate, would not be jeopardized or diminished. While the principle of "a Jewish Commonwealth in Palestine" was favored by all constituents of the Joint Committee, the San Francisco agenda ruled out any such formula at the time. We therefore sought one that would maintain and protect the status quo. Various trusteeship plans were offered by the U.S. and other delegations. To protect our Jewish interests in Palestine, we published a five-point memorandum, on the basis of which a working paper was submitted to the UN Trusteeship Committee. It contained a safeguard clause, Paragraph B 5, whereby "nothing in this chapter should be construed in and of itself to alter in any manner the rights of any state or any peoples in any territory."

Although Palestine was nowhere mentioned in this paragraph, the wording gave rise to heated debate. The issue hinged on the word *peoples*, which the Arab spokesmen endeavored to have replaced by *people*. The plural form would make all the difference for the existing and potential Jewish population of Eretz Yisrael, as our opponents well realized, whereas the singular form, *people*, could only be interpreted to mean the general population—which, in the case of Palestine, meant the Arab majority. To have that vital *s* inserted in the final text, therefore, was our chief concern.

Unable to vote on any motion in the Trusteeship Committee, we lobbied for support outside, canvasing government leaders and members of the various national delegations. On the whole, our efforts seemed to bear fruit. We had some "friends at court"—Jan Masaryk of Czechoslovakia and Field Marshal Jan Christiaan Smuts, the Prime Minister of South Africa—as well as new and younger men holding key posts in various friendly governments. Our first task, however, was to make the American delegation aware of our apprehensions and of the U.S. Administration's obligation to safeguard the existing Jewish rights in Palestine.

As Congressman Sol Bloom was an important member of the U.S. delegation to the conference, in his capacity as chairman of the Foreign Affairs Committee of the

House of Representatives, Henry Monsky and I went to see him. Initially, he advised against raising the Palestine issue because of the danger that Arab countermeasures might undermine our position. We tried to impress upon him that our rights in Palestine under the Mandate must not be imperiled. We also asked him to convey, in his various intergovernmental contacts, the disappointment and resentment that British policy had aroused among the American people. He proved to be an understanding friend.

Our next meetings were with U.S. Secretary of State Edward R. Stettinius, John Foster Dulles, and Commander Harold E. Stassen. They were, for the most part, understanding and helpful. Dulles saw Monsky, Lipsky, and me. The residuary title of some territories rested in the old League of Nations and, in this connection, he cautioned that Great Britain might claim certain areas of Palestine.

During our conversation, I took occasion to say to Dulles:

> I can speak freely to you because both the Republican and Democratic platforms state clearly and unequivocally what American policy should be. We American Jews are moral trustees for the surviving remnant of European Jewry, for whom Palestine is the only solution. Now we say to our Government, "You must safeguard their rights. You must beware lest, unconsciously, you permit a formula which might impair them."

His reply was that they were "aware of the situation" and would keep it in mind. I then reminded him of the convention between the United Kingdom and the United States (signed in London on December 3, 1924), regarding the rights of each country's government and of their respective nationals in Palestine. That convention embodied the text of the Palestine Mandate entrusted to Great Britain, and it made two important points:

> The United States and its nationals shall have and enjoy all the rights and benefits secured under the terms of the Mandate to members of the League of Nations and their nationals, notwithstanding the fact that the United States is not a member of the League of Nations. [Article 2]

> Nothing contained in the present Convention shall be affected by any modification which may be made in the terms of the Mandate, as recited above, unless such modification shall have been assented to by the United States. [Article 7]

Dulles observed that this was an additional reason for America to be especially concerned with the whole situation, but he went on to say, "We are just beginning to make peace, and it is a hard process."

Our next approach was to members of other delegations in San Francisco. When talking to them, we made it clear that the Jewish people, represented by the Jewish Agency for Palestine, would not countenance any change in its status as far as Palestine was concerned, except some measure that would fulfill the intent of the Balfour Declaration and the League of Nations Mandate by establishing a Jewish commonwealth in Eretz Yisrael.

Jan Masaryk, the Czech statesman, was an old and admired acquaintance. He told me at the conference that he would support the cause of minorities other than the (Sudeten) Germans. After having described the plight of Jewish survivors in liberated Poland, Rumania, and Bulgaria, I asked him to speak with the Soviet Foreign Minister, Vyacheslav Molotov, urging that the USSR use its good offices on our behalf. Masaryk then disclosed that Molotov had been disturbed by the recent initiative of Anthony Eden and the British Foreign Office in sponsoring the creation of the Arab League. Great Britain's efforts to consolidate anti-Soviet influences also worried the USSR.

Peter Fraser, the Prime Minister of New Zealand, was known for his pro-Zionist attitude. Henry Monsky and I went to see him, accompanied by the Reverend Maurice L. Perlzweig of the World Jewish Congress. Fraser proved to be an affable man and we had a frank discussion, outlining our misgivings about the trusteeship proposal. "The Americans," he said, "are probably thinking in terms of the Pacific area, whereas the British have to take other parts of the world into consideration—Tanganyika and Palestine, for example." He agreed to consult us before taking any action, and we urged him to see the Jewish Agency representatives as well.

Our attempt to get through to the Chinese delegation, though unsuccessful at first, resulted in a diverting interlude. At that time, China was still ruled by the Kuomintang (Nationalist) Party, headed by Generalissimo Chiang Kai-shek. As I sat in my hotel room, racking my brains to find some way of obtaining an interview with General Wu, the head of China's delegation, I suddenly hit on a possible solution to our problem. While in Canada a year or two previously, I had met that picaresque character, Morris Abraham Cohen, a London cockney by birth, whose adventurous career had led him to spend nearly twenty years in China. Suffice it to say that his political connections with the Chinese community in Edmonton, Alberta, had enabled him to strike up a friendship with the exiled Sun Yat-sen in 1908. Fourteen years later, when Sun Yat-sen became President of China, Cohen's powerful physique made him an ideal bodyguard and he moved to Peking. There, he proved useful to the Chinese leader in more ways than one, supplying excellent financial as well as military advice. After Sun Yat-sen's death in 1925, Chiang Kai-shek, his successor, ensured that he would have as his close confidant the man whose habit of wearing a revolver on either hip earned him the nickname, "Two-Gun Cohen."

For his services in helping to organize and train the Kuomintang army, this Jew from Whitechapel was awarded the rank of general. In subsequent campaigns against both the Communists and the Japanese, he became to all intents and purposes Chiang Kai-shek's Minister of War. As General MA (a Chinese cognomen he adopted from the initial letters of his Hebrew name, Moshe Avraham), "Two-Gun Cohen" was a legendary figure during the late 1920s and early 1930s. Two years after his capture by the invading Japanese in 1941, he made his way back to Canada. It was at about that time that I first encountered him in Montreal.

As a result of my brainwave, I wired "Two-Gun Cohen," urging him to fly out to San Francisco and assist us with an introduction to the inaccessible General Wu.

He promptly obliged and mentioned the fact that General Wu was a recent convert to Christianity. A few days later, we were able to call on the head of the Chinese delegation. General Wu greeted us warmly and said, "You are my spiritual brothers. There will be no true peace in the world unless justice is done to the Jewish people. History teaches us that those who persecute the Jews are destroyed, while those who befriend them prosper." Needless to say, we received China's backing for our trusteeship formula at the conference.

Jewish efforts to protect the status quo in Palestine reached a climax in the last week of May 1945, when the safeguard clause and related matters were debated at meetings of the Trusteeship Committee. As already indicated, the five Arab League representatives tried hard to force through amendments that would have changed the wording to our disadvantage. On behalf of the Jewish Agency, Dr. Nahum Goldmann wrote to Alger Hiss, secretary-general of the UN Conference, requesting that our statements of protest and clarification be circulated among the various delegations, but Hiss denied these requests. We were then compelled to expose the Arab maneuvers by turning to the American press. To make matters worse, at one stage, Rabbi Elmer Berger, executive director of the American Council for Judaism, came to the aid of the Arabs by calling a press conference at which he attacked Zionist aims and denied the very existence of a Jewish people.

Fortunately, however, the implication of the successive Arab amendments was not lost on many of the delegates, who saw pro-Zionist comments in the American press. Concerted action by the Jewish delegations in San Francisco also succeeded in discrediting Elmer Berger and his small but noisy clique. For all their privileged status as last-minute converts to the anti-Nazi cause, and in spite of their barrage of propaganda, the Arab League states suffered a resounding defeat. As ratified, the disputed clause finally read: "Nothing in the Trusteeship Chapter itself shall alter any existing rights of states or peoples or any international instruments." Most of the participants in the UN Conference were still haunted by the specter of Hitlerism. Our public-relations campaign made an impression at the time.

A detailed report on the founding Conference of the United Nations assembly was presented to the delegates of the American Jewish Conference on June 25, 1945. The three co-chairmen conveyed their impressions.

In the course of my remarks, I welcomed those provisions of the UN Charter dealing with "human rights and fundamental freedoms," but cautioned that "it would be unrealistic to think of them as an effective *safeguard* to protect the rights of minority groups. There is no provision empowering the *enforcement* of human rights." Turning next to the trusteeship issue, I observed:

> At San Francisco our right to Palestine under the Balfour Declaration and the Mandate emerged unimpaired, despite the attempts by the Arab states to introduce phrases and clauses which might have foreclosed the possibilities of the fulfillment of the Balfour Declaration on which the Palestine Mandate is based. The American delegation was foremost in safeguarding Jewish rights under the Mandate, and other nations joined, with the conspicuous exception of the Arab states.
>
> This is not an unhopeful sign for the future, yet it would be fatuous to indulge

in self-gratulations on that account. The White Paper still keeps Jews out of Palestine and the decisions regarding the Jewish Commonwealth are still in the indefinite future. Unless the Jewish people can have free access to Palestine, which spells life, liberty and happiness for millions of men, women and children, the Jewish people, who paid the heaviest toll, will have lost the War. . . . We should regard the San Francisco Conference as opening, not closing, the door to a better future.

Postwar Jewish Revival: Communities and DPs

The Allied victory in Europe came a fortnight after the opening of the UN Conference in San Francisco. While in Denver, on my way back to New York, I telephoned a special message to Congregation B'nai Jeshurun as VE-Day was about to dawn. Another four months were to elapse before the Japanese laid down their arms, after the United States had devastated Hiroshima and Nagasaki with its fearful new atomic bombs. At the end of the war in the West, European Jewry's future was uppermost in our thoughts and preoccupations. The American Jewish community, through the American Jewish Conference, felt that it was "now or never" and had joined in an all-out effort for the achievement of two supreme postwar tasks: one was to resuscitate, rehabilitate, and reconstruct the *She'erit ha-Pletah*, the surviving fragments of our people; the other, to press for the establishment of a Jewish commonwealth in Palestine.

Zionist hopes ran high. On the one hand, we wanted to achieve a solution that would eliminate once and for all the perennial physical menace to defenseless Jewish minorities by hostile majority populations. On the other hand, we also wished to give the survivors every possible opportunity for revival.

When VE-Day was celebrated on May 8, 1945, I was in London for a meeting of the Zionist General Council (Actions Committee). It was the first such gathering of the largest Zionist body, next to the Zionist Congress itself, to take place in almost six years. Deep mourning prevailed in the conference hall. Many familiar faces from Europe were missing and the Actions Committee members who came from Palestine, the United States, the United Kingdom, and other parts of the world felt the tragedy of their absence. We reaffirmed our support for the Biltmore Program, demanding a Jewish commonwealth in Eretz Yisrael as partial compensation for the catastrophe that had befallen our people. It was the least that humanity owed to those pathetic, tortured figures now being restored to life in the camps where, a short while earlier, millions of Jews had been sacrificed to the Nazi Moloch.

The record of the Arab states and populations during World War II had been, almost without exception, a meretricious one. The vast majority went on hoping for a German victory. Some openly collaborated with the Nazis, the most notorious case being that of the Mufti of Jerusalem, Haj Amin al-Husseini, who, as Hitler's honored guest in Berlin, had applauded the mass murder of Jews. By contrast, Palestinian Jewish volunteers had put up a fine showing alongside the British forces in the Middle East and in the ranks of the Jewish Brigade. We hoped that these facts would be taken into account by the postwar British Government.

The short-range situation was unclear and the long-range outlook was beclouded as we conferred in London. Great Britain was in the throes of an election campaign, and it seemed likely that the Labor Party, headed by Clement Attlee, would be swept into power. That, indeed, is what the elections brought about a couple of months later. The Zionist General Council hoped that Labor Party pledges would be fulfilled—that the British White Paper restrictions would be abolished forthwith and that the gates of Palestine would at last be opened wide to Jews. This was not to be. The new Labor Government proved no less unbending than its predecessor.

Bitter disillusionment lay in store for the Zionist movement. Ernest Bevin, who became Foreign Secretary in Attlee's cabinet at the end of July 1945, was hostile to the aims and purposes of Zionism almost from the very outset. Once the Foreign Office took over the handling of Palestine affairs from the Colonial Office, Bevin's regime turned out to be the most bitterly anti-Zionist in the entire period of the British Mandate. Delaying tactics—such as the appointment of commissions of inquiry with the clear purpose that, if their findings were negative, they would be honored and, if affirmative, ignored—were employed by Bevin to vitiate President Truman's call for the gates of Palestine to be opened to large numbers of the homeless Jewish refugees crowding the DP camps in Europe.

This kind of governmental ploy had the effect of strengthening Zionist resistance. It clearly indicated that we could expect nothing whatsoever from the Mandatory power, and that the only means of ending the misery of the Jewish DPs lay in the establishment of a sovereign Jewish State. The time of decision, we felt, must be close at hand.

Flying back to New York after the Actions Committee meetings in London, I had an opportunity to ponder the future of Zionism in America at this critical stage for World Jewry. With the war in the Pacific nearing its end, a period of far-ranging political settlements would naturally set in. It was high time, therefore, to assess the chances of our Zionist aims being fulfilled, especially with the help of the U.S. Administration.

An occasion to express these views arose a few weeks later, when I was asked to address a meeting of the National Laymen's Institute of the United Synagogue of America, held at the Jewish Theological Seminary, on June 22. Regarding the prospects of achieving a Jewish commonwealth in Eretz Yisrael, I anticipated a tough struggle ahead. In the United States, where Zionist objectives enjoyed the largest reservoir of favorable public opinion, the Government did not seem particularly inclined to force the issue with Great Britain, which still maintained its policy of appeasing the Arabs. President Truman and the majority of Congress were on our side, however, and Soviet Russia had given more than one indication that it was not opposed.

At San Francisco, the conference agenda had ruled out the possibility of any new decision favorable to the Zionist cause. "None of the Arab maneuvers succeeded. Most of the other nations sustained our position," I said. "Considering the obvious advantage enjoyed by the Arab states in being inside the conference, while the Jewish people were outside, their failure should encourage us." I expressed my belief that, in the relatively near future, we would see a considerable fulfillment of our hopes. "Dynamic faith is called for, the faith that generates action."

In July 1945, two months after the war had ended in Europe, I set out again by air from New York, first to London and Paris, and then on to Germany for a tour of the DP (Displaced Persons') camps in the U.S. zone of occupation. This mission I undertook as president of both the ZOA and the Synagogue Council of America, with the object of bringing to the half-million survivors of the Holocaust a message of fraternal greeting and hope from their fellow Jews in the United States, as well as some consignments of food.

Early in the morning of July 6, the day after my arrival in London, Dr. Weizmann telephoned and invited me to come over to Great Russell Street. I found him in his office with the familiar coterie of associates and advisers—Berl Locker, Professor Lewis Namier, Blanche Dugdale, Lavy Bakstansky, and Ivor Linton. They questioned me closely about Harry S. Truman, the new President of the United States, who was even more an unknown quantity to our friends in Great Britain than he was to most Americans. I told them what little I knew about the senator from Missouri who had been precipitated into world prominence. Weizmann conveyed particulars of his latest conversation with Field Marshal Smuts, who, he said, was as fervent a supporter of Zionism as ever, but who also thought that the British War Cabinet's stand in favor of a partition of Palestine was "no good."

Dr. Weizmann then referred to another matter. President Truman had sent Professor Earl G. Harrison, dean of the Faculty of Law at the University of Pennsylvania, on a mission to the DP camps in Germany, "to inquire into the conditions and needs" of the inmates, with particular reference to "stateless and non-repatriable persons, especially Jews." In the letter of authority that had been given to Harrison, there was no reference whatsoever to Palestine! The Harrison Report, to which I shall revert, made it quite clear that most of the Jewish DPs were adamant about going to Palestine. Its recommendations were to become a powerful weapon in the hands of the Zionist movement immediately after the war.

My four days in England included a meeting with leaders of the British Council of Christians and Jews to discuss, among other matters, the holding of an international conference in the summer of 1946. One of the highlights of my visit was the two-hour meeting I had there with Rabbi Leo Baeck, the spiritual leader of German Liberal Jewry and president of the Reichsvertretung der Juden in Deutschland during the Nazi period. For me, it was a deeply emotional experience to speak with this saintly, heroic man, who had refused to desert his Berlin congregation and who had spent the years 1943–45 in the "privileged" ghetto camp of Theresienstadt (Terezín), Czechoslovakia.

Rabbi Baeck had left Theresienstadt only a week earlier, and was now living with his daughter and son-in-law in London. He looked well, despite his advanced years and the nightmare of his ordeal. When I thanked him for the message he had sent me in 1925, on the centenary of Congregation B'nai Jeshurun in New York, he said, "May you live until its hundred fiftieth anniversary," and was amused to hear that I doubted whether my congregation would be so long-suffering.

The account Rabbi Baeck gave me of his years in Theresienstadt was both gruesome and inspiring. Two kinds of treatment awaited deportees in the Nazi camps, he said: outright murder, and death by starvation and disease. Theresienstadt had specialized in the second type of annihilation, although many of its inmates were transported to mass-extermination camps in Eastern Europe. He had been among the fortunate ones who survived. The strength to survive had come from his lectures to fellow Jews, several hundred of whom would gather nightly in a large, unlit room on top of the barracks. There, he gave courses on philosophy and Jewish history.

I asked him whether the terrible experiences the inmates had undergone made them more positive or more negative toward religion. "They became more religious," he said, "and their faith sustained them." Zionism, he added (in response to another query), was "the comfort of their souls" and Palestine was their first choice as destination once they would be liberated. Those who had children in countries other than Eretz Yisrael naturally wished to join them.

"What future do you think there will be for the Jews of Europe?" I asked.

Rabbi Baeck threw up his hands. "That chapter seems to be over," he answered somberly.

I arrived in Paris on July 10, 1945. It was to be a crowded two weeks, packed with meetings and conferences, in a city just recovering from the Nazi occupation and from the treacherous Vichy regime of Marshal Pétain, which had aided and abetted the Nazis in deporting a large section of French Jewry. The impact of the Maquisards, the French resistance fighters, was seen, heard, and felt everywhere.

Among Zionist colleagues whom I contacted in Paris were Sam Segall, Michel Topiol, and Jacques Orfus. I received an especially cordial welcome, since, apart from Chaplain Judah Nadich and Dr. Joseph Schwartz, who had been there on behalf of the Joint Distribution Committee, I was the first American Jewish leader to visit France after the liberation.

The friends whom I met painted a depressing picture of the French scene, as far as the Jews were concerned. They were deeply pessimistic about the future, a feeling heightened by the anti-Semitic slogans not yet erased from the billboards. General Charles de Gaulle, the nation's hero, was noncommittal about the Jewish "problem," and the attitude of the resistance movement was still unclear. Jews were thrown out of their apartments when they returned, and the French police stood by, indifferent to all of this. Some Jewish children had been dispatched to farms in the countryside for use as slave labor, and the farmers now refused to release them. Others had become attached to their foster parents, who urged them to stay put and avoid trouble. As in other formerly occupied countries, there were cases of Jewish children who had been baptized and whom zealous Catholics would not release to the Jewish kinfolk.

Rabbi Judah Nadich, deputy to the Chief of Chaplains in the European Theater of Operations, came in to see me, and we spoke about the Christian clergy. He said that the Cardinal Archbishop of Paris was suspected of having been a Nazi collaborator. Rabbi Nadich had done a magnificent job in Paris shortly after the liberation, organizing the other Jewish chaplains for relief work with the Jewish Welfare Board and with the Joint Distribution Committee, which provided the funds.

I had already received and quoted a report from Rabbi Nadich about the outstanding part played by Jews in the underground Maquis, known officially as the Forces Françaises de l'Intérieur (FFI). Several French Jews had held high rank and assumed posts of command in the FFI. More important, to my mind, was the role of the Organisation Juive de Combat (OJC), which grouped together the Zionist youth movements, the Jewish Scouts, and others who fought as Jews. They had rescued many Jewish children and carried out nearly 2,000 acts of sabotage during the war. In Paris, and particularly in the south of France, they had disposed of numerous enemy troops, French Nazis, and active collaborators. The OJC's part in the liberation had been of major importance, in Marseilles and Grenoble especially, and the town of Castres in southwestern France was the first to be liberated entirely by these Jewish heroes. Some of their most prominent members later settled in Israel.

An early meeting with Rabbi Jacob Kaplan, the Chief Rabbi of Paris, brought me face to face with the problems confronting the religious organizations of French Jewry. Owing to my inadequate French, we conversed in Yiddish, which the Grand Rabbin spoke with an elegant French accent. The situation, in his words, was catastrophic. One-third of the Jews in France had been deported, scores of synagogues had been destroyed or pillaged, and Jewish homes and business premises had been confiscated. An attempt was now being made to reorganize and revive the community. He called my attention to the Christian missions that were enticing Jewish children in city streets. He also sought and obtained my financial help in establishing afternoon recreational and educational programs for these youngsters. Centers for this purpose were set up in neighborhoods where the missionaries were active.

Rabbi Kaplan took me to a meeting of the Consistoire, the central religious organization of the French Jewish community. It was probably the first occasion on which that august body was greeted in *Mamme-loshen*. Léon Meiss, the president of the Consistoire, served as my interpreter. The Consistoire Central Israélite de France (CCIF) had been set up by Napoleon in 1808, when he reorganized the structure of French Jewry. It comprised local consistories throughout the land and also, until some years after World War II, in Algeria. Unlike the Board of Deputies of British Jews, founded about a half-century previously in the reign of George III, which concentrated on political issues, the CCIF dealt with religious matters only, such as the maintenance of the Chief Rabbinate and the rabbinical seminary. The French counterpart of the Board of Deputies was CRIF, the Conseil Représentatif des Juifs de France, founded in 1944, during the Vichy administration, as a roof organization of the principal Jewish institutions.

The Collège Maïmonide, a secondary school for Jewish boys, had been closed during the war. Its principal, Dr. Marcus Cohen, had been a prisoner of war in Germany, but was now about to resume his post. The school, which taught boys ages twelve to eighteen, was the only one of its kind in France, and he wanted to open it in three months' time. Some of the pupils were now orphans, he told me, and a number wanted to go to Palestine. There were no books, these having either been burned or taken away, and financial aid was badly needed. I undertook to provide such help and was able to do so, thanks to my congregation and also to the Altschul Foundation, of which I was a trustee.

All whom I met in those emotion-laden days—French Jews who had escaped Hitler's clutches, returning prisoners of war and civilian deportees, U.S. Army personnel and chaplains—had the magic words "Zionism" and "Palestine" on their lips. The *She'erit ha-Pletah* hungered for Eretz Yisrael. At the JDC offices, I was told that Jewish DPs were ready to put up with their miserable conditions for six months longer, if only they could be sure of a passage to Palestine.

Marc Jarblum, the French Zionist leader, who had been active in the underground, was a valuable source of information, particularly in regard to Socialist attitudes on the Zionist issue. During the 1920s, he had won over Léon Blum, a future Socialist Prime Minister of France, to the Zionist cause. His wife, Laura Margolis Jarblum, was an American-trained social worker who represented the JDC in Europe, under the overall direction of Dr. Joseph Schwartz. Marc Jarblum told me that he had spoken recently with Léon Blum, whom he quoted as saying, "In spite of all the problems and difficulties, I continue to believe in a Jewish State."

A group of American Jewish chaplains had come to Paris after a period of service in Germany. Among them were Rabbis Max Braude, Robert Marcus, and Joseph Shubow. Their leader, Rabbi Herschel Schacter, had been the first Jew in the chaplaincy corps to enter Buchenwald. He told me, "The American Jewish Conference should have had someone stationed over here. I was always a Zionist, but never thought much about it. Now I am aflame, after seeing these people who declare themselves stateless, so as to be able to get to Eretz Yisrael."

Bastille Day, July 14, 1945, was a memorable occasion. I was taken by friends to have a traditional Sabbath meal in a Jewish restaurant, and then to see all the resistance groups parading down the Champs Elysées. A large number of the participants were Jewish, and it was especially moving to see some of the former prisoners of war and newly liberated inmates of the concentration camps marching in their tattered garb.

The sights and sounds of Paris during that visit were unforgettable, as were many of the eyewitness stories of the war that I heard. Thousands of Jews had been deported from the old Jewish quarter, the *Pletzel*, where I heard Lamentations *(Megillat Ekhah)* recited on the eve of Tish'ah be-Av. One of my hosts was Baron Guy de Rothschild, a good friend of Chaim Weizmann. He had been to Palestine a few months earlier and was impressed by what he had seen. I went with him to a meeting of CRIF, where he interpreted what I had to say about the World Jewish Congress, the American Jewish Conference, and the Synagogue Council of America.

During my two-week sojourn in France, I finalized the arrangements for my visit to Germany, enlisting the help of U.S. Ambassador Caffery. He called in Colonel Edward ("Eddie") Warburg, a friend and colleague from New York, who was attached to the embassy and who eventually secured permission for me to enter the American zone of occupation. I went not only as president of the ZOA and of the

Synagogue Council, but also as chairman of the United Palestine Appeal and co-chairman of the UJA.

Flying over the city of Frankfurt am Main, I could see the devastation caused by incessant Allied air attacks. My first stop was in Frankfurt itself, where I met Colonel Schottland, the officer in charge of the Displaced Persons section of the U.S. military government. He told me that there were still about 90,000 Jewish DPs in the German camps—50,000 of them in the American zone, 22,000 in the British zone, and 18,000 in the French zone. Although the figures he quoted were technically correct, they did not give a true picture of the situation there. Between 500,000 and one million Jews were, in a real sense, DPs, having been displaced economically, socially, and culturally from their prewar homes. Physically, too, they were endangered. The vast majority of these unfortunate people wished only to be allowed into Palestine. There were, in any case, no other countries prepared to admit large numbers of homeless Jews.

Apart from the Jewish chaplains serving with the U.S. and British forces in Germany, there were also a few local rabbis who had made their way back after the war. I had a talk with Rabbi Neuhaus, the acting religious leader in Frankfurt, who had been in Theresienstadt. He told me that there were about seven hundred Jews (mostly survivors of the prewar community) living thereabouts; others were still emerging from their hiding places. He complained that Jews in the Frankfurt area were not receiving the treatment to which they were legally entitled as victims of the Nazis. I mentioned this matter to the U.S. military authorities, who took steps to remedy the situation. At the time, incidentally, there was no proper coordination between the various army commands in the American zone, let alone between the Americans, the British, the French, and the Russians.

While roaming through Frankfurt, I found one synagogue largely intact, although the interior, converted into a theater by the Nazis, had been gutted before they fled. Another building I visited was a storage place for Jewish books retrieved from German hands. Alfred Rosenberg, the leading ideologist of National Socialism, had organized the systematic despoilment of Jewish libraries throughout Europe and his underlings had deposited their loot here in Frankfurt. It was an astonishing and heartbreaking sight. Perhaps as many as 200,000 volumes lay around, filling three whole floors of the building. I saw folios of the Talmud, rare Jewish incunabula, Torah scrolls, ceremonial objects, and a mass of stolen antiques. Whole libraries were piled there, the bindings lacerated and pages torn out, like so many parents and children wrenched apart. Here, I reflected, was the "surviving remnant" of European Jewry's looted spiritual treasures.

Why all of this had been preserved was a complete and utter mystery. Had the Nazis intended these books to form part of some anti-Jewish museum, to symbolize the triumph of Hitler's "New Order" over Judaism, or was it merely that there had been no time to destroy them? My guide offered me an antique *Megillah* (Scroll of Esther), but I declined, saying, "This belongs to the Jewish people." The fact that no proper care was taken to guard everything aroused my indignation. I contacted the Department of Archives and Antiquities in the U.S. military government, and steps were then taken to safeguard the collections and to classify the scrolls and volumes. A great deal of the material was later identified, what could be restored to its rightful owners was handed back, and the rest of the books eventually found homes in Jewish libraries all over the world.

My tour of the American zone coincided with Earl Harrison's fact-finding mission to the DP camps, and I was able to bear out the accuracy and justice of his observations. Leaving Frankfurt, I traveled by jeep to Munich by way of Darmstadt, Mannheim, Heidelberg, Stuttgart, Augsburg, and some smaller towns. We drove along Hitler's vaunted Autobahn, sections of which had been obliterated in the fighting. Most Germans, I was told, only regretted the fact that the Führer had not managed to develop more secret weapons for mass destruction.

Chaplains Judah Nadich and Joseph Shubow were helpful in arranging my entry into the camps where Jewish DPs were housed. As civilians could not be admitted, it was necessary to provide me with some military rank for the duration of my week-long visit. I was accordingly given the designation, "Simulated Colonel." This caused me some amusement, because I had only known a few "simulated" rabbis in the past. My new status had no military uniform to back it up, but the supporting documents I received enabled me to enjoy all the courtesies and facilities extended by the U.S. Army of Occupation. An official military escort also accompanied me when I visited the places on my itinerary, including the ghastly death camp at Dachau, near Munich.

With the exception of Jewish servicemen and chaplains, and the JDC teams headed by Dr. Joseph Schwartz, I was the first American Jew to set foot in postwar Germany and to bring a word of comfort and fellowship to the survivors of the *Sho'ah*. A full report on my visit was submitted to the Interim Committee of the American Jewish Conference on October 5.

The American Jewish Joint Distribution Committee was then about to begin its mission of mercy in the refugee camps, while the United Nations Relief and Rehabilitation Administration (UNRRA) had just commenced its operations. The director-general of UNRRA was Herbert H. Lehman, who had latterly resigned as Governor of New York State to assume his new post. Lehman was a benevolent man of high principle, who, though of assimilated background, had a keen appreciation of popular Jewish feelings as a result of his political career in New York. After his term of office with UNRRA, he went on to serve for a number of years in the U.S. Senate and became a consistent supporter of the Zionist program for a Jewish commonwealth in Palestine.

Meeting the *She'erit ha-Pletah*, the surviving remnant of European Jewry, was a deeply moving experience for me and, I had reason to believe, for them also. I inspected a number of the DP camps and what I found inside was profoundly distressing. The inmates, free only in a technical sense, bore all the marks of torment, starvation, and soul-searing fright. Prolonged suffering was etched into their haggard faces. They pressed forward eagerly, inundating me with requests for help and for messages to be conveyed to kinfolk in the United States. Speaking in Yiddish, I told them of American Jewry's profound concern for their welfare and I encouraged them to hope that they would find safety at last in the Jewish homeland. The modest amount of money I had at my disposal was used to purchase a few material necessities, items that were luxuries for these bundles of skin and bone.

Who could fail to be impressed by the dignity with which they bore their grim fate, cooped up in the very places that had been an inferno for Jews? I was struck by their hunger for renewed contact with the Jews outside these camps and by their expressions of gratitude to all who had helped to liberate them from the Nazi torturers. They vied with each other in praising the heroism of a few American officers and enlisted men who had acted on their own initiative to save thousands of lives, the devotion of our Jewish chaplains and, most of all, the courageous exploits of volunteers from the Yishuv who had come to them in the uniform of the Jewish Brigade.

It was particularly distressing to hear their constant demand that Jewish DPs be moved to separate camps of their own, because of what was happening where Jews and non-Jews were kept together. Among the Polish DPs in two camps near Wetzlar that I visited were small numbers of Jews, and some had become "Marranos," afraid to reveal their true identity, knowing that this would expose them to the anti-Semitic insults and hooliganism of the Polish Gentiles. It was a macabre reminder that common suffering at the hands of the Nazis had not mitigated the effects of inbred hatred for the Jew in Eastern Europe. Generally speaking, these camps were in a miserable state. The UNRRA personnel, recruited mostly from social-service agencies, had proved inept and lacking in initiative, always waiting for official directives. Later, however, the situation improved.

There was one bright spot, for me, in this gloomy picture—the camp at Feldafing, a lakeside village facing the Bavarian Alps, some twenty miles southwest of Munich. Until recently, it had been a summer camp for the Hitler Youth, excellently equipped with dormitories and kitchen facilities, providing accommodations for about 4,000 people. A U.S. Army detachment, commanded by Lieutenant Irving J. Smith, a Jewish boy from South Bend, Indiana, arrived on the scene and commandeered this abandoned Nazi resort. With the help of a Jewish chaplain, he then "consecrated" it for Jewish purposes, bringing in large numbers of DPs whom he discovered in the area. Whatever supplies he thought necessary were transported from the neighboring town of Tutzing.

Lieutenant Smith was responsible for a splendid piece of organization, and he had a dramatic story to tell. I made a note of it at the time:

> He arrived in Tutzing on May 1, 1945, eight days before Germany capitulated to the Allied forces. He and his men found on the railroad siding a trainload of eight hundred Jews, inmates of the Mühldorf and Wald concentration camps, on their way to another destination where they were to have been killed. They were in a terrible physical and mental condition. During all of the preceding week, they had each received one-quarter of a loaf of bread and four portions of cheese.
>
> That same night, they were fed on the train, the first hot meal they had had in several weeks. The German civil and military authorities were ordered to find accommodations for them and a camp was discovered at Feldafing, some distance

away. The same night, eight hundred Germans were set to work, preparing the camp for their reception. At five o'clock on the following afternoon, the train was moved to Feldafing, after the most seriously ill had been taken to various hotels in the area. The night they arrived, the people were bathed, disinfected and provided with clean underclothing, and then fed. Each was allotted a bed.

The American Jewish officer promptly requisitioned physicians, nurses, and dentists from nearby German villages, and also mobilized local supplies of underwear, cloth, and other essentials intended for the SS. Food packages were made available by the Red Cross. He proceeded to locate more Jews in the vicinity and arranged their transfer to Feldafing from mixed camps. A community of 5,000 Jewish DPs was thus established. Lieutenant Smith then began a search for those with some vocational talent, and in this way he was able to recruit tailors, shoemakers, cooks, bakers, and even teachers.

I reached Feldafing on a Friday morning. It was a most moving experience to see groups of youngsters going over the weekly Torah portion or studying the laws of Shabbat. They told me how much they looked forward to rebuilding their lives in Eretz Yisrael. A few of the older people spoke resentfully of the Jews in the United States. "When we were in the concentration camps, and others received messages of comfort and cheer, where were you?" The articulation of their resentment was an encouraging sign of high morale.

An outdoor concert, attended by 3,000 people, was arranged during my visit. Local German carpenters were enlisted to build a wooden stage and to provide seating, a piano was brought in and army trucks beamed light on the improvised concert platform, draped with a blue and white Zionist flag. The performers, a male pianist and a female contralto, wore evening dress that had been "liberated" from a neighboring town. It was the first time since their deportation that these two artists had been able to display their talents. Everyone felt the emotional impact of this scene, which naturally affected my message of hope to the audience.

Before I left Feldafing, Lieutenant Smith called in a young Jewish violinist to play for me, in order to show what talent abounded in the camp. Dressed in overalls, the violinist chose a piece by Bach and seemed to pour out his heart as he played. It was as if those quivering strings were filling the air with an *El Malé Rahamim* prayer in memory of the man's parents, brothers, and sisters who had been turned to ashes in the Holocaust.

As a whitewashing operation, Feldafing camp became a showplace for visiting journalists, although it could hardly be described as a typical reception center for DPs. The facilities developed there included a synagogue, a hospital, a school, an open-air movie theater where stage productions also took place, and a dance hall, complete with orchestra. The deportees assembled in the camp hailed from Greece, Yugoslavia, Hungary, Rumania, Poland, Lithuania, and other parts of Central and Eastern Europe. Having lost their families and all their material possessions, they had no wish or reason to "go back home." The youngsters whom I saw there were, without exception, teenagers capable of forced labor for the Nazis. No younger

19. Biltmore Hotel Conference. At one of the sessions *(left to right):* the author, David Wertheim, Louis Lipsky, Judge Louis E. Levinthal, and Dr. Chaim Weizmann. Zionist Archives and Library, New York.

20. Joint Palestine Appeal campaign luncheon at the Grosvenor House Hotel, London, March 1944. Pictured *(left to right):* Eva, Marchioness of Reading, Dr. Chaim Weizmann *(delivering an address),* Simon Marks, the author, Vera Weizmann, Chief Rabbi Joseph H. Hertz, Aaron Wright, and Rebecca Sieff. Krongold photo, London.

21. Zionist General Council (Actions Committee) meeting in London, August 1945. Dr. Weizmann in a characteristic pose with *(left to right)* Maurice Rosetti, the author, Dr. Stephen Wise, and *(partly obscured, front)* Rabbi Wolf Gold. Krongold photo, London.

22. Zionist General Council meeting in London, 1945. Group of American delegates *(left to right)*: Judge Louis E. Levinthal, Daniel Frisch, Dr. Emanuel Neumann, Juliet Benjamin, Naomi Chertoff, Dr. Abba Hillel Silver, Judith Epstein, Dr. Stephen Wise, Rose Halprin, Meyer Weisgal, the author, Rabbi James G. Heller, Louis Lipsky, and Mendel Fisher. Krongold photo, London.

23. The author receiving his first honorary degree, at the Jewish Theological Seminary of America, October 1945. Seated between Dr. Goldstein and Provost Louis Finkelstein *(left)* are Professors Alexander Marx and Mordecai M. Kaplan; standing *(far right)* is Professor Shalom Spiegel.

24. At the American Jewish Conference, 1946. Pictured *(right to left):* Dr. Abba Hillel Silver, the author, Judith Epstein, Dr. Zalman Grynberg, Henry Monsky, Dr. Stephen Wise, and Rabbi Irving Miller.

25. At the Zionist Organization of America convention, October 1946. The author with Dr. Moshe Sneh *(center)* and Dr. Emanuel Neumann. Zionist Archives and Library, New York.

26. Meeting of the WZO Political Advisory Committee at Lake Success, 1947. Dr. Emanuel Neumann, Zvi Herman and Isaac Schwarzbart are seated to the right of the author *(standing)*, followed by Rabbi Irving Miller and Judith Epstein *(along right wall)*. Others pictured include *(right to left, along left wall)*: Rabbi Leon Gellman, Rabbi Mordekhai Nurock, Dr. Oscar Wolfsberg, Louis Segal, Dr. S. Margoshes, and Meir Grossman; *(left to right in 2d row)*: Bert Goldstein, Marion Greenberg, and Rebecca Shulman; *(left to right in 3d row)*: Joseph Schechtman and Yosef Klarman, and, nearest to the camera, Edward Gelber *(far left)*, Hadassah Samuel, and *(far right)* Denise Turover.

27. Jewish Agency reception for the author in Jerusalem, July 1947. Prominent figures at this gathering are *(left)* Arthur Hantke and *(right)* Rabbi Meir Berlin.

28. Welcoming the first U.S. envoy to the State of Israel, 1948. Pictured *(left to right):* the author, Golda Myerson (Meir), Dr. James G. McDonald and his wife, Bert Goldstein, and Moshe Shertok (Sharett). H. Pinn photo, Tel Aviv.

29. First official session of the Jewish Agency's American Section, New York, 1948. Pictured *(counterclockwise, from below, around the table):* Yitzḥak Gruenbaum, Yehudah Braginski, Yitzḥak Werfel (Raphael), Baruch Zuckerman, Rabbi Leon Gellman, Zvi Herman, Rose Halprin, Ḥayim Greenberg, Meir Grossman, Shlomo Zalman Shragai, the author, Pinḥas Rosen, Eliezer Kaplan, Gottlieb Hammer, Isidore Hamlin *(standing)*, Robert Nathan, Rabbi Wolf (Ze'ev) Gold, Maurice Boukstein, Eliyahu Dobkin, Benjamin Browdy, Berl Locker, Dr. Nahum Goldmann, Levi Shkolnik (Eshkol), Moshe Kolodny (Kol), Zvi Luria, and Shlomo Eisenberg. Alexander Archer photo, New York.

30. Amidar housing program: At signing of an agreement between Amidar and Solel Boneh, for the construction of 4,000 housing units. Pictured here are Dr. Yeshayahu Foerder *(2d from right)*, the author *(presiding)*, Meir Hartman and Yosef Saphir *(right to left of the author)*, and Shmuel Epstein *(nearest to camera, at left)*.

31. World Confederation of General Zionists KMK conference in Tel Aviv, 1949. Pictured *(left to right, standing):* Kalman Sultanik, Moshe Kol, Yosef Serlin, Yitzḥak Kubowitzki, and Yisrael Meron; *(seated)* Yitzḥak Gruenbaum, the author, Peretz Bernstein, and Dr. Yosef Rufeisen.

32. Farewell reception for the outgoing treasurer of the Jewish Agency, on completion of his year of service in Israel, August 1949. Facing the camera *(left to right):* Bert Goldstein, Eliezer Kaplan *(speaking)*, Moshe Polakewitz, Yosef Sprinzak, and the author.

33. Histadrut Ivrit of America, annual dinner, December 18, 1949. With the author and Ambassador Abba Eban paying close attention, Maximilian Moss, president of the New York City Board of Education, responds to tributes for his introduction of Hebrew studies into American public schools. Alexander Archer photo, New York.

34. Histadrut Ivrit of America. Group of leading supporters on the same occasion, at the Waldorf-Astoria, New York. Pictured *(left to right):* Harry Fierst, Samuel Fishman, Menahem Ribalow, Joseph Weiss, the author (dinner chairman), Samuel J. Borowsky, Boris Margolin, Dr. Moshe Davis, Mordecai Halevi, and Dr. Azriel Eisenberg. Alexander Archer photo, New York.

children could be found, just as there were no adults over the age of fifty. All of them pinned their hopes on starting life anew somewhere else, preferably in Palestine.

Rabbi Abraham Klausner, who later went on to serve a congregation in Boston, was one of the Jewish chaplains who did much to raise the morale of these hapless people and whose devoted efforts on their behalf won many tributes. A Lieutenant Hutter of Chicago also managed to overcome official red tape, working among Jewish DPs in the Heidelberg area. I left Germany shaken to the core by the plight of these last vestiges of once proud and famous European *kehillot*. My week in the American zone intensified my determination to fight for the only real answer to the problem of Jewish homelessness—an independent Jewish commonwealth in Eretz Yisrael.

Immediately after my visit to the camps in Germany, I sent letters to Herbert Lehman, the head of UNRRA, and to General Dwight D. Eisenhower at Supreme Headquarters, Allied Expeditionary Force in Europe (SHAEF), suggesting a number of improvements in the DP centers. Be it said to their credit that they both took heed of the representations, which must also have come from other sources, with the result that the Jewish DPs were eventually provided with separate camps and facilities in the U.S. zone of Germany.

100,000 Certificates for Palestine

After my eventful three weeks in newly liberated Europe, I returned to London on the Sunday following the British general election. Labor Party banners were, metaphorically speaking, waving everywhere in celebration of that peaceful revolution that had ousted Churchill and ushered in the Attlee administration.

Hopes ran high in Zionist circles that now, with the advent of a Labor Government, there were more favorable prospects for the achievement of our national aims in Palestine. This was the prevailing view at the London Zionist Conference, which opened on August 1, 1945. It was the first such world assembly to take place since the Geneva Zionist Congress of September 1939, and delegates from many countries arrived in a mood of expectant optimism. I came primarily as president of the ZOA, although, together with Henry Monsky and Louis Lipsky, I also participated on behalf of the American Jewish Conference. "The feeling at this [London] Conference," I noted at the time, "is that, with the Labor Party committed in our favor and the Leader of the Opposition [Winston Churchill] a friend, the outlook for the Zionist movement is a bright one." By courtesy of the U.S. Office of War Information, I broadcast a preview of the assembly, indicating its importance for World Jewry at the end of the war.

Our chief aims were to take stock of the current Jewish situation and to voice our demands to the world in view of the Jewish people's desperate needs. The real heroes of the conference were the spokesmen for the surviving remnant of European Jewry, the ghetto fighters and members of the underground, as well as representatives of the Jewish Brigade. With suppressed emotion, they told of their experiences and they reiterated our call for justice for the Jewish people. It was clear that only the Zionists had a program for Jewish revival and that Palestine alone projected a ray of light amid the fear and misery besetting the Jewish survivors in Europe.

At the opening ceremony, Rabbi Israel Brodie, Senior Jewish Chaplain to the British Forces, recited memorial prayers for the Jewish soldiers who had died in battle and for the millions of Jews annihilated by the Nazis. Dr. Chaim Weizmann, who presided, also paid tribute to the martyrs in his inaugural address. "We are meeting," he said, "in the shadow of the greatest catastrophe which has befallen the Jewish people." He went on to say that the Zionist movement needed to reformulate its policy: A Jewish State in Palestine must be one of the fruits of the Allied victory, and 100,000 immigration certificates must be made available immediately. The new complexion of the British Government should expedite the realization of all our hopes.

At the same time, however, Weizmann cautioned against undue optimism. He had tried vainly to see Churchill, who maintained that the Zionist issue could not be taken up before the Peace Conference. "It seems that England alone finds difficulty in this matter," Weizmann remarked bitterly. For his part, Clement Attlee, the new Prime Minister, apparently failed to understand "why Jews don't go to Transjordan, which is half-empty"—an ironic reference to Attlee's naïve (or willful) ignorance of conditions in the Middle East.

Dr. Stephen Wise expressed the hope that President Truman would implement pre-election resolutions by the Democratic Party platform favoring "the establishment of a free and democratic Jewish commonwealth in Palestine." Dr. Abba Hillel Silver declared that, "if necessary, British Jews must fight their Government as the Jews in the United States are ready to do," should circumstances necessitate this. "By resisting, we are saving the honor and the soul of the British Government," he affirmed. "We have nothing to lose but our illusions!"

Eliyahu Dobkin, a member of the Jewish Agency's Jerusalem Executive and head of its Immigration Department, brought a message from the liberated Jews in German DP camps. At a recent conference near Munich, he reported, a six-year-old boy from Auschwitz had been chosen to sit on the presidium as a representative of the very few children who had survived the Holocaust. Each daily session began with *Mir Zeynen Do!* ("We are Here!"), the song of the Jewish partisans, and ended with *Hatikvah*. He estimated that there were 110,000 Jewish DPs in the U.S., British, and French zones of occupation, while a further 30,000 had been transferred from Sweden and other countries; more were being discovered all the time in mixed camps and villages. Altogether, Dobkin estimated, some one and a half million Jews had survived in Europe outside of the USSR. Those who made their way back to their old homes encountered such hatred that they soon returned to the camps. "Their only hope," he concluded, "is Aliyah."

Fresh from my own recent travels in France and Germany, I was able to confirm and supplement Dobkin's report. Stressing Washington's position as one of the two main political centers in the postwar world, I urged greater representation for the

ZOA on the Zionist Executive. Among other things, I also made reference to the UN Conference at San Francisco, where representatives of American Jewry had played a part in defending Zionist interests. "What we want now," I asserted, "is not only the abolition of the White Paper but a new political dispensation."

Among the significant addresses delivered during the conference sessions were those by Moshe Shertok, who hailed the Jewish Brigade's combat record and the establishment of fifty new settlements in Eretz Yisrael since 1939, and by Dr. Emil Sommerstein, head of the Polish delegation, who observed that he and his colleagues represented "three million martyred Jews for whom death was the lightest ordeal."

Dr. Abba Hillel Silver, now again head of the American Zionist Emergency Council, was particularly critical of Weizmann's keynote speech because of the note of dejection it contained. As for the victory of the British Labor Party, he warned against Jewish reliance on promises made by statesmen or political parties. It was the task of the Zionist movement to maintain the fighting spirit of the Jewish masses and to concentrate on the establishment of a Jewish State in Palestine, not merely on the granting of certificates for a small proportion of the Jews who sought entry to the homeland. Silver reminded the delegates that a memorandum about the 100,000 certificates had been submitted to the British Government more than two months earlier, and that a similar appeal by the Jewish Agency to the British High Commissioner for Palestine in June 1944 had remained unanswered.

By the summer of 1945, it became clear that Zionist policy was no longer amenable to compromise. Both Churchill and Attlee found themselves entangled in a web of conflicting interests—the need to placate Arab rulers and a reluctance to abandon the Zionists completely. The British thought that some way might be found to separate the problem of the DPs in Europe from that of their own administration in Palestine. On the one hand, they believed that the surviving Jews ought to be resettled on the European continent; on the other hand, they held that Palestine must fit in with the strategic needs of the West. Despite the Labor Party's pre-election pledges, the developing Cold War with the Soviet Union seemed to indicate that Jewish interests in Palestine might have to be sacrificed.

At the London Zionist Conference a tough new line emerged, advocated forcefully by David Ben-Gurion and supported by most of the American delegates. "We are now in the last struggle for Jewish existence," Ben-Gurion declared. "We are powerless because we lack the one essential instrument, a State. . . . I have no faith in the *Galut*. Palestine will be another *Galut* if life and conditions there are no different from the lands of the Diaspora." He cautioned that a British Labor Government would not be the same as a Labor opposition. Pro-Weizmann moderates and anti-Weizmann activists lined up in opposing camps, and this confrontation dominated the conference sessions.

A strongly worded political resolution was finally adopted, declaring that "the remnants of European Jewry cannot and will not continue their existence among the graveyards of millions of their slaughtered brethren. Their only salvation lies in their speediest settlement in Palestine." The resolution went on to demand "Palestine, undivided and undiminished, as a Jewish State, in accordance with the original purpose of the Balfour Declaration."

A new Zionist Executive was elected by the conference, reflecting the increased importance of the ZOA and American Zionism generally. Both Stephen Wise and Abba Hillel Silver joined Louis Lipsky and Nahum Goldmann on the Executive. These four men, together with four representatives of the Zionist parties in the United States, Leon Gellman of the Mizraḥi, Ḥayim Greenberg of the Labor Zionists, Rose Halprin of Hadassah, and I on behalf of the General Zionists, now formed a committee of eight responsible for the handling of political questions and for Jewish Agency operations in North America.

Throughout the period of the London conference, from July 30 until August 29, the presence of so many Zionist leaders in the British capital was utilized to the full. Simultaneous conferences of the World Zionist Organization (Jewish Agency) and of the World Jewish Congress took place, and consultations were held with other bodies such as the American Jewish Conference and the Board of Deputies of British Jews. Firsthand reports on the Jewish position in Poland, Czechoslovakia, Belgium, and other countries were submitted by representatives of those liberated communities. I had the responsibility of participating in more than one capacity.

The principal questions dealt with were the plight of displaced, stateless, and nonrepatriable Jews in Europe, on which a memorandum was prepared for the attention of UNRRA; reparations demands to be presented to Germany, for Jewish losses as a result of the Holocaust; the forthcoming Nuremberg Trials of major Nazi war criminals; and our stand at the Peace Conference. The memorandum submitted to UNRRA called for authorization to reestablish contact between Jewish communities and DPs, the removal of Jewish DPs from camps to more congenial surroundings, consideration for special needs in the matter of food, clothing, and medical supplies, and the provision of facilities for the reemployment of Jews in useful occupations. A number of these recommendations were subsequently put into effect. The memorandum also urged that no displaced persons be repatriated against their will, and that full consideration be given to the fact that the majority of Jewish DPs wished to settle in Palestine.

Our stand in regard to the 100,000 immigration certificates was to become the focal point of conflict between the Zionist movement and the British Labor Government for some time to come. The fact that President Truman chose to intercede was a source of great encouragement.

Harry S. Truman, the former Vice-President and senator from Missouri, knew little of Zionism when he first came to the White House. Initially, he saw no immediate connection between Zionist aspirations and the relief of Jews who had survived the Nazi concentration and death camps. Palestine, for him, was the Holy Land, while the Jewish DPs—for whom he had a genuine concern—were people deserving American assistance. During the months following the war, however, he came to understand the problem of the displaced Jews of Europe as it grew more and more acute. On June 22, 1945, President Truman commissioned a special team headed by Earl G. Harrison to investigate the entire situation in the U.S. zones of Germany and Austria. There, Harrison came face to face with evidence of the Nazi atrocities, the whole scope of the Holocaust, and the difficulties confronting Jews who had managed to survive. He received considerable help and guidance from Dr. Joseph J. Schwartz, European director of the JDC, and other experts in the refugee field.

On August 1, 1945, the day on which the London Zionist Conference began its deliberations, Earl Harrison submitted his preliminary report to the President. In addition to describing what he had seen and heard, he made a number of urgent recommendations. Most of the Jews whom he had met would settle for nothing less than the Jewish homeland—"They want to be evacuated to Palestine now." Harrison therefore urged the U.S. Administration's support for the Jewish Agency request in regard to the 100,000 certificates. He was nevertheless careful to stress the humanitarian nature of this recommendation, which expressed no opinion on the overall Palestine problem.

After reading the Harrison Report, President Truman signified his approval and asked General George Marshall, the U.S. Chief of Staff, to send a résumé to General Eisenhower at SHAEF, requesting prompt, effective action. This had an immediate and salutary effect. Steps were taken to ameliorate the living conditions and general treatment of Jewish DPs throughout the U.S. zone of occupation. Jews were also granted a considerable measure of autonomy in running their own affairs in the camps.

On October 8, 1945, General Eisenhower reported to President Truman that although much still needed to be done, conditions had improved since Earl Harrison's visit in July. Eisenhower mentioned, incidentally, my recommendation "that nonrepatriable Jews be separated from other stateless people and be placed in exclusively Jewish centers." As a result, the Joint Distribution Committee was called upon to supervise the establishment of these centers "for those Jews who are without nationality or those, not Soviet citizens, who do not desire to return to their countries of origin." No Jewish or other displaced persons had been housed in their former places of confinement longer than was absolutely necessary, for medical quarantine and recovery from acute illness. General Eisenhower also stated that medical attention and adequate supplies of food and clothing were now available. Religious programs and children's schooling had been organized. The UNRRA and JDC staffs were administering more and more centers, where Jewish chaplains and agencies played an active role. In conclusion, he said, "real and honest efforts are being made to provide suitable living conditions for these persecuted people until they can be permanently resettled."

Four Jewish advisers were authorized by the U.S. War Department and UNRRA to work with the American military government in Germany. They were Judge Louis E. Levinthal, Judge Simon H. Rifkind, Rabbi Philip S. Bernstein, and Harry Greenstein. This was an important achievement for the American Jewish Conference, since the British Government had turned down a similar request by the Jewish Board of Deputies in London.

Far more important in the long term, however, was Truman's endorsement of the recommendation in Earl Harrison's report about the 100,000 certificates for Palestine. The humanitarian aspect of the problem triumphed over other considerations. At the end of August, therefore, Truman sent a personal letter to Prime Minister Clement Attlee, urging that 100,000 Jewish DPs be admitted to Palestine forthwith. This letter was resented, especially by the new British Foreign Minister, Ernest Bevin, who looked to the Americans for support in imposing a British solution of the Palestine problem. Truman's refusal to take no for an answer had much to do with the subsequent course of events, leading eventually to the positions which he adopted in November 1947 and in May 1948.

My preoccupation with Zionist affairs during this time, in Great Britain and France, was briefly interrupted when I reverted to my responsibilities as president of the Synagogue Council of America and flew to Rome for an audience with Pope Pius XII. Our talks were confined to ecumenical matters. As Cardinal Eugenio Pacelli, he had been the Vatican's secretary of state, handling foreign affairs for nearly a decade until his elevation to the pontificate in 1939. While secretary of state, he had conducted the negotiations that led to the signing of a concordat between the Holy See and the Third Reich in 1933. What little I then knew of the Pope's wartime record, primarily with regard to the Nazi "Final Solution," was far from encouraging. In any event, our meeting was brief and formal, and we did not touch on matters of substance. At the conclusion of this audience, I was received by the acting secretary of state, Monsignor Domenico Tardini, a suave Italian prelate who looked every inch the diplomat his office required him to be. In view of my religious credentials, I felt free to discuss with him several issues of mutual concern.

I began by referring to my experience, as president of the Synagogue Council, working alongside the National Catholic Welfare Conference in the struggle against restrictive U.S. immigration policies. These affected Catholics more than Jews, I pointed out, since Jews were in any case prevented from leaving Soviet Russia and very few remained in Poland, whereas many Catholics in Poland and Italy wished to, and could, emigrate to the United States.

Another sphere of common endeavour upon which I touched was the Synagogue Council's joining with Catholic bodies in the U.S. in opposing regulations that would prevent religious seminaries and parochial schools from being built in residential areas. I said that although Catholic institutions were mainly affected by these proposed measures, the Synagogue Council had joined in combating the enactment of such ordinances.

"Yes," the prelate rejoined, "but what about that Reform rabbi in California who doesn't go along with you?"

I was astonished to find that this monsignor-statesman, whose jurisdiction embraced the whole Catholic world, should be familiar with one tiny detail in a vast range of important, pressing concerns.

There were several vital matters which the protocol of my hosts did not allow me to take up with the Vatican, and I hoped that different credentials might enable me to broach them on some other, future occasion.

From Rome I returned to London for a few more days, during which I had an interesting talk with Professor Harold Laski, the left-wing British Socialist, who had recently been elected chairman of the Labor Party. As a political scientist and Socialist thinker, he wielded considerable influence over the Labor movement in Great Britain, and importance was attached to his views. Following the change of government in July 1945, Laski expressed strong support for the establishment of a Jewish commonwealth in Palestine and attacked Bevin's anti-Zionist policies. Such had also been the view of his late father, Nathan Laski, a prominent Anglo-Jewish communal leader.

Professor Laski advanced the suggestion that the Jewish Agency and Zionist Organization move their world headquarters to Washington, D.C., "so as to deal with Great Britain as a foreign government." When I asked whether, in his view, it would take special courage for the Laborites to push through their election promises on Palestine, he replied, "No more courage than it will take to nationalize the Bank of England."

He spoke of irrigation schemes for Palestine and the adjacent areas, benefiting the Arabs as well as the Jews, and stressed that Jews ought to make such a generous goodwill gesture.

On August 10, I was in Paris again and addressed a mass meeting in Yiddish. I praised French Jewry's role in the anti-Nazi resistance and spoke of the American Jewish community's deep concern—reflected in its most representative body, the American Jewish Conference—for the rehabilitation of European Jewry. The Jews in Europe, I said, should themselves be represented in that effort. Alluding to the San Francisco Conference, where we had striven to protect existing Jewish rights in Palestine under the British Mandate, I declared that we now wanted more than the status quo. "We seek a Jewish commonwealth in Eretz Yisrael and we have confidence in the support of the American people and of President Truman." I assured my audience that "American Jewry will not rest until the Jewish people will be a free people in a free world, living in a free Eretz Yisrael."

My six-week sojourn in Great Britain and Western Europe terminated on August 17, when I flew out of London with Dr. Abba Hillel Silver, Judge Louis Levinthal, Meyer Weisgal, and Mendel Fisher as fellow passengers. Among those on board our plane was Colonel Harold B. Hoskins, a senior official in the State Department's Office of Near Eastern and African Affairs (NEA), which had responsibility for dealing with the Palestine problem. Hoskins, whose links with the oil-rich sheikhdoms of the Persian Gulf region made him the watchdog of important vested interests, had been President Roosevelt's personal envoy to Saudi Arabia.

Dr. Silver and I tackled Colonel Hoskins during the flight. He was obviously sensitive about the attacks being leveled at him in Jewish circles and remarked, "There is a danger that all of this will make anti-Semites of some people, though as for myself, of course . . ."

My reply did not spare him. "I know that you have a fine Christian background and, were I a Christian, it would sit heavily on my conscience to think that I had done something which spelled death for thousands of Jews. You must try to understand why we feel so bitterly. Your policy of favoring the Arabs has sent thousands of Jews to the gas chambers."

He was taken aback for a moment and then said, "The Jews have had the run of propaganda in the United States, and I felt it necessary to present the Arab point of view. Why not have Palestine as an international state to which the Jews can come for spiritual reasons, and create a Jewish State elsewhere?"

"Have you an offer?" I asked. "Even if you had one, we would reject it because there is an affinity between the Jews and Palestine. No other people would invest such toil and love in that land."

We discussed the prospects for Jewish immigration into other countries, and I brought up the question of prevailing anti-Semitism. Hoskins could think of no effective answer and, indeed, how could there be one? Innumerable palliatives and alternatives had been proposed for generations past, but only the Land of Israel offered a home and haven for our people.

On October 5, 1945, the Interim Committee of the American Jewish Conference sent a telegram over the signatures of its three co-chairmen to President Truman. It expressed appreciation of his request, based on the Harrison Report, that Great Britain facilitate the immediate entry of 100,000 Jews into Palestine. We urged that this be regarded as an initial step toward the definitive solution of establishing a Jewish national homeland in Palestine, and we besought Truman's leadership in attaining that end.

On that same day, I presented a comprehensive report to the American Jewish Conference, describing my visits to the DP camps in Germany and covering my participation in the Zionist Conference and other meetings in London.

During October, I had the honor of being elected as an additional American member of the Zionist Executive.

One important appointment that strengthened our efforts at this time was that of Dr. Benjamin Akzin as political advisor (and, later, as secretary) of the American Zionist Emergency Council. An expert on international relations and constitutional law, Akzin had served under John W. Pehle, Jr., in the U.S. War Refugee Board. After his Aliyah in 1949, Dr. Akzin went on to achieve eminence in his field as dean of the Law Faculty at the Hebrew University of Jerusalem.

Meanwhile, as will be indicated more fully in a subsequent chapter, events were warming up in Palestine, where Ben-Gurion's policy of active resistance to the White Paper led to a temporary alliance between the Haganah and the two smaller Jewish underground movements. The warnings we had heard in London about not placing much reliance on the new Labor Government proved to be only too well founded. Over the next two years, Zionist hopes were blasted by Whitehall's delaying tactics and by increasingly repressive measures aimed against the Yishuv by the Palestine Mandatory authorities. This process began with the announcement by Foreign Secretary Ernest Bevin, on November 13, 1945, that the British and U.S.

Governments had agreed on the appointment of an Anglo-American Committee of Inquiry to investigate the problems affecting Palestine and European Jewry, and to propose measures for their solution. The upshot was that the Committee of Inquiry presented a report that was not to Bevin's liking and which he therefore chose to ignore. From that point onward, the Zionist movement plunged into its climactic struggle.

My two-year term as president of the Zionist Organization of America ended at the Atlantic City convention, which opened on November 17. In the course of my farewell address, I surveyed the ZOA's record, its successes and failures, during my wartime presidency. Concluding on a note of rededication to the cause of Jewish statehood, I said:

> No kind of public service is a bed of roses, and anyone who chooses it does so at his own risk and should not whine if he gets hurt. Yet I tell you, with all my heart, that I am deeply in your debt for having summoned me to the most difficult, the most trying, the most challenging, but the most glorious and the most rewarding commitment in Jewish life—Zionism. . . .
>
> We are an ancient people, acquainted with grief. If sufferance has been the badge of our tribe, it is not written in our Book that sufferance is our destiny. Our destiny is to be a people among peoples, standing on our feet and resting our feet upon the hallowed soil of our fathers.

After having retired from the leadership of the ZOA, I continued to serve as co-chairman of the American Jewish Conference, until its dissolution at the end of 1948.

5

The Founding of Brandeis University

My concurrent terms as president of the ZOA and of the Synagogue Council of America both expired at the end of 1945, thus substantially easing the burden of public responsibility I had carried in the preceding years. Accordingly, I was able to devote more time and effort to the affairs of my congregation. Wherever weak spots seemed to have developed, I now hastened to repair them. B'nai Jeshurun's lay leadership naturally welcomed the renewed daily contact with their rabbi and the congregation's affiliated bodies were reinforced.

An innovation I introduced in 1946, under the auspices of the men's club, was an annual Brotherhood Day award to a distinguished citizen. For a number of years past, the men's club had sponsored a Brotherhood Day service in February, when the birthdays of George Washington and Abraham Lincoln were nationally observed. The award ceremony enhanced this special service and promoted the cause of interfaith understanding in the New York community.

To mark my fiftieth birthday, in June 1946, Congregation B'nai Jeshurun tendered a dinner at which a fund was raised for the purpose of endowing a lectureship in my name at the Jewish Theological Seminary of America. Professor Louis Finkelstein, president of the Seminary, who delivered an outstanding address, presented me with a scroll commemorating the endowment. Initially, this lectureship was an annual event, the lecturers and their subjects varying from year to year. Professor Martin Buber of the Hebrew University was among those who delivered a series of lectures. The lectureship was subsequently expanded into a chair in practical theology, and its first incumbent was Rabbi Max Arzt.

The toastmaster at this fiftieth anniversary dinner was Alan Stroock, a third-generation member of my congregation and a trustee of the Seminary. Apart from Professor Finkelstein, the speakers were Judge Samuel Null, the Reverend Dr. Ralph W. Sockman, chairman of the World Peace Commission of the Federal Council of Churches, and Charles H. Silver, B'nai Jeshurun's vice-president. Among the cables and telegrams received were messages from Governor Thomas E. Dewey of New York and from Professor Selig Brodetsky, president of the Board of Deputies of British Jews, as well as two others from my good friend, the Reverend Dr. Everett Clinchy, president of the National Conference of Christians and Jews, and from Cardinal Francis Spellman of New York.

In the course of my own remarks, I said that my aim had been to function as "a full-time Jew in the service of the Jewish people." I also expressed the hope that three things would be accomplished in my lifetime: the checking of anti-Semitism as a plague to be declared "out of bounds" by humanity; the establishment of an internationally recognized Jewish State in Palestine; and a worldwide process of education whereby all men would come to appreciate the value of "the Jewish entity in civilization's mosaic."

How the "Jewish University in America" Originated

The relative freedom I now enjoyed from extra-congregational responsibilities enabled me to turn over in my mind an idea that had been filed away subconsciously for consideration at an opportune time. It had to do with a secular, broadly based university under Jewish auspices, which would represent no particular wing of Judaism but the American Jewish community as a whole. Jews and non-Jews would be admitted to its faculty and student body on merit only, and not according to any quota system. In various forms, this had been envisaged for some considerable time and had inspired a monograph entitled "A Jewish University in America," published by Rabbi Louis I. Newman in 1923.

The existing institutions of higher Jewish learning in the United States, meant primarily for the training of rabbis, did not meet this particular need. No Jewish group in American public life had so far taken the initiative in fostering a denominational college or university, similar to those sponsored by Catholics, Episcopalians, Presbyterians, Baptists, Methodists, Congregationalists, Quakers, and other Christian groups. Individual Jews had made generous contributions to such establishments, but they had never embarked upon a collective undertaking of their own in the sphere of higher education.

This was all the more regrettable in view of the unofficial *numerus clausus* barring thousands of students on religious or ethnic grounds. The unofficial quota system bore down heavily on Jews, while Black students and teachers suffered even more from the prevalent discrimination.

Obviously, one Jewish-sponsored university, open on merit only to all races and creeds, would hardly solve the problem. It would nevertheless serve as an instructive example and thus it would redound to the credit of the American Jewish community. Moreover, there would be other advantages. Scholars on the faculty would enrich the general culture and science of the American community as a whole, while making an identifiably Jewish contribution to the mainstream of knowledge.

It also occurred to me that such an institution of higher learning could play a significant part in building leadership echelons for American Jewry by developing a consciousness of its current problems, and by fostering a broad social and communal awareness among students during their college years. As yet, there was no center where this kind of in-depth training for Jewish intellectual leadership could be obtained. Furthermore, it was reasonable to suppose that a university of this type would become a cultural milieu to which illustrious Jewish scholars from many parts of the world would gravitate as visiting professors. It would provide a forum where their views could be expressed and where their learning and wisdom could be made available. I also envisioned a special relationship between such a university and the Hebrew University of Jerusalem.

There were, of course, various counterarguments—that it would be a ghetto, that non-Jewish students would join only as a last resort when rejected by other colleges, that it would serve as a pretext for other universities to refuse admission to Jewish applicants, and so forth. These were, to my mind, specious arguments. Such misgivings arose, I believed, from the desire of certain Jewish elements to "keep a low profile," to shy away from anything that savored of an assertion of Jewish identity. Chameleon-like, these complex-ridden Jews sought protection by simulating the color of their environment.

Some genuine problems, however, would need to be tackled and thrashed out, such as the type of curriculum and academic aura to be fostered at such an institution, the nature of its Jewish religious observance, exchange programs with other centers of Jewish learning, and various other matters. I nevertheless felt that these could be solved and that there was no reason to fear insuperable difficulties.

As far back as the annual convention of the Zionist Organization of America, held in Detroit toward the end of 1938, I had mentioned to a number of friends my idea of a Jewish-sponsored university in America. Other priorities, however, soon imposed themselves. What gave special urgency to such musings after the war was the demobilization of large numbers of Jews who had served in the U.S. armed forces, and the educational opportunities extended to them under the G.I. Bill of Rights.

In November 1945, during the convention of the ZOA held in Atlantic City, when my term as president was drawing to an end, I broached my proposal to a few friends and colleagues. One of them was Rabbi Simon Greenberg of Congregation Har Zion, Philadelphia, who also served as associate professor of education at the Jewish Theological Seminary of America. His response was most encouraging.

I was only too well aware of the formidable task that lay ahead. It meant translating the idea into important and difficult practical steps, such as finding a suitable campus, raising the necessary funds, planning the educational syllabus, selecting the right kind of faculty, attracting good students, and creating public goodwill.

Sooner than I had expected, a real possibility of fulfillment presented itself early in the following year. It came in a letter dated January 7, 1946, from C. Ruggles Smith, general counsel of Middlesex University at Waltham, Massachusetts. He wrote at the suggestion of Joseph Schlossberg, who thought that I might be able "to assist an institution which has been the victim of the policy of anti-Semitism motivating those organizations which control education and practice in the professions that deal with the healing arts in this country."

Joseph Schlossberg, a leader in the Jewish labor movement and at one time a member of the New York Board of Education, was a cherished friend of mine to whom I had once mentioned my interest in the idea of a Jewish-sponsored university. I learned subsequently that C. Ruggles Smith was the son of Dr. John Hall

Smith, a prominent Boston surgeon, who until his death in 1944 had been the guiding spirit of Middlesex University. Dr. Smith had devoted his life and fortune to its establishment after it had taken over the charter of a previous medical school.

My correspondent cited a number of articles in newspapers and periodicals that dwelt on the racial and religious discrimination practiced in medical and in veterinary medical education. He charged that the graduates of Middlesex University were being denied accreditation, owing to its policy of nondiscrimination in the admission of students, and he laid the blame at the door of the American Medical Association and the American Veterinary Medical Association.

Mr. Smith, on behalf of the board of trustees, then offered to turn over their responsibilities to any new group that could reestablish the School of Medicine on an approved basis. He believed that I might be in a position to enlist the support of persons who would be interested in the running of "an educational institution which would offer college and professional education in the field of the healing arts on a democratic American basis, with the elimination of racial, religious or social discrimination in the selection of students and faculty."

Soon afterwards, I received a letter from Dr. Joseph I. Cheskis, dean of the College Department and campus director of Middlesex University, proposing that the two of us meet. He was a friend of Joseph Schlossberg.

It was a tempting opportunity, yet there was one manifest drawback. To assume responsibility for a medical school from the outset was hardly the way to build up the kind of university I had in mind. I felt that a medical school, the establishment and maintenance of which would be a very costly undertaking, should be considered only some years after the successful establishment of a college of liberal arts.

At the same time, the existing campus and buildings constituted, undeniably, a valuable asset. C. Ruggles Smith estimated the value of these properties at over one million dollars, free and without encumbrance save for a mere $20,500. The university's proximity to Boston had a twofold advantage. First, the Boston area, with its institutions of higher learning, was probably the intellectual center of America. Second, Boston's large and outstanding Jewish community represented an immediate source of interest and support. Besides, the availability of charters for a school of liberal arts and for the professional schools was a most important and persuasive factor.

On the negative side, damaging publicity about Middlesex had clearly impaired its prestige. I felt, however, that this could be overcome by a change of name, which would in any case be desirable in order to give the university a Jewish connotation, and that it would come to be judged on the basis of its current record, not its past.

In mid-January 1946, a week after receiving Mr. Smith's letter, my wife and I went to look over the grounds at Waltham. Located about ten miles northeast of Boston and rising on high ground, Waltham dominates both sides of the Charles River. It has long been renowned as the home of the Waltham Watch Company. The 100-acre campus of Middlesex University offered vistas of woodland and grassy landscape. The grounds had a delightful setting and commanded a view of the city and of the river meandering on its way down to the sea.

The main college building, in the architectural style of the medieval turreted castle, contrasted with the more functional design of the School of Veterinary Medicine on the campus. Although the grounds showed signs of neglect, and in spite of some dilapidated structures and the general need of repairs, Bert and I saw the potentialities and felt that the answer to a long-cherished vision lay in the Middlesex campus.

A few weeks of intensive activity followed. The first person whom I consulted, and in whose judgment and counsel I placed unreserved confidence, was Julius Silver of New York City. An eminent lawyer, the vice-president, director, and general counsel of the Polaroid Corporation of Cambridge, Massachusetts, he had served as associate counsel of the U.S. Senate Committee on Banking and Currency. I felt that Julius Silver could give me sound general advice and guide me through the labyrinth of legal and financial problems. My faith in him proved to be fully justified.

Acting on his suggestion, we enlisted the help of George Alpert, a prominent Boston attorney, whose advice and assistance could be useful in dealing with any legal problems that might arise, as well as in enlisting the cooperation of leading Jews in the Boston community. Our preliminary contacts found a number of civic and philanthropic leaders of the Boston Jewish community well disposed toward our proposal. After probing all aspects, we resolved to go forward and bring matters to their conclusion.

The first requirement was educational sponsorship of high caliber. A number of prominent scholars, scientists, and public figures with whom I discussed the matter showed great interest, but I aimed higher. Accordingly, I made an appointment to see the greatest figure in the academic world, Professor Albert Einstein, at his home in Princeton, New Jersey.

Einstein received me in his study. We were no strangers, having already met seven years previously, when I was chairman of the board of the Palestine Pavilion at the New York World's Fair. I gave him an outline of my scheme. He heard me out attentively and then agreed that a Jewish-sponsored secular institution of higher learning was an important objective, especially in view of the current plight of Jewish students and academicians. He was especially concerned about the problem facing Jewish scholars, some of them recent arrivals from liberated Europe, who found it difficult to secure teaching positions in American institutions of higher learning.

A second interview was arranged, and Julius Silver accompanied me so as to explain to Professor Einstein the details regarding the acquisition of the campus and charter of Middlesex University.

Events followed hard upon each other with dizzying rapidity. Less than two weeks had elapsed since my receipt of the letter from C. Ruggles Smith, and much ground had been covered by the time Professor Einstein wrote me a letter of acceptance, on January 23, agreeing to become the new university's educational sponsor. Time was of the essence, as we had heard rumors that other groups, both public and private, were interested in this property for either educational or commercial purposes.

Einstein's communication was warmly encouraging. He wanted it to be made certain "that the Board and Administration will remain permanently in reliable Jewish hands." He went on to say:

I am convinced that such an institution will attract our best young Jewish people and not less our young scientists and learned men in all fields. Such an institution, provided it is of a high standard, will improve our situation a good deal and will satisfy a real need. As is well known, many of our gifted youth see themselves denied the cultural and professional education they are longing for.

I would do anything in my power to help in the creation and guidance of such an institute. It would always be near to my heart.

Fortified by this backing, Julius Silver and I proceeded to build up an effective nucleus of men to help us get the project off the ground. Our initial group comprised George Alpert; Judge Samuel Null of the Supreme Court of the State of New York; Dr. Israel S. Wechsler, professor of neurology at Columbia University; Dr. Alexander Dushkin, executive vice-president of the Jewish Education Committee of New York; Major Abraham F. Wechsler, president of the Madison Settlement House; and two men prominent in business circles and philanthropy, Milton Bluestein and Albert Rosen.

Negotiations with Mr. Smith and his colleagues at Waltham proceeded swiftly. Parallel with these talks, I made the first soundings about fund raising and met with a group of New York businessmen in my study at Congregation B'nai Jeshurun on the afternoon of January 31. The response was modest, but encouraging.

Meanwhile, our discussions with Middlesex University were going well. Dr. Cheskis took part in some of these meetings. I emphasized that it should be a source of considerable moral satisfaction to them that their principle of a nonquota institution would be safeguarded by my group.

Writing to C. Ruggles Smith on February 4, 1946, I set forth the conclusions Julius Silver and I had drawn up following our discussions with Professor Einstein, with educators and with businessmen interested in educational philanthropy. These conclusions were:

(1) To develop on the Middlesex campus a college of liberal arts and various schools for professional training, which would be open to qualified students and to faculty members without restrictions as to race, creed, or color. The aim would be to make a worthwhile contribution to American education, and its successful realization would be a "well-merited vindication of American democratic principles which have not always been paramount in the conduct of many educational institutions in our country."

(2) To secure financial support for such an enterprise, which leading educators and scientists, headed by Professor Albert Einstein, had encouraged us to believe was "a project of educational and spiritual value and significance."

(3) That Middlesex should continue to operate, with such incidental strengthening as might be required, until the new and larger enterprise which we

envisaged could be opened in October 1947. During the interim period, it would be our moral obligation to help cover the operating deficit.

Since Mr. Smith had arranged to secure the resignation of five of the seven trustees of Middlesex University, and to elect five of our group in their stead, thereby placing the university under our control, my letter concluded with the nomination of five new designees who would serve until such time as a full board would be appointed. Our nominees were George Alpert, Dr. Israel Goldstein, Judge Samuel Null, Julius Silver, and Major Abraham F. Wechsler.

A series of preparatory steps followed. With an eye to fund raising, Julius Silver and I obtained the consent of Professor Einstein to establish the Albert Einstein Foundation for Higher Learning. Next came a meeting of the trustees of Middlesex University at the Harvard Club in Cambridge, Massachusetts, on February 7. The chair was taken by the Reverend Hugh Wallace Smith, president of the board. Upon the resignation of all but one of the remaining trustees, I was elected president of the board, Julius Silver as secretary, and George Alpert as treasurer. We now constituted the executive committee, together with Dudley F. Kimball, the former treasurer, who remained a trustee and committee member.

So ended the first phase, one month after Mr. Smith's letter had reached me. Our group established a substantial basis on which to build a Jewish-sponsored secular university, and we acquired the essential instruments with which to proceed. All of this had been achieved in thirty-one days of unceasing activity, negotiations, and journeyings to and fro between New York and Boston, enlisting sponsors, obtaining Einstein's endorsement, exploring fund-raising prospects, and securing the campus and the charters.

Laying the Foundations

Our next step was to broaden the sponsorship, campaign for support, and win over public opinion. I embarked on a schedule of meetings with leading personalities, commencing in the Boston area, where, it seemed to me, the primary support should be canvassed. My first call was on Dr. Karl T. Compton, president of the Massachusetts Institute of Technology, with whom I had a frank discussion. It seemed natural to him that American Jews should seek to establish an institution of this kind, and he did not believe that it would be used by other institutions as a pretext for restricting their admission of Jewish students. Dr. Compton authorized us to use his endorsement, declaring that "this university would provide another facility for higher education at a time when existing facilities are greatly overtaxed and when all trends point toward a continual, increasing demand for higher education of the youth of our country."

A constructive proposal emerged from my talk with Dr. Daniel L. Marsh, president of Boston University, who offered an exchange of facilities and courses where either of the two institutions might have special advantages to give in certain subjects.

My interview with the Governor of Massachusetts, Maurice J. Tobin, produced an important additional endorsement. Writing from State House in Boston, he affirmed, *inter alia*, that "just as other religious denominations have established outstanding institutions which have become landmarks of American culture and scientific advancement, so may this university prove to be an eminent contribution to American civilization."

Similarly, Archbishop Richard J. Cushing, on whom I called, expressed sympathetic interest and wished our venture every success. "We Catholics," he wrote, "have solved, by founding our own Colleges, many of the problems confronting us in the effort to secure educational opportunities for our young people."

Further encouraging statements and letters were received from various quarters, and there was a gratifyingly positive reaction in the local press. An editorial in *The Boston Traveller* of April 5, 1946, thus concluded:

> It is incumbent on the general public, as well as the world of scholarship, to know and evaluate fully the fact that Middlesex hereafter will be in the mainstream of the world's intellectual tradition and that its future graduates will be full-fledged and fully honored members of the ancient company of scholars.

Some useful advice came from David K. Niles, special assistant to Presidents Roosevelt and Truman, when I consulted him. His home was in Boston and, as one active in the public affairs of his home state, he was able to recommend certain important approaches. Leaders of the Boston Jewish community, including men of national prominence, also volunteered their good offices and assistance. Communal and synagogue bodies expressed sympathetic interest.

Inevitably, as I had foreseen, there were some negative reactions as well, but public opinion was largely affirmative and, in many cases, even enthusiastic. The unfavorable arguments were precisely those which we had anticipated, and they were not difficult to answer. One valid reservation that I kept in mind, however, concerned the reopening of the medical school without regard for the huge costs involved and the availability of proper clinical facilities.

Boston, of course, constituted only the base of the pyramid of support that needed to be built up. A long round of interviews, meetings, and other promotion activities followed during the ensuing weeks, and the list of those who were persuaded to give their endorsement became long and impressive. By the summer of that year, we had received favorable resolutions from a large number of eminent public bodies and individual leaders, and we could appeal for nationwide moral and material support with the backing of nearly a hundred personalities of rank, including governors, senators and congressmen, educators, judges, clergy, authors, and labor leaders.

George Alpert and I went around the country, bringing word of our university project to communities and congregations. I was even urged to enlarge its scope by fostering a similar institution on the West Coast. Our path, however, was still strewn with difficulties. A storm blew up in Boston itself when a state senator, Edward M. Rowe, introduced a bill into the Legislature of the Commonwealth of Massachusetts to revoke that part of the Middlesex University charter authorizing it to operate a medical school, in view of the fact that its graduates were no longer eligible to be licensed in the state. Since the establishment of a medical school was not excluded from our future plans, retention of the existing charter meant that we could avoid much worry and effort later on, if we should decide to implement that aspect of our plan.

On April 1, 1946, Alpert and I appeared before the legislature's subcommittee on education, to argue against Rowe's bill. We presented our plan for a Jewish-sponsored secular university as a contribution to higher learning, and we cited the civic, religious, and educational leaders from whom we had received endorsements. In the end, our representations proved successful. Senator Rowe withdrew his bill and our charter remained intact.

Amid all this strain and tension, there was also one amusing episode. In the final stages of our negotiations with the Middlesex board of trustees, it transpired that one hangover responsibility still had to be discharged—the graduation of thirty-seven veterinarians.

With no academic official available to award the diplomas, it fell to my lot, as president of the new board, to perform those honors on May 27, 1946. The conferment of veterinary degrees was a novel experience for a rabbi, but I took it in my stride. Conditioned to begin my addresses with some appropriate text, I quoted the biblical narrative that relates how Saul, while in quest of his father's asses, was encountered by the prophet Samuel and anointed king of Israel. The humor of the situation was not lost on my audience.

Our headaches were not yet over. Every now and then, we were faced with the question as to whether it might not be advisable to seek a campus elsewhere, in view of the dubious reputation inherited from Middlesex University. Doubts were also expressed here and there as to the physical suitability of the available campus. I investigated other possibilities and came to the conclusion that we should retain what we had.

For the time being, we continued to administer the property under its Middlesex University title. The Albert Einstein Foundation was not only the financial instrument but also the policymaking body for Middlesex, and its directors served as trustees of the university. Since I headed both bodies, control was centralized.

The Foundation was incorporated under the laws of the State of Delaware on February 25, about six weeks after the campus had been acquired. Temporary income-tax exemption for gifts was obtained from the Internal Revenue Service, with permanent exemption to follow after the first year's operation. A fund-raising apparatus was set up and personnel were hired. As a temporary office, we used rooms adjoining my study, by courtesy of Congregation B'nai Jeshurun. Later on, as our operations expanded, separate and more commodious offices were leased. Our first director of fund raising was Boris Young.

The university's inaugural function took place at the Waldorf-Astoria on the evening of June 20, and was attended by sixty guests. Prior to that occasion, S. Ralph Lazarus, a senior executive of the Benrus Watch Company who headed the fund-raising campaign in New York, had brought a number of potential donors to visit Albert Einstein at Princeton. The Waldorf-Astoria function netted pledges of $350,000 from the small group present. A gift of $100,000 by Israel Rogosin, the textile magnate, headed the list of contributions.

The speeches at that dinner included a stirring address by Dr. Alvin S. Johnson, head of the New School for Social Research. All present sensed that they were participating in a pioneer and historic educational venture. The following day, approving editorial comments appeared in *The New York Times, The New York Herald Tribune,* and other dailies.

Meanwhile, various names for the college had been proposed, but none struck me as particularly suitable. I then hit upon a name that appeared to be highly appropriate—Louis D. Brandeis. The greatest American Jew of his time, liberal in his Americanism and self-affirming in his Jewishness, a Zionist par excellence, Justice Brandeis had rendered historic services to the United States and to the Jewish people, and his notable life could serve as an inspiration to American youth. He had died five years previously, in October 1941. The fact that a large part of his career had been linked with Massachusetts gave special point to associating his name with the university at Waltham. Moreover, I felt, the association of his name and philosophy would serve as a constant reminder of the need to keep the institution modest in size, but outstanding in quality.

On one occasion, while speaking with Professor Einstein, Julius Silver and I had ventured the suggestion that the university should bear his name, but he declined. He approved the linking of Brandeis's name with the university. A resolution to this effect was accordingly passed by the board of the Foundation on July 16, 1946. It expressed the hope that the new institution, Brandeis University, would constitute "a worthy memorial, dedicated as a Jewish contribution to the promotion of higher learning in America for the advancement of human culture and science, and for the advancement of understanding, goodwill and righteous living among men."

We sought and obtained the approval of the family of the late Justice Louis D. Brandeis. Mrs. Susan Brandeis Gilbert, his daughter, together with her husband and other members of the family, gave their wholehearted blessing to the project and to the name.

It now remained to set a date for the opening of Brandeis University. Applications from would-be students and faculty members were pouring in from all parts of the U.S. and from other countries. We felt that it would require at least a year to raise the minimum funds to repair and renovate the buildings, organize a faculty, and provide dormitories and a refectory. The nearest conceivable time was the fall of 1947. We planned an inaugural class of 150, with a total enrollment of about 500 students in the early years, rising eventually to a maximum of one thousand.

I felt that it would soon be necessary to appoint a president or chancellor, or possibly both, one to be the university's representative vis-à-vis the public and to take charge of fund raising, the other to be responsible for academic policy and administration. With this in mind, I made another trip to Princeton and met with

Professor Einstein and his close friend, Dr. Otto Nathan, then assistant professor of economics at New York University, to discuss the setting up of an educational advisory committee that would select an acting academic head and an advisory panel to assist him. Dr. Nathan had been chosen by Einstein to serve as his liaison with the directors of the Foundation.

In the course of our conversation, I mentioned the name of Dr. Abram L. Sachar, then director of the B'nai B'rith Hillel Foundation, as a possible candidate for the top position at Brandeis. I referred to Dr. Sachar's academic record and to his books, copies of which I later sent to Professor Einstein. Subsequently, in a conversation with Dr. Sachar, I asked if he would be interested in having his name proposed to the Educational Advisory Committee among those to be considered for the post. He promised to take the matter under advisement, but it was made clear that neither of us was entering into any formal commitment.

Meanwhile, the financial side of our program was assuming greater urgency and importance. We had the campus, the charter, the name, and a broadly representative educational sponsorship. To get our project off the ground, a fund-raising campaign of major proportions had become indispensable.

A Critical Decision

One day, as I was busily preparing for a larger fund-raising dinner to be held at the Hotel Pierre on November 19, I was startled to receive a letter from Professor Einstein, complaining that I had been guilty of breaches of confidence toward him, first, in having invited Cardinal Francis J. Spellman to take part in the program at the dinner, and second, in having approached Dr. Sachar about heading the university without the authorization of the Educational Advisory Committee. In the circumstances, Einstein wrote, he could no longer cooperate with me nor permit his name to be used in fund raising for an enterprise in which I would play an important part.

This letter came as a thunderbolt: I was completely stunned. At no time had Professor Einstein given me to understand that he wished to concern himself with the details of a program for a fund-raising dinner. As for Dr. Sachar, I had made only a tentative, exploratory approach to gauge his interest, and it had been made clear that there was no commitment on either side.

In my reply, I explained these points fully, but I could not induce Professor Einstein to modify his decision. Nor were efforts by other equally perturbed board members any more successful.

It was a bizarre situation, for which there was no precedent throughout my experience in public affairs. My contacts with Einstein had not been close enough for me to evaluate his character. Naturally, I was impressed by his standing as a great personality, a great scientist, and a great Jew, but I had had no personal knowledge of the man when I sought and obtained his patronage for the university project. It occurred to me that perhaps he had reacted in this way as a result of garbled reports by a third party serving as his advisor. Whatever lay behind this sudden démarche, the damage was done. His adamant stance brooked no compromise and rendered useless any mollifying overtures on my part.

I was now faced by an agonizing choice: either to stay on at the head of the project and risk the after-effects of Einstein's public withdrawal, or to bow out and thus ensure his continued association with it. From conversations with my colleagues, I knew that, if I chose to stay on, the majority would back me. Nevertheless, I opted for the other course, to bow out, which I felt would be in the best interests of the Brandeis University project. It was a heartbreaking decision, as I had resolved to devote the next few years to guiding the effort in its early stages until it was firmly based.

At a meeting of the board of the Foundation held in my study on September 16, 1946, I tendered my immediate resignation from all offices, including presidency of the board of trustees. This, I felt, would leave the way clear for Professor Einstein to maintain his association. My friends were not easily persuaded to agree to my withdrawal. They expressed the view that, all things considered, my continued leadership outweighed other factors. I insisted, however, that my decision was the best course to follow, and they reluctantly acquiesced.

I proposed that Ralph Lazarus succeed me as president of the board of trustees, subject to Einstein's approval, and I also seconded a motion by George Alpert and Julius Silver, which was carried unanimously, that the Boston Jewish community be given greater representation on the board of the Foundation.

Finally, I presented to the meeting a summary of what had been done during the eight busy months since Mr. Smith's letter had arrived. "I content myself," I said, "with having done some of the spadework in winning support and sponsorship for the idea, in securing and holding the premises, in establishing a Board of fine, able, devoted men, in organizing machinery for fund raising, and in attaching an important name [Einstein] to the Foundation and an important name [Brandeis] to the University."

In the course of my report, I went on to say:

> Building a university is a project not for years, but for decades. Leadership comes and goes, the idea and the institution must go on. At different stages, different men have their places and their uses. It is a source of deep satisfaction to me that I have had a part in the pioneer stage. . . .
>
> Some day, when Brandeis University will be a notable landmark in American higher education, respected as a Jewish contribution to American culture and as a symbol of Jewish dignity and self-respect, it may be worth recalling the chapter of Genesis.

In a public statement issued on September 25, I explained that my resignation had been tendered because of differences between Professor Einstein and myself, and because I believed that his association with the university project was indispensable to its success. I expressed gratitude for having had some part in "a Jewish-sponsored nonquota university, as a contribution to American higher education paralleling those made by other religious denominations."

It was gratifying to learn that, at a subsequent meeting of the board held on September 30, 1946, Dr. Otto Nathan, Einstein's representative, declared that he considered my statement to the press to have been "very dignified and generous."

Three weeks after my resignation, I wrote to a large group of friends urging their continued interest and support.

Less than a year later, in June 1947, Professor Einstein himself resigned from the Brandeis University enterprise and simultaneously withdrew his name from the Foundation. According to press reports, he resigned because a majority of the board had opposed his wish to invite Professor Harold Laski of the London School of Economics to head the university. As I commented at the time, "the circumstances of Dr. Einstein's withdrawal seem to me somewhat ironic in view of my own earlier unfortunate experience."

The board of trustees thereupon altered the name of the sponsoring body to The Brandeis Foundation. The opening of the College of Liberal Arts was set for the fall of 1948.

At one point, in the course of subsequent developments, I was approached to resume the leadership. It was evident to me, however, that my acceptance would involve a full-time commitment, necessitating the surrender not only of my Zionist responsibilities, which were dear to me, but even of my career in the rabbinate. I was invited to a meeting of the board of the Brandeis Foundation at the Waldorf-Astoria on October 13, 1947. A group of six leading Jews in the Boston area had meanwhile been elected to join George Alpert on that body. All seven of them agreed to a proposal by the New York members that I should become president of the university and of the Foundation. A committee of two was appointed to discuss the matter further with me.

I mentioned several conditions, including one bearing upon the composition of the governing board, which, it seemed to me, would have to be met in order to enhance the prospects of success for this new educational venture. These conditions were not acceptable to the Boston group. Our discussions ended at that point.

To the credit of the Boston group, it should be recorded that they shouldered their responsibilities with great devotion and success.

On April 27, 1948, it was announced that Dr. Abram L. Sachar had been appointed president of Brandeis University. I immediately offered my heartfelt congratulations on his choice, which I saw as "a good augury." It was a source of considerable satisfaction to me that my own high opinion of Dr. Sachar's qualifications for the position, which had created tension with Professor Einstein, was now fully vindicated.

Brandeis University opened its doors in the fall of 1948. It has gone from strength to strength, fulfilling in great measure the hopes and expectations that we, the initiators of the project, originally pinned upon it.

I drew some comfort from a letter Dr. Sachar wrote me on June 2, 1948, in which he stated: "You are really the father of Brandeis University. You put endless energy and devotion into the building of the concept and the corralling of its first support."

Addressing a Brandeis luncheon in Boston in November of that year, I took occasion to say:

More than two years ago, it became my privilege to wed the idea to a tangible reality by the acquisition of a campus, a charter, a name, an academic and civic sponsorship and initial funds. The two basic realities, the campus and the charter, were the cohesive forces which held the project together across the changing hands and across the intermittent heartbreaks. Then a group of noble-spirited Jewish citizens of Boston made it the passion of their lives to bring to fruition all that had been planted. Today is the vindication of the faith and the stubbornness of all who tilled and planted and hoed and weeded.

In 1951, I published a book entitled *Brandeis University: Chapter of its Founding,* which set forth in detail the story of its genesis.

On June 8, 1958, President Abram L. Sachar, conferring upon me an honorary degree, read out the following citation:

THE TRUSTEES OF
BRANDEIS UNIVERSITY
UPON THE RECOMMENDATION OF THE FACULTY
HAVE CONFERRED ON
ISRAEL GOLDSTEIN

eloquent and resourceful rabbi, rich in sympathies, a faithful servant of the Jewish people in its darkest hours and in its brightest achievements. His extraordinary energy has left its mark on the American scene, on the salvaging of the survivors of Europe's hell holes and concentration camps, and on the reconstitution of the Jewish State. The Hebrew University and the Weizmann Institute of Science in Israel, the Jewish Theological Seminary and the University of Judaism in America have all been strengthened because of his devotion and concern. A forerunner in the development of Brandeis University, with the imagination to understand the historic importance of the concept, and with the practical genius to bring the concept to the threshold of fruition. President of such a variety of world organizations that they represent a cross-section of the most vital areas in modern Jewish history. Symbol of the select few who interpret the ministry in prophetic terms, rising above individual piety to enrich communal life.

THE HONORARY DEGREE OF
DOCTOR OF HUMANE LETTERS

6

For Zion's Sake: 1946–49

During the last quarter of 1945, to resume my post–World War II story, the Zionist struggle for a Jewish State in Palestine began in earnest. The impact of the European Holocaust, the uncertain fate of Jews pouring into the DP camps in Germany, Austria, and Italy, and the British Labor Government's obvious unwillingness to fulfill its pre-election promise by repealing the 1939 Palestine White Paper—these were the major factors that led to a hardening of Jewish and Zionist opinion throughout the world.

President Truman's request that 100,000 immigration certificates for Palestine be issued to Jewish DPs was brusquely rejected by the British cabinet. Mass protest rallies were organized in many American cities, an avalanche of telegrams descended upon the White House, and British consular offices were picketed. In Madison Square Park, New York, no fewer than 200,000 people attended a vast open-air demonstration. A joint congressional resolution was passed "that the United States shall use its good offices with the Mandatory Power to the end that Palestine shall be opened for the free entry of Jews into that country, to the maximum of its agricultural and economic potentialities, so that they may freely proceed with the upbuilding of Palestine as the Jewish National Home, in association with all elements of the population and establish it as a democratic Commonwealth in which all men, regardless of race or creed, shall have equal rights." The U.S. State Department paid little heed to this resolution, which nevertheless represented one more moral victory for the Zionist cause.

Early in November, mainly on the initiative of the American Christian Palestine Committee, the International Christian Conference on Palestine took place in Washington, D.C. The delegates, who came from thirty different countries, included President Gonzalez Videla of Chile and Lorna Wingate, widow of Major General Charles Orde Wingate, the "Friend" of the Yishuv, who had died in an air crash in Burma a year previously. This conference resulted in the establishment of the World Committee for Palestine, headed by Sir Ellsworth Flavelle of Canada, which worked closely with Christian Zionists in the U.S. and began to arouse public opinion in Canada and the Latin American states.

Britain's Prime Minister Clement Attlee and Foreign Secretary Ernest Bevin were, of course, anxious to win American support for their Middle East strategy.

186

They therefore proposed the establishment of an Anglo-American commission to investigate the problem of the Jewish refugees and then recommend an acceptable solution. "All aspects" of the problem were to be looked into—a far from oblique allusion to the intransigent Arab nationalist stand on the future of Palestine. Since the whole issue had become a matter of public concern in the U.S., President Truman agreed to the British proposal, although he insisted that "Palestine" should figure in its terms of reference. With the American Zionists exerting pressure from one side and the British from the other, Truman evidently hoped that the inquiry commission would secure the 100,000 certificates from Whitehall, thereby assuring everyone of a breathing space. In the longer term, an overall solution to the Palestine problem seemed to be the proper concern of the UN.

On November 13, 1945, Attlee announced the appointment of the Anglo-American Committee of Inquiry regarding the Problems of European Jewry and Palestine, which would make on-the-spot investigations and then report on its findings.

I have always felt that the British rejection of Truman's humanitarian request for the immigration certificates, though bitterly resented by our Zionist leadership at the time, was in a sense providential, since it actually led the President to conclude that a more radical and far-reaching solution was needed—a Jewish State that would not be dependent on any outside authority to determine how many Jews should enter the country.

Meanwhile, with the gates of Palestine virtually closed to Jewish immigrants and the political situation there stagnating, Zionist activism in face of the "Great Betrayal" mounted rapidly. Overcoming previous, often violent disagreements, the Haganah, Palmah, Irgun Tzeva'i Leumi (Etzel), and Lehi ("Stern Gang") joined forces in Tenu'at ha-Meri ha-Ivri, the combined Jewish Resistance Movement, which launched a series of underground attacks on the British Mandatory regime and its installations. This campaign was intended to sabotage Whitehall's repressive policies and to serve notice that the Yishuv was prepared to fight for a Jewish State with all the means at its disposal.

On October 10, following a surprise attack on the Athlit internment camp near Haifa, some 200 "illegal" immigrants were released by the Palmah. Three weeks later, on November 1, the Resistance Movement carried out 150 acts of sabotage on the Palestine railroad system under cover of darkness, and sank a number of British patrol launches used to intercept the "coffin" ships bearing "illegals" to the shores of Eretz Yisrael. The might of the Royal Navy was hurled against these ramshackle craft with their pitiable human cargoes. Few of the refugee vessels managed to evade British security measures on the high seas and to unload their passengers at remote points along the coast of Palestine. The vast majority of "illegal" immigrants transported from European ports by Mosad Aliyah Bet—the organization handling clandestine Jewish immigration—eventually ended up in detention centers, first in Palestine and later in Cyprus. Their number was deducted from the "legal" quota of 1,500 per month. The strong-arm methods employed by the British forces when boarding the refugee ships and forcing the Jews to disembark at Haifa outraged popular feeling in the Yishuv and also made a negative impression on some members of the Anglo-American Inquiry Committee who happened to be present as the ships docked.

Scenes of violence at the quayside and of clashes between British security forces and Palestinian Jewish demonstrators filled newspaper columns and movie screens throughout the world. From the political angle, such developments cast the Attlee Government in a bad light and reinforced the Zionist position. On January 2, 1946, the American Jewish Conference, represented by Henry Monsky, submitted a memorandum to the Anglo-American Committee of Inquiry along the lines of the Palestine resolution adopted at the Conference's opening session. It called for a program of reconstruction to revive organized Jewish life in Europe, the punishment of Nazi war criminals and the payment of reparations by Germany, and also urged that a series of key measures be taken immediately to reverse Britain's Palestine policy, so that a Jewish majority might be attained in the country and a self-governing Jewish commonwealth established there.

By an odd coincidence, a statement was issued that same day by General Frederick Morgan, a British officer who had been appointed UNRRA director for the Allied zones of occupation, alleging that the flight of Jews from Eastern Europe was being contrived by "a secret, politically motivated Jewish organization." Such an announcement, with its overtones of a "world Jewish conspiracy," was reminiscent of the forged "Protocols of the Learned Elders of Zion," once utilized by Henry Ford and regurgitated by the Nazis. It called for a sharp answer. An opportunity to set matters straight presented itself at the third session of the American Jewish Conference, held in Cleveland in the middle of February. After conveying my impressions of the Jewish emergency in Europe, where more than a million of our brethren were in every sense displaced, discriminated against, and dispossessed, I went on to say:

> The British propaganda machine is seeking to build up the impression that the flight of Jews from Europe is artificially stimulated by an "organized international conspiracy." Yes, we proudly assert, there *is* an organized international effort to help Jews who are compelled to flee for their lives from the hell holes where life is intolerable. There *is* an organized effort to throw these Jews a lifeline which leads to Palestine, where they can truly live. The effort is organized, for when a house is burning the rescue must be organized; otherwise, there is panic and stampede. The effort is international, and therefore the more noble and the more likely to succeed. Europe itself might be under Hitler's heel today, and Great Britain itself might be biting the dust, if the war against Hitler had not become an organized international effort. But we resent the slur that there is a conspiracy to simulate emergency. If there *is* an ignoble, shameful conspiracy, it is the conspiracy of the British Government to force Jews to perish in Europe.

My conclusion was that the Anglo-American Committee of Inquiry, and the governments that sponsored its investigations, would earn nothing but contempt if they should fail to dismantle the DP camps before the coming fall and resettle the

Jewish refugees where they would no longer be branded as "displaced persons." On one point, however, General Morgan proved to be right. Unless a halt was called to the mass exodus, he said, half a million Jews would soon flood the Western zones of Germany. Just four months later, on July 4, 1946, Polish nationalists (aided by some Communists) organized a pogrom in Kielce, the worst anti-Jewish disturbance to occur in "liberated" Europe after World War II. Clearly, there was no longer room for Jews—over forty of whom were murdered in the pogrom—on the blood-soaked soil of Poland. Those who had survived the death camps, now joined by Jews who had secured repatriation from the USSR, fled en masse to the West.

At the sessions of the American Jewish Conference in Cleveland, Rabbi Abba Hillel Silver delivered a forceful address and Dr. Hayyim Fineman, a prominent Labor Zionist, surveyed the current position of the Jewish DPs with burning indignation and a call for action. Following the debates, a strongly worded resolution on Palestine was approved by a large majority. I was one of those who believed that the Conference should continue its active existence on a permanent footing, concurrent with "the 5 Rs arising out of the War and still in the process of being solved, namely, Resettlement, Reparations, Restitution, Reconstruction and Rehabilitation." The majority of delegates, however, felt that the Conference should continue on an interim basis only. It went on functioning until December 31, 1948, when the major participants—unwisely, to my mind—turned down a proposal to establish a permanent American Jewish Assembly as the Conference's successor.

During the first few months of 1946, the Anglo-American Committee of Inquiry was engaged in its fact-finding mission. After an initial briefing in Washington, members of the committee proceeded to London, where they met with Ernest Bevin, and then studied the position of the Jewish DPs in Germany, Poland, and other European countries. Finally, they went on to Cairo and Palestine. In Washington, the Zionist viewpoint had been presented most effectively, whereas in London and Cairo the Arab stand was expressed with much vehemence, receiving the usual support from Arabists in the British Foreign Office. Jamil al-Husseini, whose World War II record as one sympathetic to Hitler approached that of his notorious uncle, the Mufti, was among those who drew a fanciful picture of Arab involvement in the Allied war effort and who began the now familiar process of branding the Zionists and the Jews of the Yishuv as "Nazis."

The six American members of the committee were headed by Judge Joseph Hutcheson, who, despite some initial fears on our part, proved to be a fair-minded co-chairman. The six British members were headed by Sir John Singleton, a High Court judge. Bevin presumably expected that his nominees would succeed in influencing their American colleagues to "deliver the goods," but this was not to be. Like three of the Americans, Bartley C. Crum, Frank Buxton, and James Grover McDonald, Bevin's Labor protégé, Richard Crossman, M.P., was won over to the Zionist cause as a result of what the committee saw and heard. The testimony presented by Dr. Weizmann and David Ben-Gurion in Jerusalem more than balanced that of the more persuasive advocates of the Arab case. Furthermore, the plight of the Jews in the DP camps made a great impression on the committee, which learned that a poll conducted by UNRRA had disclosed that almost ninety-seven percent of these refugees pinned their hopes on settling in Eretz Yisrael.

By April 20, the Anglo-American Committee had finished its work, and its unanimous report and detailed recommendations to the U.S. and British Governments were published on May 1. Although, in the committee's opinion, Palestine was unlikely to solve the entire Jewish refugee problem, it still offered the best prospect of restoring the homeless Jews to a normal life. Accordingly, while the United States and Great Britain should seek additional places where they might be resettled, 100,000 immigration certificates for Palestine should be granted immediately to Jewish victims of Nazi and Fascist persecution. The report also recommended a return to the pre-1939 policy of the League of Nations Mandate, involving the repeal of existing restrictions on Jewish immigration and land settlement in Palestine. As for that country's future, the members of the committee believed that it should constitute neither a Jewish nor an Arab state, where one group would dominate the other, but that it should remain under British rule for an indefinite period of time.

These recommendations incensed Bevin and found no favor in Whitehall, although President Truman considered them to be acceptable. Under increasing British pressure, Truman reluctantly agreed to a quickly devised proposal by Attlee and Bevin that a new committee be appointed, comprising members of the British and American cabinets, to hammer out a detailed blueprint for the future status of Palestine. This was to result in the Morrison-Grady Scheme, to which I shall revert.

Since the Anglo-American Committee's findings had left no room for the Zionist demand that "an independent Jewish Commonwealth" be established in Palestine, Rabbi Abba Hillel Silver was inclined to condemn the whole report out of hand. He was persuaded to avoid a head-on collision with President Truman only after other Zionist leaders urged a more pragmatic course of action. In Palestine, however, there was a violent reaction to the British rejection of the committee's report. During the hours of darkness on June 17, 1946, "the Night of the Bridges," units of the Jewish Resistance Movement blew up all but one of the bridges connecting Palestine with neighboring countries. Twelve days later, on what has come to be known as the "Black Sabbath," British forces struck back with unprecedented harshness by arresting every member of the Jewish Agency Executive and the Va'ad Leumi whom they could find, together with the mayors of several Jewish cities. Religious opinion was particularly inflamed by the fact that these arrests were made on the Sabbath, which Rabbi Yehudah-Leib Fishman, one of the Jewish Agency leaders, was forced to desecrate when soldiers bundled him onto an army truck. In a vast, fortnight-long sweep, British troops combed schools, hospitals, and synagogues, cordoning off streets and residential areas, in their search for members of the Jewish underground. Thousands of suspects were rounded up and a large number of them sent to detention camps at Rafa. While hunting for arms caches in agricultural settlements, the British virtually destroyed some kibbutzim. Henceforth, too, "illegal" immigrants were no longer interned at Athlit, but shipped to camps in

Cyprus. The Mandatory government, having lost its patience with the Yishuv, seemed intent on breaking Jewish resistance and compelling Palestinian Jewry to elect a more compliant leadership.

The Jewish Agency and other arrested leaders were placed in a detention camp at Latrun, some fifteen miles west of Jerusalem, where they were interned for almost five months. Latrun, dominated by a fortress-like police station that half-trained Israeli troops would vainly try to wrest from the Arab Legion in 1948, has a biblical setting in the Vale of Ajalon. Here, Joshua inflicted a resounding defeat on the five Amorite kings who made war on his Gibeonite allies. This historical precedent was surely not lost on Moshe Shertok, Yitzhak Gruenbaum, David Hacohen, Zalman Shragai, Dr. Dov (Bernard) Joseph, and the other prominent detainees. In any event, Great Britain's repressive measures failed to break the spirit of the Yishuv and the arrested men were eventually released. Their internment was one of the major blunders that led to the termination of British rule in Palestine.

As a result of the "Black Sabbath," Jewish Agency tactics were modified and resistance eventually switched from sabotage attacks to intensified Ha'apalah, "illegal" immigration. The alliance between the Haganah and the more radical components of Tenu'at ha-Meri, the Resistance Movement, then collapsed, since both the Revisionist Etzel and the Sternists of Lehi refused to accept the change of plan. Lehi, which had been responsible for the assassination of Lord Moyne in 1944, embarked on a campaign of indiscriminate terror, while Etzel, commanded by Menahem Begin, redoubled its armed attacks on the British Government apparatus. A spectacular raid on the King David Hotel in Jerusalem, on July 22, of which Yisrael Galili and other Haganah leaders apparently had foreknowledge, resulted in the blowing up of an entire wing that housed the Mandatory government's secretariat and the headquarters of the Criminal Investigation Department. Begin and his followers have ever since maintained that the British received telephone messages warning them to evacuate all personnel prior to the explosion, but that these warnings were ignored. Others claim that no such messages were received. The melancholy fact is that, in addition to the political damage this operation brought about at the time, forty Jews as well as many British officials and Arabs were among the dead.

Once again, British retaliation was aimed against the Yishuv as a whole, although the Jewish Agency, with Ben-Gurion as its spokesman, condemned the Etzel dissidents and urged that their movement be suppressed. General Sir Evelyn Barker, who commanded the British forces in Palestine, was no friend of the Yishuv and had doggedly opposed the setting up of the Jewish Brigade in the latter stage of the war. In a furious anti-Semitic outburst, for which he was transferred to another command three months later, General Barker placed Jewish shops and homes out of bounds to British troops. "You will be punishing the Jews in a way the race dislikes as much as any," he blandly asserted, "by striking at their pockets."

Throughout that long, hot summer, as reprisals and acts of retaliation succeeded each other, it became apparent to us all that smoldering resentment in the Yishuv had given way to a thoroughly explosive situation. We had reached the point of no return. Dr. Moshe Sneh, in fact, resigned from his command of the Haganah in protest against the new line of moderation. In one way or another, the confrontation between British administrators seeking to impose their will by force and the Jews of Palestine, anxious to free themselves from that yoke, would typify the last, inglorious phase of the Mandatory regime. Ernest Bevin's policy of wholesale repression was self-defeating.

Toward Zionist Unity and Fulfillment

The King David Hotel disaster in July 1946 coincided with preliminary steps to work out a new plan for Palestine, which was becoming the last bastion of British military power in the entire Middle East. The Morrison-Grady Scheme, named for its architects, Herbert Morrison, Lord President of the Council and Deputy Prime Minister of Great Britain, and Dr. Henry F. Grady, an Assistant Secretary of State in Washington, proposed that the Mandate be transformed into a British trusteeship with its central government and a High Commissioner in Jerusalem. According to this modified version of an old Foreign Office plan, the whole of Palestine would be divided into four sectors: a miniscule "autonomous" Jewish canton restricted to a mere seventeen percent of the country; a larger Arab zone covering forty-seven percent of the area; and two British-controlled provinces of Jerusalem and the Negev. This patchwork "federation" left matters of defense, foreign policy, and revenue effectively in British hands. There was one concession to the Jews— 100,000 refugees would be admitted within twelve months if the Jews and Arabs would both agree to the scheme; if not, Great Britain would let the United Nations find some other solution to the Palestine issue.

Clearly, the Morrison-Grady Scheme had no redeeming features. If anything, it was designed to thwart the emergence of a viable Jewish State, and Morrison's official announcement of the final plan in the House of Commons, on July 31, called for some appropriate Zionist rejoinder.

Although Dr. Weizmann was in Palestine at this time, David Ben-Gurion had been out of the country for about two months and had thus escaped arrest by the British authorities on the "Black Sabbath." Fearing that Zionism now faced abandonment by the United States as well as by Great Britain, he called a special conference to be attended by members of the Jewish Agency Executive from Jerusalem, London, and New York, and by a few other Zionist leaders as well. The conference was scheduled to begin at the Royal Monceau Hotel in Paris on August 2. I was among those invited to participate.

The day after arriving in Paris, I attended a meeting of the American Jewish Conference in the offices of the World Jewish Congress on the Champs Elysées, at which the WJC and the British Board of Deputies were also represented. Various major Jewish organizations were about to assemble in Paris, where memoranda would be submitted to the UN Peace Conference, dealing with ways to safeguard the rights of Jewish communities in the UN treaties. Our main problem was how to formulate a common approach. We sought a modus vivendi with Agudat Yisrael and with the non-Zionist American Jewish Committee.

Those taking part in the preliminary deliberations were Rabbi Maurice Eisendrath, I. L. Kenen, Nehemiah Robinson, Louis Lipsky, Rabbi Stephen Wise, and I, representing the United States, and Professor Selig Brodetsky, Israel Cohen, and Alec Easterman of Great Britain. Dr. Jacob Robinson, one of our expert advisers, pointed out the necessity of using the procedural rules of the 1919 Versailles Peace Conference as precedents in the approach adopted by our nongovernmental bodies to the peace talks. It was, he said, essential to coordinate our efforts in framing a joint memorandum and a joint approach, instead of going to each nation separately, since the present conference was the last opportunity to do so.

The organizations represented at the main gathering, held at the same hotel, were the American Jewish Conference, American Jewish Committee, Board of Deputies of British Jews, Anglo-Jewish Association, National Council of the Jews of Palestine (Va'ad Leumi), Agudat Yisrael, and the Alliance Israélite Universelle. Louis Lipsky was in the chair. It was one of the rare occasions when such a galaxy of personalities holding different—and, at times, opposing—views and outlooks assembled under one roof to establish a force for Jewish unity and peace.

A joint memorandum was worked out and submitted to the UN Peace Conference. We did not, however, get very far with our proposals to this assembly of world statesmen. Other issues obscured those affecting the Jewish people.

Soon afterwards, there also took place at the Royal Monceau Hotel the meeting of some thirty top Zionist leaders which Ben-Gurion had convened. Held behind closed doors, it amounted to an agonizing reappraisal of our platform and the Yishuv's seemingly hopeless armed struggle with the British.

Leafing through the minutes of the Paris conference, I find expressions of opinion that anticipated the positions taken at the decisive 22nd World Zionist Congress held in Basle some four months later. Such views reflected the propensities of those taking part, and the following brief quotations are illustrative:

Dr. Moshe Sneh (then a General Zionist): England is dead set against us. It wants to liquidate Zionism, which was necessary to its interest when it needed the Jews to prevent an Arab State. Now it does not want a Jewish State, because the Jews are not considered a safe basis for its interests vis-à-vis Russia. . . . We must sever relations with the British and be ready to renew them only on the basis of a Jewish State in Palestine. We must turn "illegal" immigration into a tremendous movement to stir up Jews outside Palestine.

Professor Lewis B. Namier: Everything must be done to change the British plan, but not to reject it.

Rabbi Y. L. Hacohen Fishman: Partition of the country into separate states will help to save Jews.

James de Rothschild: There must be no insistence on political discussions. The issue should be the grant of 100,000 immigration certificates. The Arab states should be financially compensated if they take Arabs out of Palestine.

Berl Locker: The British Government insisted that "illegal" immigration must be halted before talks begin. Our answer should be: Yes, if you start extensive "legal" immigration. It stated that those detained in Latrun must not be delegates. Our answer: *We* decide who goes.

Eliyahu Dobkin: Jews in the Russian orbit who are able to go to Palestine now may not be allowed out in a year or so.

Simon Marks: Heroics lead nowhere. Take part of Palestine, and advance from there.

David Ben-Gurion: Banish illusions and avoid despair!

Rabbi Wolf Gold: I am opposed to partition. But if the British propose partition, it is a *gezerah* [an edict].

Rabbi Stephen Wise: President Truman believes that American unity with Britain against Russia is important. [Wise now supported partition. This was, as far as I knew, the first departure from his consistently anti-partition stance.]

Rabbi Leon Gellman: We must not wage war against Britain. We can lose both the Yishuv and the support of the Jewish world.

Rabbi Israel Goldstein: We must not overlook the impact of American Zionist Emergency Council activity on public opinion. I do not agree that Rabbi Abba Hillel Silver was justified in refusing to appear before the Anglo-American Committee of Inquiry. The world will think that had we appeared, the results would have been different. [Silver had sent a cable, requesting that he be consulted before any approach was made to Washington about the Morrison-Grady Scheme.]

Viewed in retrospect thirty-five years later, some of Ben-Gurion's opinions are of interest. He, the father of the Biltmore Program and the advocate of Zionist militancy, now expressed support for a Jewish State even if only in part of Palestine, and maintained that the Agency should not refuse to negotiate because of the continued detention of Executive members at Latrun. He suggested the following program for negotiations: (1) An immediate start to the granting of 100,000 immigration certificates; (2) enlargement of the area proposed for the Jewish population; (3) real self-government; (4) election of officers and institutions; (5) power to control immigration; (6) power to control economic life; (7) the right for the Jews to declare independence within five years; and (8) the appointment of the Jewish Agency's chosen representatives at any round-table conference.

Ben-Gurion went on to urge that the United States be told that, if there were any chance of a Jewish State, we would negotiate, but that the present British plan offered no basis for negotiation.

Eliezer Kaplan stated that the full Zionist General Council should be convened to discuss the assumption of responsibility according to Ben-Gurion's outline of proposals. He took a pragmatic line, saying that the important thing now was to provide more working opportunities and to lay the basis for autonomy, and that immigration could not be subject to the dictates of a High Commissioner.

I put forward the view that President Truman had changed his position in regard to the Jewish case as a result of the political pressure exerted by American Zionists. This was an important breakthrough because it clearly signified that the President was more concerned with American Jewish reactions than with those of the Jewish Agency. Hence, any representations made to the U.S. Administration must be coordinated with and through the American Zionist Emergency Council, as Dr. Silver had requested.

At the opening session, on August 2, Dr. Nahum Goldmann told us of a long-distance telephone call he had received from David K. Niles, President Truman's personal assistant, requesting that a member of the Zionist Executive fly to Washington and set forth the Agency's minimum demands. Ben-Gurion subsequently received a cable from Dr. Silver, asking for a policy decision in this matter for his personal guidance. We thus had to decide how we should proceed in order to inform President Truman of our attitude toward the Morrison-Grady Scheme.

The proposals made in that scheme were supposedly based on the recommendations of the Anglo-American Committee of Inquiry, to which the Attlee Government (namely, Bevin and his advisers) had taken exception.

A critical stage was reached on August 5, when Louis Lipsky was among those, including Ben-Gurion, who opposed the choice of Nahum Goldmann for the mission. He suggested that, instead of sending Goldmann, we should ask Abba Hillel Silver to conduct the negotiations.

It was now 12:30 P.M. If Goldmann were in fact to go, he would need to leave at once in order to catch the plane scheduled to depart at three o'clock. An immediate decision had to be taken, but the question was whether to vote on principles or on the specific proposal. The delegates ruled in favor of the second option.

The resolution adopted, moved by Dr. Goldmann, was that the British proposal offered no basis for negotiation and that the Executive was ready to talk only on the basis of a Jewish State established in a suitable area of Palestine. The three conditions indispensable for the establishment of a Jewish State must be the issuing of 100,000 immigration certificates, to begin at once; control of immigration, to be entrusted to the Jewish Agency in the agreed territory of the Jewish State; and full administrative and economic autonomy in the transition period.

This resolution had Ben-Gurion's covert support, as a way out of the current impasse, although he was one of two who abstained in the vote.

Once again, I strongly urged that anyone going to Washington must consult with, and obtain the consent of, the American Zionist Emergency Council or its head, and that he must appear together with a representative of the AZEC. Ben-Gurion ruled, however, that my stand in this matter was unconstitutional.

Dr. Goldmann now had only five minutes left if he was to catch the plane, and Ben-Gurion chided him for being nervous. They exchanged sharp words, and Goldmann had some difficulty in rushing off to the airport. After his departure, the Jewish Agency Executive discussed a possible venue for the forthcoming Zionist Congress. Some favored Palestine, if the situation there would improve sufficiently, while others preferred the United States. The final decision was in favor of Switzerland.

During a break that day, I had a private talk with Dr. Moshe Sneh, a member of my own General Zionist faction, who had managed to evade the British dragnet in

Palestine. With an eye to the forthcoming Zionist Congress, he was seeking a formula whereby Weizmann, Ben-Gurion, and Silver would be kept together at the helm, and damaging acrimony would be avoided.

The Paris meeting was adjourned, pending Dr. Goldmann's return from the U.S. I seized the opportunity to slip over to England, where an interfaith conference was scheduled to be held in Oxford. Delegates came from a number of countries, including the United States, Canada, South Africa, and Switzerland, and I met some old friends. Among them were Neville Laski, the British jurist, and Rabbi Israel Mattuck, the Liberal Jewish leader in London; Father Ahearn, of Boston; Rabbi Maurice Eisendrath, who had helped to found the Canadian Council of Christians and Jews while serving as a Reform rabbi in Toronto; Dr. Everett Clinchy, chief executive of the National Conference of Christians and Jews in the United States; and the Reverend W. W. Simpson, secretary of the British Council of Christians and Jews. Dr. Clinchy was mainly responsible for organizing the Oxford conference, but he had a valuable assistant in the Reverend Simpson, who was the leading ecumenical activist on the British side.

This gathering led to the establishment of the International Conference of Christians and Jews.

Upon its conclusion, I flew back to Paris with Ḥayim Greenberg, on a two-passenger aircraft. Our valises, coats, and other impedimenta made it impossible for us to move. The pilot was eager to point out the places on the coast of France where Allied armies had landed a couple of years earlier. Poor Ḥayim, buried under the luggage, could not have seen very much, but what I managed to glimpse through the window impressed me.

It was my second Tish'ah be-Av fast day in Paris: I had been there one year earlier, prior to my tour of the DP camps in Germany. After attending services at the "Rothschild Synagogue" on the Rue de la Victoire, I chatted with Chief Rabbi Isaïe Schwartz, who complained of the economic plight of French Jewry. It was gratifying to learn that the aid made available by me twelve months before had been put to good use.

Among several old acquaintances whom I was fortunate to meet again, in the interval before the Jewish Agency Executive resumed its deliberations, was the onetime Premier of France, Léon Blum. Then in his mid-seventies, he seemed remarkably well and robust after his ordeals—a Vichy-engineered "war trial" that had fizzled out, and prolonged internment by the Nazis during the war.

When I mentioned lingering Nazi and Vichyite influences in France, with their residue of anti-Semitism, he observed that it would be strange if all trace of them had vanished, but that there were, in his view, no serious complications. As for Zionism, he assured me of his warm sympathy and expressed optimism about the Jewish future in Palestine. Léon Blum recalled with gratitude the fact that the Jewish National Fund of America, during the period of my administration, had initiated the Kfar Blum project for a kibbutz in northern Palestine.

Nahum Goldmann returned from his six-day visit to Washington in a highly buoyant mood. He reported that most of the U.S. members of the Anglo-American Committee of Inquiry, led by the co-chairman, Judge Joseph Hutcheson, had spoken out sharply against the Morrison-Grady Scheme. They had decided to tell the President that this plan was a violation of their own findings and contrary to the Mandate, since it would create a ghetto in Palestine.

What was even more important, Dr. Goldmann also reported on his conversations with Dean Acheson, the U.S. Undersecretary of State, who had promised to support the demand for Jewish statehood. He then met with David Niles, an admirer of Stephen Wise and a recent convert to the Zionist cause. Niles was responsible for the arrangement of various important interviews with the U.S. Administration.

A dramatic about-face had occurred in the hitherto negative attitude of the American Jewish Committee toward the Zionist program of a Jewish commonwealth in Palestine. After a prolonged and emotional appeal by Goldmann, Judge Joseph M. Proskauer, the committee's president, changed his stand and agreed to make an appointment with his old friend, Robert P. Patterson, the U.S. Secretary of War, whose attitude on partition would be crucial. Proskauer was thus enlisted for a joint approach to the Administration. The appearance together of Goldmann and Proskauer at the meeting with Secretary Patterson was a telling demonstration of the essential unity of American Jewry behind the Zionist program.

In abandoning his previous opposition to Jewish statehood, Judge Proskauer had reacted spiritedly to critics within his own group. When one important member of the American Jewish Committee insisted, "Goldmann is taking you for a ride," the judge had retorted, "I have a responsibility to the Jewish people, not to the American Jewish Committee. If they disavow me, I shall resign and join the Jewish Agency." In the end, of course, the committee was won over to his side.

It was clear, therefore, that Nahum Goldmann's mission had been a diplomatic success. On August 12, Truman cabled Attlee, indicating his final rejection of the Morrison-Grady Scheme. He now endorsed the partition plan and instructed Dean Acheson to inform the British Government accordingly.

The special Zionist meeting concluded with a discussion about a program of noncooperation with the British regime in Palestine, organized by the Va'ad Leumi, in protest against the arrest and continued detention of the Jewish Agency leaders.

Three important factors had thus operated in favor of the Zionist case, demanding a Jewish commonwealth in Eretz Yisrael: American public support, generated under the leadership of Dr. Stephen Wise and then of Dr. Abba Hillel Silver; the support of the U.S. Congress, as expressed in its latest resolution; and the winning over of President Truman by the démarche of Nahum Goldmann, Judge Proskauer, and David Niles. The President's commitment had a vitally important bearing on subsequent developments in the UN, which reached a climax in the historic partition resolution adopted on November 29, 1947.

The new phase of the Zionist movement's political struggle was intensified after our return from Paris to the United States. On August 20, Dean Acheson received two representatives of the American Zionist Emergency Council, Abraham Tulin and Professor Milton Handler, a congregant and close friend of mine who played an important part in American Zionist affairs at this time. Acheson confirmed what we had already heard from Dr. Nahum Goldmann, namely, that President Truman, having rejected the Morrison-Grady Scheme, had made up his mind "to wash his hands of the whole Palestine problem" and to let the British worry about its solution.

In the meantime, pursuing the Weizmann-Wise line of secret diplomacy, Dr. Goldmann was endeavoring to reach an agreement with the British Foreign Secretary on the issue of partition. Ernest Bevin, however, was quite a different proposition from Harry Truman, and Goldmann's new mission was doomed to failure. On August 26, at a plenary session of the AZEC, Rabbi Abba Hillel Silver attacked the latest diplomatic maneuvers, claiming that the way in which our alternative to the Morrison-Grady Scheme had been presented was "a colossal political blunder." Infuriated over the slap in the face he had received from Dr. Goldmann, who preferred an anti-Zionist (Judge Proskauer) to be with him when he saw Robert Patterson, Rabbi Silver had insisted on resigning from the Zionist Executive.

Dean Acheson had told Handler and Tulin that the matter was now one "between the [Jewish] Agency, the British Government and the Arabs." This was an accurate assessment, since the British, in a desperate final effort to retain control of Palestine, were planning a three-sided conference in London. If nothing came of this, they would hand the problem over to the United Nations. None of us took the threat seriously at the time. Nevertheless, Rabbi Silver was correct in his forecast that the London Conference, which opened in September 1946 and reconvened in January 1947, would get nowhere and that we would find ourselves back where we started, except for the "small" matter of having "signed away our rights to a part of Palestine." He advocated intensified political pressure before the congressional elections in November, when the Democrats in fact suffered a massive electoral defeat, and he laid plans for a no less sweeping change in the Zionist leadership. Here, the forthcoming Basle Congress was his major objective.

New Hands at the Helm

When delegates from countries of the free world assembled in Basle for the opening of the 22nd Zionist Congress on December 9, 1946, seven fearful years had gone by since the last such meeting of that forum on the eve of World War II. A glance at the rows and names of those present was enough to make one realize what havoc the war and the Holocaust had wrought among the constituents of the Zionist movement. Issues of vital importance to the entire future of Zionism were debated in an atmosphere charged with somber recollections, and with a spirit of militant defiance that current British policy had engendered. This Congress was also notable for the return of the Revisionist movement, now bereft of its leader, Ze'ev Jabotinsky, after an absence of eleven years.

Most of us felt that time was running out and that notice must be served on the Mandatory power, together with all others concerned, that the Zionists, antagonized by British Government tactics, were intent on abandoning their hitherto moderate line. Dr. Chaim Weizmann's patient, diplomatic approach, which had achieved much in the past, was no longer suited to the tense situation in Palestine nor to the desperate position of the Jewish DPs in Europe.

That hardening of attitude which had emerged since the London Zionist Conference in 1945 was now on the ascendant. Opposition to the Morrison-Grady Scheme was virtually unanimous. In denouncing any form of partition, however, Abba Hillel Silver and his followers spoke for a minority. The most serious and divisive issue was that of Weizmann's continued "soft line" toward the British and his willingness to cooperate with them by attending the second round of the Whitehall-sponsored conference with the Arabs in London.

Ben-Gurion and Silver, the leading militants, headed an alliance of Zionist factions comprising a majority of the ZOA and the General Zionists, a minority of the Labor Zionists, and the whole of the Mizraḥi and Revisionist parties. Ben-Gurion spoke for a wide section of the Yishuv. Silver, now president of the ZOA and a powerful force in the American Zionist Emergency Council, went far beyond Stephen Wise in his outspoken orations, for which there was growing support and admiration in the United States. On the European scene, too, it was not difficult to muster broad support for militant action in the prevailing atmosphere, especially among the *She'erit ha-Pletah*.

Weizmann had the backing of Wise, Lipsky, Goldmann, Shertok, and Locker, who rallied over two-thirds of the Labor Zionists, a minority of the General Zionists, and the extreme left of the Zionist movement. He maintained nearly all of his traditional support among the British Zionists.

Immediately prior to the Congress in Basle, we had established the World Confederation of General Zionists.* My own sympathies, and those of the majority of my colleagues, were with Abba Hillel Silver in this central issue. The importance attached to the role of American Zionism after the war, and to Silver's own position at the Congress, was demonstrated by his election as chairman of the Political Committee.

In the course of the political debate on December 16, I drew attention to the impact of Zionist thinking on American public opinion and urged that a strong branch of the Zionist Executive be established in the United States. Such a move would prevent a recurrence of the damage suffered by the movement as a result of the "Black Sabbath" arrests in Palestine, which paralyzed a large part of the Zionist leadership. It would make easier open criticism of the Mandatory regime "without psychological restraint" or "an iron curtain of censorship." There was, furthermore, no reason to fear that President Truman would "wash his hands of the Palestine problem," since the Zionist issue had become one of the facts of American political life. "Five million U.S. citizens would not wash *their* hands of it," I said, which meant that both the Democrats and the Republicans could not afford to alienate an influential section of the American electorate.

Turning to the question of militancy, I disputed the assertion that physical resistance to an oppressor ran counter to the spirit of Jewish tradition. "A readiness

---

*On General Zionism and the Confederation, see chapter 14.

to offer resistance is the ultimate price one must pay for the birth or rebirth of a nation," I declared. "The American nation understands that principle from its own history, and American public opinion, in my judgment, will understand and support the Haganah."

As to the question of the proposed conference in London, I saw this not as a matter of principle but of tactics. We had already retreated too far and, to judge by the present composition of the Jewish Agency Executive, its representatives were likely to make more and more concessions under British pressure. For this reason, I opposed taking part in any such conference and I went on to say:

> We shall be told that the world is against us, that our powers of resistance must not be overestimated. People are asking, "Why is Mr. Bevin so eager for us to go to the Conference?" My answer is that he is confident he can wear us down. . . . I submit that we have nothing to gain by going. We have this to lose, that we ourselves may be a party to Great Britain's designs upon us. We should not appear at a mock conference staged at our expense. Where are we left? We have the Yishuv. We have the World Zionist Movement. We have the driving force of Jewish homelessness, which is heading Palestineward. We have the friendly interest of the American Government. With these weapons we must fight as best we can.
>
> We need a vigorous leadership, a collective leadership which will invigorate us and which, by its very complexion, will serve notice on Great Britain that it will have neither peace nor honor in Palestine or elsewhere until its pledge to the Jewish people will have been fulfilled.

The fact that the British were barring Eretz Yisrael to Jewish refugees, throughout this time, weighed heavily in favor of our hard-line policy. Most delegates at the Congress felt that no more good would come of the latest talks in London than was the case in 1939, when the White Paper restrictions were imposed. They therefore voted to make the Biltmore Program our official platform, and to boycott the London Conference. Chaim Weizmann, who regarded this vote as a motion of no confidence in his leadership, promptly resigned as president of the World Zionist Organization and the Jewish Agency Executive. "I hope that we shall live and continue our labors," he said, "and that, when we meet again, our National Home will be intact."

A new Zionist Executive was elected, headed by Ben-Gurion in Jerusalem and by Abba Hillel Silver in New York and Washington. The presidency of the World Zionist Organization remained vacant. I was appointed to the General Council (Actions Committee) of the WZO. Dr. Silver was also elected the Zionist movement's chief spokesman at the United Nations. He had emerged as the undisputed leader of American Zionism, capable of pursuing an aggressive public-relations campaign in Christian as well as Jewish circles, and of winning the support of both major political parties in their bid for American Jewish votes.

The 22nd Zionist Congress, held in that same tranquil Swiss town overlooking the Rhine where Theodor Herzl had issued his call for a Jewish State half a century earlier, thus marked the close of the political struggle in its initial phase. It was also the overture to the second, climactic phase, heralding the crucial deliberations at Lake Success and the still deeper involvement of the U.S. Government in the entire problem of the Middle East.

Weizmann's defeat also brought about the resignation of Dr. Stephen Wise from the American Section of the Jewish Agency Executive and his retirement from leadership in the Zionist movement. Dr. Silver's arch-opponent, Nahum Goldmann, though transferred to London, soon managed to regain a foothold in the American political arena on the strength of his international connections. He was replaced as the Agency's chief diplomat in Washington by Moshe Shertok, who found it easier to collaborate with the forceful American Zionist leader.

Superficially, the militants had gained control and had won support at Basle for the maximalist program, but their victory was by no means complete. Dr. Weizmann, who did not hide his chagrin, still had an important contribution to make in the struggle for an independent Jewish Palestine. Even Ben-Gurion realized that the Basle Congress had not eliminated either the moderate element in the Zionist Executive or the possibility of arriving at a compromise solution of the Palestine issue. Despite the majority vote, therefore, and Silver's continued objections, Ben-Gurion and Shertok made an unobtrusive appearance in London at the Whitehall-sponsored conference, which reopened on January 27, 1947.

While these talks were still pending, Arthur Creech-Jones, the new British Colonial Secretary, made a determined effort to reduce tensions and give expression to his own mildly pro-Zionist sentiments. A new British army chief was appointed, the detained leaders of the Yishuv were set free, and Creech-Jones himself went so far as to propose that, in return for a five-year moratorium on Jewish statehood, the 1939 White Paper restrictions would be lifted. Ernest Bevin, however, refused to give way on this point and insisted on his own scheme—British trusteeship leading to an Arab-dominated Palestine, with minimal concessions to the Jews. On this he "staked his political reputation." Ben-Gurion had gone to London with a few colleagues in the hope of reaching agreement on either of two alternatives: the admission of 100,000 Jewish refugees within a two-year period, followed by unrestricted Aliyah, or partition and the ending of British rule. For their part, the Arab League states—now joined by representatives of the Mufti's Palestine Arab Higher Committee—were unwilling to accept any scheme involving the slightest prospect of further Jewish immigration. Their demand was that the British "pack up and get out, leaving the Palestine Arabs to handle the situation"—with outside Arab support, should this prove necessary.

Having thus failed to satisfy either the Jews or the Arabs, Bevin gave up in despair, insisting that the Mandate was unworkable and that responsibility for Palestine should be vested in the United Nations. He made an announcement to that effect after the London Conference ended in deadlock on February 14, although Creech-Jones hinted that Britain only sought UN advice about administering the Palestine Mandate.

None of this came as any surprise to Rabbi Silver and his supporters, who had maintained all along that the British, in deference to Arab intransigence, would never reach an acceptable compromise with the Zionists. Weizmann, Goldmann, and other moderates who had believed otherwise were flabbergasted. On the one hand, they had been offered a ghetto in one tiny portion of the Jewish homeland, subject to a Palestinian Arab state in the heart of the Arab world; on the other hand, they now had to face the real possibility that the United Nations, ignoring all past pledges, might enable the British to reimpose their will on Palestine and do precisely as they liked there. For the Yishuv and the Zionist movement in general, the outlook was grim indeed.

Tension mounted throughout Palestine as soon as the breakdown of the London Conference became known. Jewish resistance activities took various forms: the Haganah intensified "Aliyah Bet" operations, while the Etzel and Lehi concentrated their attacks on British military installations. In response to executions and suicides in the Acre prison, Etzel and Lehi units carried out a daring assault on May 4, 1947, releasing some 250 detainees, including a number of Arab convicts, after blowing up part of that fortress. The familiar pattern of reprisal and retaliation dominated the months that followed. Simultaneously, as rival Arab militias trained and paraded without hindrance from the British throughout the countryside, terrorist bands operating under the banner of the Husseini clan swiftly eliminated their more moderate opponents. British security measures collapsed, resulting in dusk-to-dawn curfews, the evacuation of civilians, and the construction of fortified barbed-wire zones in Jerusalem, which members of the Yishuv derisively termed "Bevingrad" areas. Such was the climax of a quarter-century of British Mandatory rule, now doomed to end in bloodshed, ignominy, and a betrayal of trust.

After a prolonged debate at Lake Success, the UN General Assembly resolved, on May 13, to appoint its own team of investigators to review the situation in the DP camps and in Palestine. The United Nations Special Committee on Palestine (UN-SCOP), comprising eleven nominees of various member states headed by Justice Emil Sandström of Sweden, then set out on its mission. Behind the scenes, U.S. State Department and British Foreign Office bureaucrats tried to influence UNSCOP to come out in favor of Bevin's trusteeship scheme, while the Arabs sought to eliminate the Jewish refugee issue from the UN committee's agenda. Fortunately, both of these maneuvers proved unsuccessful.

One straw in the wind was the address delivered by Andrei Gromyko, the Soviet Union's delegate at the UN, which constituted an astonishing *volte-face* in the USSR's hitherto rigidly anti-Zionist position. Gromyko attacked Whitehall's handling of the Palestine Mandate, spoke angrily of the West's abandonment of European Jewry in the Hitler period, and gave a clear hint that his country would support partition and the granting of territorial independence to the Jewish people. Various reasons have been suggested for this sudden shift in Russian policy, but I have never found them especially convincing. Had the Soviets merely wished to "gain a foothold in the Middle East" by removing the British, they would have been better served by an alliance with the Arab-Muslim bloc than by espousing the "reactionary" Zionist cause. Whatever their motivation, the Russians helped to strengthen our case. On June 5, the American Jewish Conference submitted to the members of UNSCOP a memorandum similar to the one prepared for the Anglo-American Committee of Inquiry in January 1946.

Pursuing its on-the-spot investigations, the UNSCOP team arrived in Palestine in mid-June and spent a number of weeks in the Middle East. This visit coincided with various grim events which, together with the evidence gathered later in Europe, would only confirm UNSCOP's impression that British Mandatory rule must be terminated as soon as possible. Whereas the Jewish Agency spokesmen made themselves available and presented impressive testimony, the Arab Higher Committee decided to boycott the UNSCOP hearings and to organize violent anti-Zionist demonstrations throughout Palestine. Subsequently, in Beirut, Azzam Pasha, secretary-general of the Arab League, made a fatal mistake by adopting the tactics of the Mufti and his followers. His bloodcurdling threats, leveled against Jewish communities in Arab lands as well as against the Yishuv, left UNSCOP in no doubt as to the fate in store for any Jewish population subject to an Arab majority—in Palestine or anywhere else.

More evidence was forthcoming in July. The *Exodus* affair, to which I shall revert, was followed by events pointing to the peculiar ineptitude of the British authorities in dealing with Jewish resistance, whether active or passive. Three members of the Etzel ("Irgun") underground group, recaptured by the British after the mass escape from Acre at the beginning of May, were condemned to death. Two British army sergeants were then seized by Etzel as hostages, and it seemed that the three condemned Jews would be reprieved. Once the UNSCOP investigators were safely out of Palestine, however, the Etzel men were hanged. Two days later, in retaliation, the two sergeants were similarly executed by Menahem Begin's men. Although few people approved of such retribution, it did serve to highlight the bankruptcy of the British regime. Clandestine Etzel radio broadcasts in Palestine and the propaganda campaign launched by the Hebrew Committee for National Liberation, headed by Peter Bergson (Hillel Kook) in New York, exploited such grim incidents to the full. Bergson's group, repudiated and combatted by the major Zionist organizations in the United States, nevertheless succeeded in enlisting the support of Ben Hecht and other prominent American Jews who believed that only all-out war on the British would lead to the establishment of a Jewish State.

On August 31, 1947, UNSCOP concluded its deliberations. A minority (India, Iran, and Yugoslavia) favored the creation of a binational Arab-Jewish state in Palestine. The majority report, calling for partition, was backed by Canada, Czechoslovakia, Guatemala, Holland, Peru, Sweden, and Uruguay. One delegate, Australia's, favored neither solution and abstained. Among other things, the majority recommended that Great Britain's Palestine Mandate be ended at the earliest possible time and that two independent states, one Jewish and one Arab, be established, as well as a "special international regime" for the Jerusalem-Bethlehem region. All three areas were to enter an economic union. For the first two years, a total of 150,000 Jewish immigrants would be admitted to Palestine; this influx was to be limited thereafter to 60,000 Jews annually. Some aspects of the majority report

were patently unrealistic and absurd. It could hardly be expected that the Jewish
State would indefinitely subsidize the Arab state's economy, and both territories
comprised three segments linked at two points on the map. Even so, the Zionist
movement was prepared to go along with the plan. The Arabs rejected it and the
British predictably refused to be responsible for its enforcement. A final decision
was left to the UN General Assembly.

I was serving at this time as chairman of the United Palestine Appeal, which,
together with the Joint Distribution Committee and the National Refugee Service,
benefited from the funds raised in America through the United Jewish Appeal. The
general chairman of the UJA was former U.S. Secretary of the Treasury Henry
Morgenthau, Jr., who remained at its head until 1950.

Toward the middle of July 1947, my wife and I left New York for our usual
summer visit to Eretz Yisrael. Apart from the refreshment and reinvigoration this
trip would afford, my objective was to study the financial needs of the Yishuv and to
survey those activities which had been made possible through the funds of the
United Palestine Appeal.

On July 18, shortly after our arrival in Palestine, a Haganah immigrant ship,
Exodus 1947, limped into Haifa port under British naval escort. The S.S. *Exodus*,
packed with 4,500 Jewish survivors of the Nazi death camps, had fought a heroic
but hopeless battle with warships of the Royal Navy, in the course of which it had
been rammed and boarding parties, armed with machine guns, tear gas, and clubs,
had beaten the passengers and crew into submission. Three Jews were killed and
hundreds suffered injuries. Bill Bernstein, a young Jew from Brooklyn who served
as chief officer of the *Exodus*, was one of the dead.

Further violence marked the forcible removal of refugees from the *Exodus* at
Haifa, where they were herded into cages and jammed into the holds of three British
transport vessels bound for Port de Bouc, the small French harbor from which their
ship had set sail. We shared in the grief manifested by the Yishuv and in the protest
demonstrations against Ernest Bevin's heartless resolve to demonstrate the futility of
"Aliyah Bet" and to return these unfortunate people to Europe. Bevin's action was
also intended to warn the French that His Majesty's Government would not overlook
any foreign interference with British policy or cooperation with those organizing
"illegal" immigration. The French authorities, however, while ready to accept any
Jews wishing to disembark, refused to allow British troops to eject the DPs by force.
After three weeks of confinement in the Mediterranean heat, the DPs received a
final taste of Bevin's vindictive rage—transportation by sea from Port de Bouc to
Hamburg. This display of calculated cruelty not only shocked world opinion but
gave rise to an outcry in Great Britain. Even the British soldiers ordered to remove
the Jews in Hamburg, from where they were taken to detention camps, made no
secret of their distaste for such a job. As far as the British Foreign Secretary was
concerned, Holocaust survivors could languish on the hated soil of Germany, but
they would never be permitted to set foot in Palestine. How wrong he was! Less than

a year later, every one of those passengers from the ill-starred *Exodus* had freely entered the sovereign Jewish State.

The harrowing scenes on the quayside at Haifa were witnessed by stunned members of the UNSCOP commission, who drew their own conclusions. Nearby lay eighteen ships of the "Jewish fleet," part of the armada of despair impounded by the Royal Navy after attempts to ferry "illegals" to the Promised Land. This grim drama unfolded during our first few days in Eretz Yisrael.

When the three Jews killed on the *Exodus* were borne to their last resting place on July 20, I set out from Jerusalem to attend the funeral with Golda Myerson (later, Meir), who was acting head of the Jewish Agency's Political Department, and Zvi Herman, a fellow member of the Zionist Executive. We arrived just as the funeral procession was about to leave for the Haifa cemetery, with thousands of young people following on foot. Golda and I joined the mourners on the way to the cemetery and spoke at the graveside. I referred to Bill Bernstein as "a symbol of the readiness of American Jewish youth to join in the struggle for Israel's survival."

Owing to the citywide curfew, which began at 7:00 P.M., we could not leave Haifa immediately after the funeral and stayed at a hotel overnight. The Jewish residential areas were in a virtual state of siege. Throughout the day, British police vehicles patrolled the streets, with loudspeakers blaring out warnings that search-lights would be used at night to detect "illegal" craft in Haifa Bay. Every so often, Royal Navy vessels exploded depth charges to scare off the immigrant-runners and, possibly also, frogmen of the Palyam, the marine arm of the Palmah, who had sabotaged British interceptors. The dull booms of exploding mines echoed all over the city.

It was during this visit to Eretz Yisrael, in 1947, that I made a vain, perhaps naïve attempt to bring together Menahem Begin, head of the Irgun Tzeva'i Leumi (Etzel), and Yisrael Galili, the Haganah commander. Seeing Galili presented no problem. We met at the Hotel Gat Rimmon in Tel Aviv. The meeting with Begin, however, was a more complicated matter, as he was in hiding from the British. Blindfolded, I was driven in a series of cars from one place to another in Tel Aviv, until we finally came to a house where I was taken to the top floor. Once my blindfold had been removed, I came face to face with the Etzel chief, who then wore a beard.

We had a long talk, but it was fruitless and my mediation effort came to naught. I never discovered where our meeting took place, but was told years later that, as the British authorities had put a price on his head, Begin would move around and make a point of sleeping in a different place every night.

Despite recurrent outbreaks of violence, the Yishuv remained calm and went about its daily tasks. A week after our arrival, a Haganah immigrant ship landed its human cargo somewhere along the coast and all on board managed to get ashore without detection. People seemed confident that a Jewish State would very soon come into being.

On the last Sunday night in July, I was an active participant in the thrilling adventure of an immigrant vessel bringing former inmates of the DP camps from their port of embarkation somewhere in Europe. The ship's name was *Kadimah*, a word bearing various connotations in the Zionist vocabulary, such as "forward," "onward," and "eastward."

The *Kadimah* unloaded its passengers offshore at Tel Aviv, and all were brought safely to the beach—some in boats, others on the backs of Palestine-born Sabras, a few swimming ashore unaided. Fortunately, the water was warm and there were few waves, as it was a windless night. To await the landing, I had gone down from Jerusalem with Eliezer Kaplan, treasurer of the Jewish Agency Executive, Peretz Bernstein, Yitzhak Gruenbaum, and David Remez, all four of whom were to become ministers in the first Government of the State of Israel a year later.

I was moved by the sight of these young boys swimming out to the ship in order to greet and help ashore brethren of theirs who had escaped the Nazi inferno. Among the "illegal" immigrants were survivors of Bergen-Belsen. When asked to say a few words, I made the point that a Jewish National Home without Jewish ships and airplanes would be incomplete. I foresaw the development of a flourishing maritime industry.

It so happened that a ship with a similar name to that of the immigrant boat, the S. S. *Kedmah*, had been purchased in January by Zim, the fledgling navigation company that was to become Israel's shipping line. As chairman of the United Palestine Appeal, I was present when this vessel went into commission later that year. It transported passengers and cargo between Haifa and Marseilles, subsequently bringing large numbers of Olim from Europe after the establishment of the Jewish State.

At the beginning of August, I visited Haifa, where I was received by the Jewish mayor, Shabbetai Levy, and his Arab deputy. Relations between Haifa's Jewish and Arab communities were friendly, but Arab members of the Municipal Council went in fear of terrorist attack. I therefore agreed not to release a photograph taken with them on the occasion of my visit.

While touring the area north of Tel Aviv, I also visited Moshav Benei Zion, a flourishing rural settlement sponsored by the American General Zionist fraternal order of B'nai Zion. It was especially pleasing to meet and to speak with a group of twelve new settlers who had just arrived from Cyprus and were living in tents. They hailed from Bessarabia and were among the very few who had survived the Nazi death camps of Buchenwald and Dachau.

On August 9, I flew to Cyprus for a three-day visit to the British detention centers outside Famagusta, on the southwestern coast of the island. I went there primarily in my capacity as president of the World Confederation of General Zionists, to observe at first hand the morale of the Jewish detainees and the conditions under which they were kept behind barbed-wire fences, awaiting their turn to enter Palestine.

The August weather there was similar to what we had experienced in Tel Aviv. The days were swelteringly hot and humid, while the nights brought no cool breath of wind. To be with the DPs and to see them at close quarters was an emotional and depressing experience, but one accompanied by thanksgiving that they had been saved from the Nazi furnaces.

There must have been at least 15,000 Jews under detention in Cyprus. It was an infamous reminder of the suffering they had endured for years on German and Polish soil. Living conditions were generally miserable, although the food provided was adequate. I received a particularly warm welcome from the Ha-No'ar Ha-Tzioni youth group, of which Moshe Kolodny (later, Kol), who subsequently headed the Independent Liberal Party in Israel and became Minister of Tourism, was the leader. I spoke at a number of meetings, bringing messages of fellowship and cheer both from American Jewry and from the Yishuv. My theme was that "the Jews of America are working hard to get the Administration to exert its influence on the British Government, so that the Cyprus camps will be closed and all of you will be allowed to go to Palestine."

The national spirit of the detainees was evident in their standard refrain: "Tell American Jews to send their youth to Eretz Yisrael." It was heartening to find that these surviving remnants of European Jewry, though still in distress, had held on to their faith in the mission of Zionism and in *Ha-Medinah ba-derekh*, the state-in-the-making. They were as much concerned with that State's future as with their own immediate plight.

Beholding those gaunt faces, eyes still haunted by memories of the Holocaust and by grief for the near and dear ones—often whole families—who had been wiped out, I was overwhelmed by the urge of these *ma'apilim* to reach the Promised Land. Aliyah Bet was now at its height, and reports came in daily of the small craft sailing from Greek and Italian ports, only a few of which managed to evade the blockading ships of the Royal Navy.

Over and over again, people asked me how soon they might obtain entry permits for Palestine. Many of the youngsters belonged to my General Zionist constituency. I told them of my experiences at Feldafing and other camps in the American zone of Germany immediately after the war. Walking among the DPs in Cyprus, I was struck by the thought that some of them might well have been in those German camps when I visited them two years earlier, in 1945.

A valiant effort was made to keep up the morale of the detainees. Here, the devoted labors of the volunteer camp personnel, sent by the Jewish Agency and the Joint Distribution Committee, were an inspiration. They did their utmost to keep everyone occupied, to create social and cultural amenities, and to prepare the DPs for their eventual settlement in Eretz Yisrael. A democratically elected central committee was responsible for self-government in the camps. They had a library, a pharmacy (though not enough doctors), and workshops where inmates were taught carpentry and tinsmithing; a garden and smaller garden plots for the children who cultivated them; and a program of education including, for those who desired it, yeshivah instruction. The usual schedule was four hours' work and four hours' instruction. A "vacation camp" was in operation, providing ten days of rest and relaxation after six weeks of the normal routine. One remarkable feature was an art exhibit of painting and sculpture, depicting scenes in the Nazi death camps, on the ships, and in Cyprus.

Joshua Leibner and Morris Loeb of the JDC, who had accompanied me from Palestine, told some harrowing tales of the early days in these refugee camps on Cyprus. Some of the Jews were in such tatters that they ripped up the canvas of their tents to make clothes for themselves. There were many cases of psychological depression, and a variety of social problems were encountered. Offenders were punished by the only sanctions available—reduced food rations and postponement of their turn for Aliyah. A few of the more serious offenders had to be sent for trial to Famagusta and were imprisoned in the city jail. On the whole, I was told, the attitude of the local Cypriot population was very friendly, as the Cypriots were anti-British and were campaigning for their own national independence.

One aspect of my visit that afforded some amusement, mingled with a certain apprehensiveness as to the future, was the proliferation of Zionist alignments. These seemed to dominate camp life, which functioned on the same party basis as the political institutions in the Yishuv. The elected council conducted internal affairs and enforced discipline. These party distinctions among the refugees served to prepare them for their future life and integration in Eretz Yisrael.

My three days in Cyprus were a poignant, emotional experience. It was thrilling to see a *mifkad* (parade), with the marchers, some 500 young people, singing Hebrew songs. They were dressed in their best clothes. The participants filed into an amphitheater, which had been made by carving ridges in a hilltop. A choir was conducted by a man who, I learned, had once been a musical director in Bucharest. Then came the speeches. More than one called upon the Jews of the United States to help the Yishuv not only with money, but also with manpower. More than once, I heard the refrain, "The British are planning to crush our morale here, but in spite of them, we are undeterred!"

At an assembly held toward evening one day, I said:

> *Zekhut banim*, the merits of the youth, exceed in this case *zekhut avot*, the parental merits. You give us elders courage. It is now sundown, but the sun will rise and shine again tomorrow. Thus, we can be certain that the darkness of these past years will give way to the sun which will arise in our *Mizrah!*

I came away from Cyprus with much to report to the Jewish organizations concerned. One lacuna I noted was the internal administration's lack of a rabbinical authority. To judge from what I heard, this was a prime necessity. On my return to Jerusalem, I mentioned the matter to Chief Rabbi Isaac Halevi Herzog, who remedied the omission.

After that brief stay in the Cyprus camps, I resumed my journey, proceeding in a reverse direction along the immigrant route, and spent some time in Italy. There I acquainted myself with the work of Berihah ("Flight"), the clandestine Jewish organization that spirited the *ma'apilim* across the Alps and the Pyrenees by various ingenious stratagems. Mr. A. Galub was in charge of this operation, and he told me about its use of the now famous "secret roads."

It was not until my arrival in Rome that I realized Italy's importance in the programs of the International Refugee Organization (IRO), which operated in close coordination with the offices of the Joint Distribution Committee and Jewish Agency there. The IRO had then been in existence for eighteen months, taking over the work of handling the refugees which until then had been UNRRA's responsibility. One criticism of UNRRA I had voiced arose from its policy of indiscriminately helping every refugee who came along to its office without investigating his or her credentials.

According to the information I received, there were 18,000 Jewish refugees being cared for in congested barracks, with another 6,000 on their way from Austria and Germany. Hundreds of DPs arrived by day and night. Some of them were thinking of going back to Poland until the situation in Palestine cleared up. When I visited a children's home, I found there a group from Poland belonging to the Ha-No'ar Ha-Tzioni youth wing of our General Zionist Party, the strongest among the Jewish refugees. I told these youngsters about Jewish children in America and also spoke of those whom I had seen in Cyprus.

Before going on to Geneva and Paris, I had a long conversation with Chief Rabbi David Prato, in the course of which he praised the work being done by the JDC to revive and support Jewish institutions in Italy. Italian Jewry was then in the process of recovering from its wartime trauma. Rabbi Prato, a keen and active Zionist, had been Chief Rabbi of Alexandria and had then served as Chief Rabbi of Rome from 1936 until 1938. He had spent the World War II years in Palestine, resuming his former post in 1945.

A week of conferences and meetings in Paris—including a meeting of the World Confederation of General Zionists and of its Constructive Fund—preceded the sessions of the Zionist General Council in Zurich, where I functioned as chairman of the Political Commission. Delegates heard a full report of the *Exodus* tragedy from Zalman Rubashov, who (as Zalman Shazar) would become Israel's third President. He was then a member of the Jewish Agency Executive and editor of the Tel Aviv Labor daily, *Davar*. Moshe Shertok, head of the Agency's Political Department, surveyed the work of UNSCOP, which had completed its inquiries and was now preparing a definitive report on the Palestine situation and framing its recommendations to the UN.

At the beginning of September, after the Zionist General Council meeting, I went to Lyons, where a children's home under General Zionist auspices was named in my honor, in acknowledgment of my activities in the rescue of European Jewish orphans and educating them for their new life in Eretz Yisrael.

The home, a magnificent château of thirty-eight rooms, set in two acres of grounds, had accommodations for 240 youngsters. As we entered that morning, around eleven o'clock, about a hundred of the children greeted us. All were from Poland, where they had grown up in forests and churches; their survival was little short of miraculous. They welcomed us with touching little speeches. Among those who addressed them from the balcony were the Mayor of Lyons, the Chief Rabbi of the Lyons Jewish community, the General Zionist leader in France, Michel Topiol, and a Youth Aliyah representative.

Responding in Yiddish, I spoke about wartime Jewish resistance to the Nazis in France and elsewhere, also referring to the recent *Exodus* affair. I closed by saying, "The Keren Kayemet 'presented' me recently with a *'Nahalah'* in the Darom [Southern Palestine]. I would like to make a *shiddukh* [match] for you to settle on it. . . . Palestine awaits you!"

The UN Vote on the Jewish Commonwealth

Once the United Nations Special Committee on Palestine (UNSCOP) had completed its investigations and presented its majority and minority reports, the Ad Hoc (Palestine) Committee was appointed by the UN to consider these findings. Unofficial Zionist contacts with representatives of the Arab League left no doubt that the Arabs would stand by their threat to invoke economic sanctions and use armed force if the UN were to adopt either report. Neither partition nor a binational state was acceptable to the Arabs: the whole of Palestine must remain under their control. By now, as Azzam Pasha was to confess during a secret interview with David Horowitz and Aubrey (Abba) Eban in mid-October, no compromise settlement was possible. Arab nationalist feeling had reached such a peak that anyone openly favoring negotiation with the Jews would be endangering his own life.

On September 25, the UNSCOP recommendations came before the UN General Assembly's Palestine Committee. More than two months were to go by, however, before the final vote would be taken at a plenary session of the General Assembly. Meanwhile, a united Jewish front was established by the World Jewish Congress, the Jewish Agency, the American Jewish Conference, Agudat Yisrael, and the American Jewish Committee. Only two small pressure groups, each with its own axe to grind, stood apart from us—the anti-Zionist American Council for Judaism and Peter Bergson's pro-Irgun committee. Since our only hope now lay in partition, we of the Zionist leadership threw ourselves into the struggle to obtain United Nations approval for the UNSCOP majority report.

At the August meeting of the Zionist General Council in Zurich, a decision had been taken to appoint a special Political Advisory Committee—representing the World Zionist Organization as a whole—which would meet with Jewish Agency representatives at the United Nations in Lake Success (and subsequently at Flushing Meadows), in order to hear reports from our spokesmen there. Seventeen full members and a number of deputies or alternates sat on this committee, which represented the various Zionist factions—Ahdut Avodah, Aliyah Hadashah, the General Zionists, Hadassah, Ha-Shomer Ha-Tza'ir, Mizrahi and Ha-Po'el Ha-Mizrahi, Po'alei Zion, and the Revisionists. Nine of the members were from Eretz Yisrael. I was named chairman of the Political Advisory Committee and its convenor. Simon N. Herman, now a professor in the Institute of Contemporary Jewry at the Hebrew University of Jerusalem, was appointed secretary.

The committee, as its name indicated, was only a consultative body. It was not vested with any measure of authority over those who bespoke our cause at the UN, but it did serve a useful purpose in keeping the entire Zionist movement *au courant* with developments there and with the way in which representatives of the Jewish Agency Executive put the Zionist case before the world. This was no easy matter, considering that we had three separate focal points, in Jerusalem, London, and New York. The Political Advisory Committee nevertheless concentrated its Zionist effort and concern in New York, not far from the scene of action at Lake Success and Flushing Meadows.

From October to December 1947, fifteen meetings were held in the New York offices of the Jewish Agency. Among those who appeared before our committee were Rabbi Abba Hillel Silver, chairman of the Agency's American Section and the chief Zionist spokesman at the UN, Dr. Nahum Goldmann, and Moshe Shertok. They presented updated reports, answered questions, and listened to the views expressed by members of the committee in regard to matters under discussion at the UN. We were given the opportunity of attending sessions of the Ad Hoc Committee on Palestine, and of the UN General Assembly, throughout this period.

Our meetings were also attended by Zionist officials and emissaries such as Aubrey Eban, Dr. A. Lauterbach, secretary of the WZO, and Arthur Lourie. Dr. Walter Eytan prepared daily political reports. Both Eytan and Lourie would subsequently become eminent Israeli diplomats, while Eban was destined to become Israel's ambassador to the United States and to the UN, and, later, Foreign Minister. At the same time, much valuable work was done by Eliahu Epstein (later, Elath), who headed the Jewish Agency's Political Bureau in Washington. An expert on Arab affairs, he went on to become Israel's first ambassador to the United States and eventually served as president of the Hebrew University during the decade following our Aliyah.*

The fact that a majority of the Ad Hoc Committee seemed to favor partition did not mean that our victory was a foregone conclusion. A number of delegations were firmly committed to the establishment of Jewish and Arab states, respectively, in Palestine. These included half-a-dozen Communist bloc countries, which took their lead from Moscow. Arabists in the British Foreign Office and the U.S. State Department, however, were still intent on frustrating any such decision in the General Assembly. Thus, Loy Henderson, one of our old enemies, led the State Department chorus against partition, using as one of his arguments the bogeyman of a Jewish "theocratic racial state." If anything, that description could properly be applied (then as now) to most countries in the Arab world. President Truman, who apparently saw through these maneuvers, instructed the U.S. delegation to maintain its support for the UNSCOP majority recommendations. Truman's stand, which David

---

*An important contribution to Zionist history over this period is Dr. Elath's two-volume work, *Ha-Ma'avak al Ha-Medinah (The Struggle for Statehood)*. *Washington: 1945–1948* (Tel Aviv: Am Oved, 1979–82). For some additional insights, I am indebted to Dr. Zvi Ganin's *Truman, American Jewry, and Israel, 1945–1948* (New York and London: Holmes & Meier Publishers, Inc., 1979).

Niles, Herbert Lehman, and a few others had a hand in shaping, was reiterated by Eleanor Roosevelt and General John H. Hilldring, two newly appointed advisors to the U.S. delegation, and by Herschel V. Johnson, who announced the President's formal endorsement of partition at the October 11 session of the Ad Hoc Committee. Three days later, the USSR followed suit.

Early in October, with the arrival of Dr. Chaim Weizmann in New York, Abba Hillel Silver and Moshe Shertok had received some new and effective support. Despite Weizmann's address before the Ad Hoc Committee on October 18, however, President Truman's stand was not clear-cut, and the conflict between the White House and the State Department was not resolved until the eve of the crucial General Assembly vote at the end of November. In the absence of a firm American lead, several delegations began drifting toward the Arab side or adopted a noncommittal posture. On November 19, while things remained in the balance, Weizmann saw Truman and succeeded in convincing him that the Negev should form part of the Jewish State. This was no mean achievement at the time, since President Truman was becoming irritated by and resentful of the constant pressure to which we Zionists were subjecting him. Unfortunately, we had no other option, as lobbying and appeals to American public opinion were our only way of counteracting the forces ranged against us.

To avoid antagonizing the White House, Jewish Agency leaders decided to canvass the support of various uncommitted delegations at the UN, instead of asking our friends in the U.S. Administration to do so. Rabbi Silver, Moshe Shertok, David Horowitz, and Eliahu Epstein were particularly active in this campaign. On November 25, the Ad Hoc Committee on Palestine finally disposed of the minority recommendations and gave its approval to the majority plan by twenty-five votes to thirteen. At this stage, President Truman's refusal to put any pressure on the waverers made it doubtful that the necessary two-thirds majority would be secured in the General Assembly. Everything now hinged on the seventeen countries that had abstained in the Palestine Committee vote. Loy Henderson and his allies in the U.S. and British delegations were convinced that they would get their own way.

American Zionism thus faced its supreme challenge. Nothing could be left to chance, and the Jewish State for which two generations had fought so hard might never arise, simply because of one crucial vote.

In point of fact, the General Assembly was scheduled to render its decision on Wednesday, November 26. It became obvious to Dr. Nahum Goldmann, Dr. Emanuel Neumann, and our other lobbyists at Flushing Meadows that partition was doomed if the final vote were to be taken on that day. Around noon, our friends in the U.S. and Latin American delegations agreed to resort to delaying tactics, since November 27 was Thanksgiving Day, when no session of the General Assembly would be held. If, therefore, we could somehow prolong the debate and then have the actual voting postponed, it might yet be possible to change the course of events. Filibustering tactics, combined with the unofficial sympathy of UN Secretary-General Trygve Lie and Dr. Oswaldo Aranha, president of the General Assembly, brought us the vital breathing space.

From that Wednesday evening until Saturday afternoon, when the General Assembly reconvened, a last-ditch effort was made to secure the essential votes for partition. Countless talks, interviews, and long-distance telephone calls to heads of state and other influential persons led to new instructions being given to several key delegations. Every form of legitimate pressure, including the personal intercession of eminent non-Jews as well as Jews, was exercised to bring the wavering delegates over to our side.

The rest is history. On the evening of Saturday, November 29, 1947, the UN vote was recorded. Thirty-three countries voted in favor of partition, including the U.S., the USSR and the Communist bloc states (except Yugoslavia), Western Europe, the British Commonwealth, and most of the Latin American countries; thirteen (mainly Arab and Muslim) states voted against; and ten countries, including Great Britain, abstained. Apart from authorizing the establishment of Jewish and Arab states within specified boundaries, the UN General Assembly called upon Great Britain to quit Palestine by August 1, 1948 (this date was subsequently brought forward to May 14), appointed a special Palestine Commission to see to the implementation of partition, and made the UN Security Council responsible for the maintenance of peace in the Middle East. Jerusalem was to have a "special international regime," and freedom of access to the holy places of Judaism, Christianity, and Islam was guaranteed.

We had no way of knowing then that the battle had only begun and that it would be no easy matter to put the historic UN resolution into effect. Zionists and non-Zionist Jews throughout the world, united in this moment of victory, gave way to unbounded rejoicing. It was, in Abba Hillel Silver's words, an event "of incalculable significance for our people and for the history of mankind," a blessed relief for hundreds of thousands of Jewish DPs, since the achievement of statehood meant recognition of the Jews as a nation, "the end of *Galut* and the opportunity for us to ingather all the dispersed of our people."

As national chairman of the United Palestine Appeal and co-chairman of the UJA, I had been engaged in many fund-raising journeys throughout the length and breadth of the United States. Everywhere on my travels I had found tense expectancy among Jews in the weeks preceding the decisive UN vote. American Jewry was solidly behind the creation of a Third Jewish Commonwealth in Eretz Yisrael. Eddie Jacobson, a (non-Zionist) longtime Jewish friend of Harry Truman, had begun to play an important part in our ramified campaign. Before very long, he would be called upon to perform another significant task in regard to White House policy on Jewish statehood.

To the great chagrin of Dr. Stephen Wise, Louis Lipsky, and myself, it so happened that when the crucial vote was taken at Flushing Meadows on that Saturday evening, November 29, we—together with Henry Monsky and many heads of Jewish and Zionist organizations—were attending an important, previously scheduled meeting of the American Jewish Conference in Chicago. Owing to the uncertainty caused by two successive postponements of the UN vote, and because there was no clear indication that any such vote would be called for that weekend, it had been decided to go ahead with our Chicago program.

Various factions were caucusing in separate rooms when news of the passage of the resolution was telephoned to our hotel. All other matters were immediately forgotten and we ran to embrace one another, shedding tears of joy. My wife and I will never forget the emotion and euphoria that swept over us. At a public meeting that I chaired later the same day, I alluded, in my opening remarks, to the momentous event that had just taken place several hundred miles from where we were assembled:

> I am sure that every one of us, and every Jew the world over, feels a new sense of dignity as a result of the decision of the UN earlier this evening. It happened just at the time of *Melaveh Malkah,* when the Orthodox Jew was escorting Queen Sabbath out; but for the Jewish people as a whole it was a time of *Kabbalat Melukhah,* escorting the State in.
>
> We, the Jews of America, speaking through the American Jewish Conference, which represents the overwhelming majority of American Jews, pledge ourselves to keep alive—and continue to focus the consciousness and the conscience of the American people upon—the importance of giving the infant Jewish State a chance to live and flourish.
>
> We salute the Yishuv and we say to them: "Your courage, your dignity, your sacrifices have been an inspiration to all of us and have given the world a demonstration of what Jewish Palestine can do for the enrichment of human values." To the Jews in Europe, in Cyprus, in the DP camps, and to the Jews of the *Exodus* we say: "By your refusal to accept any *ersatz* for *Eretz,* you have made Zionism the irresistible solution to the Jewish problem."
>
> We salute the memory of our martyred dead. We thank God—*Shomer Yisrael*—that the time has come at long last when our national rebirth can be fulfilled in and through our generation.

The UN resolution of November 29, 1947, marked the end of one Zionist era and the beginning of another. It was not, as some have claimed, merely the outcome of political pressure (although such pressure was indeed exerted); it owed far more to pangs of conscience within the international community over the European Holocaust, the plight of the Jewish DPs, and the Yishuv's resistance to repressive British government in Palestine.

The "verdict of the nations" set the seal of fulfillment on half a century of desperate struggle, which began at the First Zionist Congress in Basle, where Theodor Herzl, in his own words, "founded the Jewish State." Fifty years after the formulation of his political program, as Herzl had predicted, there would come into being an independent Jewish commonwealth in Eretz Yisrael. The Zionist movement's dreamers, pioneers, and martyrs were thus vindicated.

On December 1, 1947, the following cable (in Hebrew) to David Ben-Gurion and his colleagues in Jerusalem was sent on behalf of the Political Advisory Committee, which I had the privilege of heading throughout this momentous period:

> Congratulations to our people and to the Executive of our Renascence Movement on achieving the end of our *Galut* and removal of alien yoke from our Homeland. Ours has been the privilege to take part in this historic struggle and to

witness at first hand the sagacity, talent, loyalty and courage of our colleagues in performing their supreme task. As we have been privileged, under your leadership, to secure recognition of the nations for our sovereignty in the Homeland, so may we be vouchsafed the Ingathering of the Exiles in their State, the uniting of our people under the flag of our Renascence, the assurance of a life of peace and brotherhood with our Arab neighbors, and our freedom among nations of the world. To you, leaders of our Liberation movement, who have raised the banner of our statehood and fought under it, the acknowledgment and blessings of our entire people are due.

My final task as chairman of the committee was to publish a statement on December 3, hailing the UN resolution, congratulating the Jewish Agency Executive on its "effective and statesmanlike conduct before the United Nations," and thanking the U.S. and Soviet Governments for their vital support. Although important areas of western Palestine (notably Jerusalem) had been excluded from the territory allocated to the Jewish State, most of us felt that even this sacrifice was justified in order to reach a permanent settlement and obtain UN sanction for the establishment of a Jewish commonwealth in Eretz Yisrael.

There was an immediate and violent reaction in Palestine to the UN partition resolution. Within twenty-four hours, the Mufti's Palestine Arab Higher Committee declared a three-day general strike, heralded by the looting and destruction of Jerusalem's commercial center on December 1. Jewish communities in various Arab states were subjected to murderous attacks by rioters, and Jewish settlements throughout the Yishuv came under hostile fire. The British, too, were furious and refused to cooperate with the United Nations or its Commission of Five. Early in December, the U.S. Government banned all arms shipments to the Middle East. In practice, this move affected only the Yishuv, since the British continued to "fulfill existing commitments" by shipping arms to Arab League states.

A particularly blatant example of British irresponsibility was Whitehall's refusal to allow members of the United Nations Palestine Commission into the country before May 1, 1948. These "Five Lost Pilgrims," as they were dubbed, sat helplessly in New York. A six-man UN team that nevertheless arrived in January to prepare the ground for this commission was thoroughly humiliated. The British administration confined the team to a Jerusalem cellar and left it to fend for itself.

Rather than maintain law and order, which would provoke a confrontation with the Arabs, Foreign Secretary Ernest Bevin decided to abandon all pretense of impartiality. As Richard Crossman, M.P., noted at the time, Bevin continually raged about Zionist tactics, which had put him to shame before the entire world, and gave vent to obsessively anti-Semitic utterances. He alleged that there was a "worldwide Jewish conspiracy run from America," which aimed to discredit him, and that the Nazis had learned their methods from "Jewish terrorists." Military experts, such as Field Marshal Bernard Montgomery, also calculated that the Arabs were bound to win any full-scale war in Palestine after the evacuation of British troops. Bevin's strategy, therefore, was to "let the Jews and Arabs fight it out" in the confident expectation that Great Britain would be asked to come back and save the Yishuv from annihilation. In this way, the British would regain their vital bases in Haifa and the Negev. During the last months of British Mandatory "government," a deliberate attempt was made to create disruption and chaos. Palestine was expelled from the sterling area and, in order to bankrupt the future Jewish State, Palestinian assets were frozen in London while the Jerusalem treasury was emptied. The railroads ground to a halt, armed bands crossing the border were left undisturbed, and, while disarming members of the Haganah, the British authorities turned money and military hardware over to local Arabs, whose commanders received advance notification of key installations their unofficial allies were about to evacuate.

The Yishuv's fight for survival passed through an initial, critical phase in the early months of 1948. Toward the end of January, an "Arab Liberation Army" began infiltrating into Palestine from Syria. Commanded by Fawzi al-Kawukji, a mercenary officer who had been active during the Arab revolt of 1936–39, it included in its ranks a motley assortment of Polish and Yugoslav Fascists, Spanish Falangists, and World War II cutthroats of the Nazi SS. Within two months, Kawukji had 7,000 men under arms in northern Palestine; further south, almost as many roamed the countryside under the able leadership of Abd al-Kader al-Husseini, the Mufti's nephew, and 2,000 Muslim Brotherhood volunteers arrived from Egypt to harass Jewish settlements in the Negev. Major highways were blockaded, Jewish Jerusalem was besieged, and isolated kibbutzim (such as those of the Etzion Bloc, between Bethlehem and Hebron) had to withstand constant attacks. The British stood by all the while, refusing to intervene. On paper, the Yishuv could call upon some 30,000 defenders—Haganah reservists, boys and girls of the Palmah, and Etzel and Lehi underground fighters—but all of them were poorly armed and half-trained. Ben-Gurion's policy was to hold on to every inch of land allotted to the Jewish State, regardless of the cost, until the British left Palestine. This strategy paid off in the end, but it involved tremendous sacrifices in terms of lives, vehicles, and supplies. As the siege of Jerusalem intensified, with Arab snipers and ambushers waylaying convoys from Tel Aviv at Bab el-Wad, Dr. Bernard (Dov) Joseph was empowered to impose rationing on the city's Jewish population.

A series of unprecedented outrages now shook the Yishuv. On February 1, the offices of *The Palestine Post* were blown up in downtown Jerusalem. Three weeks later, most of the shops and apartments in Ben-Yehudah Street were destroyed, with tragic loss of life. The perpetrators, in both cases, were British policemen who supported the (Fascist) Union Movement of Sir Oswald Mosley. A third bomb, planted by an Arab on March 11, devastated the Keren Hayesod wing of the Jewish Agency building in Jerusalem's Rehavia neighborhood. The thirteen dead included our beloved Leib Jaffe, the veteran Zionist leader and emissary.

Meanwhile, partly under the impact of this violence, President Truman's administration was having second thoughts about the partitioning of Palestine. Evidence of the Yishuv's weakness at the time, combined with anti-American demonstrations throughout the Arab world, prompted top officials in the U.S. State Department to press for some form of trusteeship instead of partition. Our opponents, notably Dean

Rusk and Loy Henderson in the State Department, found some powerful allies in the Pentagon and in James Forrestal of the Defense Department. Alarmed by the prospect of American troops having to join an international police force in Palestine, they inspired *Time* and *Newsweek* magazine stories that General George Marshall, the U.S. Secretary of State, was now at variance with President Truman's Middle East policy. Rumor had it that Zionist "intransigence" was on the point of igniting a conflagration that would engulf U.S. oil interests, hasten the advance of Soviet imperialism, and unleash a wave of anti-Semitic reaction throughout the United States. Desperate efforts were made by the American Zionist leadership to prevent the UN partition resolution from being sabotaged.

Our first intimation of what was afoot came in mid-January. Dr. Abba Hillel Silver was then consulting with Jewish Agency leaders in Palestine, and during his absence I had been appointed acting chairman of the American Zionist Emergency Council. It was my good fortune to have several effective colleagues at my side, notably Dr. Emanuel Neumann, Professor Milton Handler (who functioned also as chairman of the American Jewish Conference's Palestine Committee), and Herman Shulman, an eminent lawyer, who had helped Stephen Wise and myself to secure the Democratic Party's pro-Zionist plank at its convention in July 1944. Dr. Neumann and I went to Washington, where we met with ten influential senators and forty members of the House of Representatives. I also managed to obtain an interview with President Truman, at which certain vital matters previously reviewed with Professor Handler were discussed.

On February 5, I delivered a Zionist *"J'accuse"* at a mass demonstration organized by the AZEC in Manhattan Center, New York. The prevailing somber mood contrasted markedly with the jubilation felt by all of us only two months earlier. Deputizing for Abba Hillel Silver, I condemned international faintheartedness and British connivance with the Arabs in defying the UN. I also criticized the American Government for its failure to exert economic pressure on Great Britain and for imposing an arms embargo that hurt only Jews defending themselves against Arab attacks in Palestine. British intrigue and U.S. inertia threatened to reduce the UN partition resolution to a mere "scrap of paper." There must be an end to sabotage and obstructionism, I declared. Though handicapped, outnumbered, and besieged, the Yishuv still had the will to resist. It was high time that both the United States and the United Nations offered tangible support. "The American Government, by all moral considerations, should be hailing this valiant company of the Yishuv," I said, "upholding democracy in a sea of semi-feudalism."

Throughout this time, we were convinced that President Truman would reassert his authority and curb the State Department machinations, if only influential friends of ours (such as ex-Secretary of War Henry L. Stimson) could have a judicious word with him. Truman, however, was also beset with doubts and evidently preferred to leave matters to the bureaucrats. On February 24, Senator Warren Austin, the U.S. delegate to the UN Security Council, gave formal expression to the emerging U.S. line when he proposed that the Security Council "look into the Palestine situation," with a view to keeping the peace rather than enforcing partition. His statement in no way supported the appeals made by Trygve Lie and the UN Palestine Commission for British and Arab defiance of the United Nations to be resisted.

While in Washington, therefore, on March 2, I delivered an address before the Palaver Club in my capacity as chairman of the World Confederation of General Zionists and as chairman of the United Palestine Appeal. My theme was "Palestine, United States, and Security Council: What Now?" In the course of this forthright speech, I conveyed some of the anger we felt over British perfidy, Arab defiance of the UN, American inaction, and State Department encouragement of the attempts to sabotage partition. The latest statement by Senator Austin indicated a retreat from the November 29 resolution, which was itself a final compromise. Were the American Government to back down now in the face of Arab menaces, I said, it would "be driving the first nail into the coffin of the UN." At the instance of Senator Olin D. Johnston of South Carolina, who had introduced me to the members of the Palaver Club, the bulk of my address was inserted in the next day's *Congressional Record*.

David Ben-Gurion, the chairman of the Jewish Agency Executive, believed that an American retreat from partition would not affect the progress toward a Jewish commonwealth, provided that sufficient funds could be raised to arm the Yishuv. At Ben-Gurion's request, therefore, Dr. Silver flew back to New York for the purpose of raising money and mustering political support. The AZEC embarked on a new information campaign, but Silver was alarmed to discover a change in President Truman—he was "sulky, irritated and inaccessible to Zionist leaders." Furthermore, on the pro-Arab side, we now had to face a new and vocal opponent in Kermit Roosevelt, grandson of the late President "Teddy" (Theodore) Roosevelt, who proclaimed the incompatibility of U.S. and Zionist aims. He and the recently established (Protestant) Committee for Justice and Peace in the Holy Land made common cause with our old enemies, the American Council for Judaism, whose leader, Lessing Rosenwald, also had a following in the American Jewish Committee. Fortunately for us, however, the anti-Zionist lobby did not succeed in winning over Congress or American public opinion.

Once again, President Truman was subjected to grueling pressures. He could not fail to note the chaotic developments in Palestine, warning signals from the State Department and the Pentagon, and the Soviet-inspired coup which brought Czechoslovakia into the Communist orbit on February 25. At the same time, American Jewry was in full cry against any surrender to Arab and British intrigue. Our arguments were reinforced by Clark M. Clifford and Oscar R. Ewing, among other White House advisers, who urged the President to denounce Arab aggression, end the arms embargo, and give teeth to the UN. Clifford attacked Warren Austin's recent speech, asserting that it had undermined American morale, popular faith in the President, and the credibility of the United Nations. If the Truman Doctrine had proved effective in saving Greece and Turkey from Communism, why should it not also work in Palestine? There was no reason to suspect that a Jewish State would align itself with Moscow, as some U.S. officials had been hinting, and Arab oil embargo threats were a bluff. "They need us more than we need them," Clifford insisted. This dispute between the presidential advisers and the U.S. Administration raged on until mid-May.

On February 4, Dr. Chaim Weizmann had arrived in the United States to bolster our diplomatic offensive. Though initially reluctant to embroil himself in the political conflict, since he had no status in the World Zionist Organization and because he feared (rightly, as it turned out) that a winter in New York might adversely affect his health, Weizmann was persuaded by Joseph (Ivor) Linton to do whatever he could to stem the tide.* A cabled invitation from the Jewish Agency Executive clinched matters.

Having moved into the Waldorf-Astoria Hotel, Weizmann tried to arrange an appointment with President Truman but was told repeatedly that he was "not available." As a final resort, Truman's old friend and former business associate, Eddie Jacobson, was flown out from Kansas City and, on March 13, he succeeded in getting the President to change his mind. Apparently, Jacobson pointed at a statue of Andrew Jackson on the President's desk and said, "I, too, have a hero whom I have never met—Dr. Chaim Weizmann. He is one of the greatest Jews who ever lived, but you won't see him, just because you were upset by some American Jewish leaders!" After a moment or two, Truman replied, "You win, you bald-headed so-and-so! I will see him." When Weizmann came to the White House five days later, Truman assured him that his support for partition remained unaltered. This was certainly welcome news for those of us who had feared the worst.

On the following day, however, we were dumbfounded to hear that U.S. policy was practically the reverse. Addressing the Security Council, Warren Austin declared that his Government now favored a "temporary trusteeship" for Palestine, under UN auspices, and thought that the Palestine Commission should no longer strive to implement partition. Most United Nations delegates could not believe their own ears, and there was a violent reaction from American Jewry over this sudden betrayal. Many of us, including Abba Hillel Silver, concluded that Truman had known all along about the impending *volte-face* and that, like President Franklin D. Roosevelt, he had simply pulled the wool over our eyes.

Not until later did it emerge that Truman, far from reaching a final decision on the Palestine issue, had not even been consulted before Senator Austin dropped his bombshell. It seems likely that the President did know that some such proposal was being considered by the State Department, although he had not yet given it the go-ahead signal. It is even more probable that Secretary of State Marshall, then conveniently absent on the West Coast, knew perfectly well what Austin's speech contained. Loy Henderson, Dean Rusk, and the other antipartitionists, anticipating difficulties with Clark Clifford and David Niles if they were to request White House clearance for Austin's text, simply went over Truman's head. The President could not very well disown his UN spokesman: his hands were tied. Five days later, on March 24, the whole matter was investigated in the presence of General Marshall,

*I am grateful to Mr. Linton (since deceased) for some details included in the following pages.

now back from the West Coast. Clifford served as "chief prosecutor" and Niles and Henderson exchanged angry words, but the damage had been done.

Among the few who remained calm were Dr. Weizmann and Eddie Jacobson. Instinctively, Weizmann could not believe that Truman had had foreknowledge of Austin's "Black Friday" statement at the UN. This was a correct supposition. Indeed, having only just given his personal assurance to Dr. Weizmann, President Truman was furious with the State Department for putting him "in the position of a liar and a double-crosser." His mortification would soon work to our advantage, although we were unaware of this at the time. For the moment, however, Truman contented himself with a statement to the effect that the United States had not abandoned partition as the ultimate political solution for Palestine. A fortnight later, on April 9, Weizmann wrote to the President, thanking him for this declaration and adding that the Jewish people now had to choose between statehood and extermination. "History and Providence have placed that issue in your hand," he concluded, "and I am confident that you will yet decide in the spirit of the moral law."

While Abba Hillel Silver was assuring us that "we have lost a major battle, not the war," things were looking grim for the Yishuv. Machine guns, let alone tanks and planes, were in short supply. Ben-Gurion, fearing British intentions, called not only for armaments but also for UN and American recognition of any provisional Jewish government established in Eretz Yisrael. On March 23, four days after Warren Austin's bombshell, the Jewish Agency Executive categorically rejected any trusteeship scheme and announced its decision to set up a Jewish administration no later than May 16. By the end of March, a majority of UN delegations had expressed opposition to the State Department's démarche. For all that, British and American delaying tactics continued to be applied.

In Palestine, meanwhile, Yigael Yadin, the Haganah's chief operations officer, told Ben-Gurion that it was time to go over to the offensive. The seizure of strategic roads and hilltops from Arab marauders was a risky gamble, seeing that British forces might choose to intervene, but Ben-Gurion supported Yadin's proposal. What especially weighed in favor of his decision was the long-awaited arrival of vital arms, purchased from Czechoslovakia, which were flown in by air and smuggled into the country by sea during the first few nights of April.

Disputes between the rival Arab commands made it easier for the Yishuv to counterattack. Ignoring Arab League directives, the Mufti's undisciplined gangs acted on their own initiative, thereby disrupting the overall campaign. Abd al-Kader al-Husseini, on the Jerusalem front, worked at cross purposes with Fawzi al-Kawukji in the north. Since January, Fawzi's "Arab Liberation Army" had gained little glory for itself, failing to capture Kfar Szold and Tirat Tzvi, a religious kibbutz where the overconfident invaders lost many men. Desperate to score a victory, Fawzi laid siege to Mishmar ha-Emek on April 4, but simultaneously let the Haganah know that he would do nothing to prevent the Jews from thrashing his archrival in the foothills below Jerusalem. Operation Naḥshon (April 6–15) temporarily cleared the Tel Aviv–Jerusalem road, facilitating the passage of three vital supply convoys. It was marked by fierce fighting, particularly at Kastel, where Abd al-Kader al-Husseini met his death on April 9. This was a blow from which the Mufti's troops never recovered.

Prelude to Independence

As Operation Naḥshon got underway, on April 6, a meeting of the Zionist General Council was convened at the Levinsky School in Tel Aviv. Its major purpose was to decide whether the Yishuv should go ahead and proclaim a Jewish State when the Mandate ended and British forces were evacuated from Palestine on May 15, 1948.

My colleagues and I had arrived at Lydda (now Ben-Gurion) Airport, where we found Haganah men in civilian dress guarding the passenger terminal. Enemy agents, in the guise of porters, were also visible. A kind of armed truce prevailed at Lydda, but the twelve-mile route to Tel Aviv posed many dangers, since Arab guerillas controlling the highway had nothing to fear from the British "security forces." We could proceed in one of two ways—either by armored car or in a Piper Cub aircraft. The Piper Cub, a small plane with room for one passenger, was popularly known as a "Primus," from the Hebrew designation for the local kerosene stove that sputtered and hissed when lit.

My choice was the air route, and I sat next to the pilot, who skillfully dodged potshots from the ground by Arab snipers. After a hair-raising trip, we arrived all in one piece at our destination. Because of the obvious dangers, those members of the Actions Committee who lived in Jerusalem were forced to make a long detour by way of the Dead Sea Potash Works, from where they reached Tel Aviv in British army lorries.

A dramatic counterpoint to our deliberations was the battle for Mishmar ha-Emek, then under attack by the army of Fawzi al-Kawukji, who again failed to register a military triumph.

Under these circumstances, it was not easy to move ahead toward a declaration of independence. The risks were apparent every day. Only a very few, notably Ben-Gurion, realized the state of our defenses. He alone knew precisely how many guns, tanks, and planes the Haganah possessed, but he kept his own counsel. Those of us who were not "in the know" accepted his advice to press on regardless.

More than two decades later, while visiting Ben-Gurion at his home near the Tel Aviv seafront in 1970, I harked back to that session of the Zionist General Council at which he declined to reveal the strength of the Haganah. "Why were you so secretive?" I asked him. Many of us thought at the time that his refusal to disclose the facts had something to do with the conflict between the Haganah and the Etzel underground movement. Ben-Gurion, however, dismissed that supposition. "No, it was not that," he answered. "I did not want to have to reveal the source of our arms supplies." The fact that they had come from Moscow-oriented Czechoslovakia, in the political and diplomatic circumstances then prevailing, made it necessary to be secretive about such deliveries.

At this meeting of the Zionist General Council, I chaired the Political Committee, which had the task of drafting the fateful resolution calling for a Jewish State to be proclaimed. Zalman Rubashov, our masterful Hebrew stylist, drew up the text. It began by referring to the Palestine administration's policy, which had "departed from the spirit of the Mandate and replaced it with the selfish purpose of furthering its Middle Eastern interests." It noted the treatment of Jewish refugees, denied entry into Palestine while "striving desperately after a last refuge," and then went on:

> Now the Mandatory is proposing to destroy the very foundation of our existence and leave the country in utter chaos. To prevent this, we have resolved this day that upon the termination of the Mandatory regime, there shall be an end of all foreign rule in Palestine and that the Governing Body of the Jewish people shall come into being.

The resolution also indicated that we would turn to "the Arab citizens of the Jewish State and our Arab neighbors, offering peace and friendship, and the building of our State in common with the Arabs as equal citizens." It concluded as follows:

> Secure in the justice of our cause, we are ready to give our all for its achievement and we call upon Jews in all lands, and especially in Eretz Yisrael, to close their ranks for the accomplishment of this our sublime task.

The resolution received an overwhelming vote of approval at the closing session of the Zionist General Council meeting on April 12, coinciding with the third day of Nisan, less than a fortnight before Passover. The Jewish State was to be proclaimed a little over a month later, on Friday, May 14, 1948, one day before the British were scheduled to withdraw from the country.

I vividly recall that protracted closing session, which lasted until past midnight. Council members from abroad, especially rabbis such as I, were anxious to be home well before Passover, and we were concerned over the length of the proceedings. We were due to leave at six o'clock on the following morning and still had our bags to pack at the hotel.

At long last, Zalman Rubashov stood up and read out the final draft. I gazed around at the delegates. Many of them were slumped in their chairs, worn out by the lengthy deliberations. Everybody knew in advance what the resolution was going to say, and people awoke only in time for the virtually unanimous show of hands. I was reminded of those events nearly three decades later, when we went to see the play *1776* in New York. This dramatized portrayal of the birth of the United States included a scene where the Declaration of Independence was adopted at midnight. The members of the Continental Congress, as shown on stage, were exhausted and half-asleep as Thomas Jefferson read out the American Declaration of Independence. Remembering what I had witnessed and experienced at the Zionist Actions Committee meeting in Tel Aviv, I thought to myself, "That's how history is made!"

If the UN's authorization for a Jewish State in Palestine was not quite the same as its implementation, might this not also be true of the resolution passed by the Zionist General Council? In my chairman's report to the board of directors of the United Palestine Appeal, at a meeting held in New York on April 28, I discussed the practicableness of that resolution. Three factors—morale, economic strength, and military power—would determine whether or not statehood could become a reality. I had been impressed by the Yishuv's high morale, and independent experts had given encouraging estimates of its military power. As for the economic factor, Palestinian industry was now on a war footing and Golda Myerson had just concluded a successful UJA mission in the United States. "The embattled Yishuv looks to American Jewry and to the U.S. for economic assistance," I said. "Unless we strengthen the hands of the Yishuv, the battle may be lost. It is crucial, not only for the Jews of Palestine but for Jews throughout the world."

The military phase of our struggle had reached a decisive point. As a result of the many Arab civilian casualties at Deir Yassin, a village on the western edge of Jerusalem where Etzel and Lehi units had botched an anti-terrorist operation on April 9, Arab Palestine was now in a state of panic. A few days after that grim episode, a medical convoy bound for the Hadassah Hospital on Mount Scopus was ambushed and virtually wiped out by Arab irregulars, but this did nothing to restore our opponents' morale. Indeed, outside the Jerusalem region, Haganah, Palmah, and Etzel forces were gaining the upper hand, despite British and Arab Legion attempts to intervene. Yigal Allon had begun the conquest of Galilee, Haifa was under Jewish control, and the encirclement of Jaffa was completed on April 29.

One week earlier, Ernest Bevin had been alarmed by false press reports claiming that the victorious Jews had massacred 23,000 Arabs in Haifa. New orders were issued to British troops in a desperate attempt to retrieve Great Britain's reputation in the Arab world and salvage something from the debris. Nothing more could be done, however, for the Jews were working hard to establish their State. Following the Zionist General Council meeting in Tel Aviv, with the participation of the Va'ad Leumi (National Council of the Yishuv), two representative bodies were set up—an all-party, 37-member Provisional State Assembly (Mo'etzet ha-Am) and a 13-member Provisional State Council (Minhal ha-Am), headed by David Ben-Gurion, which was empowered to serve as an interim Jewish government until the British departure from Eretz Yisrael. The Minhal ha-Am proceeded to collect taxes, raise a national loan, and maintain essential services amid the surrounding chaos. Steps were even taken to print new "Hebrew" currency and postage stamps, the actual name of the embryonic Jewish State still requiring a final decision.

Whereas the well-disciplined Yishuv remained calm and went about its business, the Arab population was fed atrocity propaganda and could not adjust itself to the daily pandemonium. On the one hand, Arab radio stations outside Palestine exploited the Deir Yassin "bloodbath" for all they were worth and urged a mass evacuation of *Falastin*, pending the "inevitable" victory over the Zionists. On the other hand, Haj Amin al-Husseini, the Mufti of Jerusalem, ordered the Arabs to stay put. Stories of new Jewish "atrocities" and "secret weapons" turned the first trickle of Arab emigration, led by the wealthy, into a panic-stricken flood. Despite his exhortations, the Mufti had never attempted to establish a governmental framework comparable to that of the Yishuv, his principal objective being to destroy the Jewish commonwealth in embryo. With the hindsight of subsequent events, I cannot help reflecting how different the Middle East would be today if the Palestine Arab Higher Committee, instead of fleeing to Beirut and other cities across the border, had resolved to fight on and establish the Arab state authorized by the UN resolution of November 29, 1947.

By the beginning of May 1948, it was obvious that nothing short of Great Power intervention would prevent the emergence of our Medinah. In the course of a meeting with Judge Samuel Rosenman, a close friend of President Truman, on April 23, Dr. Weizmann had learned that Truman was now determined to see partition implemented and to grant recognition to the Jewish State soon after its proclamation. The President felt a moral commitment to do so for a number of reasons. His stand in favor of partition dated back to August 1946; he had made a solemn undertaking to Weizmann on March 19; and the preemptive State Department action at the UN still rankled within him. Impressed by Eddie Jacobson's hero-worship of Chaim Weizmann, Truman had also been drawn to the old warrior.

There were, furthermore, sound practical reasons for the President's decision. Having entered the White House by accident, as it were, on the death of Franklin D. Roosevelt, Truman wanted to be elected President of the United States in his own right. The 1948 election campaign was now close at hand. Eleanor Roosevelt and Clark Clifford both warned him that his chances of being voted in were far from good, because of the challenge of Henry Wallace on the left and of the Republican candidate, Governor Thomas Dewey, aided by rebel "Dixiecrats," on the right. Unless steps were taken to win over Jewish and Black voters, Harry Truman and the Democrats faced an inevitable and crushing defeat. The advice of his White House team, coupled with his resentment of the State Department bureaucrats, probably helped the President to reach a crucial decision.

At about this time, there was an almost unprecedented initiative from another part of the U.S. Administration. Dr. Nahum Goldmann, known to be one of the Zionist "doves," was called in by a high official in the State Department, who requested that the proclamation of a Jewish State be deferred for two weeks in the hope that full-scale war might be prevented. This official, probably Undersecretary of State Robert Lovett,* offered to place *The Sacred Cow*, President Truman's personal aircraft, at the disposal of our UN delegates, who would fly to Palestine and attend a round-table conference there aimed at breaking the deadlock. Accompany-

---

*Several versions of this meeting have appeared in print. According to some, the official involved was Assistant Secretary of State Dean Rusk or even the head of the State Department, General George Marshall. In his *Autobiography* (1969), Goldmann claims that it was President Truman himself who made the offer (p. 288). I have reason to believe that Dr. Zvi Ganin's version of the incident (in *Truman, American Jewry, and Israel*, pp. 183–84) is the most accurate one, although I have amplified it.

ing this suggestion was a threat of blackmail: should the Zionists not agree, economic sanctions would be imposed on the Yishuv and the State Department would publish damaging revelations of Zionist pressure tactics and American Jewish "disloyalty."

This startling development necessitated an emergency meeting of Zionist leaders in New York. Goldmann and Shertok took both the offer and the threat seriously, urging that Ben-Gurion be acquainted with the facts, while three or four others were inclined to accept the idea of a last-minute conference in Palestine, so as to avoid war with the Arabs. At the meeting held on May 4, 1948, the overwhelming majority refused to knuckle under and insisted that the blackmail attempt be ignored, endorsing Abba Hillel Silver's rejection of these State Department menaces. By then, Shertok had already told Dean Rusk that any two-week delay in proclaiming Jewish independence was out of the question.

Significantly, Dr. Weizmann, in rejecting any postponement of independence on the eve of the scheduled date, showed a firmness that surprised those of us who remembered his attitude at the 1946 Basle Congress. Ivor Linton was with him when Shertok came to say goodbye before flying back to Palestine. "Tell them in Jerusalem to proclaim the State now," said Weizmann, "otherwise, I will never live to see it." Then, turning to Linton, he added, "Nor will he, although he's much younger!"

News of successful military operations continued to reach us from Palestine and the united front of American Jewry was restored. Clark Clifford, who had succeeded David Niles as our strongest advocate in the White House, received much useful advice and assistance from Bartley Crum, Eliahu Epstein, and Max Lowenthal at this time. Clifford kept stressing that only the U.S. State Department refused to acknowledge the obvious—that partition was now a fact of life in Palestine. It would be in President Truman's own interests to extend immediate recognition to the new Jewish State, as he could thereby outmaneuver both the Russians and his Republican rival.

Our hopes and anxieties rose feverishly as we entered the second week of May. Not everything was going well for the Yishuv. Gush Etzion, a bloc of four kibbutzim in the hills near Hebron, had been resisting fierce attacks since May 4 and there was no way of reinforcing the defenders, whose casualty rate was high. Three of these settlements—Kfar Etzion, Massu'ot Yitzhak, and Ein Tzurim—were manned by Ha-Po'el Ha-Mizrahi pioneers; the fourth, Revadim, was affiliated with Ha-Shomer Ha-Tza'ir. After an epic defense, the Etzion Bloc succumbed to overwhelming onslaughts in which local forces were joined by Arab Legion tanks and artillery. Only four members of Kfar Etzion survived the bloody massacre that followed their surrender on May 13; the three other kibbutzim insisted on surrendering to the Arab Legion a day later and the settlers were made prisoners of war, although the Legion was still officially under British control. Some twenty years later, after the Six-Day War, Gush Etzion would be reestablished by a new generation of *halutzim*, including children of the original pioneers (see chapter 12).

The fall of these kibbutzim was a grave setback, since their prolonged defense had tied down considerable enemy forces. The British-officered Arab Legion now moved on beleaguered Jerusalem, where the Haganah still had no artillery. Despite all the risks involved, Ben-Gurion's provisional Government stood by its decision to proclaim the Jewish State by May 15, hoping that things would improve once the British had left Palestine. Yigael Yadin was less sanguine: true, the Arab Liberation Army had proved more troublesome than dangerous, while the Mufti's forces were in disarray, but several large and heavily equipped Arab armies stood poised on the borders of Eretz Yisrael. The Yishuv's War of Liberation had only just begun.

On May 13, Dr. Weizmann wrote to President Truman expressing his hope that U.S. recognition for the infant Jewish State would speedily be forthcoming. The world, he said, would regard it as especially appropriate "that the greatest living democracy should be the first to welcome the newest into the family of nations." Thanks to some timely intercession by David Niles, Weizmann's letter was handed in at the White House on the following morning and placed on Truman's desk.

At 8:00 A.M. on Friday, May 14, the Union Jack was lowered from the flagstaff over the High Commissioner's residence in Jerusalem as the British rearguard prepared for its last journey to Haifa. Sir Alan Cunningham's farewell broadcast, and his departure on a Royal Navy warship, brought three decades of British rule to an ignominious end. As the UN General Assembly was still debating Palestine's future, at 4:30 P.M. that same afternoon (less than eight hours before the Mandate was due to expire), David Ben-Gurion proclaimed the independence of the Jewish commonwealth, to be known henceforth as Medinat Yisrael, the State of Israel.

Overruling State Department objections, President Truman extended *de facto* recognition to "the new State of Israel" eleven minutes after the Palestine Mandate had terminated.* It was an act that simultaneously gave international legitimacy to Israel and forestalled British military intervention on the Arab side. Ivor Linton rushed into Dr. Weizmann's hotel room in New York, to bring him the news flash, but before he could utter a word, Weizmann said, "The President has given us recognition." Knowing that "the chief" had no radio in his room, Linton was astonished. "Your face told me everything!" Weizmann replied, smiling.

I was among those who sat in the Jewish Agency offices on 65th Street, near Madison Avenue, tensely awaiting the historic announcement from Tel Aviv. It reached us around 11:00 A.M. (New York time), immediately after Ben-Gurion's proclamation of the Medinah. At Congregation B'nai Jeshurun's Sabbath eve services that night, I concluded my specially composed Prayer for the Welfare of the State of Israel with the *Sheheḥeyanu* benediction. *Hallel* was recited during our services the next morning, when I devoted my sermon to "The New Star in Zion."

A giant rally took place at Madison Square Garden on Sunday, May 16, to

---

*Not, as has been stated more than once, eleven minutes after Ben-Gurion had proclaimed it.

celebrate the birth of the Jewish State. Dr. Emanuel Neumann, president of the Zionist Organization of America, chaired the proceedings. Chaim Weizmann was informed that he had been elected provisional President of Israel and made a statement to the press, after which the Waldorf-Astoria management threw a party in his honor. The next morning, a blue and white Zionist flag, provided by the Jewish Agency office in New York, was hoisted outside the hotel. Crowds gathered to gaze at the flag and a police guard was stationed next to Dr. Weizmann's suite.

Owing to his state of health, an official invitation to visit President Truman in Washington was limited to a meeting between the two leaders and to a private luncheon that Dr. and Mrs. Weizmann tendered at Blair House. Before leaving New York, Israel's new President had to decide on a suitable gift for President Truman. "Arab rulers usually give diamond-studded swords," Weizmann observed, "but I should offer something which reflects the Jewish tradition."

Professor Louis Finkelstein, chancellor of the Jewish Theological Seminary, had a small Torah scroll of his own, which he offered to Dr. Weizmann. At the White House, President Truman was visibly moved when he received the gift. Years later, incidentally, when Chancellor Finkelstein asked if the ex-President would consider donating this *Sefer* to the Seminary, Truman replied, "Oh no, it belongs to the Truman Museum at Independence, Missouri." And there it remains.

After their Washington meeting, Weizmann disclosed that Truman had reacted favorably to a request for a $100 million loan and to a plea for the U.S. arms embargo to be rescinded.

A cable from Moshe Shertok was waiting for Linton on his return to New York. Shertok, now Israel's Foreign Minister, asked Linton to become the new State's diplomatic representative in London and to improve relations with Great Britain. Three days after Israel's Declaration of Independence, *de jure* recognition was extended by the Soviet Union. It took another eight months, however, before Great Britain's Foreign Minister, Ernest Bevin, grudgingly recognized Israel *de facto* at the end of January 1949. Meanwhile, the Jewish State had been engaged in a life-and-death struggle against its enemies.

The Birth of Medinat Yisrael

The decision to proclaim the independence of a new Jewish State had not been taken lightly. On May 11, when Moshe Shertok was about to fly home from New York, U.S. Secretary of State George Marshall urged him to impress upon the Zionist leadership the dangers facing the heavily outnumbered Yishuv. In defiance of President Truman's stand on partition, Marshall and his subordinates were still looking for a last-minute trusteeship formula. Though previously one of the waverers, Shertok realized that the die had been cast. "If we throw away this opportunity," Shertok retorted, "who knows when we'll ever have another?" Fearful of how future generations might view hesitancy at this stage, he believed that the real danger was not acting, but failing to act decisively.

At about the same time, Golda Myerson, director of the Jewish Agency's Political Department, had returned from a secret rendezvous in Amman with King Abdullah of Transjordan. In this cloak-and-dagger affair, she had made the journey there and back disguised as an Arab woman. More amenable to compromise and reason than other rulers of the Arab world, Abdullah was intent on using the Arab Legion to seize control of Palestine immediately after the British evacuation. He nevertheless offered the Jews representation in a Cisjordanian parliament and the prospect of "good relations" with their Arab neighbors, thus preventing a destructive war. Such an offer was unacceptable to the Yishuv, of course, but Abdullah's comparative moderation vis-à-vis the Zionists infuriated Palestinian Arab fanatics. Little more than three years later, on July 20, 1951, he was murdered by one of the Mufti's agents after attending prayers at the Mosque of al-Aksa in Jerusalem's Old City.

On the return leg of her mission to Amman, Golda Myerson had spotted concentrations of Arab Legion armor near the borders of Eretz Yisrael. Her report to the Jewish Agency Executive raised the question of military preparedness in face of the impending enemy attack. It was one thing to defeat Fawzi al-Kawukji's "Arab Liberation Army" and the Mufti's irregulars; to hold one's own against several trained and heavily equipped armies was a very different matter. Yisrael Galili, who now commanded the Haganah, and Yigael Yadin, the chief operations officer, surveyed the position candidly on May 12. Things looked worst on the Jerusalem front, where Abdullah's Legion, having laid waste the Etzion Bloc, was intensifying the siege and bringing its artillery and tanks into action. The overall arms balance clearly pointed to an Arab victory. Yadin, however, expected the situation to improve within forty-eight hours following the British withdrawal. The Yishuv could then mobilize without hindrance, manpower and arms supplies would begin to flow into the country, and Jewish military experience, resourcefulness, and morale could affect the sway of battle. Yadin and Galili felt that the Yishuv had an even chance of withstanding a wholesale Arab invasion.

Encouraged by this military assessment, the Jewish Agency Executive proceeded to review the political situation. Shertok believed that the UN Palestine Commission, which should have taken over administrative responsibility for the country, was as good as dead and that a Jewish government must therefore hasten to fill the vacuum. Some people urged that the Zionist movement's elder statesman be consulted and a long-distance telephone call was made to New York. Dr. Weizmann's firm answer was: "Proclaim the Medinah, no matter what happens!" By the end of the day, a final decision had been taken by the Minhal ha-Am to go ahead according to schedule, rejecting all outside pressures for the postponement of Jewish independence.

With Zalman Rubashov's Actions Committee resolution as a basis, Moshe Shertok, assisted by four other members of the Jewish Agency Executive, drew up a lengthier and more elegant legal document, which was submitted to David Ben-Gurion, head of the Provisional State Council, on May 13. A handful of Council members took part in these preliminaries, one of them, Rabbi Y. L. Hacohen

Fishman, having been flown in specially to Tel Aviv from besieged Jerusalem by Piper Cub.* Working through the night of May 13–14, 1948, Ben-Gurion subsequently recast the Proclamation of Independence and introduced various changes.

At 10:00 A.M. on May 14, members of the Mo'etzet ha-Am, the Provisional State Assembly, gathered in the Tel Aviv offices of the Jewish National Fund to ratify the text of the proclamation. There were two points of contention—the lack of any reference to the boundaries of the new State, and the insertion of a reference to the Almighty. In answer to the Revisionists, who were doctrinally committed to a Jewish commonwealth on both sides of the Jordan, Ben-Gurion asserted that no frontiers had been defined in the American Declaration of Independence and that no one could foresee what the Jewish State's boundaries would be after the inevitable war with the Arabs. For their part, the religious parties—Mizraḥi, Ha-Po'el Ha-Mizraḥi, Agudat Yisrael, and Po'alei Agudat Yisrael—insisted that no self-respecting Jewish State could ignore the hand of God in this momentous time. The Marxist parties, Aḥdut Avodah and Mapam, strenuously objected to any mention of the Lord and it was only with the greatest reluctance that they agreed to a compromise formula. This laid down that the proclamation should conclude, *"Mi-tokh bitaḥon be-Tzur Yisrael . . ."*—"Placing our trust in the Rock of Israel," a deft solution to the impasse. As Ben-Gurion pointed out at the time, "Everyone has his own way of interpreting 'the Rock of Israel.'"

One other religious issue had already been settled. According to the original schedule, the State should have come into being at the stroke of midnight, when the Mandate expired. Had the independence ceremonies and the affixing of signatures to a document been held then, the first Sabbath of the Third Jewish Commonwealth would thereby have been desecrated publicly. It was therefore resolved that the ceremony be brought forward to 4:00 P.M. on Friday, which would allow time for all the arrangements to be completed before the Sabbath's commencement. Medinat Yisrael would not begin with *ḥillul Shabbat*.

From the JNF offices, members of the Provisional State Council and Assembly proceeded to the Tel Aviv Museum on Rothschild Boulevard, once the home of Meir Dizengoff, the all-Jewish city's first Mayor. Nearly 240 people witnessed the ceremony, including representatives of the Jewish Agency, the World Zionist Organization, and the Va'ad Leumi, Chief Rabbis Herzog and Uziel, and other notables. The formal Proclamation of the State of Israel covered seventeen paragraphs, beginning with the words, "The Land of Israel was the birthplace of the Jewish People," and ending with "the redemption of Israel." Its legal and historical aspects and the pledges it contained are sufficiently well known to make any detailed comment here superfluous. As soon as Ben-Gurion had finished reading out the proclamation,

---

*The following account is based, in part, on "Birth of the State," an article by my good friend, Eliezer Whartman, which appeared in the Independence Day Supplement of *The Jerusalem Post* on May 6, 1981. It was his task, in 1960, to record for posterity (and for the Israel State Archives) firsthand recollections of the thirty-one surviving signatories of Israel's Independence Proclamation.

Rabbi Fishman recited the *Sheheḥeyanu* benediction, giving thanks for the privilege of having lived to see this event, and the British White Paper restrictions on Aliyah and settlement were abolished by unanimous assent.

There had been no time for a scribe to indite the text on the special parchment scroll, and so a typewritten copy of the proclamation was attached to it, over the space reserved for the signatures. Only later could the text be inscribed—a procedure which, I believe, has no historical precedent. When the signatories were invited to come forward and append their names to the scroll, only twenty-eight of the thirty-seven State Council members were able to do so: eight were still trapped in Jerusalem, and one more was abroad. They added their names at a later stage. Ben-Gurion felt that the occasion called for the widest possible representation of the Yishuv, and he accordingly made sure that the signatories should include every leader—from Rabbi Yitzḥak Meir Lewin of Agudat Yisrael to Meir Wilner of the Communist Party, who held no position on the Jewish Agency or Va'ad Leumi executives. All of them sensed the momentous character of this ceremony betokening Jewish national rebirth.

By this time, war had erupted throughout the country and within hours Tel Aviv itself would be subjected to an Egyptian air raid as Arab forces crossed the international border and began attacking towns and settlements in the areas allocated to the Jewish State by the UN. Israel's Proclamation of Independence was heard by Jews wherever a radio set could be tuned in to the live broadcast, except in Jerusalem. There, electrical power had been cut off and only those who had a battery-powered radio were able to hear the transmission. Among them were the eight stranded members of the Mo'etzet ha-Am, Israel's provisional Government. Ben-Gurion concluded the ceremony in Tel Aviv with a stirring announcement—"Medinat Yisrael has arisen!"—whereupon the assembled audience rose to sing the Zionist anthem, *Hatikvah*. Two months later, *Hatikvah* became the designated anthem of the new State. Itzḥak Ben-Zvi, one of those who appended his signature to the Independence scroll later on, was destined to become Israel's second President; two other signatories, Ben-Gurion and Shertok, were to serve as Prime Minister. Ironically, however, Dr. Chaim Weizmann, whom the State Council elected provisional head of state on May 16, was never asked to sign the Proclamation of Independence.

Shortly before these events took place, a terse statement was made in the House of Commons to the effect that "Palestine" had been expelled from the British Commonwealth of Nations. It was a despairing gesture, calculated (along with other declarations) to regain favor with the Arabs. When, subsequently, the wounds began to heal, Israelis remembered the Balfour Declaration and other positive features of British rule. As the historian has drily remarked, such things "deserved a better epitaph than the one Bevin provided."*

During the early hours of the morning, on May 15, 1948, the armies of five Arab states—Egypt, Iraq, Lebanon, Syria, and Transjordan—invaded Israel. They were

*Howard M. Sachar, *A History of Israel* (New York: Alfred A. Knopf, 1976), p. 313.

joined by units from Saudi Arabia and other parts of the Arab world. Azzam Pasha proclaimed "a war of extermination and a momentous massacre which will be spoken of like the Mongol massacres and the Crusades." A reference to the much more recent slaughter of one-third of the Jewish people, by the Nazis and their henchmen, might have had a more devastating impact on world public opinion. It was, however, no empty threat, as Israel's civilian population would learn to its cost.

The story of what Israel terms its War of Liberation *(Milḥemet ha-Shiḥrur)*, rather than War of Independence, need not be dealt with at length in these pages. Vastly outnumbered and, at first, outclassed in terms of military hardware, the Jews of the Yishuv fought desperately to survive repeated enemy onslaughts. No UN sanctions were imposed on the aggressors, no international police force came to Israel's rescue. Instead, "both sides" were called upon to end the hostilities that the Arab states, in defiance of the United Nations resolution and of the UN's authority, had unilaterally unleashed. Israel's one "secret weapon" was the slogan, *"En Brerah,"* "No Alternative," which inspired its fighting forces and civilians.

A small, 5,000-strong "Foreign Legion" of volunteers, including some non-Jewish sympathizers, joined *Maḥal (Mitnadvé Ḥutz La-Aretz)*, originally the Foreign Volunteers section of the Haganah. They did not fight as a separate unit but were absorbed by all branches of *Tzahal (Tzeva Haganah Le-Yisrael)*, the unified Israel Defense Forces (IDF), which came into being at the end of May. Among these volunteers were 2,000 from the United States and Canada, 500 or more from Great Britain, and an impressive 700 from South Africa. Many had World War II combat experience and their skills were put to good use, especially in Israel's fledgling air force, which RAF and USAF veterans trained and commanded. The fatalities included an eminent American West Point graduate, Colonel David ("Mickey") Marcus, IDF commander on the Jerusalem front, who was accidentally shot by a sentry on June 10.

In the first month of the war, Syrian, Lebanese, and Iraqi troops invaded Galilee, while the Arab Legion gained control of the central hill country and sought to overwhelm the Jewish section of Jerusalem. The Egyptian army, in its bid to join forces with the Legion, encountered fierce resistance from kibbutzim in the Negev, several of which were either devastated, abandoned, or bypassed. Tel Aviv and other urban centers were repeatedly bombed by the Egyptian air force. In the north, Syrian tanks were repulsed at Kibbutz Deganyah and the Lebanese contented themselves with a few temporary gains.

The Arab offensive concentrated on Jerusalem, where the Old City's Jewish Quarter surrendered to the Legion after a mere 100 Jewish defenders had put up a heroic resistance. Subsequently, as we would discover, all of the Jewish Quarter's historic synagogues and institutions that had survived enemy bombardment were razed to the ground. Though pounded by Arab artillery, the New City of Jerusalem continued to hold out: Egyptian forces were unable to take Kibbutz Ramat Raḥel, on the southern flank, while the Legion's armor was routed by Jewish boys and girls who hurled flaming Molotov cocktails. New Jerusalem owed its salvation to an emergency route bypassing the main highway from Tel Aviv, which the Legion's heavy guns had made impassable. Supplies began to flow along this improvised track, which Israelis called the "Burma Road," a name borrowed from the jungle route hacked out by World War II Chindits serving under General Orde Wingate—"Ha-Yedid," "The Friend" of the Yishuv. There would be numerous occasions, in the second half of the year, when I would travel along the "Burma Road," which was finally replaced by Kvish ha-Gevurah, the "Road of Valor."

Israel had practically no air force or navy when the war began, but planes arrived in time to make retaliatory raids on Amman and Damascus. The Jewish State managed to withstand initial enemy attacks and the UN, where Abba (Aubrey) Eban served as Israel's eloquent and effective spokesman, arranged a first cease-fire, which lasted from June 10 until July 8.

During this truce, the provisional Government of Israel faced a sudden internal crisis. It arose from the attempts made by Etzel and Lehi on the one side, and by the Palmah on the other, to retain some measure of independence, despite the central role and authority of the Israel Defense Forces. On June 20, 1948, the Irgun ship *Altalena*, named for Ze'ev Jabotinsky, arrived off the coast near Kfar Vitkin, loaded with arms and more than 800 volunteers. Etzel leaders insisted on retaining at least part of the weaponry, but Ben-Gurion denied their claim and ordered them to hand everything over to the IDF. Neither side would give way and, after a Palmah unit had subjected it to bombardment, the *Altalena* blew up off Tel Aviv. Not everyone on board had escaped in time, and the combined loss of life and of precious munitions engendered considerable bitterness. The last independent Etzel and Lehi units were forced to disband in September and then merged with the IDF. Two months later, the Palmah—in which many of Israel's future generals gained battle experience—was also dissolved.

When the Arabs opened fire once more on July 9, Israel had strengthened its position and was able to score impressive victories over the invading armies. Both the Egyptians and the Arab Legion suffered heavy losses, Fawzi al-Kawukji's marauders, augmented by Wehrmacht veterans and British deserters, were routed, and the IDF prepared to recapture the Old City of Jerusalem. By July 18, as a second truce came into force, Israel held practically all of the territory allotted to the Jewish State by the UN and had secured control of another 800 square miles of Palestine.

Count Folke Bernadotte of Sweden, the UN mediator, arranged this new cease-fire, a truce in name only, which was punctuated by continual fighting until the war came to an end in 1949. Belying his humanitarian reputation, Bernadotte sought to penalize the victims of Arab aggression. He proposed a new solution to the Middle East conflict that set aside key elements in the UN partition scheme. According to the "Bernadotte Plan," Transjordan was to absorb the territory of the unborn Arab state and to engulf half of Israel, including New Jerusalem and the Negev. What remained of Israel was to be forced into a junior partnership with King Abdullah's Greater Jordan. Ben-Gurion's provisional Government refused even to discuss such a proposal, which was subsequently modified. To Israelis and Zionists, Count

Bernadotte's role as an "honest broker" appeared highly suspect. On August 1, in an act of defiance, Ben-Gurion appointed Dr. Dov Joseph military governor of Jerusalem. Three weeks later, the Zionist General Council, meeting for the first time in the independent Jewish State, began to review the entire situation and to plan for the future. I shall revert to these deliberations presently.

On September 17, while driving through the New City of Jerusalem, Bernadotte and his French aide were assassinated by unidentified gunmen, evidently members of a Leḥi splinter group. It was a senseless act of violence that gave the UN's chief representative the status of a martyr. His "Plan" immediately found enthusiastic advocates in U.S. Secretary of State George Marshall and British Foreign Secretary Ernest Bevin, who called for Israel's truncation, for Jerusalem to be internationalized, and for Israel to "take back" vast numbers of Arab refugees, whose return would have swamped the 700,000 Jews with a dangerous Fifth Column. Although this latest "solution" was firmly rejected, Israel later permitted many thousands of displaced Arabs to return to their old homes under a "unification of families" scheme. Dr. Ralph Bunche of the United States became the acting UN mediator and the fighting continued.

Enemy counterattacks were beaten back, the IDF captured Beersheba, and part of the Egyptian army was trapped in the Faluja pocket. Among the commanders prominent there was a certain Gamal Abdul Nasser, who seized power in 1954 as the new Egyptian republic's dictator. Nasser's charisma and ambition would provoke a second Arab war against Israel, the Sinai Campaign of 1956. Following the rout of the Syrians, Iraqis, and Lebanese in the north, and a stalemate with the Arab Legion on the central front, the Egyptians were vanquished in a two-week campaign (December 23, 1948—January 7, 1949) and driven back across the international border. IDF units penetrated Sinai and only evacuated El Arish under UN pressure. This withdrawal saved Egypt from complete humiliation and enabled the British to avoid total loss of face in the Arab world.

An incident that took place on the final day of Israel's campaign in the south exposed the nature of British collusion with Egypt. Five aircraft that had been surveying and strafing forward positions of the IDF were shot down by Israeli fighter pilots. On inspection, these downed aircraft turned out to be Royal Air Force planes based, presumably, in the Suez Canal zone. Once news of this hostile intervention by the RAF reached London, a political storm arose and Bevin's vindictive anti-Israel policy was torn to shreds. Winston Churchill, on behalf of the opposition Conservative Party, led the chorus of angry protest in the House of Commons. Now thoroughly discredited, Attlee's Labor Government turned tail and extended *de facto* recognition to the State of Israel before the end of January.

In effect, by resisting aggression and thrashing its assailants, Israel had implemented at least part of the UN partition resolution of November 29, 1947. One-third of the 6,000 Jews killed in the War of Liberation were civilians. Nevertheless, as previously indicated, the UN Security Council deliberately refrained from stigmatizing those responsible for the war in Palestine. Nor was the indiscriminate Transjordanian bombardment of Jerusalem, including those holy places for which the

Vatican and other Christian bodies had shown such solicitous concern, enough to arouse international anger and condemnation. This ominous development foreshadowed a gradual deterioration in the UN's moral authority, more especially in the Middle East.

On December 29, 1948, the Security Council issued a call for Israel and the Arab states to begin peace talks on the island of Rhodes. What brought the war to an end, however, was not a compelling United Nations resolution but the proven inability of the Arabs to defeat and destroy the Jewish State. An armistice agreement was signed with Egypt on February 24, 1949, when IDF forces, led by Yigal Allon, were completing their conquest of the Negev and about to occupy Umm Rash Rash (Eilat) on the Gulf of Akaba. Further armistice agreements were signed with Lebanon (March 23), Transjordan (April 3), and Syria (July 20), but other belligerent Arab countries (such as Iraq and Saudi Arabia) refused to negotiate and have remained officially at war with Israel to this very day.

From the spring of 1948, strenuous efforts were made by the American Zionist Emergency Council to galvanize public opinion, first against the State Department's trusteeship proposal and delaying tactics, and then against those conspiring to strangle the newly born Jewish State. The Synagogue Council of America played an important part in mobilizing Jewish moral and material support for Israel's cause. The foremost spokesman of the American Zionist movement throughout this time was Dr. Abba Hillel Silver, whose position vis-à-vis both U.S. and British officialdom was one of eternal vigilance. In a report to the AZEC on May 25, 1948, Silver had characteristically forthright words for the anti-Israel cabal. "Great Britain," he affirmed, "has launched the attack on Jerusalem, using the Arab Legion as its tool."

American Jewry's financial contribution to Israel was vastly more significant than its human contribution in terms of *Mahal* volunteers and Aliyah. As chairman of the United Palestine Appeal and co-chairman of the UJA, I was deeply involved in fund-raising efforts at the time. A particularly significant role was played by Henry Montor, who had been appointed first executive director of the UJA in 1939 and who had planned its record-breaking $100 million campaign in 1945. The quota was raised to $250 million in 1948, a peak year, when more and larger donations were secured in the wake of the UN partition vote and the Arab invasion of Israel. Montor was also active in the AZEC and in the United Palestine Appeal. He continued to serve with the UJA until 1951, when he resigned to become director of Israel Bonds. His successor, Dr. Joseph J. Schwartz, former executive director of the American Jewish Joint Distribution Committee, was followed by Rabbi Herbert A. Friedman, who in 1971 was succeeded by Irving Bernstein.

As previously mentioned, Henry Morgenthau, Jr., was general chairman of the United Jewish Appeal during the crucial year 1948–49, when thousands of Jewish DPs were emerging from the detention camps in Cyprus and being brought to freedom in Israel. At a meeting of the UJA board on June 27, 1948, Morgenthau reported that there were still a quarter of a million Jews in the various DP camps and that they needed food and clothing to supplement the meager allowances UNRRA provided while they were awaiting their turn to go to Israel. Others were arriving in the United States with help from the National Refugee Service.

The income of the United Palestine Appeal in 1948 was $50 million, a large sum, but not one commensurate with the vastly increased needs of the Jewish State. As chairman of the UPA, I presided at a meeting of the executive on May 24, 1948, the first to be held after the proclamation of Israel's independence. The initial phase of the War of Liberation was then at its height and Golda Myerson, whose two trips to the United States made her the "star" of our campaign, stressed the urgency of raising unprecedented amounts to cover immediate requirements. Ben-Gurion's provisional Government was determined to hold on to the entire area allocated to Israel by the UN partition plan, and this would involve enormous sacrifices on the part of the Yishuv.

Responding to her appeal, I emphasized that American Jewry was obliged to meet the challenge of this historic hour. In my statement before the UPA executive, I went on to say:

> The star of Zion shines again after a dimout of nearly nineteen centuries. The culmination of the Zionist hope is a tribute primarily to the faith and courage of the Yishuv. It is also a tribute to the faith and courage of the Jewish people. American Jewry has played a significant role, not only in the economic help which it has given for the foundation of what is now the Jewish State but also in winning the support of the American people and Government.
>
> American Jews have an urgent assignment now. They can expand or contract the economic absorptive capacity of the Jewish State, depending on the dollars which they will make available. Would it not be a bitter irony if, now that the White Paper has departed with the British regime, American Jewry, by the sin of omission, were to be guilty of imposing restrictions upon the opportunities for land purchase and immigration?
>
> While 25,000 are waiting in Cyprus, hundreds of thousands are waiting in the lands of Europe. Only the failure of American Jews to respond adequately to the United Jewish Appeal can bar them from the land of their heart's desire.

Along with the military and economic demands made by Israel's fight for survival, another major problem faced the Jewish Agency and the World Zionist Organization shortly after the establishment of the State. These two bodies had provided the interim Government and its civil service with many of their top personnel. Among these senior officials was Eliezer Kaplan, who had served with distinction as treasurer of the Jewish Agency, watching over its finances with great initiative, ability, and rigor during the previous fifteen years. Now he had been chosen to serve as Minister of Finance in Ben-Gurion's Administration. Kaplan was able to plan and implement Israel's fiscal policies, to draw up the country's initial yearly budgets, and to help secure and properly utilize the first major loans extended by the U.S. Government and by a consortium of American commercial banks.

Eliezer Kaplan's appointment as Finance Minister left vacant the post of treasurer of the Jewish Agency. My name was proposed by the Zionist leadership in the United States, headed by Dr. Abba Hillel Silver, their feeling being that my experience in the Jewish National Fund of America, the United Palestine Appeal, and the United Jewish Appeal would stand me in good stead. It was made clear to me that I would have to spend the forthcoming year in Israel. After Bert had enthusiastically agreed, and my congregation's board of trustees had given its consent, I indicated my readiness to do so. Before any final arrangements could be made, however, the recommendation had to be approved by the Zionist General Council, which met in Jerusalem toward the end of August 1948.

To many people it must have seemed strange indeed that a rabbi should be invited to assume such an office. The one historical precedent I could find was that of Don Isaac Abrabanel, the great fifteenth-century Bible commentator, philosopher and statesman, who served for a time as treasurer to the Portuguese king and as financial adviser to the rulers of Spain and Naples. He excelled in performing the *mitzvah* of *pidyon shevuyim*, redeeming Jewish captives who had been held for ransom. I saw my new task as being that of a *shali'ah*, an emissary of the Jewish people, whose mission it would be to rescue Jews from the DP camps of Europe and the *mellahs* of North Africa, and to help provide them with the chance of building a new life in Medinat Yisrael. I also made one promise to those who wondered about my financial program: the budget of the Jewish Agency during my regime would certainly exceed that of Portugal in Abrabanel's time, and the deficit would also be larger. That promise, as fate would have it, I kept!

On August 9, 1948, my wife and I left New York by air for Paris, en route to Israel. Our parental responsibilities were no longer a hindrance to any prolonged stay abroad, since our son, Avram, and daughter, Vivian, were happily married and were rearing their families. As far as our forthcoming sojourn in Jerusalem was concerned, therefore, we could look forward to the change of scene with eager anticipation.

At Athens Airport, where our plane landed on the final leg of our journey, we had a chance meeting with Dr. James G. McDonald, whom President Truman had just appointed as U.S. special representative to the provisional Government of Israel. A year later, he was to become the first accredited American ambassador to the Jewish State. McDonald had served on the Anglo-American Committee of Inquiry in 1946 and earlier, during the 1930s, he had made no secret of his pro-Jewish feelings as High Commissioner for Refugees under the League of Nations. At that time, he had assailed Hitler's Nazi regime, which he accused of planning the extermination of German Jewry.

We had always maintained a cordial relationship, and our reunion was a joyful one. McDonald told me that he had recently met Britain's Foreign Secretary, Ernest Bevin, who kept raging about the debacle of his Palestine policy. "*I* could have solved the whole problem," Bevin still insisted. President Truman had asked his new envoy to report on the situation in Israel as soon as possible. According to McDonald, the attitude of the U.S. State Department remained "problematic." Four years later, he published an interesting account of his term as ambassador, entitled *My Mission to Israel, 1948–51*.

The night we arrived in Tel Aviv coincided with the lifting of the blackout, and it was delightful to see people reveling in the lights of the city. It was a subdued form of rejoicing, however, for no one could forget the losses so far incurred in Israel's War of Liberation. Too many young lives had been sacrificed in the fighting, and civilian casualties had also been high. In the battle for Jerusalem alone, thousands had been killed and wounded.

Prior to the meeting of the Zionist General Council, a conference of the World Confederation of General Zionists took place on August 20. It was the first to be held on the soil of an independent Jewish State. The leaders present included Dr. Nahum Goldmann, Yitzhak Gruenbaum, Rose Halprin, Moshe Kolodny (later, Kol), Dr. Emanuel Neumann, Dr. Isaac Schwarzbart, and Rabbi Abba Hillel Silver. I was called upon to preside. A week later, I also addressed a conference of the General Zionist Party in Israel. It was then confronted with the problem of welding together various disparate elements, which would part company and form separate parliamentary lists in the following year. On the one hand, Dr. Abraham Granovsky, Moshe Kolodny, and Felix Rosenblueth (later, Pinhas Rosen) represented the generally pro-Labor wing of the movement; on the other hand, Ihud Ezrahi, the Citizens' Union, which took a more right-wing line, was headed by Yosef Saphir, Avraham Krinitzi, and Oved Ben-Ami, the mayors of Petah Tikvah, Ramat Gan, and Netanyah. The first group was to emerge as the Progressive Party, the second as the General Zionists, forerunners of the Liberal Party, which now belongs to Israel's ruling Likud alliance. Although I continually insisted that one powerful and united General Zionist "center party" was needed, it proved impossible to bridge the widening gulf between these two political factions (see chapter 14).

The first meeting of the Zionist General Council (Actions Committee) after Israel's establishment was held in Jerusalem during the fortnight commencing August 22, 1948. It was opened by Yosef Sprinzak, chairman of the Actions Committee.

Dr. Abba Hillel Silver, chairman of the American Section of the Jewish Agency, spoke about our political work in the United States and delivered a masterly *tour d'horizon* of events since November of the previous year. "If there is a Jewish State in Palestine today," he said, "it is due overwhelmingly to the initiative and the determination of the Jewish people here. They created it and they have defended it." He nevertheless pointed out that this achievement had also been made possible "by the extraordinary efforts and unfailing devotion of unnumbered Jewish men and women in many parts of the world, especially the United States."

Dr. Silver went on to review the American Zionist movement's fight against those hostile elements that had sought to "scuttle" partition and to impose a "solution" more acceptable to Britain and the Arabs. There had been a conspiracy within Government circles in Washington, "backed by a powerful oil lobby, by British propaganda, by pro-Arab Near East missionary groups in the United States, and spearheaded by Forrestal and Henderson," which almost succeeded in destroying Zionist hopes. Fortunately, however, we had found ready allies in America and in the United Nations, who helped to neutralize such maneuvers. President Truman had also "reversed the policy of the American Government and brought it back to the main highway from which it had been detoured." By recognizing Israel, Truman had "brushed aside all the accumulated legal rubbish and clumsy political artifices, redeemed the honor and integrity of the United States, and imbued the gallant builders and defenders of Israel with new hope and courage." Dr. Silver now felt confident that Israel would receive a full measure of political and economic support from the U.S. "The arch-foe of Zionism in the State Department, Loy Henderson, head of the Near East Division, is no longer there. The appointment of James G. McDonald as head of the United States Mission to Israel is definitely a gesture of goodwill and friendly cooperation."

In conclusion, Dr. Silver affirmed that the American Zionists realized that the struggle was not yet over and that Israel was still under the threat of renewed Arab attack. Final victory, in both the military and the political spheres, had yet to be achieved. The Jews of Israel could not be expected to meet the war bill from their own modest resources; the Jews of the United States would have to make a greater financial contribution. "We have heretofore done not a little," he said. "We shall have to do much more."

Israel's new Finance Minister, Eliezer Kaplan, former treasurer of the Jewish Agency, spoke of the problems and costs involved in defending the Medinah, establishing a governmental apparatus and public services, and in supplying the population with food and other vital necessities. He also emphasized the budgetary requirements of Aliyah.

Not surprisingly, many of the speeches were marked by a note of jubilation over a great turning point in Jewish history and the military achievements of *Tzahal*. David Ben-Gurion, however, sounded a note of caution. While agreeing with Rabbi Meir Berlin (later, Bar-Ilan) that the events so far witnessed had been nothing short of miraculous, he warned that Israel could not rely on miracles in the immediate future. Despite the official truce, war was still being waged and the State was not yet secure. "We are a people of twelve million," he said, "but only 700,000 stand in the breach. We do not want to die like heroes. No one at the UN will sit *shiv'ah* in mourning for us." The consolidation of Israel as a sovereign state would require no less effort and sacrifice than its creation had demanded, and the fulfillment of Zionism was a more difficult undertaking than any achievement of victory over the Arabs. Ben-Gurion named the three major tasks ahead as security, immigration, and agricultural settlement. For these, World Jewry must be mobilized. He made clear his own view of the historic turning point: "No leadership outside Eretz Yisrael can mobilize the Jewish people."

The resolutions adopted by the Zionist General Council reflected his views.

I was the first to be given the opportunity of speaking after the reports. Before commenting on the addresses we had heard, I briefly referred to the work of the Political Advisory Committee, which had sat with the Jewish Agency's representatives at the United Nations. One of our most critical decisions, not to delay proclamation of the Jewish State, had disregarded "a suggestion from very high quarters" in the U.S. Administration that no action be taken in this matter until a delegation of both Arabs and Jews could discuss it in Palestine, after being flown over from New York. Despite the nervousness of one or two people on our side, we had voted overwhelmingly to reject the firmly worded "invitation." If anything, Dr. Silver's review had understated American Zionism's achievements in regard to the UN and its refusal to be intimidated by powerful opponents.

I then contrasted Palestine's atmosphere of insecurity and foreboding in April, when the last Actions Committee meeting had taken place, with the gladdening scene in a resurgent State of Israel. "It would be less than human," I said, "not to indulge in the expression of thanksgiving." There were protests from the Revisionist delegates when I congratulated Israel's provisional Government on exercising its "firm authority" against internal threats (an oblique reference to the *Altalena* affair) and upheld its right to suppress "any group which, by force of arms, tries to undermine the authority of the Central Government." I went on to say:

> Now a new cycle begins for the Zionist movement, a cycle in which the Jewish people the world over will be a full partner with those who are citizens of Israel. We are one people with one destiny. The dangers which confront us are common dangers and the opportunities which beckon are common opportunities. Jews throughout the world are eager to make their contribution. They understand that the Zionist program has not yet been fulfilled with the establishment of the Jewish State, but that the Jewish State has created a fact which makes possible the fulfillment of the other part of the Zionist program—the solution of Jewish national homelessness.

The Jews of the West, particularly America, I said, would undertake the responsibility for underwriting the mass Aliyah of two million of their brethren in Europe and Arab lands who wished to come to Israel as soon as possible. Another priority was Zionist education abroad, to strengthen the forces of Jewish survival in communities threatened by assimilation, which now menaced Jews in the liberal democracies as well as in totalitarian states. I believed that Israel itself would benefit from a *Golah* that was "not only strong numerically but also strong in Jewish spirit and in Jewish consciousness." Enormous enthusiasm had been aroused among Jews everywhere following the establishment of Medinat Yisrael:

> Let me tell you, as one who comes in contact with American Jews rather broadly, non-Zionists as well as Zionists, that they feel a deep sense of gratitude to you in Israel because you have raised their prestige in the eyes of their own non-Jewish neighbors. A hundred Anti-Defamation Leagues cannot accomplish a fraction of what has been accomplished by the people of Israel in bringing new dignity to the name, "Jew," throughout the world.

My prediction was that there would be a fifty-percent increase in income from the 1948 campaign of the United Jewish Appeal, and I expressed our appreciation of

Golda Myerson's invaluable assistance during recent months. In answer to Eliezer Kaplan's request for aid, I saw fit to recommend new financial schemes and supplementary resources: as Dr. Emanuel Neumann had stressed at the ZOA convention in July, American Jews were ready for capital investments in Israel. Opportunities must be given for industrial development in the private sector as well as in that of the Histadrut labor federation. Underscoring this point, I declared that "the Jewish capitalists of America don't want to come here to make fortunes, but to make firm the fortunes of Israel. Upon the twin foundations, the right of labor to be strong and organized and the right of private initiative to exercise its talents, there can develop a model for democratic commonwealths throughout the world."

In conclusion, I said:

> Whereas, four months ago, we left the Actions Committee with confidence in our hearts, a confidence based on faith, today we feel a confidence based not only on faith but on facts. . . . We are certain, not only *be-emunah shelemah*, with faith, but with knowledge, that those who plot against us will be frustrated, that the world will see a deathless people living as a sovereign nation upon its ancient soil.

The most controversial issue debated at this meeting of the Actions Committee was *Hafradah*, a clear separation of the functions to be undertaken henceforth by Israel's Government and by the World Zionist Organization and Jewish Agency. American Zionists especially pressed for such a division of responsibilities, believing that the WZO now had a legitimate role to play that, for sound and very practical reasons, could not be assumed by a sovereign Jewish State. To my mind, however, rigid formulas were inadvisable at this stage. Dr. Emanuel Neumann, president of the Zionist Organization of America, made two specific recommendations. International relations and security matters obviously belonged to the province of the Government, while Aliyah, cultural, and organizational matters should be left in the hands of the Jewish Agency. On this, there was fairly wide agreement. What aroused a storm was his proposal that members of the Government should be debarred from holding any position on the WZO and Jewish Agency executives.

Ben-Gurion and his colleagues resisted Neumann's proposal. Many of us, looking at the issue from a different angle, found it difficult to understand his strenuous objections. Was it not more prestigious to be an Israel cabinet minister than the head of some department in the WZO or the Jewish Agency? How could one begin to compare the power and responsibilities of the Israel Government with those of the World Zionist Organization?

Speaking before the Actions Committee, I urged the adoption of a level-headed, pragmatic approach to these questions, declaring that it was "only sheer common sense that we follow the direction indicated by practical considerations, as long as those considerations remain." In six months or a year from now, things might look different and prove easier to work out. "Few, if any," I said, "would question that, in the long range, the heart of the Zionist movement must be in Jerusalem. Only

Jerusalem can command spiritual authority. This is not, nor should it be, a matter for dispute."

On the first point, Ben-Gurion and his allies raised no serious objections. They appreciated the financial role of the WZO and accepted *Hafradah* in respect of the Jewish Agency's promotion of ties between Israel and Diaspora Jewry. The functions of the Zionist Organization were to include responsibility for immigration, absorption, agricultural settlement, Youth Aliyah, economic development, education in the Diaspora, and overseas information. To augment the income received from the UJA and Keren Hayesod *magbit* campaigns, efforts would also be made to raise substantial loans abroad. Furthermore, according to a widely publicized Actions Committee resolution, all funds were to be used for the humanitarian needs of Israel and not for security requirements or political purposes.

On the second point, however, we at first made little headway. Ben-Gurion was not prepared to grant any sharing of Zionist authority or to acknowledge any form of equal partnership with leaders of the Zionist movement who chose to remain in the *Golah*. As opposed to Silver and Neumann, he objected to the whole idea of Diaspora Zionism's retention of control over the fund-raising apparatus, and he evidently feared that the ZOA would bring its political clout to bear in the WZO and the Jewish Agency Executives. Before long, indeed, Ben-Gurion was to cold-shoulder the Zionist hierarchies overseas and to campaign against any Zionist "monopoly" of fund raising for Israel. Yet Emanuel Neumann was no less determined to win this battle. We American Zionist leaders had reason to fear that anti-Zionist groups, such as the American Council for Judaism, would charge us with dual loyalty if *Hafradah* were not to become a reality.

Ben-Gurion finally gave way and those Zionist leaders who had been appointed to ministerial posts in Israel's provisional Government resigned from the Jewish Agency Executive.

Thus, on the one hand, Israel's sovereignty was preserved while, on the other hand, the World Zionist Organization was invested with rights and obligations that justified its continued existence in the era of the independent Jewish State. Inevitably, some adjustments had to be made because the sums needed for Aliyah and absorption rapidly exceeded the budgetary resources of the Jewish Agency, while both the Agency and the WZO soon discovered that they had no status when it came to negotiating for loans from foreign governments and banks. The new division of responsibilities would also have a long-term effect on the Keren Hayesod (see chapter 13).

Ben-Gurion's reluctant agreement to the implementation of *Hafradah* did not put an end to this contentious issue. It dragged on, in fact, for several more years and its after-effects are still with us. At the 23rd Zionist Congress, held for the first time in Jerusalem, on August 14–30, 1951, the aims and tasks of Zionism were redefined as "the consolidation of the State of Israel, the Ingathering of the Exiles in Eretz Yisrael and the fostering of the unity of the Jewish people." This "Jerusalem Program," subsequently amplified in 1968 (see chapter 12), replaced the Zionist movement's original Basle Program, which had been outdated by the emergence of the Jewish State. In time, as American Jews increasingly looked to Israel for political guidance and viewed Jerusalem as the center of Zionist authority, the ZOA lost much of its former power.

One resolution passed by the 23rd Congress demanded that legal status and recognition be extended by Israel to the World Zionist Organization, thus enabling both the WZO and the Jewish Agency to maintain their independence as bodies charged with the historic mission of bringing Jews to their Land and settling them there, and of developing spiritual and cultural ties between Israel and the Diaspora. This resolution inspired a Law of Status, which Israel's Knesset formally adopted on November 24, 1952. Two years later, a special "Covenant" *(Amanah)* was entered into by the Government of Israel and the World Zionist Organization Executive, whereby the immigration and absorption of Olim would remain the specific responsibility of the WZO and of its instrument, the Jewish Agency for Israel.

A prolonged debate also took place on the role of Zionism outside the State. Ben-Gurion had no time for Zionists, more especially Zionist leaders, who would not honor their ideological commitment through Aliyah. To him, Zionists content to live in the *Golah* were no better than other Diaspora Jews. Younger Israelis who had fought in the War of Liberation, and those who took part in later campaigns, also tended to deride such people as exponents of an empty *Tziyyonut*. Thus, in June 1968, at the 27th Zionist Congress meeting in Jerusalem, Israeli delegates and their supporters from other countries forced through a resolution obligating Zionist leaders abroad to accept a personal commitment to Aliyah. A number of U.S. delegates, particularly members of Hadassah, strongly opposed this resolution, which was entered into the record but, in effect, consigned to limbo.

The bitterness engendered by wrangling over *Hafradah* at this Actions Committee meeting fortunately gave way, at the very end, to broad agreement on essentials. On September 2, after my election as treasurer of the Jewish Agency in succession to Eliezer Kaplan, I sensed a new confidence in the Zionist movement and spoke of the contribution I hoped to make in the work that lay ahead:

> For years now, I have heard the challenge hurled at American Zionists: "Come here, share our responsibilities, we need you and we welcome you!" These challenges have been on my conscience for a long time. I have been waiting for an opportunity to meet them, not only as an individual Jew but as an American Zionist.

Ten days later, before returning to New York, I was delighted to cement a tie of friendship dating back more than forty years to my childhood in Philadelphia. At the *ḥeder* conducted by Samuel Markowitz, one of my classmates had been Isidore Whartman. Now his son, Eliezer, was to be married in Israel. The ceremony, in which I participated, took place at a synagogue in Tel Aviv and I made the journey from Jerusalem and back by way of the "Burma Road," which had been open to traffic since early June. Eliezer Whartman and his wife, Drora, have remained beloved friends of ours ever since.

As I wound up my affairs back home in New York, during the fall of 1948, I was conscious of the many knotty problems that Bert and I would undoubtedly have to face in the course of a year's Zionist service in and on behalf of Medinat Yisrael. A leave of absence had been granted by my congregation, B'nai Jeshurun, and my duties there were left in the capable hands of my young associate, Rabbi David H. Panitz, who had assisted me during the preceding two years.

Toward the end of 1948, it became clear that the days of the American Jewish Conference were numbered. As mentioned earlier, I had been one of those who favored its establishment as a permanent representative "parliament" of American Jewry, for the purpose of safeguarding the religious and civil rights of Jews at home and abroad. The dramatic pronouncement of the United Nations on November 29, 1947, had the effect of lessening enthusiasm for any such permanent body among its potential constituents. After an effective operation of five years, the American Jewish Conference was wound up on December 31, 1948, and presented its final report a month later.

My farewell address as national chairman of the United Palestine Appeal was delivered in Chicago, on November 6, 1948, before some 3,000 delegates who attended the UPA's annual convention. It was the first UPA conference to be held since the establishment of Medinat Yisrael. I was succeeded by Herman L. Weisman. As a major beneficiary of the nationwide UJA campaign, the United Palestine Appeal (later renamed United Israel Appeal) now had an even greater responsibility for financing Israel's immigration and settlement program. Fifteen thousand Olim per month were entering Israel at the time.

While reporting on what had been achieved during my period of chairmanship, I also bore in mind what awaited me in Israel as the newly elected treasurer of the Jewish Agency. "United Palestine Appeal conferences have been many," I began, "but this one is unique and historic: since last we met, nineteen centuries of Jewish prayers have been answered. The Jewish State is here! 'A new light shines upon Zion—and already it sheds its glory upon all of us.' If we American Jews are deriving benefits of dignity and inspiration from this new light, we appreciate it the more because we have had a share in helping the new dispensation come to pass." Ours was only one contribution, however, and certainly not the most important. The lion's share belonged to all who had fought in and for the Jewish homeland:

The charter from the United Nations would have remained a scrap of paper, had it not been for Kfar Etzion and Tirat Tzvi, Mishmar ha-Emek and Deganyah, Negbah and Nitzanim, Kfar Szold and En Gev—to mention a few of the score of battlefields—and the crown of Jewish resistance, Jerusalem. We honor the dead and hail the living. We send our reverent, fervent, loving salute to Israel and to its military and civilian leaders, headed by President Chaim Weizmann and Prime Minister David Ben-Gurion. . . . Those of us who have had the privilege to be in Israel lately have felt the sense of the miracle.

Ahead of us there were still military and political dangers, I continued, and American Jews should not relax their vigilance. Above all, however, lurked the danger of economic stress, for Israel, surrounded and boycotted by intransigent foes, had yet to receive appropriate aid from "the most affluent of its friends" and was under tremendous strain. The burden of responsibility for solving Jewish national homelessness must be placed on the shoulders of World Jewry, not only those of the infant Jewish State. There was, I said, no longer a White Paper to bar Olim; the only barrier was financial limitation, and the Jews of America were capable of lifting it. Approximately 100,000 Jews had arrived in Israel since January 1, 1948, and of these only four percent did not require financial assistance from the Jewish Agency. At the current rate of immigration, a vastly increased budget of $240 million or more would be required, of which three-quarters would have to come from the Jews of America.

In the United States, our efforts had now shifted from the political to the economic front. "It should be obvious," I continued, "that to the extent to which Israel is relieved of the cost of absorbing the new immigration, to that extent it is free to devote its resources to the military requirements. A large and rapid immigration strengthens Israel against future contingencies." It was my belief that the same zeal and self-sacrifice that American Jewry had devoted to political campaigns in the past would guarantee the success of this new economic task. "The United Palestine Appeal is the immediate instrument, and this conference is the immediate occasion for sounding the call."

I ended my address on a personal note, expressing my sense of privilege in having headed the UPA during two years that were "the most productive financially and the most epoch-making politically." A record total of well over $100 million had been raised, "small in comparison with present needs, but twice as large as the largest amount raised in any corresponding period in the past."

I concluded with the following words of farewell:

> As I leave for Israel, I want to feel that the Treasurer of the Jewish Agency will have no reason to complain that American Jews are not doing as much as they could do. I imagine the people in Israel expect that when, for the first time, an American Jew is entrusted with the Treasury of the Jewish Agency, he will have the full backing and support of American Jewry. If I fail, dear friends and colleagues, it will be your failure. . . .
>
> Rachel need no more weep for her children, because in Zion and throughout Israel there is hope for the despondent, a home for the homeless, freedom for the fettered, dignity for the rejected, a place for the displaced, a center for the dispersed, a heritage for the disinherited, and a promising future for a people of tragic present and glorious past.

On the eve of our departure for Israel, a dinner was arranged in my honor, sponsored by the Zionist Organization of America and the United Palestine Appeal. Hayim Greenberg, the newly appointed chairman of the Jewish Agency's Department for Education and Culture in the Diaspora, who was one of the speakers, treated his audience to a memorable quip: "A nation which made shepherds into kings can make rabbis into treasurers and economists."

A Year in the Jewish Agency "Cabinet"

The passing of time has not altered my belief that the year I spent in Israel, when the State was still in its infancy, was the most interesting, the most difficult, and, in many respects, the most important and the most fruitful in my public career. The responsibilities the treasurer of the Jewish Agency had to undertake were enormous at a time when the War of Liberation still raged, despite the official truce, and when vast numbers of Jews were arriving from various parts of the world. Immigration reached a peak with 251,000 Olim, adding one-third to the population of the Jewish State. Thus, while the fighting continued, Ashkenazi DPs from Europe and Sephardi-Oriental Olim from North African and Near Eastern countries presented Israel with overwhelming absorption problems. In addition to the existing transit camps, mostly inherited from the British, two dozen new reception centers were set up for these immigrants, most of whom needed every kind of assistance from the outset, and often for a considerable period thereafter. There were, unfortunately, many social cases and only five percent of the newcomers could be absorbed in agricultural settlements, although ninety-six new *yishuvim* were in fact established during that initial year. It was a situation fairly bristling with complexities.

Despite its meager resources, and the fact that it was still nursing the grievous wounds inflicted by its Arab attackers, Israel made heroic efforts to solve the problems it faced. Considerations of security, employment needs, and utilization of land to feed the expanding population impelled the Jewish Agency to step up agricultural settlement at this time. Nearly one hundred *yishuvim*, which had been destroyed or badly damaged during the war, were restored. Yet although income from Zionist fund-raising campaigns around the world proved to be woefully inadequate, few Israelis ever contemplated restricting the tide of immigration. Even before the Law of Return promulgated by the Knesset in 1950, almost everyone insisted that Aliyah was one of the pillars of Jewish statehood and that the human needs of those seeking to enter the gates of a free and independent Israel must be the overriding consideration.

The cost of absorbing immigrants, 350 Israel Pounds ($1,000) per capita, meant that some 250,000 Olim in the budgetary year ending September 30, 1949, would require 85 million Israel Pounds ($240 million), exclusive of the JNF budget for land purchases. If the actual Aliyah figures vastly exceeded our original expectations, why did the Jewish Agency take such a financial risk? My treasurer's report of May 5, 1949, to the Actions Committee provided an explanation:

> It was the Zionist thing to do, to establish the homeless in the Jewish National Home as soon as possible, to place no obstacles in the way of Jews who could escape then and who might not be able to escape later, and to add the strength of numbers to this young new nation as quickly as possible.

Jews throughout the world had to understand that military victories would be empty unless the gates of Israel were kept open for all who wished to enter.

From its budget the Jewish Agency had to cover not only the cost of a huge program of immigration and absorption, as well as land settlement, but also work in fields such as education, organization, and youth activities. Other assignments that came within the treasurer's purview included the supervision of purchase contracts in Israel and abroad, control of expenditure and the payment of outstanding debts, currency exchanges and the arrangement of bank loans (to which I shall revert). Last, but by no means least, came the task of playing an active role in fund-raising campaigns throughout the Diaspora. Here, my principal sphere of activity was the English-speaking countries, from which the bulk of Jewish Agency income has always been obtained. Some seventy percent was contributed by American Jewry.

The post of treasurer had been built up by my immediate predecessor, Eliezer Kaplan, who established a tradition of being not only a fiscal officer but also an administrator in charge of all the Jewish Agency budgets. As such, he carved out for himself a position of influence in determining how the money should be spent. The ingrained habit of equating financial decisions with whatever Kaplan had in mind proved hard to break, but I persevered. Another of the difficulties confronting me was a political one. First, Eliezer Kaplan, though now Israel's Minister of Finance, had retained a seat ("without portfolio") on the Jewish Agency Executive, which gave him the right and opportunity to keep an eye on developments within the Zionist Organization. Second, I, a General Zionist, had been selected to work with a Finance Minister who belonged to the dominant Mapai Labor Party, whose financial resources were overstrained, and who had held my portfolio for many years. There were, no doubt, some who expected a good deal of friction to develop.

Fortunately, however, the relationship between Kaplan and myself proceeded smoothly and transcended narrow party interests. The groundwork I managed to lay during my year in Israel was evidently appreciated.

Needless to say, the very act of leaving our home in New York and setting up house temporarily in Jerusalem was no easy matter in November 1949, while hostilities with the Arabs continued. Bert and I were grateful to Ḥayyim Vinitzky of the Jewish Agency, a fine public servant, who helped us overcome some of the initial problems of settling in and acclimatization.

Though aware of the nature and scope of my task, I soon realized that the experience I had gained in the United States covered only one side of Zionist financial operations. My work in the Jewish National Fund, UJA, and United Palestine Appeal had been limited to *raising* funds, for the most part, rather than *spending* them. The treasurer of the Jewish Agency must be engaged in both. I had therefore to learn on the job what was, for me, the more difficult assignment of working out budgets with the heads of the Jewish Agency's respective departments. In this I was fortunate to have the daily help and cooperation of David Baharal, director-general of the treasury, and of the deputy director-general, Yeḥiel Giladi.*

---

*I am greatly obliged to Mr. Giladi, who later (after the death of David Baharal) assumed the post of director-general of the Treasury Department, for some important statistical data contained in these pages.

I saw myself as a bridge between the Medinah and American Jewry, from whose ranks increased financial support would be expected. I also looked forward to a period of close and fruitful cooperation with the Government of Israel.

Hafradah, the division of functions between Government and Jewish Agency departments, had not affected the "party key" system determining which officials should head the respective departments of the Jewish Agency. The majority of the key posts were held by members of Mapai, others by General Zionists or by leaders of Mizraḥi and Ha-Po'el Ha-Mizraḥi. Among those ideologically close to me were Dr. Abraham Granovsky, chairman of the Keren Kayemet Le-Yisrael, Arthur (Menaḥem) Hantke, managing director of the Keren Hayesod, Moshe Kol, head of Youth Aliyah, and Zvi Herman, director-general of the Immigrant Absorption Department. Both the Keren Hayesod and the Keren Kayemet enjoyed some measure of autonomy within the Jewish Agency framework. Prominent among the Mapai department heads were Eliyahu Dobkin (organization and information), Levi Eshkol (agricultural settlement), Dr. Dov Joseph (legal adviser), and Eliezer Kaplan. The Mizraḥi's Rabbi Wolf (Ze'ev) Gold headed a special department for the development of Jerusalem, while Zalman Shragai and Yitzḥak Werfel (later, Raphael) of Ha-Po'el Ha-Mizraḥi served, respectively, as Jewish Agency Executive member without portfolio and as head of the Immigration Department.

Some of these Zionist leaders subsequently went on to achieve eminence in the Government or in other spheres of national life. Thus, Levi Eshkol would later become Minister of Finance and then Prime Minister; Dov Joseph, whose book, *The Faithful City*, reflected his experiences during the War of Liberation as military governor of Jerusalem, became Minister of Justice; Moshe Kol would subsequently become Minister of Tourism; Zalman Shragai was to head the Aliyah Department after having served as Mayor of Jerusalem; and Yitzḥak Raphael would end his public career as Minister of Religious Affairs. My predecessor as treasurer of the Jewish Agency, Eliezer Kaplan, Israel's Minister of Finance, was for a short time Deputy Prime Minister before his death in 1952.

The chairman of the Jewish Agency Executive in Jerusalem at that time was Berl Locker, a veteran Labor Zionist whose career in Mapai embraced many years of political activity. I had first met him during my visit to Great Britain in February and March 1944, and again when attending the London Zionist Conference in the following year. He was one of Weizmann's faithful quartet of advisers, the others being Professor Selig Brodetsky, Blanche Dugdale, and Professor Lewis Namier. Berl Locker had many important connections in the British Labor Party. A skillful debater, noted for his wit and his fund of stories, he was a good colleague and leader. His wife, Malkah, continues to be a woman of letters, a personality in her own right, and a splendid hostess. It could not have been easy for Berl Locker to follow in the footsteps of David Ben-Gurion by assuming the chairmanship of the Executive at such a momentous stage in Jewish and Zionist history.

One of the Jewish Agency departments to which I devoted particular attention was that concerned with Jerusalem's reconstruction and development. Its head, Rabbi Ze'ev Gold, had a very effective director-general in Meir Grossman, the onetime Revisionist leader who had broken with Jabotinsky and formed the Jewish State Party. I made a point of involving the city's first Jewish Mayor, Daniel Auster, in our discussions. Jerusalem had only just emerged from the ravages caused by prolonged Arab siege and bombardment; its main business area, adjoining Ben-Yehudah Street, was in shambles and badly in need of restoration. When I began my work as treasurer of the Agency, a substantial part of the mass immigration was being directed to Jerusalem and new industries were obviously required in order to provide employment opportunities for the many Olim.

I drew up a five-year development program for the city, embracing not only the reconstruction of Ben-Yehudah Street in downtown Jerusalem but also the establishment of a new industrial center on what was then its periphery. There, premises would be made available at moderate rentals for small and medium-sized enterprises, such as printing houses and handicraft industries. One of our most ambitious schemes was the planning of a large convention center, which would provide facilities for Zionist Congresses and other international gatherings and for concerts by the Israel Philharmonic Orchestra. This convention center, better known today as Binyanei ha-Umah, was eventually completed in the late 1950s.

Speaking at the Orion Theater on March 13, 1949, the first anniversary of the Ben-Yehudah Street explosion, I stressed the need for "visible improvements which would inspire new confidence in the city's population." The chief priorities were housing, better roads, commercial development, and the transfer to Jerusalem of Government and Jewish Agency departments and personnel. It was, I said, "the universal conviction of the Jewish people that Jerusalem must be the capital city of the Jewish State," and I expressed the hope that this official status would be confirmed within the next twelve months. On December 10, 1949, however, the UN General Assembly called for the establishment of "an international regime" over the whole of the divided city. Both Israel and Jordan opposed the internationalization scheme, which became a dead letter. On December 26, sessions of the Knesset were resumed in Jewish Jerusalem, "Israel's eternal capital," as it was designated in a Government proclamation.

Ever since May 14, 1948, a Council of State had functioned as Israel's provisional Government and Dr. Chaim Weizmann had served likewise, as President, in a provisional capacity. These interim arrangements had, of course, necessitated the transformation into governmental ministries of the various departments and bureaus that had previously functioned under the aegis of the Va'ad Leumi, the Jewish Agency, and the Mandatory regime.

Following Israel's first general election, on January 24, 1949, twelve parties gained seats in the Knesset, where the total number of elected members remained fixed at 120. The largest factions to emerge from the voting were Mapai, the Israel Labor Party, with 46 seats; Mapam, the left-wing Socialists (19); the United Religious Front, comprising Mizrahi and Ha-Po'el Ha-Mizrahi, Agudat Yisrael and Po'alei Agudat Yisrael (16); and Herut, the Freedom Party, successor to the old Revisionists (14). Owing to the split between General Zionists and Progressives, our middle-of-the-road Zionist factions could only manage to gain twelve seats between them. When the first Knesset assembled on February 14, Weizmann was elected President of the State and Yosef Sprinzak became Speaker of the Knesset. Having been sworn in three days later, President Weizmann called upon David Ben-Gurion, as head of the largest parliamentary group, to form a government. This he proceeded to do on the basis of a coalition between Mapai and the United Religious Front. Israel's first constitutional Government was officially installed on March 10, 1949.

It was exhilarating to be in Israel at such a time. *De jure* (to replace *de facto*) recognition was extended by the United States and, on May 11, Israel was elected a member state of the United Nations. One final act of historic justice took place toward the end of my treasurership at the Jewish Agency, on August 17, 1949. According to his last will and testament, Theodor Herzl had stipulated that his remains be laid to rest in Vienna until the moment would come for the Jewish people to reinter them in the Land of Israel. By Government decree, this wish was fulfilled and, after a solemn lying-in-state in Tel Aviv, the remains of the Zionist movement's founding father were reinterred in a hilltop cemetery on the western outskirts of Jerusalem, which subsequently received the designation, Mount Herzl. Close by his tomb, which bears the simple Hebrew inscription, "Herzl," a special museum was established. The twentieth day of Tammuz, marking the anniversary of his death, is now a national *Yahrzeit* memorial day in Israel.

Soon after Dr. Weizmann had been elected President, my wife and I went to visit him at his home in Reḥovot. He was half-blind by then and ailing; moreover, he felt unhappy about the inactive role assigned to him as President. The titular status and ceremonial functions of an Israeli head of state were a far cry from what Weizmann had once enjoyed as president of the World Zionist Organization. Real power lay in the hands of the Prime Minister, David Ben-Gurion. Yet he still managed to retain his acerbic Weizmannesque humor. When Bert and I congratulated him on his richly deserved honor and asked him how he felt, Weizmann replied with a punning Yiddish phrase: *"Man zogt mir az ikh bin a 'symbol,' tzimbel ikh"*—"They tell me I'm a symbol, so I play the cymbals." It was apparent that he was not enjoying his high office and that he found much greater satisfaction in his continued scientific work.

As for Ben-Gurion, there was no mistaking his deprecating attitude toward the Zionist movement. Once, when we were having a conversation over lunch, he observed that three factors were operative on the world Jewish scene—Medinat Yisrael, the Jewish people, and the World Zionist Organization. It was his opinion that the Israel Government should take over responsibility for *Klitah*, the absorption of immigrants, and that the WZO should confine itself to *Hasbarah* and *Ḥalutziut*, information work and pioneering settlement. Clearly, Ben-Gurion's heart was not in the Zionist Organization, but since it existed, he recognized that it had somehow to fit into the scheme of things.

My responsibilities as treasurer of the Jewish Agency entailed frequent meetings with Prime Minister Ben-Gurion and with Finance Minister Kaplan, as well as with other members of the Government. One of my most important functions was to negotiate loans for the Jewish Agency, since our current income was insufficient to meet all our requirements. In this connection, we developed an ongoing contact with the Anglo-Palestine Bank (soon renamed Bank Leumi Le-Yisrael), which was then headed by an eminent Dutch-born economist, Eliezer S. Hoofien. I frequently met with him and his associates, Dr. Ernst Lehmann and Mr. H. Margolis. Two other senior officials of the bank had played a leading role in German Zionism and, later, in Eretz Yisrael—Dr. Aharon Barth in the Mizraḥi and Dr. Yeshayahu (Herbert) Foerder as secretary of the German Zionist Organization. Barth, who became general manager of Bank Leumi, served from 1946 as chairman of the Zionist Congress court, while Foerder, who became chairman of the board in 1957, went on to become a Member of Knesset representing the Progressive Party.

One particular difficulty we faced was the lack of a guiding hand behind the Zionist movement's fund-raising campaigns and administration in Western Europe. David Baharal, my director-general, believed that Eran Laor, an experienced Zionist emissary, was the right man for the job. Laor had just resigned from the Israel Ministry of Transport, where he had served for a year as controller of shipping, his task having been to reestablish Israel's maritime links with other countries following the disruption caused by the War of Liberation.

In February 1949, when Eran Laor and I met in Tel Aviv, I asked him to spend a year in Europe as our representative there. He agreed to do so and set up the Treasury Department's office in Geneva, where many other Jewish organizations were based. Laor proved successful in establishing credit for us, largely on the strength of the good name and backing of the United Jewish Appeal, and he remained in Europe, discharging a number of vital tasks and responsibilities, not for the period of twelve months I had requested but for the next twenty-five years.

Although we did manage to obtain some loans from Swiss banks, mostly they were negotiated in the United States, where I had the valuable assistance of Gottlieb Hammer, the enterprising executive director of the Jewish Agency in New York, and of Maurice Boukstein, the Agency's very able legal adviser. As controller of the Palestine Pavilion at the New York World's Fair in 1939–41, Hammer had worked under Meyer Weisgal and then moved to the Jewish National Fund of America, where he functioned in a similar capacity.

There is an amusing story relating to Eliezer Kaplan's application for a substantial loan from the Chase Manhattan Bank. Winthrop Aldrich, the bank's president, invited him to attend a meeting of his board in New York and, after introducing him, said, "You should know, Mr. Kaplan, that when a loan of this size is being considered, we ask the applicant to produce all the financial statements issued by his enterprise over the past ten years."

"In that case," Kaplan answered, "I would have to go back not ten years but nineteen centuries, and I doubt if the records are still available."

The president of the Chase Manhattan Bank then turned to the members of his board and said, "Gentlemen, you may remember that six months ago we made a similar loan to the Bethlehem Steel Corporation. If we could do it then for Bethlehem, let's do it now for Jerusalem!"

A number of problems made it necessary for me to travel back and forth between Jerusalem and New York in the course of the year. For one thing, as co-chairman of the United Jewish Appeal, I still had ongoing obligations in respect of planning the campaign and addressing UJA meetings in the United States. Despite marked increases in the overall fund raising, our existing contract with our partners, the Joint Distribution Committee, resulted in a shortage of money needed to pay for the vast program of Aliyah absorption in Israel. The negotiations over who should receive what percentage of the total income derived from the UJA campaign were mainly between the JDC and the United Palestine Appeal, which I headed as national chairman. These two organizations, however, also agreed on the allocation of certain amounts to the National Refugee Service, whereas the Jewish National Fund was permitted to conduct a separate campaign of its own, subject to a fixed ceiling. Another question that arose involved the U.S. law forbidding tax-exempt donations to be used for governmental purposes overseas. We feared that our transfer of UJA contributions to Israel might be misinterpreted, unless it could be demonstrated that such funds would be utilized in an approved manner, and here again I was called upon to help rectify matters.

The several trips I made across the Atlantic on Jewish Agency business enabled me to spend short spells with my congregation. During one such visit, B'nai Jeshurun arranged a fund-raising dinner for the United Jewish Appeal. On my return trip, I stopped off in London to launch the Joint Palestine Appeal there.

Throughout the period of my treasurership, I was constantly engaged in a battle with fellow members of the Jewish Agency Executive who pressed for larger budgetary allocations for their departments. They obviously had no choice in the prevailing circumstances, whereas I had the unenviable task of trying to raise more and more money through direct contributions or bank loans abroad. I well remember a meeting of the Jewish Agency in New York, on February 4, 1949, which was attended by members of both the Jerusalem and the American executives. Berl Locker, the chairman of our Jerusalem section, was handling a debate on the budget when he took occasion to remark, "Goldstein fights not only with us but with himself as well. That is the fate of all treasurers!"

Occasionally, there were also bright spots. Golda Myerson, on one of her fund-raising visits to America in the spring of 1948, had accompanied me when I went to see David Dubinsky, head of the International Ladies' Garment Workers Union. A colleague of mine in the leadership of the New York Liberal Party, David Dubinsky was also a friend of Israel and a keen supporter of Israel's labor federation, the Histadrut. He arranged for the ILGWU to lend the Jewish Agency a million dollars for one year. When that period of grace expired, early in March 1949, Gottlieb Hammer and I made another visit to Dubinsky's office in the hope of renewing or at least extending part of the loan. I can well imagine what must have crossed Dubinsky's mind when we telephoned to say that the two of us were on our way to see him. Past experience in such matters may have led him to fear that we could not repay the money and would plead for some additional time. At any rate, there was a somber, apprehensive look on his face when we were shown into his office.

"David," I said, "we owe you money—and we've come to pay you."

With a howl of glee, Dubinsky started to punch buttons on his desk. Doors were flung open and suddenly an assortment of vice-presidents and other officials of the ILGWU poured into the room. "I told you it would be all right!" Dubinsky shouted at the top of his voice. "Where's the photographer?" In a trice, the photographer appeared and handed a comb to the union's president so that he could straighten his unruly hair before a picture was taken of the Jewish Agency treasurer presenting him with a one-million-dollar check in repayment of the loan.

After things had quieted down, I said, "Well, David, you didn't expect to get paid, but you got the money. Now I'm asking for another favor." It was not difficult, on the spot, to obtain a new loan of half a million dollars.

Apart from visits to the United States, my duties also necessitated periodical trips to Europe. One especially memorable journey was on the maiden flight of El Al, Israel's fledgling national airline, from Lod (Lydda) to Rome. Finance Minister Eliezer Kaplan was our distinguished fellow passenger. Our plane, fitted only with bucket seats, was not really suited to regular passenger service, but the pride we felt in this latest achievement of Israel more than compensated for any discomfort.

During my tour of Western Europe in June and July 1949, I spent some time in Germany so as to ascertain the feasibility of closing down the DP camps there. At that time, there were still 13,000 Jewish displaced persons in the American zone alone. Compared with what I had seen of the country three years earlier, in July 1945, West Germany was scarcely recognizable. The economy was booming, and so was the black market.

The aim of the Jewish Agency was to have the DP camps emptied and dismantled as soon as possible. This was the theme of an address I delivered before the Central Committee for Jewish Displaced Persons in Munich on July 1. Prominent among the Holocaust survivors in Germany was Josef Rosensaft, a legendary figure, who had led Jewish resistance to the anti-Zionist administration in the British zone and who was active in "Aliyah Bet" and Beriḥah operations. He later served as president of the World Federation of Bergen-Belsen Survivors. The condition of these Jewish DPs was far better than when I had last seen them, although one still encountered a variety of psychological problems resulting from the torture inflicted by the Nazis. My talks with leaders of the Jewish DPs, as well as with the rank and file, indicated that morale was generally high. Within a few months of this visit, the camps in Germany were discontinued.

On my way back to Israel, I made a brief stop in Marseilles to inspect some of the chartered ships used for transporting Olim, and had useful meetings with the Jewish Agency officials who were in charge. Marseilles then had a Jewish community of 20,000, which helped the emigrants housed in local transit camps. These camps were well organized, with vocational training centers and even a kindergarten run by an Israeli girl, who taught the children Hebrew songs. Adults were studying the rudiments of the Hebrew language. One heartening feature was the attention paid by medical teams to the health of Jews arriving from North Africa. No one could proceed to Israel without an authorization signed by one of the Jewish Agency physicians.

High on my list of priorities during the first year of Israel's statehood was the housing program. Because of the mass immigration, unprecedented anywhere else in the world as regards the proportion of newcomers to the existing population, a housing crisis of unmanageable proportions faced the country. Initially, efforts were made to refurbish abandoned Arab houses in Jerusalem, Haifa, Jaffa, Lod, Ramleh, and other towns. Such existing accommodation was quickly exhausted. All kinds of miserable and inadequate substitutes were then pressed into service—"tent cities," huts built of asbestos sheets, corrugated iron, canvas and wooden blocks, and the ubiquitous *ma'abarot*, ugly transit camps in which many luckless Olim were compelled to remain, often for years on end. The financial support our fund-raising campaigns managed to elicit abroad proved hopelessly unequal to the call of this emergency.

In a desperate effort to relieve the plight of vast numbers of Olim, the Jewish Agency, together with the Government of Israel, founded Amidar ("My People Dwells"), the Israel National Housing Company, which began its operation in March 1949. I became the first president of Amidar, and I appointed Meir Hartman as director-general. Our purpose was to expedite the provision of low-cost housing on a vast scale, enlisting the aid of building corporations such as Rassco and Solel Boneh. Amidar was established with a basic capital of five million Israel Pounds, one half of which would be provided by the Jewish Agency and the other half by the Government, the Keren Kayemet, and public housing companies.

At the outset, we set ourselves a target of 40,000 dwellings, but only about half that number of units—enough for 60,000 people—could be made available in the first year. According to our provisional estimate, 100,000 new dwellings would be required by the end of 1950. Ours was nevertheless a comprehensive housing scheme that did much, if not enough, to solve a grave social problem in the years to come. "Inadequate as it is in proportion to the need," I said in a press statement released on March 10, 1949, "a low-cost national housing program which, within one year, provides housing for seven percent of the population represents a larger housing program than is being undertaken by any other nation, great or small."

Amidar was supervised by a twenty-two-man board of directors who included Finance Minister Eliezer Kaplan, Dr. Abraham Granovsky (later, Granott), chairman of the Keren Kayemet, David Horowitz, director-general of the Finance Ministry, and Levi Eshkol, head of the Jewish Agency's Agricultural Settlement Department. Apart from Meir Hartman, the executive managers were Dr. Yeshayahu Foerder, director of Rassco; Dr. Georg Landauer of the Palestine Agricultural Housing Corporation; Selig Lubianiker of the Histadrut's housing company; and Ya'akov Reiser, head of the Jewish Agency's Technical Department.

As a preliminary step toward liquidating the *ma'abarot*, we placed orders for 4,000 prefabricated wooden houses to be imported from Sweden and for 2,000 more to be manufactured locally. Contracts were signed for 9,000 housing units built of concrete and stone. All of this involved a race against time and a long financial struggle. There was a good deal of skepticism in the Israel press each time we announced a new building project, but visible progress was made and we were eventually able to increase the average living space per family from thirty-two square meters to an area twice that size.

An amusing incident occurred at one stage, related to a new concrete pouring machine used in Texas, the "Tourneau-layer," named for its inventor. We heard that it was able to pour a concrete house in one day, on a prepared site, and that the concrete took only a few more days to harden. The cost of such a machine was not within our budget, but thanks to a private loan we succeeded in acquiring one Tourneau-layer, which began pouring scores of concrete dwellings in the Haifa Bay area. Though far from attractive in appearance, they were sturdy units and they filled an immediate need. It so happened that a Jordanian reconnaissance plane spotted our Tourneau-layer, which, seen from the air, looked rather like an enormous gun. At once there was a headline in an Arab newspaper, warning that Israel had the world's biggest long-range cannon in its possession.

Since 1949, Amidar has become a ramified nonprofit institution playing a major role in the field of absorption, and extending facilities both for rental and for purchase of greatly improved housing units. One of its most successful projects, the splendid Afridar quarter in Ashkelon, resulted from an investment agreement which, as treasurer of the Jewish Agency, I signed with representatives of the South African Jewish community.

The fact that I also served as president of the World Confederation of General Zionists throughout this time added to the dimensions of my overall task. A number of those with whom I worked in the Agency, Amidar, and other public bodies were General Zionist colleagues and they included Dr. Ludwig Pinner, who headed the Middle Class Colonization Department of the Jewish Agency. Conscious of the responsibilities I had assumed, I encouraged fellow General Zionists to foster the establishment of agricultural settlements and kindred projects in the Medinah.

My wife and I visited a number of kibbutzim and moshavim during our year in Israel. On January 27, 1949, we participated in the *aliyah la-karka* (groundbreaking) ceremony of Gesher ha-Ziv, a Labor-affiliated kibbutz north of Nahariyah, close to the Lebanese border, where olive trees grew in profusion. Bert had been a guiding force in the American branch of Habonim, a ḥalutzic movement that was sending young people to establish or join new pioneering settlements. In the course of the ceremony there was a pleasant diversion when a small Piper Cub plane flew over us and dropped a message of greetings. It had been sent by my colleague on the Executive, Levi Eshkol, who headed the Settlement Department, and the gesture evoked much appreciative applause.

Our World Confederation of General Zionists played its part in fostering and assisting various cooperative settlements throughout the country. Among these were a kibbutz, Ha-Solelim, in central Galilee, the original founders of which were American ḥalutzim of our Ha-No'ar Ha-Tzioni youth movement. Appropriately enough, its name, Ha-Solelim, meant "trailblazers." Ezra Shapiro, a Zionist leader from Cleveland, was with me at the ground-breaking ceremony on July 21, 1949. The Confederation also aided several moshavim, notably Moshav Benei Zion, which was established in 1947, with help from the American Order of B'nai Zion, whose name it bears; Moshav Udim, not far from Netanyah; Kfar Sh'muel, in the Judean foothills, named in honor of Rabbi Stephen S. Wise; and Talmei Yafeh, a moshav shitufi in the southern coastal plain. Talmei Yafeh ("Furrows of Jaffe") commemorates the director of the Keren Hayesod, Leib Jaffe, who was one of the victims of the Arab terrorist outrage at the Jewish Agency building in Jerusalem, on March 11, 1948.

Just as Gesher ha-Ziv became our favorite kibbutz, a place where Bert and I still like to spend a few days' vacation, so did Moshav Udim exert a special attraction for me among the moshavim. The very name, Udim, meaning "brands plucked out of the fire" (Zechariah 3:2), reminds one of the fact that the youngsters who founded this moshav in 1948 had survived the wartime Nazi terror in Yugoslavia. They served their apprenticeship and acquired their first experience of agricultural work on the soil of Kfar Benei Zion, where they lived in tents for a year. As soon as a land allocation was granted to them nearby, they proceeded to establish their own settlement.

Udim remains endeared to me as "the steam-shovel village," because that appliance, used in building the moshav, was a gift I secured from a friend in Chicago. After their first houses had been constructed, the young moshavniks hired out their steam shovel to another pioneering group, thus earning sufficient income to keep them solvent until their fields yielded abundant crops. A combination of hard work and fertile land (part of which had to be reclaimed from a malarial swamp) enabled these admirable *halutzim* to establish Udim's economy on a sound basis. They developed a mixed farming system and also grew flowers for export. Perhaps the best tribute to these pioneers and their way of life is the fact that, in course of time, their children—having grown up, married, and raised families of their own—were anxious to combine forces with their parents and applied for more land.

Some years after the establishement of Moshav Udim, when I saw that the settlers there now included a number of traditionally minded families, I approached my congregation in New York and secured funds for the building of a synagogue. A number of Yemenite families became fully integrated in the moshav and one such villager now conducts the services there. Other joyous events, such as circumcision, Bar Mitzvah, and wedding ceremonies, are also celebrated in Udim's synagogue. To my great delight, and that of my congregation, it was named "Bené Yeshurun."

A highlight of the year was Passover, the first to be celebrated in an independent Jewish State. Shortly before the festival, by courtesy of Israel's broadcasting service, Kol Yerushalayim, talks I had recorded were transmitted locally and to the Jews of the United States.

On Passover eve, April 13, we participated in the *Seder* held at Afikim, one of Israel's largest and most thriving kibbutzim, situated at the southwestern corner of

Lake Kinneret, the Sea of Galilee. Not only was our attendance at this *Seder* an introduction to Passover celebrations in the Land of Israel, it was also our first experience of its observance on a secular kibbutz. More than one thousand members, *haverim* and *haverot*, took their places in the huge dining hall, while several hundred guests were accommodated in a specially constructed temporary annex. Bert and I had the good fortune to be seated alongside two founder members of the kibbutz, Yosef and Leah Yizre'eli. In addition to the *Seder* service and the Passover meal, the evening's program was to include festive songs and dances. The pioneers who founded Kibbutz Afikim had mostly come with the last organized group to leave Soviet Russia in the 1920s, and their settlement was seventeen years old, having been established in 1932. We looked forward with keen interest to our *Seder* in this unusual setting.

The *Haggadah* placed before us had been specially devised for the kibbutz movement to which Afikim belonged—Iḥud ha-Kvutzot ve-ha-Kibbutzim, affiliated with Mapai. The text included various emendations, customary among nonreligious circles, such as references to the present time and place, as well as to past events, and hymns of praise to the "Spring Festival," *Ḥag ha-Aviv*. After leafing through the pages of my *Haggadah*, I turned to my neighbor, Yosef Yizre'eli, and asked him, "Where is *Ha-Kadosh Barukh Hu*, the Almighty, blessed be He, in all of this? Does He have to find His way into Afikim by 'Aliyah Bet'?"

With a somewhat patronizing look, Yizre'eli replied, "Please have a little patience. Look further on."

A few pages farther along, to be sure, I did find Him. Among various passages from rabbinic lore, there was quoted the beautiful *Aggadah* (*Megillah* 10b) that relates how, when the hosts of Pharaoh were perishing in the Red Sea, the ministering angels wanted to sing a hymn of praise, but the Holy One stopped them with the reproach, "My creatures are drowning, and you would sing?"

Mrs. Yizre'eli then turned to me. "We came from an anti-religious background in Russia," she said, "but we would like our children to acquire some kind of Jewish religious knowledge and inspiration. We know that they are missing something of value and importance, but we don't know how to give it to them. If only some of your American rabbis would come to live with us here and teach our children, so that they may come to love and appreciate those beautiful concepts and ceremonies of our tradition."

It was a challenge I subsequently tried to convey when speaking with colleagues of mine in New York, and I have continued to hear it and repeat it ever since.

Following World War II, the Jewish Agency drew up plans for the establishment of special youth villages in which Jewish children, whether orphans or not, would be housed, cared for, and enabled to make a new start in Israel. I had taken a great interest in these plans and had visited several homes for Jewish children abroad, particularly in France. The most promising future for these children, and for tens of thousands more in all parts of the world, lay in Israel, the Jewish homeland, where they could be reared and guided—Jewishly and humanly—toward useful lives, both as human beings and as citizens of Medinat Yisrael. Moshe Kol, head of the Jewish Agency's Youth Aliyah Department, was a tower of strength in leading and administering these endeavors.

On August 16, 1949, a new youth village, known locally as *Ḥavvat ha-No'ar ha-Tzioni*, the "Zionist Youth Farm," was established in Katamon, an outlying southwestern area of Jerusalem, and named in my honor. This installation, maintained by Youth Aliyah with additional support from the World Confederation of General Zionists, was intended to accommodate youngsters from the age of twelve to eighteen. Here, children of various cultural backgrounds, some with parents and others without, were offered a congenial home environment and the advantages of secondary education and vocational training.

When I first cast eyes on the spot, it was a rock-strewn, almost treeless portion of the Judean hillscape. Standing on a nearby hillock was the Monastery of St. Simon, a Greek Orthodox institution, where forty Jewish boys had lost their lives when it was stormed and captured from Arab marauders in the early summer of 1948. One of the Haganah commanders in that operation, Ze'ev Schickler, had been an active Zionist from his early days in Poland, prior to his Aliyah. He, his wife, Hadassah, and some of his comrades set their hearts on the building of a youth village close to the monastery hill where so many of their fellow combatants had fallen. There were a few abandoned stone cottages farther down the slope. Here, the first batch of forty children was accommodated. Schickler and his skeleton staff occupied another derelict structure. The whole area was a rocky wilderness on the outskirts of Jerusalem, bereft of water, electricity, or roads. Together with his staff and pupils, Schickler set to work clearing away the stones, preparing the site for construction, maintaining essential services, and doing guard duty, since the embryonic *Ḥavvah* lay only three or four kilometers from the Jordanian border.

In the course of my address at the foundation-laying ceremony, I emphasized the vital role of Youth Aliyah and the important educational task that the Israel Goldstein Youth Village would be called upon to fulfill. Like its predecessors in Kfar Glickson, Magdiel, Nitzanim, and Tel Yitzhak, this village would not be conducted on narrow political lines but would impart the widest Jewish values, "setting national interests above party interests and creating a sense of all-embracing Jewish unity." The composition of its board of management would reflect this broad outlook. While expressing my appreciation of the honor accorded to me in the naming of Jerusalem's *Ḥavvah*, I also looked forward to its significant development in the future.

The dedication ceremony took place five months later, on January 23, 1950. Among the distinguished gathering were Justice Minister Pinhas Rosen, representing the Government; Knesset Speaker Yosef Sprinzak; Dr. Abraham Granott, chairman of the Keren Kayemet; Jerusalem's Mayor, Daniel Auster; and Moshe Kol, the head of Youth Aliyah. A welcome visitor whom Dr. Granott brought with him was Bartley Crum, who had been one of our staunchest friends on the Anglo-American Committee of Inquiry in 1946. Hearty "Mazal Tov!" greetings were exchanged with this eminent American well-wisher. At the center of attention were the Youth

Village's new residents—children from thirty-two different lands, ranging from Ecuador to Malaysia. They staged a play telling about the Hebrew poet, Saul Tchernichowsky, who had often walked over this hilly terrain, and recalling how the area encompassing the village had been conquered during the War of Liberation.

Ze'ev Schickler, its founding director, was the guiding inspiration of the *Havvah* until his untimely death in 1977. He had an able assistant in his wife, Hadassah, an educator in her own right, and their son, Mikhah, grew up there. Lonia Liebergall, the able secretary, who was in effect the Youth Village "mother," and a devoted staff worked faithfully at their side from the earliest days. Youth Aliyah, our World Confederation of General Zionists, Hadassah, and other women's Zionist organizations have been a consistent source of encouragement and support.

Over the years, this Youth Village underwent dramatic changes. Today, many hundreds of children, boys and girls, are enrolled, nearly half of them day pupils from adjoining underprivileged neighborhoods in the city. Most of the residents are new immigrants or the children of recent Olim. The vocational-training program embraces carpentry and metal work for the boys and sewing, weaving, and home economics for the girls, as well as several unusual crafts, such as electronics, flower growing, wood carving, ceramics, typewriting, and watch repairing. The drama and music groups are of a high standard.

With Jerusalem's growth and expansion, the setting of the Youth Village has changed beyond recognition. It is today a verdant spot in a burgeoning urban environment.* Its graduate students have contributed to Israel's national life and development while retaining their interest in their alma mater, part of the Yesodot chain of five youth villages affiliated with Ha-No'ar Ha-Tzioni. Bert and I continue to visit our adopted "grandchildren" there and their dedicated staff, deriving constant satisfaction from this creative enterprise.

I can recall many interesting experiences, personal and otherwise, which fell to my lot during that year in Israel. One evening toward the end of our stay, Esther and Reuven Rubin came to see us and we were delighted to offer our congratulations on his appointment as Israel's first minister to Rumania. On another occasion, it was my privilege to address an audience of 3,000 Israeli soldiers. Although I had spoken to many Jewish servicemen over the years, both in the United States during World War II and in Europe shortly after the war, it was especially thrilling to stand before such a gathering of the IDF, our own Jewish army.

Unhappily, there were sad occasions as well. The Holocaust of European Jewry, observed annually on Yom Ha-Sho'ah, was an omnipresent factor in the life of the Medinah. Plans had been laid immediately after World War II, in London, for the establishment of the Martyrs' and Heroes' Remembrance Authority, which would perpetuate the record of Jewish persecution and mass murder during the Hitler era. Steps were then taken for such material to be collected in Germany and elsewhere and to be placed in the authority's archives. The War of Liberation temporarily brought a halt to such activities in Israel, but in 1949 the first basis was laid for Yad Vashem, a large and uniquely impressive memorial in Jerusalem, to house the .

*See also chapter 15.

35. Dedication of the Israel Goldstein Zionist Youth Village in Katamon, Jerusalem, January 23, 1950. Pictured *(left to right):* Dr. Abraham Granott, Yitzḥak Kubowitzki, Pinḥas Rosen, Ze'ev Schickler *(speaking)*, the author, Mayor Daniel Auster, and Bertha Schoolman.

36. Congregation B'nai Jeshurun's 125th Anniversary celebration, November 1950. The author accepts a scroll presented by the Rev. Dr. Everett Clinchy *(3rd from left)* on behalf of the National Conference of Christians and Jews. Also pictured: Jacob Sincoff and Charles H. Silver *(2d and 4th from left)*, Rabbi David Panitz, and Cantor Jacob Schwartz *(1st and 2d from right)*. Herbert S. Sonnenfeld photo, New York.

37. The Middlesex University campus at Waltham, Mass., prior to its acquisition by Brandeis University. Fairchild Aerial Surveys, Inc. photo, Boston, Mass.

38. With the Jews of Igni Nishnain in the Atlas Mountains, during visit to Morocco in November 1953. William Bein, the local JDC director, stands next to the author.

39. Conference on Jewish Material Claims against Germany. Negotiations on behalf of Jewish victims of the Nazis. Presidents of major American Jewish organizations visit the U.S. State Department in Washington, April 2, 1952. Pictured *(left to right)*: Frank Goldman (B'nai B'rith), Dr. Nahum Goldmann (World Jewish Congress), Jacob Blaustein (American Jewish Committee), Adolph Held (Jewish Labor Committee), and Dr. Israel Goldstein (American Jewish Congress). Nate Fine photo.

40. The Jewish Conciliation Board of America celebrates the 25th anniversary of Dr. Goldstein's presidency, New York, January 1954. U.S. Supreme Court Justice William O. Douglas addresses the gathering, which includes General David Sarnoff and Louis Richman *(2d and 3rd in front row, next to the author)*, and Dr. David W. Petegorsky *(in background, between Shad Polier and Judge Justine Wise Polier)*. Herbert S. Sonnenfeld photo, New York.

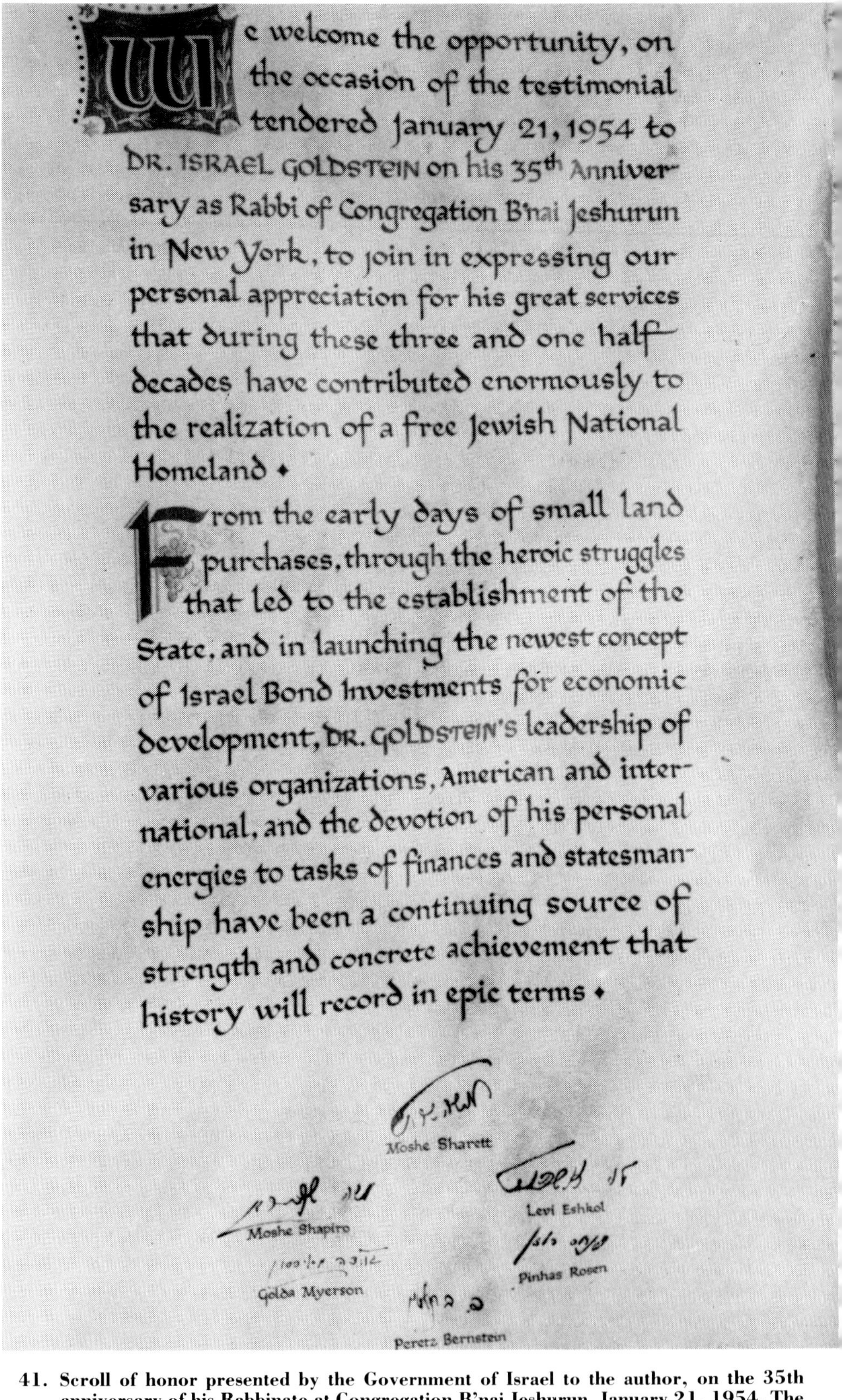

We welcome the opportunity, on the occasion of the testimonial tendered January 21, 1954 to DR. ISRAEL GOLDSTEIN on his 35th Anniversary as Rabbi of Congregation B'nai Jeshurun in New York, to join in expressing our personal appreciation for his great services that during these three and one half decades have contributed enormously to the realization of a free Jewish National Homeland ✦

From the early days of small land purchases, through the heroic struggles that led to the establishment of the State, and in launching the newest concept of Israel Bond Investments for economic development, DR. GOLDSTEIN'S leadership of various organizations, American and international, and the devotion of his personal energies to tasks of finances and statesmanship have been a continuing source of strength and concrete achievement that history will record in epic terms ✦

Moshe Sharett

Moshe Shapiro

Golda Myerson

Levi Eshkol

Pinhas Rosen

Peretz Bernstein

41. Scroll of honor presented by the Government of Israel to the author, on the 35th anniversary of his Rabbinate at Congregation B'nai Jeshurun, January 21, 1954. The signatories are headed by Israel's Prime Minister, Moshe Sharett. Hutmann-J. K. Ben-Josef photo, Jerusalem.

42. American Jewish Tercentenary, 1954. At banquet in Recife, Brazil, with Professor Gilberto Freire *(at microphone)* presiding, September 4, 1954.

43. American Jewish Tercentenary. With Dr. Jaap Meijer *(back to camera)* and other local residents in the historic 17th-century Tzedek Ve-Shalom Synagogue of Paramaribo, Surinam, September 7, 1954. Foto Ter Laag Jr., Paramaribo, Surinam.

44. American Jewish Tercentenary. Affixing memorial plaque honoring Jewish pioneers, at ruins of old synagogue of *Joden Savanne*, Surinam, September 8, 1954. Foto Ter Laag Jr., Paramaribo, Surinam.

45. American Jewish Tercentenary banquet at the Waldorf-Astoria Hotel, New York, October 20, 1954. Pictured *(left to right):* Mayor Robert F. Wagner, Judge Edgar Nathan, Jr., Joseph N. Willen, the author, Ralph E. Samuel, and President Dwight D. Eisenhower.

46. State of Israel Bonds. Shomrim Society members of the New York Police Department with the author *(3rd from right)*, Chaplain Isidor Frank *(5th from left)* and "Torch of Freedom" at the Statue of Liberty, December 1954.

47. State of Israel Bonds. Rally at Madison Square Garden, New York, May 1951. Israel's Prime Minister, David Ben-Gurion, flanked by Grover Whelan *(left)* and by Benjamin Browdy and the author *(right)*, receives a tumultuous ovation. Alexander Archer photo, New York.

48. With Authorine Lucy and Roy Wilkins, executive secretary of the National Association for the Advancement of Colored People, at a Civil Rights campaign rally in Madison Square Garden, New York, May 1956.

49. Israel's President, Itzhak Ben-Zvi, receiving the Stephen S. Wise award of the American Jewish Congress, Jerusalem, May 2, 1956. Pictured next to him are his wife, Raḥel Yannait Ben-Zvi, and the author. State of Israel photo, Government Press Division.

50. Israel Goldstein Synagogue on the Givat Ram campus of the Hebrew University in Jerusalem. General view of Synagogue. Werner Braun photo, Jerusalem.

51. Israel Goldstein Synagogue. The author, delivering his address at the dedication ceremony, August 7, 1957. Ross photo, Jerusalem.

52. Israel Goldstein Synagogue. Among those present at the dedication ceremony are: front row *(left to right)*, Bernard Cherrick, Professor Joseph Klausner, the author, President Itzḥak Ben-Zvi, Religious Affairs Minister Ḥayyim Moshe Shapira, and Mayor Gershon Agron; at end of 2d row *(extreme right)*, Edward Gelber. Ross photo, Jerusalem.

53. "Salute to Israel" in Philadelphia. With guest of honor, former President Harry S. Truman, and Herbert H. Lehman. Alexander Archer photo, New York.

54. "Salute to Israel" in Philadelphia, marking tenth anniversary of the State, April 24, 1958. Rally in Independence Square, with the author delivering an address and, seated on the dais, Governor George Leader of Pennsylvania *(extreme left)*, Israel Ambassador Abba Eban *(3rd from left)*, and Chief Justice Earl Warren *(2d from right)*. Alexander Archer photo, New York.

central archives and serve as a focus of attention in regard to everything related to the Holocaust. Yad Vashem took its name from a verse in the Book of Isaiah (56:5), which speaks of "a monument and a memorial" to be established forever in the house of the Lord, and this is precisely what the Israeli institution has endeavored to be—a center of records, research, and ceremonies on appropriate occasions. At Yad Vashem, schoolchildren, tourists, and other visitors can obtain an overwhelming impression of the catastrophe that befell the Jewish people, while receptions are held for Righteous Gentiles who saved Jews from their would-be murderers.

As treasurer of the Jewish Agency, I joined Yad Vashem's first board of directors and thus helped to plan the center, which now occupies an impressive site on the western outskirts of Israel's capital.

The death in New York of Rabbi Stephen S. Wise, on April 19, 1949, affected me deeply. We had more than one bond in common, beginning with the fact that his early rabbinical post had been at Congregation B'nai Jeshurun, from 1893 to 1900. I had often invited him to occupy my pulpit. As a younger colleague, I had shared my Jewish and American interests and commitments with him, especially in the Zionist movement. At a memorial assembly held in Jerusalem on April 24, 1949, I paid tribute to Stephen Wise as a courageous and inspiring leader of American Jewry, World Jewry, and the American Zionist movement. In the United States, he had fought corruption and reactionary social attitudes; as a spokesman for his people, he had shunned apologetics. For the most part, in both Jewish and Zionist affairs, we had been on the same side. Such a valiant warrior would be hard to replace.*

As I had anticipated before leaving New York, the balance sheet of the Jewish Agency for the period of my service reflected a considerable excess of expenditure over income.** Less than sixty percent of the year's income was derived from fund-

---

*For a more detailed appreciation of Stephen Wise, see chapter 17.
**The breakdown for the year 5709 (1948–49) was as follows:

Income	
Fund-raising campaigns abroad	IL 18,520,291
JDC grant for transportation of Olim	3,230,437
Other grants by organizations overseas	2,796,482
Realization of assets and levies	2,169,718
Loans	6,452,184
	IL 33,169,112

Expenditure	
Aliyah	IL 4,527,788 (13%)
Absorption	14,741,605 (42%)
Housing	3,132,021 (8.8%)
Youth Aliyah	3,210,551 (9%)
Agricultural settlement	7,422,166 (21%)
Education and culture	624,092 (1.8%)
Administration and miscellaneous	1,508,455 (4.4%)
	IL 35,166,678

raising campaigns abroad, almost one-fifth of the IL 33 million ($93 million) re-
ceived being made up of long-term and other loans. Expenditure amounted to some
IL 35 million ($98.5 million), of which fifty-five percent related to Aliyah and
Klitah, from the processing of immigrants abroad to their absorption in Israel.
Housing and Youth Aliyah both accounted for about nine percent of Jewish Agency
outgoings, agricultural settlement for more than twenty percent, while education
and culture (with less than two percent) received the smallest allocation. In spite of
the deficit, my colleagues and I felt that this money had been well spent. The
financial demands and pressures from all sides were enormous at a time when
Israel's population had increased by fifty percent over the May 1948 total. What
helped us to win through was the knowledge that, in bringing such vast numbers of
Olim to the Medinah, we were engaged in a vital and historic task.

My term as treasurer of the Agency expired on September 1, 1949, when I
handed over my portfolio to Yitzhak Gruenbaum, who was appointed to succeed me.
I felt grateful for the privilege of having lived and labored in Medinat Yisrael during
its first year, and especially in Jerusalem, Israel's historic capital, when almost
every day something new and significant was happening.

At a farewell reception for Bert and myself tendered by the World Confederation
of General Zionists on August 21 and attended by many of Israel's leaders, I
summed up my experience and my feelings after the many arduous months that had
preceded:

> As Treasurer of the Jewish Agency, I have had what almost amounts to an
> impossible assignment—the proper absorption of great numbers of Olim arriving
> in a country which was just emerging from its War of Liberation and struggle for
> independence. Yet that assignment had to be undertaken because of one categor-
> ical imperative, *"En Brerah,"* "No Alternative!" The economic burden of a huge
> immigration and absorption program will be felt for many years to come, but
> Israel will also reap great benefits therefrom in the spheres of agriculture, indus-
> try and defense.
>
> One sometimes hears an expression of pessimism regarding the future of our
> Medinah and suggestions that Jews abroad may in time look upon it with a degree
> of indifference. I absolutely reject such gloomy prophecies. The aura surrounding
> the fulfillment of Jewish hopes after 1,900 years of exile will not be dissipated.
> Nor will the Zionist ideal—so profoundly rooted in Jewish hearts—wane, as long
> as World Jewry is menaced by all forms of anti-Semitism and as long as Medinat
> Yisrael itself will remain conscious of its responsibility to be a light to the Jews
> and a light to the nations.
>
> *Shalom u-le-hitra'ot!* Farewell and *au revoir!* It is the earnest desire of my wife
> and myself that we will some day return to make our home among you here in
> Jerusalem.

Twelve years later, that hope was fulfilled.

7

A Jewish Window on the World: 1949–54

My return to Congregation B'nai Jeshurun in New York, after nearly a year's absence in Israel, marked the renewal of my former commitments in American Jewish life and service. They would be punctuated by other forms of service to the wider Jewish community at home and abroad. Though no longer a member of the Jewish Agency's Jerusalem Executive, I retained my seat on the American Section and continued to discharge my responsibilities as president of the World Confederation of General Zionists. It was saddening to note, upon our return to the U.S., the gap Rabbi Stephen Wise's death had left in American Jewish and Zionist affairs.

B'nai Jeshurun was the constant amidst the variables, but those variables constituted an ongoing challenge. The resumption of a familiar rabbinical routine also provided the occasion for a *ḥeshbon ha-nefesh*, personal stock-taking. On the one hand, I felt that our son and daughter had received less of my time and attention that were their due over the years. On the other hand, some congregational families must have felt the prolonged lack of their rabbi's ministrations, even if complaints never reached my ears. There was at all times a degree of competition between the congregational responsibilities of my rabbinate and the broader claims of my public career: had I been forced to choose between them, I would undoubtedly have opted for the larger sphere of activity, as my congregants perhaps realized. Nevertheless, to the best of my ability, I discharged my duties wholeheartedly, extending help and guidance to those who sought pastoral aid, while I occupied myself with the pulpit, the religious school, and the manifold organizational duties of a large and active congregation.

In time, I believe, the members of Congregation B'nai Jeshurun developed an understanding and appreciation of my outlook. Not only did they come to accept it with good grace, they also took pride in my extra-congregational involvements. Perhaps this was because I took them into my confidence and taught them to appreciate the exigencies of Jewish life the world over. At the same time, they realized that I made every effort to be with them at both congregational and family celebrations. My first reports upon returning from abroad were usually to the congregation. Indeed, it was my practice to devote a Rosh Hashanah sermon to a *tour d'horizon* of the world Jewish scene, including the achievements of Medinat Yisrael and the Zionist movement. My annual "Rabbi's Report," and the "Rabbi's Column" in *B'nai Jeshurun Topics*, the weekly newsletter dispatched to congregants, included excerpts from my sermons and from addresses delivered outside the synagogue in which I dealt with current Jewish and Zionist issues. This process had gained momentum during World War II, and large numbers of the congregational family became involved in many forms of Zionist activity.

It was, therefore, a source of particular satisfaction when, in December 1949, at the conclusion of thirty years in my ministry to the congregation, I was elected rabbi for life. There was an additional proviso that, upon my retirement, I would be designated rabbi emeritus. The sentiments expressed in that resolution were, for me, a very great reward.

Closely related to my rabbinical tasks at B'nai Jeshurun was, of course, my participation in the work of the Synagogue Council of America. On November 2, 1949, several weeks after our homecoming, I addressed its membership on "The Synagogue in Israel and in America." The date happened to coincide with Balfour Day, the thirty-second anniversary of the Balfour Declaration. Drawing comparisons and contrasts based on my recent experience of daily life in Israel, I stressed the central role of the Jewish calendar, public observance of Shabbat and *Kashrut*, and problems involving rabbinic law in the Medinah. There was no inclination to press the Synagogue-State issue at this early stage, and I foresaw a strengthening of Orthodoxy in Israel as a result of Aliyah from traditionalist Jewish communities in Muslim lands.

Many more youngsters, though fewer women, attended synagogue in Israel than in the United States—an impression I had formed after visiting many houses of worship, ranging from the colorful Oriental to the dignified and Western, such as the Yeshurun Congregation, "Ashkenazic in liturgy and Sephardic in accent, which is the nearest approximation to a Great Synagogue in Jerusalem." At times, I observed, the Israeli synagogue became the focus of national emotions, as when prisoners returned from captivity in Transjordan or when two battle-scarred Torah scrolls rescued from Kfar Etzion were escorted to the Yeshurun's *bimah* by the Chief Rabbis. Joyful dancing had followed spontaneously, I recalled, and "the synagogue that night was the expression and the possession of all the people."

As to the future, I believed that Israel's very existence guaranteed the continuity of synagogue life there, whereas in America not even the survival of the Jews as Jews could be taken for granted. As I saw it, while non-Orthodox forms of worship would develop and arouse controversy, the American brand of Reform had no prospect of gaining favor in the Jewish State. It was far more likely that synagogue centers on the Western pattern would eventually make a revitalizing contribution to religious life in Israel, and any American group sponsoring such a project would eventually build up an impressive constituency.

Finally, I alluded to fanaticism, both ultra-Orthodox (of the Neturei Karta variety) and antireligious. "The tourist coming for a brief visit," I said, "is likely to be impressed most sharply by the extremes and to complain about them." Fanatical secularists were less vocal and conspicuous in Israel than in the United States, where the Freethinkers Society of America bombarded Jews with protest literature on the eve of Yom Kippur. The founding fathers of Israel's kibbutzim had to a considerable degree been in revolt against Jewish tradition, but now their children and grandchildren were in quest of spiritual roots. With our own experience at Afikim in mind, I urged American rabbis to undertake a new form of *halutziut*—by spending their sabbatical year (or a longer period) in a kibbutz or moshav, where they would integrate themselves into the life of the settlement, win the confidence of its members, and, together with them, seek ways of shaping a congenial pattern of religious belief and observance.

Having come back to New York in time for the High Holy Day season, toward the end of September 1949, one of my first steps was to begin planning the congregation's one hundred twenty-fifth anniversary celebrations the following year. It deserved to be marked as an important milestone in the life of B'nai Jeshurun and, as had been the case twenty-five years earlier (in connection with the centenary observances), it needed to be utilized for the purpose of strengthening congregational loyalties and impressing our image upon the larger community.

Since 1925, the presidency of the congregation had been held, successively, by Charles W. Endel, Isidor S. Schweitzer, and Jacob Sincoff. They gave leadership not only to B'nai Jeshurun itself, but also to important community-wide undertakings—philanthropic, civic, and Jewish. Similar qualities were displayed by the chairman of the board, Samuel Blumberg, Vice-President Charles H. Silver (who later succeeded to the presidency), and Morris J. Bernstein, who became executive vice-president and voluntary director of B'nai Jeshurun's Community Center. Both the men's club and the sisterhood continued to flourish, as did our various youth groups.

The Community Center met a host of congregational needs—weekday services, children's services on Sabbaths, festivals, and High Holy Days, overflow services on the High Holy Days, religious instruction classes and meetings of the youth affiliates. It also accommodated wedding and Bar Mitzvah celebrations, as well as numerous social, philanthropic, and cultural groups outside the congregational umbrella. The principals of our religious school were, over the years, Goodman A. Rose, Julius Silver, Albert H. Gordon, Milton B. Perlman, Rabbi Samuel M. Segal, Israel Taslitt, Augusta Saretsky, and Dr. Herbert Greenberg.

Very helpful to me, behind the scenes, was my faithful and competent personal secretary, Mrs. Abraham Solomon, who began working with me in 1924 as Mimi Moskowitz. She continued to be helpful, after Bert and I made our Aliyah, combining devoted service with sound judgment. Miss Janet White was also of assistance to me in handling public relations for special events in the congregation and in the Jewish Conciliation Board of America.

As a result of the congregation's expanding activities, it had been deemed necessary by the board—with my full consent and appreciation—to appoint an assistant rabbi in 1946. The choice fell upon David H. Panitz, a graduate of the Jewish Theological Seminary. He and his wife, Esther, brought impressive dimensions of Hebraic and general culture to B'nai Jeshurun. Rabbi Panitz supervised the religious school and guided the youth activities, often delivered sermons, and ministered to a large number of congregational families on both joyous and sorrowful occasions. He organized the Adult Institute of Jewish Studies, established a Bar Mitzvah brotherhood and a leaders' training fellowship group, and gave valuable assistance to the men's club, sisterhood, Parents-Teachers' Association, Young People's League and Young Judea Club. His efforts gained wide recognition in Jewish and Christian circles alike.

During the period of my service in Israel, Rabbi Panitz carried the full burden of the daily ministry. Rabbi Simon Greenberg, provost of the Jewish Theological Seminary and at that time also professor of homiletics, graciously consented to deliver weekly sermons, refusing to accept any honorarium for his services. The congregation and I were deeply grateful both to Rabbi Greenberg and to Chancellor Louis Finkelstein for their important helpfulness, while I was serving in Israel. The important responsibilities Rabbi Panitz undertook at my side and the weight he shouldered during my absences were subsequently assumed by his successor, Rabbi William Berkowitz.

We continued to enjoy the inspiring cantorial art of the Reverend Jacob Schwartz, who was elected cantor emeritus on his retirement in 1951, after nearly thirty-five years of faithful and distinguished service. He died shortly thereafter. His successor, Cantor Robert H. Segal, formerly of Congregation Ohabei Shalom in Brookline, Massachusetts, had appeared in many of the *Eternal Light* programs sponsored by the Jewish Theological Seminary of America.

Having been named associate rabbi in 1949, David Panitz brought his career at B'nai Jeshurun to a climax one year later, when he collaborated with me in planning and supervising the congregation's one hundred twenty-fifth anniversary. He also edited a souvenir booklet incorporating a brief history of congregational life since its centenary in 1925.

Jacob Sincoff, president of the congregation at this time, was assuming a major role in the American Zionist leadership and in fund-raising efforts for Israel. His successor, Charles H. Silver, held important civic posts as president of New York City's Board of Education and as president of Beth Israel Hospital.

Congregation B'nai Jeshurun's one hundred twenty-fifth anniversary observances commenced at the end of October 1950 and extended over a period of two months. They were modeled on its centennial a quarter of a century earlier, and both the "mother" congregation, Shearith Israel, and the "daughter" congregation, Shaaray Tefila, participated. An exhibit of historical memorabilia was arranged, and a series of symposia on Jewish themes and an evening of liturgical music formed part of the celebrations. Educational programs organized in conjunction with these events presented, among other speakers, Rabbi Bernard J. Bamberger, Israel Chipkin, Dr. Moshe Davis, Dr. Solomon Grayzel, and Rabbi Arthur Lelyveld. Among the many other personalities of national and international repute, both Jewish and Christian, who took part in the congregation's anniversary program were Mrs. Eleanor Roosevelt; General Lucius Clay; the Reverend Dr. Everett R. Clinchy, president of the National Conference of Christians and Jews; the Honorable Oscar R. Ewing, U.S. federal security administrator; Bishop Charles K. Gilbert; Rabbi Elias L.

Solomon; Dr. Nahum Goldmann, president of the World Jewish Congress; Abba Eban, Israel's ambassador to the United States and its chief delegate to the UN; Berl Locker, chairman of the Jewish Agency Executive in Jerusalem; Senator Herbert H. Lehman; Rabbis Simon Greenberg and David de Sola Pool; Chancellor Louis Finkelstein; Robert R. Nathan; Mrs. Samuel W. (Rose) Halprin, president of Hadassah; and Mrs. Irving M. Engel, president of the National Council of Jewish Women.

Citations were presented to the congregation by the United Synagogue of America and by the National Conference of Christians and Jews. Greetings were extended by President Harry S. Truman, President Chaim Weizmann, Governor Thomas Dewey, and the Synagogue Council of America. President Truman's message was the following:

> It is a pleasure to send hearty congratulations and warmest personal greetings to Congregation B'nai Jeshurun on attaining the 125th milestone in the history of its activities.
>
> An institution which has carried on its work in the community for a full century and a quarter has thereby demonstrated abundantly the value of its mission.
>
> My anniversary message to the Congregation will be found in the word of the Lord to Micah: "And what doth the Lord require of thee, but to do justly, and to love mercy, and to walk humbly with thy God?"

Special greetings were also transmitted by Kol Zion La-Golah, Israel's overseas radio service. In New York, a program in the *Eternal Light* radio series was devoted to the occasion, and Rabbi Panitz appeared on television. A radio message I recorded was broadcast to Europe by The Voice of America.

Thus, Congregation B'nai Jeshurun's one hundred twenty-fifth anniversary celebration was a worthy sequel to its centenary observance, enhancing its already splendid reputation.

The recipient of our men's club Brotherhood Day award for 1951 was Roger W. Straus, the Jewish co-chairman of the National Conference of Christians and Jews and one of its founders. Among those who received this award over the years were Father George B. Ford, General John H. Hilldring, Paul G. Hoffman, the Reverend John Haynes Holmes, John J. McCloy, Governor Theodore R. McKeldin of Maryland, General David Sarnoff, and Walter White, executive secretary of the National Association for the Advancement of Colored People.

In June 1951, Rabbi Panitz accepted a "call" to the pulpit of Congregation Adas Israel in Washington, D.C. I had the honor of speaking at his installation there in the following November. We have remained good friends and colleagues across the years.

Much excitement was occasioned by the arrival in New York harbor of two Israeli warships, the *Haganah* and the *Misgav Yehudah*, on the first stage of a goodwill mission to the United States. Their officers and crews attended Sabbath eve services at our synagogue on May 4, 1951, and were then invited to a festive dinner we arranged in their honor at B'nai Jeshurun's Community Center.

Just over a week later, on May 12, the first U.S. ambassador to the State of Israel,

James G. McDonald, was the main speaker at our congregational observance of Israel's third Independence Day. On April 18, 1953, a Sabbath morning, the Yom Ha-Atzma'ut address was delivered by Golda Meir, Israel's Minister of Labor.

A staunch Christian friend of mine over the years was Pierre van Paassen, the internationally renowned journalist and author, who rendered important services to the Jewish people and to the cause of Zionism. An ordained minister of religion and an impassioned Christian Zionist, he accepted my invitation to speak from the pulpit of Congregation B'nai Jeshurun on several occasions.

In 1954, I published *Mourners' Devotions*, a booklet containing the afternoon and evening services, the *El Malé Rahamim* memorial prayer and an essay on "The *Kaddish:* Its Origin and Meaning." It also included a brief selection of mourning laws and customs, together with appropriate readings in English.

One melancholy event in the religious life of American Jewry was the death in 1952 of Rabbi Bernard L. Levinthal, dean of the Orthodox rabbinate in the United States. It was my sad privilege to deliver one of the eulogies at the memorial exercises in Philadelphia on October 23 of that year. As mentioned in my opening chapter, Rabbi Levinthal had been the founder of Yeshivat Mishkan Yisrael, where I studied as a boy. Of his four sons, all of whom I knew well, Israel Herbert graduated from the Jewish Theological Seminary and went on to become rabbi of the Brooklyn Jewish Center, president of the Rabbinical Assembly, and a preacher of great distinction. Louis, my classmate at the University of Pennsylvania, attained eminence as a judge in Philadelphia, as president of the ZOA, and as chairman of the board of governors of the Hebrew University.

I recalled the impression Rabbi Bernard Levinthal's scholarly discourses made upon me when he visited the Niezhiner *Shul*. He was no superficial *darshan*, but addressed himself to the mind rather than to the heart. As head of the United Orthodox Hebrew Congregations of Philadelphia, he was *Rav ha-Kolel*, all-inclusive in more than one sense. Like his famous teacher, Rabbi Isaac Elhanan Spektor of Kovno, he displayed breadth and comprehensiveness in his learning, in his outlook on Jewish problems, and in his knowledge of world affairs. He was a man of love, peace, scholarship, even temper, communal vision, wide sympathies, and practical wisdom. My father had belonged to his circle of close friends.

Strengthening Ties with Israel

The renewed involvement in congregational and Jewish communal affairs did not lessen my preoccupation with Zionist matters and the welfare of Israel. When the Jewish National Fund celebrated its fiftieth jubilee in 1951, I gladly accepted an invitation to serve as chairman of the committee that planned a program of festive events to mark the occasion throughout the United States. A more demanding new commitment, however, was the campaign for Israel Bonds.

As treasurer of the Jewish Agency, I had been only too well aware of the extent to which Israel's meager resources were drained by mass immigration, the housing crisis, food shortages, and the need to provide Olim with employment. All of these factors had vastly increased the Jewish State's burdens after a costly and prolonged War of Liberation. Moreover, once the euphoria aroused by that war and its aftermath began to decline, fund-raising campaigns for Israel also plunged downward from their 1948 peak. Early in 1950, this alarming development prompted leaders of the United Jewish Appeal to seek fresh sources of financial aid in the United States, where the loans we had obtained from Government and private agencies proved to be inadequate.

The motive forces behind this search for a new financial reservoir were Henry Montor, executive vice-chairman of the UJA, and four Israeli leaders—Prime Minister David Ben-Gurion, Finance Minister Eliezer Kaplan, Labor Minister Golda Meir, and Jewish Agency Chairman Berl Locker. At Ben-Gurion's urgent request, some fifty American Jewish notables attended a five-day conference at the King David Hotel in Jerusalem, which opened on September 3, 1950. They were a representative cross-section of the world's largest Jewish community, and the array of Israel Government and Jewish Agency leaders seated around the table was even more impressive. Teddy Kollek was one of the chief organizers of the conference. Ben-Gurion's four-point program, which the assembled delegates adopted unanimously, called for an intensified UJA campaign to underwrite immigration and absorption costs; increased loans and grants-in-aid from governmental sources abroad; private investment capital to foster Israel's economic development; and the establishment of an Israel Bonds organization as the primary instrument for raising $1.5 billion within three years from overseas investors.

The first steps toward launching an Israel Bonds drive in the United States were taken six weeks later, when Golda Meir flew to Washington in order to confer with leaders of the principal American Jewish organizations and communities. A new organizational framework then came into being, with Henry Morgenthau, Jr., as chairman of the board of governors, Rudolf G. Sonneborn as president, and Henry Montor as vice-president and executive director.

Following the passage by the Knesset of a law authorizing the flotation of Israel's first Government bonds, Ben-Gurion came to America in May 1951 for the purpose of launching the Israel Bond campaign. It was his first visit to the United States as Prime Minister and scenes of mass enthusiasm awaited him. In New York, two million people greeted Ben-Gurion with a ticker-tape parade along Broadway, and a capacity audience of 20,000 packed Madison Square Garden for the inaugural Israel Bond rally. Such demonstrations of mass support for Israel also accompanied his coast-to-coast tour of the major American cities. As a direct result of this visit, sales of Israel Bonds totalled $52 million in the opening year.

It was my privilege to serve as chairman of the executive committee for Israel Bonds in New York, where my wife became chairman of the women's division. On June 13, 1951, a dinner in support of the campaign was held at B'nai Jeshurun's Community Center, under the chairmanship of Jacob Sincoff, and bonds to the value of more than one million dollars were purchased. Subsequently, Madison Square Garden was the venue for annual Israel Bond rallies during the Ḥanukkah festival, and for "City of the Ages," a pageant sponsored by State of Israel Bonds in celebration of Jerusalem's three thousandth anniversary, on the evening of October 20, 1953.

Rabbi Abba Hillel Silver was appointed to succeed Henry Morgenthau, Jr., as chairman of the board of governors in 1955, when Abraham Feinberg became president and Dr. Joseph J. Schwartz took over Henry Montor's responsibilities. Louis H. Boyar, who headed Israel Bonds after the death of Rabbi Silver in 1963, was later succeeded by Samuel Rothberg, a founder member of the organization, who had served as national campaign chairman from 1955.

By 1970, some two million people, including non-Jewish friends of Israel, had purchased bonds in well over thirty different countries, eighty-five percent of the total having been sold in the United States. Thanks to this investment scheme, large-scale development had been made possible in Israel's agriculture and industry, housing program, tourist sector and in the exploitation of the country's natural resources. On the thirtieth anniversary of the establishment of State of Israel Bonds, the sum of $57.5 million was realized at a dinner in New York—the largest amount ever to be raised by a Jewish organization anywhere in the world at a single function.

By August 1981, cash receipts from the Israel Bond drive had amounted to more than $5 billion, a truly staggering figure. Every bond presented for redemption has been paid in full, with interest.

I take pride in the fact that it fell to my lot to have had a share in this activity, which has brought such great benefits to Medinat Yisrael. While the United Jewish Appeal for outright gifts continued as the principal fund-raising instrument providing for the needs of immigration, absorption, and agricultural settlement in Israel through the Jewish Agency, the Israel Bond campaigns were an important additional source of revenue for Israel's development program.

Many Jewish leaders have been involved in both.

During the early 1950s, as mentioned in my previous chapter, *Hafradah*—the division of functions between the Zionist movement and the Government of Israel—was the subject of discussions and debates at meetings of the Zionist General Council and in other forums. A closely related issue was the whole question of Zionist ideology after the establishment of the State. Many of us rejected Ben-Gurion's occasional derogation of the Zionist movement, believing that Zionists and a strong Zionist movement were needed to defend Israel's position abroad, to foster Aliyah, Jewish education, and Hebrew culture, and to help safeguard meaningful Jewish survival in the Diaspora.

Soon after my return to New York, the American Section of the Jewish Agency Executive set up the Committee on Zionist Problems, which I headed, for the purpose of clarifying basic proposals to be discussed at the forthcoming Zionist Congress. Maurice M. Boukstein, legal adviser to the Jewish Agency in New York, drew up a preliminary memorandum on the status of the Agency. Although our proposals for a reformulated Zionist program, submitted to the Jewish Agency Executive in January 1950, had no binding force, they did constitute the first attempt to clarify and, if possible, to find a solution for problems confronting the World Zionist Organization. In 1952, Maurice Boukstein negotiated with Prime Minister Ben-Gurion the legal basis for the WZO-Jewish Agency "Status Law" passed by the Knesset. He also drafted the agreement that resulted in the reconstitution of the Jewish Agency for Israel in 1971.

The 23rd Zionist Congress, held in Jerusalem during the second half of August 1951, was the first to have the capital of the independent Jewish State as its setting. For many of the delegates who had never previously been in Israel, it was a thrilling and inspiring occasion. Here, at last, they could rejoice over the achievements of the Medinah and, at the same time, learn at first hand about its current problems. The central issue before this Congress was, of course, the status and function of the Zionist movement. What emerged from the debates was the (first) Jerusalem Program, to which I have previously referred.

In the course of my address, on August 15, as chairman of the World Confederation of General Zionists, I emphasized American Jewry's undiminished moral and material support for Israel and the continued validity of a strong and influential Zionist movement in the Diaspora. I thought it regrettable that this historic Congress should have aroused only moderate interest in Israel itself, and attributed this to the Israel Government's own studied indifference. I also expressed firm disagreement with those who were advocating the abolition of Zionist parties in the *Golah*. "It is," I said, "legitimate for Jews in the Diaspora to wish for Israel to be built on the kind of pattern which appeals to them, yet not to interfere in the internal politics of Israel. No one questions the right of Socialists in France, for example, to support their fellow Socialists in England."

Well over a year later, I was in Israel again for a meeting of the Actions Committee and for a study of the latest developments there. An atmosphere of mourning and solemnity hung over the land, as Dr. Chaim Weizmann, Israel's first President, had died at his home in Reḥovot while I was on my way from New York. Our plane arrived in time for me to attend the funeral on November 11, 1952.

My thoughts aboard the aircraft were naturally dominated by this uniquely sorrowful event. It marked the end of an era, which had begun five and a half decades earlier with the dramatic impact of Theodor Herzl's *Jewish State*. Whereas, however, Herzl rose from the outer fringe of his people to become enshrined in the hearts and minds of Jewry, Weizmann came to the forefront of Jewish leadership from the heartland of Eastern European traditional life. His career was three-dimensional, embracing Zionism, science, and statesmanship, and he was accepted as the *Resh Galuta*, the exilarch of his time. In securing the Balfour Declaration from Great Britain, he brought the fulfillment of the Zionist dream an important step forward. Trial and error were no less characteristic of his political approach than of his technique in the laboratory. For Chaim Weizmann, it was always a question of timing. The patience and moderation that often caused many of us to become restive had undeniable and enduring results in the Hebrew University, the Keren Hayesod, and the enlarged Jewish Agency, all of which he fathered.

Although I had not always followed Weizmann, making no secret of my disagreements with him, I had acknowledged his greatness, his total dedication to the Jewish people, his unfaltering Zionist commitment, and his unexcelled place in modern Jewish history. Our personal relationship was never affected by political differences. In a letter of congratulations I wrote to him on May 18, 1948, following his election as provisional head of the new State, I said:

> No honor has ever come more appropriately to any man. . . . Your Presidency is both a symbol and a signal—a symbol of Jewish faith which surmounts all obstacles, and a signal that the Jewish Republic of Israel will be a beacon of enlightenment, liberalism, humanity and goodwill.

Like Balfour, Lloyd George, Woodrow Wilson, Roosevelt, Smuts, and Churchill, Weizmann was a statesman in the grand manner. All of these giants had wedded national and international vision, combining charm, culture, determination, and a conservative temperament with intellectual and spiritual power, liberalism in social matters, and qualities that inspired popular confidence and loyalty. What George Washington had been to the United States, Chaim Weizmann was to Israel—the father of his country.

During the flight from New York, I sat next to Meyer Weisgal, Weizmann's longtime friend and aide. I happened to remark that Israel's first President would presumably be buried on Mount Herzl, in Jerusalem. Weisgal then told me that this was not part of the official plan. A couple of years earlier, Weizmann had stood on the balcony of his Reḥovot home and, looking over the vista of orange groves set against the hills and valleys of Ephraim beyond, he had pointed to a spot in his garden and said, "Here is where I want to lie."

We arrived in Reḥovot early in the morning, some hours before the burial service was scheduled to take place. Thousands of people, young and old, continued to file past the flag-bedecked coffin, as they had been doing for the previous forty-eight hours. During that time, more than a quarter of a million men, women, and children came to attest their love and their sense of grief. It was a moving and impressive spectacle.

As I walked with Rose Halprin and Zalman Shazar in the funeral cortege, Shazar disclosed that Weizmann, in one of the deliriums of his last days, had cried, "Pack my bags! I have to go to America to raise money."

The funeral was a simple one, and no eulogies were pronounced. The coffin was of plain black wood, draped with the flag of Israel and a *tallit*. The Ashkenazi Chief Rabbi, Dr. Isaac Halevi Herzog, intoned a prayer and the Sephardi Chief Rabbi, Ben-Zion Uziel, recited *Kaddish*. Together with my fellow members of the Jewish Agency Executive, I stood at the graveside as earth was deposited on the lowered coffin by the chief mourners—Vera Weizmann, the President's widow; their son, Benjamin; Weizmann's surviving brothers and sisters; Simon and Miriam Marks; Prime Minister David Ben-Gurion; and Knesset Speaker Yosef Sprinzak. It was as if the eyes of the world were focused on that spot.

Only the military personnel gathered there seemed out of keeping with Weizmann's pacifist character. The twenty-one-gun salute fired at the end also struck me as somewhat incongruous. Yet, on further reflection, it had to be admitted that such honors were being accorded not to an individual, but to the first President of the Jewish State.

Proceeding to Jerusalem, I derived much satisfaction from the sessions of the Zionist General Council, the best I had attended in recent years. No ideological wrangling marred the fortnight of deliberations. Practical matters figured high on the agenda. A $120 million budget was under discussion, the largest so far in the Zionist movement's history, and an unprecedented fifty percent of this was earmarked for agricultural settlement. The *ma'abarot*, those grim transit camps, were on the point of liquidation. Some Olim from Oriental countries who had at first gravitated to the cities were now thinking seriously of moving to rural areas. A third encouraging development was a drop in the rate of emigration, which had reached four percent of the influx but had begun to decline. There was also evidence of a growing recognition that middle-class settlement should be encouraged, and an increasing awareness that importance needed to be attached to Aliyah from English-speaking countries, which would bring immigrants with technical and professional skills to the Medinah.

All in all, I found much to inspire hope and confidence as Israel's fifth Independence Day drew near. My tour of the country was enough to arouse fresh enthusiasm. From the new land wrested from the Huleh marshes and the port development in Haifa to the tapping of mineral deposits in the Negev and the new ports taking shape at Ashdod and Eilat, it was clear that Israel was growing sturdily and that exports would some day contribute to a vibrant national economy. The struggling little State was on its way to economic viability.

Broader Jewish Responsibilities

Side by side with my Zionist and pro-Israel activities, other kindred national and international Jewish commitments claimed me during the early 1950s. According to a much-quoted rabbinic maxim, *Kol Yisrael arevim zeh ba-zeh*—"All Jews are sureties for one another" (*Shevu'ot* 39a). That fundamental premise, which underlay Jewish national existence and survival down the ages, had also inspired the creation of a new and representative international body, the World Jewish Congress, in 1936.

Its origins went back to the Comité des Délégations Juives, established in 1919 to safeguard Jewish rights after World War I and to speak for the Jewish people before the League of Nations at Versailles. In its present form, however, the World Jewish Congress emerged from an assembly of 280 delegates representing Jews in thirty-two different countries, which was convened in Geneva by Rabbi Stephen Wise and Dr. Nahum Goldmann. Rabbi Wise served as president of the WJC from 1936 until his death thirteen years later, in 1949, when Dr. Goldmann took over as acting president, after having functioned as chairman of its Executive Committee.

At the time of its establishment, the World Jewish Congress was an energetic response to the menace of Hitlerism. It set about mobilizing the Jewish people and organizing its defenses, protests, and anti-Nazi measures, often in the face of hesitation and fearfulness on the part of some prominent Jewish bodies. Its warnings that Nazism threatened not only Jews but Christendom, democracy, and civilization itself were unfortunately, for the most part, unheeded.

Through its affiliated Jewish communities and major representative bodies in sixty-five countries, and because of the place it occupied after World War II among nongovernmental organizations under the aegis of the United Nations, the WJC has assumed a unique role in world Jewish affairs. It was active in rescue operations during the last stages of the Nazi Holocaust, and its fund of expert opinion and war-crimes documentation provided noteworthy data and testimony for the Nuremberg Trials. Since then, World Jewish Congress efforts have been directed toward relief and rehabilitation programs for Jewish refugees, the indemnification of Jews victimized by the Nazis, the reconstruction of Jewish communal life in Europe, and the fight against neo-Nazi manifestations and anti-Semitism. The WJC also developed relations with non-Jewish (mainly Christian) bodies, and has come to the support of endangered Jewish communities in the Arab world and the Communist bloc, often intervening successfully with governments when such Jews faced abuse or discrimination. At all times, the WJC has rejected the "colonial" approach displayed by some organizations that felt obligated to watch paternalistically over the interests of small and weak Jewish communities in the Diaspora.

From the very beginning, complete support was given by the World Jewish Congress to the Zionist struggle for a Jewish commonwealth in Eretz Yisrael. Such a commonwealth was regarded as an instrument for the solution of perennial Jewish homelessness, as well as a means for stimulating a Jewish cultural renascence in the Diaspora. Founded on the concept of the unity of the Jewish people, the WJC has extended the fullest moral support to Israel, believing that Israel and Diaspora Jewry need one another in the interests of Jewish physical and cultural survival.

The World Jewish Congress arranges periodical plenary assemblies, vested with overall authoritative powers, and administers its affairs through four bureaus—in North America, Latin America, Europe, and Israel. A research division, the Institute of Jewish Affairs, operates in London.

Soon after my return to New York in 1949, Dr. Nahum Goldmann, then acting president of the WJC, invited me to assume the chairmanship of its Western Hemisphere Executive, and I accepted. One of our tasks was to keep a watchful eye on some of the Latin American countries, where internal political conflicts were mounting, and to guard against the dangers posed by reactionary elements which, in the name of national security, sought to impose regimentation, to suppress basic liberties, and to arouse suspicion and hostility toward persons of foreign birth.

In December 1951, I paid a week-long visit to Great Britain in my capacity of chairman of the Western Hemisphere Executive, in order to address a series of meetings in London and the provinces. Hosting my tour was the British Section of the World Jewish Congress, headed by Eva, Marchioness of Reading. She presided at the fifteenth anniversary conference of the British Section, which took place on December 8. The speakers included a distinguished Anglo-Jewish spiritual leader, the Reverend Dr. Abraham Cohen of Birmingham's Singers Hill congregation, who held office as president of the Board of Deputies of British Jews and as vice-president of the WJC's British Section.

My address dealt, *inter alia*, with the question of German reparations and the resurgence of neo-Nazism. I urged that Jewish citizens of Great Britain and the United States request their respective governments to encourage West Germany to make full and proper settlement with Israel and with Jewish victims of the Nazis. I spoke of the neo-Nazi danger then threatening Jews in Argentina and other parts of Latin America, where Hitlerite literature was being disseminated on a vast scale. Alluding to the role of the World Jewish Congress at the time, I went on to say:

> What do we have to offer?—A sense of Jewish brotherhood, a belief in the equality and status of all Jewish communities, an affirmation of that Jewish dignity which comes from cooperative efforts by all Jewish communities in the service of great Jewish causes.
>
> We have to cope with Nazi propaganda in Latin American countries, often in cooperation with Arab communities and pro-Arab groups there. There are occasional attacks on the status and economic position of Jewish communities. . . .
>
> The position of Jews in the Diaspora depends to a large degree on the success or failure of the State of Israel. Hence, the central task of every Jewish generation is to build up Medinat Yisrael for the common good of the Jewish people. It is no use creating a psychology of fear and flight among Jews, but even the best *Galut* remains *Galut*.

Subsequently, at a press conference arranged at Grosvenor House, I dwelt on the efforts made by West Germany's Chancellor, Konrad Adenauer, to make amends to the Jewish people. Whatever reparations might be paid out by the German Government, I said, would not, however, diminish the German people's responsibility for the horrors perpetrated by the Nazis. They would merely serve to restore, in part, what had been plundered from millions of Jews during the Hitler era. I also pointed out that the American Jewish community was eager that there should be close cooperation between the United States and Great Britain in safeguarding peace in the Middle East, since the security of that area was vital to the peace of the world. American Jews, I said, viewed with alarm any shipment of military hardware to the Arab states, which were exploiting anti-Israel feeling among the Arab masses in order to divert attention from their economic misery and exploitation.

While in London, I had a number of meetings with Jewish and non-Jewish personalities, including the Marquess of Reading, Undersecretary of State for Foreign Affairs, Viscount and Lady Samuel, Professor Selig Brodetsky, Chief Rabbi Israel Brodie, Isaac Wolfson, and Sir Herbert Emerson, the UN High Commissioner for Refugees. Chancellor Adenauer had held a press conference at the Dorchester Hotel a day after mine, and Lord Reading was impressed by his evident sincerity. I told him about American Jewish representations to the U.S. State Department about German reparations to the Jewish people.

Isaac Wolfson outlined to me his plan for a "cathedral synagogue" in Jerusalem, which would cost an estimated £2 million sterling; apart from his own contribution, he intended raising money from wealthy friends in various parts of the world. It eventually took shape as Hechal Shlomo, the center of Israel's Chief Rabbinate. Work on the Jerusalem Great Synagogue began only about three decades later; it was completed in 1982.

From London, I set out on a visit to the major provincial Jewish communities of Manchester, Liverpool, and Glasgow, where I spoke mainly of World Jewish Congress activities. On my return to the British capital, I paid a courtesy call on Israel Ambassador Eliahu Elath and his wife, whom we had known well in New York during the years of Zionist political struggle for a Jewish State, when Elath (then known to us as Eliahu Epstein) had served as the political representative of the Jewish Agency.

My final engagement before returning to the United States was a dinner, held at the Savoy Hotel on December 13, to celebrate the fifteenth anniversary of the British Section of the WJC. Addresses were delivered by the Marquess of Reading and Herbert Morrison, M.P., Britain's previous Foreign Secretary. In my address, I described what the World Jewish Congress meant to American Jewry and the importance of its work at the UN and in various parts of the world.

There seemed to be a general appreciation of the fact that, with the lessening of British influence, American Jewry would assume the leading role in Diaspora Jewish affairs.

Through my association with the World Jewish Congress, I came closer to the American Jewish Congress. The origins of the American Jewish Congress dated back to the end of World War I and, like the WJC, it owed its establishment to the farsighted leadership of Rabbi Stephen Wise. During the 1930s, the American Jewish Congress played a valiant part in the fight against Nazism and in aid programs for Jewish refugees. It mobilized public opinion, helped to organize a boycott of German goods, and had also been a leading force in the establishment of the World Jewish Congress, for similar aims and purposes on an international scale.

In January 1952, I was elected president of the American Jewish Congress, succeeding Rabbi Irving Miller, who went on to head the ZOA. My Jewish service hitherto had been of a predominantly Zionist nature. As an American Jew, I felt an obligation to become more involved in Jewish and general matters affecting the American scene. In 1953, I was elected for a second term. Three years later, in 1956, my acceptance of a third term as president required an amendment to the constitution, which had limited the holding of that office to two terms only. My responsibilities in the American Jewish Congress also meant a deeper involvement in the affairs of the World Jewish Congress, since the former body was the latter organization's principal constituency.

At the time of my first election to the presidency, in 1952, the other leading figures in the American Jewish Congress were Shad Polier, chairman of the Executive Committee; Rabbi Morton M. Berman of Temple Isaiah Israel in Chicago, chairman of the Administrative Committee; and Justine Wise Polier, chairman of the Women's Division. Dr. David W. Petegorsky served as executive director and Rabbi Isaac Toubin as associate executive director.

Dr. Petegorsky, an ordained rabbi, was widely acknowledged as the most penetrating and constructive mind in American Jewish public service. After a brilliant academic career at Yeshiva University in New York and at the London School of Economics, he taught for some time at Antioch College in Ohio and entered Canadian Government service. In 1942, he became Dr. Emanuel Neumann's assistant in the American Zionist Emergency Council. He made his reputation as an outstanding executive in the American Jewish Congress, which he joined in 1945, at the instance of Rabbi Stephen Wise. Petegorsky's colleagues admired his intellect, his Jewish learning, political acumen, and broad humanity, his impatience with all forms of social injustice, and his literary and oratorical gifts. It was in no small measure because of his influence that the American Jewish Congress embarked on a postwar campaign of social liberalism and enlightenment, vigorously countering racism, religious bigotry, and every kind of discrimination, while it championed civil rights and liberties for Americans of every creed and color.

Deeply involved in the promotion of Jewish culture and Jewish spiritual values, David Petegorsky was totally dedicated to the cause of the Jewish people and to the welfare of Israel. His untimely death in July 1956, at the age of forty-one, was a severe blow to all of us. At the request of his wife, Carol, who was herself actively involved in Jewish social service, I had the sad privilege of delivering the eulogy at his funeral.

The growing menace of neo-Nazism, to which I had drawn attention during my visit to Great Britain in December 1951, became especially oppressive in the course of the months that followed. On June 19, 1952, as president of the American Jewish Congress, I submitted a formal statement to the Foreign Relations Committee of the U.S. Senate, warning that unconditional acceptance of "the new Germany" within the Western democratic community must result in disaster unless strict controls would be established to curb resurgent Nazi tendencies in the Federal German Republic. Our statement contended that the occupying Allied Powers had set a bad example by their halfhearted pursuit and prosecution of Nazi war criminals. This had made it possible for many Germans to condemn the Nuremberg War Trials as "judicial crimes perpetrated by the victors against the vanquished." Not only had various ultranationalist, Nazi-type movements begun to spring up once more on German ground, but a situation had arisen where some eighty-five percent of key officials in the West German Foreign Office had Nazi records—an even higher proportion than obtained in the Hitler period. The conclusion of our statement was that "reeducation" in West Germany had been a total failure and that no one need be surprised to discover anti-Semitism clothed in respectability over there.

Two complementary, sometimes competitive strands of concern and commitment—Jewish and civic—agitated the American Jewish Congress. On the civic and political side, concern for the rights of the Black population was a major preoccupation, and the *amicus curiae* briefs over which Leo Pfeffer and Will Maslow maintained effective vigilance were of great importance. On the other side, where stress was laid on Jewish values and the centrality of Jewish education, rabbis such as Dr. Joachim Prinz made a vital contribution, although a few eminent laymen, such as Professor Horace M. Kallen, also played a significant part. I naturally tended to lean heavily in that direction.

During my six years as president of both the American Jewish Congress and the Western Hemisphere Executive of the World Jewish Congress, one of my principal objectives was to help develop a better organized American Jewish community and to link it organically with the world Jewish community. It seemed anomalous that other and smaller *kehillot*, such as British Jewry, should have been able to achieve a modicum of central organization, whereas in the United States attempts in that direction, such as the recently defunct American Jewish Conference, had been abortive. The best we American Jews had managed to do was to bring together our leading organizations on a purely *ad hoc* basis, whenever some emergency situation arose. Except for such sporadic efforts, it had been a monotonous story of duplication, confusion, and waste of valuable energy. The nearest approximation to a central Jewish body was the National (Jewish) Community Relations Advisory Council, organized in 1948, of which the American Jewish Congress was a leading constituent.

As president of the Congress, I was associated with those who, during the years 1950–54, fought Senator Joseph R. McCarthy's assault on American liberalism. Under the cloak of an anti-Communist crusade, McCarthy and his aides created an atmosphere of hysteria in the United States, utilizing smear tactics in their "witch hunt" against writers, artists, intellectuals, movie stars, and others holding even moderately advanced political and socioeconomic views. I had the honor to appear on McCarthy's list of "dangerous radicals," and was one of the 120 prominent Americans who issued a public statement denouncing the wholesale vilification of U.S. citizens who opposed him. Among the signatories, incidentally, was a leading Hollywood actor of the time named Ronald Reagan. The American Jewish Congress was in the vanguard of liberal resistance to McCarthyism, which the U.S. Senate— to its lasting credit—finally consigned to oblivion.

Similarly, we were in the forefront of the struggle against the McCarran-Walter "omnibus" immigration bills in 1952. These bills, presented simultaneously in the Senate and the House of Representatives, were based on a national-origins quota system that was undisguisedly racist in character, discriminating against Eastern Europeans, Asiatics, Blacks, and, in fact, anyone whose origin was other than "Nordic." As an editorial in the March 12, 1952, issue of *The Washington Post* observed, such harsh measures disfavored the victims of political or racial persecution, permitted summary deportation and denaturalization in certain cases, and barred access to a land that, culturally and spiritually as well as physically, had been built upon the flow of immigrants to its shores. What was needed, according to the *Post*, was "a selective immigration policy welcoming the best of alien applicants." The American Jewish Congress joined a dozen other religious, civic, and veterans' organizations in opposing the McCarran-Walter bills, which masqueraded as liberal legislation. Congressman Francis E. Walter of Pennsylvania, one of the two principal sponsors of the Immigration and Naturalization Act, had no hesitation in declaring that the American Jewish Congress and its president were among his first adversaries.

At about this time, I secured an interview with President Dwight D. Eisenhower and indicated our concern over the bills submitted to both Houses of Congress. After listing their many objectionable features, I pointed out one astonishing anomaly. Whereas, according to the proposed legislation, entry to the United States would be denied to persons "who have been convicted by Communist governments of violating Communist laws," the "Nordic" loophole would allow Nazis and Fascists into the United States. Indeed, certain U.S. Government agencies subsequently turned a blind eye to the Nazi record of many European immigrants and permitted them to become naturalized citizens, as a team of investigators was to discover nearly thirty years later. The battle ended in defeat for opponents of the McCarran-Walter Act, but for the first time Americans were made aware of the yawning gap between their country's democratic ideals and its immigration practices.

We also took a firm stand against attempts to break down the traditional American separation between Church and State through placing religious instruction on the syllabus of public schools, the denial of unemployment insurance benefits to Jewish Sabbath observers, and similar measures. In the field of civil rights, we were prominently involved in antidiscriminatory activities regarding education, employment, and housing. Our efforts were directed toward guaranteeing the Black American equality in law and in fact. The American Jewish Congress gave important assistance to the National Association for the Advancement of Colored People in its legal battles to outlaw all forms of segregation, and in other assaults on the strongholds of prejudice. Our program was thus dictated by a belief in social justice, not only for our fellow Jews but for all members of American society.

Another major involvement of the American Jewish Congress was in the consolidation of the State of Israel, keeping it strong and viable through the mobilization of economic and moral support from Jews and non-Jews in the United States. We worked hard to counter Arab propaganda and to expose Arab blackmail tactics directed against Jews in America and elsewhere. Such often little-known forms of discrimination included the systematic boycott of Jewish business firms and other companies trading with Israel, the denial to Jews of travel visas for Arab countries, the exclusion of American Jewish personnel from the U.S. base in Saudi Arabia, and the dissemination of anti-Jewish hate literature by Arab diplomats and "students" working in collaboration with American Nazis and other professional anti-Semites.

On the occasion of my previously mentioned interview with President Eisenhower, I alluded to these worrying developments and urged that the U.S. Administration extend a generous aid program to Israel. While expressing a warm interest in its welfare, the President seemed largely unaware of the Arab policies and maneuvers, aimed against Israel's very existence. Anyone reading newspaper reports at the time would have been aware that the future Egyptian dictator, Gamal

Abdul Nasser, was a sabre-rattler and that *fedayeen* terrorists were making regular incursions into Israeli territory. President Eisenhower appeared to be ill-informed about the Middle East situation. It had long been apparent that Eisenhower's general inclination was to let the U.S. State Department proceed with the formulation and conduct of foreign policy, with minimal interference by the White House.

As early as 1953, it was evident to representative American Jewish bodies, and to their listening posts in Washington, that Secretary of State John Foster Dulles and his top aides were the ones who determined U.S. foreign policy. When matters came to a head three years later in Operation Kadesh, the Sinai Campaign of 1956, the intemperate American attitude toward Israel's defensive war against Egypt was dictated by Dulles, not Eisenhower.

Compensating Hitler's Victims

A historic task in which the World Jewish Congress played a leading role during the 1950s was the securing of reparations and restitution payments from the Federal German Republic to compensate Jewish victims of the Hitler regime. Dr. Nahum Goldmann, president of the WJC, was and remained the moving spirit in that great undertaking, through which the Jewish people secured a degree of material recompense from the nation at whose hands incalculable death, destruction, and despoliation had been suffered.

Thanks largely to Dr. Goldmann's stature and skill, negotiations with the German Chancellor, Dr. Konrad Adenauer, and his aides resulted in large sums being made available to Israel, to Jewish communities in the Diaspora, and to tens of thousands of Jews who had either fled from Nazi Germany or had survived the European Holocaust. For the millions who perished, there could be no compensation. For the survivors, however, a modicum of financial reparations was achieved. The text one often heard invoked at this time was, "Hast thou killed, and also taken possession?" (I Kings 21:19).

The achievement was not that of any one man or organization, as much useful spadework had been done by various people ever since the end of World War II. Jewish policy regarding both individual and collective compensation had, in fact, been adumbrated even before the defeat of the Third Reich. At the height of the war, together with other Allied nations, the United States had asserted the right to declare invalid all transfers of property in enemy-controlled areas. In line with this declaration, and with a Joint Chiefs of Staff directive, the newly appointed U.S. military governor, General Lucius D. Clay, gave priority to the task of securing a restitution law for the U.S. zone of occupation. He envisaged a comprehensive piece of legislation that would restore to those victimized by racial, religious, or political persecution the property confiscated from them (in the German *Länder* comprising the U.S. zone) or which had been transferred under duress. The property belonging to those who had died without heirs would be turned over to successor organizations representative of the former owners, for the relief, rehabilitation, and resettlement of surviving members of those persons' groups. Before very long, however, General

Clay realized that there was no likelihood of such a law (embodying the minimal provisions he felt it should contain) being enacted by the German authorities, and he therefore decided to promulgate such a law of restitution in his capacity as military governor.

In practice, unfortunately, legislation of this kind fell short of the mark because most of the looted property—and the plunderers—could not easily be traced. Credit was nevertheless due to the U.S. authorities, notably General Clay and High Commissioner John J. McCloy, for their sympathetic handling of the problem. Despite certain limitations, the law promulgated by the military governor was a shining example that the British and French authorities in their zones of occupation eventually decided to emulate. The Russians, however, steadfastly refused to acknowledge either individual or collective Jewish demands for restitution.

On March 31, 1946, under the provisions of the American law, the Jewish Restitution Successor Organization (JRSO) was designated as legally entitled to heirless and unclaimed Jewish property in the U.S. zone of occupation. That same year, the JRSO was incorporated under the New York State Membership Corporation Law, the incorporators being a number of Jewish organizations headed by the American Jewish Conference, the Jewish Agency, the Joint Distribution Committee, and the World Jewish Congress, together with the Board of Deputies of British Jews. By virtue of their importance, the Jewish Agency and the JDC nominated one representative each who alternated annually as president and chairman of the executive committee of the JRSO. Monroe Goldwater of the JDC and I served in these capacities. Property worth close to $250 million in the U.S. zone alone was restored to its former owners, and an additional $25 million in heirless assets proved recoverable. The proceeds were used for the relief of Holocaust survivors in Israel and to aid distressed Jews still living in Germany. Many Jewish cultural treasures—Torah scrolls, books, objets d'art, and ritual items—were also rescued and distributed to Jewish communities in various parts of the world.

Benjamin B. Ferencz, a New York lawyer who had been an adviser in the U.S. War Crimes Commission at the Nuremberg Trials, served ably as director-general of the Jewish Restitution Successor Organization. The JRSO's headquarters were established in Nuremberg toward the end of 1948. Two others associated with the JRSO at this early stage were Saul Kagan of New York and Salomon Adler-Rudel, a onetime director of the Berlin Jewish community's welfare department, who headed the Jewish Agency's international relations division. Adler-Rudel had worked with the International Refugee Organization (IRO) with regard to Jewish DPs, and he later directed the Leo Baeck Institute in Jerusalem. From 1950, Maurice M. Boukstein, the Jewish Agency's legal adviser in New York, served as an additional representative of the Agency in the JRSO, which influenced and guided the establishment of similar bodies in the British and French zones of Germany.

Despite the JRSO's successful operation, involving the return of identifiable property, the vast majority of Jews who had suffered under the Nazis still had no way of receiving compensation. Within five years of its defeat, moreover, West Germany was benefiting from an "economic miracle" while former Jewish DPs—

dispossessed, needy, and often permanently disabled—struggled to make a living in Israel's towns and rural settlements, and in other countries. Clearly, the time had come for some broader, more comprehensive legislation that would indemnify all persons entitled to redress.

The idea of negotiating directly with the Federal German Republic was first broached by Dr. Noah Barou, a Labor Zionist leader in Great Britain who had been one of the founders of the World Jewish Congress. The contacts he established with West German diplomats in London prepared the ground for subsequent negotiations aimed at what Dr. Nahum Goldmann considered "a more realistic approach." Even then, however, very few Jews were prepared for talks of any kind with a German Government; to overcome that psychological barrier required a great deal of agonized reconsideration.

Meanwhile, Israel pursued matters with the Allied Powers only. On March 12, 1951, Foreign Minister Moshe Sharett informed them of a Jewish claim for global compensation amounting to $1.5 billion, which the Germans would be asked to pay to the State of Israel in respect of rehabilitation programs for half a million Jewish refugees from Europe, at a per capita cost of $3,000. Two-thirds of this sum would be claimed from the Federal German Republic (West Germany) and the remaining third from the (Communist) German Democratic Republic. As chairman of the Jewish Agency, Nahum Goldmann was asked to set up a new body, representative of the world's leading Jewish organizations, to support Israel's demands. These may have had a tenuous legal basis, since no Jewish State had existed during the Hitler era, but the moral case was undeniable.

As a result of Dr. Barou's efforts, preliminary discussions took place confidentially with Herbert Blankenhorn of the West German Foreign Ministry, and their initial outcome was encouraging. On September 27, 1951, Chancellor Adenauer informed the Bundestag that his Government was ready to provide compensation for victims of the Nazis and to negotiate with Israel and representatives of Diaspora Jewry. Dr. Adenauer solemnly acknowledged that "unspeakable crimes were perpetrated in the name of the German people which impose upon them the obligation to make moral and material amends."

Immediately after this announcement, Dr. Nahum Goldmann convened a meeting of twenty-three major Jewish organizations in New York. From this assembly, on October 25, 1951, the Conference on Jewish Material Claims against Germany was to emerge, headed by an executive committee with Goldmann as its chairman. The countries represented included the United States, Israel, Great Britain, France, Argentina, Canada, South Africa, and West Germany itself. As president of the American Jewish Congress and of the Western Hemisphere Executive of the WJC, I was invited to join a five-man presidium comprising, apart from Nahum Goldmann and myself, Jacob Blaustein, president of the American Jewish Committee, Frank Goldman, president of the B'nai B'rith, and Adolph Held, chairman of the Jewish Labor Committee. Our function was mainly to provide advice and guidance, during the negotiations with the West German Government, in regard to claims submitted by individual victims of the Nazis and by Jewish communities outside of Israel.

Moses A. Leavitt, executive vice-president of the American Jewish Joint Distribution Committee, was one of our principal negotiators. Maurice M. Boukstein served ably as legal adviser to the Claims Conference, while Saul Kagan, its first executive director, continued in that position for eleven years and served thereafter as treasurer. My term as one of the vice-presidents continued until 1969.

Israel appointed its own team of negotiators, headed by Dr. Giora Josephthal, the treasurer of the Jewish Agency, and Dr. Felix E. Shinnar. Nahum Goldmann was, however, empowered to act also for the Israel Government. On December 6, he had a fruitful and moving interview with Chancellor Adenauer at Claridge's Hotel in London, details of which were kept secret at the time but communicated by telephone to Israel's Foreign Minister, Moshe Sharett, in Paris.

The Claims Conference had two principal objectives. The first was to obtain funds for the relief, rehabilitation, and resettlement of Jews who had suffered persecution by the Nazis, and to help rebuild Jewish communities and institutions devastated under their regime. The second was to secure indemnification for injuries inflicted upon individual victims of Hitlerism and restitution for properties confiscated by those responsible for the "Final Solution."

A critical stage was reached in January 1952, when the issue of German reparations was debated in Israel's Knesset. Whereas neo-Nazis in West Germany denied the facts of the Holocaust and thus any Jewish right to compensation, many people in the Jewish world—including some survivors of the *Sho'ah*—strongly objected to the whole notion of accepting "blood money" from the Germans. Bitter speeches were delivered in the Knesset, especially by members of the Herut Party, whose leader, Menaḥem Begin, also spoke at violent street demonstrations in Jerusalem. Various emotional arguments were put forward by those opposed to any contacts and negotiations with Germany, who warned that restitution payments would be a form of exoneration of Nazi Germany's crimes against the Jewish people. My colleagues and I, however, insisted that material reparations in no way served to extenuate such crimes and that they would only permit those who had been deprived of their property and professional opportunities to obtain a minimum of legal redress. In the end, the Knesset voted by a small majority in favor of negotiations.

Once the bill had been passed, a negotiating team was appointed by the Claims Conference and various expert advisers were called upon to assist. They included Dr. Jacob Robinson, an authority on international law and the Holocaust, who was in charge of drafting the reparations agreement, and his brother, Dr. Nehemiah Robinson, director of the Institute of Jewish Affairs in New York, who served as chief consultant on indemnification procedure. Dr. Siegfried Moses, Israel's first State Comptroller, chaired the Advisory Committee of the United Restitution Organization in Israel, while Benjamin Ferencz became the Claims Conference's director for Germany. His other responsibilities included the United Restitution Organization, which he served as director of operations.

Representatives of the Israel Government and the Claims Conference began their negotiations with West Germany at The Hague on March 20, 1952. Moses Leavitt of the JDC headed our delegation. For a short time, however, in the absence of Dr.

Nahum Goldmann, I served as acting chairman of the Claims Conference. While the talks were proceeding, my colleagues and I of the presidium stayed in nearby Wassenaar and maintained daily contact with the negotiators. Threats by extremists were not infrequent, and our quarters had to be guarded by the Dutch police. Any letters and packages addressed to us were examined and opened before we handled them, for fear that they might contain explosives. On one occasion, the police intercepted a letter bomb that had been mailed to Nahum Goldmann.

The negotiations dragged on for half a year, mainly because of problems on the West German side that Federal Chancellor Adenauer and his closest associates could not easily overcome. Indeed, Professor Franz Boehm and Dr. Otto Küster, the chief German delegates, publicly castigated the delaying tactics of their own Government and Dr. Küster resigned in protest. Their stand was a demonstration of rare moral courage that augured well for the final outcome of the talks.

After many delays, the reparations agreement was signed in Luxembourg on September 10, 1952. In terms of U.S. currency, Israel was to receive $714 million in goods, for which a special Israel Purchasing Mission in Cologne would place orders. The significance of this for the economy of the Jewish State could scarcely be exaggerated. A further sum of $110 million was allocated to the Claims Conference for the benefit of Jews who had been persecuted by the Nazis. We called for the enactment of laws which would provide individual victims of Hitlerism and their heirs with indemnification, and a total of $4 billion was subsequently earmarked for that purpose. The signatories to the agreement were Chancellor Konrad Adenauer, on behalf of the Federal German Government; Foreign Minister Moshe Sharett, for the Government of Israel; and Dr. Nahum Goldmann, on behalf of the Claims Conference.

In retrospect, it cannot be denied that this was a great and historic achievement, even more for its ethical than its economic significance. In contrast to the Arab states, which made last-minute attempts to prevent the ratification of the agreement, U.S. Secretary of State Dean Acheson and British Foreign Secretary Anthony Eden jointly declared their support of our demands. The principal credit has rightly been given to Konrad Adenauer and Nahum Goldmann, but an enduring debt of gratitude is also owed to many other people. On the Jewish side, there were our patient negotiators and expert advisers; on the German side, there were Economics Minister Ludwig Erhard, Foreign Secretary Walter Hallstein, and other loyal friends, as well as Erich Ollenhauer, leader of the Bundestag's Social Democratic opposition, whose votes more than compensated for those of Government coalition members who said "no" or abstained.

Contrary to the expectations of both sides, the yearly allocations (payable over fourteen years until 1966) eventually exceeded the amounts agreed upon in Luxembourg severalfold. This is mainly attributable to the provisions of a Federal Restitution Law, first enacted in 1953, which went through several extensive revisions and which, offering compensation for loss of life, injuries, and other infringements of human rights, indemnified persons who had been victimized because of "race," religion, and political views. In short, therefore, victims of the Nazis have been compensated either for personal wrongs inflicted by the Nazis or for their confiscated possessions.

One of the most difficult problems facing the Claims Conference involved the use of restitution funds so that the effect on Jewish life would be of enduring value. A policy was formulated whereby the needs of the moment would not adversely affect plans for the distant future. The reconstruction of post-Holocaust Jewry could not begin and end with the sums doled out by German officialdom. Looking beyond the immediate horizon, we developed cultural and educational programs in some thirty countries, awarding grants to 250 Jewish communities and institutions, mainly in Europe. More than 160 Jewish schools were built or expanded, yeshivot were subsidized, books and periodicals began to appear, and creative research was made possible through the award of scholarships and fellowships. To ensure that there would be a permanent historical record of the *Sho'ah*, appropriate sums were also made available to Yad Vashem in Jerusalem, YIVO in New York, the Wiener Library in London, the Centre de Documentation Juive Contemporaine and the Memorial to the Unknown Jewish Martyr in Paris, and kindred institutions. At a later stage, in 1965, Dr. Nahum Goldmann played a major role in the establishment of the Memorial Foundation for Jewish Culture.

Encouraged by the success of our negotiations with the Federal German Republic, we decided to make a similar approach to the Austrian Government. The Committee on Jewish Claims against Austria was set up, comprising the organizations represented in the Claims Conference and the Association of Jews in Austria and Abroad. Our case was, however, weakened by postwar Allied declarations that Austria had been a "victim of Nazism" and by Israel's own refusal to enter any claims against the authorities in Vienna. I headed a delegation that met with the Austrian Chancellor, Leopold Figl, when he visited New York in May 1952, but his response was most discouraging. The new Chancellor, Dr. Julius Raab, and other Government leaders received our delegation in Vienna about a year later, on June 17, 1953, but these talks and subsequent contacts produced no tangible results. A press statement, issued by the Austrian embassy in Washington on July 12, made glib reference to "a sincere desire to see justice done to all Nazi victims," but insisted that Austria had "no legal or moral obligation to indemnify or compensate for wrongs that it did not commit and could not prevent, because it was itself a victim of circumstances." The suggestion was that such claims be lodged with West Germany.

Apart from the fact that Hitler and many of his Nazi henchmen, including Adolf Eichmann, had been Austrians, we remembered all too well the enthusiasm with which Austria's population had greeted the *Anschluss* of 1938. Austria's population felt and behaved like a faithful section of the "Greater Reich" until the end of World War II.

Negotiations with the Austrians dragged on until 1955, when a wholly inadequate agreement was reached. It provided for the establishment of an indemnification and relief fund, which, after many delays, began to operate in 1962. With understandable reluctance, West Germany undertook to pay half of the compensation.

In connection with the reparations and restitution agreement signed by the West German Government, I had occasion to say:

It brought into being a new moral standard in international affairs affecting the Jewish people—namely, that no nation can despoil its Jewish population without being held accountable before the bar of justice. . . . The amounts total only a meager fraction of what had been despoiled, and there could be no material compensation for the lives which were destroyed. Nevertheless, what has been accomplished marks a historic milestone in international morality.

An Anxious Year

On the Jewish and Zionist world scenes, 1953 proved to be an anxious and eventful year. Ever since 1948, when enthusiastic crowds greeted Israel's first diplomatic representative, Golda Meir, in the synagogues of Moscow, Stalin and his Communist bloc associates had been regarding Israel and Jews behind the Iron Curtain with grave suspicion. Their brand of Marxism-Leninism allowed no room for international Jewish solidarity. An ominous development, in November 1952, was the Slánský Trial in Czechoslovakia. Fourteen members of the Czechoslovak Communist Party leadership were accused of conspiring against the state; eleven of them, including Rudolf Slánský, the party's secretary-general, were Jews. The show trial was conducted in a virulently anti-Zionist, anti-Israel, and anti-Semitic atmosphere, the Jewish origin of leading defendants being repeatedly emphasized, as were their alleged Zionist sympathies and connections, although virtually all of the arraigned Jews had been lifelong anti-Zionists.

Espionage charges were also leveled against Israel's first diplomats in Prague and two Israeli citizens working there were arrested, forced to act as witnesses for the prosecution and then sentenced to terms of imprisonment. Slánský and seven other Jewish defendants were sentenced to death and were executed, together with Foreign Minister Vlado Clementis and the two other non-Jewish "Titoists." Several years elapsed before the victims were "rehabilitated" and the survivors released from prison.

This trial set off a chain reaction of anti-Jewish hysteria in the Communist world, which reached its grim height in the "Doctors' Plot" of January 1953. Nine eminent Moscow physicians, six of them Jews, were arrested, interrogated, and terrorized into admitting their supposed responsibility for administering poison to two top Soviet leaders who had died several years earlier. They also reportedly confessed to having attempted the murder of several army chiefs of the USSR. Most of these "terrorists" were stated to have links with the "Joint" (JDC), which the Soviet media branded as an "international Jewish bourgeois nationalist" arm of U.S. espionage and intelligence. Israel's condemnation of the planned new show trial, followed by a bomb incident at the Soviet legation in Tel Aviv on February 9, prompted the Soviet Union to break off diplomatic relations with "the bloodthirsty Zionist mad dogs." By the middle of that month, Israel, Zionism, and the "Joint" were being bracketed together with Wall Street and Western imperialism at the top of Moscow's hate list, and the JDC found itself "implicated" in the Slánský Trial. Panic swept over Russian Jewry, which saw itself threatened by a mass pogrom.

The "Doctors' Plot" gave rise to an international outcry and an emergency conference of major Jewish organizations, summoned by the World Zionist Organization, was scheduled for March 10–12, 1953, in Zurich. The convenors were Dr. Nahum Goldmann and Berl Locker, co-chairmen of the WZO and Jewish Agency Executives. Primarily, the conference was intended to review recent grave events in Eastern Europe, to focus world public opinion on their anti-Jewish implications, to reject the baseless charges of a "Zionist conspiracy" against the Communist bloc states, and to demand that a commission of international jurists be permitted to attend the forthcoming trial in Moscow. A call was also issued to the Soviet Union and its satellites to allow all Jews so desiring to exercise their right of emigration to Israel, failing which, the issue would be brought before the United Nations.

It became my severalfold assignment, as chairman of the Western Hemisphere Executive of the World Jewish Congress, president of the American Jewish Congress, and a member of the American Section of the Jewish Agency Executive, to leave for Europe early in March, proceeding first to West Berlin.

In the wake of the Slánský Trial, East Germany's Communist regime had adopted a tougher line toward the 2,500 Jews living there at the time and 500 of them had fled to West Berlin in the space of one month. The local Jewish community was taking care of the refugees, utilizing funds provided by the JDC. Although the Hebrew Immigrant Aid Society expressed readiness to cover their travel expenses, the newcomers were not candidates for Aliyah.

My visit provided an opportunity for talks with the Social Democratic Mayor of West Berlin, Ernst Reuter, and other personalities, Jewish and non-Jewish. I also spoke with a number of the Jewish refugees from East Germany, who referred to the anti-Jewish prejudice manifest there and the police surveillance to which they had been subjected. Whether through lethargy or as a result of official pressure, Jewish culture in East Berlin was at a low ebb: virtually no Jews maintained religious observance, while Hebrew education and Zionist activity were outlawed. There was, furthermore, practically no contact with Jews and Jewish life in the free world. In view of the situation, the West Berlin authorities were less rigid in their screening of Jews who had fled from the Eastern sector. Generally speaking, most Germans with whom I spoke proved contrite about the Nazi Holocaust. They either disclaimed all knowledge of what had happened to the Jews while Hitler was in power, resenting any attempt to discuss such matters, or else they excused themselves by saying that no one could do anything about it at the time.

While in Berlin, I visited the site of the bunker in which Hitler had taken his own life as the Third Reich was collapsing around him. It was just one month before the tenth anniversary of the Warsaw Ghetto Uprising, and I could not help reflecting that our Holocaust heroes and martyrs had gained a posthumous victory in their desperate battle for Jewish freedom and dignity.

On the eve of the scheduled Zurich conference, as I was about to leave for Switzerland, news of Stalin's sudden death reached the outside world. Because of the uncertain position thus created, it was resolved to call off the assembly of Jewish leaders, pending further developments and the emergence of what might, hopefully, be a different type of Soviet regime. An official announcement from the Kremlin, on April 3, stated that the accused physicians had been innocent of the charges preferred against them and that they had been freed. Diplomatic relations with Israel were restored on July 20, after which the USSR raised its legation in Tel Aviv to embassy level. Three years later, at the Communist Party's Twentieth Congress, Secretary Nikita Khrushchev disclosed that Stalin had been responsible for the fabricated "Doctors' Plot," yet no attempt was ever made to apologize for its stridently anti-Jewish overtones.

In the spring of 1953, as mentioned previously, the Committee on Jewish Claims against Austria was hard at work, trying to secure some positive response to its demands. Among those involved in these negotiations, which dealt with the heirless property of Jews who had been murdered by the Nazis, was Abraham S. Hyman, administrative director of the World Jewish Congress in New York. As a U.S. Army major in 1946, he had been assigned to advise the American military governor, General Lucius Clay, on the restitution law enacted in the U.S. zone of Germany. Before joining the staff of the WJC, he had served from November 1950 until May 1953 as general counsel of the U.S. War Claims Commission.

Our delegation arrived in Vienna in mid-June. Outwardly, the Austrian capital seemed unaffected by the chaos of the war years and by its political division between the Western and Soviet occupying forces. Jewishly, however, it was a saddening shadow of the past. Less than 6,000 Jews remained in what had once been a center of our religious life and culture.

On the evening of June 15, two days before our second inconclusive approach to the Austrian Government on the reparations issue, I spoke at a public meeting organized by the Jewish community of Vienna. In the course of my brief address, I said:

> One cannot be here in Vienna without thinking of Theodor Herzl, and one cannot think of Herzl without recalling gratefully that, after the *Megillat Eikhah* [Lamentations of Jeremiah, recited on the fast of Tish'ah be-Av], there has come a *Shabbat Naḥamu* ["Sabbath of Consolation" following Tish'ah be-Av] in the establishment of the State of Israel. It is good to know that the Jewish community of Vienna today takes pride in and feels affection toward Israel and that, on the recent occasion of Israel's fifth Independence Day, three thousand Jews—half of your entire Jewish population—came to the celebration. This demonstrates the extent to which our Medinah is fulfilling the function which, in his day, Yehudah Halevi defined as "the heart" maintaining the pulse of the Jewish people.

Only a few weeks later, I went to Switzerland for the third Plenary Assembly of the World Jewish Congress, which was held in Geneva during the week commencing August 4. It was an eminently representative Jewish conference, with delegates arriving from more than fifty countries, including such small and distant communities as Aden and Japan. Israel's delegation was a large one and included fourteen Knesset members. Among our American delegation, which I had the privilege to head, were Rabbi Morton M. Berman, Rabbi Max (Mordecai) Kirshblum, Dr. David Petegorsky, Shad Polier, Rabbi Joachim Prinz, Louis Segal, and Dr. Joseph Tenenbaum. A number of us were members of the Organization Commission and five of our delegation were elected to the presidium.

The absence of Rabbi Stephen Wise, the WJC's late president, was keenly felt. Dr. Nahum Goldmann, who had served as acting president for nearly four years, was elected to the presidency. I was reelected as a co-chairman of the WJC Executive and as chairman of the Western Hemisphere Executive. My designated co-chairmen, Dr. Noah Barou of London and Dr. Aryeh Tartakower of Jerusalem, were appointed to serve as chairmen of the European and Israel branches of the Executive respectively.

When the Plenary Assembly opened, the international status of the WJC was reflected in the presence of representatives of many governments and of UN agencies. The director of the Human Rights Division of the United Nations, speaking on behalf of the Secretary-General of the UN, declared in his address that no organization had made a greater contribution to the cause of human rights through the UN than the World Jewish Congress. Similar tributes to the WJC's standing and achievements were paid by spokesmen for UNESCO and other international bodies.

The issues that dominated the week's proceedings and on which various resolutions were passed included the role of the UN, the need for all governments to ratify the Convention on Human Rights, protection of and assistance for refugees, and the expansion of the World Jewish Congress. The problems of Israel, Jewish cultural activity, the menace of neo-Nazism and anti-Semitism, and recent threats to Jewish communities behind the Iron Curtain were high on the Assembly's agenda. Jewish delegates from Eastern European lands were conspicuously absent, but their perilous situation was in everyone's thoughts. Profound disquiet was expressed over the supply of military hardware to Arab states by certain governments. Another resolution deplored the fact that the status of Jerusalem, Israel's natural capital, should have become a matter of international controversy. The Assembly noted with satisfaction the agreements signed lately by the Federal German Republic, the State of Israel, and the Claims Conference. It went on to express the hope that both Austria and the German Democratic Republic would follow the West German example.

In the course of my address on "Israel and the Jewish People," delivered before the WJC Plenary Assembly, I singled out three major positive factors making for Jewish survival. These were the Jewish State, whether as an aspiration or a reality; *Torah u-mitzvot*, the religio-ethical content and the mores of Judaism; and the sense of Jewish unity, transcending all geographical and social divisions. "Whenever and wherever these three factors have been intertwined," I said, "the ideal conditions for Jewish survival have existed." Anti-Semitism was only an external, negative type of contribution to *kiyyum ha-am*, the survival of our people. After a rapid survey of post-Holocaust Jewry's situation in the world, I went on to ask—and to answer—a series of questions:

> What have the Jews of Israel and the Jews of the world the right to expect of each other in fulfillment of the basic Jewish commitment and obligation, *kiyyum ha-am*, which binds us all together?
> What has Israel the right to expect of World Jewry?
> It has the right to expect a steady sense of attachment and commitment to its welfare, expressed in moral and material support and in contributions of skill and manpower. A small State surrounded by Arab neighbors will always require a hinterland of Jewish attachment and support. . . .
> What has Diaspora Jewry the right to expect of Israel?
> Thoughtful Israelis are themselves beginning to project this question upon the nation's consciousness. The Jewish people looks to Israel for specifically Jewish nourishment, that it be a cultural-spiritual fountainhead to nourish arid Jewish areas in other lands. The craving for Torah from Zion, Torah in the broadest sense, is almost everywhere.

While berating those phobia-ridden, ignorant Jews of the Diaspora who disavowed their need for any Zion-centered inspiration, I also expressed alarm over "in-growing tendencies among some of the native-born Israeli youth" and the ignorance about Jewish life abroad manifested by Israelis of all ages. Better information services would arrest these trends and help Jews in Israel and the *Golah* to understand each other.

In conclusion, I said:

> The interaction and the interrelationship between Israel and Diaspora Jewry is cardinal to the survival of both. Here, the World Jewish Congress has an important role to fulfill, complementary to that of the World Zionist Organization. The suggestion heard occasionally, that the Zionist Organization take over the functions of the World Jewish Congress, is fraught with danger. The tasks of winning support for Israel and of seeking to protect local Jewish rights require two separate organizations.
> Although these two purposes are not identical, they are complementary. Because the WJC program lays so much stress on Israel, and because Zionists have been its founders and leaders, Zionists everywhere should see in the World Jewish Congress the natural medium for their participation in the protection of Jewish rights on an international scale and in the promotion of the unity of the Jewish people. Medinat Yisrael, the World Zionist Organization and the World Jewish Congress are the three pillars, each with its own special competence and purpose, upon which rests the edifice of Jewish representation before the world.

In 1949, the American Jewish Congress instituted an annual Stephen S. Wise award for outstanding service to the Jewish and general community. During my term as president, I had the honor of presenting such awards to various deserving recipients, among them Herbert H. Lehman, Walter Clay Lowdermilk, Louis

Lipsky, and Yosef Sprinzak. In 1956, Israel's second President, Itzḥak Ben-Zvi, received the award and in 1957 it went to Golda Meir.

At an American Jewish Congress dinner held in New York on November 9, 1953, Harry S. Truman received the Stephen Wise award "for his consistent and courageous leadership in the cause of Civil Rights during his term of office as President of the United States." McCarthyism was rampant at the time and, in his response, Truman declared that the nation was "losing ground in the matter of freedom of thought and freedom of speech." The bogey of Communism was, he said, "being manipulated by a few so as to cause a nationwide wave of hysteria," but he pledged his support for those resisting smear tactics and assaults on individual liberty. Harry Truman's commitment to the Zionist program and, subsequently, to Israel was of a piece with his political liberalism in American affairs.

Toward the end of November 1953, I began a week-long visit to Morocco, in order to study the plight of Moroccan Jewry with a view to relief measures, especially through the fostering of emigration to Israel.

The half a million Jews then living in North Africa represented the largest source of potential Aliyah. There were some 200,000 Jews in French Morocco, hemmed in by eight million Muslims. The principal *kehillot* existed in the cities of Casablanca, Fez, Marrakesh, Meknès, and Rabat, where the Jews mostly inhabited separate quarters known as *mellahs;* they had nothing apart from their misery to lose by departing for some friendlier shore. Penury, filth, and disease reigned in these Moroccan ghettos, and the infant mortality rate approached fifty percent. Like other non-Muslims, Jews were denied full citizenship and they were condemned to live as wards of the Sultan, Sidi Muhammad Ben Youssef.

In Casablanca, I inspected the Jewish Agency installations and the relief activities conducted by the Joint Distribution Committee. I also visited the Jewish schools conducted by the Alliance Israélite Universelle and the Otzar Hatorah, as well as the vocational training schools of ORT. Much of the time I was accompanied, guided, and translated by Mr. Jules Braunschvig, vice-president of the Alliance Israélite. I also enjoyed the hospitality of Mr. Z. Schulman, chairman of the Zionist Federation. I met with all the leaders of the city's Jewish community to discuss Aliyah problems as well as the local philanthropic and educational programs.

From Casablanca I proceeded to Marrakesh, where the conditions of Jewish life were similar.

We then undertook what proved to be my most interesting single experience in Morocco. I was accompanied by the JDC's director in Morocco, William Bein, who also supervised its operations in other North African countries, and by Mr. and Mrs. Z. Schulman of Casablanca, and a Mr. Elkayam of Marrakesh. Our destination was Igni Nishnain, an isolated Jewish hamlet in the Atlas Mountains, some fifty kilometers south of Marrakesh, which Jews from the West had never previously visited. All thirty-four families (or 145 souls) in this community were Arabic-speaking and had only a slight knowledge of Hebrew.

After an hour's drive from Marrakesh, our party was met by an Arab guide, whom we followed up a narrow pass in single file for about twenty minutes. It was a difficult climb, during which we saw hardly anything in front of us. Then, at last, we came in sight of a number of mud and stone hovels. I could not help wondering about the kind of primitive people whom we would find in such a place.

As we approached, a familiar and delightful sound greeted our ears—the sound of Jewish children reciting prayers in unison. Guided by their voices, we found our way to the synagogue and went inside. There were about twenty-five very small children seated on the floor and chanting *Mah Tovu*—"How goodly are thy tents, O Jacob." Their teacher also sat on the ground, facing the two rows of children. They were reading the words from a sheet torn out of a prayer book and pasted on a board, which was passed around from hand to hand. The tiny, poverty-stricken community could not afford more than one or two prayer books. On the wall I saw a Jewish National Fund blue and white box and poster. Thus, we were greeted with the ancient Biblical words and the modern JNF appeal.

Ours was the first visit to Igni Nishnain by an outside group. Within minutes, dozens of older people congregated around us, headed by the Ḥakham, the most learned man, and the sheikh, the richest among them, whose surname was Ben-Lulu. Having come unexpected and unannounced, we introduced ourselves and explained our purpose, to prepare them for Aliyah.

A community had existed on this hilltop for centuries. One tombstone I saw there was 473 years old. They had a tradition that a *shali'aḥ*, an emissary, once came from Jerusalem to collect money. They eked out a livelihood by working for Arab farmers—planting, ploughing, and threshing grain.

In simple Hebrew, I explained to the men, women, and children milling eagerly around us that I brought "Shalom" greetings from Eretz Yisrael. I asked if they would send their children to Israel, and they cried out in chorus that all of them, not only the children, were ready to leave at once. It was not easy to make them understand that it would take some time to arrange matters.

William Bein had brought gifts—a *Ḥummash* (Pentateuch), which was especially welcome since theirs was worn out; Hebrew manuals; a layette for the mother with the youngest infant and another for a woman who was about to give birth; and a hundred cakes of soap. The JDC planned to send in a nurse, who would come for a few days weekly to teach the mothers the essentials of hygiene. Although most of the children were healthy, there were a few blind ones among them, victims of the trachoma prevalent in Morocco.

Walking through the village, we found that bread was baked in outdoor ovens and saw places where olives were being beaten to extract the oil and where wheat and corn were being threshed. In one corner, women were weaving a rug; elsewhere they were spinning wool. The huts were clean, both inside and out.

Two of the elders took me into a cave where, it seemed, they stored religious books, scrolls, and ritual articles. They presented me with an old *Megillah* (Scroll of Esther) and a shofar (animal horn blown on High Holy Days).

I was told that the villagers married early, and that men were allowed two wives.

All of them appeared to be in fairly good health, because of the mountain air, although it was surprising to learn that some "elderly" folk were no more than thirty years of age.

At the home of the sheikh, we were given a meal consisting of bread, hard-boiled eggs, Arab tea, and (to my astonishment) whiskey. They implored us to remain and offered to slaughter a chicken if we would stay for a few hours, or a sheep if we would remain overnight. In spite of these inducements, we explained that we had to go.

The love of Zion was deeply implanted in these simple Jews. A few months later, Igni Nishnain's entire community was transplanted to Israel by the Jewish Agency, after having received aid from the JDC in the interim.

Years later, I visited these people in their new abode, the settlement of Avivim in northern Israel. The children whom I heard singing in that remote Moroccan hamlet had grown up. The boys were serving in the army. The girls were busy with domestic chores and some of the older ones had married and were already proud mothers. Some time thereafter, alas, Avivim suffered a murderous attack by Arab terrorists who had infiltrated from Lebanon.

The Aliyah of Moroccan Jewry continued. It is today one of Israel's foremost constituencies, beset with absorption problems but also abundant in achievements, having contributed much to the nation's defense, agriculture, and industry. David Levi, a onetime Oleh from Morocco, is now a prominent member of the Israel cabinet and serves as Deputy Prime Minister.

The night before my departure for the United States, a dinner was tendered in my honor by the Casablanca Jewish community, in conjunction with representatives of the JDC, ORT, OSE, and the Alliance Israélite Universelle. I gave an eyewitness account of how Moroccan Jewish immigrants had been integrated into the society of Israel, and explained what still remained to be done. As my audience was also eager to hear about religious life in Israel, I recalled that Rabbi Y. L. Hacohen Maimon, the eminent Mizraḥi leader, was once asked, "What about irreligion and atheism in Israel?" He replied, "I have not seen it, because I have not looked for it." I then went on to say, "In Israel, you will find whatever you look for. Having lived in Jerusalem for the best part of a year, I must have attended services at forty different synagogues because I was interested in seeing the colorful diversity of religious observance in the capital of our Medinah."

This visit to Morocco was fresh in my mind when I arrived in Israel soon afterwards. On December 23, I had the pleasure of addressing several hundred members of the Association of Americans and Canadians in Israel at ZOA House in Tel Aviv. It marked the beginning of an association with the AACI which has lasted for well over two decades.

Eminent Contemporaries

The multiple Jewish and Zionist activities in which I was involved during the late 1940s and early 1950s brought me into contact with several of the world's leading statesmen. Perhaps a closer view of a few such personalities—Konrad Adenauer, Golda Meir, Dwight D. Eisenhower, and Harry Truman—may be of interest and relevancy at this point.

Some months after the signing of the reparations agreement with the Federal German Republic, a group of us representing the Claims Conference met with Chancellor Konrad Adenauer in his suite at the Waldorf-Astoria in New York. Headed by Dr. Nahum Goldmann, our delegation comprised, apart from myself, Jacob Blaustein, Jules Braunschvig, Adolph Held, Moses Leavitt, and Rudolph Kallman. Speaking on our behalf, Dr. Goldmann expressed appreciation for the Chancellor's decisive part in negotiating the agreements with Israel and the world Jewish organizations concerned.

We were aware not only of the German Chancellor's vital role in these negotiations, but also of his impeccable anti-Nazi past. He had been dismissed from his post as Bürgermeister (Mayor) of Cologne in 1933, and had subsequently undergone arrest and imprisonment by the Hitler regime. Adenauer, deeply sensitive to his own countrymen's responsibility for the Holocaust, had come forward eagerly with an offer of reparations and restitution to the Jewish people.

In reply to Dr. Goldmann's opening remarks, Chancellor Adenauer stressed that the reparations agreement had been a matter of the heart and conscience for him. As an eyewitness who lived in Germany throughout the Hitler era, he knew well enough what unspeakable crimes had been committed against the Jewish people. While recognizing that money could not atone for what had taken place, he nevertheless believed that some measure of tangible amends had to be made as a matter of elementary justice. Dr. Adenauer then went on to speak highly of Nahum Goldmann's role in the negotiations and of the way in which serious obstacles had been overcome during the preliminary stages.

The impression of Chancellor Adenauer that I gained in the course of this meeting was of a devout Christian and upright man whose unenviable task it would be to create a new moral order out of the wrack and ruin that Nazism had bequeathed to postwar Germany. He had to cope with tremendous difficulties, yet dealt with even the most contentious and problematic issues in a firm, courageous, and compassionate manner. His behavior and the personal example he set when handling the reparations and restitution problems, and in striving to make his fellow Germans feel conscience-stricken about Nazi barbarism toward the Jews, was an earnest of his own moral integrity. He keenly desired to establish diplomatic relations with Israel, and from secret contacts we eventually proceeded toward "normalization." In 1966, a year before his death, Adenauer paid a visit to Israel as the Government's honored guest.

The fifth anniversary of Israel's Proclamation of Independence fell in the same week of April 1953 when our interview with Dr. Adenauer took place. Golda Meir (formerly Myerson), then Minister of Labor, was in the United States and attended the special Sabbath services held at my synagogue to mark Yom Ha-Atzma'ut. A huge crowd assembled to greet her, and hundreds of people had to be content with listening to her address over the amplifiers installed in our Community Center, adjoining the synagogue.

Golda Meir was a remarkable combination of talents and qualities. She had a goodly measure of the *Yiddishe Mamme* in her, yet few men could excel her in strength of character. She was at once logical and intuitive; lacking patience for details, she knew how to delegate secondary responsibilities to other people, thereby leaving herself free to make the major decisions. Every mission she undertook proved to be a resounding success.

Golda inspired loyalty in her subordinates and the wholesome respect of her colleagues. With almost unerring instinct, she went to the heart of a problem. She had her pet affections and her pet aversions, and she loved to be loved—who doesn't? With Golda, however, this was more than usually the case.

A week later, I was received at the White House by President Eisenhower. This interview, on April 28, had been arranged with the help of Governor Theodore McKeldin of Maryland, through the kind offices of Judge Simon Sobeloff, a prominent figure in Baltimore's Jewish and general community. As mentioned previously, issues related to the McCarran-Walter Act, civil rights and Israel's security headed my agenda.

I took occasion to remind the President of our meeting in England early in 1944, when he was preparing for the Allied invasion of Europe. I had come to see "Ike" as chairman of the Jewish Section of British War Relief in the United States. Later, during my visit to the DP camps in Germany after the liberation, I had sent him a memorandum about the need to provide separate facilities for Jewish DPs instead of herding them with anti-Semitic non-Jews, and I recalled our expression of gratitude to him for his prompt and effective measures.

Then I brought up the objectionable racist aspects of the discriminatory McCarran-Walter Immigration Act. President Eisenhower observed that he had not been conscious of anti-Semitic prejudice in Abilene, Kansas, where he was reared, and that it was only when he came east that he encountered it. My answer was that places such as Abilene were exceptional. Where anti-Semitism existed, it needed to be tackled in order to protect the American way of life. The President concurred.

Touching on the subject of Israel, I thanked him for the reassuring Government statements about continued economic aid to the Jewish State, but voiced concern over recent expressions of Arab belligerence, which clashed with the U.S. Administration's desire for peace and stability in the Middle East. President Eisenhower displayed a constructive interest in Israel's welfare, but as already indicated, he relied on his senior advisers, who evidently made the major foreign-policy decisions.

When I returned to the anteroom, I found Secretary of State John Foster Dulles waiting to see the President. I later heard that Dulles had sent in a note to "Ike," stressing that he was in a hurry. Eisenhower's disinclination to rush me must have indicated his interest in our topics of conversation.

As I was about to leave the President's outer office, his administrative assistant, former Governor Sherman Adams of Massachusetts, invited me into his room for a chat, which ranged over the entire Israel-Arab problem. When he touched on the Arab refugee issue, I repeated the statement I had made to President Eisenhower— that Israel had offered a generous contribution to a resettlement fund—and added that the Arab governments, to judge by their treatment of these refugees, were displaying no genuine concern for them at all. Obviously, their purpose was to keep the refugee issue alive, so as to exploit it as a source of political capital against Israel.

Sherman Adams then made an interesting and original suggestion—that instead of top members of the U.S. Administration making lightning visits to countries in the Middle East, skilled diplomats should spend considerable periods of time in those lands, including Israel, to instill the idea that America had a sincere interest in their welfare, agricultural development, and economic prosperity. Such an approach, he believed, would do much to promote better relations and to bring about an enduring peace in the region.

This idea, I said, was certainly worth exploring, but I felt that one important consideration ought to be borne in mind. The U.S. economic-aid program was intended primarily to strengthen the cause of democracy. Israel, which possessed all the features of a democratic state and society, deserved more of America than any of the Arab states, which could in no way be described as democratic. As for peace and stability in the Middle East, who needed to preach these values to Israel? For Israel, peace was like the breath of life; for the Arabs, turmoil and war drums seemed preferable. "Our Government," I concluded, "must know where the pressure for peace has to be applied."

Three meetings with former President Harry S. Truman enlivened the year for me. He was a remarkable man, frank and breezy in manner, yet gifted with a shrewd perception—a typical "show me" Missourian. Our first meeting in 1953, which his friend, Abraham Feinberg of New York, arranged, was at the Waldorf-Astoria on July 3. I went to see him there in order to set the date for the function at which he was to receive the annual Stephen S. Wise award of the American Jewish Congress. He looked very fit and relaxed, and I remarked that some of us whose leadership responsibilities were incomparably more limited would do well to learn from him how best to retire from high office. Smiling, he replied that many people who never learn that secret end up "being carried out feet first."

As we sat talking, a pleasant domestic interlude occurred when Mrs. Bess Truman came into the room and asked her husband for a dollar to buy something.

Harry Truman was characteristically forthright in his pronouncements. As one of his partisans, I told him that we all hoped nonetheless for the success of President Eisenhower's Administration, yet Eisenhower evidently did not realize that, if he looked beyond Congress into the hearts of the American people, he would find tremendous forces prepared to rally around him. Truman said that his successor had the reputation of being a great executive, but did not seem to be alert to the public-relations factor with which an American President has to cope.

He went on to express his fear that McCarthyism's next phase would be a descent into anti-Semitism. A brochure Truman had just written identified various reactionary epochs in American history and we were, he said, now living in such an epoch.

Turning to Israel, Truman mentioned "a stupid speech" that John Foster Dulles had made in Egypt. As one deeply interested in matters pertaining to the Middle East, the ex-President had met with experts whose recent survey proved that exploitation of that area's oil reserves, combined with a linkup of the Tigris and Euphrates with the Mediterranean, would bring great prosperity to the entire region. He believed that Israel, with its fund of economic expertise, could play an important part in developing this plan.

The American Jewish Congress dinner honoring Harry Truman was held on November 9, 1953, at the Roosevelt Hotel in New York. America's former President came with his wife, Bess, and their daughter, Margaret. The function was attended by a cross-section of American Jewish and non-Jewish leadership, including Dr. Ralph Bunche, Professor James G. McDonald, Dr. Channing B. Tobias, Lloyd Garrison, and delegates to the American Jewish Congress convention from all parts of the United States. Justine Wise Polier was in the chair. Rabbi Abraham A. Neuman, president of Dropsie College, Philadelphia, delivered the invocation. I presented the guest of honor with a plaque recording his selection for the Stephen S. Wise award on the basis of "his consistent and courageous leadership in the cause of Civil Rights during his term of office as President of the United States." That cause was the theme of Truman's brief address in response to the presentation.

During the dinner, he asked me about the musical origin of *Hatikvah*, the Zionist and Israeli anthem. I explained that the melody was popularly associated with a theme from *Vltava*, one of six symphonic poems making up the cycle, *Má Vlast* ("My Country"), by the nineteenth-century Czech composer, Bedřich Smetana. The theme is a common one in Eastern Europe, however, and musicologists have established a direct link between the melody of *Hatikvah* and a Rumanian folk song. Harry Truman observed that it seemed to reflect the tragedy of the Jewish people throughout the ages, and that he had noticed the prevalence of the minor key in many Jewish songs, both religious and secular.

He also told me of his deep admiration for the late Dr. Chaim Weizmann and his statesmanship. Mrs. Truman mentioned some traditional Jewish dishes she had enjoyed at the homes of her Jewish friends.

There was an amusing human sidelight at the dinner table. Truman noticed the huge plaited *hallah*, over which a blessing had been recited before the meal was served, and he asked me about its significance. I explained that this kind of bread was prepared for Jewish households in honor of the Sabbath and festivals, adding that the present occasion was also a festive one for us. He then asked if he could take a piece of *hallah* home with him after the dinner. I cut off a generous portion from the end, wrapped it in a napkin and presented it to him. Reverently, and with repeated words of thanks, he stowed it away in his pocket as a souvenir of a function that obviously meant a great deal to him.

In February 1954, I again spent some time with Truman when he was in New

York to receive an honorary degree from one of the universities. Our conversation, at the Waldorf-Astoria, where he was staying, provided further insight into his unaffected simplicity and modest character. In response to the congratulations I offered, he thanked me and said, "Let me tell you, Dr. Goldstein, that I would give all my honorary degrees for just one degree which I earned." It is no secret that his family could not afford to send him to law school and so, after attending night classes for two years in Kansas City, he worked in a lawyer's office. In 1922, he was elected judge of the county court in Jackson, Missouri, and he became presiding judge there, in an administrative capacity, two years later. That was the start of a career that would take Harry Truman to the White House.

Some Nostalgic Occasions

Amid the hurly-burly of my daily rounds during the mid-1950s, there were a few events of personal or general significance that afforded an opportunity for tranquil relaxation and nostalgic remembrance.

On January 17, 1954, as mentioned in an earlier chapter, the Jewish Conciliation Board of America observed my twenty-fifth anniversary as its president with a function at the Jewish Educational Alliance in the heart of New York's Lower East Side, whence most of the Board's original clients had come. Justice William O. Douglas of the U.S. Supreme Court delivered the principal address and General David Sarnoff, head of the Radio Corporation of America and NBC, presided. It was a warm and homelike gathering.

Four days later, Congregation B'nai Jeshurun arranged a dinner to mark my thirty-fifth year as rabbi. It took place in the ballroom of our Community Center. Jacob Sincoff, president of the congregation, chaired the proceedings; Samuel Blumberg, chairman of the board of trustees, was the toastmaster; and Professor Louis Finkelstein, chancellor of the Jewish Theological Seminary, delivered the main address. I was delighted to receive a bronze likeness of myself, fashioned by the promising young Boston-born Jewish sculptor, Robert Berks, who was later to achieve nationwide eminence in his artistic field.

Hundreds of congratulatory messages were received from organizations and individuals, both Jewish and non-Jewish, in the United States, Canada, Great Britain, and Israel. One was from ex-President Harry Truman and another came from Israel's President, Itzhak Ben-Zvi. On behalf of the Government of Israel, Dr. Michael Simon, its Chief of Protocol, ceremonially presented me with a scroll bearing the signatures of Prime Minister Moshe Sharett and Ministers Peretz Bernstein, Levi Eshkol, Golda Meir, Pinhas Rosen, and Moshe Shapira. The scroll was encased in a beautiful silver receptacle embossed with the insignia of the State of Israel, which Dr. Simon referred to as my "Field Marshal's baton." It is one of my most treasured possessions.

Among those present at the dinner, I was especially glad to see my good friend, James G. McDonald, the first U.S. ambassador to Israel, who had rendered outstanding services to the Jewish people since the 1930s.

While finding such observances a source of personal gratification, and rejoicing in the warm tributes they evoke from close friends, colleagues, and associates, I have always regarded them as opportunities for meditation and self-examination. The results are often sobering.

Year by year, until our final departure for Israel in 1960, the second *Seder* night was always marked by an extended family gathering in our New York home, at 300 Central Park West. A congregational *Seder* took place on the first night of Passover at B'nai Jeshurun, where I conducted the celebration. We invariably had a large number of special guests at our second *Seder*, representing a broad cross-section of the Jewish and non-Jewish communities—visiting Israeli and Zionist leaders, civic and labor personalities, Christian clergymen, Blacks and Hindus, writers and artists. Among those who came to our second *Seder* at various times were Eleanor Roosevelt, Mayor Robert F. Wagner, Sholem Asch, Isaac and Vera Stern, Kedar Nath Das Gupta, André Maurois, Langston Hughes (the Negro poet), Father George B. Ford, Dr. Everett R. Clinchy (executive director of the National Conference of Christians and Jews), Ada Maimon, Alex Rose, and the Reverend Donald Harrington (minister of New York's Community Church). Both Alex Rose and the Reverend Harrington were leaders of the Liberal Party in New York, which had my political allegiance.

Our practice was to use the Reconstructionist *Haggadah*, because of the references it contained to the contemporary struggle for freedom by various oppressed racial and economic groups. Black guests would often ask permission to take their copy home with them as a meaningful souvenir of the Passover celebration they had attended.

On one occasion, Ada Maimon—abetted by Eleanor Roosevelt—"stole" the *Afikoman* (portion of the *matzah* reserved for the end of the meal) and "held it for ransom," in accordance with time-honored Jewish family custom. The price she asked for its return was an epidiascope. Without knowing exactly what this was, I agreed to the exchange and then discovered that she had inveigled me into giving her an expensive type of projector for teaching botany. A guest from my congregation promptly offered to share the "redemption fee" with me, in return for the privilege of escorting Ada Maimon and Eleanor Roosevelt home. Some time later, while visiting Israel, I was shown the epidiascope at the Ayanot Agricultural School, where Ada Maimon was principal. The pupils had decided to name it *Afikoman*, by way of recalling how this apparatus was originally acquired!

At another second *Seder*, in 1955, we placed on the table—but refrained from opening—a bottle of *kasher* wine that had been left unused at the wedding of David and Paula Ben-Gurion in New York, in 1916. We had managed to acquire this bottle from the Mizrachi Wine Company, our own suppliers, who had provided the liquor for B-G's *simḥah*. I once mentioned our possession of this unique bottle in a letter to Ben-Gurion, knowing that the story would appeal to him.

The American Jewish Tercentenary

In the late spring of 1952, plans were first laid for the observance of the three hundredth anniversary of Jewish settlement in North America, scheduled to take place in 1954. A small nucleus of planners was formed, comprising representatives of the American Jewish Historical Society and the American Jewish Committee. A short while later, some other national Jewish leaders were invited to participate, and I welcomed the opportunity of becoming actively involved in this important program. Ralph E. Samuel, a vice-president of the American Jewish Committee, became chairman of the newly formed American Jewish Tercentenary Committee and brought in Judge Samuel Rosenman to head its team of program planners.

The historical background, of course, was the arrival in New Amsterdam harbor, on September 12, 1654, of a group of twenty-three Jews who had set sail from the port of Recife when Portuguese troops regained control of Brazil from the Dutch. The basic historical facts were well known to us, as was the origin of North America's first Jewish congregation, Shearith Israel, which the Sephardi newcomers later founded on Mill Street, now part of downtown New York, near the Battery and Bowling Green. The patroons and burghers of New Amsterdam, headed by the Dutch administrator, Peter Stuyvesant, displayed prejudice and hostility in their treatment of these Jews and were at first inclined to expel them from the colony. Even after the Dutch West India Company intervened in their behalf, it took some time before they were admitted to the body politic. Following the surrender of New Amsterdam to the British in 1664, however, the civil and religious status of the embryonic *kehillah* underwent a marked improvement.

It seemed rather odd to me when the Tercentenary Committee began its work that this historic observance should be regarded as the exclusive preserve of two American Jewish organizations and a limited number of Jewish individuals, however eminent they might be. The program committee, which was to devise a central theme for the tercentenary observance and recommend various forms of celebration, had already been "elected" on an *ad hoc* basis and was scarcely representative of the American Jewish community as a whole. It consisted of Judge Benjamin V. Cohen, who, like Judge Rosenman, had been one of President Franklin D. Roosevelt's inner circle of advisers; Adolph Held, chairman of the Jewish Labor Committee; William S. Paley, chairman of the Columbia Broadcasting System; David Sarnoff, president of the Radio Corporation of America and the National Broadcasting Company; Benjamin Sonnenberg, a public-relations expert; Rear-Admiral Lewis L. Strauss, chairman of the U.S. Atomic Energy Commission; and Herbert Bayard Swope, the noted editor and consultant.

Before long, an opportunity arose for me to criticize this anomalous "appropriation" of American Jewry's three hundredth anniversary. Judge Rosenman invited me to have lunch with him one day in September 1952, for the purpose of hearing my ideas about the forthcoming celebration. After the death of President Roosevelt, Judge Rosenman had served President Truman in a similar advisory capacity. He told me over lunch that his father had been an immigrant from Russia who settled in San Antonio, Texas, and earned his livelihood as a peddler. Rosenman himself was an outstanding jurist and liberal, who provided Roosevelt with his political slogan of the "New Deal." Like Henry Morgenthau, Jr., he did not disguise his Jewish loyalties and had, in fact, proved helpful to the Zionist cause while serving at the

White House in 1948. In the course of our talk, he also spoke of his profound gratitude to America for the opportunity given him to attain the high position of counsel to two successive Presidents.

In regard to the tercentenary observance, I ventured to suggest that the people who had been chosen so far were, for the most part, not active in American Jewish life or prominent in synagogue and congregational affairs. Had men such as these been in command of American Jewish strategy two or three generations earlier, I remarked, there might not be a Jewish community in the United States today to celebrate its tercentenary. I therefore urged that a more representative cross-section of American Jewry be brought into the picture—labor groups and industrialists, religious leaders and educators, Zionists and non-Zionists, Ashkenazim and Sephardim.

I also felt that the celebration should be self-affirming and dignified, not motivated by the usual "hush-hush" approach favored in certain Jewish quarters. It would be a grave mistake to proceed in this way, on tiptoe. Had we not pursued a forthright Jewish policy, I told my host, the Jewish State might never have come into being, nor would laws against discriminatory practices have been entered into the statute books of the United States.

Finally, I proposed that two permanent monuments be created in honor of the tercentenary. One was an authentic volume of American Jewish history, to be prepared by qualified scholars (Professor Salo W. Baron was eventually chosen to head this project); the other was a building in Washington, D.C., to house important documents related to American Jewry and to religious rights and freedoms.

Judge Rosenman listened carefully to what I had to say and took my strictures in good part. It was agreed that I would attend further meetings with the larger group.

Throughout the ensuing discussions, I continued to speak out against any apologetic approach to the American Jewish Tercentenary. We should behave like any other group of American citizens holding this type of celebration, I said. Moreover, two important aspects were not covered by the proposals submitted heretofore. The first was a proper emphasis on Israel, the establishment of which had been the greatest single event in nineteen centuries of Jewish history. Both American Jewry and the American Government and people had played a tremendous part in bringing it about, hence the need for Israel to be reflected prominently in our celebration. The other missing aspect was Jewish education and values, the promotion of which should also be stressed as the key to Jewish survival. "We must do what we can," I urged, "to make sure that, in 2054, there will be a strong and vital Jewish community in America to celebrate the next centenary milestone in its history."

The planning conference of the American Jewish Tercentenary Committee took place in New York over the weekend of April 11–12, 1953. By that time, the original nucleus had grown to a membership of 300, with a representative steering committee. Among those who addressed the Saturday night session were Herman Wouk, the prominent author and Orthodox layman; Rabbi David de Sola Pool of Congregation Shearith Israel, the oldest synagogue in North America; and two Nobel Prize laureates, Professors Selman A. Waksman and Isidor I. Rabi. The

Sunday luncheon program, at which Judge Simon Rifkind presided, included Leon H. Keyserling, the economist, Judge Joseph Proskauer and myself as speakers.

I had prepared two different addresses, one of a controversial nature, but David Bernstein, the Tercentenary Committee's executive director, was in favor of my delivering the milder one and I accepted his advice. It dealt with the past half-century's impact on American Jewry, highlighting a few of the notable successes and failures. After posing some questions about the future, it ended on a note of thanksgiving.

My speech evoked a handsome statement on Israel from Judge Proskauer. This was a bold gesture on his part, considering that one of his American Jewish Committee associates on the platform was none other than Lessing Rosenwald, president of the vehemently anti-Zionist American Council for Judaism. Proskauer's tribute to Israel cemented a broad front of Zionists and non-Zionists, allied against the anti-Zionist element, within the context of American Jewry's three hundredth anniversary celebration.

At the time of my election as an associate chairman of the American Jewish Tercentenary Committee, I was also president of the American Jewish Congress and chairman of the Western Hemisphere Executive of the WJC. This fortunate conjunction of posts and responsibilities tied several threads together, enabling me to convey the message of the tercentenary to other Jewish communities and to strengthen the bonds of Jewish peoplehood by bringing back greetings to the Jews of the United States.

There were three special foci of interest: Israel, the ancestral Jewish homeland; the mother community in Holland, which had provided and helped the earliest Jewish settlers in the New World; and the first historic Jewish population centers in Central and South America. The route taken on my "sentimental journey into the past" could roughly be described as an enormous triangle, with its base stretching from North to South America and its two sides extending to the Netherlands and to Israel in the Old World.

My wife accompanied me on the preliminary leg of this trip, which began in the Caribbean. Our first stop was Kingston, the capital of Jamaica in the British West Indies. There were about 1,500 Jews on the island, mostly in Kingston, and they were planning a tercentenary celebration of their own to commemorate the first Jewish settlement, which followed the British conquest of Jamaica in 1655. Their synagogue, a merger of previously separate Sephardi and Ashkenazi congregations, no longer maintained Orthodox ritual. The rate of intermarriage was high and the superficial Jewish education given to children seemed unlikely to prevent rapid assimilation.

I delivered a sermon before the United Congregation of Israelites on Friday evening, March 12, 1954. After referring to the fact that the Reverend Henry S. Jacobs, one of my predecessors in the rabbinate of Congregation B'nai Jeshurun (from 1874 to 1893) and first president of the New York Board of Jewish Ministers, had been born and reared in the Jamaican community, and served his novitiate there, I emphasized the significance of this particular day, *Shabbat Zakhor*, the Sabbath of Remembrance. It must serve not only to remind us of "the Hamans and Hitlers who sought to destroy our people," but also to remember and aid our less fortunate brethren, as well as to drive home the lessons of Jewish experience in exile. Jews had contributed in various ways to Columbus's voyage across the ocean, I said, and in the New World he discovered they had found providential sanctuary and freedom. "The various branches of the scattered household of Israel must feel united by a bond of common responsibility," embracing one faith, one people, and one destiny, which in our time had acquired a historic new dimension in Medinat Yisrael.

From Kingston we went on to St. Thomas, in the Virgin Islands, which came under U.S. rule in 1917. Here were born two early American statesmen— Alexander Hamilton, who became Secretary of the Treasury in George Washington's first Administration, and Judah Philip Benjamin, who held office, successively, as Attorney General, Secretary of War, and Secretary of State in the Confederate Government during the American Civil War. Hamilton, I recalled, had one Jewish parent, while Judah P. Benjamin was fully Jewish. In the course of my address before Congregation Berakhah Ve-Shalom in St. Thomas, on March 26, I took occasion to mention the "bit of help" that B'nai Jeshurun, then a struggling infant in New York, asked and received from this well-established Jewish community in 1825. No more than fifteen Jewish families remained in St. Thomas when we were there, although they still had a rabbi, Moses D. Sasso.

A special event of Jewish communal interest occurred during our visit to St. Thomas. It was the farewell banquet tendered in honor of the outgoing Governor of the Virgin Islands, Morris Fidangue de Castro, who had held that office for a number of years, much to the proud delight of his fellow Jews. The gift presented to him by the Legislative Council at that function was a painting of the beautiful and historic Sephardi synagogue at St. Thomas, to which he was deeply attached. The present building, erected in 1833, replaced an earlier one destroyed in a fire.

Our visit to Sosúa, on the northern shore of the Dominican Republic, the other half of the island of Hispaniola shared with Haiti, coincided with Purim. When President Roosevelt convened the Evian Conference in 1938, the President of the Republic, General Rafael L. Trujillo, had offered Sosúa as a place of agricultural settlement for Jewish refugees from Europe. It received an initial grant from the American Jewish Joint Agricultural Corporation (Agro-Joint), a subsidiary of the JDC. More than 22,000 acres were made available by Trujillo, but not all of this land was utilized at the beginning. There was considerable opposition to this project within the Zionist movement, as it seemed likely to divert potential Olim from Palestine.

Somewhat to our surprise, we found a flourishing Jewish colony in Sosúa, which enjoyed a high reputation throughout the Dominican Republic for its excellent meat and dairy produce. We were met upon our arrival by the head of the community, Señor Alfred Rosenzweig, who had come from Vienna in 1940. The 180 Jewish residents whom we found there in 1954 represented a veritable *Kibbutz Galuyyot*, an "ingathering of exiles" from places as far afield as Germany, Austria, Hungary, and Shanghai. Among them, to our astonishment, were also a few families from Israel who, it seemed, had been driven abroad by domestic and other problems at home. During World War II, there had been as many as 600 Jews in Sosúa, but their numbers had declined steeply since then. More than two-thirds had left, mostly for the United States. There were two smaller *kehillot* in Santo Domingo and Santiago.

Since the Jews of Sosúa were quite well-off, with a cooperative boasting a turn-over of $600,000 annually and each settler farming twenty-five acres, I thought it strange that so many should have left. The chief reason for this, I discovered, was the absence of any meaningful Jewish future for the younger generation. Throughout the Caribbean region, assimilation and intermarriage posed the greatest danger to Jewish life and continuity. Old Sephardi families had long disappeared, leaving only their aristocratic surnames among the Christian population. Even some of the recent Ashkenazi settlers had married Dominican women, and I saw children in the Sosúa community with dusky, negroid features.

During our stay there, I took occasion to visit the local Jewish school, where religious instruction was meager and Hebrew was not included in the syllabus. I stressed the need for the community leaders to provide their children with an adequate knowledge of Hebrew, and urged the Israeli Yordim to make themselves useful as Hebrew language teachers. All of these Jews, I said, should begin plan-ning their future in Israel. The first priority was a more intensive religious training, since "Jews, surrounded by a non-Jewish environment, do not survive as Jews by force of inertia, but only by force of the Jewish will to live, translated into a program of Jewish survival."

Soon after our return to New York, we left for Israel, where I had to attend meetings of the Zionist General Council and the Jewish Agency Executive, which were scheduled to take place in July. There was much gratifying interest in the American Jewish Tercentenary, to which the Israeli press devoted considerable attention.

Our tour of the country that month included a visit to the seaside town of Ashkelon, where the Amidar housing corporation, set up by the Jewish Agency during my term as its treasurer, had launched the Afridar residential project in cooperation with South African Jewry. President Itzhak Ben-Zvi and his wife, Rahel Yannait, were at their summer home, adjoining the house in which their son and his family lived, so Bert and I took the opportunity of calling on them. It was an extremely hot day and I had my jacket and tie over my arm when Israel's head of state came out to receive us.

"Mr. President," I said, "if protocol demands a jacket and tie, here they are, all ready to put on." He smiled briefly, in his usual reserved way, and replied, "Save them for your visit to Bet Ha-Nasi, the President's House in Jerusalem!"

Itzhak Ben-Zvi gave the impression of being a dry, somewhat distant person, but this impression did not do him justice. His natural modesty made him appear to be a scholar rather than a statesman and politician, although he had spent many decades in public life. I had first met him years earlier, during the British Mandate period, when he served as president of the Va'ad Leumi, virtually the head of Palestinian Jewry. He and David Ben-Gurion, fellow law students in Constantinople prior to World War I, had left for the United States shortly after the outbreak of hostilities in the Near East. Three years later, they had returned to Palestine in the ranks of the Jewish Legion.

His wife, Raḥel Yannait, was a Zionist leader in her own right. She had striven mightily to promote agricultural education for young women and established a farm school in North Talpiot, Jerusalem, which she conducted successfully for many years. After the death of her husband in 1963, she became the moving spirit in Yad Itzḥak Ben-Zvi, the institute specializing in research into the history of Oriental Jewish communities. Ben-Zvi had been the author of various scholarly works on that subject, including *The Exiled and the Redeemed* (1958).

At the Actions Committee meeting on July 29, I dealt with relations between American Jewry and Israel, with particular reference to the tercentenary:

> The twenty-three Jews who sailed into the harbor of New Amsterdam in September 1654 little dreamed that they were opening up a path which would become a highway to millions of Jews, in the years and generations to come. They were refugees from parts of the new continent, where already Jewish communities had flourished. . . . They fled from Brazil when that land changed hands and religious freedom was abrogated and religious persecution was substituted. After them came streams of other refugees across the generations, escaping religious, racial and political persecution, down to the recent chapter of our own time.
>
> American Jews, for the most part, are refugees or the offspring of refugees. There are no *yaḥsanim* [people who can boast of an especially distinguished pedigree]. The most "aristocratic" and the least "aristocratic" are alike refugees, only a few generations removed.

That same evening, the Zionist General Council, assembled in Jerusalem, passed an impressively worded resolution extending greetings to the American Jewish community "on the occasion of its observance of the three hundredth anniversary of the first settlement of Jews" in North America. I took the resolution back home with me, together with messages from President Ben-Zvi, Prime Minister Moshe Sharett, and Chief Rabbi Isaac Halevi Herzog, to be read out at a meeting of the WJC's Western Hemisphere Executive in New York, which was scheduled for mid-October.

A few hours before the passage of this tercentenary resolution, Actions Committee members had attended a moving ceremony at Yad Vashem, then under construction on Har ha-Zikkaron, the Mount of Remembrance, in Jerusalem. A law enacted by the Knesset, on August 19, 1953, had brought into being the Martyrs' and Heroes' Remembrance Authority (Yad Vashem), to which an area of land was allocated near Mount Herzl. Within the next few years, a complex of buildings arose there, housing a museum of the Holocaust and of Jewish resistance to the Nazis, a synagogue, a Hall of Names perpetuating the memory of Holocaust victims, a library, archives, a research center, and a Hall of Remembrance (Ohel Yizkor), where the Eternal Light (Ner Tamid) burns and martyrs' ashes are preserved in a vault. Yad Vashem demonstrates to all who come there that the six million shall not remain nameless and that they will never be forgotten.

On the way back to New York, I stopped over in Holland to bring a message of goodwill from American Jewry to Queen Juliana and the Dutch royal family and to the Government and people of the Netherlands. Appropriately, our tercentenary message recalled with gratitude that "Holland was the mother of religious tolerance in the Western Hemisphere" and that "the Bible, which has influenced the Dutch people so deeply, was the spiritual foundation of American democracy."

Dr. Willem Drees, Prime Minister of the Netherlands, received me cordially when I called on him at his office in The Hague on August 10. He was interested to learn that the twenty-three Jewish refugees from Brazil who arrived in New Amsterdam had been preceded two months earlier by a Dutch Jew, Jacob Barsimon, who came directly from Holland early in July 1654. I also mentioned other Jewish groups fleeing Brazil that had found refuge under the Dutch flag in Surinam and Curaçao. Upon learning that it was my intention to visit these two Dutch colonies in the West Indies within the next few weeks, Prime Minister Drees was kind enough to advise their Governors of my impending trip.

The conclusion of my message had referred to the recent dedication of a youth and children's village in Israel bearing the name of Queen Juliana. In the official statement Dr. Drees asked me to convey to American Jewry on the occasion of the tercentenary dinner scheduled to be held in October, he emphasized the continued felicitous relationship between Holland and the Jewish people, which he stated as follows:

Less than fifteen years ago, the Dutch people were horrified and incensed at the persecution that befell the Jewish community of the Netherlands under the German occupation. The history of those days tells of the solidarity of the Dutch people with their suffering Jewish brethren.

The bond between Holland and the State of Israel remains to this day, I would add, one of the shining examples of close friendship between nations that could be emulated with advantage by many other nations.

The Pioneer Trail

On September 1, 1954, I resumed my "sentimental journey," setting out for Recife in Brazil, Surinam (Dutch Guiana), and Curaçao. The seventeenth-century founders of the North American Jewish community had taken months to reach New Amsterdam by ship; I was able to proceed in the reverse direction, by air, in a matter of hours.

Recife, capital of the Brazilian state of Pernambuco, where the story began, was my first port of call. Among the original Portuguese settlers there were "New Christians" (Marranos) and others of Jewish descent who were active in commerce, especially the production and marketing of sugar. Many of them married into "Old Christian" (non-Jewish) families and achieved prominence. As a result of the Dutch conquest of Pernambuco in May 1630, Dutch Brazil became the one area in Latin America where Jews could openly practice their religion and establish a ramified communal life. Jewish immigrants came in fairly large numbers from Holland and were joined by some of the "New Christians," who formally reverted to Judaism. A synagogue, K. K. Tzur Yisrael, was consecrated by the Jews of Recife in 1636 and two religious schools were opened. Six years later, the growing needs of the community brought the first ordained rabbi to the New World—Isaac Aboab da Fonseca of Amsterdam. He was accompanied by the scholarly Moses Rafael de Aguilar and many more Jewish immigrants. By 1645, the local *kehillah* reached its zenith, numbering some 1,500 persons or fifty percent of the European civilian population, and it had become famous as "the Jerusalem of the New World."

Nine years of Portuguese guerila warfare, commencing in 1645, severely affected the Recife community, which had declined to about 600 when the Dutch finally surrendered in January 1654. A number of Jewish prisoners of war were executed by the enemy or shipped back to Portugal for trial by the Inquisition. With the fall of Recife, most professing Jews either returned to Holland or sought refuge in Curaçao, Barbados, and other parts of the Caribbean. Among them, of course, were those who arrived in New Amsterdam. Crypto-Judaism was still alive in Brazil a century later, but no trace of the old Sephardic community now remains. The present *kehillah* dates only from the early twentieth century and comprises Ashkenazim of East European (mainly Rumanian) descent.

A degree of historical irony accompanied the warm reception extended to me on my arrival by the Governor of Pernambuco, Dr. Etelvine Lins de Albuquerque, the Prefect (Mayor) of Recife, and other Brazilian notables. It so happened that my visit coincided with nationwide festivities celebrating "the three hundredth anniversary of the overthrow of Dutch oppression," and the streets of Recife were festooned with bunting in honor of that event. What had brought about the mass flight of Jews from Brazil, where so many had fought and suffered for the Dutch cause, was a reason here for widespread rejoicing. I nevertheless accepted an invitation to view the battlefields on which "the yoke of the Dutch" was finally broken, realizing that time has a way of dulling the edge of such incongruities.

There were about 1,300 Jews in Recife at the time of my visit. I toured local Jewish institutions and was impressed by the all-day elementary school, where ninety percent of the community's children were said to be enrolled. Israel and Zionist themes occupied an important place in the curriculum, and Yiddish was also taught. Dr. V. Winterstein, director of the World Jewish Congress in Brazil, came up from Rio de Janeiro to greet me and he escorted me on my tour of Recife.

While visiting the city's historical museum, we gathered that the museum's head, a noted scholar, was eager to promote research into Jewish antiquities of the colonial period. I urged the leaders of the *kehillah* to establish a local Jewish historical society in order to foster such research, and there was an immediate positive response.

One of my hosts told me a curious firsthand story about a Jewish visitor from overseas who met a Catholic dignitary at the airport on his way to an ecclesiastical conference in Rio. The latter introduced himself as Bishop Toledano, whereupon the visitor pointed out that this was a typically Jewish surname. He then learned that the bishop's father had been a Dutch Jew; his mother, an ardent Catholic, had raised her son in the Christian faith after the death of her husband. Only some years later, following his ordination, did the son find out about his Jewish antecedents. This prompted him to take an interest in Judaism. As evidence, Bishop Toledano delved into his valise and produced a bag containing a *tallit* and a pair of *tefillin* (prayer shawl and phylacteries). It was most intriguing to hear of such a latter-day "Marrano."

A farewell banquet held in my honor on September 4 was attended by leaders of cultural, social, and political life in Recife and the state of Pernambuco. One of Brazil's outstanding intellectuals, Professor Gilberto Freire, chaired the proceedings. It was gratifying to hear a number of warm statements concerning the Jewish contribution to civilization and to Brazil, and some glowing tributes to Israel. More than one speaker remarked that, when the Jews left Recife three centuries previously, Brazil and Portugal had suffered a grave loss.

I was intrigued by Professor Freire's reference to the "New Christians" and the minority of Jews who remained in Pernambuco when the majority left for other shores after the Dutch capitulation. "There are," he said, "anthropological grounds for the fact that some of us, whose ancestry dates back to those far-off days, are sometimes taken by 'Nordic' Europeans to be people of Jewish descent. In Portugal and in Spain, members of the Jewish race had already undergone considerable mixture with Nordic and Moorish elements before the European colonists first arrived in America."

Professor Freire then went on to speak of early Brazilian history under the Portuguese and to express his regret that seventeenth-century Recife had not retained as citizens men such as Rabbi Isaac Aboab da Fonseca. "Had they stayed here and had their successors been comparable men of learning," he said, "the Recife of today would be a more brilliant city." After dwelling at length upon the influence of Sephardic culture and the Hispanic civilization that shaped future cultural life in Brazil and Latin America, he concluded that "Brazil was the first dazzling center of Jewish efflorescence in the New World."

On the morning after the banquet, I was the guest of Professor Freire at his home on the outskirts of Recife. As I was admiring his extensive library, he pulled out a volume from one of the shelves and said, "This book arrived from England only a few weeks ago. You may be interested in having a look at it." It was a genealogical study of one of Anglo-Jewry's prominent families. I opened a page at random and came across some details concerning a seventeenth-century ancestress of that family named Esther Pereira. The name "Esther" had been given to her because she was born on Purim, and there was a verse dedicated to her memory. What startled me, however, was the similarity of her family name to that of my host. I turned to him and said, "Professor Freire, the name Pereira may well have been borne by your ancestors, since in Hebrew the letter *F* becomes *P* merely by the insertion of a dot."

My host was even more startled than I had been. "There is a tradition in our family that Jewish blood flows in our veins." he explained, "and this has always been a matter of pride. Now you come from New York, visit my home, and I show you this book. You open it at a certain page and discover someone who may well have been one of my ancestors. This must surely be the finger of God!"

Before my departure, the Governor of Pernambuco and the Prefect of Recife handed me written messages to convey to Governor Thomas E. Dewey of New York State and Mayor Robert F. Wagner of New York City, respectively. I was also entrusted with greetings in Yiddish that the Recife *kehillah* wished to transmit to the Jewish community of New York.

En route from Recife to Surinam, I spent a few hours in Belém (a contracted form of "Bethlehem"), capital of the state of Pará, in northeastern Brazil. A port on the estuary of the Pará river, one of the Amazon's tributaries, Belém then had a Jewish community of some 250 families, almost all of them Sephardim from North Africa. The first Jews to settle there arrived in the early nineteenth century and established a synagogue in 1824. At the time of my brief visit, these Moroccan Jews maintained two synagogues and three cemeteries, but they had no rabbi and Jewish communal life there was at a low ebb.

In Paramaribo, the chief city and capital of Surinam, an official luncheon was tendered me by the Dutch Governor, Dr. J. Klaasesz. This followed a reception arranged by the local Jewish community. The Governor and his lady showed rare consideration, providing a special meal, of which the *pièce de résistance*, surrounded by elaborate silverware, was an unopened can of Rokeach's *kasher* meat placed before each guest. I thought this a memorable token of their hospitality.

It seemed that only the coastal region of Dutch Guiana had been developed, the rest of Surinam being jungle. The population totaled about 250,000 and mainly comprised American Indians, Creoles, Hindus, Indonesians, and "Bush Negroes," people of mixed African and Creole descent. There were about 500 Jews in Surinam, roughly one-sixth of the European element.

Surinam boasts the oldest continuous Jewish settlement in the Western Hemisphere. The first Jews arrived there from Holland and other places as early as 1639, when the territory was ruled by the British. A second group came from England in 1652 and, fourteen years later, a large contingent arrived from Cayenne and British Guiana. They were headed by Joseph Nuñez de Fonseca, known popularly as David Nassi, and had originally left Dutch Brazil in 1654. These newcomers moved some ten miles up the Surinam river and established a settlement that became known as *Joden Savanne*, "the Jewish Plain." Benefiting from their previous farming experience, they successfully cultivated sugarcane, coffee, tobacco, and other tropical crops.

When Surinam fell to the Dutch in 1667, the Jewish settlers were regarded as such industrious citizens that every effort was made to prevent them leaving. Their religious freedom, guaranteed by the British in 1665, was subsequently reconfirmed by the Dutch authorities. The colony's second synagogue was built in *Joden*

Savanne in 1685 and, by the end of the seventeenth century, nearly 600 Jews lived thereabouts, including some immigrants from Germany. Despite the abolition of slavery and a decline in the sugar trade, the Jewish population grew steadily until the beginning of the twentieth century, when the community numbered 1,500. By then, there were more Ashkenazim than Sephardim in the territory. During World War II, several hundred Jewish refugees from Europe found refuge in Dutch Guiana, although most of them later dispersed to other parts of North and South America. Some moved to Holland.

Surinam's Jewish community differs markedly from other *kehillot* in Latin America because of the ability of many of its members to trace their ancestry back to the seventeenth century. A glance at some of these decendants of the early Jewish settlers, however, is enough to make one realize that there has been a good deal of intermarriage with the native population.

There are two old-established congregations in Paramaribo—Tzedek Ve-Shalom, the original Sephardi house of worship, and Neve Shalom, the Ashkenazi synagogue founded in 1734. Since, at the time of my visit, there were no longer enough Jews to utilize these two synagogue structures to a sufficient extent, the congregational elders had hit on a neat solution to the problem. Throughout the year, congregants worshiped alternately in both synagogues. A similar arrangement governs use of the "Spanish" and "Levantine" synagogues in Venice.

Jewish religious activities, I found, were subsidized by the Dutch Government. No full-time rabbi ministered to the Jews of Surinam, although the Sephardim had a *ḥazzan*, Isaac J. Bueno de Mesquita, who was away when I arrived. The Ashkenazim were fortunate to have the services of Dr. Jaap Meijer, a graduate of the rabbinical seminary in Amsterdam, who held a Government post as a high-school teacher. He fulfilled certain rabbinical functions and gave religious instruction to the Jewish community's children.

On September 7, an impressive evening service took place at Congregation Tzedek Ve-Shalom in honor of the American Jewish Tercentenary. Dutch, American, and Israeli flags adorned the exterior of the synagogue, which was illuminated for the occasion. My address was devoted to the theme, "In the Footsteps of the Pioneers." The entire official hierarchy of Surinam attended the service, including the Governor, the locally elected Prime Minister, the U.S. consul, local Christian clergy, and leaders in all walks of life. This representative gathering was a tribute to the status of the local Jewish community. Prayers for the Netherlands royal family and Government and for Israel were recited. Dr. Meijer extended greetings in Dutch and in Hebrew, and I responded in Hebrew and in English.

Pointing up my reference to treading "in the footsteps of the pioneers," my hosts accorded me that privilege by organizing a cruise the following day to the old, abandoned settlement of *Joden Savanne.* Our journey up the Surinam river took five hours, enabling me to see the tribal villages along our route, some of them inhabited by Bush Negroes who still practiced voodoo. We also saw the bauxite mining and shipping installations operated by Alcoa (the Aluminum Company of America).

Surinam is thought to be the world's largest single producer of bauxite, which constitutes the territory's chief source of income.

The site of *Joden Savanne* had been chosen by the original Jewish settlers because of its elevation and suitability for farming. It was continuously inhabited for almost 150 years, until a fire destroyed the synagogue there in 1832. The Jewish community thereupon moved back to the capital, Paramaribo. All that remains of the former synagogue are portions of the walls and the *Mah Tovu* steps, on which congregants once recited "How goodly are thy tents, O Jacob, thy dwelling places, O Israel!" before entering their house of worship.

I learned that Jews from Paramaribo still came here to recite memorial prayers before the High Holy Days and on other solemn occasions. We affixed a commemorative tablet in honor of the pioneers on the ruined wall of the synagogue.

A few hundred yards away, through tropical jungle, lay the old cemetery, where we visited the grave of David Nassi, who had led the group that founded the settlement in 1666. Memorial prayers were recited and brief addresses were delivered by the head of the Jewish community and myself.

The sight of these gravestones heightened the irritation I felt over the inadequate Jewish education available in Paramaribo and the lack of an organized fund-raising campaign for Israel. Turning to our pilgrimage group, I said:

My mood is solemn, because I am thinking about the Jewish future of your community. Will an epitaph soon be written for Jewish life in Surinam? Will the Judaism to which your ancestors, who lie here, were dedicated come to an end? Were the Jewish community in Surinam to disappear because of Aliyah to Israel, I would bless the day; but that does not seem to be the prospect. I trust that you will think seriously about it and, in the meantime, do all you can to give your children a meaningful Jewish education and conduct a meaningful annual *magbit* for Israel, which, in itself, is a vitalizing Jewish exercise. Thus, you will prove worthy of your ancestors, whose memory we have honored here today.

My parting words must have left a sour taste in the mouths of my hosts, particularly Dr. Meijer. He nevertheless promised to convey my remarks at the cemetery to the entire Jewish community of Surinam.

Before my departure, I was asked to take home with me greetings from the Governor and the Prime Minister of Dutch Guiana on the occasion of the American Jewish Tercentenary.

The island of Curaçao in the Netherlands Antilles, formerly known as the Dutch West Indies, was the last port of call in my "sentimental journey." At its height, in the eighteenth century, the island's Jewish community had been the largest and the wealthiest in the Western Hemisphere, but there were barely 800 Jews to be found there at the time of my visit, less than one percent of the total population.

The earliest Jewish settlers arrived in Curaçao around 1650, sixteen years after the Dutch had wrested the island from Spain. They immediately founded the nucleus of a synagogue, out of which the historic Congregation Mikveh Israel was to develop. In 1654, some of the Jewish refugees from Brazil came ashore and remained on the island. A cemetery was acquired and branch synagogues were established. The first Sephardi *Ḥakham* took up his rabbinical duties in 1674. Protected by the Dutch West India Company, Curaçao Jewry flourished and made its mark in trade and shipping. A few Jews commanded ships and distinguished themselves in naval battles with privateers. They contributed generously to local causes, and three Jews served as president of the Colonial Council in the nineteenth century. Thereafter, their numbers began to decline.

The many disputes that beset the Jewish community are a fair indication of vitality as well as testiness. There were repeated secessions from the mother congregation, Mikveh Israel, the last of which culminated in the establishment of a Reform temple, Emanu-El, in 1864. At the time of my visit, these two congregations were entirely separate, but I learned subsequently that they amalgamated as a Liberal synagogue in 1963. Between the two World Wars, Ashkenazi Jews from Eastern Europe began to settle in Curaçao, where they set up their own communal structure. An Ashkenazi congregation, Sha'arei Tzedek, was founded in 1959.

This island community enjoys the distinction of having received the first charter of religious liberty in the New World, according to the provisions of which Jews were permitted to desist from work on the Sabbath.

Close connections prevailed between this *kehillah* and those of North America. Among the old-established Jewish families in the United States that originated from Curaçao were the Touros of Newport, Rhode Island, who founded Congregation Yeshuat Israel. In 1720, Congregation Shearith Israel in New York and, in 1756, Congregation Yeshuat Israel in Newport appealed to the affluent Jewish community of Curaçao for assistance in building their synagogues. Rabbi Raphael Ḥayyim Carigal, an emissary from Hebron, visited the island in 1762 and remained there for two years as *Ḥakham*. It was some time later, in 1773, that Rabbi Carigal arrived in Newport and so impressed Ezra Stiles, with whom he subsequently maintained a correspondence.

On my arrival at the airport, I was welcomed by a representative Jewish delegation, with Rabbi I. Jessurun Cardozo of Congregation Mikveh Israel at their head. In responding to the greetings they extended, I lightheartedly remarked that one of the purposes of my visit would be to ascertain whether the old congregational records showed a repayment by my own congregation, B'nai Jeshurun, of the sum Mikveh Israel had advanced in 1825 to help build our first synagogue in New York.

Unfortunately, my stay in Willemstad, the capital of Curaçao, had to be limited to an afternoon and an evening, but I had time to meet with the Acting Governor, Mr. V. D. Valk, and the Prime Minister of the Netherlands Antilles, Dr. M. F. da Costa Gomez. I learned from our conversations that Peter Stuyvesant, the Governor of New Amsterdam in 1654 (when the twenty-three Jewish immigrants arrived from Pernambuco), had lost his leg in battle while serving in an earlier post as Governor of Curaçao.

My tour of the local Jewish historical sights included a visit to the old cemetery, where many beautifully sculpted gravestones were obviously suffering from the fumes emitted by the island's huge oil refinery. An odd criterion determined where a Jew or Jewess was buried in this graveyard. One section was reserved for Sephardim who, on reciting the benediction over wine, conclude with "*boré p'ri ha-gefen*," and another section was appointed for Ashkenazim, who pronounce the words, "*boré p'ri ha-gofen*." How strange that such a shibboleth should have divided one Jewish community from another!

Rabbi Cardozo, a devoted Zionist, headed a Hebrew-speaking circle on the island and encouraged Aliyah to Israel. A *magbit* campaign was organized each year, but the response to this appeal was not commensurate with the financial resources of the local *kehillah*. As elsewhere, I discovered plentiful evidence of intermarriage. Rabbi Cardozo told me of a case in which the children of such a mixed union had been sent to a youth village in Israel for a year; upon their return to Curaçao, these youngsters no longer felt comfortable in their home environment. They now wished to go back to Israel, where they were not made to feel "different."

A culminating experience of interest for me was the meeting arranged by the community, on the evening of September 9, at the beautiful synagogue of Congregation Mikveh Israel. This structure, the fourth house of worship built by the early Jewish settlers, had been completed and consecrated in 1732. It is the oldest surviving synagogue in the Western Hemisphere, and takes as its model the renowned and magnificent Portuguese synagogue of Amsterdam, consecrated in 1675. The floor was covered with sand, a reminder of Israel's first sanctuary in the wilderness and a sign of mourning for the Temple in Jerusalem.

The assembly, which took place outdoors on the patio of Congregation Mikveh Israel, was attended by the Acting Governor, the Prime Minister, the mayor, the U.S. consul, and members of the *kehillah*. In the course of my address, I reviewed the historical connection between North American Jewry and the communities of Latin America and the Caribbean, which were its "alma mater." I also dwelt on present-day ties and their common interest in and attachment to Medinat Yisrael. Later that evening, I spoke briefly in Yiddish and Hebrew to members of the Club Union, the social center of Ashkenazi Jews who had immigrated more recently to Curaçao from Eastern Europe. The Prime Minister took the occasion to pay his first visit to this Jewish club. Both he and the Acting Governor entrusted me with messages of greeting to the American Jewish Tercentenary.

My last stop on the homeward journey to the United States was the island of Aruba in the Netherlands Antilles. Jewish settlement there dated from 1753. Most of the sixty Jewish families living on the island in 1954 had arrived within the past two or three decades from Holland and from Central and Eastern Europe. There was time to meet only a few of these families before I boarded my plane for Miami and New York.

Brief though it was, this ten-day trip—the second and more important stage of my "sentimental journey" into American Jewry's past—had been a rewarding and meaningful experience. Some of the important lessons that could be drawn from it were outlined in my Kol Nidré sermon delivered before Congregation B'nai Jeshurun in New York on October 6. There were, I said, two current schools of thought regarding the future of Jewish life outside Israel. The first cited many historical precedents to argue that there would be no enduring Jewish existence in the *Golah*, even in the United States. Dutch Zionists whom I had met during my summer visit to Holland could not understand why American Jewry should be making a *Yom tov* of 300 years in Diaspora. Their attitude made sense in the light of the Nazi Holocaust. Curiously enough, however, those who took a more positive view of Judaism and Jewish life in the Diaspora included some Israelis. Professor Ben-Zion Dinur, Israel's Minister of Education, who was present in our synagogue when I spoke, thought that time should be allocated to the American Jewish Tercentenary in schools throughout the Medinah. I also inclined toward this second viewpoint, but with certain reservations:

> Recently, I have seen old communities in the Caribbean which provide an object lesson of Judaism in decline, when left to the forces of inertia. There are Cohens and Levys who have been Catholics and Protestants for generations. There are old synagogues where today not even a *minyan* appears on the Sabbath, where there are no organized religious schools for the children, and where the most impressive communal feature is the cemetery. While there is life, however, there is hope. Perhaps they can be revived if the Jews of the United States and the Jews of Israel are determined to meet this challenge and to supply properly qualified teachers and rabbis.

The Jews of the United States themselves, I added, had no reason for complacency, since only twenty-seven percent of Jewish children in our own country were receiving even the most meager form of Jewish education. "Operation Survival" meant that far greater support must be given to local institutions of higher Jewish learning, the promotion of Jewish culture and scholarship, and an attitude that would encourage young men to "choose Torah as a career."

In a detailed report submitted to the Western Hemisphere Executive of the World Jewish Congress on October 14, 1954, I summed up my general impressions of the overseas tours I had undertaken at the outset of this tercentenary year. Such visits by representatives of American Jewry should be continued in the future, I urged, as they strengthened Jewish morale and heightened the sense of Jewish fellowship among the communities of Central and South America. The role of Medinat Yisrael in enhancing their local prestige was everywhere apparent. A goodly part of my status in the eyes of non-Jewish leaders during these tours had consisted of my Zionist credentials. I felt especially grateful for the opportunity of bringing to these *kehillot*, which had seen better days and were now mainly in a state of decline, an expression of U.S. Jewry's indebtedness to them for the moral and material aid rendered by their forebears when they were in a position to do so, and for their notable contribution to the history of Jewish communal life in North America.

Public observance of the American Jewish Tercentenary was signaled by a number of functions throughout the United States. The Synagogue Council of America arranged a special service of thanksgiving in the synagogue of Congregation Shearith Israel, New York, where Professor Salo Baron delivered a keynote address.

On October 20, the tercentenary dinner was held at the Hotel Astor in New York, with President Dwight D. Eisenhower as the guest of honor. About 1,800 people attended and Ralph E. Samuel took the chair. I delivered a short prayer. The messages from Israel's President, Itzhak Ben-Zvi, Prime Minister Moshe Sharett, and Chief Rabbi Isaac Halevi Herzog drew enthusiastic applause. Other messages of greeting, which I had brought from the Prime Minister of the Netherlands, Dr. Willem Drees, and from various dignitaries in Brazil and the Caribbean, were also warmly appreciated.

President Eisenhower's speech dealt mostly with current world problems, and proved disappointing. He could have said much more about the Jewish contribution to the United States, and his remarks about Israel left much to be desired. He merely gave an assurance that the U.S. Administration would "see to it" that arms supplied to countries in the Middle East would not be used for aggressive purposes, ending with the usual expression of friendship for Israel and the other nations of the region.

During the dinner, I chatted with Bernard Baruch, who said that "Israel is getting a raw deal." He told me that he would try to see the President the following day, in order to take up the matter. Bernard Baruch had already spoken with Winston Churchill, but he remarked that the British statesman was surrounded by "politicians."

One much-appreciated item on the program was the singing of "God Bless America" by the immensely popular U.S. composer, Irving Berlin, who prefaced it with the remark, "I am a refugee, the son of a rabbi, and I came here just over sixty years ago." Another highlight was a musical contribution by the West Point Jewish Chapel Choir. Some forty young men from that renowned military academy sang various religious songs, including one in Hebrew, *Se'u She'arim*, "Lift up your heads, O ye gates" (Psalm 24:7–10). It was moving to hear it chorused by those Jewish lads in U.S. Army uniform.

I continued a while longer to be occupied with tercentenary events. They included a radio message in the *Eternal Light* series, a speech at the Israel Bonds Hanukkah celebration in Madison Square Garden, and addresses before the New York Federation of Jewish Philanthropies and the annual conference of the Jewish National Fund in Washington, D.C. On January 31, 1955, while attending a session of the WJC Executive in Paris, I spoke on "American Jewry and its European Origins" before the Culture Council of the Paris Jewish community. It was also my pleasure to pay tribute to the chairman of the American Jewish Tercentenary Committee, Ralph E. Samuel, at a function in New York on May 10, 1955, and to hand him a volume containing messages of greeting in six languages from fifty-seven different Jewish communities throughout the world. My final assignment was to speak at Carnegie Hall, on June 1, when the three hundredth anniversary celebrations officially concluded. The address I delivered on that occasion included a brief statement of my credo as an American Jew. The following is an extract:

I believe that the American in me merges congenially with my Jewish tradition, seeing that the Old Testament was revered by the original colonies as a model and pattern for the individual and the commonweal; and the Jew in me adds an extra dimension to my Americanism, seeing that the difficult but inescapable role of the Jew, by the very nature of his being a persistent minority, has challenged, evoked and defended decency, liberalism and civilization in every society in which he has lived.

I believe that the best hallmark of the Jew and his most valuable credential is his religion. . . . Torah is the mind and soul of Israel across time and space. And Torah can flourish in America if American Jewry wills it.

I believe that the State of Israel has a special destiny as the natural habitat of Jewish survival, as a light to the nations, as a gifted young sister democracy to the United States, and as the corporate demonstration of Jewish capacity to write a new page worthy of the Old Testament, which will be a vitalizing influence upon Jewish life everywhere. . . .

I believe that the exalted words of Isaiah, Chapter 66, can find fulfillment both here and in Israel, "For as long as the new heavens and the new earth which I make shall endure before Me, saith the Lord, so shall your offspring and your name endure."

Toward the end of 1955, my congregation generously sponsored the publication of a volume containing the various tercentenary addresses I had delivered on four continents. It appeared in New York under the title, *American Jewry Comes of Age*.

Rallying Support for Israel

On the international scene, grave new problems faced the World Jewish Congress and its ancillary bodies during the latter half of 1954. Stalin's death and the new Soviet regime headed by Nikita Khrushchev brought little or no improvement to the situation of more than two million Jews in the USSR. Hebrew culture and Zionist activity were rigorously suppressed, while what passed for Yiddish literature and culture was made to serve as a tool of Soviet propaganda. Attendance at synagogue, except by a meager number of older, retired folk, was fraught with danger, and Jewish religious instruction of the young was an indictable offense. Not even during the worst days of Czarism had Judaism in Russia undergone such wholesale repression.

When an opportunity presented itself in September of that year to raise these matters with a select committee of the U.S. Congress, I did so on behalf of the American Jewish Congress and attached a series of documented research reports on the fate of those whom Elie Wiesel was to dub, some twelve years later, "The Jews of Silence." We had reached the melancholy conclusion that Soviet policy, if unchanged, would result in the extinction of any distinctive Jewish life behind the Iron Curtain, despite the possibility of "détente" and "coexistence between East and West." Russian Jewry lay under the menace of cultural genocide, in defiance of international law, world public opinion, and the Soviet Union's own constitution.

At the same time, enormous political and economic difficulties confronted Israel. Ambassador Abba Eban gave us a briefing on the situation in the course of a breakfast meeting on September 17. Among those present were Irving M. Engel, who had recently succeeded Jacob Blaustein as president of the American Jewish Committee; Rose Halprin; Philip Klutznick, president of B'nai B'rith; Louis Lipsky; Rabbi Irving Miller, president of the American Zionist Council; I, as president of the American Jewish Congress; and Henry Montor, who directed the American Financial and Development Corporation for Israel, which was responsible for the State of Israel Bonds campaign.

During the preceding weeks, U.S. Secretary of State John Foster Dulles had called in Ambassador Eban several times and seemed anxious to ease relations with American Jewry over policy toward Israel. Recent speeches by one top official in the State Department, Henry Byroade, whom we regarded as decidedly pro-Arab, had infuriated Jews in the United States, and Dulles was reported to have issued instructions that no more speeches of a "sensitive" nature were to be made without his prior approval. This sudden démarche by the Secretary of State may well have been influenced by a pressing domestic concern—the forthcoming Congressional elections in November.

Eban had told Dulles that Israel, being the only small country in the Middle East that did not belong to any regional defense system, must therefore be given appropriate military aid by the United States. Moreover, he argued, it required a firm guarantee of its borders from the United States, since no existing document—not even the tripartite "guarantee" of 1950—was comparable to the treaty between Great Britain and Jordan, whereby an attack on the latter would be regarded as an attack on the former as well. Eban wanted to secure this kind of binding commitment from the United States.

Opinions at the breakfast meeting were divided. Some of those present were nervous about organizing any public protest that might antagonize Republican circles on the eve of the elections. Henry Montor and I, however, favored a return to the methods adopted in 1946 and 1947—mobilizing public opinion throughout the country. I urged that this was a legitimate procedure in a democracy, and that previous experience had taught us that even friends in the Government sometimes required "needling."

Further briefing sessions with Ambassador Eban took place in the first half of October 1954, when the latest political developments affecting Israel were reviewed. The upshot was that the heads of sixteen major national Jewish organizations went as a delegation to Washington, D.C., on October 25, for an interview with Secretary Dulles at the State Department. The fact that the group's spokesman, Philip Klutznick, held no official Zionist position stressed the all-embracing Jewish character of our deputation.

A memorandum we then submitted called upon the U.S. Government to refrain from arming the Arab states as long as they refused to make peace with Israel. It also urged that nothing be done to impair the balance of power in the Middle East, and that Israel be invited to join Western defense planning in that area. Our memorandum further called attention to the discrepancy between President Eisenhower's renewed affirmation of concern for Israel's welfare and the current

State Department policy, which was "neither equitable nor impartial" and which, we averred, did not serve America's own national interests.

Through this high-level meeting in Washington a pattern was set for the development of a significant relationship between successive U.S. Administrations and the organized American Jewish community, on all matters concerned with policy toward Israel. That relationship survived various strains and stresses over the years, and the united front of American Jewry vis-à-vis Government officialdom in Washington has continued ever since to prove its worth.

A significant political development on the American scene, which could be taken as a straw in the wind indicating popular discontent with the Republican Administration, was the Democratic victory that elected Averell Harriman as Governor of New York State, on November 2, 1954. The Liberal Party contributed in no small measure to Harriman's victory, and I was glad, as an official of that party, to have taken an active part in the election campaign.

There was a widespread feeling that Jewish resentment against the Eisenhower Administration's Middle East policies had much to do with the Republican candidate's defeat. Significantly, however, Jacob K. Javits was returned as Attorney General of New York State on the Republican ticket, defeating the Democratic candidate, Franklin D. Roosevelt, Jr. What evidently counted with many voters was Javits's outstanding pro-Israel record, which enabled him to gain a personal triumph, overcoming the anti-Republican backlash.

With a closely divided Congress, in which the Democrats controlled both the Senate and the House of Representatives by a small majority, we were hopeful that the U.S. Government would now take that situation as a warning that it was expected to do something constructive for Israel at long last.

8

To Live in Peace: 1954–58

The period of the mid-1950s was notable for growing social restlessness in the United States, for Cold War friction between East and West in Europe, and for an upsurge of nationalism in Egypt that would result in the second Israel-Arab war. Led by Egypt's charismatic young dictator, Gamal Abdul Nasser, the Arab world not only would not make peace with Israel but refused to accept the existence of the Jewish State and sought every means to undermine and, if possible, destroy it. Since the armistice agreements of 1949, this open hostility had stopped short of a declaration of war, but warlike acts did occur. By 1955, gangs of *fedayeen* crossing the southern border with Egypt, especially from the Egyptian-controlled Gaza Strip, were leaving a bloody trail behind them in Israeli settlements and villages. This rapidly became a grave menace to the nation's security.

Both this paramilitary threat and the tangled political situation were a source of deep concern to Israel's friends and well-wishers abroad, not least in the United States. The American Section of the Jewish Agency Executive met frequently to consider ways of countering the unfriendly influences in the U.S. State Department and of persuading the Eisenhower Administration to adopt a more positive and helpful approach to the Medinah. We were particularly incensed by the fact that Israel continued to be denied U.S. arms shipments, while the Arab states could obtain large quantities from a variety of sources.

One meeting of the Jewish Agency Executive, held in New York on December 24, 1954, was attended by Levi Eshkol, Israel's Minister of Finance, who was taking part in the negotiations his Government was then conducting with Eric Johnston, President Eisenhower's special envoy, over the allocation of water resources between Israel and the neighboring Arab states. Eshkol had just appeared as guest of honor at the Hanukkah festival organized by Israel Bonds at Madison Square Garden, where he presented a special Hanukkah Torch of Freedom to the people of New York City. It was accepted by Ira Guilden, chairman of the Greater New York Campaign for State of Israel Bonds, who has since played a major role in developing the campus and facilities of Boys' Town in Jerusalem.

More than 20,000 purchasers of Israel Bonds, to the value of $2.5 million, were crammed into the vast auditorium. In my opening remarks, as chairman of the Hanukkah festival committee, I urged that American policy in the Middle East

317

should not leave Israel to fend for itself against hostile neighbors who spurned its outstretched hand of peace. One-sided arms allocations and the exclusion of Israel from regional defense systems sponsored by the Great Powers were scarcely calculated to defend the vital interests of the one democracy in that part of the world. "It is essential," I concluded, "that American bipartisan policy, which helped Medinat Yisrael to be born, should now help it to live in peace and security."

Levi Eshkol's survey of the economic position, presented at the Jewish Agency Executive meeting on the following day, was comparatively sanguine. He reported that there was virtually no unemployment in Israel, that it could absorb 25,000–30,000 Olim per year, that irrigation of former desert areas was proceeding at a satisfactory pace, and that more new settlements were being established on the borders.

When the Agency's American members discussed the political situation a week later, concern was expressed over a pamphlet on Israel that had just been published by the State Department. A great deal of anti-Israel prejudice could be detected in this "balanced" and "dispassionate" presentation, and we decided upon some appropriate action.

The complexion of the new U.S. Congress gave grounds for anxiety. Senator Walter George of Georgia, chairman of the Senate Foreign Relations Committee, was no friend of Israel, and his counterpart in the House of Representatives, Congressman James P. Richards of South Carolina, favored continued arms supplies to the Arabs. Indeed, on his return from a fact-finding visit to the Middle East, Congressman Richards had declared that Israel was no more significant to the United States than any Arab land and that all of these countries were morally on a par. Geopolitical considerations, it seemed, meant more than ideological ones.

Dr. Nahum Goldmann and Avraham Harman, Israel's consul general in New York, spoke at a meeting of the Western Hemisphere Executive of the World Jewish Congress in the first week of January 1955. Goldmann outlined his long-cherished plan for a body similar to the WJC that would become the non-Zionist section of the Jewish Agency. In his far-ranging survey, Harman reported on the Arab propaganda onslaught against Israel, the arms-shipment crisis, and Egypt's blatant defiance of the UN resolution on freedom of passage through the Suez Canal. He also touched upon the show trials of Jews then being held in Cairo, following what became known in Israel as the security "mishap" *(Meḥdal)* or the Lavon Affair.

These were some of the issues that preoccupied us in those uneasy days and gave rise to widespread anxiety among American Jews.

As has often been the case over the years, a few tranquil interludes occurred in the midst of my tense Zionist responsibilities. The University of Judaism, established in Los Angeles under the wing of the Jewish Theological Seminary, decided to extend its program to New York and to organize postgraduate courses for rabbis and educators, as well as for social workers and civic leaders. Chancellor Louis Finkelstein of the JTS took the first step in this direction when he offered me a visiting professorship in contemporary Jewish history for the 1954–55 academic year. With the help of Professor Moshe Davis, I worked out a plan for the course and inaugurated it on November 1, 1954. A number of Jewish scholars from overseas also participated in this lecture series.

At the end of January 1955, the S.S. *Dagan*, built in Hamburg under West Germany's reparations agreement with Israel and the first ship in Zim's fleet of passenger and cargo vessels, arrived in New York harbor on its maiden voyage. It had an all-Israeli crew. Yosef Goldansky, its captain, was the first recipient of a master's license from the Israel Government. He had previously served as captain of the S.S. *Negbah*, which brought many refugees to Israel. The arrival of the *Dagan* caused a good deal of excitement among the Jews of New York, and I participated in the welcoming ceremony. The officers and crew attended Friday evening services at Congregation B'nai Jeshurun and were our guests at a Shabbat dinner.

In response to the increasingly serious problems confronting Israel, fifteen leading Jewish bodies in the United States had joined together in 1954, to set up what became known officially as the Conference of Presidents of Major American Jewish Organizations. Unofficially, it was dubbed "the Presidents' Club." Nahum Goldmann presided at the outset, and I was a member of the original nucleus. We met in New York during the second week of January 1955 in order to finalize our plans for coordinated action aimed at the strengthening of peace and security in the Middle East.

Some 500 community leaders from all parts of the United States, representing sixteen different organizations, attended the inaugural session of the Presidents' Conference, which was held at the Shoreham Hotel in Washington, D.C., over the first weekend of March 1955. The number of organizations represented had risen to twenty-four when the Conference later became a permanent body. Its proclaimed objective was to express, among other things, the disquiet felt by American Jewry over the erosion of Israel's security position.

Philip Klutznick presided at the opening session on Saturday night, March 5, when Nahum Goldmann drew up a roster of demands for presentation to the State Department. "While we do not hold the Administration guilty of ill will," he said, "we question its methods in sending arms to Arab states without making it a condition that they negotiate peace with Israel." He also reiterated our criticism of the Administration for excluding Israel from the Middle East defense system. Assistant Secretary of State George V. Allen, who spoke that evening, said nothing of consequence, merely indicating that his chief, John Foster Dulles, would issue an official statement.

The next day's panel included Israel's Finance Minister, Levi Eshkol, who reviewed the country's economic position; Norman S. Paul, Near East regional director of the Foreign Operations Administration, who favored grants-in-aid and technical assistance to Israel; and John D. Jernagen, Deputy Assistant Secretary of State, who made it clear that the U.S. Government would not accede to our demands in the military sphere.

The luncheon session on Sunday at which I presided was addressed by Rabbi Maurice N. Eisendrath, the energetic president of the Union of American Hebrew Congregations (Reform); by Rabbi Philip Bernstein, a onetime adviser on Jewish affairs to the SHAEF commander, Dwight D. Eisenhower, and now chairman of the American Israel Public Affairs Committee; and by Abba Eban, Israel's ambassador to the United States and its chief delegate at the UN.

Generally hailed as "the most important gathering of American Jewish leaders since the establishment of Israel in 1948," the Washington conference served as an impressive demonstration of American Jewish solidarity with the Medinah. Although it failed to obtain any meaningful assurances from the State Department, all the participants recognized the value of such a representative body, not as some fitful response to an emergency but as an expression of ongoing concern and responsibility.

Abundant opportunities arose for the Presidents' Conference to make its voice heard. Only a few days before the Washington sessions took place, Israeli and Egyptian army units in the Gaza Strip area had been locked in the fiercest fighting since 1949. Ambassador Eban called for an immediate discussion by the UN Security Council of Israel's complaint about Egypt's "continuous violation of the General Armistice Agreement and the resolutions of the Security Council, endangering international peace and security." He listed a number of specific acts of violence. This threatening situation naturally overshadowed our discussions at the Shoreham Hotel.

A delegation representing the "Presidents' Club" subsequently flew to Washington for a long talk with George V. Allen at the State Department. It comprised Nahum Goldmann, Philip Bernstein, Adolph Held, and myself. We soon came to the conclusion that Allen's approach was more forthright and constructive than Henry Byroade's had ever been. He left us in no doubt, however, that Secretary Dulles made all the foreign-policy decisions. As a result of this talk, we concentrated our pressure on two major issues: arms supplies to Middle East states, which neglected Israel's vital needs, and the Byroade policy of keeping Israel isolated and excluded from regional security pacts.

Among the top officials with whom I discussed the Administration's attitude toward Israel were the U.S. Solicitor General, Judge Simon E. Sobeloff, and President Eisenhower's Cabinet Secretary, Maxwell M. Rabb.

Some improvement in the situation became evident. Abba Eban reported that U.S. aid to Israel, amounting so far to $430 million, had been administered with great skill and had not only strengthened and stabilized the economy of the Medinah, but also contributed to its military preparedness. We were informed that Israel now had more confidence in American Jewry's ability to influence the direction of U.S. Government policy in the Middle East. No other Jewish community in the world seemed capable of exerting such political pressure on its government.

Jewish Life in Southern Europe

While on a mission to Europe for the World Jewish Congress in the summer of 1955, my wife and I visited Italy, Switzerland, Yugoslavia, and Turkey. My aim was to look into the state of Jewish communal life, in Yugoslavia and Turkey particularly, to assess the needs of these *kehillot* so as to be able to enlist the help of the World Jewish Congress and the World Zionist Organization, and to bring a message of fellowship from the Jews of the United States.

Upon my arrival in Belgrade, the capital of Yugoslavia, I was welcomed by Dr. Albert Vajs, professor of law at Belgrade University and chairman of the Federation of Jewish Communities, and by Professor Calderon, the Federation's secretary.

Agricultural production had dropped since the abandonment of collectivization two years previously, and the Yugoslav Government had launched a campaign for increased productivity, encouraging farmers with the promise of various incentives. Certain foodstuffs were in short supply, resulting in high prices and long lines outside the stores.

As far as the surviving postwar Jewish community was concerned, I learned that 8,000 Yugoslav Jews had left to settle in Israel, and that there were then about 6,500 Jews in the country out of a general population of some thirteen million. Whereas one in ten people in the non-Jewish population had been killed during World War II, the Nazis had murdered eighty percent of the Jews. Under President Tito's Communist regime, private business ventures were naturally outlawed, but the economic situation of the Jewish community was tolerable. Most Yugoslav Jews were either in the professions, such as law, medicine, and engineering, or salaried officials in Government employment and various state enterprises.

Dr. Vajs accompanied me on a visit to Belgrade's Ashkenazi synagogue, which the Nazis had converted into a military brothel during the occupation. Both the Government and the JDC had provided funds for its restoration after the war. Prior to their retreat, the Nazis had blown up the Sephardi Great Synagogue, but this was rebuilt and reconsecrated after the liberation. We also visited the Jewish cemetery outside Belgrade, where a well-kept section reserved for Jewish partisans included a magnificent stone memorial executed by the famous Yugoslav sculptor, Ivan Meštrovič.

My host told me that the official and public attitude toward Yugoslav Jewry had been tolerant and friendly, on the whole, although this record had been marred by the cruelty of Ustaše Fascists and Nazi sympathizers in Croatia during the occupation. Many non-Jews provided help and shelter for hunted Jews at that time, and at least 2,000 Jews had fought heroically in Tito's partisan army. Dr. Vajs showed me a book in which this patriotic activity was described in much detail. Postwar relations between Jews and non-Jews were exemplary, I heard, and the type of anti-Semitic prejudice so widespread in other parts of Central and Eastern Europe was virtually unknown in Yugoslavia. Many intellectuals took a keen interest in Israel and in the constructive role some of their former countrymen were playing in its development.

Zionist activities were neither banned nor subject to restriction. This was in remarkable contrast to the situation in other Communist states. Prior to my arrival, a successful fund-raising campaign had resulted in 50,000 trees being subscribed to the Martyrs' Forest in Israel, a tribute to the Yugoslav Jews who had perished in the Nazi Holocaust. It was heartening to learn that many non-Jews had contributed to the project.

Dr. Vajs, who headed the Yugoslav Section of the World Jewish Congress, was a highly respected leader of his community. We had already met some months earlier in New York, while he was on a Government mission to the United States. I made a point of telling him about Moshav Udim, settled by young immigrants from Yugoslavia, in which I had taken a special interest, and reported that it was progressing well. A touching indication, both of Yugoslav Jewry's links with Israel and of the esteem in which Dr. Vajs was held, manifested itself after his death in 1964, when a forest in Israel was dedicated to his memory.

During that all-too-brief visit, I conferred with the Executive Committee of the Federation of Yugoslav Jewish Communities. Religious life was parlously weak, and one solitary rabbi still ministered to the entire *kehillah*, in Sarajevo. They stressed the need for rabbis and teachers, and I expressed my regret at not having seen their children and young people. I promised to bring their problems to the attention of the World Jewish Congress and the Claims Conference. It was heartrending to see the condition to which Jewish life had been reduced in a part of the world where vibrant and proud communities had existed without interruption for nearly 2,000 years.

I had a particularly good meeting with Rodoljub Čolakovič, one of the four Vice-Presidents of Yugoslavia, who was in charge of cultural affairs. My original intention was to obtain an interview with President Josip Broz Tito and an appointment had, indeed, been made for me to visit him at his summer residence in Brioni, but my wife's illness while we were in Venice obliged me to cancel it. Dr. Vajs, who set up the meeting with Vice-President Čolakovič, served as translator and Zvi Locker of the Israel embassy accompanied us.

At the beginning of our talk, I said that Yugoslavia was in various ways a bridge between East and West and paid tribute to the efforts made by the Government and people of that country to reduce tensions and improve relations between various states in the area. The Vice-President frankly averred that his fellow Serbs, in the old days, had made the mistake of oppressing national minorities living in their midst. The present situation, he went on, showed that a healthier attitude now prevailed and that the atmosphere was conducive to fruitful intergroup relationships.

I next turned to Israel, "the firstborn child of the United Nations," and expressed appreciation for Yugoslavia's friendship and for the idealism that had brought thousands of Yugoslav Jews to the new State. Vice-President Čolakovič declared that his country based its Middle East policy on moral principles. He had a great admiration for Israel and told me, with obvious pride, that his volume of war memoirs, *Fire in the Forest*, was being translated for publication in Israel.

When I called on U.S. Ambassador Crittenberger, he observed that President Tito was determined to "sit on the fence," and that it was in America's interest to "play along with him" in order to keep the Iron Curtain rolled back as far as possible. Tito's neutralism was to find expression, of course, in the Bandung Conference of 1955, at which a "nonaligned bloc" of Afro-Asian states emerged under the leadership of Tito, Indian Prime Minister Jawaharlal Nehru, and Egypt's Gamal Abdul Nasser. Thereafter, Yugoslav relations with Israel deteriorated rapidly, although economic links between them were preserved.

One other leading personality whom I met in Belgrade was Moša (Moshe) Pijade, an old comrade of Tito's, who retained his sense of Jewish identity. During the Nazi occupation, he had been one of the chief organizers of the Communist partisans and, after the liberation, he served as President of the Serbian Republic and as Chairman of the Yugoslav National Assembly. Moša Pijade also represented his country at the postwar Peace Conference and helped to draft Yugoslavia's constitution.

As we were in the middle of our conversation, he suddenly asked, "Why don't you send me some *matzot* for *Pesah*?" I promised to do so and had a consignment forwarded to him, but I had no way of knowing if the *matzot* ever reached their destination. Yugoslavia's Jewish Vice-President died only two years later.

The responsibilities that had summoned me to Europe involved consultations on various important issues in Switzerland. I attended a meeting of the Executive Board on Jewish Material Claims against Austria, which took place in Zurich, and then spent a couple of days in Vulpèra with Dr. Nahum Goldmann, who was accompanied by the Reverend Dr. Maurice Perlzweig and Alec Easterman, two senior officials of the World Jewish Congress, and by Dr. Gerhart Riegner, the WJC's secretary-general in Geneva. We discussed the convening in Geneva of a summit conference of world Jewish organizations, in which Philip Klutznick of B'nai B'rith, delegates from various rabbinical groups, and other U.S. representatives were to participate.

During my short stay in Switzerland, I met Josef ("Yossel") Rosensaft, president of the World Federation of Bergen-Belsen Camp Survivors, whose efforts for the rehabilitation of Jewish DPs in the German camps had already been common knowledge when I visited the American zone in July 1949. Bergen-Belsen had been the first Nazi concentration camp liberated by the Allies, and the horrors that British troops witnessed on their arrival gave rise to worldwide shock and indignation. One of the first to enter it was the Reverend Leslie Hardman, a Jewish chaplain with the British forces, who later recorded his impressions in *The Survivors* (1958). After the liberation, Yossel Rosensaft led the struggle for separate Jewish camps in Germany and went on to head the Central Jewish Committee for the British Zone. As increasing numbers of Jewish DPs arrived from Eastern Europe bound for Eretz Yisrael as "legal" or "illegal" immigrants, he boldly voiced their Zionist protests and demands. This campaign reached its height at the time of the *Exodus* episode in 1947.

A man of resourcefulness and wit, Yossel told me an amusing story of his encounter with the British general who took charge of Bergen-Belsen following its liberation. This officer was leaning back in his chair, with his boots resting on the desk, when Rosensaft came into the room. Taking his cue from the general, Yossel sat down and put his feet up as well. "Where are your manners?" asked the commander in outraged tones. "I'm so sorry, I was only trying to be polite," Rosensaft answered. "Seeing that you had your feet on the desk, I naturally thought this formed part of British etiquette."

Not until three years after the war, when the last Jewish inmates had left and the camp was scheduled for closure, did Yossel leave Bergen-Belsen. His wife, Hadassah, a physician, was also a "graduate" of the camp and their son, Menaḥem, was born there. The three of them have dedicated their lives to aiding the survivors and keeping alive the memory of the Nazi Holocaust.

En route to Israel, we spent a week in Istanbul, the former capital of the Ottoman Empire, where we saw a great deal of the Jewish community and its institutions. Since the sweeping reforms of Kemal Atatürk in the 1920s, when secularization hit all religious groups, Turkish Jewry had been weakened considerably. Although a large measure of internal autonomy had been restored to the Jews in 1949, they were still forbidden to join "foreign" international bodies such as the World Zionist Organization and the World Jewish Congress. Sephardim formed a majority on the Jewish Community Council of Istanbul, but there was a substantial Ashkenazi congregation, which included the descendants of Russian Jews who had fled to Turkey after the abortive revolution of 1905.

At the time of our visit, Rabbi Raphael Saban was *Ḥakham Bashi* of the Sephardi congregations and Henri Soriano was president of the Community Council. I was able to gain some insight into the general position when two lay leaders of the *kehillah* visited us at our hotel and, later, at an official reception tendered by Chief Rabbi Saban and his religious associates. On *Shabbat Ḥazon*, coinciding with July 23, the Sabbath preceding Tish'ah be-Av, we spent some time with pupils of one of the Jewish schools, where about 400 pupils were enrolled. Most of them came from poor families, as the wealthier Jews sent their children to Turkish or foreign schools. The largest synagogue in Istanbul, Neveh Shalom, had been built in 1949 and seated 2,000 worshipers. Those members of the community whom we met were obviously well-to-do. They were extremely cautious in their statements. They also exercised restraint in their cultivation of Jewish and Zionist contacts.

Chief Rabbi Saban, then in his eighty-second year, was an imposing figure. He wore a long ceremonial robe and a gold chain of office, at the end of which dangled a tablet inscribed with the Ten Commandments. At the outset of our conversation, I greeted him in the name of the American Jewish Congress and the World Jewish Congress. Recalling my year's residence in Jerusalem as treasurer of the Jewish Agency, I mentioned some of the many synagogues I had visited there as a worshiper and referred to the fact that I had often gone to the Turkish congregation in Jerusalem's Sha'arei Ḥesed quarter, adding that Turkish Jews were known to have become well adjusted to life in Israel. I also took occasion to mention the Jewish Conciliation Board in New York and its mode of operation. Chief Rabbi Saban then informed me that the Istanbul Jewish community administered an arbitration court, which was, however, mainly preoccupied with questions of marriage and divorce.

The chief purpose of my conversations with the Jewish leaders at this reception was to impress upon them the need to improve the standard of Jewish education in Istanbul. I ventured to suggest that much more could be done in that respect, and I urged them to make greater demands on the Jewish Agency and the World Jewish Congress for the supply of guidance and qualified teachers. Greater financial support, I urged, should be secured from the wealthier members of the community. The lay leaders present stated that the Turkish authorities did not look with a kindly eye upon large-scale assistance from outside bodies such as the Jewish Agency and the WJC. Conditions, they said, were now much better than they had been ten years previously and would, in all likelihood, continue to improve.

Responding, I cautioned that gradualism was not the right policy when Jews everywhere were caught up in a race against time. I advised that a more vigorous tempo be maintained in the battle for Jewish survival, and I urged that greater stimulus be given to Aliyah.

We then proceeded to the city hall for a meeting with the Mayor of Istanbul, who was surrounded by a "cabinet" of municipal commissioners. There, I was introduced as president of the American Jewish Congress; there was no reference to the WJC, for reasons I understood. Back at our hotel, I was awaited by leaders of the Ashkenazi congregation, who asked me to help them find a rabbi, half of whose salary they were willing to defray. It was their hope that the other half might be provided by outside sources. Like their Sephardi brethren, they were timid and cautious in their statements to me. When I inquired whether it would be in order to say something about Israel before this gathering, the Ashkenazi *parnas* replied emphatically in an undertone, "No!"

On the following afternoon, prior to our departure, Bert came with me to an official reception tendered by both Jewish communities, Sephardi and Ashkenazi. Only one other woman was present. I had been told that around 30,000 Jews had left Istanbul for Israel, representing more than fifty percent of the *kehillah*, and that some 2,000 of them had come back. In my response to greetings by the lay leaders, who spoke in French, I said that the quality of an enlightened government could best be judged by the position of Jews living under it. Since Turkish Jewry was free to provide its children with a sound Jewish education, I asked: "Are you using that freedom to the full?" My final remark was another challenging question: "You have the right to emigrate to Israel. Are you using that right fully?"

Refreshment from the Spiritual Center

It was with a feeling of uplift and relief that we set foot in Israel once more after our dispiriting experiences in communities of the Diaspora. The Zionist General Council was scheduled to meet in Jerusalem during the third week of August, and Bert and I had time before then to "socialize" with our many friends and to tour parts of the country we had either not visited on previous trips to Israel or had not seen for a long while past.

A cause to which I gladly devoted considerable time was Brit Ivrit Olamit, the World Hebrew Union, of which the U.S. branch is known as Histadrut Ivrit of

America. The second World Hebrew Congress, held in Jerusalem at the beginning of August 1955, was an occasion for summing up the work done since its inaugural convention.

Addressing the plenary session on behalf of the American Section of the Jewish Agency Executive, I criticized the World Zionist Organization and its Jerusalem and New York executives for not giving greater financial support to the dissemination of the Hebrew language and culture. Mindful of those countries where the danger of assimilation was most acute, I urged that more Hebrew teachers be sent from Israel to Jewish communities abroad and that more energy be expended on programs and methods. "If we apply to the Aliyah of Hebrew in the Jewish world the kind of practical approach which we have applied to physical Aliyah," I said, "we may find that every successive Hebrew Congress will constitute a new milestone of substantial progress toward our goal."

Prime Minister Moshe Sharett addressed the opening session of the convention. His appearance there and his message were a source of encouragement to the delegates.

On August 7, I attended the dedication of Bar-Ilan University at its campus in Ramat Gan. This new institute of higher learning, sponsored by the American Mizrahi Organization, was named in honor of Rabbi Meir Bar-Ilan (Berlin) of blessed memory, who had been the acknowledged leader of the World Mizrahi movement. Professor Pinkhos Churgin, former dean of the Teachers' Institute at Yeshiva University, New York, presided at the opening ceremony. One of the foremost Hebrew educators in the United States, and a veteran religious Zionist, Professor Churgin had made Aliyah in order to establish and consolidate the fledgling Bar-Ilan University, which he served thereafter as first president. It was regarded with some disfavor in certain Government and Jewish Agency circles. The Jewish Agency Executive did not send an official representative to the dedication exercises. I decided, however, to participate, as I felt that Bar-Ilan University would fulfill a useful purpose within the framework of Israeli higher education.

In the course of my address at Ramat Gan, I said:

> A university in Israel founded under religious auspices will, I think, be not only understood but even appreciated in the United States, since the leading American universities, beginning with Harvard, were established under religious auspices. It will not be enough, however, for such an institution of higher learning to be religious. Its primary justification will have to be its academic quality. . . .
>
> It has been said that an institution is the lengthened shadow of a man. I feel privileged to have been among those who knew Rabbi Meir Bar-Ilan of blessed memory. In his personality were combined *Torah* and *Ḥokhmah*, religion and worldly culture, the twin pillars upon which this University is to rest.
>
> The human race has reached a stage, the atomic stage, when the ultimatum of Sinai becomes humanity's last chance for survival—"Accept the moral law, or perish!" The *Torah-Ḥokhmah* alliance, in its broadest sense, becomes therefore not an option but an imperative.

Following the death of Pinkhos Churgin in 1957, Rabbi Joseph H. Lookstein of Congregation Kehilath Jeshurun in New York succeeded him as chancellor. A former president of the (Orthodox) Rabbinical Council of America and of the New York Board of Rabbis, "Joe" Lookstein was also a noted educator, having served as professor of homiletics and practical rabbinics at Yeshiva University and having founded the Ramaz Hebrew day school attached to his congregation. Under his leadership, Bar-Ilan University expanded rapidly. It is now the third largest institution of higher learning in Israel, with a distinguished faculty, thousands of students, a wide range of departments in the arts, sciences, and Judaica, major research programs, and important publications to its credit.

A week or so after the exercises at Ramat Gan, the first plenary meeting of the Zionist Actions Committee took place in Jerusalem. It was heartening to hear a plea for increased Aliyah from leaders of North African Jewry. "One hundred thousand Jews want to come to Israel," they said. "Please take in as many as you can." Never before had the spokesmen of such a large Jewish community made this kind of appeal to Medinat Yisrael and to the World Zionist Organization. It pointed up not only Israel's unique role as the lifeline for Jews in need of the Medinah, but also the vital, ongoing partnership between Medinat Yisrael and the Zionist movement in all parts of the Diaspora.

Another session was devoted to the twentieth anniversary of Mosad Bialik, the publishing house of the WZO, and to Mosad Ha-Rav Kook in Jerusalem. Various Jewish literary works were reviewed and evaluated on this occasion. I observed that "the same people who had listened with pained attention in the morning to the story of the need for physical Aliyah, and who are grappling with the demands of that problem, listened with pride in the evening to the story of an Aliyah of the Jewish spirit."

New Issues and Concerns

For some time past, Dr. Nahum Goldmann had been giving serious thought to the creation of a permanent roof organization of Jewish bodies that would be representative of World Jewry in all matters pertaining to Jewish communal and individual rights. Exploratory talks aimed at the formation of such an organization had taken place in Paris early in February 1955, and I had been one of the participants. As previously mentioned, further discussions took place in Switzerland during the summer. Nahum Goldmann's idea was to set up an international forum similar to the Presidents' Conference in the United States, and to draw into it bodies such as the B'nai B'rith that had remained outside the World Jewish Congress.

After my return to New York in the autumn, a meeting took place at Goldmann's home and those present included, apart from me, Shad Polier, Philip Klutznick, Maurice Bisyger, and Frank Goldman of B'nai B'rith; Jacob Patt of the American Jewish Labor Committee; and Barnett (later, Lord) Janner, the Labor M.P. and president of the Board of Deputies of British Jews, who had formerly headed the British Zionist Federation.

From these and subsequent discussions, there eventually emerged, in 1958, the international Conference of Jewish Organizations, better known as COJO. Its first meeting, held in Rome, was convened by Nahum Goldmann, Philip Klutznick, and (representing the Zionist Executive) Avraham Harman. It was not until 1967, however, that the WZO formally joined COJO. It brought together an imposing array of Jewish bodies in the United States and Canada, Europe, Latin America, South Africa, and Australia. At the outset, COJO served as an advisory, coordinating organization aiming to prevent needless duplication of effort. It functioned on a two-year trial basis until 1960, when a meeting in Amsterdam elected Dr. Goldmann as chairman, with Label Katz of B'nai B'rith as co-chairman.

Thereafter, high-level meetings of COJO took place annually. Their purpose was, in Goldmann's words, "to create a kind of Jewish world parliament that, while not having the right to make binding decisions, would provide a world forum for all shades of Jewish opinion, from the Lubavitcher Rebbe to committed Jewish Communists." Among the issues to which COJO addressed itself were the fate of Soviet Jewry and the plight of Jews in Arab lands, problems affecting Jewish communities in Latin America, the security of Israel and the Arab boycott issue, Jewish education and ways of preserving Jewish life and culture, civil rights, and relations with the Vatican.

COJO fulfilled a useful purpose for some time, but its effectiveness was not a lasting one.

From August 1955, Arab belligerency vis-à-vis Israel assumed new and graver dimensions. In his attempt to gain ascendancy over the Arab world, Nasser had orchestrated a chorus of hate against both Israel and the Western Powers, seeking a rapprochement with the Communist bloc at variance with his "neutralism" and "nonalignment." In addition to a vicious propaganda campaign against Israel, which contained many Nazi-inspired anti-Jewish overtones, the Egyptian dictator had organized a worldwide boycott of trade with Israel, the denial of free passage through the Suez Canal and the Straits of Tiran to all ships bound to and from Israeli ports, and the dispatch of *fedayeen* gangs to carry out acts of murder and sabotage against civilian targets inside Israel.

Proceeding one step further on the road to open war, Nasser concluded a massive arms deal with the Soviet Union, which was transacted officially with Czechoslovakia. This brought unprecedented shipments of military hardware to Egypt, including the latest Soviet-built Mig planes, and upset the precarious balance of power in the Middle East, which had been maintained hitherto by the West. Although Israel managed to purchase arms from the French Government, neither the U.S. nor Great Britain seemed disposed to intervene. A delegation representing the "Presidents' Club" went to Washington and met with Secretary of State John Foster Dulles. His attitude was more friendly than at any time in the past, but he gave no assurances about providing Israel with arms to restore the balance or about the negotiation of a security pact.

On November 2, David Ben-Gurion, who had succeeded Moshe Sharett as Prime

Minister, presented his new cabinet and began to grapple with the menacing situation. A military alliance between Egypt and Syria had already been initialed, *fedayeen* attacks had multiplied, and regular Israeli and Egyptian forces were exchanging fire on the Sinai border. A week later, in a Guildhall speech that echoed a suggestion made by Dulles in late August, Sir Anthony Eden, Britain's Foreign Secretary, proposed that Israel's borders undergo modification in order to placate neighboring Arab states, several of which both Great Britain and the U.S. were even then arming to the teeth. Ben-Gurion firmly rejected Eden's proposal.

The publication of Ben-Gurion's statement coincided with a huge rally at Madison Square Garden on November 15, calling for Israel's security to be preserved. It was held under the auspices of the American Zionist Council, representing all Zionist groups in the United States, and co-sponsored by labor organizations as well as major national Jewish bodies. Among those who addressed the 20,000 people gathered there were Rabbi Irving Miller, chairman of the American Zionist Council, who presided; Dr. Nahum Goldmann, as chairman of the Jewish Agency Executive; Rabbi Abba Hillel Silver; New York's Mayor Robert F. Wagner; Rabbi Abraham F. Feldman, president of the Synagogue Council of America; Nathan Chanin, chairman of the Administrative Committee of the Jewish Labor Committee; and I, as president of the American Jewish Congress.

"The United States played an important part in the establishment of Israel," I said, "and it should play an important part in seeing to it that Israel's existence is secured. It must be secured not only by supplies of arms, but by a guarantee against aggression by its neighbors. The same kind of guarantee can be given to its neighbors as well. Such a guarantee against aggression can, if necessary, be unilateral— a declaration by the United States alone, or in concert with other powers, that it will not tolerate aggression by one of the Middle East nations against another."

A resolution was adopted at the rally, calling for the immediate negotiation of security treaties and urging the U.S. Administration to provide Israel with all the weapons necessary for its legitimate defense. "The highest interests of justice and the security of free democratic nations everywhere," the resolution affirmed, "demand that America shall act firmly and decisively before it is too late."

I was invited to repeat my speech in Pittsburgh, Boston, Newark, and other cities. In Pittsburgh, an impressive, outspoken address was delivered that same night by Mayor David Lawrence, a Catholic, who wielded considerable power inside the Democratic Party.

Tension in the Middle East continued to mount during the first few months of 1956. For their part, President Eisenhower and Secretary of State Dulles showed no inclination to counter the Soviet Union's escalating military involvement, through its support for Nasser's warmongering, and contented themselves with pious declarations. State Department policy was an astonishing example of diplomatic inertia. Dulles and his associates gave the appearance of subscribing to the belief that a complex problem would eventually disappear if it were ignored long enough. They turned a deaf ear to all the frantic pleas for defensive arms that Israel, its supporters in Congress, and the American public directed toward them. Only one answer came from the Eisenhower Administration—a warning that no "hasty action" should be taken by the besieged Jewish State.

Our efforts to bring about a softening in the attitude adopted by top officials at the White House and the State Department were unremitting, but they proved fruitless. Throughout the year, they seem to have remained blind and unresponsive to obvious dangers. Subsequent events demonstrated the utter folly of this policy line, which not only imperiled Israel's existence but also worked against American and Western interests in the Middle East.

As early as mid-January 1956, my colleagues and I tried to arouse Washington, the American press, and public opinion to a realization of the menace Nasserism posed for the free world's security, as well as for Israel's. It was to no avail. Eisenhower and Dulles turned a deaf ear. Confronted by this gloomy situation, Jewish leaders in the United States awaited the outcome of such inaction with alarm and foreboding.

The Domestic Scene

Side by side with these responsibilities and anxieties, I continued to participate in liberal social and political endeavors on the wider American scene. Believing the objectives of the labor movement to be consonant with the humane ideals of Judaism, I had long given active support to trade unionism, both from the pulpit and from lay platforms. Thus, on December 6, 1955, I spoke before the historic merger convention of the American Federation of Labor and the Congress of Industrial Organizations. It was a great day for organized labor, I said in my address, and I hailed the labor movement as "the most reliable and the most effective force against Communism," as well as "the most convincing of all arguments for the American system of democracy." Nevertheless, I felt bound to utter some words of caution regarding democratic procedure and racial and religious equality, both within the unions and outside their sphere of activity. I condemned the smear campaigns that were charging union leaders with racketeering and dictatorship, and the Taft-Hartley Law, which represented no less a threat to organized labor than hired thugs and tear-gas bombs had been in previous years.

Toward the middle of January 1956, I flew to London in order to attend the plenary session of the World Jewish Congress, at which the position of North African Jewry figured high on the agenda. I brought greetings from the American Jewish Congress and, while in London, addressed one of the first functions held to mark the tercentenary of the resettlement of the Jews in the British Isles. As president of the American Jewish Congress and associate chairman of the American Jewish Tercentenary Committee, I extended congratulations to the 420,000 Jews of Great Britain on the occasion of this anniversary.

With its centralized organizational structure, Board of Deputies, Chief Rabbinate, and largely Orthodox complexion, British Jewry bore little resemblance to the far less organized, though vastly more numerous Jewish community of the United

States. Following a directive by Chief Rabbi Israel Brodie, synagogues throughout the country observed the first Sabbath of the year, Saturday, January 7, 1956, as Tercentenary Sabbath. The celebrations continued with a central service of dedication and thanksgiving, held on March 22, at the historic Spanish and Portuguese Synagogue, Bevis Marks, built in 1701. It was attended by a large congregation of both Ashkenazim and Sephardim. Other services were held in the leading provincial communities. A culminating event was the tercentenary banquet at London's Guildhall, on May 29, when His Royal Highness Prince Philip, the Duke of Edinburgh, representing Queen Elizabeth, proposed a toast to the Anglo-Jewish community and showed his familiarity with Jewish religious practice by donning a *kippah*. Viscount Herbert Samuel, elder statesman of the Liberal Party, delivered the response. The Jewish Tercentenary Council also arranged various exhibitions and published a commemorative volume.

Back home in New York, at the biennial convention of the American Jewish Congress in mid-April, I was drafted for a third term as president. Another member of the Goldstein family, my sister-in-law, Fannie, played an active role in the AJC at this time. She became secretary of the Philadelphia chapter the following October.

One of the issues raised in my address at the New York convention was the need for Jews to support the National Association for the Advancement of Colored People and the campaign against racial segregation in the United States. Subsequently, at a civil rights rally in Madison Square Garden, New York, on May 24, I stressed that religious or racial minorities constituted the bulk of American society. "This diversity of composition is the strength and the richness of America. It is not a melting pot as much as it is an orchestra. Hence, the protection of the integrity, equality and security of any group is a protection for all groups. . . . We are all of us members of a mutual insurance company, for we are of one another."

Immediately after the convention in New York, my wife and I flew to Israel to attend the 24th Zionist Congress, which opened in Jerusalem on April 24. Meetings of the Jewish Agency Executive preceded this Zionist Congress, which was the first to take place in Binyanei ha-Umah, Jerusalem's splendid new convention center.

The delegates were troubled, of course, by the ominous situation facing Israel at the time, although the World Zionist Organization could do little about that. Wrangling, ostensibly on ideological grounds but actually over personality clashes, may well have reflected the tension we all felt during the fortnight-long assembly. At the forefront, however, were internal issues that had implications for the Zionist movement as a whole. One of these resulted from the schism within my own General Zionist camp. Two separate General Zionist parties had emerged in Israel. The divergent trend was soon to lead to the creation of a World Union of General Zionists—politically oriented to the right, as distinct from our centrist World Confederation of General Zionists.

Aliyah and settlement properly received considerable attention at the Congress. The issue that most preoccupied representatives of all the Zionist factions was a proposal for the merger of the Keren Hayesod and the Keren Kayemet Le-Yisrael into a single body. Dr. Chaim Weizmann, before his death, had favored such an amalgamation. While the KKL (Jewish National Fund) had registered some important successes and achievements since the establishment of the Medinah, these were mostly secured through funds provided by the Government. Weizmann had therefore contended that, unless the JNF at least doubled its income from sources of its own, it might as well join forces with the Keren Hayesod and the United Israel Appeal.

My position was at variance with this proposal. Entering into the thick of the debate, I urged that the JNF should retain its distinctive character, not least because of its Zionist educational programs, and that the instrument which raised the funds should have a decisive say in determining how they were to be spent. Moreover, since the United Jewish Appeal in America was not a wholly Zionist operation, there was all the more need to maintain and strengthen the Jewish National Fund as a Zionist instrument with a universal appeal. "You cannot—you must not—merge a Zionist with a non-Zionist fund," I warned. "You will lose an army of workers, some of whom are among our best Zionists. It is proposed to call the new fund 'Keren Yisrael,' or something similar. Why give up a name with such a beautiful tradition as Keren Kayemet Le-Yisrael?" Structural reforms or organizational streamlining would not benefit the JNF, I urged, nor would they strengthen Zionism.

To the satisfaction and relief of many of us, the merger proposal was finally dropped.

The Congress elected Dr. Nahum Goldmann to the presidency of the World Zionist Organization, a post that had remained vacant for ten years since the resignation of Dr. Weizmann in 1946. I was reelected to the Zionist Executive. Some time previously, Dr. Goldmann had asked me to take on the chairmanship of the Jewish Agency's American Section, but I declined, as it would have entailed too much work and responsibility. My acceptance of a third term as president of the American Jewish Congress reinforced this decision.

Dr. Emanuel Neumann and Rose Halprin, who headed the two opposing groups within the General Zionist orbit, were contenders for the chairmanship of the American Section. A neat arrangement devised to overcome the difficulty was that Nahum Goldmann, as the newly elected president of the WZO, would also assume the position in New York, leaving an acting chairman to function there while he was abroad. Rose Halprin was appointed to serve first as alternate chairman of the Jewish Agency's American Section.

Our stay in Jerusalem made it possible for Bert and myself to attend the laying of the cornerstone for the Israel Goldstein Synagogue at the Hebrew University on May 6. It was a gift by my congregation in New York to mark my sixtieth birthday. One of the messages received on the occasion came from Charles H. Silver, president of B'nai Jeshurun, who headed the committee of friends responsible for securing the necessary funds.

The ceremony took place on a knoll at the western edge of the Givat Ram campus, then still in its early stage of development. Those present included the president of the university, Professor Benjamin Mazar; the Deputy Minister of Religious Affairs, Dr. Zerah Warhaftig; Gershon Agron; Mortimer May, president of the Zionist Organization of America; Dr. Nahum Goldmann; Moshe Kol, the head of Youth Aliyah; Rabbi and Mrs. David de Sola Pool; and Reuven Rubin, the artist. On behalf of the Hebrew University, Bernard Cherrick read the text of a scroll that was deposited with the cornerstone.

An eminent participant was Chief Rabbi Isaac Halevi Herzog, who had accepted the invitation when assured that the synagogue would be conducted on Orthodox lines. Although both my congregation and I were not Orthodox, I felt that since the university was of a semigovernmental character, its chapel should be Orthodox, as long as no other house of prayer existed on the campus.

The dedication ceremony, of which I shall have more to say, took place in August the following year.

I was particularly moved by my old friend Gershon Agron's address. He referred to our boyhood days in South Philadelphia and brought back memories of our early efforts for Zionism at that time. Gershon had recently become Mayor of Jerusalem, heading a Mapai-led coalition with Ahdut Avodah, the Progressives, and Agudat Yisrael.

Shortly thereafter, while touring the Galilee region in northern Israel, we visited Peki'in, a village where Jews have lived continuously since ancient times. Only two Jewish families still remained there, and one of them took care of the old synagogue. We saw a fragment of a Torah scroll reputedly more than a thousand years old. Recent Olim from Morocco had been settled in a nearby moshav, and these thirty families were employed by the Keren Kayemet in an afforestation project. We visited the Huleh swamp area, where drainage was still underway, and also stopped at an archaeological dig in Bet She'arim and at the artists' village of En Hod.

Traveling south to the Lachish region, we met Sam Hamburg, an American Jew, who had successfully introduced cotton growing into Israel and was helping to plan the development of an area that would have Kiryat Gat as its population center. We lunched at Kibbutz Hafetz Hayyim, a thriving Orthodox settlement affiliated with Po'alei Agudat Yisrael.

These trips were a welcome source of education and refreshment. They enabled us to see the progress made in reclaiming land from centuries of neglect and in unearthing the glories of the past from the accumulated debris of millenia.

One of my most pleasant assignments during that visit to Israel was the presentation of the Stephen S. Wise award of the American Jewish Congress to President Itzhak Ben-Zvi. The ceremony, held on May 2, included a bouquet of tributes in which Levi Eshkol, Moshe Sharett, Yosef Sprinzak, and Sephardi Chief Rabbi Itzhak Nissim participated.

Following our return to New York, I once more entered the political fray on Israel's behalf. A prominent friend of our cause at that time was Senator Stuart H. Symington, a ranking member of the Democratic Party, who occupied a position of influence on the Senate Armed Services Committee. Together with Maurice Perlzweig of the World Jewish Congress and Will Maslow of the American Jewish Congress, I went down to Washington for discussions with a number of congressmen and State Department officials. Arms shipments to Saudi Arabia, the effect of the Arab boycott on Jewish business interests in the United States, and related matters figured on our agenda. We were joined by Aaron Goldman, chairman of the Washington Jewish Community Council, who represented the National (Jewish) Community Relations Advisory Council.

Senator Symington was the first person whom we called upon in Washington, D.C. He expressly favored American arms supplies to Israel and other forms of aid, because, in his view, Israel was one of the few reliable allies of the U.S. in the Middle East. He coupled Turkey with Israel in that category. No other states in the region deserved consideration, he told us, and even Great Britain could not be relied upon in the event of a war breaking out in that area. The senator added that he expected to make a speech on this issue shortly, and that his would not be the only voice raised on Israel's behalf.

These overtures formed part of our ongoing effort to concentrate the attention of Congressional and public circles on the pan-Arab menace to Israel and the West. As the months went by, with the approach of new elections in November 1956, we also made presentations of our case before leading political forums, especially at the Democratic and Republican national conventions held in August.

On behalf of the American Jewish Congress, I went to Chicago with Julian Freeman of the National Community Relations Council,'in order to attend a hearing of the Democratic Platform Committee, chaired by Representative John W. McCormack. We intended to present our case regarding the Arab campaign of boycott and discrimination aimed at Jews throughout the world, including the United States. Isaiah L. ("Si") Kenen, executive director of the American Israel Public Affairs Committee and one of the most effective pro-Israel lobbyists, was already there working on the Israel plank when we arrived. The atmosphere at the hearing was a friendly one. Congressmen Emanuel Celler of New York and John E. Moss of California, Mayor David Lawrence of Pittsburgh, and several other sympathetic Democrats figured on the Platform Committee panel. Before the adjournment, a pro-Israel plank had been circulated in the House by Representatives Emanuel Celler and Abraham Multer of New York, Thomas J. Dodd of Connecticut, James Roosevelt of California, and Edith Green of Oregon. It was laid before the Platform Committee by Congressman Dodd.

Vicious attacks on both Jewish and non-Jewish supporters of Israel had previously been made at the hearing by Clarence L. Coleman, Jr., president of the American Council for Judaism, and by Alfred Lilienthal, the notorious pro-Arab apologist. They were sharply criticized by the chairman, Representative McCormack, and by other members of the Platform Committee. Lilienthal's speech had been an especially offensive anti-Zionist diatribe.

Before turning to my brief, I offered the following short comment:

Mr. Lilienthal's appearance before you is a demonstration that democracy permits even those who are wrong to express their views. It is important, however, to evaluate those views as representing the opinions of an aberrationist fringe. American Jewry almost unanimously, and the great majority of the American people, want to see Israel strong and vital.

The Democratic plank as adopted was clear-cut and favorable. It included a pledge to supply Israel with arms and an unambiguous statement on the Arab refugees, undertaking to support "large-scale projects for their resettlement in countries where there is room and opportunity for them."

Upon my arrival in Chicago for the Democratic Party convention, I had telephoned Senator Adlai Stevenson, then at his farm in Libertyville, and read to him the plank we wished to put forward, urging that he give it his support. Stevenson told me that he would not interfere with the platform's formulation, but it was clear that it would not be made final without having first been submitted for his approval.

The Republican Party convention, held shortly thereafter, made no pledge of arms to Israel. Its platform did, however, contain a firm undertaking to defend that country against attack. "We regard the preservation of Israel as an important tenet of American foreign policy," it declared. "We are determined that the integrity of an independent Jewish State shall be maintained. We shall support the independence of Israel against armed aggression."

Nasser's warmongering speeches and propaganda were then approaching a hysterical crescendo in Egypt, as the flow of military equipment from the USSR encouraged his belligerent posturing. Subsequent events were to justify our worst fears and misgivings, and our disenchantment with the do-nothing policies of the Eisenhower-Dulles Administration.

Meanwhile, two or three events in the communal sphere and in my personal life brought some welcome diversion. The New York Board of Rabbis, with which I had long been associated, observed its seventy-fifth anniversary in April and May 1956. I was designated chairman of the Board's celebration. Then came my sixtieth birthday, which was marked by a series of functions arranged to help causes particularly dear to me. Among these were the launching of a special fund for the benefit of the American Jewish Congress, which had been announced at its convention in April, and the establishment of the synagogue named for me at the Hebrew University in Jerusalem, to which reference has already been made. A third "gift" was the raising of nearly one million dollars for the United Jewish Appeal at a dinner held on June 6, under the joint auspices of the American Jewish Congress and Congregation B'nai Jeshurun. Many leading Jewish and Christian personalities in American life attended, and messages of greeting came from all parts of the world and from friends and colleagues in Israel, headed by President Itzhak Ben-Zvi.

One additional project, a source of much gratification to me personally, was the publication in the following year of a volume of essays dealing with the general, Jewish, and Zionist developments marking the period through which I had lived and served.* The book was edited by Harry Schneiderman, former editor of *The American Jewish Year Book* and coeditor of *Who's Who in World Jewry*. The contributors included more than a score of eminent scholars, religious leaders, and public figures, American and Israeli, Jewish and non-Jewish. Professor Louis Finkelstein wrote the foreword. An international committee of sponsors lent additional prestige to this book.

On June 18, the date of my sixtieth birthday, Bert and I celebrated the occasion by a visit to the city of my birth, Philadelphia. We were joined there by my brother, Isaac, and sister, Sarah, who accompanied us on a nostalgic tour of our early stamping grounds. We visited Gratz College, both the original and the later sites; Dropsie College, where I stepped in for a few minutes to see the president, Dr. Abraham Neuman; the Litt Brothers' emporium, where I had worked for a spell after leaving high school, earning eight dollars weekly in the stoves department; and the Horn and Hardart automat, which had been a favorite haunt for light refreshments on the way home from Gratz College.

Our next stop on this family pilgrimage was the Niezhiner *Shul*, which had been our childhood abode. Still standing nearby was the Polish Catholic church, where we had occasional fights with the young Poles: they showered us with stones, but we gave back as good as we got. The former site of the Niezhiner *Shul* on South Third Street, where I was born, had long since been transformed into a church with a Black congregation. The synagogue, in its subsequent location on Second Street near Catherine, was in good repair and I took the opportunity to have a long look at the attic that had once been our home. We made arrangements for a plaque in memory of my parents to be affixed under the *Ner Tamid*, the Eternal Light.

The tour conjured up memories of places that no longer existed. The elementary school at Third and Catherine Streets, which I had attended almost half a century earlier, was now a vacant lot. The Hebrew Education Society, where I had first made contact with Yiddish speakers and Yiddish literature, had been turned into business premises. Southern High School, in the process of demolition, was scheduled to make way for a handsome new structure. The University of Pennsylvania campus remained more or less intact.

Our final stop was at the Mount Judah cemetery, where Isaac, Sarah, and I visited the graves of our parents. My father had gone to his eternal rest at the age of sixty-eight, on January 6, 1934, my mother on December 30, 1945, at the age of seventy. Bert's father had also passed away in 1945, but her mother was then happily still with us. She lived on until 1960.

It was an emotionally satisfying day, climaxed by a family celebration in the evening, for which a welcome surprise guest—our daughter, Vivian—also arrived.

One melancholy event that midsummer, to which passing reference has already been made, was the untimely death, at the age of forty-one, of David W.

Two Generations in Perspective: Notable Events and Trends 1896–1956 (New York: Monde Publishers, Inc., 1957).

Petegorsky, the brilliant executive director of the American Jewish Congress. I had the sad privilege of eulogizing him at the funeral. He was succeeded by his friend and associate director, Isaac Toubin, also a rabbi by training, who brought to his office an abundance of intellectual gifts and administrative skills, together with a deep concern for the well-being of the American Jewish community.

The autumn of 1956 was dominated by the approaching U.S. Presidential election. As honorary vice-chairman of the Liberal Party of New York State, which, as usual, had thrown its weight behind the Democratic Party, I was involved in the work of the Platform Committee. Our efforts resulted in the adoption of good planks on Israel and against the Arab boycott.

I had been chosen to nominate Adlai Stevenson as our candidate for the Presidency at the Liberal Party's state convention. In a speech delivered in Manhattan Center on September 11, I hailed him as "a statesman in the noble tradition of Woodrow Wilson and Franklin D. Roosevelt." Much to our chagrin, Dwight D. Eisenhower, the Republican candidate, defeated Stevenson in a close contest, thus returning to the White House for a second term.

There was a piquant incident at about this time, when the Stephen S. Wise award of the American Jewish Congress was presented to *The New York Times*. Arthur Hays Sulzberger, the president and publisher of that great newspaper, accepted the award at a meeting chaired by Judge Simon Soboloff of Baltimore. Justine Wise Polier and I were the speakers and Sulzberger responded. Over luncheon, I told him that Julius Haber (in his book, *The Odyssey of an American Optimist*) had referred to Arthur's father, Cyrus L. Sulzberger, as one of Theodor Herzl's early supporters. I myself recalled him as an eminent philanthropist, benefactor of the Hebrew University, and onetime vice-president of the Federation of American Zionists, who had also done much for the rehabilitation of Russian Jewish immigrants in the United States. Arthur Sulzberger assured me, however, that his father had never been a Zionist, since he opposed the whole idea of a Jewish nation-state. Yet I knew that Cyrus had kept in his possession the classic portrait of Herzl gazing at the Rhine from his hotel balcony in Basle. Haber was probably closer to the truth.

The Second Israel-Arab War

Throughout the summer of 1956, as Gamal Abdul Nasser's shadow lengthened over the Middle East, *fedayeen* attacks on Israel were intensified. Israel's Foreign Minister, Moshe Sharett, still favored reliance on the UN to achieve a peaceful solution, but Prime Minister David Ben-Gurion placed more trust in Israel's own defensive capability and so, in June, Golda Meir was asked to take over Sharett's portfolio.

Meanwhile, the United States and Great Britain, having become disillusioned with the Egyptian dictator, withdrew their offer of financial assistance for Nasser's cherished project of a high dam on the Nile at Aswan. On July 26, Nasser retaliated by nationalizing the Suez Canal and seizing the assets of the Suez Canal Company to finance the construction of his dam. The British and French Governments, headed by Sir Anthony Eden and Guy Mollet, began making secret preparations for military intervention in the Canal Zone. Israel received considerable shipments of heavy armaments from the French, who were especially infuriated with Nasser because of his open support for the National Liberation Front (FLN) rebels in Algeria, where a full-scale war had been raging for some time.

The Middle East crisis came to a head in October, when Egypt—defying the UN Security Council resolution calling for "free and open transit through the Suez Canal"—intensified its blockade of shipping bound to and from Israeli ports, while mounting heavy guns at the Straits of Tiran in order to isolate Eilat, Israel's outlet to the Red Sea and the Indian Ocean. A joint Arab military command, under an Egyptian chief of staff, was established by Egypt, Syria, and Jordan. Nasser and his allies proclaimed their intention to "restore the rights of the Palestinian Arabs" by force and to "liquidate the Zionist enemy." On October 27, Ben-Gurion informed his cabinet of an impending preemptive attack by IDF forces to catch the Arabs off balance before their war preparations could be set in motion. Israel's objective was to wipe out the terrorist bases in the Gaza Strip, to destroy Egypt's military concentrations on the southern border, and to reopen the Straits of Tiran.

What followed requires no elaboration here. The Sinai Campaign, known in Israel by its code name, *Mivtza Kadesh* ("Operation Kadesh"), resulted in a feat of arms that astonished the world. It lasted from October 29 until November 5, and within the first 100 hours Israeli paratroops, infantry, and armored brigades had swept through the Sinai peninsula, driving most of the Egyptian forces back across the Suez Canal. Only in a few places, such as the Mitla Pass, did General Moshe Dayan's troops encounter serious resistance, as many Egyptian officers simply panicked and abandoned their men. Israeli aircraft achieved mastery of the skies.

On October 30, Great Britain and France issued an ultimatum calling upon Israel and Egypt to cease fighting and withdraw to positions ten miles distant from either side of the canal. That same evening, however, they vetoed an American-sponsored Security Council resolution demanding that Israel withdraw from Sinai. Western unity was shattered for the moment, pointing to the bankruptcy of State Department foreign policy. Unlike Israel, Egypt rejected the Anglo-French ultimatum. Accordingly, on the following day, British and French planes bombed Egyptian airfields and military installations, while the IDF continued its advance. By November 3, Israeli forward units had reached and halted at the agreed points short of the Suez Canal. Two days later, as IDF forces occupied Sharm el-Sheikh (commanding the Straits of Tiran), British and French paratroops landed at Port Said and Port Fuad. The second Israel-Arab war had come to an end.

It was a comparatively simple task for Dag Hammarskjöld, the UN Secretary-General, to arrange a cease-fire, but the issue of a withdrawal proved to be far more complicated. Although the Soviet Union had joined forces with the United States in denouncing Anglo-French-Israeli "collusion" and "aggression," Bulganin and Krushchev were unable to intervene effectively on Nasser's side because of the anti-Communist revolution in Hungary during the first week of November. Ironically enough, while massive international pressure was exerted against Nasser's opponents, the UN General Assembly contented itself with passing empty resolutions condemning Soviet intervention in the affairs of a member state, Hungary, where the popular bid for freedom was brutally suppressed by Russian troops. Even before then, however, the USSR had warned Egypt that it would not risk a third World War over the Suez issue. Nasser was advised to make peace with Great Britain and France, if not with Israel.

On November 8, Israel agreed to a demand for UN Emergency Force troops to be stationed at various strategic points, provided they would take effective control. A phased withdrawal of IDF units, begun at the end of the month in the face of violent criticism by Prime Minister Ben-Gurion's opponents in the Knesset, allowed for their eventual replacement by United Nations Emergency Force (UNEF) troops in the Gaza Strip area and, later, at Sharm el-Sheikh, when the last Israeli soldiers there pulled back in March 1957. For their part, Great Britain and France also reluctantly agreed to evacuate their troops from the Canal Zone on December 22, 1956. Nasser learned nothing from his defeat, however, and nursed his revenge.

While the fighting was at its height, a series of emergency meetings had taken place in New York, involving the American Executive of the Jewish Agency, the Presidents' Conference, and other major Jewish bodies. One meeting of the Agency Executive was attended by Teddy Kollek, then director-general of the Prime Minister's Office in Jerusalem, and Avraham Harman of the Israel Foreign Ministry. A brief visit by Foreign Minister Golda Meir enabled us to receive some firsthand information about the war and its effects on civilian life in the Medinah. IDF casualties amounted to 171 dead, 817 wounded, and four captured. The Egyptian losses had been at least 3,000 dead and thousands more wounded, with about 7,000 prisoners in Israeli hands.

Speaking on "Israel's Moral Case" at a meeting of the Presidents' Conference in New York, on November 26, 1956, I recalled that when the United Nations nine years earlier had authorized the establishment of a Jewish State in Palestine, that august body had taken no steps to implement its own resolution, which had been a high moral peak in UN history. Nor had sanctions been imposed upon the Arab states that attacked the infant Medinah. Despite this record of brazen defiance, I said, the Arabs were now "hugging the UN for dear life." Most disturbing of all was the ambivalence of the two Great Powers. "Where were they when the UN was being defied by the Arabs? Why did they not then summon emergency sessions to name the aggressors and to propose sanctions?" We all knew, of course, that a double standard applied in the UN to everything connected with Israel.

After the termination of "Operation Kadesh," David Ben-Gurion had resisted U.S. pressure for a complete and unconditional Israeli withdrawal from all occupied territory, braving explicit threats by Secretary of State Dulles to impose sanctions if Israel did not evacuate its troops forthwith. On February 9, 1957, David Sarnoff told me that he was working on a comprehensive proposal he intended submitting to President Eisenhower, whereby Israel would receive the assurance of effective U.S. support in the event that Egypt would resume its blockade and acts of aggression against the Jewish State. On the basis of such a firm undertaking, he hoped, Israel would find it possible to comply with the UN demand for a final withdrawal from the Gaza Strip and Sharm el-Sheikh. Golda Meir, who was in New York at the time, informed me that Sarnoff's proposal might well be acceptable, but that it would only act as a deterrent if Nasser were to learn of its contents.

On February 11, Dulles conferred with Israel's ambassador, Abba Eban, and handed him an *aide-mémoire* that went some way toward allaying the anxieties felt by Jerusalem. Meanwhile, prominent and influential Republican senators joined forces with their Democratic colleagues in opposing the use of coercive tactics against Israel.

President Eisenhower, however, encouraged by Secretary Dulles, maintained American pressure on the Israelis. Eisenhower decided to call in his onetime chief of staff, General Walter Bedell Smith, a former director of the Central Intelligence Agency and Undersecretary of State, who was known to have channels of communication with Ben-Gurion.* General Smith, though now in private business, continued to serve as an unofficial adviser to Eisenhower and favored strong military support for America's allies. He had a particularly close friend in Abraham F. Wechsler, an active New York Jewish philanthropist, who was a longtime friend and congregant of mine. When the President and the Secretary of State asked him to intercede, Bedell Smith made clear his view that Ben-Gurion would probably agree to a withdrawal if a personal assurance were to be authorized by Eisenhower stipulating that the Suez Canal would be opened to Israeli shipping on Nasser's own recognizance.

"I will call Ben-Gurion now, if you will give me your word on this, Mr. President," Bedell Smith declared. Eisenhower and Dulles thereupon gave him their verbal guarantee that such an assurance would be forthcoming, and he then telephoned Ben-Gurion, who acceded to the arrangement.

On March 1, Golda Meir informed the UN General Assembly that, on the basis of the American *aide-mémoire* of February 11 and other international undertakings, Israel would complete its evacuation of the remaining areas. Subsequently, however, when Nasser resumed his blockade of Israel-bound vessels through the Suez Canal, no serious attempt was made to implement the Presidential guarantee. In anger and frustration, General Bedell Smith severed his links with the Administration. He held Dulles to be primarily responsible for what had occurred.

Nevertheless, there were some tangible compensations for Israel. *Mivtza Kadesh* had demonstrated to the world that the Jewish State was a dangerous foe and a valuable ally, harboring no expansionist aims (since the IDF withdrew from Sinai), but wishing only to be left in peace in order to work out its own problems and potentials. The free world might have been wiser, of course, had it permitted Nasser to reap the whirlwind which he so richly deserved. In fact, however, Western maritime nations, headed by the United States, went on record in support of unrestricted freedom of navigation through the Red Sea and the Straits of Tiran. While accepting the new arrangement, Israel gave formal notice that any interference with

*For the following information, I am indebted to Abraham F. Wechsler of New York.

its maritime trade and shipping in the future would constitute an act of war. Ten years of relative peace were to follow.

There also emerged one important gain on the economic front. Through its Red Sea port of Eilat, Israel was able to develop valuable trade links and diplomatic ties with many countries in Asia and Africa. Within a year or two of "Operation Kadesh," a whole series of commercial agreements and technical aid programs spread Israel's name and reputation to parts of the world where few people had known anything of that enterprising little state before its victorious Sinai Campaign.

A *"Tour d'Horizon"* of the Jewish World

The last steps taken by Israel in regard to the military withdrawal from Sinai were very much in the news when I arrived in Jerusalem early in March 1957 to attend a meeting of the Jewish Agency Executive. It was mostly concerned with aspects of the immigration and absorption program. Eastern Europe and North Africa were the principal reservoirs of anticipated and potential Aliyah at that time. An influx of 7,000 Olim monthly was expected and the necessary financial and administrative preparations had to be made.

We paid a Shabbat call on President and Mrs. Ben-Zvi. He had just returned from Sabbath morning services in a nearby synagogue, where he had observed the *Yahrzeit* memorial for their son, who had fallen in the War of Liberation in 1948. Soon he would be on his way to the weekly Talmud *shi'ur* he attended. Raḥel Yannait Ben-Zvi participated in a Talmud study session for women during the week. Truly, a remarkable Presidential couple, I reflected.

Members of the Jewish Agency Executive had occasion to visit David Ben-Gurion while I was in Israel. As so often, we found him engrossed in Bible study. There was a huge map of the world spread across the wall, with Israel a tiny spot on it marked in blue. Aliyah was our first—and last—topic of conversation. Ben-Gurion felt that a population of four million Jews was a realistic possibility for Israel. An army of half a million would then make the State impregnable to enemy attack for at least another twenty-five years. "I'm the Minister of Defense," he added, "but I can tell you that Aliyah is no less vital and important."

He then went on to speak about the alliance with France that had been forged during the recent Sinai Campaign. Without minimizing its significance, he believed that the combination of circumstances that had brought it about would in all probability not be repeated. Turning to relations with the USSR, Ben-Gurion said, "We are a small country. Even though we are well aware of Soviet unfriendliness toward us, we cannot be hostile to the Russians." Before our group left, he returned to his well-known thesis that "one who does not make Aliyah to Israel is not a Zionist."

While on a hurried visit to Eilat, I remembered something Ben-Gurion had mentioned about the need for a railroad link from the north of the country to Israel's Red Sea port. He was a great believer in road and rail links and also favored the development of an internal waterway. It was impressive to see how Eilat had grown since my last visit there four years earlier. There was a great deal of construction work underway in the harbor, and the first oil pipe was being laid as the giant oil tanks neared completion.

When my official business in Israel had been concluded, I stopped off in London en route for New York, to attend a meeting of the World Jewish Congress Executive at the home of Israel Sieff. Apart from the usual WJC *tour d'horizon* of the Jewish world scene, my visit afforded a welcome opportunity to lunch with "the family"—Israel Sieff, Simon Marks, Harry Sacher, Michael Sacher, Marcus Sieff, and Dr. Alec Lerner. Nowhere else in the world is there such a family unit as this, combining wealth, culture, nobility of character, philanthropy, and Zionism, coupled with a wholehearted devotion to Great Britain.

Before flying on to the United States, I also had a chat with Isaac Wolfson, who spoke proudly of his son, Leonard, as an outstanding businessman and a warmly committed Jew who was beginning to share his father's constructive interest in Israel. The development of Jewish day schools in the British Isles met with Isaac Wolfson's enthusiastic approval and support. He told me that he was planning to take a group of leading men from the business world to Jerusalem for the dedication of Hechal Shlomo, the Supreme Rabbinical Center in Israel and headquarters of the Union of Israel Synagogues. He had built this structure on Jerusalem's King George Avenue as a memorial to his late father, Solomon (Shlomo) Wolfson.

My speedy return to New York was primarily in response to an urgent call from a member of Congregation B'nai Jeshurun who wished me to officiate at the funeral of his wife. Objectively, perhaps, I need not have interrupted my journey abroad—while I was engaged in the "business" of the Jewish people—yet on this occasion, as on others, I felt that my congregational claims had a high priority.

Resuming my tour overseas, I flew back to Israel and found that preparations were already being made for the tenth anniversary celebrations of the independent State. Teddy Kollek came to see me for a discussion of the observance to be held in the United States.

For some time past, I had felt that a street in Jerusalem should be named for Dr. Stephen S. Wise, preferably close to the youth hostel bearing the name of his wife, Louise. I talked the matter over with my old friend, Gershon Agron, then Jerusalem's Mayor. He reacted favorably, and my suggestion was implemented. The site chosen, however, was in the vicinity of the Hebrew University's Givat Ram campus, since the Louise Waterman Wise Youth Hostel happened to have been built in the Orthodox neighborhood of Bayit Vegan, and not all of the residents there would have welcomed the naming of a street for a Reform rabbi!

At a reception for Dr. Nahum Goldmann in Jerusalem, he took me aside and asked me to give serious thought to becoming the head of a new organization in which the Keren Hayesod and the Keren Kayemet would be combined. I saw no reason, however, for changing the view I had espoused at the Zionist Congress in April of the previous year.

While in Israel, I also visited Kiryat Gat, to see the new youth center which, on the initiative of the New York United Jewish Appeal, had been established there in my name. Teenage boys and girls received vocational training at the center, preparing them to earn a useful livelihood. The site was especially meaningful to me, as I had first visited the area when the future development town of Kiryat Gat was still on the drawing board, with an imported cotton gin waiting to be used. Several years later, the textile plant of Polgat (combining the names of Pollak and Kiryat Gat) was established there by Israel Pollak, an industrialist whom I came to know during the 1960s, when I was world chairman of Keren Hayesod and he headed our *magbit* in Chile.

Ongoing responsibilities in my congregation kept me busy that spring, but the agenda of the American Jewish Congress also made frequent demands upon my time. The matters of concern included Nasser's anti-Jewish measures in Egypt, Jewish restitution claims from the West German and Austrian Governments, developments in North Africa, and Jewish education in New York City. At a special meeting of the Presidents' Conference, we heard an analysis by Foreign Minister Golda Meir of the way in which UN Secretary-General Dag Hammarskjöld had handled Israel's withdrawal from Sinai.

One of our most gratifying experiences in the wake of the recent Middle East conflict was a session that a number of my colleagues and I had with several leading Republican and Democratic senators. Rabbi Philip Bernstein, Rose Halprin, I. L. Kenen, Rabbi Irving Miller, Dr. Emanuel Neumann, and Bernard Trager accompanied me. Senator Lyndon B. Johnson, a Texas Democrat, made a particularly strong impression on us. He was unreservedly pro-Israel and condemned the double standard of dealing one way with small, weak nations and another way with large and powerful ones. Senator Johnson believed that President Eisenhower ought to apply the same pressures and tactics to Egypt that he did to Israel. Another friend of ours, Senator Hubert H. Humphrey of Minnesota, observed that whereas Harry Truman had proved capable of overruling his own State Department, Eisenhower had listened only to his inner circle of foreign-policy advisers, who "kept pumping him full of anti-Israel prejudice."

Another interesting encounter during this time was with Mohammed Ben Barka, leader of the Istiqlal (Independence Party) in Morocco, when he visited the United States. Justine Wise Polier and I met him in the company of Eleanor Roosevelt, who had just returned from a tour of Morocco. Conditions there were simply appalling, she said, and Muslims and Jews both suffered from the country's impoverishment. True to her noble, humanitarian character, Mrs. Roosevelt was anxious to do everything possible to relieve their plight. In her talks with Sultan Muhammad V and various Moroccan notables, she had urged them to permit a larger Jewish emigration to Israel. The opposition Istiqlal Party eventually assailed Zionist activity in Morocco and demanded the banning or restriction of Aliyah, but Ben Barka himself claimed to be well disposed toward the Jews.

My commitment to the Hebrew movement in the United States found expression in an address I delivered at the annual dinner of Histadrut Ivrit of America, held on April 7, 1957, at the Sheraton-Astor Hotel in New York. "There is no case in history," I said, "where a Jewish community has survived without a vital Hebraic culture." It was regrettable that relatively few in the United States were active in the promotion of Hebrew. Prior to 1948, Jews could have furnished, as an alibi, their total involvement in the struggle for the establishment of a Jewish State in Palestine. Now, however, there was no valid excuse for the low priority given to Hebrew language programs. The American Zionist organizations were chiefly responsible for this state of affairs. In New York City alone, two-thirds of the Jewish children attending Jewish schools received not even a smattering of Hebrew language instruction. Throughout the United States, only 33,000 children attended Jewish day schools. American Jewry, I declared, could take no comfort from these statistics.

I went on to castigate the majority of American Jewish leaders for their continued neglect of this essential activity:

> How do they visualize the American Jew of fifty years hence? Are they content to see a generation whose knowledge of Hebrew will consist of an ability to read the *Shema Yisrael* and the *Kaddish* in transliteration? The Zionist movement has a major responsibility to prevent the threat of Jewish cultural bankruptcy in American Jewish life, but it is the responsibility of all Jews and of all Jewish leaders. No American Jew has the right to be called a Jewish leader unless he feels and exercises a sense of concern for Jewish education and Hebrew culture.

My wife and I made a return visit to Israel in the summer. At the King David Hotel in Jerusalem on July 25, I took much pleasure in presenting the Stephen Wise award to Golda Meir. In the course of my remarks, I referred to a question that had often intrigued me:

> What is the secret of Golda's power? The answer, I believe, is moral force. It shines through her, to the credit of Israel as well. Israel's case is essentially a moral case. Therefore, its most effective advocates are those who speak with moral conviction. Indeed, it may be said that Israel's cause has been, and will continue to be, the touchstone of the moral caliber of the United Nations.

The high point of this trip was the dedication of the completed Israel Goldstein Synagogue on the Givat Ram campus of the Hebrew University, an event to which Bert and I had been looking forward eagerly ever since the laying of the cornerstone fifteen months earlier. The ceremony took place on the morning of Wednesday, August 7, 1957, in the presence of President and Mrs. Itzhak Ben-Zvi and a large and distinguished congregation. Those in attendance included justices of the Israel Supreme Court, leading rabbis, members of the Jewish Agency Executive, Hebrew University professors and scholars from abroad, as well as a number of visitors from the United States. The participation of my beloved teacher, Professor Mordecai M. Kaplan, was a particular joy. Among other friends who came were Professor Cecil Roth, the eminent Jewish historian of Oxford, Dr. Aryeh Tartakower, and my longtime Zionist colleague, Rose Halprin.

Messages of greeting were sent by Chief Rabbi Itzhak Nissim, Governor Averell Harriman of New York and Mayor Robert F. Wagner, David Sarnoff, Herbert

Lehman, the presidents of several American universities, Chancellor Louis Finkelstein of the Jewish Theological Seminary, the New York Board of Rabbis, and my own congregation, B'nai Jeshurun, which had made a major contribution to the building of the new synagogue. A special message came from President Dwight D. Eisenhower.

The University Synagogue was of unusual design, built as a hemisphere on a platform supported by eight pillars and covered by an elliptical dome. The interior was illuminated by natural light that flowed upward and along the rising cupola, creating a remarkably striking effect. Seating was arranged in a circular fashion. The Ark was austere, shaped like a pillar. A library formed part of the building, and a *bet midrash* was added to it in December 1974. This structure inspired one design for a series of Israel postage stamps on modern architecture, issued in 1975.

The service of consecration began with *Mah Tovu*, sung by Cantor Robert H. Segal, my colleague at B'nai Jeshurun in New York, whom I was especially pleased to welcome. Addresses were then delivered by Professor Benjamin Mazar, president of the Hebrew University; Ḥayyim Moshe Shapira, Israel's Minister of Religious Affairs and Social Welfare; and Gershon Agron, the Mayor of Jerusalem. Mine was the concluding address. Prayers on the dedication of the synagogue and for the welfare of Israel were recited by Bernard Cherrick, the university's director of organization and information, whom I had first met in London during World War II. To conclude the service, Professor Joseph Klausner, a venerable figure with a worldwide reputation in Jewish scholarship, slid back the doors of the Holy Ark, at which point all present joined Cantor Segal in chanting *Va-yehi bi-neso'a ha-aron*, "When the Ark of the Covenant set forward" (Numbers 10:35–36). The singing of *Kedushah* and the national anthem, *Hatikvah*, by the male choir of Kol Zion La-Golah, Israel Radio's overseas service, and the unveiling of an inscribed plaque at the entrance by my wife, concluded the proceedings.

Prior to my address, I felt bound to recite the *Sheheḥeyanu* blessing in thankfulness for the privilege of having been honored by the construction of this unique house of worship. After an expression of thanks to all who had made it possible, I stressed the synagogue's role as a carrier of religion and an abode of democratic Jewish fellowship linking Jews throughout the world. I continued as follows:

> My friends in the United States have felt, and I trust the feeling is generally shared in Israel, that a university, particularly the Hebrew University, is not complete without a house of worship on its premises. When American Jews think of Israel, and especially of Jerusalem, the Holy City, they think primarily of its historic religious connotations. It is to be hoped that this Synagogue will have a functional value in the life of the University's students and faculty.
>
> Let this Synagogue serving the Hebrew University, which is an offspring of the Zionist movement, be a reminder of the role which the Synagogue has played as the "alma mater" of Zionism. Eighteen hundred years before there was a Zionist Organization there were Zionists. Sentiment alone might never have created the Jewish State, but without the millenial Synagogue-cradled sentiment the practical program might never have found an adequate constituency.

May this Synagogue, an integral part of the University, symbolize the truth that Science and Culture without Religion—*Da'at* without *Da'at Elohim*—threatens to become man's undoing. It is, in the end, Religion which is concerned with the aims and goals, the eternal values of human life and conduct. . . .

The gifted architects, Heinz Rau and David Resnick, have so designed the structure that a straight line running east would lead from this Synagogue to *Har ha-Bayit*, site of the ancient Temple not many kilometers away. The geometric line is a symbol of the psychometric line which unites us with *Har ha-Bayit* and our ancient past. The axis formed by this psychometric line needs to become the axis for a world of justice and of peace.

Israel's Tenth Anniversary

As a native son of Philadelphia, cradle of American nationhood, I felt an additional surge of wistful sentiment with the approach of the tenth anniversary of Israel's independence in 1958, when it was decided to observe the climax of this celebration in Philadelphia's Independence Square. No more appropriate decision could have been taken, since Philadelphia was the birthplace of American independence. The proclamation of Medinat Yisrael had taken place on the fifth day of Iyyar, which coincided with May 14. Yom Ha-Atzma'ut in 1958 was to be celebrated on April 24, in accordance with the Hebrew lunar calendar.

Prime Minister David Ben-Gurion had sent Meyer Weisgal from Israel to help organize American Jewry's observance of the tenth anniversary. Herbert H. Lehman was the general chairman and I served as administrative chairman of the committee appointed to supervise the planning and arrangement of the various events. A panel of leading personalities from all walks of life was assembled on our letterhead. During the months preceding the festivities, we met frequently.

One of our first steps was to extend an invitation to U.S. Vice-President Richard M. Nixon. He received me on the morning of February 9, 1958, at his office in the Senate Building on Capitol Hill. I took the occasion to discuss with him a number of matters of concern then to the American Jewish Congress in regard to the legislative program for that year, as drafted by the Eisenhower Administration. These included civil rights, Federal education grants, U.S. ratification of the International Convention on Genocide, and the initialing of the Convention on the Rights of Stateless Persons, which was being delayed.

The Vice-President was amiable and surprisingly well informed. He knew of my recent trip to Rome and that I had spent the last week of January attending sessions of the Claims Conference and meetings of the newly formed Consultative Organization and Coordinating Committee of the World Jewish Congress. I told him about the report I had given to Cardinal Octaviani and Monsignor Tardini regarding common areas of cooperation among Protestants, Catholics, and Jews in the United States. I also mentioned having received an account of his recent discussions with leaders of the "Presidents' Club," who had been greatly impressed with his friendly attitude toward Israel.

I asked Nixon if he would be able to visit Israel during the tenth anniversary celebration. He was doubtful, as this would mean that he would have to visit other countries in the region as well, and he had no time to spare. He nevertheless noted the date on which our program would begin in the United States, so as to issue an appropriate statement on Israel. In fact, however, he failed to do so, nor did he accept our subsequent invitation to be the principal speaker at a gala dinner in New York scheduled for May 19. We felt at the time that this was all part of the Administration's decision, masterminded by our "friends" in the State Department, to remain aloof from Israel's *simḥah*.

Later that month, the committee organizing our tenth anniversary celebrations made its bow with a luncheon at the Hotel Pierre in New York for some 200 leading personalities in the nation's artistic, literary, political, civic, and philanthropic life. Herbert Lehman was the host at this function. The speakers, apart from Lehman and myself, were Governor Averell Harriman, Mayor Robert F. Wagner, Ogden Reid, publisher of *The New York Herald Tribune*, and William Hart Benton, publisher of the *Encyclopaedia Britannica*.

Herbert H. Lehman was one of the outstanding personalities who ever graced the general American and Jewish public scenes. His dignity stamped him as a born aristocrat. He had been a founder of the Joint Distribution Committee. He served as Lieutenant Governor of New York State for four years, until the election of Franklin D. Roosevelt as President in 1932, when he succeeded him as Governor and then served for five successive terms. After having occupied the post of first director-general of UNRRA from 1942 to 1946, Lehman entered the U.S. Senate as a Democrat and remained there until his resignation in 1956. A liberal in the full sense of the term, and a fierce opponent of McCarthyism, he was a man of broad humanitarian outlook who served both his country and the Jewish people with devotion and distinction.

We had met often before, but our association in the Israel tenth anniversary program enabled me to discern his sterling qualities at closer range. Then in his eightieth year, he enjoyed robust health and displayed enviable vigor. He reacted with patience and wisdom to difficulties that would have ruffled many younger men.

The U.S. Administration continued to be ambivalent, if not downright evasive, in responding to our various proposals. The Post Office refused to issue a special postage stamp to mark Israel's tenth anniversary year, while the State Department balked at the suggestion that a special emissary, other than the American ambassador, represent the Government at the main celebration in Israel.

Fortunately for our plans, Israel was not without loyal friends in Washington. Arrangements were made for the session of April 23 in the Senate to be opened with a prayer by Rabbi Philip Bernstein, chairman of the American Israel Public Affairs Committee, and for a prayer in the House of Representatives to be delivered by me, on behalf of the anniversary committee. Senator Jacob K. Javits (Republican) and Congressman Emanuel Celler (Democrat), together with I. L. Kenen, were responsible for these observances in Congress. Both Houses unanimously passed resolutions extending good wishes to Israel. The resolutions, sponsored by Senators Knowland and Johnson and by Representative McCormack, respectively, were adopted without debate.

Senator Javits and Congressman Celler presided at a festive luncheon held thereafter. Some two dozen leading members of both Houses attended, and Ambassador Abba Eban responded to the toasts. That same afternoon, a number of gratifying speeches were delivered in Congress by Jewish and non-Jewish representatives.

In my own congregation, the tenth anniversary of Medinat Yisrael was marked by a special service of thanksgiving at which the principal speaker was James G. McDonald, first U.S. ambassador to Israel.

On Sunday, April 27, a crowd of about 40,000 gathered under lowering skies at the Polo Grounds in uptown New York to participate in a mass "Salute to Israel." It was a star-studded event, punctuated by many glowing tributes. Outstanding addresses were delivered by General Moshe Dayan, Governor Averell Harriman, Eleanor Roosevelt, Thomas E. Dewey, Abba Eban, and George Meany, the American labor leader.

Celebrations reached a climax on April 29 with the assembly at Independence Square in Philadelphia. The symbolism linking that site with the present occasion was inescapable. A tight schedule had been arranged. Two special parlor cars conveyed our group from New York to Philadelphia. Bert and I were fortunate to travel in the car with former President Harry S. Truman and former Senator Herbert H. Lehman. Truman was in excellent form—we spent much of the journey chatting about our grandchildren!

At a press conference held on our arrival, Truman declared:

> Well, I'm happy to be here for the celebration of the Tenth Anniversary of the birth of Israel, the young republic which has made good and for which I have the kindliest feelings. I know something about the history of Israel. I know something about the promises which had been made to Israel. I know something about the people who had gone through more suffering and more travail and trouble than any other people . . . they have survived it, and that's one of the greatest things in the history of the world.
>
> Present in the Middle East today are Soviet influence and power. This need not have come to pass—and I know what I'm talking about. It could have been avoided, but there's no point in talking about what might have been. *Our* influence needs to be felt. We're for freedom, progress, prosperity and peace for all the peoples of the Middle East. I see no advantage in talking about any settlement which is based on the idea of requiring Israel to give up any of her territories or any of her rights as a free and sovereign, independent nation.

A luncheon at the Warwick Hotel, chaired by Frederick R. Mann, a Philadelphia Jewish notable, was without speeches. Chief Justice Earl Warren appeared there to grace us with his company. We then proceeded to the assembly point. The weather looked unpromising until the ceremony began, whereupon the sun broke through the clouds and continued to shine on us.

After a brief pause at the Liberty Bell, our party mounted the platform overlooking the immense plaza, where some 5,000 people had congregated. Rabbi Abraham A. Neuman, president of Dropsie College, delivered the invocation. I then introduced Herbert Lehman, whose speech was followed by those of Harry Truman and Chief Justice Warren. These were inspiring addresses, delivered before a highly responsive and enthusiastic audience. As usual, Truman's remarks were forceful and emphatic:

> We are here today to celebrate the establishment of the State of Israel ten years ago. . . . I am proud to have been the first to recognize the State of Israel. I did it because I knew that in doing so I was expressing not only the fundamental wishes of the American people, but the high traditions of the United States of America.
>
> History has justified the re-creation of the State of Israel because historical claims and the claims of humanity both pointed in the same direction. Our Government must make it clear that Israel is not *on* the bargaining table, as far as we are concerned, but is *at* the bargaining table and a full member of the group of nations in the Middle East.

He felt that the Arab states "would be easier to deal with when they learn they cannot negotiate Israel out of existence or make any backstairs deals with the Soviet Union or the United States."

All in all, it was a most impressive occasion. The highlight of the rally at Independence Square was a two-way transatlantic telephone conversation with Prime Minister David Ben-Gurion in Israel, when Ambassador Eban first handed the instrument to Herbert Lehman and then to Harry Truman.

That same evening, back in New York, Christopher Fry's *The Firstborn*, a play about Moses, had its premiere at Carnegie Hall, under the sponsorship of the America-Israel Cultural Foundation. It had an excellent cast, a well-written script, and, of course, a captivating theme, but somehow it lacked sparkle. Later, the entire company was flown to Tel Aviv, thanks to Meyer Weisgal, who had been behind the production, but the Israeli press and public gave the play a halfhearted reception. It ran only for a week at the Habimah Theater.

The concluding event in the United States was a gala dinner at the Waldorf-Astoria, New York, on May 19. There was a roster of distinguished speakers, including Justice Felix Frankfurter, Henry Steele Commager, the historian, Lewis Mumford, and Nahum Goldmann. Edwin Rosenberg took the chair and I opened the proceedings.

Had I been asked for a considered opinion of the tenth anniversary program as a whole, I would have said that it was dignified but not exciting. The U.S. Administration kept a discreet distance from the celebrations, but with a State Department rigidly controlled by John Foster Dulles, what else could one have expected?

Some Retrospective Judgments

The American Jewish Congress held its annual convention at the Carillon Hotel in Miami Beach on May 14–18, 1958. It was my last appearance as president since assuming that post almost seven years previously. Mingling with the delegates following our arrival, I discovered that there was a move afoot to draft me for an additional term. I promptly appeared before the nominating committee in order to make it clear that I would not accept any such proposal, and I urged that Dr. Joachim Prinz be approached to succeed me as president.

The closing banquet was notable for the fine addresses delivered by U Thant, Burma's ambassador to the United States (and later Secretary-General of the UN); Governor Mennen Williams of Michigan; Ambassador Abba Eban of Israel; and Governor William Stratton of Illinois, who brought greetings from the Presidents' Conference, which was then meeting close by in Miami.

In my president's report, the swan song of my tenure, I could not avoid painting a rather gloomy picture of the current world situation and of its Jewish components. The period under review had been characterized by a precarious balance between the potentials of peace and war.

The following were some of the observations in my farewell address:

> The United Nations Organization, always a forum but not always a force, does not yet hold the key to world peace.
>
> The two giant power blocs, led by the United States and the Soviet Union, respectively, continue to glower apprehensively at each other, neither of them willing to assume the risk of taking the first step which would involve reliance upon the good faith of the other. The uncommitted part of the human race, in its desperation, tends to grasp at peace slogans without examining too closely the substance behind them.
>
> In a time of world tension, the lot of the Jewish people is a seismograph, reflecting the conditions in every area. Among these is the position of the three million Jews of the Soviet Union, who have oscillated between Stalin's terror and Khrushchev's uneasy toleration. Forty years of the Soviet regime have all but withered their spirit, all but liquidated their uniquely Jewish culture and their religious life. Another such forty years may spell their doom as Jews. Only emigration to Israel can save them. . . .
>
> The one million Jews of Western Europe and the British Commonwealth enjoy freedom and economic security, but their future as Jews is challenged by assimilation and intermarriage.
>
> The nearly half a million Jews of Morocco, Tunis and Algeria, secure in their religious practices, face an uncertain political and economic future between indigenous counter-pressures, and many of them will find the solution to their manifold perplexity only in Israel.
>
> The 600,000 Jews of Latin America, among whom memories of the old European homesteads still stir, are temporarily secure, but keep one eye open to the threat of political instability, and the leaders are beginning to worry about inroads of assimilation among the youth. . . .
>
> For Israel, every one of these seven years has been a new test, a new milestone of progress and a new source of pride and stimulation to Jewish communities everywhere. Israel's population of two million makes it the third largest Jewish community in the world, and dynamism ranks it as the first. Never has an infant grown so fast in the face of so many obstacles.

The major portion of my address, however, was devoted to the state of American Jewry, its problems, potentials, and prospects. To judge from the criteria of education, employment, and housing, I said, anti-Semitism in the United States had declined to its lowest point in many years. The American Jewish community had grown and prospered; its philanthropies, both for local and for overseas needs, had expanded; its religious and secular institutions had multiplied. There had been a movement of middle-class Jewish families to the suburbs, while synagogue affiliation and religious-school education had registered an increase.

I then issued a caution that still holds good in the 1980s. "The complexion of American Jewry fifty years hence depends upon its leadership today. Ten thousand Jews of leadership caliber in the United States can determine the spiritual and cultural future of millions of Jews a generation or two from now. What matters, therefore, is to take up one's position among those who do the steering, not the drifting."

My survey covered the record of the American Jewish Congress in defending civil rights and in protecting minority groups and individual liberties in the United States. A forthright stand had been taken by the AJC against all forms of state-imposed segregation—in the public schools, transportation, recreational facilities, and public building—and this stand had culminated, after a twenty-year battle, in the historic U.S. Supreme Court decision of May 1954 outlawing segregation in American schools. The Congress had also played an active part in resisting McCarthyism, which threatened to undermine the foundations of a free and just society. In the sphere of religious liberty, it was no exaggeration to state that the American Jewish Congress had become "the staunchest and the most effective defender of the separation of Church and State" in the United States.

I referred to our multiple programs, which included steps taken in regard to Sunday observance laws, compulsory recitation of the "Lord's Prayer" in public schools, the insertion of a religious question in the national census, child adoption across religious lines, distribution of Bibles to public-school pupils, religious criteria in appointing and assigning probation officers and in film censorship, joint Christmas-Hanukkah celebrations, religious symbols on public property, financial aid for religious institutions and attempts to bar them from residential areas.

A significant part of my address was devoted to the AJC's unswerving support for Israel. In this connection, I referred to its annual dinner, organized in support of the United Jewish Appeal, which had become an outstanding event in the UJA campaign calendar. I also mentioned our fight against the Arab anti-Israel boycott. In April 1956, the American Jewish Congress had published the first comprehensive study of Arab boycott operations, which revealed the U.S. Administration's acquiescence in such discriminatory practices. Both major political parties had subsequently adopted planks condemning this type of discrimination against American citizens, and had urged the Government to resist it.

So ended a term of service I regard as one of the important endeavors and privileges of my public life.

It was a pleasant change in my routine a few weeks later to attend the commencement exercises at Brandeis University. For my wife and me, this was our first visit to the Waltham campus after a long absence, during which Brandeis University, under Dr. Abram L. Sachar, had developed remarkably.

I had been chosen to receive an honorary degree there, on June 8, 1958, and the other recipients included Ambassador Abba Eban, Professor Harry Wolfson, and the presidents of several colleges of high caliber. Abraham Feinberg, who played an important part in the United Jewish Appeal and in Israel Bonds, was chairman of the board of trustees at the time. William Mazer, a leading member of the board of trustees, and our gracious host, showed us around the beautiful campus. George Alpert, who had carried a major responsibility for the fledgling institution years earlier, offered his congratulations at the luncheon. President Sachar, after reading out the citation and handing me the diploma at the exercises, whispered into my ear, "I'm so happy that the record has been set right!"

This was not altogether the case, unfortunately, as the citation stopped short of acknowledging my role as the founder of Brandeis University (see chapter 5). Still, it was a gracious gesture that I much appreciated.

The success enjoyed by Brandeis University vindicated my faith in the whole enterprise. It had nevertheless been my hope that such a Jewish-sponsored university might become the first in a chain of similar colleges established in or near cities with a large Jewish population and a distinguished academic tradition.

Moreover, despite Brandeis University's academic achievements, a tribute to Dr. Sachar's presidency and to the devotion and generosity of its trustees, I believed that it had failed in one important respect to fulfill the hopes I had originally placed in it—namely, in regard to the Jewish dimension. My fondest wish had been that Brandeis would foster special ties with the Hebrew University in Jerusalem, and that it would aim primarily to train Jewishly knowledgeable and Jewishly motivated leaders for the American Jewish community.

Perhaps these hopes will yet be fulfilled.

The clamorous needs and demands of *Klal Yisrael* responsibility left precious little time for retrospective musings. High on our list of priorities was the administration of funds made available to the Claims Conference by the Federal German Republic for the rebuilding of Jewish life and institutions in the many countries where Jewish refugees from Nazi Germany had found a haven.

On June 22, I joined a delegation of American Jewish leaders who called upon West Germany's President Theodor Heuss during a visit he was paying to the United States. Although our main purpose was to express our appreciation of the President's fine democratic spirit and for the outcome of negotiations on Material Claims, much of the discussion revolved around the dangers of anti-Semitism and neo-Nazism in postwar Germany.

In reply to our assorted observations, Dr. Heuss declared that there was no anti-Semitic danger in his country and nothing to worry about on that score. My private feeling was that there were probably too few Jews left in Germany to provoke widespread hostility. He felt confident that there would be no resurgence of Nazism in the Federal Republic, since people there knew only too well how disastrous such "experiments" had been. On this point, my feeling was that human memory had often proved all too fickle and selective. Dr. Heuss averred that the German people wished to bring about a reunification of their country, but assured us that they were not prepared to go to war for the achievement of that end.

I came away from this meeting with the distinct impression that the German President, however well-meaning, was either deliberately soft-pedaling various undercurrents in his country or unwilling to admit the misgivings which he felt regarding the future.

The Austrian Government, as previously mentioned, continually evaded its obligations and responsibilities toward former Jewish citizens. On September 16, 1959, a delegation headed by Jacob Blaustein called on Dr. Bruno Kreisky, Austria's new Foreign Minister, and presented a memorandum urging that the Austrian indemnification law be extended in scope. The law then provided only for meager payments, in compensation for internment in Nazi concentration camps. What we sought was a measure akin to the broader German indemnification law.

In his initial response, Dr. Kreisky told us that the specific points we had raised were not within his jurisdiction as Foreign Minister, and that, in any case, he ruled himself out as an adjudicator—because of his Jewish origin! Upon accepting his Government portfolio, Kreisky had stipulated that he would not deal with two policy matters—the claims of Austrian Jews and the Concordat with the Vatican—since in either case he anticipated criticism, whichever way he acted. He advised us to take up the issues in a memorandum to the Austrian Finance Minister, Dr. Reinhold Kamitz, who was in New York at the time.

Kreisky went on to speak at length and with much feeling about Austria's obligations. He pointed out that he himself had been arrested on two successive occasions during the 1930s—once as a Socialist, when the Fascist regime took control in 1934 after the assassination of Chancellor Engelbert Dollfuss, and later, as a Jew, after the *Anschluss* in 1938. Hitler had come to power in Germany "by legal means," Kreisky maintained, and it could thus be said that the German people had voted him in as their Führer. In Austria, however, he had seized power: *ergo*, the Austrian people had not voted him in and could not be held responsible!

This future Chancellor stated, in conclusion, that whatever the present-day Austrian Government might agree to do would be based entirely on humanitarian considerations, and not out of a sense of responsibility for what had happened after 1938.

That approach reminded me of what a perceptive American author, John Gunther, had once written in his excellent book, *Inside Europe*, published before World War II: "Vienna's familiar lassitude [*Schlamperei*], product of the warm, sirocco-like *Föhn*, enveloped politics in a fog of languor."